Heresy and Inquisition in the Middle Ages
Volume 6

HERESY IN LATE MEDIEVAL GERMANY

Heresy and Inquisition in the Middle Ages
ISSN 2046–8938

Series editors
John H. Arnold, Faculty of History, University of Cambridge
Peter Biller, Department of History, University of York
L. J. Sackville, Department of History, University of York

Heresy had social, cultural and political implications in the middle ages, and countering heresy was often a central component in the development of orthodoxy. This series publishes work on heresy, and the repression of heresy, from late antiquity to the Reformation, including monographs, collections of essays, and editions of texts.

Previous volumes in the series are listed at the back of this volume.

Heresy in Late Medieval Germany

The Inquisitor Petrus Zwicker
and the Waldensians

Reima Välimäki

THE UNIVERSITY *of York*

YORK MEDIEVAL PRESS

First published 2019

A York Medieval Press publication
in association with The Boydell Press
an imprint of Boydell & Brewer Ltd
PO Box 9, Woodbridge, Suffolk IP12 3DF, UK
and of Boydell & Brewer Inc.
668 Mt Hope Avenue, Rochester, NY 14620–2731, USA
website: www.boydellandbrewer.com
and with the
Centre for Medieval Studies, University of York
www.york.ac.uk/medieval-studies

ISBN 978-1-903153-86-4

A CIP catalogue record for this book is available
from the British Library

The publisher has no responsibility for the continued existence or accuracy
of URLs for external or third-party internet websites referred to in this book,
and does not guarantee that any content on such websites is, or will remain,
accurate or appropriate

This publication is printed on acid-free paper

To my wife Henna, and to our daughter Aune

Contents

List of Illustrations ix

Author's Note x

Acknowledgements xi

List of Abbreviations xii

Introduction 1
    Earlier research 9
    Sources and how to read them 12

1   Petrus Zwicker and the Career of an Inquisitor at the Turn of
    the Fifteenth Century 22

2   The Inquisitor Writes 38
    The *Refutatio errorum*: a draft-like treatise on Waldensians 39
    Different redactions of the *Refutatio errorum* 41
    Structure of the *Refutatio errorum* 48
    On purgatory 50
    Boethius and Pseudo-Ezekiel 60
    The *Cum dormirent homines*: polemical biblicism 64
    Auctoritas and authorities in late medieval culture 71
    New institutions 81
    Sicut verba sonant: monastic and scholastic versus literal
    dissident reading 85
    Polemics for the Church in crisis 98

3   The Inquisitor's Practice and his Legacy 104
    The texts in the enigmatic collection *Processus Petri* 106
    Waldensians and how to interrogate them 116
    De vita et conversacione 119
    Articuli Waldensium 125
    The remains of Zwicker's manual in Austria 138
    The transformation of the inquisitor's manual 149
    The last revisions and a priest sentenced after a copying
    mistake 164

4   Communicating Faith 171
    Inquisitor as preacher and performer 172
    Citations and public penance 184

Contents

From polemics to pastoral theology: Ulrich von Pottenstein   194
Johlín of Vodňany: preaching and propaganda against
Waldensians in Bohemia   207

5   The Dissidents, the Clergy and the Church   217
    Virgin Mary venerated and denigrated   218
    The clergy devalued, the clergy elevated   225
    The worst priest and the holiest layman   235
    The absence of the Schism   243

Epilogue: The Consolation of Inquisition   257

Appendix 1: Manuscript Descriptions   262

Appendix 2: Chapters and Titles of the *Cum dormirent homines*
according to Jacob Gretser (1613/77)   290

Appendix 3: The Circulation of the *Processus Petri* together with the
Cum dormirent homines   292

Appendix 4: Inquisitors' Manuals of St Florian and Linz   293

Appendix 5: Collation of Formularies in St Florian, MS XI 234 and
Würzburg, UB MS M. ch. f. 51   295

Bibliography   296

Index   328

Illustrations

Table 1. Redactions of the *Refutatio errorum*   43–44

Table 2. The *Refutatio errorum* with the *Processus Petri*   114

Figure 1. Petrus Zwicker wrote some of the protocols himself. The protocol from Katharina Hagen's interrogation (16 March 1394) shows Zwicker's handwriting; the eschatocol is written by an anonymous notary. Herzog August Bibliotek Wolfenbüttel, MS. Guelf. 348 Novi, fol. 37r   137

The author and publishers are grateful to all the institutions and individuals listed for permission to reproduce the materials in which they hold copyright. Every effort has been made to trace the copyright holders; apologies are offered for any omission, and the publishers will be pleased to add any necessary acknowledgement in subsequent editions.

Author's Note

A word on nomenclature. As modern convention demands, I have used primarily local forms of place names, with the exception of major cities with conventional English names, such as Munich, Vienna or Prague. Stettin is an exception. Although recent studies have used the Polish name Szczecin,[1] I use the name Stettin for the simple reason that the German-speaking Hanseatic city of Stettin is a different historical entity from the post-war Polish city. There is no hard and fast rule for naming persons whose careers traversed the multi-lingual Central Europe of the late Middle Ages. For the key characters Petrus Zwicker and Martinus of Prague I have used their Latin first names. Otherwise German personal names, such as Ulrich von Pottenstein, are given in their German form. When the use of a local or Latin form would be confusing, I have anglicized the names, as with William of Auvergne or Matthew of Kraków.[2] For Czech persons I have used local forms, but without attempting to use the Czech genitive: thus we have Jan of Jenštejn (instead of Jan z Jenštejna). The names of deponents, witnesses and other persons known only from trial documents and formularies are given as they are written in the sources, but only one variant of each name is used. In the case of well-known individuals such as Bernard Gui I have used the established forms. My policy has been to translate Latin. I have however left untranslated a few Latin passages where the sole purpose of citation is to help the investigation of authorship and textual dependence.

---

[1] See e.g. G. Modestin, 'The Anti-Waldensian Treatise *Cum dormirent homines*: Historical Context, Polemical Strategy, and Manuscript Tradition', in *Religious Controversy in Europe, 1378–1536*, ed. M. Van Dussen and P. Soukup (Turnhout, 2013), p. 215.

[2] Cf. S. Mossman, *Marquard von Lindau and the Challenges of Religious Life in Late Medieval Germany: The Passion, the Eucharist, the Virgin Mary* (Oxford, 2010), p. v.

Acknowledgements

This book saw its beginning in the research group 'Modus vivendi' of the Department of Cultural History at the University of Turku. I am forever indebted to Marjo Kaartinen, Meri Heinonen, Marika Räsänen and Teemu Immonen, as well as the whole Cultural History faculty and graduate students for their invaluable comments and guidance. At different stages of the research, many brilliant scholars have read and commented on the manuscript or parts of it, or offered their help with the sources. Peter Biller is not only the ultimate expert one could hope for this book, but also the most generous, kind and helpful person, and this book would not be here without him inexhaustibly ushering it towards its goal. He and John H. Arnold form a wonderful, helpful and lightning-quick editorial team in all matters heretical. In addition, special gratitude is owed to Jennifer K. Deane, Étienne Doublier, Jochen Johrendt, Richard Kieckhefer, Adam Poznański, Miri Rubin, Lucy Sackville, Hannu Salmi, Kirsi Salonen, Peter Segl, Sita Steckel, Pekka Tolonen, Werner Williams-Krapp and David Zbíral. I also wish to thank Caroline Palmer at Boydell & Brewer for being a very patient and understanding editor. I have the warmest memories of my research periods abroad, at the Finnish Institute in Rome and at the Bergische Universität Wuppertal. The personnel at the manuscript departments of the libraries housing Zwicker's manuscript have always been most helpful and promptly provided all materials I have asked for.

This book would not have been possible without financial support from various institutions: the Finnish Doctoral Programme of History, the Academy of Finland project 'Modus Vivendi', TUCEMEMS, Villa Lanten Ystävät ry and Turku University Foundation.

Throughout the years, my friends and family have stoically borne the presence of Petrus Zwicker in our conversations. Finally, the largest debt of gratitude is owed to my wife Henna Ylänen, who is forever my equal partner and companion, my best friend and greatest love. She has borne the heaviest burden of this book, especially as the final stages were completed after our daughter Aune was born and completely changed our life – so much for the better.

List of Abbreviations

BAV   Vatican City, Biblioteca Apostolica Vaticana.

Biller, 'Aspects'   P. Biller, 'Aspects of the Waldenses in the
                             fourteenth Century, Including an Edition of their
                             Correspondence' (unpublished Ph.D. dissertation,
                             University of Oxford, 1974).

Biller, *Waldenses*   P. Biller, *The Waldenses, 1170–1530: Between a Religious
                             Order and a Church*, Variorum CS 676 (Aldershot,
                             2001).

Bivolarov,   V. Bivolarov, *Inquisitoren-Handbücher. Papsturkunden*
  Inquisitoren-   *und juristische Gutachten aus dem 13. Jahrhundert*
  Handbücher   *mit Edition des Consilium von Guido Fulcodii*, MGH
                             Studien und Texte 56 (Wiesbaden, 2014).

BSB   Munich, Bayerische Staatsbibliothek.

BSSV   *Bollettino della Società di Studi Valdesi – Bulletin de la*
                             Société d'Histoire Vaudoise.

Cameron, *Waldenses*   E. Cameron, *Waldenses: Rejections of Holy Church in*
                             Medieval Europe (Oxford, 2000).

DA   *Deutsches Archiv für Erforschung des Mittelalters.*

Döllinger, *Beiträge II*   J. J. I. von Döllinger, *Beiträge zur Sektengeschichte des*
                             Mittelalters. Zweiter theil. Dokumente vornehmlich zur
                             Geschichte der Valdesier und Katharer (Munich, 1890).

FRB   *Fontes Rerum Bohemicarum.*

Gerson, *Œuvres*   Jean Gerson, *Œuvres complètes*, ed. P. Glorieux, 10
  complètes   vols. (Paris, 1960–73).

HAAB   Weimar, Herzogin Anna Amalia Bibliothek.

HAB   Wolfenbüttel, Herzog August Bibliothek.

Halm, *Catalogus*   K. Halm, G. Von Laubmann, and W. Meyers.
  codicum   *Catalogus codicum latinorum.* Catalogus codicum
                             manuscriptorum Bibliothecae Regiae Monacensis,
                             vols. III.1–3 and IV.1–4 (vols. III.1–2, 2nd edn)
                             (Munich, 1873–94).

JEH   *Journal of Ecclesiastical History.*

Kieckhefer,   R. Kieckhefer, *Repression of Heresy in Medieval*
  Repression   *Germany* (Liverpool, 1979).

KMK	Prague, Knihovna Metropolitní kapituly (the Metropolitan Chapter Library). Now part of the Presidential archives (Archiv Kanceláře prezidenta republiky).
Kurze, 'Zur Ketzergeschichte'	D. Kurze, 'Zur Ketzergeschichte der Mark Brandenburg und Pommerns vornehmlich im 14. Jahrhundert: Luziferianer, Putzkeller und Waldenser', *Jahrbuch für die Geschichte Mittel- und Ostdeutschlands* 16/17 (1968), pp. 50–94.
LLT-A; LLT-B	Library of Latin Texts – Series A & Series B; Brepolis, Brepols Publishers, <http://clt.brepolis.net/llta/Default.aspx>.
Martin von Amberg, *Gewissensspiegel*	Martin von Amberg, *Der Gewissensspiegel*, ed. S. N. Werbow (Berlin, 1958).
Matěj of Janov, *Regulae*	*Mathiae de Janov dicti Magister Parisiensis Regulae veteris et novi testamenti*, ed. V. Kybal, 5 vols. (Prague, 1907–26).
MGH	Monumenta Germaniae Historica.
Modestin, *Ketzer in der Stadt*	G. Modestin, *Ketzer in der Stadt: der Prozess gegen die Straßburger Waldenser von 1400*, MGH Studien und Texte 41 (Hanover, 2007).
Moneta, *Adversus Catharos et Valdenses*	Moneta (Cremonensis), *Monetae Adversus Catharos et Valdenses: libri quinque*, ed. T. A. Ricchini (Rome, 1743).
Neumann, 'Výbor'	A. A. Neumann, 'Výbor z předhusitských postil', *Archiv literární* 2 (1922), 60–75, 94–102, 121–43, 184–9, 216–22, 233–40, 250–5, 287–90, 319–26, 356–60, 366–76.
NKCR	Národní knihovna České republiky (National Library of the Czech Republic).
NLM	*Neues Lausitzisches Magazin.*
OÖLA	Linz, Oberösterreichisches Landesarchiv.
OÖLB	Linz, Oberösterreichische Landesbibliothek.
ÖNB	Vienna, Österreichische Nationalbibliothek.
PAN	Polska Akademia Nauk Biblioteka.
Parmeggiani, *Consilia*	R. Parmeggiani, *I consilia procedurali per l'Inquisizione medievale (1235–1330)* (Bologna, 2011).

Parmeggiani, *Explicatio*	R. Parmeggiani, *Explicatio super officio inquisitionis: origini e sviluppi della manualistica inquisitoriale tra Due e Trecento* (Rome, 2012).
Patschovsky, *Anfänge*	A. Patschovsky, *Die Anfänge einer ständigen Inquisition in Böhmen. Ein Prager Inquisitoren-Handbuch aus der ersten Hälfte des 14. Jahrhunderts*, Beiträge zur Geschichte und Quellenkunde des Mittelalters 3 (Berlin, 1975).
Peter von Pillichsdorf, *Fragmentum ex Tractatu*	'Fragmentvm ex Tractatv Petri de Pilichdorff contra pauperes de Lugduno. Ex M.S.C. Monasterij Tegernseensi', in *Lucae Tvdensis episcopi, Scriptores aliqvot svccedanei contra sectam waldensivm*, ed. J. Gretser, in *Maxima bibliotheca veterum patrum et antiquorum scriptorum ecclesiasticorum*, ed. M. de La Bigne, 27 vols (Lyon, 1677), XXV, 299E–302F.
PL	*Patrologia Latina, Patrologiae: cursus completus series Latina*, ed. J.-P. Migne, 221 vols. (Paris, 1844–64). *Corpus Corporum repositorum operum Latinorum apud universitatem Turicensem*. University of Zürich, <http://www.mlat.uzh.ch/MLS/index.php?lang=0>.
Quellen, ed. Kurze	*Quellen zur Ketzergeschichte Brandenburgs und Pommerns*, ed. D. Kurze (Berlin, 1975).
Quellen, ed. Modestin	*Quellen zur Geschichte der Waldenser von Straßburg (1400–1401)*, ed. G. Modestin, MGH Quellen zur Geistesgeschichte des Mittelalters 22 (Hanover, 2007).
Quellen, ed. Patschovsky	*Quellen zur böhmischen Inquisition im 14. Jahrhundert*, ed. A. Patschovsky, MGH Quellen zur Geistesgeschichte des Mittelalters 11 (Weimar, 1979).
Quellen, ed. Patschovsky and Selge	*Quellen zur Geschichte der Waldenser*, ed. A. Patschovsky and K.-V. Selge (Gütersloh, 1973).
Quellen, ed. Utz Tremp	*Quellen zur Geschichte der Waldenser von Freiburg im Üchtland (1399–1439)*, ed. K. Utz Tremp, MGH Quellen zur Geistesgeschichte des Mittelalters 18 (Hanover, 2000).

Refutatio, ed. Gretser	'Refvtatio Errorvm, Quibus Waldenses distinentur, incerto auctore', in *Lucae Tvdensis episcopi, Scriptores aliqvot svccedanei contra sectam waldensivm*, ed J. Gretser in *Maxima bibliotheca veterum patrum et antiquorum scriptorum ecclesiasticorum*, ed. M. de La Bigne, 27 vols (Lyon, 1677), XXVI, 302G–307F.
Schmidt, 'Actenstücke'	C. Schmidt, 'Actenstücke besonders zur Geschichte der Waldenser', *Zeitschrift für die historische Theologie* 22 (1852), 238–62.
Scriptores contra sectam waldensium, ed. Gretser	*Lucae Tvdensis episcopi, Scriptores aliqvot svccedanei contra sectam waldensivm*, ed J. Gretser, in *Maxima bibliotheca veterum patrum et antiquorum scriptorum ecclesiasticorum*, ed. M. de La Bigne, 27 vols (Lyon, 1677), XXVI, 252–312.
TIF	*Thesaurus Iuris Franconici Oder Sammlung theils gedruckter theils ungedruckter Abhandlungen, Dissertationen, Programmen, Gutachten, Gesätze, Urkunden etc. etc., welche das Fränkische und besonders Hochfürstlich-Wirzburgische Geistliche, Weltliche, Bürgerliche, Peinliche, Lehen-, Polizey- und Kameralrecht erläutern etc.*, ed. J. M. Schneidt, 12 vols. (Würzburg, 1787–94).
Utz Tremp, *Von der Häresie zur Hexerei*	K. Utz Tremp, *Von der Häresie zur Hexerei: 'wirkliche' und imaginäre Sekten im Spätmittelalter*, MGH Schriften 59 (Hanover, 2008).
Werner, 'Nachrichten'	E. Werner, 'Nachrichten über spätmittelalterliche Ketzer aus tschechoslowakischen Archiven und Bibliotheken', *Wissenschaftliche Zeitschrift der Karl-Marx-Universität Leipzig. Gesellschafts- und sprachwissenschaftliche Reihe* 12 (1963), 215–84.
Zwicker, *Cum dormirent homines*	Zwicker, Petrus, [*Cum dormirent homines*] '[Pseudo]-Petri de Pilichdorf contra Haeresin Waldensium Tractatus', in *Lucae Tvdensis episcopi, Scriptores aliqvot svccedanei contra sectam waldensivm*, ed. J. Gretser, in *Maxima bibliotheca veterum patrum et antiquorum scriptorum ecclesiasticorum*, ed. M. de La Bigne, 27 vols (Lyon, 1677), XXV, 277F–299G.

Introduction

On 13 February 1393, Peter Beyer from Bernwalde, accused of Waldensian heresy, was interrogated by the inquisitor Petrus Zwicker in the Pomeranian town of Stettin. During his detailed deposition Peter Beyer provided a small but revealing detail about how laymen sympathetic to Waldensian beliefs experienced their situation in the 1390s. Beyer was apparently a sort of trustee of the Waldensian Brethren, who as itinerant lay confessors and preachers formed the intellectual and spiritual nucleus of the Waldensian movement. Peter Beyer hosted the Brethren and donated money to them, and also took care of some cash on their behalf. However, some time before his interrogation he had improvised with some of the funds actually intended for the Brethren. Peter Beyer 'had given four marks to the poor – for God – after he had heard that there was disruption among the sectaries'.[1]

The disruption or destruction Beyer referred to was caused by the intensification of proceedings against the Waldensians in German-speaking Europe. After being declared heretics in 1184, mainly because of their disobedience to ordained clergy rather than for doctrinal divergence, the Waldensians had been persecuted to a greater or lesser degree throughout the High Middle Ages. Over the years the Waldensian groups had developed into a distinct religious movement, characterized by lay preaching and confession, literal imitation of apostolic life and disapproval of clerical hierarchy and the Church's material possessions.[2] Until the late fourteenth century the Waldensians had enjoyed a relative lack of attention and persecution in many

---

[1] '4, postquam audiverit, disturbacionem fieri inter sectarios, dederit pauperibus propter deum'; *Quellen*, ed. Kurze, p. 172. On the financial arrangements of the Waldensians, see Biller, *Waldenses*, ch. VII.

[2] For overviews of medieval Waldensianism, see Cameron, *Waldenses*; G. Audisio, *The Waldensian Dissent: Persecution and Survival, c. 1170–c. 1570* (Cambridge, 1999); J. Gonnet and A. Molnár, *Les Vaudois au Moyen Âge* (Turin, 1974). Various aspects of medieval Waldensians' lifestyle and doctrine are covered in the collection of articles, Biller, *Waldenses*. The forthcoming Brill *Companion to the Waldenses*, ed. M. Benedetti and E. Cameron, will include several chapters on medieval Waldensianism.

German regions, but this came to an end with the inception of an unprecedented series of inquisitions and other proceedings against them.[3]

The persecution had devastating effects on the Waldensian communities, and it also reshaped how heresy was perceived, refuted and repressed. Previous studies have demonstrated that the *inquisitio heretice pravitatis* (inquisition of heretical wickedness) was not a static power structure controlling deviance in medieval Christendom.[4] It was a reflective discourse, a changing set of laws and rules, practices and instructions, technologies of speech, theology and bureaucracy. In addition, the self-understanding of its representatives, the inquisitors, developed over time. Christine Caldwell Ames has studied how churchmen – and particularly Dominicans – came to understand the inquisition as a pious enterprise, as a fulfilment of Christ's promise to bring a sword. She has shown how this understanding was forged not as arid academic theology but through negotiation by men who were themselves conducting very real repression, or were at least personally connected to those who were persecutors of dissidence.[5] Some years before Ames, John H. Arnold had already demonstrated how over the course of the late thirteenth and early fourteenth centuries the focus of the interrogations in the southern French inquisitions shifted from actions that proved deponents' heresy, such as donating money or adoring a heretic, to an emphasis on individuals' faith and confession about themselves and their personal transgressions.[6]

---

[3] For an overview of the persecution of German Waldensians at the end of the fourteenth century, see Modestin, *Ketzer in der Stadt*, pp. 1–12; J. M. Kolpacoff, 'Papal Schism, Archiepiscopal Politics and Waldensian Persecution (1378–1396): The Ecclesio-Political Landscape of Late Fourteenth-Century Mainz' (unpublished Ph.D. dissertation, Northwestern University, 2000), pp. 247–61. Kieckhefer, *Repression*, pp. 53–73, is a classic but now outdated. See also a recent but unpublished dissertation: E. Smelyansky, 'Self-Styled Inquisitors: Heresy, Mobility, and Anti-Waldensian Persecutions in Germany, 1390–1404' (unpublished Ph.D. dissertation, University of California, Irvine, 2015).

[4] On criticism of the concept of the medieval inquisition as an institution or judicial body, see especially Kieckhefer, *Repression*, pp. 3–10; E. Peters, *Inquisition* (New York, 1988), pp. 67–71; R. Kieckhefer, 'The Office of Inquisition and Medieval Heresy: The Transaction from Personal to Institutional Jurisdiction', *JEH* 46 (1995), 36–61. H. A. Kelly has pointed out that it is a common misconception that the judicial process *inquisitio* was developed especially to prosecute heresy, or that it was especially fitting for it; see H. A. Kelly, 'Inquisition and the Prosecution of Heresy: Misconceptions and Abuses', *Church History* 58 (1989), 439–51; H. A. Kelly, 'Inquisitorial Due Process and the Status of Secret Crimes', in *Inquisitions and Other Trial Procedures in the Medieval West* (Aldershot, 2001), pp. 407–27.

[5] C. C. Ames, *Righteous Persecution: Inquisition, Dominicans, and Christianity in the Middle Ages* (Philadelphia, 2009), pp. 3–5 and passim.

[6] J. H. Arnold, *Inquisition and Power: Catharism and the Confessing Subject in Medieval Languedoc* (Philadelphia, 2001), pp. 98–107; J. H. Arnold, 'Inquisition, Texts and Discourse', in *Texts and the Repression of Medieval Heresy*, ed. C. Bruschi and P. Biller (York, 2003), pp. 63–80.

This book explores how inquisition into heresy was once again reshaped in a very particular setting: the repression and conversion of the Waldensian heresy in German-speaking Europe at the turn of the fifteenth century. It reveals the ways in which the manuals, formularies and polemical treatises of inquisitors of heresy from the previous century and half were deployed and revised. It also looks at the effects of this process, how it redefined both heretics and good Christians in late medieval Europe. This process featured the application of old tools in a new setting as well as genuine innovations, and the phenomenon was characteristically both pastoral and doctrinal.

The central figure in this process was the Celestine provincial Petrus Zwicker, and it is around his career and literary works that this study has been structured. Zwicker took up the office of inquisitor of heresy in several German dioceses between 1391 and 1404, interrogating and converting hundreds, probably thousands of Waldensians. In 1395 he composed a thorough polemical treatise against the Waldensian heresy, known as the *Cum dormirent homines*, 'When men were asleep'. Through his extensive inquisitions Zwicker was one of the main forces in the persecution of German Waldensians in the 1390s,[7] and his treatise, which is still extant in approximately fifty manuscript copies, is undoubtedly the most influential and important late medieval text on the Waldensian heresy.[8]

Like so many medieval agents and writers, however, Zwicker should be understood as inseparable from his inquisitorial *familia* (household): co-inquisitors, notaries, commissaries and servants. Caterina Bruschi has warned us not to forget the importance of the inquisitors' *familia*, who did much of the background work, even if it is the person of the inquisitor that fascinates us.[9] Her warning is applicable to Zwicker and his entourage. For example, during his career Zwicker cooperated and interacted with another important inquisitor of heresy, Martinus of Amberg (or Prague),[10] to such a

---

[7] Kieckhefer, *Repression*, pp. 55–6; Kurze, 'Zur Ketzergeschichte', pp. 69–70; Cameron, *Waldenses*, pp. 139–40; G. Modestin, 'Peter Zwicker (gest. nach dem 7. Juni 1404)', in *Schlesische Lebensbilder* 10, ed. F. Andreae (Breslau, 2010), pp. 25–34; Modestin, *Ketzer in der Stadt*, p. 3; Utz Tremp, *Von der Häresie zur Hexerei*, p. 141.

[8] Biller, *Waldenses*, p. 237; G. Modestin, 'The Anti-Waldensian Treatise *Cum dormirent homines*: Historical Context, Polemical Strategy, and Manuscript Tradition', in *Religious Controversy in Europe, 1378–1536*, ed. M. Van Dussen and P. Soukup (Turnhout, 2013), pp. 211–29 (p. 211).

[9] C. Bruschi, '*Familia inquisitionis*: A Study on the Inquisitors' Entourage (XIII–XIV Centuries)', *Mélanges de l'École française de Rome – Moyen Âge* 125 (2013). Bruschi has studied French and Italian papal inquisitors, who could have dozens of *familiares*, resources that far exceed those Zwicker or other contemporary German inquisitors had at their disposal. Nevertheless, her general remark about the importance of the *familia* applies.

[10] Although S. Werbow, the editor of Martin von Amberg's German penitential manual *Der Gewissensspiegel*, was cautious about identifying the author with the inquisitor Martinus, they are generally considered to be one and the same person.

degree that it is impossible to distinguish who first composed certain pieces in the compilation of inquisitorial formulas transmitted under Petrus Zwicker's authorship.[11] In Stettin Zwicker was assisted by Nikolaus von Wartenberch, a Celestine monk described as his sub-delegate, and at least two public notaries, as well as the lay servants Paulus de Ens and Peter de Tuntorp.[12] In the diocese of Passau Zwicker worked with his commissary Fridericus, a monk at Garsten and parish priest of Steyr, as well as a notary, Stephanus Lamp, who later became an inquisitor of heresy himself. These local associates very probably participated in compiling texts on heresy and assisted in the dissemination of Zwicker's works. As these works spread, the circle of actors that must be taken into account also increases to include copyists, compilers and translators and others who adapted his texts. The most important of these were the Austrian canon and writer of pastoral theology, Ulrich von Pottenstein, who translated Zwicker's treatise into German vernacular, as well as Johlín of Vodňany, a priest who preached against the Waldensians in early fifteenth-century Prague. Rather than looking only at Zwicker, I shall investigate the ways in which a whole group of people – Zwicker and the circle of other actors around him or influenced by him – reshaped the battle against dissent, and in so doing brought Waldensian heresy onto the public stage and gave it a prominent role in the religious-political debates of the later Middle Ages.

The circumstances in which Zwicker and his colleagues and companions operated were extraordinary and they produced an equally extraordinary response. The circumstances included: inside information provided through the conversion of leading members of the Waldensian movement, amounting to a remarkable breakthrough in knowledge; the febrile and polemical spiritual atmosphere of the Great Western Schism (1378–1417); the nascent reform movement; religious controversies in Prague; and the rise of new normative theological literature with a pastoral emphasis. Out of the coincidence, collision and coalescence of all these things there emerged a new definition and understanding of heresy and inquisition. Waldensian heresy came to be seen as a set of errors that attacked virtually every aspect of late medieval Catholic Christianity, errors that could be refuted through theological polemic and minute inquiry into individual heretics, their instruction and conversion.

See S. N. Werbow, 'Einleitung', in *Der Gewissensspiegel*, ed. S. N. Werbow (Berlin, 1958), pp. 9–31 (p. 12); S. N. Werbow, 'Martin von Amberg', in *Verfasserlexikon* 6, pp. 143–50; R. E. Lerner, *The Heresy of the Free Spirit in the Later Middle Ages* (Berkeley, 1972), p. 101; A. Patschovsky, 'Straßburger Beginenverfolkungen im 14. Jahrhundert', *DA* 30 (1974), 56–198 (p. 91); Kieckhefer, *Repression*, p. 133, n. 13.

[11] On this so-called *Processus Petri* collection, see Chapter 3.

[12] See *Quellen*, ed. Kurze, pp. 235, 250, 257, and the discussion in Kurze, 'Zur Ketzergeschichte', pp. 72–4. On the notaries, see D. Kurze, 'Bemerkungen zu einzelnen Autoren und Quellen', in *Quellen*, ed. Kurze, pp. 12–56 (pp. 23–5).

This view acquired literary expression in Petrus Zwicker's polemical writing in the 1390s. The first to be on the receiving end of the stick were the Waldensian communities scattered around Central Europe, as the inquisitors – above all Petrus Zwicker and Martinus of Prague, men equipped with extensive and precise descriptions of heresy and equally detailed inter-rogatories – inquired into the beliefs of laymen with a depth and attention to minute particulars that were unprecedented in the Empire. Then there were further effects and ramifications, as the anti-heretical messages of Zwicker's treatises and the shorter texts produced in the course of the persecution were translated, rearranged and preached at the turn of the fifteenth century. Waldensian heresy became a tool to discern, label and blacken other radical and critical movements and persons, above all those attacking the clergy.

The structure of the book is as follows. It does not follow a strict chronological path, because the processes it deals with were simultaneous, overlapping and recurrent, and as a consequence it has to zig-zag back and forth between *c.* 1380 and 1410. Chapter 1 discusses Petrus Zwicker's life and career, and provides an outline of the persecution. Chapter 2 concen-trates on polemical writing, above all how Zwicker revived and at the same time revolutionized the type of polemics that had prevailed in the thirteenth century, doing this in the light of the late fourteenth-century emphasis on the authority of the Scriptures. Chapter 3 explores how Petrus Zwicker and Martinus of Prague reformed the mode of interrogation, and at the same time inquisitorial manuals. Chapter 4 turns to the public dissemination of the anti-heretical message, first through the inquisitors' own actions and then in translations and sermons carried out and delivered by others. Finally, Chapter 5 describes how the revised perception of Waldensianism was used to survey and label dissident beliefs and the grey area between heresy and orthodoxy, and how repression of heresy functioned as a way of handling the trauma caused by the Great Schism.

As a whole, this study maps out a remarkable development which is most easily grasped through use of the phrase 'the pastoralization of heresy'. This was a process whereby Catholic perception of the Waldensian heresy and responses to the problems posed by the existence of heretics were redefined at the turn of the fifteenth century. It was manifested in the polemical treatises, judicial proceedings, inquisitorial formulas and questionnaires, sermons, and the condemnations, penances and absolutions written and performed in German-speaking Europe during this period. In addition to being an object of canon-legal inquiry, Waldensian heresy increasingly came to be perceived and treated as a pastoral problem. As much as in the courtroom, the battle-field against heresy was in the preacher's pulpit, at the writer's desk or at the altar of the church. Heretics could and should be converted. Priests should be better informed and prepared. And laymen should be warned against the danger of heresy, so that the enemy of faith would not triumph 'while good Christians were asleep', *cum dormirent homines*.

Pastoralization happened in three forums, each dealt with in Chapters 2–5 below. In the anti-heretical polemics written by Petrus Zwicker, pastoralization manifested itself through the revival of the doctrinal and debating polemical style of the early and mid-thirteenth century,[13] but in an updated form that engaged with contemporary questions of authority and biblical interpretation. In the inquisitions of heresy it meant a shift from action-oriented, legal inquiry towards penitential confessions of the deponents' beliefs and correction of their transgressions. This is similar to the development John H. Arnold, and more recently Irene Bueno, have identified as happening in the southern French inquisitions by the early fourteenth century,[14] but I argue that in German-Bohemian inquisitions the change happened later. Though Petrus Zwicker and Martinus of Prague were crucial in this, similar tendencies are visible in inquiries carried out by others. Finally, pastoralization meant a spillover of the anti-heretical message from inquisitors' texts and polemical treatises into pastoral theological genres: catechetic treatise and postil. Each of these phenomena had its own chronology and history, and none of them on their own would justify the claim that is being made here about 'pastoralization'. But their interaction, overlapping and mutual reinforcement does, and the consequent transformation of how heresy was perceived and treated – its pastoralization – make late medieval Germany a time and place of extraordinary significance in the history of medieval heresy.

Pointing out such a development implies that there was a preceding period when heresy was not seen primarily as pastoral or doctrinal problem. I see this as having happened in the shift from persuasion, public debate and polemical intellectual engagement between Catholics and dissidents to violent coercion that first occurred in the Albigensian Crusade (1209–29), and then to legal inquiry as the judicial procedure of inquisition was implemented through heresy trials and the apparatus of penances and punishments was set in place.[15] The will to persuade and convert heretics never disappeared, of course, and inquisitors almost always preferred a penitent convert to an obstinate martyr. Nevertheless, heretics and their punishment were increasingly seen through the legal and theoretical framework created for and by the

---

[13] L. J. Sackville, *Heresy and Heretics in the Thirteenth Century: The Textual Representations* (York, 2011), pp. 13–40.

[14] Arnold, *Inquisition and Power*, pp. 98–107; I. Bueno, *Defining Heresy: Inquisition, Theology, and Papal Policy in the Time of Jacques Fournier*, trans. I. Bolognese, T. Brophy and S. Rolfe Prodan (Leiden, 2015), pp. 104–18.

[15] Cf. J. K. Deane, *A History of Medieval Heresy and Inquisition* (Lanham, 2011), pp. 30, 53, 90, 101, 111. On the first stages of inquisition of heresy, see the collection of articles *Die Anfänge der Inquisition im Mittelalter. Mit einem Ausblick auf das 20. Jahrhundert und einem Beitrag über religiöse Intoleranz im nichtchristlichen Bereich*, ed. P. Segl (Cologne, 1993); W. Trusen, 'Der Inquisitionsprozess. Seine historischen Grundlagen und frühen Formen', *Zeitschrift der Savigny-Stiftung für Rechtsgeschichte. Kanonistische Abteilung* 105 (1988), 168–230.

inquisitors of heresy. The heretics were dealt with predominantly in judicial terms, with reliance on an ever-increasing body of legislation and procedural commentaries for inquisitors of heresy.[16]

In addition to legal guidelines, this inquisitorial framework gradually standardized the assessment of what it meant to be involved in heresy, including thereafter not only the public advocates of heresy but also its supporters and sympathizers. This went side by side with the corresponding penitential and punitive measures, such as public and private penance, imprisonment and the confiscation of property. Inquisitors, partly restrained by the requirements of the legal process, increasingly employed concrete action against the suspected heretic instead of engaging in detailed discussion of matters of faith.[17]

There were also changes within anti-heretical literature: polemical treatises gave way to systematic and technical inquisitors' manuals. The great majority of the polemical treatises discussing heresy from a learned and doctrinal perspective originate from the turn of the twelfth and thirteenth centuries and from northern Italy between 1230 and 1250. After that the disputational style becomes rarer and the descriptions of heresy and its refutation are incorporated into manuals or compilations, the most important in German-speaking Europe being the large composite work by the so-called Anonymous of Passau, written in the 1260s.[18] Sometimes descriptions of heresy were incorporated into general theological works, such as Martinus of Krems's (d. 1338) *Expositio misse*. Nevertheless, Paul Ubl is forced to sum up his survey of refutations of heresy by Austrian theologians in the thirteenth and early

---

[16] The emergence, growth and organization of canon law on heresy, its commentaries and legal consultations and their compilation in inquisitors' manuals in the thirteenth and early fourteenth century have been covered in several recent and thorough studies. See Bivolarov, *Inquisitoren-Handbücher*; Parmeggiani, *Explicatio*; Parmeggiani, *Consilia*; R. Parmeggiani, 'La manualistica inquisitoriale (1230–1330): alcuni percorsi di lettura', *Quaderni del Mediae Aetatis Sodalicium* 6 (2003), 7–25; L. Paolini, 'Inquisizioni medievali: il modello italiano nella manualistica inquisitoriale (XIII–XIV secolo)', in *Negotium Fidei. Miscellanea di studi offerti a Mariano d'Alatri in occasione del suo 80 compleanno*, ed. P. Maranesi (Rome, 2002), pp. 177–98. On secular law and heresy, see S. Ragg, *Ketzer und Recht: die weltliche Ketzergesetzgebung des Hochmittelalters unter dem Einfluss des römischen und kanonischen Rechts* (Hanover, 2006).

[17] Arnold, *Inquisition and Power*, p. 19–47 and passim; see also T. Lentes and T. Scharff, 'Schriftlichkeit und Disziplinierung. Die Beispiele Inquisition und Frömmigkeit', *Frühmittelalterliche Studien* 31 (1997), 233–52 (p. 249).

[18] Sackville, *Heresy and Heretics*, pp. 13–14, 39–40, 138; *Heresies of the High Middle Ages*, ed. W. L. Wakefield and A. P. Evans (New York, 1991), pp. 59–62, 633–8; A. Patschovsky, *Der Passauer Anonymus: ein Sammelwerk über Ketzer, Juden, Antichrist aus der Mitte des 13. Jahrhunderts*, MGH Schriften 22 (Stuttgart, 1968); M. Nickson, 'The "Pseudo-Reinerius" Treatise, the Final Stage of a Thirteenth-Century Work on Heresy from the Diocese of Passau', *Archives d'histoire doctrinale et littéraire du moyen âge* 42 (1967), 255–314.

fourteenth century by concluding that all in all heresy appears very seldom in their theological texts, despite the reputation of Austria as a hotbed of heresy – until Zwicker's treatise changes the situation.[19] It seems therefore that although many of the polemical authors of the mid-thirteenth century, such as the Dominicans Moneta of Cremona and Peter of Verona, were also inquisitors,[20] the establishment of inquisition in fact brought an end to the debating and disputational polemical treatise – until the late fourteenth-century invigoration of anti-Waldensian polemic in Germany.

The timing was not accidental. The reinvention of a particular polemical style was connected to the atmosphere of crisis and reform in the period of the Great Western Schism. The battle against heresy was a reaction to the insecurity created by the division of Christendom, and the texts written against Waldensians formed one aspect of fundamental debates about authority, Church and salvation. The refutation of an established heresy offered an arena for reflection on issues such as the dignity of the priesthood and the Scriptures as the basis of Catholic cult. The office of inquisitor with its related preaching and the performance of public penance made it possible to disseminate these reflections to the level of parish churches and individual believers.

The doctrinal and pastoral emphasis in Zwicker's texts toned down anti-heretical rhetoric: heretics were no longer accused, for example, of worshipping Lucifer and having sex orgies, a common suggestion in many fourteenth-century texts, as also in some later French and Italian trials.[21]

---

[19] K. Ubl, 'Die Österreichischen Ketzer aus der Sicht zeitgenössischer Theologen', in *Handschriften, Historiographie und Recht: Winfried Stelzer zum 60. Geburtstag*, ed. W. Stelzer and G. Pfeifer (Munich, 2002), pp. 190–224 (pp. 210–20).

[20] Sackville, *Heresy and Heretics*, pp. 14, 17; cf. P. Biller, 'Moneta's Confutation of Heresies and the Valdenses', *BSSV* 219 (2016), 27–42 (p. 29); Biller points out that information about Moneta as inquisitor is late and anecdotal. In a later article Sackville mentions Moneta's participation in the early years of the Dominican inquisition in Lombardy, but stresses that at the time preaching and debate characterized anti-heretical activity in northern Italy: see L. J. Sackville, 'The Textbook Heretic: Moneta of Cremona's Cathars', in *Cathars in Question*, ed. A. Sennis (York, 2016), pp. 185–207 (pp. 223–4).

[21] Kurze, 'Zur Ketzergeschichte', pp. 52–66; A. Patschovsky, 'Waldenserverfolgung in Schweidnitz 1315', *DA* 36 (1980), 137–76; A. Patschovsky, 'Der Ketzer als Teufelsdiener', in *Papsttum, Kirche und Recht im Mittelalter. Festschrift für Horst Fuhrmann zum 65. Geuburtstag*, ed. H. Mordek (Tübingen, 1991), pp. 317–34; N. Cohn, *Europe's Inner Demons: The Demonization of Christians in Medieval Christendom* (London, 2000), pp. 51–61; P. Biller, 'Why no Food? Waldensian Followers in Bernard Gui's *Practica inquisitionis* and *culpe*', in *Texts and the Repression of Medieval Heresy*, ed. C. Bruschi and P. Biller (York, 2003), pp. 127–46 (pp. 143–4); P. Biller, 'Bernard Gui, Sex and Luciferanism', in *Praedicatores, inquisitores I. The Dominicans and the Medieval Inquisition. Acts of the 1st International Seminar on the Dominicans and the Inquisition, 23–25 February 2002*, ed. A. B. Palacios (Rome, 2004), pp. 455–70; Utz Tremp, *Von der Häresie zur Hexerei*, pp. 275–353.

However, this did not mean greater tolerance – this dilution of heresy into problems such as anticlericalism or denying the validity of indulgences and papal power had the potential to bring more people under the scrutiny of the inquisitors.

Even more importantly, the representation of the Waldensian heresy as a complete, coherent sect opposing nearly every aspect of the Catholic faith served to strengthen the Church, which by the end of the fourteenth century was being criticised even by its loyal sons. For example, in the mid-1390s, when Zwicker was putting all his effort into defending the legitimacy of indulgences, another perfectly orthodox cleric, the Dominican master Heinrich von Bitterfeld, was preaching in Prague against the sumptuous indulgences granted by the Roman pontiff Boniface IX.[22] In this time of crisis the Waldensian heresy functioned as a necessary adversary of and counterpart to the Catholic Church; exhaustive and minutely detailed refutation of Waldensian doctrine was an opportunity to parade the fundamental orthodoxy of the Catholic faith, which remained incorruptible even if some representatives of the Church at times failed to live up to the ideal. The texts demonstrating that criticism of (for example) indulgences or sacramentals was Waldensian and therefore heretical and corrupt functioned at the same time to stabilise and reinforce the holiness of these Catholic practices, which were at times doubted by far larger groups of believers than those sympathetic to the Waldensians.

Earlier research

Although less well-known outside specialist circles than the battle against the Cathars in southern France, the series of trials of German Waldensians at the turn of the fifteenth century belongs to the major episodes of repression of dissidents in the Middle Ages. The foundations of scholarship on this subject were laid in the studies and publications of sources by late nineteenth-century German medievalists.[23] In the 1960s and 70s several studies on sources of

---

[22] F. Machilek, 'Beweggründe, Inhalte und Probleme kirchlicher Reformen des 14./15. Jahrhunderts (mit besonderer Berücksichtigung der Verhältnisse im östlichen Mitteleuropa)', in *Kirchliche Reformimpulse des 14./15. Jahrhunderts in Ostmitteleuropa*, ed. W. Eberhard and F. Machilek (Cologne, 2006), pp. 1–121 (p. 45); V. J. Koudelka, 'Heinrich von Bitterfeld OP (†. *c.* 1405), Professor an der Universität Prag', *Archivum Fratrum Praedicatorum* 23 (1953), 5–65 (pp. 12, 44–8).

[23] Especially W. Wattenbach, 'Über Ketzergeschichte in Pommern und der Mark Brandenburg', *Sitzungsberichte der Preussichen Akademie der Wissenschaften, philos.-histor. Klasse* 1 (1886), 47–58; H. Haupt, 'Ein Beghardenprozess in Eichstädt vom Jahre 1381', *Zeitschrift für Kirchengeschichte* 5 (1882), 487–98; H. Haupt, *Der Waldensische Ursprung des Codex Teplensis* (Würzburg, 1886); H. Haupt, 'Waldenserthum und Inquisition im südöstlichen Deutschland seit der Mitte des 14. Jahrhunderts',

German and Bohemian Waldensians and their persecution were published, the most important being Dietrich Kurze's discovery of additional protocols from the inquisitions in Stettin 1392–4, and the subsequent edition.[24] At the end of the 1970s Richard Kieckhefer finished his influential overview, the *Repression of Heresy in Medieval Germany*.[25]

Peter Biller's dissertation from 1974 not only treated its actual topic, the correspondence between the converted Austrian Waldensians and the Lombard Brethren, but also established Petrus Zwicker's authorship of the *Cum dormirent homines*.[26] However, many of Biller's results became available, in updated form, to the scholarly community only with the publication of his collected essays in 2001.[27] Biller's conclusions about the sources, manuscript tradition and structure of the *Cum dormirent homines* are fundamental to the topic. Biller also established that Zwicker possessed an extraordinary insight into the Waldensianism of his day, that his treatise is one of central sources on late medieval German Waldensians and, despite its polemical approach, that it informs us about the heretics, not only the views of their persecutors.[28] This book is, however, the first comprehensive study on all the known texts from Zwicker's circle, as well as the underlying principles and guidelines that directed the genesis of these works.

The scholarship of the past two decades has disentangled the outlines of the persecution of Waldensians at the turn of the fifteenth century. The repression of Waldensians in Mainz (1390–3), Fribourg (1399) and Strasbourg (1400) have all received thorough studies with accompanying editions of sources, by Jennifer Kolpacoff Deane,[29] Kathrin Utz Tremp[30] and Georg Modestin[31] respectively. Thorough case studies have established the variety

---

Deutsche Zeitschrift für Geschichtswissenschaft 3 (1890), 337–411; W. Preger, *Beiträge zur Geschichte der Waldesier im Mittelalter* (Munich, 1877); Döllinger, *Beiträge II*.

[24] Kurze, 'Zur Ketzergeschichte'; *Quellen*, ed. Kurze; G. Gonnet, 'I Valdesi d'Austria nella seconda metà del secolo XIV', *BSSV* 111 (1962), 5–41; A. Molnár, 'Les 32 errores Valdensium', *BSSV* 115 (1964), 3–4; A. Molnár, 'Les Vaudois en Bohême avant la Révolution hussite', *BSSV* 116 (1964), 3–17; A. Molnár, 'La Valdensium regula du manuscrit de Prague', *BSSV* 123 (1968), 3–6; Werner, 'Nachrichten'; Patschovsky, *Anfänge*; *Quellen*, ed. Patschovsky.

[25] Kieckhefer, *Repression*.

[26] Biller, 'Aspects'.

[27] Biller, *Waldenses*.

[28] Ibid., ch. XVI.

[29] Kolpacoff, 'Papal Schism'; J. K. Deane, 'Archiepiscopal Inquisitions in the Middle Rhine: Urban Anticlericalism and Waldensianism in Late Fourteenth-Century Mainz', *Catholic Historical Review* 92 (2006), 197–224.

[30] K. Utz Tremp, *Waldenser, Wiedergänger, Hexen und Rebellen. Biographien zu den Waldenserprozessen von Freiburg im Üchtland (1399 und 1430)* (Fribourg, 1999); *Quellen*, ed. Utz Tremp.

[31] Modestin, *Ketzer in der Stadt*; *Quellen*, ed. Modestin.

of motives behind individual trials,[32] and several articles have shed new light on Bohemian pre-Hussite heresy.[33]

There has been a recent revival of interest in Petrus Zwicker. Peter Segl has studied Austrian Waldensians around 1400 based on Zwicker's inquisitions,[34] and Modestin has published both a biographical article and an essay on the *Cum dormirent homines*.[35] In the field of Latin philology Adam Poznański has explored Zwicker's treatise from the point of view of rhetorical theory.[36] There is also a recent but so far unpublished dissertation on the so-called itinerant inquisitors Martinus of Prague, Heinrich Angermeyer and Petrus Zwicker, and their interaction with different authorities.[37] A forthcoming *Companion to the Waldenses* will include a chapter by Peter Biller on Waldensians in Brandenburg and Pomerania, offering an up-to-date overview on the people Zwicker interrogated in 1392–4.[38]

What has been lacking is an exploration of the worldview that lay behind

---

[32] L. Schnurrer, 'Der Fall Hans Wern. Ein spätmittelalterlicher Elitenkonflikt in der Reichstadt Rothenburg ob der Tauber', *Jahrbuch für fränkische Landesforschung* 61 (2001), 9–53; G. Modestin, 'Der Augsburger Waldenserprozess und sein Straßburger Nachspiel (1393–1400)', *Zeitschrift des Historischen Vereins für Schwaben* 103 (2011), 43–68; E. Smelyansky, 'Urban Order and Urban Other: Anti-Waldensian Inquisition in Augsburg, 1393', *German History* 34:1 (2016), pp. 1–20.

[33] I. Hlaváček, 'Zur böhmischen Inquisition und Häresiebekämpfung um das Jahr 1400', in *Häresie und vorzeitige Reformation im Spätmittelalter*, ed. F. Šmahel (Munich, 1998), pp. 109–31; P. Soukup, 'Die Waldenser in Böhmen und Mähren im 14. Jahrhundert', in *Friedrich Reiser und die 'waldensisch-hussitische Internationale' im 15. Jahrhundert*, ed. A. de Lange and K. Utz Tremp (Heidelberg, 2006), pp. 131–60; E. Doležalová, 'The Inquisitions in Medieval Bohemia: National and International Contexts', in *Heresy and the Making of European Culture: Medieval and Modern Perspectives*, ed. A. P. Roach and J. R. Simpson (Aldershot, 2013), pp. 299–311.

[34] P. Segl, 'Die Waldenser in Österreich um 1400: Lehren, Organisationsform, Verbreitung und Bekämpfung', in *Friedrich Reiser und die 'waldensisch-hussitische Internationale' im 15. Jahrhundert*, ed. A. de Lange and K. Utz Tremp (Heidelberg, 2006), pp. 161–88.

[35] Modestin, 'Zwicker'; Modestin, 'The Anti-Waldensian Treatise'.

[36] A. Poznański, 'Traktat Piotra Zwickera Cum dormirent homines – uwagi wstepne', in *Fortunniejszy był język, bo ten i dzis mily*, ed. I. Bogumil and Z. Glombiowska (Gdańsk, 2010), pp. 98–105; A. Poznański, 'Ad retorquendum erroneos articulos: środki retoryczne w późnośredniowiecznych pismach antyheretyckich', in *Kultura pisma w średniowieczu: znane problemy nowe metody*, ed. A. Adamska and P. Kras (Lublin, 2013); A. Poznański, 'Reakcja Kościoła na kryzys ortodoksji w średniowieczu Piotra Zwickera traktat Cum dormirent homines', in *Ecclesia semper reformanda: kryzysy i reformy średniowiecznego Kościoła*, ed. T. Gałuszka, T. Graffand and G. Ryś (Kraków, 2013), pp. 195–210. These are unfortunately available only in Polish, which has prevented their wider reception by the scholarly community.

[37] Smelyansky, 'Self-Styled Inquisitors'. I wish to thank Dr. Eugene Smelyansky for kindly providing access to his work. The chapter treating the trials at Augsburg in 1393 has been published: see Smelyansky, 'Urban Order and Urban Other'.

[38] P. Biller, 'Waldensians by the Baltic', forthcoming in *Companion to the Waldenses*, ed. M. Benedetti and E. Cameron (Leiden, forthcoming).

the persecutions, and that is what is provided in this book. It describes and explains this worldview and its transformation: how the spiritual geography of the late medieval Church, facing schism, crisis and nascent reform, facilitated and we could even say required the persecution of dissidents, and how this persecution in turn rearranged the spiritual geography, where worldly and otherworldly concerns, political motives and spiritual salvation overlapped.[39] This is underpinned by work on and exploitation of little-used or hitherto unknown manuscripts, beginning in the following chapters with the demonstration that Petrus Zwicker was the author of the treatise the *Refutatio errorum* (*Refutation of Errors*) – regarded until now as anonymous – and the redating of Zwicker's inquisitions in Upper Austria.

Sources and how to read them

The sources of this study consist primarily of the materials written for the repression of the Waldensian heresy in German-speaking Europe in the last years of the fourteenth and the first years of the fifteenth century, as well as earlier texts that functioned as their model, sources and inspiration. These are examined in the light of other contemporary works such as general theological and pastoral treatises, sermons and canon law. The form and length of the texts ranges from single sentence remarks in the margins of manuscripts to the catechetic encyclopaedia by Ulrich von Pottenstein, which if ever published would easily fill 2,500 modern pages. Some of the sources, such as the documents from the Strasbourg inquisition in 1400,[40] are available in critical scholarly editions that satisfy the requirements of the most demanding scholar. Others are accessible only in unedited manuscripts, including an important inquisitorial formulary compiled by Zwicker in Upper Austria after 1395,[41] or sentences of inquisition in Regensburg in 1395.[42] Many circulate in early modern or nineteenth- and early twentieth-century printings of varying quality. Often the version in print is neither the closest to the original nor the most widely circulated redaction, as is the case with the treatise *Refutatio errorum* explored below in Chapter 2.

Here, I shall briefly explain the crucial issues in the long reception and edition history of texts Zwicker wrote and used as his sources. The central

---

[39] The term 'spiritual geography' is adopted from Ames, *Righteous Persecution*, pp. 3–5, 13, 145 and passim.

[40] *Quellen*, ed. Modestin.

[41] St Florian, Stift St Florian, MS XI 234, fols. 88ra–90vb.

[42] Vienna, Österreichische Nationalbibliothek, MS 3748, fols. 145r–155v. Kieckhefer provided transcripts of these documents in his dissertation, but never published them. See R. Kieckhefer, 'Repression of Heresy in Germany, 1348–1520' (unpublished Ph.D. dissertation, University of Texas at Austin, 1972), pp. 433–76; he kindly provided a copy when I was finishing this book.

source for the whole study is Zwicker's treatise against Waldensians written in 1395. It is undeniably the most important anti-heretical text of the period – in terms of length and popularity as well as the expertise of its author. The treatise is usually known today as the *Cum dormirent homines*, after its initial quotation from the Gospel of Matthew (13:25). It became one of the most popular anti-heretical treatises of the Middle Ages, with around fifty manuscripts containing Zwicker's *Cum dormirent homines* or parts of it still extant.[43] Because of a mistake by the seventeenth-century editor of the work, Jesuit Jacob Gretser, for over three centuries the *Cum dormirent homines* was attributed to Peter von Pillichsdorf, a Viennese university professor and theologian contemporary with Zwicker. Although the attribution had been doubted since the late nineteenth century,[44] it was Peter Biller who showed in his dissertation (1974) and subsequent publications, through both external and internal evidence, that it was Zwicker, not Pillichsdorf, who wrote the treatise.[45]

There is no modern edition of the text. As Gretser's edition corresponds closely to the main manuscript tradition of the *Cum dormirent homines*, the references are primarily to the most easily accessible printed edition, a reprint of Gretser's edition in the series *Maxima Bibliotheca Veterum Patrum*.[46] When a variation relevant to my analysis occurs, I will refer to the manuscripts in question. The manuscripts produced in Zwicker's lifetime or immediately afterwards have provided the most important reference point, but unfortunately they are all of relatively poor textual quality with obvious scribal mistakes.[47] Descriptions of the manuscripts used in this study are provided in Appendix 1.

There is another treatise, the *Refutatio errorum*, which clearly is a representative of the same era and state of knowledge as the *Cum dormirent homines*, although the text itself does not contain an indication of the date of composition. It was also edited by Gretser,[48] and thus far has mostly been treated as the work of an anonymous author, except by Peter Segl,

---

[43] Most of these manuscripts are listed in Biller, *Waldenses*, pp. 264–9. For an updated description of manuscripts, see Appendix 1.

[44] Preger, *Beiträge*, pp. 188–9; Kurze, 'Bemerkungen zu einzelnen Autoren und Quellen', pp. 31–2; P. Uiblein, 'Die ersten Österreicher als Professoren und der Wiener Theologischen Fakultät (1384–1389)', *Wiener Beiträge zur Theologie* 52 (1976), 85–101 (p. 101, n. 91); P. Burkhart, *Die lateinischen und deutschen Handschriften der Universitäts-Bibliothek Leipzig. Band 2, Die theologischen Handschriften; Teil 1 (MS. 501–625)*, Katalog der Handschriften der Universitätsbibliothek zu Leipzig 5 (Wiesbaden, 1999), p. 252.

[45] Biller, 'Aspects', pp. 354–62; Biller, *Waldenses*, ch. XV.

[46] Zwicker, *Cum dormirent homines*.

[47] Seitenstetten, Stift Seitenstetten, MS 213, fols. 108v–133r; St Florian MS XI 234, fols. 93ra–112rb; Gdańsk, Polska Akademia Nauk Biblioteka, MS Mar. F. 295, fols. 191ra–211ra.

[48] *Refutatio*, ed. Gretser.

who tentatively proposed Zwicker's authorship and encouraged further study on the subject.[49] The text bears many similarities to the *Cum dormirent homines* and they are often preserved in the same manuscripts.[50] The edition by Gretser is incomplete, which has discouraged the study of the *Refutatio*. The printed version has ten chapters, but stops abruptly in the middle of the tenth chapter.[51] The complete text comprises twelve chapters, in four different redactions, and the version that has the most extensive manuscript circulation differs significantly from the printed edition. In Chapter 2 I propose that the similarities in style, contents and composition of the *Refutatio errorum* and the *Cum dormirent homines* are so remarkable that Petrus Zwicker can be confirmed as the author of both texts. Where possible, I follow the same policy as with *Cum dormirent homines* and refer to the printed edition when the quoted texts can be found there. When referring to unedited parts, I use the best available exemplar of each redaction.[52]

The best glimpse into Zwicker's work as inquisitor and his interaction with the interrogated is provided by the protocols of the Stettin inquisition of 1392, now preserved in Herzog August Bibliothek Wolfenbüttel.[53] These protocols have been available since 1975 in a scholarly edition by Dietrich Kurze, although mostly in summarized form. A total of 195 protocols of the more than 450 original ones have been preserved, some of them in fragments.[54] The protocols are a valuable source, since at times they include reflections on the inquisitor's office and the expectations of the intellectual capacities and theological understanding of those accused of heresy. Kurze's decision to edit the protocols selectively, leaving out the inquisitorial formula and often the repeated answers from most of the depositions, has serious shortcomings,[55] and where there is obscurity I have resorted to the manuscripts. The references are primarily to Kurze's edition, and when referring to original protocols both manuscript folio and the corresponding passage in the edition are provided.

Besides the inquisitions of Stettin, none of Petrus Zwicker's depositions or

---

[49] Segl, 'Die Waldenser in Österreich', p. 185, n. 102.

[50] Biller, *Waldenses*, pp. 252–3, 263–9; Biller, 'Aspects', pp. 354–6.

[51] Gretser evidently noticed this, as the end of the text is marked with the words 'Hactenus manuscriptum exemplar' ('The manuscript exemplar [goes up] to this point'); see *Refutatio*, ed. Gretser, p. 307G.

[52] Redaction 1: Gdańsk, PAN MS Mar. F. 295; Redaction 2: Augsburg, Staats- und Stadtbibliothek, MS 2° Cod 185; Redaction 3: Prague, NKCR MS XIII. E. 7; Redaction 4: Augsburg, StaSB, MS 2° Cod 338.

[53] Wolfenbüttel, HAB MS Guelf. 403 Helmst; and MS. Guelf. 348 Novi.

[54] *Quellen*, ed. Kurze, pp. 73–261.

[55] See the contemporary review of the edition by A. Patschovsky, '[Review:] Quellen zur Ketzergeschichte Brandenburgs und Pommerns. Gesammelt, herausgeben und eingeleitet von Dietrich Kurze', *DA* 34 (1978), 589–90; P. Biller, 'Editions of Trials and Lost Texts', in *Valdesi medievali. Bilanci e prospettive di ricerca*, ed. M. Benedetti (Turin, 2009), pp. 23–36 (p. 29).

other original court room documents have been preserved.[56] The information about trials in the diocese of Passau and elsewhere in Austria and Hungary comes from the compilation of documents providing guidelines to the inquisition of the Waldensians. This compilation, or rather group of different compilations, usually included questionnaires (interrogatories), copies of sentences and lists of Waldensian errors. In nineteen manuscripts, the compilation has been copied jointly with the *Cum dormirent homines*, and Peter Biller, from whom I have adopted the name *Processus Petri* (*Peter's Procedures*) for the compilation, used the shared manuscript tradition of the texts as a proof of Zwicker's authorship of the *Cum dormirent homines*.[57] The history of different texts in the compilation and the different versions of the *Processus Petri* will be analysed in Chapter 3. Among other things, I will propose that the manuscript XI 234 from Stift St Florian includes a copy of a manual used by Zwicker or his commissary at the inquisitions in the diocese of Passau in 1390s, and for the first time the contents of this manual will be properly analysed. Parts of the *Processus Petri* have been printed since the seventeenth century, usually based on a single manuscript. References are always to the best generally available edition, singled out in Chapter 3 in relation to each component of the compilation.

As my purpose is to track down changes in inquisitorial practice in texts that were revised, compiled, separated and recompiled, I have chosen a method that stresses the textual history: the Überlieferungsgeschichtliche Methode,[58] practised in German scholarship when analysing the production and distribution of medieval literature as well as the editions of texts. The intent is to make the different historical layers of the text (*Textgeschichte*) clearly visible.[59] Whereas another influential method, new or material philology,[60] is

---

[56] With the possible exception of extant fragments from the inquisition in Trnava, 1400. These small fragments, preserved in a fifteenth-century book binding from Zwicker's home monastery of Oybin, do not allow us to establish whether or not they are from an original trial deposition or later copies. See NKCR, MS VII. A. 16/4. Edited in J. Truhlář, 'Inkvisice Waldenských v Trnavě r. 1400', *Česky časopis historický* 9 (1903), 196–8.

[57] Biller, *Waldenses*, pp. 233, 253–4, 263–9, 271, 286; Biller, 'Aspects', pp. 354–6, 360–1.

[58] Driscoll translates it as 'history of transmission', but the term is best left untranslated as *terminus technicus*; see M. J. Driscoll, 'The Words on the Page: Thoughts on Philology, Old and New', in *Creating the Medieval Saga: Versions, Variability, and Editorial Interpretations of Old Norse Saga Literature*, ed. J. Quinn and E. Lethbridge (Odense, 2010), pp. 85–102 (p. 93).

[59] The method of Überlieferungsgeschichte and its relation to the new philology have been discussed in W. Williams-Krapp, 'Die überlieferungsgeschichtliche Methode. Rückblick und Ausblick', *Internationales Archiv für Sozialgeschichte der Deutschen Literatur* 25 (2000), 1–21; R. L. R. Garber, *Feminine Figurae: Representations of Gender in Religious Texts by Medieval German Women Writers, 1100–1475* (New York, 2003), pp. 6–7, offers an English overview of the method.

[60] For a relatively recent and accessible overview of the new philology programme, see Driscoll, 'Thoughts on Philology', pp. 90–1.

based on the concept that every version of a text is an independent work, the Überlieferungsgeschichtliche Methode with its emphasis on *Geschichte*, history, traces textual history and aims to document it in editions. However, this book is not philological and the goal is not an edition: I study the mutation of the *Processus Petri* in the course of its reception in order to understand how and why it acquired the form it did, and how the text was possibly interpreted by contemporaries.

To grasp the effects of Zwicker's works one has to move beyond the history of transmission and revisions, into *Wirkungsgeschichte*, the history of reception. An important part of the pastoralization of heresy was dissemination of the anti-heretical message outside inquisitorial manuals and polemical treatises. Here the most important and the least studied evidence is the translation of the *Cum dormirent homines* in the catechetical work by Ulrich von Pottenstein, written in the first decade of the fifteenth century. The connection between the *Cum dormirent homines* and Ulrich von Pottenstein's *oeuvre* was pointed out by Hermann Menhardt long ago, in 1953, although he accepted the false attribution of the *Cum dormirent homines* to Peter von Pillichsdorf.[61] Menhardt's work has not been further developed, even though Peter Segl suggested this in an article.[62] The language and the reception of Ulrich's work have been studied by Gabriele Baptist-Hlawatsch,[63] while Baptist-Hlawatsch has edited the first chapter of the *Decalogue* and Gerold Hayer the *Pater noster* (Our Father) part.[64] However, most of the chapters concerning heresy are in unedited parts, above all in expositions of the Creed and Decalogue. Probably because of its enormous size, over 1,200 manuscript leaves, Ulrich's treatise never existed in a single manuscript. For the same reason it will probably never be edited in its entirety. The sections discussing heresy have been the topic of a dissertation project that terminated unfinished at the beginning of the 2000s. I am very grateful to the former project leader, Professor Dieter Harmening, with whose permission I was able to consult the transcripts

---

[61] H. Menhardt, 'Funde zu Ulrich von Pottenstein (etwa 1360–1420)', in *Festschrift für Wolfgang Stammler: zu seinem 65. Geburtstag dargebracht von Freunden und Schülern* (Berlin, 1953), pp. 146–71 (pp. 159–70); see also G. Baptist-Hlawatsch, *Das katechetische Werk Ulrichs von Pottenstein: Sprachliche und rezeptionsgeschichtliche Untersuchungen* (Tübingen, 1980), p. 6; D. Schmidtke, 'U. v. Pottenstein', in *Lexikon des Mittelalters* VIII (Munich, 1997), pp. 1200–1.

[62] Segl, 'Die Waldenser in Österreich', pp. 186–8.

[63] Baptist-Hlawatsch, *Das katechetische Werk*.

[64] U. von Pottenstein, *Dekalog-Auslegung: das erste Gebot: Text und Quellen*, ed. G. Baptist-Hlawatsch (Tübingen, 1995); G. Hayer, 'Paternoster-Auslegung: nach der Handschrift a X 13 des Erzstiftes St. Peter zu Salzburg kritisch herausgegeben und eingeleitet. 1, I. und III. Teil' (unpublished Ph.D. dissertation, University of Salzburg, 1972); G. Hayer, 'Paternoster-Auslegung: nach der Handschrift a X 13 des Erzstiftes St. Peter zu Salzburg kritisch herausgegeben und eingeleitet. 2, II. Teil' (unpublished Ph.D. dissertation, University of Salzburg, 1972).

prepared by Christine Wolf from Vienna, Österreichische Nationalbibliothek, MS 3050.[65]

Alongside the works written in the end of the fourteenth century, one must also take into account treatises written in the previous century that were still in active use and which were also later copied, together with fourteenth-century texts. These treatises were very probably used by Petrus Zwicker himself.[66] The first is a compilation against the enemies of the Church (heretics, Jews and the Antichrist) by an unknown author, who was probably a Dominican writing in the Austro-Bavarian diocese of Passau in the 1260s. Today the author is commonly referred to as the Anonymous of Passau. Both the manuscript and edition history of the treatise of the Anonymous of Passau are complex and confusing, and it is often difficult to know what version each edition represents.[67] Another widely circulating treatise was the *De inquisitione hereticorum* (*On the Inquisition of Heretics*) that Wilhelm Preger attributed to the German Franciscan David of Augsburg, an attribution considered to be very doubtful. The text is difficult to date, but Lucy Sackville gives a *terminus post quem* of 1253.[68]

The third treatise, far more uncommon in the late-fourteenth-century German or Austrian monastic libraries than the previous two, was the lengthy refutation of Cathar and Waldensian heresies written by Dominican Moneta of Cremona in 1240s, entitled *Adversus Catharos et Valdenses* (*Against the Cathars and Waldensians*).[69] Peter Biller has suggested that Zwicker probably used a copy of Moneta's treatise, accessible to him in the library of the Benedictine monastery of Garsten in Austria, Zwicker's base of operation in the mid-1390s.[70] In Chapter 2, I will demonstrate that this manuscript, nowadays Linz, Oberösterreichische Landesbibliothek, MS 296, was indeed the one Zwicker resorted to, not only when he was at Garsten but earlier, when composing the *Refutatio errorum* (or, alternatively, that Zwicker also wrote the *Refutatio* while at Garsten).

Further texts probably familiar to Zwicker were works by the Waldensians themselves. *Liber electorum* (the *Book of the Elect*) describes Waldensian history

---

[65] I am also grateful to the Digitisation Project of Kindred Languages of the Finnish National Library, which kindly provided OCR and OCR user interface for the early New High German text of Wolf's transcript, which I would otherwise have been forced to retranscribe manually.

[66] Biller, *Waldenses*, pp. 256–61, 272–3.

[67] Patschovsky, *Der Passauer Anonymus*; Nickson, 'The "Pseudo-Reinerius" Treatise'; Sackville, *Heresy and Heretics*, p. 138.

[68] Sackville, *Heresy and Heretics*, p. 139; I have resorted to the edition of the long redaction: 'Der Tractat des David von Augsburg über die Waldesier', ed. W. Preger, *Abhandlungen der historischen Classe der königlich bayrischen Akademie der Wissenschaften* 14 (1879), 203–35.

[69] The text is available in an eighteenth-century edition; see Moneta, *Adversus Catharos et Valdenses*.

[70] Biller, *Waldenses*, pp. 259–61.

from their own point of view and was very likely written in Italy between c. 1335 and the 1350s.[71] In addition to the *Liber electorum*, we have polemical correspondence between the Austrian Waldensian Brethren converted to Catholicism and the Lombardian Brethren. Peter Biller has dated this correspondence to the late 1360s and pointed out that a copy of it was available to Zwicker at Garsten.[72] These texts have been edited by Peter Biller in his unpublished dissertation.[73] Somewhat later an unknown author composed a short treatise, the *Attendite a falsis prophetis* (*Beware of False Prophets*), probably written in the 1370s and at the latest c. 1390, which also influenced the *Cum dormirent homines*.[74]

How is the cultural historian to interpret theological polemics and other texts written by an inquisitor? The study of medieval polemical treatises has been strongly influenced by the idea that the use of literary archetypes, *topoi*, was often haphazard, repetitive and routine-like, and that the descriptions of heresy are first and foremost literary constructions of the inquisitors and other Catholic authors.[75] While I wholeheartedly share the view that

---

[71] On the work, see ibid., ch. XII.

[72] Ibid., p. 256.

[73] Biller, 'Aspects', pp. 264–353.

[74] R. Cegna has edited the text, but wrongly attributed it to the Dominican Johannes of Gliwice and wrongly dated it to 1399; see his 'La condizione del valdismo secondo l'inedito "Tractatus bonus contra haereticos" del 1399, attribuibile all'inquisitore della Silesia Giovanni di Gliwice', in *I Valdesi e l'Europa* (Torre Pellice, 1982), pp. 39–66. Patschovsky has commented that there are no grounds whatsoever for either the attribution or the dating; see A. Patschovsky, 'Ablaßkritik auf dem Basler Konzil: der Widerruf Siegfried Wanners aus Nördlingen', in *Husitství – Reformace – Renesance. Sborník k 60. narozeninám Františka Šmahela*, ed. J. Pánek, M. Polívkaand and N. Rejchrtová (Prague, 1994), pp. 537–48 (n. 15). F. M. Bartoš, 'Husitika a bohemika několika knihoven německých a švýcarských', *Vestník královské ceské spolecnosti nauk. Trída filosoficko-historicko-jazykozpytná* 5 (1932), 1–92 (pp. 32–3) and, following him, A. Molnár have attributed the work to Konrad Waldhauser, a German reform preacher active in Prague in the mid-fourteenth century; see A. Molnár, *Storia dei valdesi 1. Dalle origini all'adesione alla Riforma (1176–1532)*, 2nd edn (Turin, 1989), p. 158, n. 29. I have been unable to confirm this attribution. This would date the treatise to the 1360s, which seems improbable in the light of its contents and manuscript circulation. It is likely that there is confusion between the treatise and Waldhauser's sermon on the same bible verse; cf. *Quellen*, ed. Patschovsky, pp. 125–6. Biller pointed out the similarity of topics treated in *Attendite a falsis prophetis* and *Cum dormirent homines*; see Biller, 'Aspects', pp. 261, 365; Biller, *Waldenses*, p. 290. Biller regards the treatise as anonymous. The references are to my own transcript from St Florian MS XI 152, fols. 48v–50v.

[75] To my knowledge this tradition began with the classic essay by Herbert Grundmann, published in 1927 and republished in H. Grundmann, 'Der Typus des Ketzers in mittelalterlicher Anschauung', in *Ausgewählte Aufsätze* (Stuttgart, 1976), pp. 313–27. Peter Biller in particular has argued that the inquisitorial literature is a valuable source on heresy if read carefully, and that deconstruction of these sources has gone too far. Biller's article also summarizes much of the discussion on the topic.

polemical texts on heresy are above all literary compositions corresponding to the expectations of erudite, orthodox clergy, I suggest it is a mistake to regard – and therefore overlook – what was attributed to heresy and heretics as mere rhetoric. Rather, I endorse a more pliant understanding of the medieval concepts of *topos* or *locus*, as proposed, for example, by Teemu Immonen. The *topos* should not be thought of as a textual convention that self-evidently obscures historical facts. Rather, in a very concrete way *topos/locus* is a place: a jumping-off point to various, perhaps even contradictory, interpretations and explanations of a concept. 'A place – *topos, locus* – was where the plurality of meanings of a certain concept was situated in the forest of meanings.'[76] In the case of anti-heretical literature this means that an author could pick from a variety of metaphors, some of which could lead to several different interpretations in the minds of contemporary readers. Thus a careful reading of the metaphors can reveal what aspects of heresy were stressed by certain authors or during certain periods, and consequently what the function of heresy was in contemporary culture. This view resembles Lucy Sackville's on reading descriptions of heresy: instead of a static *topos*, she has tracked the layering and accumulation of certain elements in thirteenth-century literature, as well as the adaptation of these elements to the purposes of the text.[77] As my intention is to explore both the changes in approaches to heresy and the effects these changes had on the Church that initiated the persecution as well as those it persecuted, it is necessary to perceive *topoi* as tools to discern and categorize, and eventually to reshape the reality, not as something that veils and distorts it.

See his 'Goodbye to Waldensianism?', *Past and Present* 192 (2006), pp. 3–33. An important collection of essays arguing for the invention of heresy by Catholic authors is *Inventer l'hérésie? Discours polémiques et pouvoirs avant l'Inquisition*, ed. M. Zerner (Nice, 1998). In recent years Mark G. Pegg and R. I. Moore have provided the most influential critical reading of this type, which considers the dualist heresy in Languedoc to be a polemical literary construction. See esp M. G. Pegg, 'On Cathars, Albigenses, and Good Men of Languedoc', *Journal of Medieval History* 27 (2001), 81–95; M. G. Pegg, *The Corruption of Angels: The Great Inquisition of 1245–1246* (Princeton, 2001); R. I. Moore, *The War on Heresy* (London, 2012); R. I. Moore, 'The Cathar Middle Ages as an Historiographical Problem', in *Christianity and Culture in the Middle Ages: Essays to Honor John Van Engen*, ed. D. C. Mengel and L. Wolverton (Notre Dame, 2014), pp. 58–86. For an opposing interpretation and evidence, see esp. C. Bruschi, *The Wandering Heretics of Languedoc* (Cambridge, 2009); C. Taylor, 'Evidence for Dualism in Inquisitorial Registers of the 1240s: A Contribution to a Debate', *History* 98 (2013), 319–45; C. Sparks, *Heresy, Inquisition and Life-Cycle in Medieval Languedoc* (York, 2014). The recent anthology *Cathars in Question*, ed. A. Sennis (York, 2016), contains essays by the most important proponents of the debate on Catharism, but without resulting in a synthesis of views.

[76] T. Immonen, 'Building the Cassinese Monastic Identity: A Reconstruction of the Fresco Program of the Desiderian Basilica (1071)' (unpublished Ph.D. dissertation, University of Helsinki, 2012), p. 15.

[77] Sackville, *Heresy and Heretics*, pp. 9, 175, 177 and passim.

There are two further caveats about the interpretation of inquisitorial sources. Firstly, Waldensianism as a uniform doctrinal system exists either as a construction by inquisitors and polemicists or as a reconstruction by historians. When the protocols of the Stettin inquisitions of 1392–4 claim that somebody believed in something 'from the teachings of the heresiarchs'[78] (*ex doctrinis heresiarcharum*), it is the inquisitor Petrus Zwicker's concept and language we read. In a loose dissident group dispersed over a large geographical area and held together by annual or rarer visits by the Brethren, variation of doctrine and opinions was inevitable. Indeed, as Gabriel Audisio has pointed out, it was the inquisitors who needed to catalogue and who were anxious about the apparent syncretism of the dissidents, and historians who often perceive this syncretism from a distance; but the Waldensians themselves were probably far less aware of it or interested in it.[79]

However, we should not overstate this division and variation. There is convincing evidence, discussed in detail by Peter Biller, that Waldensians had a distinct identity and sense of history, and that there was communication between different groups as well as continuity of doctrine.[80] There was also cohesion inside the particular group studied here, the German Waldensians at the end of the fourteenth century, even if they represent geographically distant and socially diverse groups, ranging from the farmhands of the Pomeranian countryside to Swiss merchant families. The strongest common denominator for all these dispersed brothers and sisters in faith was the same Waldensian Brethren who visited them all and were responsible for the pastoral care and education of their flock.[81] There was also migration between different Waldensian communities: key witnesses in the Strasbourg process in 1400 were five women, among whom there were probably refugees from Augsburg, where trials took place in 1393.[82] Thus, there existed a dissident group professing a religious identity distinct from that of mainstream Catholicism. Its members understood this very well: they called themselves 'the known' (die Künden/*notos*), and those outside their group 'the strangers' (die Fremden/*alienos*).[83]

---

[78] *Quellen*, ed. Kurze, pp. 148, 155.

[79] Audisio, *The Waldensian Dissent*, p. 44.

[80] Biller, 'Goodbye to Waldensianism?'. On Waldensian sense of identity, see also G. Audisio, 'Le sentiment de supériorité dans les minorités: l'exemple vaudois (xve–xvie siècle)', *BSSV* 194 (2004), 25–36.

[81] For example, the Brethren Konrad von Saxony and Klaus von Solothurn appear in depositions both in Stettin and in Strasbourg; see Kurze, 'Zur Ketzergeschichte', pp. 79–80; see also Modestin, *Ketzer in der Stadt*, p. 121. In Fribourg no names of Brethren are mentioned, but there are references to their German and Bohemian origin; see *Quellen*, ed. Utz Tremp, p. 53.

[82] *Quellen*, ed. Modestin, p. 2.

[83] The distinction is prominent in Stettin protocols and discussed e.g. in Cameron, *Waldenses*, p. 131.

The second caveat relates to the interpretation of documents of inquisition. It is especially postmodern linguistic criticism of sources that has produced valuable insights into how to read (or not to read) the biased minutes of interrogations that were conducted by inquisitors intent upon their own particular truth, and translated from the vernacular into Latin by long-dead notaries.[84] After a period of extreme suspicion about anything written by the inquisitors, recently there has been a clear tendency towards more moderate interpretation of these sources, and acknowledgement that while sometimes inquisitors sought only to confirm existing suspicions, some were genuinely interested in 'fishing out' new transgressions and learning about heresy. Many trials fell in between the two extremes, and not all evidence of heretical doctrine is based on inquisitors' presuppositions that had been forced upon deponents either by physical coercion or discursive power.[85]

With great caution I follow this moderate way of reading, though I do not see any fundamental contradiction with the earlier criticism. John H. Arnold, one of the scholars who has embraced the postmodern, in particular Foucauldian, approach to inquisitors' sources, has also reminded us that we should not be content to state that the past is unattainable, and be 'hypnotized by the chasm of epistemological aporia'. The strength of academic historians working with archival sources is their recognition of the messiness and complexity of the human condition, and of the fact that the dialogue between the archive and postmodern theories can produce historiography which at its best is self-reflective and intelligent.[86] This messiness and complexity are very much present in the depositions of late-medieval German Waldensians, and they deserve to be explained rather than dismissed as unfathomable.

---

[84] The discussion began in the 1960s and was intense in 1990s and 2000s. I have been influenced especially by Arnold, *Inquisition and Power*; Arnold, 'Inquisition, Texts and Discourse'.

[85] H. A. Kelly, 'Inquisitorial Deviations and Cover-Ups: The Prosecutions of Margaret Porete and Guiard of Cressonessart, 1308–1310', *Speculum* 89 (2014), 936–73 (pp. 938–9); Taylor, 'Evidence for Dualism in Inquisitorial Registers of the 1240s', p. 329; Sparks, *Heresy, Inquisition and Life-Cycle in Medieval Languedoc*, pp. 24–6; Bruschi, *The Wandering Heretics of Languedoc*, pp. 11–49.

[86] J. H. Arnold, 'Responses to the Postmodern Challenge; or, What Might History Become?', *European History Quarterly* 37 (2007), 109–32 (pp. 127–8).

1

Petrus Zwicker and the Career of an Inquisitor at the Turn of the Fifteenth Century

Petrus Zwicker was an exceptionally successful inquisitor and polemicist, but he was an unlikely man to become an inquisitor. He was not a Dominican or Franciscan friar, to whom the inquisition of heresy was commonly entrusted; neither was he a secular cleric or a canon regular, whose pastoral obligations made them suitable for the task. He was a Celestine monk from the monastery of Oybin, founded by Emperor Charles IV in 1369,[1] and between 1394 and

---

[1] The history of the Oybin monastery is based mainly on nineteenth-century works, with a few later contributions mainly on the art history and archaeology of the castle and monastery. See C. A. Pescheck, *Geschichte der Cölestiner des Oybins* (Zittau, 1840); M. O. Sauppe, 'Geschichte der Burg und des Coelestinerklosters Oybin [I]', *NLM* 62 (1886), 88–110; M. O. Sauppe, 'Regesta castri et monasterii Oywinensis', *NLM* 63 (1888), 370–7; M. O. Sauppe, 'Zur Geschichte des Klosters Oybin im 15. Jahrhunder', *Neues Archiv für Sächsische Geschichte* 13 (1892), 315–22; M. O. Sauppe, 'Geschichte der Burg und des Coelestinerklosters Oybin [II]', *NLM* 79 (1903), 177–240; M. O. Sauppe, 'Geschichte der Burg und des Coelestinerklosters Oybin [III]', *NLM* 83 (1907), 110–95; K. Mutke, 'Die schlesischen Besitzungen des Coelestinerklosters Oybin', *Zeitschrift des Vereins für Geschichte Schlesiens* 48 (1914), 34–73; F. Günther, *Die Klosterkirche Oybin* (Berlin, 1959); J. E. Fries, 'Ausgrabungen in der mittelalterlichen Burg- und Klosterruine Oybin', *Arbeits- und Forschungsberichte zur Sächsische Bodendenkmalpflege* 44 (2002), 179–90; R. Němec, 'Die Burg- und Klosteranlage Oybin. Die Entwicklung der Handelswege im Lausitzer Gebirge im Lichte der Territorialpolitik Karls IV. und ihre Bedeutung für die Erbauung des Kaiserhauses und die Stiftung des Coelestinerklosters', *Burgen und Schlösser* 44 (2003), 241–51; R. Němec, 'Architektur als identitätstragendes Herrschaftsinstrument. Kunsthistorische Betrachtungen der Residenzanlagen Karls IV. am Fallbeispiel der Burg- und Klosteranlage Oybin', *NLM* 128 (2006), 9–30; R. Němec, 'Die Burg- und Klosteranlage Oybin im Kontext der regionalen und höfischen Architektur Karls IV. zur Verbreitung des Stils der Prager Veitsdomhütte', *Umění* 59 (2011), 102–25. The Celestines of Oybin have been taken into account in Christian Speer's studies on the devotional practices of the urban elite in Görlitz. However, almost all his sources are decades after Zwicker's time. See C. Speer, 'Die Bedeutung der Cölestiner für die Frömmigkeitspraxis städtischer Eliten im Spätmittelalter', in *Česká koruna na rozcestí. K dějinám Horní a Dolní Lužice a Dolního Slezska na přelomu středověku a raného novověku (1437–1526)*, ed. L. Bobková (Prague,

1404 he was the provincial of the order in Germany. The German province of the Celestines, consisting only of the monastery in Oybin and a smaller house in Prague, came into being as a result of the Schism. It was created under the Italian main monastery of S. Spirito del Morrone in order to prevent the German Celestines from slipping under the influence of the French party in the order.[2]

The Celestines were an eremitic order founded by Pietro da Morrone in the mid-thirteenth century. They came to prominence after their founder was unexpectedly nominated as Pope Celestine V in an odour of sanctity in July 1294, his rapid resignation after five months in office and his death in 1296. He was canonized in 1313, and soon after this the Celestines acquired their name.[3] They were supposed to exclude themselves from the world and secular tasks, and their constitutions strictly regulated the acceptance of assignments from outsiders, with the exception of those ordered by kings and cardinals. Even then the service could be continued beyond three years only with the permission of the general chapter.[4] Therefore it is no wonder that Petrus Zwicker and Nikolaus von Wartenberch, who assisted Zwicker in Stettin, are the only Celestines known to have held the office of inquisitor of heresy.[5] (Whilst the practice of inquisition into heresy is particularly associated in modern scholarship with the Dominican order, it should be noted that, from its inception, it was a tool wielded by Franciscans, bishops and secular priests as well.)

As there are no letters of commission surviving from Zwicker's first known duty as inquisitor in Erfurt 1391, it is impossible to know by whose orders Zwicker first assumed the office of inquisitor, but a connection to the

---

2010), pp. 294–338; C. Speer, *Frömmigkeit und Politik: Städtische Eliten in Görlitz zwischen 1300 und 1550* (Berlin, 2011).

[2] K. Borchardt, *Die Cölestiner: eine Mönchsgemeinschaft des späteren Mittelalters* (Husum, 2006), p. 126. Borchardt follows Sauppe and mistakenly gives Zwicker's years in office as 1391–7; cf. Sauppe, 'Geschichte der Burg und des Coelestinerklosters Oybin [II]', p. 212. The first time Zwicker refers to himself as provincial is in March 1394, in a preface to a protocol: 'frater Petrus provincialis fratrum ordin(is) Celestinorum per Alamaniam, inquisitor pravitatis heretice'; *Quellen*, ed. Kurze, p. 235. If the description, drawn from a since lost manuscript from the Moravian city archives is to be trusted, Zwicker still had this title in 1404; Biller, 'Aspects', p. 372; see also A. A. Neumann, *České sekty ve století 14. a 15.: Na základě archioních pramenů podává* (Velehrad, 1920), p. 6*. According to the sentence of Andreas Hesel in Vienna, Zwicker was provincial at least until March 1403: Würzburg, Universitätsbibliothek, MS M. ch. f. 51, fol. 27v: 'nos frater [Petrus] prouincialis Religiosorum fratrum ordinis celestinorum per alcmaniam inquisitorem [sic] heretice prauitatis'.

[3] Borchardt, *Die Cölestiner*, pp. 13–47.

[4] Ibid., pp. 257–8.

[5] C. Caby, who has extensively studied the Celestines and other eremitic orders, confirmed my hypothesis. She has not uncovered any other Celestine monk who would have held the office. Discussion with C. Caby in Rome, May 2015.

archbishop of Prague, Jan of Jenštejn, is probable. The archbishop had taken action against Waldensians already in the 1380s, and he had consecrated the church of the Oybin monastery in 1384.[6]

The superiors of the order seem to have approved this anomalous German inquisitor, and Zwicker's commission was acknowledged in the communication between Oybin and the mother house in Italy. On 20 September 1397 subprior Ulrich von Rorbach visited Aquila and acquired 'in the name and in place of prior and brethren of Monastery of the Holy Ghost in Oybin' a witnessed and confirmed copy of privileges granted by Pope Celestine V to the monastery of S. Spirito del Morrone and houses attached to it in 1294.[7] The visit corresponds with the election of the new abbot Nicolao d'Aversa in autumn 1397. And in January 1398, in the sentences declared in the diocese of Passau, Zwicker holds the title 'brother Petrus, provincial of the religious brothers of the order of the Celestines, assigned to his province of Germany by the venerable father, brother Nicolaus de Aversa, abbot of the principal monastery of Santo Spirito prope Sulmona in the diocese of Valva and the whole order mentioned above'.[8]

Zwicker was the highest official of his order in Central Europe, but as sources for Oybin's early period are very scarce, very little is known of him as provincial. A rare glimpse of his monastic duties is the confederation of prayer (*Gebetsbrüderschaft*) Zwicker formed between Oybin and the Austrian Benedictine monastery of Gleink in 1397.[9] Another administrative document,

---

[6] Biller, 'Waldensians by the Baltic'; on the consecration of the monastery church see Sauppe, 'Geschichte der Burg und des Coelestinerklosters Oybin [II]', p. 210.

[7] The letter was edited in the early eighteenth century in J. B. Carpzov, *Analecta Fastorum Zittaviensium Oder Historischer Schauplatz Der Löblichen Alten Sechs-Stadt des Marggraffthums Ober-Lausitz Zittau*, 5 vols. (Zittau, 1716), III, 158–63, The original, which in Carpzov's time was in the city hall of Zittau, has since been destroyed, probably in the city fire of 1757. Apparently Caprzov aimed for an exact transcription, since he also drew the seal at the end of the document: see p. 163. The contents of the document, with the obvious exception of the protocolla and escatocolla added in 1397, correspond for the most part to the papal letter of 1294 edited by Borchardt, *Die Cölestiner*, pp. 377–84 [U2].

[8] 'Quoniam nos frater petrus provincialis religiosorum fratrum ordinis celestinorum a venerabili patre fratre Nicolao de Aversa Abbate principalis Monasterii sancti spiritus prope Sulmanam [sic] valvensis dyocesis necnon tocius religionis prefate per eius provinciam alamanie deputatus.' Cited according to Munich, BSB MS Clm 5338, fol. 239v; cf. Haupt, 'Waldenserthum und Inquisition', p. 404. Nicolao d'Aversa was abbot from 1397 to 1400, and effectively acting as such between 1398 and 1400. He was elected in 1397 in Capua by a group of sixteen monasteries from Terra di Lavoro, which were protesting against the extension of the term of office for vicar Antonio da Roccaraso; Borchardt, *Die Cölestiner*, p. 130. Because Zwicker was commissioned by him already by January 1398, when Nicolao was still struggling for power, there must have been someone from Oybin present at his election, almost certainly subprior Ulrich.

[9] OÖLA, Stiftsarchiv Gleink, MS Nr. 2, p. 78. The notice from the early modern

where we see Zwicker acting as the head of a monastery rather than as an inquisitor, was written in Prague between February 1400 and February 1404 (the last part of the year is illegible, but the notarial instrument was issued during the papacy of Boniface IX, who died 1 October 1404).[10] It is a notarial copy of a contract, commissioned by Zwicker from a public notary in Prague. The copy has been preserved only as a fragment in the binding of a manuscript, but it appears to be a contract where the arms-bearer or squire (*armiger*) Michalík of Břvany (north-western Bohemia) and his wife Anne sell their property (*curia*) to the brethren in Oybin for the price of 3,600 groschen of the money of Prague (*grossorum monete pragensis*). The original was issued by Vilém Zajíc of Hazmburk, provost in Litoměřice. There are three remarkable things in this document. Firstly, Zwicker ordered a legally valid copy of the contract, 'lest its copy get lost or in whatever other way cannot be kept, through the chance of accident on account of the interruption (?) of roads or other dangers'.[11] This shows not only the restlessness of the times, but outside the documents of inquisitions it is yet another indication of Petrus Zwicker's wandering lifestyle in the first years of the fifteenth century. Secondly, that the copy was issued and probably preserved in Prague witnesses Zwicker's personal presence in the Bohemian capital at the time.[12] It is important in relation to the circulation of Zwicker's texts in Bohemia and their use by the preacher Johlín of Vodňany, discussed in the subsequent chapters. Finally, Zwicker's title in the document reads 'dominus petrus prouincialis Ordinis Celestinorum necnon Inquisitor heretice prauitatis'. The legal act itself, however, did not presuppose the authority of inquisitor; it was done as the provincial of the order. Yet it seems that by 1400 the office of inquisitor had become an integral part of how Petrus Zwicker presented himself and was seen by others. For contemporaries, he was 'Petrus Inquisitor' (Peter the Inquisitor), as the title of his short treatise on the *Pater noster* states in a manuscript from St Florian.[13]

There are some pieces of information about Petrus Zwicker from the time before his inquisitorial career, rather more than those usually available for fourteenth-century clergymen. According to the established biography,[14]

---

chronicle was discovered by Peter Segl, who kindly provided me with copies. See also Segl, 'Die Waldenser in Österreich', p. 183; Modestin, 'Zwicker', p. 30.

[10] Peter Biller was first to notice the notarial instrument's connection to Zwicker. See Biller, 'Waldensians by the Baltic' [forthcoming].

[11] NKCR MS IV. B. 4, fragment from the binding: 'ne ipsius copia casu fortuito propter viarum distermina [?] et alia pericula amittatur aut quouismodo alio haberi non possit.'

[12] Besides the document, there is nothing else in MS IV. B. 4 that would suggest a provenance in Oybin. See the description at the *Manuscriptorium* [consulted 18 October 2017.]

[13] St Florian MS XI 96, fol. 298r. See also below in Chapter 2.

[14] Modestin, 'Zwicker'; P. Segl, 'Zwicker, Peter', in *Lexikon des Mittelalters* IX (Munich, 1998), pp. 732–3; Segl, 'Die Waldenser in Österreich', pp. 165–6.

Zwicker was born in Wormditt, East Prussia (now Orneta in Poland), spent two decades as the schoolmaster at the town school of Zittau and received the degree of bachelor from the Faculty of Arts at the University of Prague in 1379. In 1381 he entered the nearby Celestine monastery of Oybin.

This narrative, which is repeated in the latest scholarship,[15] contains a crucial inconsistency: that Zwicker was a schoolmaster at Zittau for almost two decades before he entered the university. If this is true, Zwicker must have been about 40 years old when he graduated in 1379. Even though late medieval scholars quite often returned from the office of schoolteacher to university, this was usually related to taking up an office on the teaching staff of the university or continuing their own studies in the so-called higher faculties of theology, medicine or law.[16] The bachelor of liberal arts was, however, a basic academic education and the students usually young boys in their teens. At the fourteenth-century University of Prague the students generally entered the faculty of arts at an age of between 14 and 16 and graduated as masters at the age of 20.[17] Even if Zwicker was above the average age when he entered the university, it is highly improbable that a schoolmaster with over fifteen years of teaching experience would study the basics of logic with boys barely older than those he used to educate.

The information about Zwicker's university education and his position as schoolmaster comes from two independent sources. The medieval book of deans of the faculty of arts recounts that on the feast of St Vitus (15 June) in 1379 'Petrus Czwycker' received the bachelor's degree.[18] The accounts mentioning him as a schoolmaster and then entering the monastery in 1381 are based on Johann Carpzov's early eighteenth-century historiographical work, which states that Zwicker was born in Wormditt, was schoolmaster in Zittau from the 1360s and entered Oybin in 1381 and became provincial by 1395.[19] A more precise year, 1363, is given for the beginning of Zwicker's post as schoolmaster

---

[15] Including, in addition to the above-mentioned biographical surveys, P. Biller, 'Intellectuals and the Masses. Oxen and She-Asses in the Medieval Church', in *The Oxford Handbook of Medieval Christianity*, ed. J. H. Arnold (Oxford, 2014), pp. 323–39 (p. 323); Smelyansky, 'Self-Styled Inquisitors', p. 42.

[16] K. Wriedt, 'Schule und Universitätsbesuch in norddeutschen Städten des Spätmittelalters', in *Bildungs- und schulgeschichtliche Studien zu Spätmittelalter, Reformation und konfessionellem Zeitalter*, ed. H. Dickerhof (Wiesbaden, 1994), pp. 75–90 (p. 89).

[17] F. Šmahel, *Die Prager Universität im Mittelalter: gesammelte Aufsätze* (Leiden, 2007), p. 252.

[18] *Liber decanorum facultatis philosophicae universitatis Pragensis, ab anno Christi 1367, usque ad annum 1585* (Prague, 1830), I, 187; this notice was not connected to Petrus Zwicker until a hundred years later in J. Prochno's 'Regesten zur Geschichte der Stadt und des Landes Zittau 1234–1437', *NLM* 114 (1938), 1–421 (p. 6, no. 435).

[19] Carpzov, *Analecta Fastorum Zittaviensium*, III, 107–8; Sauppe, 'Zur Geschichte des Klosters Oybin im 15. Jahrhunder', p. 315; Sauppe, 'Geschichte der Burg und des Coelestinerklosters Oybin [II]', p. 211; Prochno, 'Regesten 2', p. 12, no. 462.

in nineteenth-century scholarship, based on a tradition that likewise goes back to Carpzov.[20] While Carpzov had access to some sources that were lost in the city fire of 1757,[21] here he obviously refers to a notice in the annals (*Jahrbücher*) of the town notary Johannes von Guben. It is a note written when one of Guben's followers, Conradus Wiszinbach, accepted the duties and book of the notary in 1395. Conradus probably wrote down his life story himself, and for some reason also mentioned Zwicker, whose career had overlapped with his own:

> Note. AD 1395, on the vigil of the Annunciation of holy Mary the Virgin, Johannes Hertil left the office of city notary, who [Johannes] succeeded Johannes Gubin, of pious memory, in the office written above. And there was received in his place Conradus Wiszinbach, born in Eschwege, a city of Hessen. At an earlier time he was for three years second teacher and cantor of [serving under] the rector of this school [the school of Zittau], master Petrus Czwicker from Wormditt, now in the monastery of Oybin Provincial of the Order of Celestines. Then, after master Petrus entered the Order [of Celestines], the same Conradus was rector of the school and notary of the city of Löbau for eleven years. Then, in the year and on the day written above, he received the office of notary of this city.[22]

This contradicts the account by Carpzov, who states that Conradus was Zwicker's *locatus* from 1370 till Zwicker left the school in 1381.[23]

If we dismiss Carpzov's version, the contradiction between Zwicker's graduation date and his career in Zittau and Oybin disappears. After gaining

---

[20] T. Gärtner, 'Die Zittauer Schule bis zur Gründung des Gymnasiums', in *Festschrift zur dreihundertjährigen Jubelfeier des Gymnasiums zu Zittau am 9. und 10. März 1886* (Zittau, 1886), p. 3; J. Müller, 'Die Anfänge des Sächsischen Schulwesens', *Neues Archiv für Sächsische Geschichte und Altertumskunde* 8 (1887), 1–40, 243–71 (p. 252).

[21] See e.g. J. G. Zobel, 'Beitrag zur geschichte des Klosters Oybin bei Zittau', *Neue Lausizische Monatsschrift*, zweiter Theil, achtes Stück (1802), 102–24 (p. 103). See also the letter of privileges brought from the Celestine mother house in 1397 mentioned above.

[22] *Scriptores rerum lusaticarum* 1 (Görlitz, 1839), p. 2: 'Nota. A.D. MCCCXCV in vigilia annunciacionis sancte Marie virginis dimisit notariam ciuitatis Johannes Hertil, qui successit in officio prescriptum Johannem Gubin, pie memorie: et loco sui acceptatus fuit Conradus Wiszinbach, natus de Esschenwege, ciuitate Hassie, qui prius tempore rectoris scole huius, magistri Petri Czwickers de Wormpnijt, ciuitate Pruszie, nunc prouincialis in monasterio Oywin, ordinis Celestinorum, fuit locatus et succentor tribus annis; dejnde postquam magister Petrus intrauit ordinem, fuit idem Conradus rector scole et notarius ciuitatis Lobauie vndecim annis; deinde anno et die prescripto acceptauit notariam huius ciuitatis.'

[23] Carpzov, *Analecta Fastorum Zittaviensium*, III, 108: 'Dessen Locatus und Succentor in der Schulen war an 1370 Conradus de Weissenbach von Eichwege aus Hessen, welcher nach des Magistri Petri Abzuge ebenfalls die schule verlassen, und zu Loebau in der Schule als Ludimoderator, zugleich aber auch aufm Rath-Hause als Notarius Elff Jahr gedienet, bis er an 1395. zu, Stadtschreiber Dienste dieser Stadt, Vocation erhalten.'

the basic academic degree in the summer of 1379 Zwicker could well have joined the majority of bachelors seeking a career in the service of cities, courts and the Church administration,[24] and achieved the position of schoolmaster in Zittau around 1380. It is much more credible that a young man from Eastern Prussia would first end up studying in Prague and then receive an office at a town belonging to the archdiocese of Prague, than vice versa. At the time Prague was a popular university city among students from central and northern parts of Europe,[25] and thus a natural choice for a Prussian seeking an ecclesiastic career. If Zwicker assumed the post of a schoolmaster soon after his graduation, there would be time for Conradus's three-year teaching period under Zwicker before the former accepted the position of schoolmaster and notary in Löbau around 1383 or 1384 (ending some eleven years before 1395) and the latter entered the religious order. This would also mean that Zwicker joined the Celestines a little later than assumed, but in any case by 1385. It is also possible that Zwicker later acquired the higher academic degree of master: Conradus calls him *magister* (master), and he appears as such in the short *Pater noster* treatise attributed to Zwicker.[26] I consider this improbable, though not impossible. I have not found his name anywhere else among the graduates or teaching staff of the University of Prague, nor do the inquisitorial documents ever describe him as a master. The few references can be interpreted as honorific rather than academic titles. *Magister* was, even in the late Middle Ages, a rather vague title and in addition to academic masters it could refer to bachelors, schoolmasters or at times even uneducated scribes.[27]

We must keep in mind Zwicker's formative study years in Prague when we try to understand his worldview and anti-Waldensian programme. Zwicker studied in Prague, by then the crown jewel of Bohemia under the Emperor Charles IV.[28] When thinking about devotion in late fourteenth-century Prague, it is easy to look back from the Hussite revolution and seek the roots

---

[24] Šmahel, *Die Prager Universität im Mittelalter*, p. 252.

[25] Ibid., p. 220.

[26] St Florian MS XI 96, fol. 298r: 'Dicta magistri petri Inquisitoris'. See also the manuscript BSB MS Clm 15125, fols. 170ra, 208vb, where the *Processus Petri* is called *tractatus waldensium magistri petri*. That Zwicker had a master's degree has been proposed or speculated about by Haupt, 'Waldenserthum und Inquisition', p. 345; Sauppe, 'Geschichte der Burg und des Coelestinerklosters Oybin [II]', p. 211; Modestin, 'Zwicker', p. 26; Biller, 'Intellectuals and the Masses', p. 323.

[27] J. Schmutz, *Juristen für das Reich: die deutschen Rechtsstudenten an der Universität Bologna 1265–1425* (Basel, 2000), pp. 124–9; R. Gramsch, *Erfurter Juristen im Spätmittelalter: die Karrieremuster und Tätigkeitsfelder einer gelehrten Elite des 14. und 15. Jahrhunderts* (Leiden, 2003), p. 218, n. 80; J. Barrow, *The Clergy in the Medieval World* (Cambridge, 2015), p. 209.

[28] Biller presents the connection of Zwicker, Prague and Charles IV's architectural, artistic and devotional programmes in Biller, 'Waldensians by the Baltic'. I have had the fortunate opportunity of discussion with him and developing the idea further.

of the biblicist and Eucharist-oriented Bohemian reform movement.[29] Biblical-moralistic, anti-authoritarian movements existed in Prague, but it was also a city of magnificent palaces, newly renovated and decorated churches and numerous relics. Prague was a centre of Marian devotion, where Charles IV had provided for twenty-four sacristans, thirty choirboys and twelve psalmists to sing the praises of the Virgin in St Vitus's Cathedral,[30] and where a few decades later Archbishop Jan of Jenštejn introduced the feast of the Visitation.[31] The Church in all its sacramental glory, richness of liturgy and holiness of matter that Petrus Zwicker defended in his treatises was very much the Church Charles IV and Bohemian prelates had envisioned in the previous decades. But the emperor had died in 1378, and the times were much more troubled in the 1390s. This image of the Church was challenged from different sides, and between them Petrus Zwicker set himself to defend faith against its enemies.

It will probably remain a mystery why a Celestine monk was called from his mountain monastery to prosecute heretics. Yet even this mountain recluse was very much a result of Charles's devotion and politics. In the France of Charles V (1364–80), the austere Celestines were seen as effective intercessors, and the order became closely bound up with the court.[32] The Emperor Charles IV had been raised in the French court and was related to Charles V,[33] and it was from France he brought the Celestines to Bohemia in 1366. The monks were settled in a new imperial castle that was built on Mount Oybin near Zittau. The emperor granted extensive privileges to the monastery in its founding charter issued in Lucca in 1369, and placed it under the mother house of S. Spirito in Sulmona. The castle was to remain forever in the possession of the Bohemian crown.[34] In the eyes of contemporaries the Celestine monastery was intimately connected to the emperor. The Prague chronicler Beneše of Weitmil wrote how 'at that time the lord Emperor Charles founded a new monastery in his castle Oybin facing Zittau, and placed there monks who are called Celestines, and provided sufficient means for their living and support'.[35] Richard Němec has demonstrated how the monastery

---

[29] On this danger, based on largely mythical historiographical constructions, see P. Soukup, 'Die Predigt als Mittel religiöser Erneuerung: Böhmen um 1400', in *Böhmen und das Deutsche Reich: Ideen- und Kulturtransfer im Vergleich (13.–16. Jahrhundert)*, ed. E. Schlotheuber and H. Seibert (Munich, 2009), pp. 235–64 (pp. 235–241).

[30] F. Machilek, 'Praga caput regni: zur Entwicklung und Bedeutung Prags im Mittelalter', *Studien zum Deutschtum im Osten* 17 (1982), 67–125 (pp. 83–4).

[31] See Chapter 2.

[32] Borchardt, *Die Cölestiner*, pp. 76–82.

[33] F. Seibt, *Karl IV: ein Kaiser in Europa 1346–1378*, 4th edn (Munich, 1979), pp. 115–20.

[34] Sauppe, 'Geschichte der Burg und des Coelestinerklosters Oybin [II]', pp. 208–10; Borchardt, *Die Cölestiner*, pp. 94–6; Němec, 'Architektur als identitätstragendes Herrschaftsinstrument', pp. 16–19.

[35] 'Kronica Beneše z Weitmile', ed. J. Emler, *FRB* IV, p. 534.

church was built using the stylistic language and form of Prague's St Vitus. It thus referred to a specific style promoted by Charles IV, and the whole castle and monastery complex was intended to represent the emperor's authority in a potentially restless area.[36] Petrus Zwicker was the prior of a monastery that was associated with the Bohemian crown and the House of Luxemburg, and also perhaps – in the middle of the crisis of the 1390s – with more prosperous and glorious times.

The only problem with Zwicker's biography as sketched above is whether at the time of his first commission in 1391 as inquisitor of heresy in Erfurt, together with Martinus of Prague, he had reached the age of 40 years, the minimum age for someone to become an inquisitor of heresy since the constitutions of Clement V. It is possible that he was in his thirties and thus underage, but exceptions to the rule were not unknown.[37] No inquisitor's commission has survived from Erfurt: the only source describing the inquisition is the so-called short list of converted Waldensians, transmitted mostly within the *Processus Petri* compilation.[38] This is the starting point of the careers of men whom Richard Kieckhefer in his influential book characterized as the primary persecutors of Waldensians in the period and as 'itinerant inquisitors', including Zwicker, Martinus of Prague (Martin von Amberg) and Heinrich Angermeyer. According to Kieckhefer, these inquisitors acted independently, primarily on their own initiative, following the traces of the Waldensians revealed by converts and requesting episcopal authorization as the trials proceeded. None of them was a papal inquisitor or a mendicant friar.[39] The interpretation has since been widely accepted and often repeated.[40]

---

[36] Němec, 'Architektur als identitätstragendes Herrschaftsinstrument', pp. 24, 26–7; Němec, 'Die Burg- und Klosteranlage Oybin im Kontext der regionalen und höfischen Architektur Karls IV'.

[37] Clem. 5.3.2. The decretal was also copied into the inquisitors' manual used by Zwicker (see Chapter 3); OÖLB, MS 177, fols. 60r–v. By contrast, the minimum age for commissioned judges according to canon law was 20; see Hostiensis, *Summa Aurea*, 5 vols. (Venice, 1574), I, 283. In the thirteenth century the minimum age of 20 applied to papal inquisitors; Bivolarov, *Inquisitoren-Handbücher*, p. 262. Later the age limit was at times relaxed, e.g. in the first century of the Spanish Inquisition; J. Pérez, *The Spanish Inquisition: A History* (New Haven, 2005), p. 114.

[38] Quoted here from BAV MS Pal. lat 677, fol. 54 v: 'Postea tamen anno domini 1391 per dominum martinum de amberg et fratrem petrum celestinum omnes in erfordia sunt conuicti et conuersi abiurati et cruce signati' (Afterwards, however, in AD 1391 all of them were convicted in Erfurt by lord Martinus of Amberg and Brother Petrus the Celestine, and converted, and they abjured and were marked with the cross [sentenced to wear crosses on their clothes as punishment]). On the lists of converts, see Chapter 3.

[39] Kieckhefer, *Repression*, pp. 55–7. A similar but less pronounced view had already been given by Patschovsky, 'Straßburger Beginenverfolkungen im 14. Jahrhundert', pp. 117–18.

[40] Cameron, *Waldenses*, p. 139; Modestin, *Ketzer in der Stadt*, pp. 3–9; Modestin, 'The Anti-Waldensian Treatise', p. 213; Utz Tremp, *Von der Häresie zur Hexerei*, pp. 279–80;

Even though the title of my study includes the name of one of these men and another, Martinus of Prague, is often discussed, I am less inclined to reconstruct the persecution of the German Waldensians at the turn of the fifteenth century around the personalities of these three inquisitors. Rather than seeing the years 1390–1404 as marking a distinctive campaign against Waldensians, I would regard this activity as an intensification of a process that started in the 1360s and lasted at least until the rise of the Hussite movement in the second half of the 1410s: the period saw disruption and dissolution among the Waldensians, their voluntary or forced conversion to Catholicism and increased consciousness and counter-reaction on the Catholic side. The crisis of the German Waldensians began with the conversion of the Austrian Brethren and believers in the late 1360s – an event that facilitated a polemical correspondence between the converts and the Lombard Waldensian Brethren and probably formed the basis for the later inquisitorial campaigns and anti-Waldensian polemics by Catholic authors.[41]

The accumulating of texts against Waldensians in Austrian and southern German libraries seems to support this. Not only did the letters of the 1368 circulate, but they were followed by an anonymous treatise, the *Attendite a falsis prophetis*, probably written in the 1370s and and at the latest around 1390. The polemical response reached its peak with the *Cum dormirent homines* in 1395.[42] The conversion of the 1360s was repeated in 1390–1 and two complementary lists of names of converts were compiled, the shorter having eleven or twelve and the longer twenty names.[43] The converts provided more inside information about the Waldensian movement, and the texts written by the generation active in the 1390s, above all by Zwicker, make use of the earlier material but with significant expansion, revisions and systematization.

M. Lambert, *Medieval Heresy: Popular Movements from the Gregorian Reform to the Reformation* (Oxford, 2009), p. 175.

[41] Biller, *Waldenses*, p. 233; see also Gonnet and Molnár, *Les Vaudois au Moyen Âge*, pp. 150–2; on the intellectual stagnation of the Waldensian movement, see A. Patschovsky, 'The Literacy of Waldensianism from Valdes to c. 1400', in *Heresy and Literacy, 1000–1530*, ed. P. Biller and A. Hudson (Cambridge, 1994), pp. 112–36 (pp. 134–6); and on their inner crisis concerning the legitimacy of lay apostolate, see K. Utz Tremp, 'Multum abhorrerem confiteri homini laico. Die Waldenser zwischen Laienapostolat und Priestertum, insbesondere an der Wende vom 14. zum 15. Jahrhundert', in *Pfaffen und Laien, ein mittelalterlicher Antagonismus? Freiburger Colloquium 1996*, ed. E. C. Lutz and E. Tremp (Freiburg, 1999), pp. 153–89 (pp. 166–7 and passim); Modestin, *Ketzer in der Stadt*, p. 3. Kieckhefer, *Repression*, p. 57, also considered that the ultimate reason behind the inquisitorial campaign and its special character lay in the disruption within the Waldensian movement itself.

[42] Biller, *Waldenses*, pp. 290–1. On the dating of the *Attendite a falsis prophetis*, see above, p. 18, n. 74.

[43] Biller, *Waldenses*, ch. XIV; Kurze, 'Zur Ketzergeschichte', pp. 79–80, n. 152. See also Chapter 3.

One can also point out corresponding continuity in inquisitorial activity and responses by the authorities, without denying that they culminated in the 1390s. Martinus of Prague prosecuted beguines in Strasbourg as early as 1374,[44] and he was the inquisitor against Waldensians in Regensburg in the early 1380s.[45] These trials may have been a response to the letter of 1381 by the archbishop of Prague, Jan of Jenštejn, where he, as papal legate, urged the bishops of Bamberg, Regensburg and Meissen to nominate inquisitors against Waldensian heretics.[46] In the same year, Jenštejn expressed his concern over Waldensian heresiarchs in the diocese of Olomouc.[47] The archbishop himself held heretics in custody, most likely Waldensians, and Master Matthew of Kraków preached about their errors to the citizens of Prague in January 1384.[48] There is also a tradition of Bohemian inquisitors in Austria. Zwicker's predecessor in the diocese of Passau was Henricus of Olomouc, whose documents Zwicker must have used since he made several references to sentences from them.[49] Henricus could have been active already in the 1360s, so it was possibly he who was responsible for the conversion of the Austrian Brethren around 1368, as Biller suggested.[50] Neither was Zwicker the first to go to Hungarian dioceses: a certain Elisabeth who abjured to Zwicker in Buda in 1404 had been converted by the same Henricus of Olomouc.[51]

Without doubt Petrus Zwicker and Martinus of Prague were ardent converters of Waldensians and defenders of the Catholic faith, and their co-operation is impressive. After Erfurt they first acted independently of each other, Zwicker in Stettin in 1392–4 and Martinus in Würzburg in 1391. The inquisition in Würzburg, where nine Waldensians were sentenced to bear crosses, is clearly an aftermath of the Waldensian Brethren's conversion:

---

[44] Patschovsky, 'Straßburger Beginenverfolkungen im 14. Jahrhundert', pp. 89–91.

[45] Modestin, *Ketzer in der Stadt*, p. 6; *Quellen*, ed. Modestin, no. [88]; H. Finke, 'Waldenserprocess in Regensburg, 1395', *Deutsche Zeitschrift für Geschichtswissenschaft* 4 (1890), 345–6; Haupt, 'Waldenserthum und Inquisition', pp. 348–9; Biller, 'Aspects', p. 138.

[46] *Concilia Pragensia = Prager Synodal-Beschlüsse*, ed. C. Höfler (Prague, 1862), pp. 26–7; cf. a new critical edition, *Pražské synody a koncily předhusitské doby*, ed. J. V. Polc and Z. Hledíková (Prague, 2002), p. 215; Kieckhefer, 'Repression of Heresy in Germany, 1348–1520', p. 174.

[47] J. Loserth, 'Beiträge zur Geschichte der husitischen Bewegung I. Der Codex Epistolaris des Erzbischofs von Prag Johann von Jenzenstein', *Archiv für österreichische Geschichte* 55 (1877), 267–400 (p. 368).

[48] *Quellen*, ed. Patschovsky, pp. 318–23.

[49] BSB MS Clm 15125, fols. 205ra–rb; 206va; cf. ed. in. Haupt, 'Waldenserthum und Inquisition', p. 404; St Florian MS XI 234, fol. 90vb; Würzburg UB, MS M. ch. f. 51, fol. 29r, cf. ed. in Haupt, *Der Waldensische Ursprung des Codex Teplensis*, pp. 34–5.

[50] Biller, 'Aspects', p. 226; on Henricus of Olomouc, see Haupt, 'Waldenserthum und Inquisition', pp. 368–9; Gonnet and Molnár, *Les Vaudois au Moyen Âge*, pp. 150, 157; Segl, 'Die Waldenser in Österreich', pp. 176–7; Modestin, 'The Anti-Waldensian Treatise', pp. 225–6.

[51] Neumann, *České sekty ve století 14. a 15.*, p. 6*; Biller, 'Aspects', p. 372.

the short notice about the incident describes how Martinus 'ordered and prescribed by God, came to Würzburg having been informed and instructed about them by other heretics in the different parts of the world'. Impressed by his expertise, Bishop Gerhard von Schwarzburg commissioned Martinus to conduct the inquisition in his town.[52] The co-operation of the two inquisitors continued a few years later. Both men were commissioned as inquisitors in the diocese of Passau, probably around 1395. Martinus probably never acted as inquisitor there, for the sentences from Passau (1395–8) are all authored by Zwicker alone, and the unedited formulary that has the commission of inquisitors also includes Zwicker's commission to Fridericus, parish priest of Steyr, to act as his sub-delegate because of the heavy burden of the office.[53] It appears that Martinus was meanwhile busy in Prague, where he was inquisitor in September 1396,[54] and in Nuremberg and Bamberg in the spring of 1399.[55] In September 1400 Zwicker and Martinus were inquisitors in the diocese of Esztergom, in what is now Trnava in Slovakia, but only short, fragmentary records of their activity there have survived.[56] The rest of their common career is preserved in the formularies of the *Processus Petri*. In January 1401 they sentenced heretics to do public penance by wearing crosses in Ödenburg (now Sopron, Hungary) in the diocese of Győr,[57] and finally in February of the same year they were at Hartberg in Steiermark, in the archdiocese of Salzburg, where three women ended up on the pyre as relapsed heretics and opponents of the inquisitors.[58]

Nevertheless, rather than seeing them as zealous, self-styled heretic-hunters, I would situate them within the tradition of Bohemian inquisitors

---

[52] 'Ac officium inquisitionis ad personas predictas fuit commissum Domino deuoto Martino de Bohemia, qui ab aliis haereticis in diuersis mundi Partibus eductus et instructus fuit de illis, et Deo ordinante et disponente venit Herbp.' See *TIF*, 1. Abschnitt, 17. Heft, pp. 3263–6 (quotation p. 3265); for corrections of several mistakes in the edition, see H. Haupt, *Die religiösen Sekten in Franken vor der Reformation* (Würzburg, 1882), pp. 23–4; see also Kieckhefer, 'Repression of Heresy in Germany, 1348–1520', p. 502. The only manuscript containing the note is Würzburg, Staatsarchiv MS 6, fol. 28r. See the description in A. Ruland, *Die Ebracher Handschrift des Michael de Leone*, Besonderen Abdruck aus dem 'Archiv des historischen Vereines dür Unterfranken und Aschaffenburg' Band XIII. Heft 1 (Würzburg, 1854), pp. 65–6.

[53] St Florian MS XI 234, fols. 88ra–vb. See Chapter 3 below for detailed discussion.

[54] Modestin, *Ketzer in der Stadt*, p. 7; Soukup, 'Die Waldenser in Böhmen', p. 140; *Quellen*, ed. Patschovsky, p. 129.

[55] Neumann, *České sekty ve století 14. a 15.*, p. 6*; *Deutsche Reichstagsakten unter König Wenzel, Abt. 1–3 (1376–1400)*, 2nd edn (Göttingen, 1956), Abt. 3, p. 88; Modestin, *Ketzer in der Stadt*, p. 7.

[56] Presently with the shelf mark NKCR MS VII. A 16/4. Edited in Truhlář, 'Inkvisice Waldenských v Trnavě r. 1400'.

[57] Ed. in Haupt, 'Waldenserthum und Inquisition', pp. 401–3.

[58] Ed. ibid., pp. 408–11.

sent outside the formal jurisdiction of the metropolitan see.[59] Alexander Patschovsky observed a similar phenomenon with regard to the Bohemian Dominican inquisitors who were operating in Silesia in the 1390s, an area which – contrary to the wishes of Emperor Charles IV and the archbishops of Prague – had remained a part of the Polish diocesan structure. The inquisition of heresy enabled a degree of control that was not possible for Prague at the level of the conventional Church hierarchy.[60] Even if Martinus went to Würzburg on his own initiative, Petrus Zwicker's commission in Stettin seems to be more closely linked to the Bohemian Church. No letter of commission has survived, but the protocols reveal that he was authorized by the archbishop of Prague and the bishops of Cammin, Lebus and Brandenburg.[61] At the time the archbishop was the same Jan of Jenštejn who had called for repression of Waldensianism a decade earlier, and the bishop of Cammin was in Prague as well. Since 1387 the diocese had been divided over a struggle between the candidate of the diocesan chapter and the local duchy, Bogislaw of Pommern-Volgast, and the nominee of Pope Urban VI who was supported by King Wenceslaus, Johannes Brunonis. Johannes was never consecrated, but in the early 1390s when he used his power *in spiritualibus et temporalibus* (in spiritual and temporal things) this was through auxiliary bishops as well as the archdean of Stolp and provost of Cammin, while Johannes simply stayed back in Prague, getting on with his job as King Wenceslaus's chancellor.[62] Although the names of the bishops are not

---

[59] As in fact proposed earlier by Gonnet and Molnár, *Les Vaudois au Moyen Âge*, p. 157.

[60] A. Patschovsky, 'Über die politische Bedeutung von Häresie und Häresieverfolgung im mittelalterlichen Böhmen', in *Die Anfänge der Inquisition im Mittelalter*, ed. P. Segl (Cologne, 1993), pp. 235–51 (pp. 240–2); A. Patschovsky, 'Spuren böhmischer Ketzerverfolgung in Schlesien am Ende des 14. Jahrhunderts', in *Historia docet. Sborník prací k poctì šedesátých narozenin prof. PhDr. Ivana Hlaváèka*, ed. M. Polívka and M. Svatoš (Prague, 1992), pp. 357–87 (p. 363 and passim).

[61] *Quellen*, ed. Kurze, p. 235: 'frater Petrus provincialis fratrum ordin(is) Celestinorum per Alamaniam, inquisitor pravitatis heretice a reverendis in Christo patribus et dominis, Pragensi, Lubucensi et Caminensi, archiepiscopo et episcopis constitutus'. Zwicker's commission in Brandenburg is revealed in the protocol of Petrus Lavbruch from Angermünde (21 March 1394), where Zwicker is called 'inquisitore heretice pravitatis per diocesim Brandenburgensem et adhuc non revocato' (inquisitor of heretical wickedness for the diocese of Brandenburg, and until now not revoked [from this office]). It seems that he had received the commission from Bishop Dietrich II (1365–93), and was not sure if it applied under the new bishop, Heinrich von Bodendieck (1393–1406), as he absolved Petrus Lavbruch 'auctoritate, quia non revocatus suo scire, et eciam spe ratihabicionis per episcopum nunc existentem' (by authority, because to the best of his knowledge not revoked, and in the expectation of ratification by the current bishop); *Quellen*, ed. Kurze, p. 253.

[62] J. Petersohn, 'Johann Brunonis', in *Die Bischöfe des Heiligen Römischen Reiches 1198 bis 1448. Ein biographisches Lexikon*, ed. E. Gatz (Berlin, 2001), p. 263; J. Petersohn, 'Bistum Kammin', in *Die Bistümer des heiligen römischen Reiches*, ed. E. Gatz (Freiburg im Breisgau, 2003), pp. 267–72; J. Petersohn, *Die Kamminer Bischöfe des Mittelalters:*

mentioned in the protocol, it was obviously Johannes Brunonis, not the more or less ousted Bogislaw, who commissioned Petrus Zwicker. The provost of Cammin and Johannes Brunonis's vicar-general, Philipp von Helpte, witnessed two hearings in Stettin.[63]

Again, the ghost of Charles IV looms in the background. With the exception of the diocese of Cammin, Zwicker's inquisitor's commission in 1392–4 matched the area that – after the long hoped-for acquisition of Brandenburg in 1373 – belonged either to Bohemian crown lands or Luxemburg patrimonial dominions.[64] Bishop Dietrich II of Brandenburg (1366–93) was Charles's ally, and in 1374 the emperor had even attempted to add the dioceses of Brandenburg, Lebus and Havelberg to the legation of the archbishop of Prague, already covering the dioceses of Regensburg, Bamberg and Meissen.[65] Although this plan came to naught, and although the House of Luxemburg's political expansion to the north ended with the death of Charles IV,[66] it is necessary to remember that during his northern inquisitorial campaign Petrus Zwicker operated in an area long aspired to by both the Bohemian Crown and the Church, and where they had a network of allies. One should not, however, imagine a unified front of Bohemian ecclesiastical politics at this point: Archbishop Jan of Jenštejn and King Wenceslaus were involved in a bitter struggle with each other.[67] Interestingly enough, Zwicker was commissioned both by the archbishop and by the king's chancellor. Yet simultaneously representing two rivals and enemies while working for the greater good of the Church was probably something easily reconciled in Petrus Zwicker's mind. As we shall see in the following chapters, his goal was in every way to bypass the struggles and factions of his times by stressing the fundamental unity of the Church.

In addition to these personal links, inquisitorial praxis and the ownership of manuscripts link Zwicker intimately with the Bohemian tradition of inquisition of heresy. He owned, used and partly reproduced a Bohemian inquisitors' manual, as will be discussed in detail in Chapter 3. I would also

---

Amtsbiographien und Bistumsstrukturen vom 12. bis 16. Jahrhundert (Schwerin, 2015), pp. 60–2.

[63] *Quellen*, ed. Kurze, pp. 78, 112.

[64] On Charles IV and Brandenburg, see H. Stoob, 'Kaiser Karl IV. und der Ostseecraum', *Hansische Geschichtsblätter* 88 (1970), 163–214 (pp. 180–207); Seibt, *Karl IV*, pp. 279–85.

[65] Z. Hledíková, 'Die Prager Erzbischöfe als ständige Päpstliche Legaten. Ein Beitrag zur Kirchenpolitik Karls IV', *Beiträge zur Geschichte des Bistums Regensburg* 6 (1972), 221–56; E. Wetter, 'Die Lausitz und die Mark Brandenburg', in *Karl IV., Kaiser von Gottes Gnaden: Kunst und Repräsentation des Hauses Luxemburg 1310–1437*, ed. J. Fajt, M. Hörsch, A. Langerand and B. D. Boehm (Munich, 2006), pp. 341–9 (p. 344).

[66] K. Conrad, 'Herzogliche Schwäche und städtische Macht in der zweiten Hälfte des 14. und im 15. Jahrhundert', in *Deutsche Geschichte im Osten Europas*, ed. W. Buchholz (Berlin, 1999), pp. 127–202 (p. 162).

[67] R. E. Weltsch, *Archbishop John of Jenstein (1348-1400): Papalism, Humanism and Reform in Pre-Hussite Prague* (The Hague, 1968), pp. 40–78.

separate Petrus Zwicker and Martinus of Prague, both of whom enjoyed the support of the highest ecclesiastical and secular officials throughout their careers, from Heinrich Angermeyer, who really does appear to have been a 'self-styled' inquisitor. Because of this Angermeyer ran into conflict with the bishop of Würzburg; in November 1394, in the case of Hans Wern from Rothenburg ob der Tauber, the bishop quickly replaced the 'Ketzermeister' with his own inquisitor, vicar-general *in spiritualibus* Walter Schubel.[68]

There is also good reason to ask whether concentrating on those inquisitors active in the southern and eastern parts of German-speaking Europe gives a false impression of the trials (and of Waldensianism) as a whole. As Jennifer Kolpacoff Deane has observed, the first urban persecution of the Waldensians began in 1390 as part of the new archbishop Conrad von Weinsberg's campaign against local heresy and anticlericalism, and this predates the appearance of Zwicker and Martinus in Erfurt in 1391.[69] In Swiss Fribourg in 1399, matters were entrusted to the papal inquisitor, the Dominican Humbert Franconis, and the guardian of the Franciscan convent at Lausanne, Aymo of Taninges,[70] and in Strasbourg in the following year the city council took matters into their own hands.[71] Because these significant trials were all conducted very differently from those of Zwicker and Martinus of Prague, Georg Modestin, albeit subscribing to the 'itinerant inquisitor' thesis, has remarked that their activities are not the complete picture, and he is inclined to speak of a series of individual trials rather than a continuous wave of persecution.[72]

Neither did the end of Zwicker's inquisitorial career after 1404 – and most likely his life also – mean the end of inquisitions into Waldensian heresy. The last trials he was responsible for were one against a man called Andreas Hesel in Vienna in 1403[73] and the already mentioned abjuration of Elisabeth in Buda in 1404. After that, according to local early modern tradition, Zwicker died at the Benedictine monastery of Garsten and was buried there.[74] But the

---

[68] The different political and personal implications in the trial of Hans Wern have been thoroughly studied, with additional archival discoveries, in Schnurrer, 'Der Fall Hans Wern'; Angermeyer was a bit more succesful in Augsburg and Dinkelsbühl in 1393; see Modestin, *Ketzer in der Stadt*, pp. 8–9; Modestin, 'Der Augsburger Waldenserprozess', pp. 50–68; C. Bürckstümmer, 'Waldenser in Dinkelsbühl', *Beiträge zur bayerischen Kirchengeschichte* 19 (1913), 272–5; A. F. von Oefele, *Rerum Boicarum scriptores*, 2 vols. (Augsburg, 1763), I, 620.

[69] Deane, 'Archiepiscopal Inquisitions', pp. 205–6 and passim.

[70] *Quellen*, ed. Utz Tremp, p. 208.

[71] Modestin, *Ketzer in der Stadt*, pp. 17–27.

[72] Ibid., pp. 9–10; Modestin, 'The Anti-Waldensian Treatise', p. 213.

[73] The sentence has been preserved in a single manuscript, Würzburg, UB MS M. ch. f. 51, fols. 27v–28v.

[74] Peter Segl has listed the various handwritten early modern chronicles of the local tradition; Segl, 'Die Waldenser in Österreich', p. 166, n. 88. I have myself consulted the chronicle of Seraphin Kirchmair, *Chronicon sive Annales percelebris monasterii B. Virginis Mariae in Gärsten*. Göttweig, Stiftsbibliothek, MS 811 (rot), fol. 30r.

trials against Waldensians continued. In February 1408 the *Landeshauptmann* Reinprecht II of Wallsee received oaths of truce (*Urfehde*) and abjuration of all heresy from a widow and her three children who had been imprisoned because of their heresy – the father of the family had been burned.[75] In 1410 Bishop Georg von Hohenlohe, the same who had commissioned Zwicker, denounced 'Wiklefiten' in Griesbach and Waldkirche; it is more likely that the heretics were Waldensians than genuine supporters of John Wyclif, even though Jerome of Prague had preached in the area.[76] In another document from May 1418, Stephanus Lamp, Zwicker's notary in the 1390s, is mentioned as the inquisitor who had ordered the imprisonment of two brothers in Gleink,[77] and he held the title at least until 1419,[78] implying continuity in the office of inquisition in the diocese of Passau. In Brandenburg a man called Jakob Schröder was executed in 1411 for denying the legitimacy of death sentence, the description of his heresy explicitly mentioning that 'in this error they are Waldensians and Cross-Brethren (flagellants)' (*in isto errore sunt Waldenses et Crucifratres*).[79]

Although the trials and other measures of repression were to a degree more sporadic in the 1380s and early fifteenth century, and although there were no inquisitors with comparable careers or fame, one should not isolate the inquisitions of Petrus Zwicker and Martinus of Prague from their predecessors and followers. Zwicker especially became such a monumental figure in the repression of heresy because he was an innovative, original and determined inquisitor and polemicist, but within the established tradition and earlier models. To understand the downfall of German Waldensians at the turn of the fifteenth century, we must study Petrus Zwicker. At the same time we must keep in mind that his success depended on his ability to ride the waves of much broader anti-heretical sentiments and anxiety over the state of the Church.

---

[75] Vienna, Österreichische Staatsarchiv, Haus-, Hof- und Staatsarchiv, Allgemeine Urkundenreihe, 1408 II 17; cf. M. Doblinger, 'Die Herren von Walsee. Ein Beitrag zur österreichischen Adelsgeschichte', *Archiv für österreichische Geschichte* 95 (1906), 335–578 (p. 399); Segl, 'Die Waldenser in Österreich', p. 175, n. 57. The document does not mention the dates of the trial or the length of their imprisonment, nor does it refer to any inquisitor, but nothing indicates that the sentences took place a decade earlier when Zwicker was responsible for the prosecutions. The trials and punishments are probably post-Zwicker. On the same day another similar document was prepared for a certain Hanns Schalderhart, likewise imprisoned for heresy. The document is preserved in the same archival location.

[76] Haupt, 'Waldenserthum und Inquisition', pp. 349–50; A. Schmid, 'Georg von Hohenlohe', in *Die Bischöfe des Heiligen Römischen Reiches 1198 bis 1448. Ein biographisches Lexikon*, ed. E. Gatz (Berlin, 2001), pp. 560–1; cf. T. A. Fudge, *Jan Hus: Religious Reform and Social Revolution in Bohemia* (London, 2010), pp. 148–9. See also R. Välimäki, 'Old Errors, New Sects: The Waldensians, Wyclif and Hus in the Fifteenth-Century Manuscripts', in *Golden Leaves, Burned Books*, ed. G. Müller-Oberhäuser and T. Immonen (Turku, 2019) [forthcoming].

[77] OÖLA, Stiftsarchiv Gleink, 1418 V 19; Segl, 'Die Waldenser in Österreich', p. 182.

[78] OÖLA, Stiftsarchiv Garsten, 1419 III 8.

[79] Excerpt from Stephan Bodecker's *De decem preceptis*; *Quellen*, ed. Kurze, pp. 267–8.

2

The Inquisitor Writes

Item dicunt quod ex institucione ecclesie nichil tenentur credere nisi textui biblie.[1]

And they say that nothing from the institution of the Church is worth believing if not from the text of the Bible.

Waldensian articles from the 1390s.

In 1395 Petrus Zwicker rewrote the Waldensian heresy. There is no doubt that the *Cum dormirent homines* was his most important work. It is also the most important anti-Waldensian text of the later Middle Ages, in terms of length and popularity as well as the expertise of its author. It was not, of course, conceived overnight. The composition of a long treatise such as the *Cum dormirent homines* was an arduous process, and included several phases. This chapter demonstrates that in addition to the finished treatise, an early version of Zwicker's polemic against the Waldensians has been preserved in a shorter polemical text, known as the *Refutatio errorum*, often copied together with the *Cum dormirent homines* and treating material very similar to the themes discussed in the longer treatise. This text has been known, acknowledged and cited by scholars, but not properly studied, and its author was previously unidentified. On the basis of both codicological and internal evidence, presented here for the first time, we can be relatively certain that the text originated from the hand of Petrus Zwicker – or rather, that its early version was compiled in the circle around him, probably before the completion of the *Cum dormirent homines* in 1395. Recognizing the shared origin of the two treatises underlines the uniqueness of the latter work, which can be regarded as the finalized product of Zwicker's anti-heretical literary endeavours. Studying what was preserved, changed and left out in this process of compilation and revision brings to light a revival of the thirteenth-century polemical style combined with contemporary emphasis on the authority of the Scriptures. These were the literary characteristics of this pastoralization

---

[1] Augsburg, UB MS II. 1. 2° 78, fol. 245va.

of heresy. Zwicker not only compiled existing knowledge on Waldensianism, but also aimed higher. He created a polemical treatise matching the style and vigour of the thirteenth-century anti-heretical treatises and directed against the enemy he deemed the worst threat to the Church: the Waldensians. It was intended for an audience wider than inquisitors, and the sheer number and diffusion of the surviving manuscripts show it was a howling success. Its result was clerics using pastoral weapons, fighting heresy as preachers from the pulpit.

The Refutatio errorum: *a draft-like treatise on Waldensians*

The anonymous *Refutatio errorum* gives a view of Waldensianism very similar to that of the better-known *Cum dormirent homines*, and it is clearly representative of the same era and state of knowledge. It has been less commented on by scholars than the *Cum dormirent homines*, quite likely because the only available printed version, edited by Jacob Gretser together with the *Cum dormirent homines* (1613/1677), is obviously incomplete. As already stated, it has ten chapters, but the text stops abruptly in the middle of the tenth chapter.[2] In his studies on the *Cum dormirent homines* Peter Biller does not suggest any author or dating for the *Refutatio*, but seems to hold the view that the two treatises were not written by the same author, that is Zwicker. In fact, Biller uses the common manuscript tradition of *Refutatio errorum* and *Cum dormirent homines* as an argument against the attribution of *Cum dormirent homines* to Peter von Pillichsdorf, the author suggested by Gretser in his seventeenth-century edition. Biller suggests that the now lost Tegernsee manuscript, which included treatises by both Zwicker and Pillichsdorf and consequently led Gretser to propose Pillichsdorf as the author of both these treatises, is a parallel case to that of the several manuscripts including the *Cum dormirent homines* and the *Refutatio*. These too were two different treatises but treated as one by both medieval scribes and modern compilers of manuscript catalogues. Biller does not state anything explicit concerning the authorship of the *Refutatio*, calling it and Zwicker's treatise only 'two tracts on similar material'.[3]

They do indeed cover very much the same material, and because of this Peter Segl has tentatively proposed that these two treatises originated from the same hand.[4] Euan Cameron describes the treatise very vaguely, but evidently treats it as a product of the 1390s, at one point calling it 'a

---

[2] Gretser evidently noticed this, as the end of the text is marked with the words 'Hactenus manuscriptum exemplar'. *Refutatio*, ed. Gretser, p. 307F.

[3] Biller, *Waldenses*, pp. 252–3, quotation p. 252.

[4] Segl, 'Die Waldenser in Österreich', p. 185, n. 102.

third treatise from Zwicker's circle'.[5] Patschovsky has also associated the *Refutatio* loosely with Zwicker, without making any definite claims about its authorship.[6] There is also a medieval attribution of a sort, a reference to Zwicker's achievements as inquisitor, inserted at the beginning of the treatise in some manuscripts: 'It is to be noted that brother Petrus called back to faith around six hundred of the above-mentioned heretics in one year.'[7] This is no guarantee of Zwicker's authorship, but it demonstrates that some medieval copyists made a connection between the *Refutatio* and Zwicker.

The *Refutatio errorum*, preserved in one form or another in nineteen manuscripts,[8] is one of those medieval texts that persistently defies all attempts at classification. This is true of many texts on heresy, as those trying to categorize writing on heresy have been forced to concede. For a historian's purposes perhaps the most applicable and the most recent categorization is offered by Lucy Sackville in her study on thirteenth-century textual representations of heresy. Sackville divides texts into four generic groups: polemical texts, texts designed for edification, canon-legal texts and inquisition literature. But, as Sackville herself points out, the division is in large part for convenience, and 'there is a great deal of overlap between these genres at their outer edges'.[9]

The *Refutatio errorum* is the type of text that crosses the outer edges of different genres, including some characteristics of polemical literature, and is too crude to be actually considered a polemical treatise, such as the *Cum dormirent homines* or Moneta of Cremona's long work against Cathars and Waldensians. Yet it is more than a simple collection of Bible quotations and other references on specific questions, like the so called *Summae auctoritatum* (*Summae of Authorities*) composed to aid preachers.[10] In addition, it bears a resemblance to texts included in inquisitors' manuals or collections of inquisitorial formularies such as lists of errors, interrogatories and short descriptions on heresy, two examples being the *De vita et conversacione* (*On the Life and Conduct*) transmitted in the *Processus Petri* compilation and the still earlier description on the Waldensians, the *De vita et actibus* (*On the Life and Doings*).[11] The *Refutatio* is, however, more polemical and doctrinal than these types of texts.

---

[5] Cameron, *Waldenses*, pp. 140, 142–3.

[6] *Quellen*, ed. Patschovsky, p. 27, n. 42.

[7] See n. 30 below.

[8] For the manuscript descriptions, see Appendix 1.

[9] Sackville, *Heresy and Heretics*, pp. 10–11.

[10] Ibid., pp. 42–53; see also W. L. Wakefield, 'Notes on Some Anti-heretical Writings of the Thirteenth Century', *Franciscan Studies* 27 (1967), 285–321 (p. 300). Wakefield has remarked that the *summae auctoritatum* too sometimes approached the status of a full treatise, when some compilers added more sources and explanatory sentences.

[11] On the text, with an edition, see P. Biller, 'Fingerprinting an Anonymous Description

It does not seem reasonable to categorize the *Refutatio errorum* into one genre or another, but for clarity's sake it could be described as a short treatise on heresy. It includes Waldensian propositions, some description of heretical practices and Catholic counter-arguments, some of which are carefully formulated, others mere lists of biblical references. Above all the *Refutatio errorum* is a practical text. Manuscripts usually begin by simply stating that it treats Waldensian errors. For example in the earliest reliably datable *Refutatio* manuscript, written in Bohemia in 1404, the opening words are:

> It is to be noted that the errors of Waldensian heretics are to be opposed with these and other Catholic scriptures. Firstly because they say that their heresiarchs, who they call 'brethren' and in confessions address as 'lord', are the true successors of Christ's disciples.[12]

This opening resembles various lists of heretical errors circulating in late medieval manuscripts. A common exposition of Waldensian errors begins thus: 'These are the articles, with which the Catholic faith is contradicted. Firstly, because such men hear confessions, who are not sent by the Church nor ordained.'[13] Like this exposition of heretical errors, the *Refutatio* goes straight into the business, without any rhetorical tags or the usual opening of a polemical treatise, a prologue or an exposition of a biblical quotation proclaiming the apocalyptic danger posed to the Church by heretics. An opening like this was not used only in anti-heretical treatises, of course – it can be encountered in a great variety of sources from papal bulls to sermons. Precisely because polemical style demanded such rhetoric, it seems reasonable to assume that the compiler of the *Refutatio* did not necessarily intend his work for wider circulation. The opening of the tract would rather suit a text intended originally for personal or a limited circle's use, as a summary of Waldensian doctrine with applicable counter-arguments.

Different redactions of the Refutatio errorum

To further complicate the study of this text, the only available printed editions are based on a text that is anything but representative of the manuscript

---

of the Waldensians', in *Texts and the Repression of Medieval Heresy*, ed. P. Biller and C. Bruschi (York, 2003), pp. 163–207.

[12] 'Notandum quod erroribus hereticorum waldensium est istis et alijs scripturis katholicis obuiandum. Primo quia dicunt heresiarchas suos, quos fratres nominant et in confessione domino [sic] appellant, esse veros discipulorum cristi successores.' Gdańsk, PAN MS Mar. F. 295, fol. 211ra–rb.

[13] 'Sunt autem hii articuli, quibus fidei katholice contrariantur. Primo quia audiunt confessiones non missi ab ecclesia, nec ordinati.' The Waldensian articles are treated in detail below. A critical edition of the text is in Werner, 'Nachrichten', pp. 267–1; these words, p. 267.

tradition of the *Refutatio*. As noted, Jacob Gretser printed the tract in the seventeenth century from a manuscript that ends abruptly in the middle of Chapter 10. Gretser's manuscript was from the Swabian Augustinian house of Diessen, and it is nowadays in the Bayerische Staatsbibliothek with the shelfmark Clm 1329. The tract was printed again, from the same manuscript, in the collection of texts on heresy by Ignaz von Döllinger, published in 1890.[14] New editions usually offer better versions of the edited text and clarify its history, but unfortunately the situation in the case of the *Refutatio* has been the opposite. From the point of view of German *Editionswissenschaft*, Döllinger's printing is an abomination. Long sections are left out without notice, the order of the chapters is mixed up and finally a paragraph that is not to be found in the manuscript is added at the end.[15] Therefore it is Gretser's edition, not Döllinger's misleading one, that must serve as a starting point for a study of the *Refutatio*.

In Table 1 the different redactions of the *Refutatio errorum* are presented. The division is based on my own comparison of the manuscripts mentioned in the table. The analysis shows that the version printed by Gretser and Döllinger is neither the most common nor the closest to the *Cum dormirent homines*, but it is Redaction 1 that must be the point of reference for any further study. This, the longest version of the text, also includes components, that have disappeared from the later revisions, which are extremely enlightening on how materials were compiled (and what they were) when a treatise on heresy was composed. Thus Redaction 1 represents the most extensive and widespread version of the text, which also has the earliest manuscripts that can be dated with certainty. Redaction 2 is an early revision of the text, extant in only one manuscript. Redaction 3 is somewhat later and a shorter version, and finally Redaction 4 represents the version printed by Gretser and preserved in one imperfect and one complete manuscript. Two Bohemian manuscripts that contain only a few sentences from the beginning of the first chapter have been excluded from the table, as it is impossible to determine the redaction of the treatise in these cases.[16]

---

[14] Döllinger, *Beiträge II*, pp. 331–44.

[15] Although Döllinger's collection has been widely used simply because it includes a huge number of texts collected in two volumes, its quality and edition principles were criticized even when it was published. However, Döllinger himself, at the time over 90 years old and approaching death, was perhaps not so much to blame as his publisher and editors. In the late nineteenth century Döllinger was the famous president of the Bavarian Academy of Sciences, and his earlier works were edited and published at a fast pace. The manuscript of *Beiträge zur Sektengeschichte des Mittelalters* was actually based on Döllinger's notes from 1839. See H. Fuhrmann, *Ignaz von Döllinger: ein exkommunizierter Theologe als Akademiepräsident und Historiker* (Leipzig, 1999), p. 22.

[16] Prague, NKCR MS X. B. 2, fol. 168rb; Wrocław, BU MS I F 707, fol. 154ra.

As stated, the longest version of the text is in Redaction 1, which is also the most common. It is the version that appears in some of the earliest datable manuscripts, and it was copied throughout the fifteenth century. A Gdańsk manuscript, Mar. F. 295, was written in 1404.[17] Another Gdańsk manuscript, Mar. F. 294, is more difficult to date, but both its provenance and watermarks indicate an origin in the 1410s. Leipzig Universitätsbibliothek, MS 602 is a little later, the part including the *Refutatio errorum* and *Cum dormirent homines* being finished in 1421. Augsburg Universitätsbibliothek, MS II. 1. 2° 127 probably originates from the second quarter of the fifteenth century, while University of Pennsylvania Library MS Codex 76 was written in the second half of the century. All in all, of the seventeen[18] copies of the treatise, thirteen have this long redaction.

Table 1. Redactions of the *Refutatio errorum*

The chapter division differs from manuscript to manuscript. For the sake of clarity the structure and numbering present in the printed text (Gretser 1613/1677) and Augsburg Staats- und Stadtbibliothek, MS 2° Cod 338 have been used as a reference point. The black shading indicates the first four chapters that appear in the same order in all redactions (with the exception of Chapter 1 in Redaction 2). The *Refutatio errorum* includes the following propositions of the Waldensians:

1. Waldensian lay Brethren were legitimate successors of the Apostles.
2. Critique of the Church's and the clergy's property.
3. Critique of the clergy's worldly lifestyle.
4. Denial of invocation and honouring of the saints and the Virgin Mary.
5. Invalidity of church buildings, ornaments, vestments and their dedications as well as church music.
6. Denial of the ecclesiastical hierarchy and authority of the papacy.
7. Illegitimacy of constitutions given by the prelates of the Church.
8. Illegitimacy of excommunication.
9. Invalidity of indulgences.
10. Denial of the existence of purgatory.
11. Sinfulness of all forms of oaths and oath-taking.
12. Sinfulness of all forms of killing.

---

[17] For more information about the datings and provenances, see Appendix 1.
[18] Excluding the two short excerpts, see above.

Redaction 1	Redaction 2	Redaction 3	Redaction 4
Gdańsk, PAN MS Mar. F. 294; PAN MS Mar. F. 295; Leipzig, UB MS 602; Augsburg, UB MS II. 1. 2° 127; Herzogenburg, Stiftsbibliothek, MS 22; UPenn MS Codex 76; Wrocław, BU MS I Q 43;[19] Vienna, ÖNB MS 1588; Prague, KMK MS C LX; Wiesbaden, Hessische Landesbibliothek, MS 35; Michelstadt, Kirchenbibliothek, MS I. Db. 685; Trier, Stadtbibliothek, MS 680/879; Würzburg, UB MS M.ch.f. 186.[20]	Augsburg, StaSB MS 2° Cod 185	Prague, NKCR MS XIII. E. 7	*Refutatio*, ed. Gretser (1613/1677); BSB MS Clm 1329; Augsburg, StaSB MS 2° Cod 338
1	–	1	1
2	2	2	2
3	3	3	3
4	4	4	4
10	10	10	5
11	11	–	6
12	12	–	7
5	5	–	8
6[21]	6	–	9
7	7	–	10
8	8	–	11[22]
9	9	–	12

Redaction 2, extant in only one manuscript, Augsburg Stadt- und Staatsbibliothek, MS 2° Cod 185, is probably an early revision. The part including heresy texts has been an independent fascicule. It is difficult to date, but watermarks indicate either the last years of the 1390s or around 1410.[23] One can safely assume that the text was composed before 1415. In

---

[19] The text breaks off abruptly in the middle of the middle of the chapter on purgatory, but the order of the chapters implies that the manuscript belongs to Redaction 1.

[20] The end of Chapter 3, Chapter 4 and the beginning of Chapter 10 (Purgatory) are missing due to the loss of a leaf. Chapter 12 (on homicide, number 7 in the manuscript) has revisions not found elsewhere.

[21] The chapter on the ecclesiastical hierarchy and the authority of the papacy is significantly longer in Redactions 1 and 2.

[22] Chapters 11 and 12 of Redaction 4 are only in the manuscript Augsburg, StaSB MS 2° Cod 338.

[23] See Appendix 1.

many ways Redaction 2 resembles the text in Redaction 1. Both have the same chapter order and similar, long chapters on purgatory and the ecclesiastical hierarchy. These are lacking or are significantly shorter in Redactions 3 and 4. In addition, MS 2° Cod 185 has numbered chapters, as do Redactions 3 and 4, whereas numeration is rare in Redaction 1.[24] However, Redaction 2 cannot represent the manuscript tradition common to all other versions because it lacks the usual first chapter on Waldensian heresiarchs. Instead, some remarks on purgatory form this chapter.

Redaction 3 is likewise represented by only one manuscript, Prague, NKCR XIII. E. 7, and the text is of poor quality, including many omissions and mistakes. It has only five chapters, the fifth chapter being on purgatory. Even though the text is significantly shorter than those in other manuscripts, the Prague manuscript seems to be complete, as the scribe closes the text with the sentence 'et sic est finis huius Tractatus' (and thus is the end of this treatise).[25] It appears to be a further revision based on Redaction 1. It has the same chapter order, and the chapter on purgatory follows the text of Redaction 1 until it breaks off in the middle of the sentence at the end of the treatise.[26] It is possible that the exemplar used to produce this copy was already imperfect. As the scribe has clearly intended to close the treatise here, I have counted the manuscript as a separate redaction, but it could equally be regarded as an imperfect exemplar of Redaction 1. The manuscript XIII. E. 7 is a theological compilation, including texts by different hands. After the *Refutatio* the manuscript includes an interrogatory of heretics according to the decrees of the Council of Constance as well as a treatise against Jan Hus by Stanislaus of Znoyma (d. 1414).[27] The heresy texts were therefore compiled together at some point after the Council, which of course does not exclude the possibility of the texts on Waldensians having existed independently earlier. Whatever the case, one can assume that Redaction 3 was composed in the first decades of the fifteenth century in the context of Bohemian religious reform and conflict.

---

[24] Würzburg, UB MS M. ch. f. 186 has numbering. In Trier, Stadtbibliothek MS 680/879, Wiesbaden, Hessische Landesbibliothek MS 35 and Vienna, ÖNB MS 1588 some chapters are numbered, but most are not.

[25] NKCR MS XIII E. 7, fol. 187r.

[26] Ibid.: 'Item bonorum et malorum alii sunt summe *clementes* [or *celestes*], alii vero summe mali, descendunt ad infernum. Non summe mali in limbum ergo assimili etc. Et sic est finis huius Tractatus.' Cf. Gdańsk, PAN MS Mar. F. 295, fol. 214va: 'Item bonorum et malorum. Alii sunt summe boni, alii summe mali, et illi descendunt ad infernum, non summe mali in lymbum, ergo assimili summe boni ascendunt in celum, sed non summe boni vadunt ad alium locum et illud purgatorium dicitur.'

[27] NKCR MS XIII E. 7. *Interrogationes haereticorum secundum decretum concilii Constantiensis*, fols. 187 bis r–187 ter v, continuation fols. 192r–193r; *Tractatus de ecclesia* by Stanislaus of Znoyma fols. 195r–252r. See also the description in Appendix 1.

Finally, Redaction 4 is significantly later. The manuscript 2° Cod 338 of Augsburg Stadt- und Staatsbibliothek was composed after the mid-fifteenth century, the parts including the texts on Waldensians probably in the 1460s. The incomplete copy in Bayerische Staatsbibliothek, MS Clm 1329, which is very similar to the Augsburg manuscript until the text breaks off in Chapter 10, is more difficult to date. The compilation includes texts from the late fifteenth and early sixteenth centuries, and the fascicule including the *Refutatio* is probably also from the late fifteenth century. Interestingly, it is precisely these late manuscripts that refer to Petrus Zwicker at the beginning of the treatise: 'It is to be noted that brother Petrus called back to faith around six hundred of the above-mentioned heretics in one year.'[28]

From the survey of the manuscripts mentioned in Table 1 it is evident that Redaction 1 is the most representative of the manuscript tradition of *Refutatio errorum*. The extant copies bear witness to its circulation already in the first years of the fifteenth century. The geographical distribution is wide, including manuscripts of southern German and Austrian, Bohemian (Gdańsk, PAN MS Mar. F. 295), Prussian (Vienna, ÖNB MS 1588) and Silesian (Wrocław, BU MS I Q 43) provenance. In contrast, Redaction 2 consists of one manuscript of Augsburg provenance, a copy that once belonged to the Augustinian canons of Heilig Kreuz in Augsburg. Redaction 3 includes one manuscript from Prague, and Redaction 4 is represented by two late manuscripts from the diocese of Augsburg.[29]

Given the main goal of this chapter, inquiry into the relationship between the *Refutatio errorum* and the *Cum dormirent homines*, Redaction 1 becomes even more relevant, as it is the version that appears together with the *Cum dormirent homines*. In the eight known manuscripts including both treatises, the *Cum dormirent homines* is always accompanied by Redaction 1. Moreover, when the two treatises appear together they form one unit. In all eight[30] manuscripts, including both the *Cum dormirent homines* and the *Refutatio errorum*, the scribes have copied the two texts (at least initially) as one work either without noticing or without indicating that they considered them separate tracts. The division between the two works is particularly inconspicuous in manuscripts where the scribe has not used any titles or otherwise

---

[28] 'Et notandum quod frater petrus infra spacium unius anni de predictis hereticis reuocauit ad fidem circa sex centos etc. 'Augsburg, StaSB MS 2° Cod 338, fol. 159r, cf. BSB MS Clm 1329 fol. 216r and *Refutatio*, ed. Gretser, p. 302G.

[29] BSB MS Clm 1329 comes from the library of the Augustinian Canons in Diessen. Augsburg, StaSB MS 2° Cod 338 has a provenance in the monastery of St George in Augsburg, also belonging to the Augustinian Canons. However, one should not make too hasty conclusions about a specifically Augustinian manuscript tradition. MS 2° Cod 338, or at least parts of it, belonged to the physician Johannes Hörlin until he donated the book to the monastery in 1474. See the donation note at fol. 1r.

[30] Excluding NKCR MS X. B. 2 and Wrocław, BU MS I F 707, which have only the first few lines of the *Refutatio*.

indicated chapter breaks in either of the treatises. In one manuscript the *Cum dormirent homines* ends and the *Refutatio errorum* begins in the same line:

> iuravit veritatem, et tu illud dampnas. [*end of CDH*] No-
> tandum quod erroribus hereticorum waldensium.[31]

That the scribes were not simply sloppy, but really considered these two texts to be one work, is best illustrated in Wrocław, BU MS I Q 43. The compiler(s) of the manuscript had a unique way of rubricating the *Cum dormirent homines*. Beginning from the chapter treating the invocation of Virgin Mary, the rubricator has enumerated different Waldensian errors, for example 'They say that the blessed Virgin cannot pray for us. The first heresy.'[32] It is remarkable that this count of heresies continues uninterruptedly from the *Cum dormirent homines* to the *Refutatio errorum*. The last chapter of the *Cum dormirent homines* has the rubric 'On oath-taking follows the sixteenth heresy'.[33] The rubricator has missed the first chapter of the *Refutatio*, but the second chapter has been given the title 'They say that the priests are not legitimate successors of Christ, because they own goods. The seventeenth heresy',[34] and the count goes up to twenty-one. As the scribe and the rubricator have meticulously followed the division of the chapters and gone to the trouble of counting and rubricating different Waldensian errors, the only credible explanation for the assimilation of the two treatises is that the exemplar the scribe had in front of him also represented these texts as one work.

Indeed, it appears that the reason for the mistake is not the carelessness of the scribes copying two treatises, one long and one short, on similar material, as Biller has suggested.[35] There is a significant manuscript tradition that treats these works as one unit. The colophon of one manuscript points out that 'there are two treatises', but the scribe's failure to separate them when he produced his copy proves that the exemplar he used did not do so. Indeed, in the manuscript in question the transition from the *Cum dormirent homines* to the *Refutatio errorum* is quite indiscernible, no more obvious than some transitions between different chapters in the two treatises. The colophon at the end of the two texts, 'The treatise against the errors of Waldensian heretics

---

[31] Gdańsk, PAN MS Mar. F. 294, fol. 220va.

[32] 'Item dicunt, quod beata virgo non potest pro nobis orare. Primus heresis.' Wrocław, BU MS I Q 43, fol. 48r.

[33] 'Item de iuramento sequitur xvi[us] heresis.' Wrocław, BU MS I Q 43, fol. 72r.

[34] 'Item dicunt sacerdotes non esse legittimos successores christi, quia possident bona, xvii[us] heresis.' Wrocław, BU MS I Q 43, fol. 74r.

[35] Biller, *Waldenses*, p. 252. Biller gives two examples of this mistake, Augsburg, UB MS II. 1. 2° 127 (Biller cites the old shelfmark Schloss Harburg, MS II.1. 2°127) and Leipzig, UB MS 602. However, this feature is more or less prominent in all the eight manuscripts studied here.

ends, and there are two treatises',[36] seems to have been written later, possibly by a different hand, than the two or more in the text itself. The reader (or corrector) who wrote this colophon had thus correctly noticed that there were two different texts, and wanted to point this out to readers precisely because the manuscript made this observation very difficult.

The above observations on the manuscript tradition and different redactions of the treatise *Refutatio errorum* lead to the following conclusions. Firstly, the existence of several different redactions and significant differences in the content of some chapters indicate that the *Refutatio errorum* was further revised and rearranged quite soon after it was written, and probably by different authors. However, I am convinced that the core of it originated from the quill of Petrus Zwicker, as the further analysis below shows. Secondly, of the *Refutatio*'s different versions, the manuscripts of Redaction 1, significantly different from the Redaction 4 partly edited by Gretser, have the widest circulation. Not only is its geographical dispersion greater, but it includes the earliest reliably datable manuscripts. Any further study of the treatise should take the manuscripts of this group as the starting point. Thirdly, there is significant interdependence between Redaction 1 of the *Refutatio errorum* and the *Cum dormirent homines*. In the manuscripts including both treatises, the *Cum dormirent homines* is accompanied by Redaction 1 of the *Refutatio*. Thus the study of the relationship of these two treatises should proceed from Redaction 1. I will now pursue this and look more closely at the structure of the two treatises, examples from the chapter on purgatory and the use of sources.

Structure of the Refutatio errorum

The first clear connection between the two treatises is the general similarity of the topics handled and the similar structure. Even though the disposition of chapters at first sight seems to differ, there are certain sections which suggest that the *Cum dormirent homines* was revised from the *Refutatio errorum*. The similarity in composition is even more obvious if the division of chapters in the printed edition is disregarded and attention is focused on the smaller sections within these chapters as they appear in the longest and most common Redaction 1, which are comparable to chapters of the *Cum dormirent homines*. An example here is Gdańsk, PAN, Mar. F. 295, a manuscript written in Bohemia in 1404, including both the *Cum dormirent homines* and the *Refutatio*. It is compared to the disposition of *Cum dormirent homines* in Gretser's edition.[37] The bulk of the Waldensian articles of faith,

---

[36] 'Explicit tractatus contra errores Waldens[sium] Hereticorum, et sunt duo tractatus.' UPenn MS Codex 76, fol. 362r. Cf. Biller, *Waldenses*, pp. 252, 266.

[37] The division of chapters and their respective titles in *c.* fifty manuscripts of the *Cum*

namely arguments concerning the priesthood, especially Waldensian accusations regarding the lifestyle of the prelates, the cult of saints and purgatory were dealt with in the same order in both treatises. In the *Refutatio*, accusations against the bad example of proud, avaricious and fornicating priests (fol. 211va) are followed by denial of invocation and honouring of the saints and the Virgin Mary and assertion that only God created and saves man and thus only He is to be honoured and praised (fols. 211vb–213ra). Treatment of purgatory and burial in cemeteries follows (fols. 213ra–215rb). The topics and their order correspond with Chapters XVI–XXII of Gretser's text of the *Cum dormirent homines*.[38]

One could of course argue that the *Cum dormirent homines* as a whole has a quite different disposition from the *Refutatio errorum* and that the division of the chapters was not stable even within the manuscript tradition of the *Refutatio errorum*. This is true, but that is why this block is significant. Even when the chapters of the *Refutatio errorum* could be and were reorganized by subsequent scribes and compilers, and by Zwicker himself when composing *Cum dormirent homines*, there still exists this consistent group of sections – and many of them extensive, important articles such as invocation of saints and purgatory – which were treated in the same order and in a similar way in both treatises. There is a close connection between the two works, much more profound than the usual borrowing and reordering of material.

There are nevertheless some major differences between the texts. One is that the history of the Waldensian heresy, the refutation of the Waldensian claim to be a movement originating from the time of Pope Sylvester, is absent in *Refutatio errorum*, whereas it occupies a conspicuous place in *Cum dormirent homines* in the arguments against the legitimacy of the Waldensian Brethren's ministry. Right at the beginning of the *Cum dormirent homines* Zwicker shows the reader that the Waldensians were not an apostolic church hidden since the times of the donation of Constantine, but instead a movement founded by a certain 'Petrus Waldensis' almost 800 years after Sylvester.[39] In fact, Zwicker is very confident in proclaiming the Waldensians as a new sect, and does not, unlike some earlier authors, consider their own version of history as a threat to the legitimacy of the Roman Church.[40] As Biller has convincingly argued, Zwicker most likely acquired his exceptionally accurate knowledge of Waldensian history from texts written by the Waldensians themselves: the *Liber electorum* and the polemical correspondence of the Austrian converts to Catholicism and the Lombard Brethren. As mentioned, both these texts were

---

dormirent homines obviously varies considerably. The division in Gretser's edition, based on three manuscripts, is in my opinion a better reference point than any single manuscript.

[38] See Appendix 2 for a list of the *Cum dormirent homines*'s chapters.

[39] Zwicker, *Cum dormirent homines*, p. 278C–D.

[40] See Chapter 5.

at his disposal in the library of the Benedictine monastery in Garsten, Upper Austria, where he resided while pursuing heretics in the diocese of Passau.[41]

As the description of Waldensian history is to be found in the *Cum dormirent homines* but is lacking in the *Refutatio errorum*, although most aspects of the Waldensian doctrine are treated in both treatises, it could mean that the author of *Refutatio* was not interested in Waldensian history. However, this is unlikely, as the origins of the Waldensians play a prominent role in almost every significant treatise circulating in late medieval Germany: it appears in the treatise of Anonymous of Passau, in the *De inquisitione hereticorum*, it is discussed by Moneta of Cremona and also by Peter von Pillichsdorf.[42]

Neither can it be assumed that Zwicker compiled the *Refutatio* before he could make use of Waldensian sources. The compiler of *Refutatio errorum* had direct access to the treatise of Moneta of Cremona, which was relatively rare north of the Alps, as will be demonstrated below. This treatise was at Zwicker's disposal in the same library of Garsten as the Waldensian texts.[43] This lack of discussion on the origins of heresy, a typical feature of the full-fledged polemical treatises, further implies that the text is a draft-like compilation of arguments against Waldensian errors, not a honed and finished treatise. It is a compilation intended to provide material for someone preaching against heretics or arguing, convincing and converting them in the inquisitions. This compilatory nature, collecting different and sometimes incongruent sources in the articles on Waldensian heresy, is well demonstrated in the chapter on purgatory.

On purgatory

The question of the existence of purgatory and continuation of penance after this life is a fitting topic for comparison. It occupies a central position in both treatises and long chapters are dedicated to it. Purgatory was a key focal point in the doctrinal debate between Catholicism and Waldensianism, and many other important points of contention are more or less connected to it: indulgences and all forms of intercession on behalf of the dead, burial according to Church rites and even the invocation of the saints. Purgatory, having

---

[41] See Biller, *Waldenses*, pp. 256–7, 261.

[42] *Quellen*, ed. Patschovsky and Selge, p. 19; 'Der Tractat des David von Augsburg', ed. Preger, pp. 205–6; Moneta, *Adversus Catharos et Valdenses*, pp. 402–3; Peter von Pillichsdorf, *Fragmentum ex Tractatu*, p. 300G–H; See also P. Tolonen, 'Medieval Memories of the Origins of the Waldensian Movement', in *History and Religion: Narrating a Religious Past*, ed. B.-C. Otto, S. Rau and J. Rüpke (Berlin, 2015), pp. 165–85.

[43] Biller, *Waldenses*, 256–61. It is also possible that Zwicker actually brought these texts to Garsten, which then became their late medieval repository. This possibility is discussed below.

established its position in the spiritual geography of Latin Christendom as late as the thirteenth century, had obviously been – and was to remain – a doctrine under discussion. It is even possible to say, following Jacques le Goff, that the doctrine of purgatory was honed against the dissidents who opposed it.[44] The Waldensians were definitely among the groups who opposed the place of purgation in the Christian universe. They started attacking the concept of post-mortem purification of the soul even before the doctrine was fully developed, and consequently the theology of purgatory was developed also against this opposition.[45]

The chapter on purgatory in the *Refutatio errorum* is worth considering in detail because it is only partially printed in Gretser's edition, which breaks off in the middle of the chapter. In addition, the purgatory chapter in Redactions 1 and 2 is significantly longer than even the full chapter of Redaction 4 (whose end is a lacking in Gretser's edition). The complete Redaction 4 text on purgatory of approximately 1,700 words can be found in the Augsburg, Staats- und Stadtbibliothek MS 2° Cod 338, fols. 166v–169r. In comparison, Gdańsk, PAN MS Mar. F. 295, fols. 213ra–215rb, which will serve here as the exemplar manuscript, has almost 2,800 words in the corresponding chapter. Thus most of the scholars who have studied the *Refutatio* have seen a significantly shorter discussion about purgatory than that included in the majority of the manuscripts.[46] The text of the long redaction is intriguing, including both striking similarities to the *Cum dormirent homines* as well as enigmatic and unique sections.

One of the most obvious similarities in the argumentation and structure of the purgatory chapters in the two respective treatises is that the Waldensian denial of the possibility of penance after death in purgatory, and thus the denial of any chance for the living to intercede on behalf of the dead, leads to further errors. The *Refutatio* promises a total of four errors ('ita ex vno errore fiunt quatuor') derived from the Waldensian position that there are only two roads after death, either to hell or to heaven. However, only three errors are provided (this applies to all redactions of the *Refutatio*): firstly, there are no venial sins ('quod nullum sit veniale peccatum'); secondly, when the guilt of the sin is forgiven the punishment is also taken away ('quando dimittitur culpa dimittitur et pena'); and thirdly, the intercession of the Church does not

---

[44] J. Le Goff, *The Birth of Purgatory* (Chicago, 1986), p. 169.

[45] On the denial of purgatorial fire after death by Waldensians already in the 1190s, see Le Goff, *The Birth of Purgatory*, p. 170. On Waldensian believers denying the existence of purgatory as early as the first half of the thirteenth century, see e.g. Cameron, *Waldenses*, pp. 75–6; Molnár, *Storia dei valdesi (1)*, pp. 296–7.

[46] Some scholars working with manuscripts have duly noted the disparity between Gretser's printed edition and the manuscript copies: for example, E. Werner in his study of NKČR MS XIII. E. 7 (Redaction 3) in the 1960s: see Werner, 'Nachrichten', pp. 237–8, n. 84b.

profit the dead ('suffragia ecclesie pro mortuis non prodesse').[47] After this the argumentation is less clear, as instead of discussing Waldensian errors various parables proving the need of purgatory and benefits of its existence are provided. In the end the author apparently returns to the point, as he declares: 'From this error the heretics conclude that it would be of no use to bury the body of a dead person in the cemetery.'[48] 'From this error' must refer to the main article discussed in the chapter, namely, that there are only two routes and no possibility of penance after death, as there are no Waldensian propositions presented immediately before this statement about cemetery burial. Thus it seems that the denial of ecclesiastical burial is the intended fourth error.

The first two errors appear also in the *Cum dormirent homines*, formulated in a similar way: that there is no venial sin, and that whenever God forgives sin, he also releases from punishment.[49] However, the third error mentioned in the *Refutatio*, that the intercessions of the Church do not help those already dead, is not stated here explicitly. This does not mean that Zwicker left this out of the *Cum dormirent homines*, quite the opposite. The question of *suffragia ecclesie* is integral to the whole concept of purgatory, and it is discussed in greater detail than in the *Refutatio*, but remarkably enough, in the same order, that is after the specifically mentioned first and second errors. And, exactly as in the *Refutatio*, it is followed by a section on ecclesiastical burial, but now appearing as an independent chapter.[50]

The development of the argumentation and changes in the composition, trivial as they might at first seem, reveal a great deal about Petrus Zwicker's writing process, and consequently, about authorship and its limits in late medieval polemical treatises. First of all, this structure is not Zwicker's invention. Neither is the source the treatise by Moneta of Cremona, whose significant impact on both the *Refutatio* and the *Cum dormirent homines* will be discussed below. The origin of this formulation, or at least a probable source for Zwicker, is the Anonymous of Passau, whose work was widely circulated and easily available in late fourteenth-century German libraries. Peter Biller has argued that Zwicker knew this work, but he has not provided any concrete examples of Anonymous of Passau's influence from Zwicker's works.[51] This thirteenth-century treatise has a very concise chapter on the condemnation of purgatory by Waldensians, and the author proposes that 'From the error of purgatory three errors arise.' The errors are the same as

---

[47] Gdańsk, PAN MS Mar. F. 295, fol. 213rb–va.

[48] 'Ex hoc errore inferunt heretici, quot non sit vtile corpus defuncti hominis sepeliri in cyminterio'; Gdańsk, PAN MS Mar. F. 295, fol. 215rb.

[49] Zwicker, *Cum dormirent homines*, p. 287A: 'Primus, quod nullum sit peccatum veniale, Secundus, quod quandocunque Deus dimittit culpam, dimittat et poenam.'

[50] Ibid., pp. 288A–289H.

[51] Biller, *Waldenses*, p. 272.

the first three proposed in the *Refutatio:* the non-existence of venial sins, the release from punishment caused by sin at the same time when sin is forgiven, and that intercessions do not help the dead. Moreover, the phrasing of these articles is very close to that of the *Refutatio.*[52]

It seems plausible that this structure was first adopted by Zwicker when compiling the *Refutatio,* and he used it almost as it was, but added a further error, the denial of ecclesiastical burial, which then in the course of compiling and combining different elements almost lost its connection to the other three errors. Consequently the structure was further elaborated by Zwicker in the course of writing the *Cum dormirent homines:* only the two closely connected propositions about venial sins and the release from punishment together with sin were kept together. The intercessions by the Church on behalf of the dead are discussed as an independent topic and burial in the cemetery became a separate chapter – and a remarkably long one – as a consequence. However, the basic structure, borrowed and reworked into the *Refutatio* from the work by the Anonymous of Passau, remained in the background.

The purgatory chapter reveals a further common source of the *Refutatio errorum* and the *Cum dormirent homines.* That is the treatise by Moneta of Cremona, which, as stated above, was relatively rare north of the Alps. Peter Biller has demonstrated that Zwicker used it as a source for the *Cum dormirent homines,* and that in the medieval library of Garsten there is a copy that Zwicker probably used.[53] The proof that Moneta's treatise was directly used in the composition of *Refutatio errorum* is that there are passages that come directly from Moneta's treatise. The similarity is too close to be caused simply

---

[52] *Quellen,* ed. Patschovsky and Selge, p. 102, with my emphasis: 'De errore purgatorii surgunt tres errores: **Primus, quod nullum peccatum sit veniale, sed mortale.** Contra Proverb. (24,16): *Sepcies in die cadit iustus.* **Secundus error: Cum dimittitur culpa, dimittitur pena.** Ex hoc datur occasio libere peccandi, et sacramentum penitencie evacuatur; Mt. (4,17): *Penitenciam agite!* Luc. (3,8): *Facite dignos fructus penitencie!* **Tercius error, quod suffragia non prosint.** Quod est sevire in mortuos; Ecc. (Eccli. 7,37): *Mortuo ne prohibeas graciam!* Si ad preces sororum Lazarus suscitatur, ergo ad preces sanctorum dimittitur pena purgatorii; Mt. (12,31–32): *Qui dixerit blasphemiam in spiritum sanctum, non remittetur ei, neque in hoc seculo neque in futuro.* Ergo aliquod peccatum remittitur in futuro' (On the error about purgatory, three errors arise. **First, that there is no venial sin, just mortal.** Against: Proverbs (24:16), 'For a just man shall fall seven times in a day'. **Second error: when guilt is remitted, punishment is remitted.** From this a pretext is afforded for sinning freely, and the sacrament of penance is made empty. Matthew (4:17): 'Do penance!' Luke (3:8): 'Bring forth therefore fruits worthy of penance!' **Third error, that offerings are of no value.** Which is to behave savagely towards the dead. Ecc. (Ecclesiasticus 7:37): 'Restrain not grace from the dead'. If Lazarus is raised in response to the prayers of sisters, the punishment is likewise remitted in response to the prayers of the saints. Matthew (12:31–32): 'Whoever shall speak blasphemy against the Holy Ghost, it shall not be forgiven him neither in this world, nor in the world to come.' Therefore, some sin is remitted in the future.)

[53] Biller, *Waldenses,* pp. 256–61.

by the common subject matter, and they feature only in Moneta's text and the *Refutatio errorum*, not in the *Cum dormirent homines*.

The clearest example is the exposition of the parable in 1 Corinthians 3:12–15 on trying with fire the foundation built by each man.[54] The parable is used as evidence to support the existence of purgatory in all three treatises, and the *Refutatio errorum* follows more closely the example set by Moneta's treatise than the *Cum dormirent homines.* All three treatises begin by quoting the parable, and all explain that gold, silver and precious stones are good deeds and that wood, hay and stubble are venial sins. However, only Moneta and the *Refutatio* say that gold corresponds to the most optimal good deeds (*optimi mores*), silver very good deeds (*meliores/mediocres*) and precious stones 'only' good (*boni*). In the *Cum dormirent homines* Zwicker speaks only of meritorious deeds (*opera meritoria*). The wording in the *Refutatio* is very close to Moneta's treatise, and it is certainly borrowed directly from there.

Moneta, *Adversus Catharos et Valdenses*, p. 372:
Per aurum intelliguntur optimi mores, per argentum meliores, per lapides pretiosos boni; ista enim non cremantur ab igne, scilicet aurum, argentum et lapides pretiosi, similiter nec bona opera. Modo quaero, quid intelligis per lignum, foenum, et stipulam? Ista enim cinerabilia sunt ab igne; ergo per ista tria intelliguntur peccata. Sed nunquid mortalia? Non: dicitur enim de eo, qui secum habet ista, quod detrimentum patietur, ipse autem salvus erit: sic tamen quasi per ignem.

Refutatio errorum, Gdańsk, PAN MS Mar. F. 295, fols. 214ra–rb:
Uel per aurum intelliguntur optimi mores, per argentum mediocres, per lapides boni. Ista enim non cremantur, sed purgantur ab igne, similiter nec bona opera. Hec enim edificacio est tantum perfectorum, qui venialiter aliquando peccant, feruore caritatis ita absumitur in eis peccatum. Sicut gucta aque in camino ignis. Et ideo non portant secum cremabilia, intelliguntur peccata venialia, ut patet per hoc quod dicit detrimentum pacietur, non dicit eternum supplicium. Vnde Subdit: ipse saluus erit, sic tamen quasi per ignem purgatorium.

---

[54] 1 Corinthians 3:12–15: 'Si quis autem superædificat super fundamentum hoc, aurum, argentum, lapides pretiosos, ligna, fœnum, stipulam, uniuscujusque opus manifestum erit: dies enim Domini declarabit, quia in igne revelabitur: et uniuscujusque opus quale sit, ignis probabit. Si cujus opus manserit quod superædificavit, mercedem accipiet. Si cujus opus arserit, detrimentum patietur: ipse autem salvus erit, sic tamen quasi per ignem.' Trans. according to Douay-Rheims: 'Now if any man build upon this foundation, gold, silver, precious stones, wood, hay, stubble: Every man's work shall be manifest; for the day of the Lord shall declare it, because it shall be revealed in fire; and the fire shall try every man's work, of what sort it is. If any man's work abide, which he hath built thereupon, he shall receive a reward. If any man's work burn, he shall suffer loss; but he himself shall be saved, yet so as by fire.'

Zwicker, *Cum dormirent homines*, p. 287B:
Vbi per aurum, argentum, lapides preciosos, intelliguntur opera meritoria,
Per lignum, foenum, stipulam opera non meritoria, sed venialia.

The comparison also shows that Linz, OÖLB MS 296 was indeed the manuscript Zwicker used. All three treatises include the argument that here Paul declared the existence of future penance instead of penance in this world, because the words are in the future tense. Slightly different verbs are chosen for each treatise, but it is notable that the *Refutatio* has verb forms that correspond almost exactly to those in the Linz manuscript.

Moneta, *Adversus Catharos et Valdenses*, 373:
Praeterea. Verba Ap. omnia de futuro sunt: manifestum erit, declarabit, revelabitur; quare ergo audes dicere de praesenti intelligi?

Moneta, *Adversus Catharos et Valdenses*, Linz, OÖLB MS 296, 230vb:
Preterea, uerba apostoli, omnia sunt de futuro scilicet **manifestum erit, declarabit, reuelabitur, in igne detrimentum pacietur, saluus erit**; quare ergo audes dicere de presenti intelligi?

Refutatio errorum, Gdańsk, PAN MS Mar. F. 295, fol. 214rb:
Vbi notandum, quod omnia verba, que ibi ponuntur sunt de futuro scilicet **manifeste erit, declarebitur, reuelabitur, detrimentum pacietur, in igne saluus erit**. Et ita patet, quod de iudicio futuro intelligitur et non de presenti.

Zwicker, *Cum dormirent homines*, pp. 287H–288A:
Contra, omnia praedicta verba S. Pauli, scilicet, manifestum erit, ignis probabit, mercedem accipiet, detrimentum patietur, saluus erit : Omnia, inquam, sunt futuri temporis, non praesentis.

However, the *Cum dormirent homines* and the *Refutatio* have common features that are not found in Moneta's text. Zwicker explains the difference between mortal and venial sins, saying that sinning mortally is not at all constructive, but destructive, whereas the wood, hay and stubble symbolize venial sins. There are subtle differences, as in the *Refutatio* Zwicker speaks only of those who 'prefer the world to God' ('mundum deo preponerent'), and claims that this destroys the foundation. In the *Cum dormirent homines* he refers specifically to mortal sins, which destroy 'if not the foundation, at least the building' ('et si non fundamentum, tamen edificium').[55] This whole argument of destruction is absent from Moneta's text.

The use of this parable from 1 Corinthians is not in itself surprising in a polemical work defending purgatory. Paul's words on trial by fire were one of the main biblical verses in support of purgatory, and their interpretation developed in the course of the Early and High Middle Ages.[56] They can

---

[55] Gdańsk, PAN MS Mar. F. 295, fol. 214rb; Zwicker, *Cum dormirent homines*, p. 287B.
[56] Le Goff, *The Birth of Purgatory*, p. 43.

also be found in other works against the Waldensians. For example, in the *Attendite a falsis prophetis*, a short treatise known to Zwicker, the same parable is discussed, but only in passing to argue that it refers to purgatory, not hell, because in hell nothing is tested or purified any more.[57] The argumentation in Moneta's text, the *Refutatio* and the *Cum dormirent homines* is nevertheless similar down to the details and demonstrates the affinity of the three treatises.[58]

The obvious use of Moneta's treatise in the *Refutatio* further endorses Zwicker's authorship, as the number of persons who had both access to Moneta's work and an interest in writing such a treatise in the 1390s must have been very limited. This would also suggest that the *Refutatio errorum* was composed before the *Cum dormirent homines*, as the direct assimilation of passages from Moneta would have been impossible, or at least extremely unlikely, if the *Refutatio* had simply been a further redaction of the *Cum dormirent homines*. This could imply that Zwicker also wrote the *Refutatio* around 1395 at Garsten, where he had access to the copy of Moneta's work, at one time bound together with a copy of the Waldensian history *Liber electorum*, as suggested by Biller.[59] Could Zwicker have possessed this work already before that? There are hardly any medieval library catalogues from Garsten, and the information about the medieval book collection is mainly based on Seraphin Kirchmayern's catalogue from 1631, where Moneta's treatise is listed.[60] The Garsten copy of Moneta is from the fourteenth century and of Italian provenance, but there is no indication as to how it ended up

---

[57] St Florian MS XI 152, fol. 49v: 'Item 1. Cor. 3. Si cuius opus arserit, detrimentum patietur. Ipse tamen salvus erit, sic tamen quasi per ignem, videlicet purgatorii, quia Apostolus per ignem nolebat tribulacionem presentis vite, sicut ipsi dicunt, sed purgatorium designare. Item ibidem uniuscuiusque opus quale sic ignis probabit, videlicet purgatorii, quia in inferno nichil probatur, nec purificatur.'

[58] Another example of the direct influence of Moneta's treatise to the *Refutatio* is within the debate on customs, rituals and legislation declared by the modern Church. One passage in the *Refutatio* comes directly from Moneta, albeit in summarized form: 'The Church of the Jews that has lesser power.' References to the Bible, the books of Esther and Maccabees, are the same. This passage is absent from the *CDH*. Moneta, *Adversus Catharos et Valdenses*, p. 445: 'Specialiter autem dicendum est de Valdensibus, quod si **Ecclesiae de Judaeis, quae minoris potestatis fuit, licuit aliqua constituere praeter legem Dei**; multo fortius Ecclesiae, quae nunc est, licet aliqua ordinare praeter Christi doctrinam, dummodo non sit contra Christum. Quod autem Ecclesia Veteris Testamenti aliqua ordinaverit **patet Estheri [9:] v.17**. & seq. ubi Judaei constituerunt decimam quartam diem mensis Adar, idest Martii solemnem, in qua desierant hostes suos caedere. **Item I.Machab. cap.4.v.59**.' Cf. *Refutatio*, Gdańsk, PAN MS Mar. F. 295, fol. 216vb: 'Item ecclesie de iudeis qui minoris fuerat auctoritatis et potestatis licuit constituere preter legem dei; hester ix°. Item primi macha ii° et iiii° etc.' My emphasis.

[59] Biller, *Waldenses*, pp. 256–61. Nowadays manuscripts Linz, OÖLB MS 292 (*Liber electorum* and the correspondence) and 296 (Moneta's treatise).

[60] *Mittelalterliche Bibliothekskataloge Österreichs. Band 5. Oberösterreich*, ed. H. Paulhart

at Garsten. It is therefore not out of the question that it belonged to Zwicker and he brought it to Garsten, as he did with the Bohemian inquisitor's manual Linz MS 177.[61] This would expand the probable time frame for the composition to 1391–5, from the beginning of Zwicker's first appearance as inquisitor of heresy to the composition of the *Cum dormirent homines*. The history of the manuscript circulation appears to support this. There are no Austrian copies of the *Refutatio errorum*, whereas both the *Cum dormirent homines* and the *Processus Petri* compilation had wide transmission there. It is thus possible that Zwicker composed the *Refutatio errorum* in the early 1390s, before starting the inquisition in the diocese of Passau in 1395.

All this does not, of course, rule out the possibility that someone used both Moneta's and Zwicker's work and compiled his own collection on heresy. Indeed, when comparing two texts on similar material and at least one of them is of uncertain date, it is difficult to be definitive about which came first. However, it is difficult to imagine the need to rework the *Cum dormirent homines* into a miscellaneous compilation such as the *Refutatio*. The latter is too long to be a practical summary, which becomes more evident when it is compared to an actual summary produced from the *Cum dormirent homines*. In MS 4511 of the Austrian National Library there is a very concise two-folio list of the main points in Zwicker's long treatise.[62] This text could have been used as a memory aid, whereas the *Refutatio errorum* is too long and too tangled to be useful for this purpose.

On the other hand, it is easy to see how the process of revision and rewriting could have proceeded in the opposite direction, from the source texts to the *Refutatio* and finally to the *Cum dormirent homines*. Zwicker had at his disposal various earlier treatises, some of them outdated or inconvenient in style, such as the treatise by the Anonymous of Passau, some of them too massive or on different heresies, such as Moneta of Cremona's *Adversus*

(Vienna, 1971), pp. 19–24. Linz, OÖLB MS 296, fol. 1r: 'Catalogo librorum monasterii Gärstensis inscriptus a. 1631. No. I D.'

[61] See *Quellen*, ed. Patschovsky, pp. 87–94. One cannot definitely exclude the possibility that Zwicker only had access to Moneta's treatise at Garsten, which would mean that both his treatises were written there. The earlier Italian provenance of Linz, OÖLB MS 296 may support this. On the provenance, see esp. fol. 334va: 'Iste liber est fratris Ambrogii de V[erona] ordinis servorum sancte Marie; Veneciis emptus duc[atis] 2' (This book is of Ambrose of V[erona], of the Order of Servites of Holy Mary; bought at Venice for 2 ducats). This has been noted by Patschovsky in *Quellen*, ed. Patschovsky, p. 87, n. 292. Garsten had the means and motivation to acquire manuscripts such as this. In the course of the fourteenth century, especially in its first half, Garsten had bought manuscripts from the intellectual and spiritual centres of its day. There are several manuscripts of Italian provenance and at least one – including *Postilla super epistolas* by Bertrand de la Tour – that was produced in Paris and ordered specially for the monastery by Abbot Erhard (1353–65.) See *Mittelalterliche Bibliothekskataloge Österreichs* (5), ed. Paulhart, p. 20.

[62] ÖNB MS 4511, fols. 159r–160v.

Catharos et Valdenses, and some perhaps not comprehensive enough, like the short treatise *Attendite a falsis prophetis*. He first assembled a compilation from different sources and organized it under corresponding Waldensian errors. This was then further reworked into the full treatise *Cum dormirent homines* to satisfy the need for an up-to-date polemical work aimed particularly at refuting the practices of the Waldensians.

That the *Refutatio errorum* is indeed a rather miscellaneous compilation becomes evident in certain passages that differ significantly from the rest of the treatise, both in their style and contents. These have been neglected, probably because they do not appear in the version printed by Gretser. The best example is in the purgatory chapter of Redaction 1, where, after discussing the existence of hell, heaven and purgatory based on scriptural evidence, the text suddenly turns into a natural-historical argumentation about the possibility of a fire capable of cleansing and punishing incorporable souls. The existence of purgatory is endorsed by the existence of miraculous fires in the corporeal world:

> It is to be noted, that there is fire that burns water, which is called Greek fire. And there is fire which neither wind nor rain can extinguish, and that kind of fire was once in the temple of Venus in torches, where the asbestos stone shone and burned, which once kindled, is never extinguished by wind or rain, and has the colour of lead and iron. And there is fire, which the common people call burning fire, which consumes nothing but itself. In the land of Sicily, there is fire that does not harm bodies.[63]

The logic behind these and other biblical instances of miraculous fires is obscure until it is proposed that if divine justice has created such wondrous things, how much more proper it is to create something that can punish the impious.[64] Yet even with this clarification the listing of these miraculous examples stands out from the rest of the treatise.

This contrast is explained by the source of this passage. It was adopted from the treatise *De Universo* (*On the Universe*) by William of Auvergne, thirteenth-century scholar and bishop of Paris. William was an important, if already slightly old-fashioned theologian of his time. He was also an influential figure in the development of the concept of purgatory, both as continuation of earthly penance and as a place where real fire corporeally

---

[63] Gdańsk, PAN MS Mar. F. 295, fol. 215ra: 'Ideo notandum, quod est ignis qui aquam comburit, qui vocatur grecus ignis. Et est ignis, qui nec vento nec pluuia potest exstingwi, qualis fuit quendam in templo veneris in lampade [sic], in qua lucebat, et ardebat abestus [sic] lapis, qui semel accensus nunquam exstingwi vento nec pluuia et est liuidi et ferriginei [sic] coloris. Et est ignis qui wlgo aqua ardens dicitur, qui nichil consumit nisi seipsum. Item est ignis in terra Sicilie, que corpora non ledit.'

[64] Ibid., 215ra: 'Quanto forcius pro torquendis uniuersis impijs tale quid ac maiora et mirabiliora facere decet iusticiam eius?'

tortures souls.[65] Zwicker did not, however, resort directly to William of Auvergne's work. Although the examples of miraculous fires, as well as a discussion on the possibility of existence of any fire capable of purifying and punishing incorporeal souls, originate in William's theology, the formulation in the *Refutatio* follows closely to the *Tractatus fidei* of Benedict of Alignan, bishop of Marseille.[66] This large treatise 'against diverse errors', completed by 1261, has been neglected in the scholarship of heresy despite its medieval popularity. The *Tractatus fidei* circulated in several late fourteenth and early fifteenth-century manuscripts in German-speaking Central Europe,[67] and it is very plausible that Zwicker had access to the treatise. Its use as a source of the *Refutatio* is further evidence of the *Tractatus*'s importance, and its influence in the late-medieval anti-heretical literature merits further study.

That this passage from the *De Universo/Tractatus fidei* does not end up in *Cum dormirent homines* is most likely a result of the rhetorical and argumentative choice Zwicker makes in composing his main work: to get rid of every explicitly extra-biblical reference and resort exclusively to the Scriptures. He almost succeeds, but there is a single lapse. It is a stroke of luck for a modern scholar, as it is yet another piece of evidence of the close affinity between these two treatises.

[65] On William's theology of Purgatory, see Le Goff, *The Birth of Purgatory*, pp. 241–5.

[66] Gdańsk, PAN MS Mar. F. 295, fols. 214vb–215ra: 'Qualiter autem ignis siue affliccio corporalis purgare possit animas, que sunt incorporales. Nota, quod anime humane delectantur et molestantur a corporibus et per illa delectabilia corporalia inflammant animas desideriis et irretiunt voluptatibus in tristalia [sic] contristant easdem. Vnde non est mirandum, si ignis sit aliquis qui animas in corporibus et a corporibus fedatas torquere valeat.' Cf. Benedict of Alignan, *Tractatus fidei*, in Paris, Bibliothèque nationale, MS Lat. 4224, fol. 293ra: 'Si queratur qualiter ignis siue afflictio corporalis purgare possit animas qui sunt incorporales. Respondetur, quod anime humane delectantur et molestantur a corporibus et per illa, nam delectabilia corporalia, inflammant animas desideriis et capiunt et irretiunt voluptatibus, et instabilia contristant easdem. Vnde non est mirandum, si sit ignis aliquis qui animas in corporibus et a corporibus separatas torquere ualeat.' Cf. also fol. 293rb: 'Notandum quod est ignis qui aquam comburit, qui uocatur ignis grecus [...]. Item est ignis qui nec uento nec pluuia potest extingui, qualis fuit quondam in templo ueneris in lampade, in qua lucebat et ardebat asbestus lapis, qui semel accensus, non extinguitur uento nec pluuia, qui lapis est liuidi ac ferruginei coloris. Est et ignis qui uulgo dicitur aqua ardens, qui nichil consumit nisi seipsum [...; 293va:] Est et ignis in terra sycilie, qui corpora non ledit.' Cf. n. 63 above. Cf. Guillaume d'Auvergne, *Opera omnia: quae hactenus reperiri potuerunt*, 2 vols. (Paris, 1674), I, 680.

[67] See a forthcoming article, J. H. Arnold, 'Benedict of Alignan's *Tractatus fidei contra diversos errores*: A Neglected Anti-Heresy Treatise'. I thank John H. Arnold for pointing out these passages in the *Tractatus* and for sending me the manuscript of his unpublished article.

Boethius and Pseudo-Ezekiel

Among the similar passages of the *Cum dormirent homines* and the *Refutatio errorum* there are two short quotations that deserve special attention, because they provide further evidence that Petrus Zwicker wrote the *Refutatio errorum*. The first is from Boethius's *De consolatione Philosophiae*, and it appears in both treatises in the context of a debate about honouring and invoking the saints. In the *Refutatio errorum* it refutes the proposition 'the heretics say: but it is written: you will adore God, your lord, and serve only Him'.[68] In the *Cum dormirent homines* it appears as a response to the same claim 'the Waldensian heretics say that only God is to be praised'.[69]

Refutatio errorum, ed. Gretser, p. 304G

Respondetur, verum est, adoratione latriae, solus Deus est adorandus. Sed adoratione duliae omnes hi adorandi sunt, et eis seruiendum, ad quos dixit Psalmista. **Ego ante dixi, Dij estis, et filij excelsi omnes. Et Boethius in lib. de. consolat. Omnis beatus, Deus. Et si natura quidem vnus est Deus, participatione vero nil prohibet esse quamplurimos.**

Zwicker, *Cum dormirent homines*, pp. 284F–H

Sic filij Dei, Dij sunt, et vocantur. Ioan.10. Nonne in lege vestra scriptum est? **Ego dixi Dij estis, et filij excelsi omnes. Boëtius: Omnis beatus Deus; natura quidem vnus est Deus, participatione vero nihil prohibet esse plurimos.**

The reference to Boethius is practically a direct quotation from the *De consolatione Philosophiae*: 'omnis igitur beatus deus. sed <deus> natura quidem unus; participatione uero nihil prohibet esse quam plurimos.'[70] Richard Green has translated the sentence as follows: 'Thus everyone who is happy [*beatus*] is a god and, although it is true that God is one by nature, still there may be many gods by participation.'[71] In both the *Refutatio errorum* and the *Cum dormirent homines* the word *beatus* should be translated as 'blessed', as the quotation is used to support the doctrine that the saints in heaven participated in the divinity of God, and therefore invoking the saints was not idolatry as the worship was ultimately directed to God. The distinction between *adoratio latriae*, worship due to the Holy Trinity alone, and *adoratio duliae*, veneration

---

[68] 'Item dicunt haeretici; Tamen scriptum est; Dominum Deum tuum adorabis, et illi soli servies. Ergo non est sancto alicui serviendum', *Refutatio*, ed. Gretser, p. 304F.

[69] Zwicker, *Cum dormirent homines*, p. 283F. The whole chapter is the longest of the treatise, covering pp. 283F–286D.

[70] Boethius, *Philosophiae consolatio* 3.prosa 10.76–7 (LLT-A).

[71] Boethius, *The Consolation of Philosophy*, trans. R. Green, 4th edn (Indianapolis, 1962), p. 63.

given to a creature, is also used in the both texts. In the concise *Refutatio errorum* these concepts appear immediately before the Boethian quotation, and in the longer and more complex text of the *Cum dormirent homines* they appear later in the chapter dealing with Waldensian scepticism about images: 'Indeed, faithful Catholics bend their knee, and celebrate, honour and adore this image not as God, but because of God the Redeemer, with veneration given to a creature (*cultu duliae*), not with worship due to the Trinity alone (*latriae*).'[72]

The significance of this quotation is not only in its similar placing and function in the argumentation of both treatises, but above all in its peculiarity. In the *Cum dormirent homines* it is the single explicit reference to any author or work besides the Bible and liturgy.[73] Zwicker resorts almost solely to biblical arguments, and this has caused scholars to conclude that he intended to meet the Waldensians on their own ground, refuting them with the help only of the Bible because the Waldensian theology was based on literal biblicism. The Boethius quotation has gone mostly unnoticed by scholars. Biller claims that the *Cum dormirent homines* 'is tightly organised and written exclusively against the Waldensians. Its *auctoritates* (authorities) are exclusively biblical, and there are a few proverbial tags.'[74] Only Adam Poznański has noted this reference.[75] There is no reason to dispute that Zwicker avoided using *auctoritates* outside the Bible and did so in order to convince his adversaries, a matter that is analysed further below, but this makes the exception to the rule, the single quotation from Boethius, even more puzzling.

Boethius, of course, was a well-known author in the Middle Ages. He was widely read and commented on, and by the late Middle Ages the readership

---

[72] 'Fideles vero Catholici genua flectunt, imaginem ipsam non vt Deum, sed propter Deum redemptorem, cultu duliae, non latriae colunt, honorant, et adorant.' Zwicker, *Cum dormirent homines*, p. 297B.

[73] Even references to liturgy are limited to mentioning the hymn celebrating the Annunciatio, *Mittit ad Virginem*. Zwicker, *Cum dormirent homines*, p. 283C, but quoted here from Seitenstetten, MS 213, fol. 114rb: 'cuius insignem annunccia-cionem melodiatis voci[b]us leta per orbem sancta canit mater ecclesia: Mittit ad Virginem non quamvis angelum sed fortitudinem suam archangelum amator hominis' (Whose glorious annunciation the holy Church, rejoicing, sings with melodious voices throughout the world: 'The lover of mankind sends to the Virgin not any angel but his strength, the archangel'). For a second comment on liturgical books, see Zwicker, *Cum dormirent homines*, p. 294F: 'Ergo ordinationes Missarum, et omnium orationum et signorum agendorum et dicendorum, sunt rite et rationabi-liter institutae, sicut de ipsis speciales libri et bene magni sunt conscripti' (Therefore the orders of masses and of all prayers and gestures that are to be performed and said have been instituted according to rite and reason, as indeed special and rather large books have been composed about these things). Cf. Biller, *Waldenses*, p. 274, n. 15.

[74] Biller, *Waldenses*, p. 245, see also pp. 240, 259, 261, 274; Segl, 'Die Waldenser in Österreich', p. 185; Modestin, 'The Anti-Waldensian Treatise', pp. 218, 221–2.

[75] Poznański, 'Reakcja Kościoła', pp. 201–2.

of the *Consolatio* extended beyond clerical circles and the work was trans-
lated into several European vernaculars. In the 1390s it belonged to the
curriculum of the Faculty of Arts at the University of Vienna.[76] Glynnis M.
Cropp sees Boethius, writing while imprisoned and aspiring to the Supreme
Good, offering a model to be imitated in times of stress and oppression.[77]
In addition to the copies of the work itself, the authoritative passages of
Boethius's treatise, including the one cited by Zwicker, were easily available
in the popular florilegium *Auctoritates Aristotelis* (*The Authorities of Aristotle*).
Zwicker, however, seems to refer to the full work, not to a florilegium.[78]

Therefore, quoting Boethius would not be surprising, not even worth
mentioning if the *Cum dormirent homines* were not completely devoid of
any other references to patristic authors. The programme of eschewing any
extra-biblical authors is so conspicuous that it cannot be accidental. Neither
would Zwicker have run out of arguments in his defence of the cult of saints,
since the chapters treating this question are among the most extensive in
the treatise, supported by a solid flow of biblical quotations. Possibly the
quotation from the *Consolatio* is a remnant from the reworking of the *Refutatio
errorum* into the *Cum dormirent homines*, not a conscious attempt to bolster
the argument in the chapter defending the veneration of the saints. There
are many other non-scriptural sources that are supressed and feature only
implicitly behind the arguments, as we shall see below. However, it is worth
mentioning that Zwicker was apparently fond of Boethius and the *Consolatio*.
He quotes Boethius in his only known work not connected to heresy and
inquisition,[79] a short exposition on the *Pater noster* in a manuscript from St
Florian, entitled *Dicta magistri petri Inquisitoris* (*The Dicta of Master Petrus the
Inquisitor*), to demonstrate how all peoples of the world have the same origin,
ruled by one Father.[80] It is thus possible that Boethius remained in the biblicist
Cum dormirent homines not by accident but as a reference to a beloved author.

---

[76] *Acta facultatis artium universitatis Vindobonensis 1385–1416*, ed. P. Uiblein (Graz,
1968), pp. 137–8.

[77] G. M. Cropp, 'Boethius in Translation in Medieval Europe', in *Translation: An
International Encyclopedia of Translation Studies*, ed. H. Kittel, J. House and B. Schultze
(Berlin, 2007), pp. 1329–37 (p. 1329).

[78] J. Hamesse, *Les Auctoritates Aristotelis: une florilège médiéval* (Louvain, 1974), p. 290:
'Omnis beatus est deus, sed natura unus est deus, participatione vero nihil prohibet
plures esse.' Zwicker's wording both in the *Refutatio* and in the *Cum dormirent
homines* is closer to the full work of Boethius than to the excerpt. In adition, in
some manuscripts of the *Refutatio*, the reference to Boethius is more accurate than
that offered by the florilegium, see e.g. Gdańsk, PAN MS Mar. F. 295, fol. 213ra: 'Et
Boecius de consolacione in 3° libro prosa x^a: Omnis beatus deus; natura quidem
vnus est, participacione sed vero nichil prohibet esse quam plurimos.'

[79] The existence of this work was first recognized by Biller, *Waldenses*, p. 274.

[80] St Florian, MS XI 96, fol. 298r: 'Boecius 3 de consolacione metro 6°: omne genus
hominum in terris simili surgit ab ortu vnus, enim rex pater est vnus cuncta
ministrat.' Cf. Boethius, *Philosophiae consolatio*, 3.carmen 6.1–2 (LLT-A).

There is a further quotation that demonstrates that Petrus Zwicker wrote the *Refutatio errorum*. It is a misquotation from the Old Testament Book of Ezekiel:

Sed dixerit quis, sufficit ut peccator dimittat peccatum suum et conuertatur ad dominum. Iuxta illud Ezech. xiiii°; in quacumque hora peccator ingemuerit etc.[81]

Ezekiel 33:12 was commonly used in medieval discussions of penance, especially of deathbed penance, when debating whether last-minute conversion and repentance by a lifetime sinner was enough to guarantee his or her salvation.[82] The context in the *Refutatio errorum* is essentially the same: is it enough that the penitents simply repent their sins and turn towards God, or must they orally confess their sins and do penance? However, the quotation here is not a direct quotation from Ezekiel, certainly not Chapter 14 or 24 as indicated in the manuscripts, but rather an adaptation of 33:12.[83]

There is a peculiar verb *ingemuerit* ('he would lament') that is not to be found in Ezekiel in the standard Vulgate. Nevertheless, it is used in the *Tractatus de Penitentia*, the part of Gratian's *Decretum* treating penance.[84] But in Zwicker's texts the quotation comes from the *Decretum* via another text that presents this quotation in exactly same form: the legal consultations on the case against the goldsmith Heynuš Lugner in the late 1330s or early 1340s, transmitted in two manuscripts, a Bohemian inquisitor's manual Linz MS 177, owned by Zwicker, and another, St Florian, MS XI 234, which is copied from the first manuscript:[85]

---

[81] Gdańsk, PAN MS Mar. F. 295, fol. 214vb. 'But should someone say that it is enough that a sinner abandons his sin and turns towards the Lord. Concerning this, Ezekiel 14 [sic], at whatever hour the sinner would lament etc.' Cf. Augsburg, StaSB MS 2° Cod 338, fol. 168v: 'Si dixerit quis: Sufficit vt peccator peccatum suum dimittat et conuertatur ad dominum. Iuxta illud Ezech 24: In quacumque hora peccator ingemuerit etc.' The printed edition by Gretser breaks off before this passage.

[82] A. A. Larson, *Master of Penance* (Washington, DC, 2014), pp. 44–5.

[83] Vulgata Clementina, Ezekiel 33:12: 'Tu ítaque, fili hóminis, dic ad fílios pópuli tui: Justítia justi non liberábit eum, in quacúmque die peccáverit, et impíetas ímpii non nocébit ei, in quacúmque die convérsus fúerit ab impietáte sua: et justus non póterit vívere in justítia sua, in quacúmque die peccáverit.'

[84] D. 1 de pen. c. 32: 'Hoc idem probatur auctoritate illa prophetica: "In quacumque hora peccator fuerit conuersus, et ingemuerit". Non enim dicitur: ore confessus fuerit, sed tantum: "Conuersus fuerit, et ingemuerit, uita uiuet, et non morietur."' See also Larson, *Master of Penance*, p. 45.

[85] Linz, OÖLB MS 177, fols. 100r–108r; St Florian, MS XI 234, fols. 127vb–132va. The text has been edited in *Quellen*, ed. Patschovsky, pp. 256–312, see also p. 149. See further discussion on Zwicker's ownersip of the Linz manual and the relationship between the two manuscripts in Chapter 3.

In contrarium est Ezechielis verbum: In quacumque hora peccator ingemuerit, omnium peccatorum suorum non recordabor.[86]

The quotation is not repeated in the *Cum dormirent homines*. Perhaps Zwicker's increased attention to the Scriptures and emphasis on their authority made him spot the mistake and remove the erroneous reference to Book of Ezekiel, or maybe the quotation was simply lost during revision. Because the Pseudo-Ezekiel/*Decretum* quotation appears only in the *Refutatio errorum* and is almost certainly copied from a very specialized and rare text that was in Zwicker's possession, it is the final evidence proving that the *Refutatio errorum* was compiled and written either by Petrus Zwicker or somebody belonging to the inquisitor's *familia*.

The evidence above also establishes that the *Refutatio errorum* was written by the same author as the *Cum dormirent homines*. In other words, Petrus Zwicker.[87] The author draws directly from sources to which Zwicker had access, but which were otherwise rare, namely Moneta of Cremona's *Adversus Catharos et Valdenses* and the legal consultations of Bohemian inquisitors. Therefore it is impossible for the *Refutatio* to be a summary of the *Cum dormirent homines*. Rather, it represents an earlier version of Zwicker's writing against heresy, and was probably written before the longer treatise. It lacks the rhetorical finesse and structural cohesion of the *Cum dormirent homines*. Instead, biblical verses, other authorities and their expositions are simply compiled under twelve Waldensian errors. The updated, polished *Cum dormirent homines* did not completely displace the draft version. On the contrary, ten of the surviving nineteen copies of the *Refutatio* are bound together with the *Cum dormirent homines*. The reason for that might be that the *Refutatio* included certain discussions, for example on the Church's legislation and Waldensian abhorrence of killing, which Zwicker left out of the *Cum dormirent homines* when he polished his most original contribution to anti-heretical literature: a work that almost exclusively employs the Bible to establish and emphasize the scriptural foundation of every doctrine, ritual and practice in late medieval Catholicism.

The Cum dormirent homines: *polemical biblicism*

Of all the texts written against the Waldensians in the late Middle Ages, the *Cum dormirent homines* enjoyed by far the greatest success. Peter Biller has

---

[86] *Quellen*, ed. Patschovsky, p. 267: 'Against is the word of Ezekiel: in whatever hour the sinner would lament, I shall not remember any of his sins.'

[87] In addition, recent results of computational authorship attribution confirm Zwicker's authorship. See R. Välimäki et al., 'Manuscripts, qualitative analysis and features on vectors. An attempt for a synthesis of conventional and computational methods in the attribution of late medieval anti-heretical treatises', in *Digital, Computational and Distant Readings of History: Emergent Approaches within the New Digital History*, ed. M. Fridlund, M. Oiva and P. Paju (Helsinki, 2019) [forthcoming].

rightly pointed out that with its extensive manuscript circulation, almost fifty extant manuscripts,[88] it was a major contribution to the literary perception of Waldensian heresy in German-speaking Europe, an extensive area, in the fifteenth century.[89] It was disseminated quickly after it was composed in 1395. The earliest known extant copy was written around 1400 in Weitra, Lower Austria,[90] in 1404 we have the first *Cum dormirent homines* manuscript of Bohemian provenance[91] and in the 1410s it was copied as far north as Pomerania.[92] The popularity lasted: the work circulated in the Council of Basel, whence it spread beyond the German-language area, into the college of Navarre in France.[93] Most surviving copies are from the mid- and late fifteenth century, preserved in the collections of Austrian and German religious

---

[88] My count is forty-seven medieval manuscripts. HAB MS Guelf. 431 Helmst, fols. 7ra–8rb, 10ra–14rb, 26ra–48vb includes excerpts from three different copies, and counting it thrice would raise the number of manuscrips to forty-nine. ÖNB MS 4511, fols. 159r–160v includes a summary of the main points of the text. In addition, Biller points to the existence of an eighteenth-century transcription based on an unidentified older text in Leipzig, UB MS 2106 (fols. 22r–81v, *Waldensium articuli*). Another manuscript that survived to the seventeenth century is the Tegernsee manuscript used by Gretser, which is not identifiable as any of the surviving manuscripts. Moreover, the monastery of St Aegidien in Nuremberg owned a copy, according to the 1440s library catalogue. See Biller, *Waldenses*, pp. 243 5, 263 9; *Mittelalterliche Bibliothekskataloge Deutschlands und der Schweiz*. Bd. 3, Tl. 3–4, ed. P. Ruf (Munich, 1961), p. 477; See also Appendix 1. Of the manuscripts listed there, Würzburg, UB I. t. f. 234, part 7 was previously unknown to scholars, and ÖNB MS 5393 has been only recently discovered and described in S. Rischpler and M. Haltrich, 'Der Codex 5393 der Österreichischen Nationalbibliothek und seine lokalhistorische Verortung', *Mitteilungen des Instituts für Österreichische Geschichtsforschung* 120 (2012), 307–20 (pp. 315, 317–20). Adding together the extant manuscripts, excerpts from them, the summary in the Vienna manuscript, post-medieval copies and medieval or early modern references to lost manuscripts, there are traces of fifty-two to fifty-three medieval copies of the *Cum dormirent homines*. Unlike the *Refutatio errorum*, the manuscript tradition of the *Cum dormirent homines* is relatively consistent; only three manuscripts (Augsburg, UB MS II. 1. 2° 129; Salzburg, St Peter, MS bVIII 9; Würzburg, UB I. t. f. 234, part 7) have a somewhat shortened version of the treatise, revised after 1425.

[89] Biller, *Waldenses*, p. 286.

[90] Seitenstetten, MS 213. Based on the watermarks, the heresy fascicule in ÖNB MS 5393 is possibly contemporary to or even predates the Seitenstetten manuscript. Information from Adam Poznanski. See manuscript description in Appendix 1.

[91] Gdańsk, PAN MS Mar. F. 295.

[92] Gdańsk, PAN MS Mar. F. 294, part of the old library collection of St Mary's in Danzig. The manuscript is not a copy from the older PAN, Mar. F. 295, which was donated to the library of St Mary's only in 1479.

[93] Paris, Mazarine, MS 1683 (1185). Basel was a major centre for the exchange of ideas on heresy and especially witchcraft, see M. D. Bailey, *Battling Demons: Witchcraft, Heresy, and Reform in the Late Middle Ages* (University Park, 2003), pp. 6, 28, 55, 57, 80, 96, 141. Interestingly in the fifteenth-century context, Zwicker's treatise was devoid of any demonizing rhetoric and rumours of devil worship.

houses.[94] Although Zwicker's treatise was never printed in the incunabula era, it was copied until large-scale manuscript production waned.[95] In fact, one of the latest copies is from the very end of the fifteenth century, bound into the end of an incunabula compilation codex.[96]

The full recognition of the importance of the *Cum dormirent homines* was hindered for a long time due to the already noted mistake by its seventeenth-century editor, Jacob Gretser.[97] He falsely attributed the *Cum dormirent homines* to Peter von Pillichsdorf, theologian at the University of Vienna. Although the attribution had been under suspicion for decades,[98] and Zwicker considered its probable author, Zwicker's authorship was not confirmed until the evidence presented by Peter Biller in his dissertation (1974): this evidence was not fully published until 2001.[99] Since then there has been a renewed interest in Zwicker and his work, most notably Georg Modestin's work on the manuscript tradition and Adam Poznański's on the treatise's rhetorical devices.[100] In addition, Zwicker's polemical work has often been used in studies on the late medieval Waldensians and their

---

[94] Georg Modestin observed this predominance of Austrian and south German Benedictine and Augustinian houses in his survey of the manuscript tradition of *Cum dormirent homines* and concluded that the treatise had circulated in the network of these orders and congregations. See Modestin, 'The Anti-Waldensian Treatise', pp. 223–4. Modestin builds upon the list and short descriptions of the *Cum dormirent homines* manuscripts in Biller, *Waldenses*, pp. 263–9. Modestin's proposition needs, however, some adjustment. While some of the manuscripts preserved in these religious communities were probably copied there, that certainly does not apply to all manuscripts in their collections. Several *Cum dormirent homines* manuscripts had previous owners and only later ended up in monastic libraries through donations. See the manuscript description in Appendix 1 for details and updates to datings and provenances proposed by Biller and Modestin.

[95] Manuscript production in late medieval Europe reached its peak in the 1460s and 1470s and then declined as printing spread, see U. Neddermeyer, *Von der Handschrift zum gedruckten Buch: Schriftlichkeit und Leseinteresse im Mittelalter und in der frühen Neuzeit: quantitative und qualitative Aspekte*, 2 vols. (Wiesbaden, 1998), I, 163 and passim.

[96] Würzburg, UB I. t. f. 234, part 7.

[97] Utz Tremp, *Von der Häresie zur Hexerei*, pp. 299–300.

[98] As early as 1877 there was suspicion about Gretser's attribution. Preger discussed the treatise in the context of Zwicker's inquisitions, without directly proposing that he was the author, Preger, *Beiträge*, pp. 188–9, 229–31. Later Zwicker's authorship was, with reservations, proposed by Kurze, 'Bemerkungen zu einzelnen Autoren und Quellen', pp. 31–2; Uiblein, 'Die ersten Österreicher', p. 101, n. 91; Burkhart, *Die lateinischen und deutschen Handschriften der Universitäts-Bibliothek Leipzig*, p. 252.

[99] Biller, 'Aspects', pp. 354–62; Biller, *Waldenses*, pp. 237–69.

[100] Modestin, 'The Anti-Waldensian Treatise'; Poznański, 'Traktat Piotra Zwickera'; Poznański, 'Reakcja Kościoła'; Poznański, 'Ad retorquendum erroneos articulos'.

persecution[101] and in several articles on Waldensianism published by Biller himself.[102]

The *Cum dormirent homines* is a relatively long treatise of approximately 20,000 words, which has thirty-six chapters in the seventeenth-century edition by Jacob Gretser.[103] The first part of the treatise (up to Chapter XIII) covers the history, organization and geographical distribution of the Waldensians (especially Chapters I, VI, and X–XII). It also compares their illicit, secret ministry with the (perceived) unity, continuity and public preaching of Catholic Christianity.[104] This is undeniably the most interesting part for historians of Waldensianism, because Zwicker's largely reliable view of Waldensian history and practices is presented here.[105] Yet it comprises only a small part of the work. Most of the treatise is dedicated to the refutation of single Waldensian propositions by using biblical argumentation to attack Waldensian reading of the Scriptures and providing an authoritative Catholic interpretation. Some chapters, such as those on the invocation of the Virgin Mary and the saints (XIX–XX), treat at length Catholic doctrines that were widely – albeit not uniformly – condemned by the Waldensians. Others, for example that on the supposed condemnation of excorcism (XXXVI), hardly ever feature in trial depositions. The treatise, especially the refutation of Waldensian articles of faith, has a disputational framework. A heretical article is proposed and Catholic counter-arguments with supporting quotations from the Scriptures are presented, followed by heretical objection to them and the final settling of the argument with a Catholic response. Unlike in many previous treatises, including Zwicker's own *Refutatio errorum*, where the heretical opinions are usually presented in the third person – 'the heretics say' (*dicunt heretici*) – the *Cum dormirent homines* addresses Waldensian heretics/heresiarchs mainly in the second person. Therefore Zwicker, after contradicting the supposedly Waldensian opinion that priests cannot exorcize demons with an example of Paul driving off spirits in the Acts of Apostles, continues: 'What do you say to this, you Waldensian heretic? Is not your

---

[101] Cameron, *Waldenses*, pp. 125–44; Segl, 'Die Waldenser in Österreich'; Utz Tremp, *Von der Häresie zur Hexerei*, pp. 297–307; Smelyansky, 'Self-Styled Inquisitors', pp. 135–77.

[102] Biller, 'Bernard Gui, Sex and Luciferanism', p. 455; Biller, 'Goodbye to Waldensianism?'; P. Biller, 'Bernard Gui, Peter Zwicker, and the Geography of Valdismo or Valdismi', *BSSV* 200 (2007), 31–43; Biller, 'Intellectuals and the Masses'; Biller, 'Waldensians by the Baltic'.

[103] The number and division of chapters vary from manuscript to manuscript, and some have practically none. For the sake of clarity the division of Gretser's edition is used. The chapter division of his edition and a translation of the titles is provided in Appendix 2.

[104] This unity was, of course, in Zwicker's time mainly wishful thinking. The relationship of this idealistic vision to the reality of the Church is discussed in Chapter 5.

[105] See esp. Biller, *Waldenses*, pp. 271–91; Tolonen, 'Medieval Memories', pp. 181–2.

confusion at the door? For these authorities [*auctoritates*] are clearly against you.'[106] The *auctoritates* Zwicker is referring to are here, as throughout the *Cum dormirent homines*, exclusively biblical, with the single exception, as we saw above, of Boethius's *De consolatione Philosophiae*.

Peter Biller has recognized the source for this style as the *Adversus Catharos et Valdenses* of Moneta of Cremona, which offered a general model for formal exposition of heretical doctrine and its refutation on the basis of Scripture alone. As discussed above, Zwicker accessed a copy of Moneta's treatise, as well as the Waldensian historiographical text *Liber electorum* at the latest while lodging at the Benedictine monastery of Garsten in 1395. There is no doubt that Zwicker had these works at his disposal when he wrote the *Cum dormirent homines*. This literary enterprise most likely took place at Garsten or somewhere else in Austria in 1395, where Zwicker was commencing inquisitions at the time.[107] The dating of the treatise is commonly accepted and unquestioned, and it is based on the proclamation in the chapter on indulgences (Chapter XXX): 'Now, as this is written, in the year of our Lord 1395, approximately 1362 years have passed since Christ suffered for us.'[108]

Even though Zwicker's work is relatively well known, its almost unique, omnipresent and obviously conscious biblicism remains insufficiently addressed. As already mentioned, Zwicker refrained from quoting any patristic or medieval authors to support his arguments, with the sole exception of a single sentence from Boethius. Waldensian propositions are refuted with the help of scriptural evidence only. This idiosyncrasy of Zwicker's writing has not gone unnoticed. Biller has proposed that Zwicker imitated Moneta's treatise in resorting only to the Scriptures,[109] and Segl has suggested that Zwicker dismissed the tradition of the Church Fathers because he knew that Waldensians did not accept it.[110] According to Modestin, Zwicker holds to the Bible 'as if he wanted to counter his opponents on their own Biblicist grounds'.[111]

All these explanations are to some extent true, but they do not fully address

---

[106] Zwicker, *Cum dormirent homines*, p. 297E: 'Quid dicis ad haec Waldensis haeretice? nonne confusio tua in foribus est? Quia haec sunt manifeste contra te.' Exorcism is one of the themes that exist mainly in literary polemic, not in inquisitions. It is very doubtful that it was an important point of disagreement for Waldensian Brethren.

[107] See the dating of the inquisitions in Upper Austria in Chapter 3.

[108] Zwicker, *Cum dormirent homines*, p. 295D: 'Iam, sicut scribitur, anno domini MCCCXCV, mille trecenti sexaginta duo anni, vel circiter elapsi sunt, postquam Christus passus est nobis.' First pointed out by Preger, *Beiträge*, pp. 188–9; see also Biller, *Waldenses*, p. 262; Modestin, 'The Anti-Waldensian Treatise', p. 212. The remainder of thirty-three years refers of course to the supposed age of Jesus at the Crucifixion.

[109] Biller, *Waldenses*, pp. 259, 261.

[110] Segl, 'Die Waldenser in Österreich', p. 185, n. 102.

[111] Modestin, 'The Anti-Waldensian Treatise', p. 222.

the singularity of Zwicker's biblicism and the complex interpretations of biblical authority in anti-heretical polemic and in more general religious disputes at the turn of the fifteenth century. Moneta was undeniably a model for Zwicker's polemical style, but his influence does not sufficiently explain the almost complete exclusion of non-biblical authors. First of all, Moneta himself often resorted to patristic and modern *auctoritates* and even classical philosophers, as we will see. Moreover, Zwicker's choice is almost unique in late medieval polemical literature, where not only Christian theologians but also ancient authors were habitually used by all parties to provide arguments.

The biblicist style was not so much an imitation of Moneta's style but an innovation in the new intellectual and spiritual atmosphere of the late fourteenth century. It is contemporary and parallel to the elevated status of the Scriptures in John Wyclif's theology,[112] in writings of other prominent university theologians of the time such as Heinrich Totting von Oyta and his followers,[113] and – more importantly in this context – in the Bohemian reform movement, whose early forms influenced Zwicker. Later in the fifteenth century this 'late medieval reform-biblicism' would be manifested in the Hussites' commitment to nothing but the 'law of God' and the war-cries of the peasant rebels of the Upper Rhine region.[114] In the last decade of the fourteenth century, however, it was still confined to academic circles and expressed in debate and theological treatises. Zwicker's treatise is a manifestation of this intellectual current in an anti-heretical polemical tractate. This biblicism responded not only to the Waldensian claim of authority but also to the need to find a purely scriptural basis for Catholic practices in times when the Church was divided in schism and under constant criticism.

Despite the emerging emphasis on the Bible's authority, the decision to omit even the patristic commentators is highly exceptional, although not unique in medieval polemical literature. I shall discuss the precedent of Richard FitzRalph later. The Latin fathers, especially Ambrose, Augustine,

---

[112] The most recent and comprehensive treatment of scriptural authority in Wyclif's thought is I. C. Levy, *Holy Scripture and the Quest for Authority at the End of the Middle Ages* (Notre Dame, 2012), pp. 54–91.

[113] A. Lang, 'Das Verhältnis von Schrift, Tradition und kirchlichem Lehramt nach Heinrich Totting von Oyta', *Scholastik* 40 (1965), 214–34.

[114] B. Hamm, *Religiosität im späten Mittelalter: Spannungspole, Neuaufbrüche, Normierungen*, ed. R. Friedrich and W. Simon (Tübingen, 2011), p. 10. On the meaning of the 'law of God' among the Hussites, see T. A. Fudge, 'The "Law of God": Reform and Religious Practice in Late Medieval Bohemia', in *The Bohemian Reformation and Religious Practice 1*, ed. D. R. Holeton (Prague, 1996), pp. 49–72. 'Der spätmittelalterliche Reformbiblizismus' is a concept of K. H. Lauterbach, *Geschichtsverständnis, Zeitdidaxe und Reformgedanke an der Wende zum sechzehnten Jahrhundert: das oberrheinische 'Buchli der hundert capiteln' im Kontext des spämittelalterlichen Reformbiblizismus* (Freiburg im Breisgau, 1985); English translation in B. Hamm, *The Reformation of Faith in the Context of Late Medieval Theology and Piety: Essays by Berndt Hamm*, trans. R. J. Bast (Leiden, 2004), p. 10.

Gregory the Great, Hilary and Jerome, were known in Western Europe throughout the Middle Ages, and even authors who rarely quoted them directly built upon their thought. The medieval theologians placed the fathers between Scripture and its ordinary commentators, and the early fathers were considered to have possessed special insight into the word of the Bible.[115] Even Luther, for all his reputation as the champion of 'die shrifft on alle glosen' ('Scripture without any glosses'),[116] did not exclude the early fathers from his authorities, although he deemed their words must be judged against the text of the Bible.[117]

Zwicker's *sola scriptura* principle, which he never explicitly formulates as such, was, however, very different from that of the Protestant reformations more than a century later. Berndt Hamm has stressed the fundamental difference between late medieval religiosity and the reformed confessions, although he himself has found evidence of 'normative centering' already in fifteenth-century religious thought and practice. According to Hamm, what in the reformations became the 'sole' central points (*solus Christus*, *sola gratia*, *sola scriptura*, *sola fide*; Christ alone, by grace alone, by Scripture alone, by faith alone) always included in its late medieval expressions a plurality of meanings and actors; the grace of Christ was mediated by his compassionate mother sitting at the foot of the cross. It was 'komplementare Alleinigkeit' (complementary exclusivity).[118] Similarly, the biblical quotations Zwicker employs work as an umbrella for the opinions of the doctors of the Church. The biblical argumentation and interpretation in the *Cum dormirent homines* carries with it the whole medieval commentary apparatus.

Here, I argue, lies a reason for the appeal of Zwicker's treatise and an explanation of its success in the decades following its production. It assumes

---

[115] The canon of the fathers as received in the medieval Church is listed in the *Decretum*, D. 15 c. 3. See also L. J. Elders, 'Thomas Aquinas and the Fathers of the Church', in *The Reception of the Church Fathers in the West: From the Carolingians to the Maurists*, ed. I. Backus, 2 vols. (Leiden, 1996), I, 337–66 (pp. 338–40); Levy, *Holy Scripture*, pp. 23–4; I. van 't Spijker, 'Beyond Reverence. Richard of Saint-Victor and the Fathers', in *Les réceptions des Pères de l'Église au Moyen Âge: le devenir de la tradition ecclésiale*, ed. N. Bériou, R. Berndt, M. Fédou, A. Oliva and A. Vauchez, 2 vols. (Münster, 2013), I, 439–64 (pp. 441–2).

[116] Luther to his opponents in 1521, cit. in H. Schilling, *Martin Luther: Rebell in einer Zeit des Umbruchs*, 2nd edn (Munich, 2012), p. 144.

[117] See e.g. L. Grane, *Modus loquendi theologicus: Luthers Kampf um die Erneuerung der Theologie (1515–1518)* (Leiden, 1975), pp. 177–8; M. Schulze, 'Martin Luther and the Church Fathers', in *The Reception of the Church Fathers in the West: From the Carolingians to the Maurists*, ed. I. Backus, 2 vols. (Leiden, 1997), II, 573–626.

[118] Hamm, *Religiosität im späten Mittelalter*, pp. 5–9, 37–39; for English translation of the concept, see B. Hamm, 'Normative Centering in the Fifteenth and Sixteenth Centuries: Observations on Religiosity, Theology, and Iconology', trans. J. M. Frymire, *Journal of Early Modern History* 3 (1999), 307–54 (p. 328); Mossman, *Marquard von Lindau*, p. 34.

the highest authority of the medieval culture, the Bible, and with it represents as uncontested and God-given the ecclesiastical practices that in the late medieval world were constantly scrutinized and questioned. Sticking to biblical passages, however embedded in commentary they might be, also means that Zwicker's work necessarily stays at pastoral-theological level and avoids most of the scholastic jargon.

Auctoritas *and authorities in late medieval culture*

When Petrus Zwicker decided to exclude practically all explicit reference to any *auctoritas* outside the biblical books, he made a strong statement about the authority of his arguments. Only in theory was authority absolute and uncontested in the medieval worldview: it flowed down from God through the hierarchy decreed by him. In practice it was as much questioned and disputed as at any time in human history. Precisely because of this negotiated authority Albrecht Classen has seen its study as the key to the culture of a given time.[119] In the disputes over heresy and orthodoxy it was not only the authority of the Scriptures, the foundation of the Christian faith, but also the authority of its interpretations and interpreters that was under scrutiny. The authority of the Bible and its commentators is the key to understanding Zwicker's position against the Waldensians. The Latin word *auctoritas* could mean both an author and/or his authority, usually both combined. *Auctoritas* had initially meant the quality by which a person can be trusted. Consequently it came to apply to the person himself, and further to the writings expressing the will of this authoritative person. Ultimately certain texts came to be regarded as *auctoritates* that could be invoked in theological arguments. The Scriptures, of course, were the principal authority in matters of doctrine, but the general opinion was also that the Church Fathers had been inspired by the Holy Spirit and had thus attained a level of insight out of reach of later masters.[120]

In order to comprehend how the medieval doctrinal debates arose and lasted for decades or centuries, one has to realize that despite forceful claims of authority by different entities, such as the papacy, church councils or universities, there was no institution in the later Middle Ages that could give a definitive decision on which text, interpretation or doctor had the status of an *auctoritas*. Moreover, each discipline had its own authoritative texts. The decrees of canon law were *auctoritates* for the canonists, but

---

[119] A. Classen, 'Introduction: The Authority of the Written Word, the Sacred Object, and the Spoken Word: A Highly Contested Discourse in the Middle Ages. With a Focus on the Poet Wolfram von Eschenbach and the Mystic Hildegard von Bingen', in *Authorities in the Middle Ages: Influence, Legitimacy, and Power in Medieval Society*, ed. S. Kangas, M. Korpiola and T. Ainonen (Berlin, 2013), pp. 1–24 (p. 5).

[120] Levy, *Holy Scripture*, pp. 23–24; see also p. 00, n. 117 above.

theologians claimed superiority in matters of faith on the basis that they had the knowledge and privilege to interpret the ultimate authority of Scripture.[121] As a consequence, antagonists could elevate different texts to the unquestionable status of an *auctoritas*, thus leaving the argument unresolved. Heresy too was discussed in the context of different, if partially separate and partially overlapping, spheres of authority. In the legal consultations for the case of goldsmith Heynuš Lugner of Brno, the heresy and orthodoxy of Heynuš's acts and beliefs are determined with reference to canon law, not to the Bible.[122] Zwicker was familiar with legal authorities. The consultations of Brno were at his disposal in the fourteenth-century manual of inquisition owned by him, and they were further copied into Zwicker's own manual, preserved in a copy at the library of St Florian.[123] Some authors cited scriptural, theological and legal authorities side by side, as did Zwicker's contemporary colleague, canon and inquisitor of heresy, Wasmud von Homburg from Mainz, in his *Contra beckardos, lulhardos et swestriones* (*Against Beghards, Lollards and Sisters*) (1398).[124]

In theory there should have been no problem in citing also classical (pagan) texts as moral authorities and using them in religious disputation. A good example is the manual of virtues and vices, *Summa de vitiis et virtutibus* (*Summa of Vices and Virtues*), written by the Dominican William Perald in the first half of the thirteenth century and popular throughout the later Middle Ages. In the prologue of the virtues part Guillelmus notes, based on the words of Augustine in the *De doctrina christiana* (*On Christian Doctrine*), that he wishes to collect information on virtues not only from the Scriptures, but from the works of philosophers, which should not be shunned but put into proper use in the service of the Christian faith.[125] It is illustrative that when Jean Gerson called for the bypassing of human legislation and various canons in favour of divine law so that the Great Western Schism could be ended, only a few lines earlier he quoted Cato, Terence, Aristotle and Valerius Maximus as moral authors in interpreting the true sense of human legislation.[126]

This position was – to a degree – maintained also by the Oxford theologian John Wyclif, despite his medieval and modern reputation of adhering to a

---

[121] Levy, *Holy Scripture*, pp. xiii, 42–5, 73, 200–4; J. Scott, 'Theologians vs Canonists on Heresy', in William of Ockham: Dialogus Latin Text and English Translation, http://www.britac.ac.uk/pubs/dialogus/frmIntro1d1.html.

[122] *Quellen*, ed. Patschovsky, pp. 259–312.

[123] Linz, OÖLB MS 177, fols. 100r–108r; St Florian, MS XI 234, fols. 127vb–132va.

[124] 'Tractatus contra hereticos Beckardos, Lulhardos et Swestriones des Wasmud von Homburg', ed. A. Schmidt, *Archiv für mittelrheinische Kirchengeschichte* 14 (1962), 336–86 (p. 341).

[125] Guilelmus Peraldus, *Summa virtutum ac vitiorum* (Lyon, 1554), Prologus, p. 14. Similarly, also: Thomas Aquinas, *Summa theologiae* 2a 2ae, qu. 167 art. 1 arg. 3 (LLT-A).

[126] Gerson, *Œuvres complètes*, V, pp. 177–8.

radical *sola scriptura* principle. According to Ian C. Levy, Wyclif cites biblical and legal commentary tradition extensively in his works and subscribes to the Augustinian position that when non-Christian sources concur with the Scriptures, they contain truths of faith, even though they cannot be proper *auctoritates*.[127] Even the Lombard Waldensians, admonishing their converted Austrian Brethren in 1360s, cited not only patristic authors and Bernard of Clairvaux, but also Seneca and Horace.[128] Moneta of Cremona, a likely model for Zwicker's biblicism, does indeed use scriptural evidence as his primary reference and authority, but he also quotes the full array of authors pertaining to his liberal arts education, from Aristotle to Muslim and Jewish commentators, from Church Fathers to High Medieval theologians.[129] Most of these authors are, however, employed in philosophical questions not related to the Waldensians but directed against Cathars, such as the problem of evil and the immortality and nature of the soul.[130] Moneta's argumentation against the Waldensians relies on the Scriptures, with only a few exceptions.[131] Another possible source of inspiration for Zwicker could have been the treatise by the Anonymous of Passau, where Waldensian propositions are refuted mainly with biblical quotations. But although the Anonymous deploys extra-biblical authorities sparingly, he does nevertheless use them: references include common law (*ius commune*) and decrees of the Church, Augustine and Gregory the Great.[132] Compared to his sources, and even to his opponents, Zwicker's decision to argue on a biblical basis alone is

---

[127] Levy, *Holy Scripture*, pp. 60, 63, 78.

[128] Biller, 'Aspects', pp. 277 (Augustine, Jerome and Seneca); 279 (Gregory, pseudo?); 278, 282 (Bernard); 279 (Pseudo-Chrysostum); 298 (Horace).

[129] I have not made a systematic survey of authors cited by Moneta, but the following examples demonstrate that he did not only cite the Bible: Philo (p. 7) Aristotle (pp. 24–5, 70, 347, 418, 425, 428–9, 480–1, 487–94 and passim); Augustine (pp. 37–8, 243, 285, 352, 417–18, 451, 478, 485, 505, 513, 558); Ambrose (pp. 144–5, 350, 486–7); Anselm of Canterbury (pp. 37–8, 419); Avicembron (Solomon ibn Gabirol) (p. 418); Avicenna (Ibn-Sīnā) (pp. 136, 418, 505); Boethius (pp. 418, 429, 488, 499, 503–5); Pseudo-Dionysius the Areopagite (pp. 489, 501, 505, 490–1, 496); Gregory the Great (pp. 417–19, 323); William of Auvergne (p. 422); John of Damascus (pp. 418, 504); 'Doctor Parisiensis' (Alain of Lille?) (p. 421); page numbers according to Moneta, *Adversus Catharos et Valdenses*.

[130] References to the above-mentioned authors were probably a reaction to contemporary heretics' citations of both ancient and medieval authors. On Italian Cathars and written culture, L. Paolini, 'Italian Catharism and Written Culture', in *Heresy and Literacy, 1000-1530*, ed. P. Biller and A. Hudson (Cambridge, 1994), pp. 83–103; see also Sackville, *Heresy and Heretics*, p. 28.

[131] Moneta invokes canon law when defending the continuity of the Church from Pope Sylvester and Augustine in demonstrating the Church's right to own property, explicitly directed against Waldensians; Moneta, *Adversus Catharos et Valdenses*, pp. 410, 446, 451.

[132] *Quellen*, ed. Patschovsky and Selge, pp. 101–2.

extraordinary, although it builds upon earlier tendencies to refute heresy with *auctoritates* that all parties acknowledged.

None of the authors cited above, of course, deemed commentaries – let alone classical texts – to have authority equal to that of the Bible, whose divine authority always superseded any secular text.[133] Moneta divides his arguments into *auctoritates* and *rationes*, that is theological authorities from the Scriptures and rational arguments supporting them. This structure had been used already in anti-heretical polemic by Peter the Venerable in the twelfth century and Alain of Lille at the turn of the thirteenth,[134] and its emergence can be traced back to the need for rational apologetics in scholastic theology, especially in the justification of faith to non-Christians.[135] By the time of Moneta, Scripture belongs to the *auctoritates* and philosophical expositions to the *rationes*.[136] Thus he shared the usual view of late medieval theologians that the Word of God was testimony (*testimonium*) that was proof in itself, while everything else was derivative.[137] The scholastic method of *auctoritates* and *rationes* is visible also in the *Cum dormirent homines*,[138] but Zwicker never explains his methods of argumentation as explicitly as Moneta. The testimony of Scripture is referred as *auctoritates*[139] or *testimonium*.[140] Biblical quotations

---

[133] R. Szpiech, *Conversion and Narrative: Reading and Religious Authority in Medieval Polemic* (Philadelphia, 2013), p. 67.

[134] C. Vasoli, 'Il "Contra haereticos" di Alano di Lilla', *Bullettino dell'Istituto storico italiano per il medio evo e Archivio muratoriano* 75 (1963), 123–72 (p. 123); M. Dreyer, '… Rationabiliter infirmare et … rationes quibus fides [innititur] in publicum deducere: Alain de Lille et le conflit avec les adversaires de la foi', in *Alain de Lille, le docteur universel: philosophie, théologie et littérature au XII siècle*, ed. J.-L. Solère, A. Vasiliu and A. Galonnier (Turnhout, 2005), pp. 429–42 (pp. 435–7).

[135] A. Lang, *Die Entfaltung des apologetischen Problems in der Scholastik des Mittelalters* (Freiburg im Breisgau, 1962); Szpiech, *Conversion and Narrative*, pp. 69–70.

[136] In the chapter treating the immortality of the soul: 'Nunc accedamus ad secundam partem hujus capitis, quae pars in duas dividitur, secundum duos modos probandi animae immortalitatem, quorum unus est ex testimonio Scripturarum, alius est ex rationibus; et iste duplex est, unus est ex communibus, & transcendentibus rationibus, alius autem est ex propriis; sunt autem isti duo modi noti, ex his, quae tradita sunt in Logica' (Now let us proceed to the second part of this chapter, which part is itself divided into two, in accord with the two ways of proving the immortality of the soul. One of these is from the testimony of the Scriptures, the other is from arguments. One of the latter is from general and transcendant arguments, the other however is from individual – for these are the two ways that are taught in logic). Moneta, *Adversus Catharos et Valdenses*, p. 422; see also pp. 107, 417; cf. p. 419, where God's ability to both combine and divide spirit and matter is demonstrated 'ex praedicta auctoritate Gregorii [Gregory the Great]'.

[137] Cf. the Carmelite Thomas Netter, writing in the 1420s, who regarded the Bible as *testimonium* (testimony) and the words of the saints as mere *testes* (witnesses): Levy, *Holy Scripture*, p. 134.

[138] Noted also by Poznanski, 'Traktat Piotra Zwickera', p. 103.

[139] Zwicker, *Cum dormirent homines*, pp. 281B, 283G, 296C.

[140] Ibid., pp. 282G, 289D, 291F.

are at times explicated through *exempla* and logical arguments. For example, engaging with the claim that invocation of saints is in vain because in every case they want what God wants, Zwicker argues:

> Likewise when you say: whatever God wants, also all the saints want, thus only God is to be invoked. Here you are mistaken, and you are unaware that with these words you argue against yourself. Because when you say, whatever God wants, all the saints want, you would also say correctly by saying the words turned around: whatever all the saints want, God wants it. Otherwise there would not be the will of God and saints, which is false.[141]

In the *Refutatio errorum* the use of *rationes* is somewhat more explicit. Defending purgatory, Zwicker proceeds from biblical quotations to rationalizing arguments by stating 'and it can be demonstrated by rational arguments [*rationibus*]'.[142] He is also more committed to the conventional method of strengthening his argument with examples from the natural world. This was a practice that was unhesitatingly advocated also by those theologians, such as Heinrich Totting von Oyta, who in the late fourteenth century spoke for the Bible's primacy in theological discourse.[143] In the *Refutatio*'s long redaction chapter on purgatory, discussed above, there is a lengthy passage of reasoning about purgatorial fire: how can corporeal fire torture incorporeal souls? This is first answered with natural-historical anecdotes about miraculous fires, paraphrased from William of Auvergne's *De Universo*, such as Greek fire or burning asbestos stone in the temple of Venus. Yet, even here, there is a quick return to scriptural authority: 'But they know more [fully] those things that are proved by the authority of Scripture. Exodus 3[:2]: fire was in a bush, but it was not burnt.'[144]

Both the *Refutatio errorum* and the *Cum dormirent homines* can thus be described as systematic polemical refutations of heretical doctrine according to biblical *auctoritates* and supporting *rationes*. They resemble the polemical treatises of the early thirteenth century more than later inquisitorial texts,

---

[141] Ibid., p. 286D: 'Item quando dicis: Quidquid vult deus, hoc volunt omnes sancti: ergo solus Deus est invocandus; Erras. Et nescis, quod his verbis tibimet concludis, quando dicis; Quidquid vult deus, hoc volunt omnes sancti; recte diceres conuersum sermonem dicendo; Quidquid volunt omnes sancti, hoc vult etiam deus. Alias non esset eadem voluntas Dei et sanctorum, quod falsum est.' Cf. also p. 287A: 'Sed quia Waldenses haeretici persuasionibus huiusmodi cum rationibus veritatis non poterant obsistere' (But because the Waldensian heretics could not block persuasions of this sort with the arguments of truth).

[142] Gdańsk, PAN MS Mar. F. 295, fol. 214rb: 'Item rationibus potest ostendi.'

[143] Lang, 'Das Verhältnis von Schrift', pp. 220–1. Matěj of Janov, eager propagator of the Bible's principality, did not shun the use of mythological parables such as that of the Chimera in his sermons. See a sermon against the corruption of the prelates, ed. in Neumann, 'Výbor', 72.

[144] Gdańsk, PAN MS Mar. F. 295, fol. 215ra: 'Sed plus illa sapiunt, que scripturarum auctoritate probantur. Exo. iii°: Ignis erat in rubo, non tamen comburebatur.'

a resemblance that undoubtedly owes much to Moneta's treatise. Their peculiarity is the biblicism, still nascent in the *Refutatio* but fully developed in the *Cum dormirent homines*, where patristic authors are almost completely excluded and *auctoritates* are stressed at the expense of *rationes*.

There is one more piece of evidence that demonstrates how peculiar Zwicker's dismissal of patristic testimony was: the additions made by later readers. An owner of one Bohemian manuscript, most likely parish priest Martinus of Plana in the first half of the fifteenth century, was so disturbed by the lack of patristic quotations that he made his own addition to his copy of the *Cum dormirent homines*. In the middle of the chapter on the necessity of obedience to all priests, including those living in sin, there is an added leaflet written by a later hand, entitled 'De obedientia' (On obedience). It is simply a collection of biblical and patristic authorities supporting the position defended by Zwicker in his treatise, that one must be obedient towards his or her superiors whatever their conduct. There are several references to Augustine and Gregory the Great, collected to provide some *auctoritates* not used by Zwicker.[145] This is not the only example. In another manuscript, references to Gregory's *Dialogues* and Augustine's *Contra epistulam Manichaei quam vocant Fundamenti* (*Against the Epistle of Manichæus, Called Fundamental*) have been added in the upper margin in support of purgatory.[146] In addition, in his translation of the *Cum dormirent homines* for his catechetic treatises Ulrich von Pottenstein supplies Zwicker's text with patristic commentary.[147]

Consequently, I propose two considerations in Zwicker's decision to exclude the extra-biblical *auctoritates*: the first of them relating to the

---

[145] NKCR MS XIII. E. 5, fol. 159r–v.

[146] Augsburg, UB MS II. 1. 2° 129, fol. 144v: 'Nec Wal[denses] credunt reuelacionibus multis de purgatorio ut experimentiis de quibus gregorius 4° dyal. nec curant magnam auctoritatem ecclesie christi cuius auctoritas est maior auctoritate sacre scripture, vnde augustinus contra epistolam fundamenti ego non ewangelio [crederem] nisi catholice ecclesie me commoueret auctoritas que ecclesia habuit tot viros doctissimos et in tali fide mortuos et claris miraculis approbatos.' (Nor do the Waldensians believe the many visions of purgatory as [real] experiences – on which see Gregory, 4th [book, ch. 39] of the *Dialogues* – nor do they care for the great authority of the Church of Christ, whose authority is greater than that of holy scripture. Whence Augustine, *Against the Epistle* […] *Fundamental* [ch. 5]: 'I would not believe the Gospel, except as moved by the authority of the Catholic Church', which Church has had so many very learned men and so many who have died in that faith and have been proven by glorious miracles). Cf. Augustine, *Contra epistolam Manichaei*, PL 42, 176. Gregory's exempla in Book 4 of the *Dialogues* were precursors of the medieval exempla about purgatory: Le Goff, *The Birth of Purgatory*, p. 90.

[147] For example the chapter on burial invokes Augustine's and Jerome's commentaries on the Gospel text, see Ulrich von Pottenstein, *Credo* 27M (ÖNB MS 3050, fols. 104va–105ra). A commentary from Gregory the Great is inserted in the middle of a chapter on the Virgin Mary and saints: see ibid., 33H (fol. 255va).

controversial status of patristic authorities among the Waldensians, and the second pertaining to contemporary doctrinal discussions that did not strictly concern the Waldensian heresy. Regarding the first reason, the Waldensians and the Church Fathers: as demonstrated above, the Waldensian Brethren quoted patristic sources in their correspondence. In addition to that, Moneta's treatise provides information on how Valdesius, when promising obedience to the pope (Alexander III), had accepted the teachings of four fathers: Ambrose, Augustine, Gregory and Jerome.[148] Other sources demonstrate that early Waldensians had indeed referred to different patristic texts, much like their counterparts in the 1360s.[149] In some Catholic treatises this was interpreted as though the heretics distorted the teachings of the fathers to support their own arguments, discarding aspects of that teaching that undermined their beliefs. This view was held by the mid-thirteenth-century author of the *De inquisitione hereticorum* as well as by the later anonymous polemicist in the *Attendite a falsis prophetis*, both works in general circulation in German-speaking Europe at the end of the fourteenth century.[150] Some sources claimed that the Waldensians denied the validity of patristic authority altogether. Matthew of Kraków stated this in a sermon given in Prague in 1384,[151] and the sole authority of the Scriptures was likewise attested in one of the many error lists composed against Waldensians in the last decade of the fourteenth century.[152] Petrus Zwicker himself wrote in his letter to the Austrian dukes in 1395, that 'they condemn and reject all words and sayings of the holy doctors Augustine, Jerome, Gregory, Ambrose and all others, with the sole exception of those which appear to be for the consolation of their sect'.[153] Zwicker knew that Waldensians resorted to the fathers, but was also aware of the disputed status of their authority. His omission of patristic references may simply have been a decision to bypass the whole controversy.

---

[148] Moneta, *Adversus Catharos et Valdenses*, p. 402; Gonnet and Molnár, *Les Vaudois au Moyen Âge*, p. 391; Molnár, *Storia dei valdesi (1)*, p. 275; C. Papini, *Valdo di Lione e i poveri nello spirito* (Turin, 2002), pp. 75–6.

[149] Molnár, *Storia dei valdesi (1)*, p. 275.

[150] 'Der Tractat des David von Augsburg', ed. Preger, p. 209 (*De inquisitione hereticorum*); St Florian, MS XI 152, fol. 49v (*Attendite a falsis prophetis*).

[151] *Quellen*, ed. Patschovsky, p. 320. The sermon is discussed in Chapter 4.

[152] Augsburg, UB MS II. 1. 2° 78, fol. 245va: 'Item dicunt quod ex institucione ecclesie nichil tenentur credere nisi textui biblie; Item dicunt se non obligari ad credendum miraculis sanctorum, quantumcumque ab ecclesia approbatis, nisi in textu biblie exprimantur' (Item, they say that they are bound to believe nothing by the ordinance of the Church except the text of the Bible. Item, they say that they are not obliged to believe in the miracles of the saints, however much they may be approved by the Church, unless they are related in the text of the Bible).

[153] P. Segl, unpublished collation of Zwicker's letter: '[73] Item dampnant et reprobant omnia verba et dicta sanctorum doctorum, Augustini, Ieronimi, Gregorii et Ambrosii et omnium aliorum, illis solis exceptis, que aliqualiter sonant ad confortaconem sue secte.' Cf. Preger, *Beiträge*, p. 249.

A difficulty in analysing the basis for Zwicker's biblicism is that unlike many other writers, he does not explain how it relates to *auctoritates* or to his own arguments. Moneta, who attacked both Waldensians and Cathars, reminds his reader that the *auctoritates* from the Old Testament can be used only against the Jews and the Waldensians, not Cathars, who accept only the New Testament.[154] Since Zwicker was arguing solely against the Waldensians, it might seem that he could simply have proceeded on the basis of the whole Bible. However, the matter was not so straightforward, as parts of Scripture were still problematic. Moneta, Matthew of Kraków and the anonymous author of the *Attendite a falsis prophetis* all acknowledged that the Waldensians did not accept the Books of Maccabees as part of the biblical canon,[155] and we must assume that Zwicker too was aware of this. However, he desperately needed Maccabees to prove that intercession on behalf of the dead was ordained in the Bible. In fact, after quoting 2 Maccabees he proclaims that prayers for the dead are manifestly decreed in Scripture.[156] This automatic acceptance of the canonical status of Maccabees is not accidental, but part of a careful biblicist argumentation whose credibility rests on certain unquestioned presuppositions. A similar example is the unquestioning acceptance of apostolic tradition not written down in the biblical canon when Zwicker refutes Waldensian secret ministry by contrasting their flight from the inquisitors with the courage of Peter and Paul in front of Emperor Nero.[157] Moreover, unvoiced presuppositions abound in Zwicker's interpretation of Scripture, as we shall see below.

Another motivation for Zwicker's biblicism can be found outside the realm of anti-Waldensian literature, which, despite Zwicker being an inquisitor, was not his whole world. The status of Scripture vis-à-vis other sources of religious authority was discussed within the reform movement in the archdiocese of Prague, and not without controversy. The primacy of Scripture as a model for Christian devotion had been emphasized already in the 1360s and 1370s by the reforming preachers Konrad Waldhauser and Jan Milíč of Kroměříž, whose principal opponents were the mendicant orders,[158] and

---

[154] See e.g. Moneta, *Adversus Catharos et Valdenses*, p. 460, about defending holy images with examples from the Old Testament: 'Ista possunt dici Judaeis, & Valdensibus; sed Catharis non nisi ex parte; illa enim testimonia Veteris Testamenti non recipiunt.'

[155] Moneta, *Adversus Catharos et Valdenses*, p. 373; *Quellen*, ed. Patschovsky, p. 321; St Florian, MS XI 152, fol. 49v.

[156] Zwicker, *Cum dormirent homines*, p. 288D–E.

[157] Ibid.

[158] H. Kaminsky, *A History of the Hussite Revolution* (Berkeley, 1967), pp. 9–23; J. Nechutová, *Die lateinische Literatur des Mittelalters in Böhmen* (Cologne, 2007), p. 254; Soukup, 'Die Predigt als Mittel religiöser Erneuerung', p. 242. The conflict between the mendicants and the secular clerics in Prague has been extensively treated in C. Ocker, 'Die Armut und die menschliche Natur: Konrad Waldhauser,

whose influence touched the students at the University of Prague, Zwicker's alma mater.[159] After them, the special status of the Bible was most elaborately explicated by Matěj of Janov in his massive *Regulae veteris et novi testamenti* (*Rules of the Old and the New Testament*), written around 1387–92.[160] The core of Janov's message is reversal of the current deplorable state of the Church through Christocentric devotion, achieved mainly through frequent communion of the laity.[161] Although the topic of frequent lay communion, much debated in Prague at the end of the fourteenth and the beginning of the fifteenth century,[162] was not an issue in anti-Waldensian polemic, Janov's work has two features that are extremely interesting in relation to the *Cum dormirent homines*. Firstly, Matěj of Janov makes hardly any use of patristic literature in his argumentation, although he does not deny its edifying value.[163] However, unlike Zwicker, he explains his decision:

> In these writings of mine I do not use the characteristic words of the doctors, but instead the words of the most holy Bible. And even though I interposed the sentences and truths of a great many doctors, I have not pursued their intercessions expressly in this book, because the words and doctrines of the doctors have their place, after all, in a great many books.[164]

Secondly, Janov is hostile to what he regards as 'inventions' (*adinventiones*) and 'human traditions' (*traditiones hominum*), feeling that saints, relics and images have distracted the laity from devotion of what is truly important, that

---

Jan Milíč von Kroměříž und die Bettelmönche', in *Die 'neue Frömmigkeit' in Europa im Spätmittelalter*, ed. M. Derwich and M. Staub (Göttingen, 2004), pp. 111–29; O. Marin, *L'archevêque, le maître et le dévot: genèses du mouvement réformateur pragois: années 1360–1419* (Paris, 2005), pp. 233–324.

[159] Nechutová, *Die lateinische Literatur*, pp. 253, 257.

[160] On the dating, see J. Nechutová, 'Matěj of Janov and his Work *Regulae Veteris et Novi Testamenti*: The Significance of Volume VI and its Relation to the Previously Published Volumes', in *The Bohemian Reformation and Religious Practice 2*, ed. Z. V. David and D. R. Holeton (Prague, 1998), pp. 15–24 (pp. 20–1).

[161] Nechutová, 'Matěj of Janov', pp. 22–3.

[162] See e.g. J. Kadlec, *Studien und Texte zum Leben und Wirken des Prager Magisters Andreas von Brod* (Münster, 1982), p. 16; D. Holeton, *La Communion des tout-petits enfants: étude du mouvement eucharistique en Bohême vers la fin du Moyen-Âge* (Rome, 1989), pp. 19–27; D. R. Holeton, 'The Bohemian Eucharistic Movement in its European Context', in *The Bohemian Reformation and Religious Practice 1*, ed. D. R. Holeton (Prague, 1996), pp. 23–47.

[163] Nechutová, *Die lateinische Literatur*, p. 260, points out this idiosyncrasy in Matěj of Janov's literary work.

[164] Matěj of Janov, *Regulae I*, pp. 13–14: 'In istis ergo scriptis meis non sum usus propriis verbis doctorum, sed tantum verbis sacratissime biblie. Et licet sentencias et veritates doctorum plurimum interposuerim, tamen non institi eorum allegacioni expresse in hoc libro, tum quia verba et doctrine doctorum habent sua loca, id est libros plurimos.'

is Christ.[165] This is the opposite view to that held by Zwicker, who defended these very things and refuted the view that they were new inventions without scriptural basis.

Even if Zwicker did not actually read Matěj's work, he must have been aware of its general implications. On 18 October 1389, a synod of Prague archdiocese had forced three men to revoke heretical, erroneous or controversial articles, much of which included popular opposition to excesses or malpractices in the cults of the saints, and particularly the cult of the Virgin. One of the men was Matěj of Janov, and two others, Jakub of Kaplice and a priest called Andreas, were also secular clergy but far less prominent figures. Janov admitted only that he had preached some things that perhaps were not right and could be misunderstood. Therefore he confirmed his Catholic faith by reaffirming that he would uphold Catholic doctrine and practice, including veneration of relics and the belief that the saints in heaven could intercede on behalf of sinners, and accept that the images of Christ and saints did not constitute a danger of idolatry. The other two were accused of more serious transgressions, including desecration of the Virgin's statue.[166] These revocations bear a striking resemblance to Waldensian errors, to the extent that in a fifteenth-century manuscript they are transmitted together with the *Refutatio errorum*.[167] Janov again appeared in front of the archiepiscopal court in 1392, when he was twice questioned over statements in his books.[168]

Accusation of such a public figure as Janov made for a high-profile trial and it would be strange if Petrus Zwicker, who within a few years was inquisitor of heresy as well as head of a significant monastery in the archdiocese, were unaware of the controversy over the opinions of Janov and his supporters. For this reason I suggest that Zwicker's work was written and read not merely as an anti-Waldensian treatise, but as a work defending the Catholic faith in general. Its biblicism should be understood as an orthodox, conventional reaction to more radical ideas that were based on the primacy of Scripture. Instead of discarding the existing practices and traditions, Zwicker set out to demonstrate that they were rooted in the Bible. If Matěj of Janov and other reform-minded preachers saw that Prague's many relics, churches rich with treasures and the sumptuous liturgy that was celebrated in them led the simple people away from the Scriptures, Petrus Zwicker saw them as instruments of salvation and piety, especially for the laity: 'the images are

---

[165] Matěj of Janov, *Regulae* II, pp. 145–6, 149; Nechutová, 'Matěj of Janov', p. 16.

[166] *Documenta Mag. Joannis Hus vitam, doctrinam, causam in Constantiensi concilio actam et controversias de religione in Bohemia anni 1403–1418 motas illustrantia*, ed. F. Palacký (Prague, 1869), pp. 699–702.

[167] NKCR MS XIII. E. 7. Revocations at fols. 188r–190v, *Refutatio errorum* [R3] at fols. 179v–187r.

[168] Nechutová, 'Matěj of Janov', p. 19.

thus books for the laity, who, not knowing the Scriptures, sometimes achieve greater devotion and grace than a great scholar from the study of books'.[169]

New institutions

The flow of biblical passages in the *Cum dormirent homines* is sometimes torrential and often exhausting. At times Zwicker lists dozens of places in the Bible that support the Catholic interpretation and undermine the Waldensian position. He does this especially in the chapters handling ecclesiastical practices that Waldensians deemed to be later inventions, such as church buildings, images, church music or canonical hours. There, the inquisitor probably felt the need to collect every possible piece of scriptural evidence he could come up with. The chapter defending canonical hours begins with a reflection on the heretical accusations:

> The Waldensian heretics say that canonical hours and all other prayers are invalid and vain, with the sole exception of the Our Father. They even say that nothing else is to be prayed than the Our Father, and that everything else that is said and read in Mass is not divine but of human institution, with the sole exception of the words of consecration and the Our Father.[170]

Zwicker continues by arguing that when instituting the Our Father, Christ did not mean to exclude other prayers. The major part of the chapter is basically a list of both Old and New Testament examples of prayers and petitions other than the Lord's Prayer.[171] The crucial assertion comes after that, in a short section that in many manuscripts and in Gretser's edition is separated into its own chapter:

> That the institution of canonical hours is not human but divine is shown by the Scriptures. Psalm 98 [sic, 118:164]: 'Seven times a day I have given praise

---

[169] Zwicker, *Cum dormirent homines*, p. 297B–C: 'Sunt ergo imagines libri Laicales, qui nescientes scripturas, quandoque maiorem deuotionem & gratiam percipiunt, quam quandoque magnus literatus ex lectione librorum.'

[170] Ibid., p. 293F: 'Item dicunt Waldenses haeretici, Horas Canonicas, et omnes alias orationes, irritas et inanes, excepto solo Pater Noster: imo dicunt, plane nihil aliud orandum esse, quam Pater Noster, et quod omnia alia, que dicuntur et leguntur in Missa, non sint institutionis diuinae, sed humanae, solis verbis consecrationis, et Pater noster exceptis.' Scepticism towards 'extra' orations is common with late fourteenth-century Waldensians. See e.g. the Mainz error list, Kolpacoff, 'Papal schism', p. 284: 'duodecimus, quod salutatio angelica non debet dici quia non est oratio nec a deo ordinata, sed a sacerdotibus inventa' (12th, that the Angelic Salutation [Hail Mary] should not be said, because it is not a prayer nor ordained by God, just invented by priests).

[171] Zwicker, *Cum dormirent homines*, pp. 293G–294C.

to thee', and Acts 3[:1]: 'Now Peter and John went up into the temple at the ninth hour of prayer.'[172]

On this scriptural basis, according to Zwicker, the Church has then instituted the seven canonical hours in memory of Christ's passion and its seven moments and instruments.[173] Forced to admit that the actual canonical hours observed in the Roman Church are later institutions, Zwicker claims that their fundamental and essential foundation is in the word of the Bible and the passion of Christ.

Zwicker attempts here, with a direct appeal to the Bible's authority, to circumvent the difficult question of the extent to which the Church had the right to institute new feasts, liturgical practices or canon law. The debate over 'new institutions' was itself nothing new. After the conversion (or apostasy, depending on one's point of view) of several Austrian Brethren to Catholicism in the 1360s, their Lombard counterparts accused them, among other things, of having defected because of the 'endless opinions' (*opiniones infinite*), referring to the ever-growing legislation and practices of the Roman Church. Johannes Leser, one of the Austrian converts, answered that they are not 'opinions' but 'apostolic institutions, to be venerated by all devout Christians', and 'not invented by human study but delivered by the inspiration of the Holy Spirit'.[174] Leser thus interpreted the status of the 'new' institutions in the same way that Zwicker did. As the latter was familiar with the correspondence, he probably knew of this former discussion, although it does not appear to have been his direct source.

Other possible sources were also available, for direct invocation of the Bible's authority in the face of 'novelty' accusations was by no means confined to the polemics against Waldensian heresy. The archbishop of Prague, Jan of Jenštejn, was confronted by his diocesan clergy, who were often

---

[172] Ibid., p. 294D: 'Institutionem Horarum Canonicarum non humanam, sed diuinam fore, probatur per scripturam. Psalm. 98. [sic] Septies in die laudem dixi tibi. Item, Act. 3. Petrus autem et Ioannes ascenderunt in templum ad horam orationis nonam.'

[173] Ibid., p. 294D–E.

[174] Biller, 'Aspects', pp. 302–3: 'Quod vero infertis quod opiniones infinite faciunt nos apostatare – respondemus: non sunt opiniones sed apostolice instituciones, a cunctis cristianis devotis venerande, non ex humano studio invente sed ex sancti spiritus inspiracione tradite. Hoc dico de usu et ordine ecclesie et ministrorum ecclesie longe ante Silvestrum Papam institute. Beati qui in hiis bene conversantur, ve autem eis qui in hiis fuerint negligentes' (Let us reply [to] the accusation that you actually make, that infinite opinions make us apostatize. They are not opinions but apostolic institutions, to be venerated by all devout Christians, not invented by human study but delivered by the inspiration of the Holy Spirit. I say this about the use and order of the Church and the ministers of the Church, instituted a long time before Pope Sylvester. Blessed are those who conduct themselves well in these things, woe to those who will have been heedless).

at odds with their uncompromising prelate, when instituting the feast of the Visitation of Mary in his archdiocese in summer 1386, inspired by a vision he had supposedly seen already in 1378.[175] The opposition was led by Master Adalbertus Ranconis de Ericinio (Vojtěch Raňkův of Ježov) in the cathedral chapter.[176] The opposing party claimed that the archbishop had instituted novelties that had no foundation in tradition or the Scriptures. Jenštejn's own sermon, dating probably to the same summer of 1386, includes some of the arguments:

> Here the complainers say disparagingly that I cannot institute a feast in my diocese without the permission of the Highest Pontiff, and, moreover, that it is without doubt erroneous and savours of heresy, and that I should not proclaim such a superstitious feast and invent unaccustomed novelties. [...] And once more I deny that this feast is superstitious and erroneous, and on the contrary I think that it is Catholic; and to say otherwise savours of heresy; for he who says that this feast is superstitious is certainly with these [words] claiming that the Gospel is superstitious.[177]

Jenštejn refers here to the fact that the Visitation is mentioned in the Gospel of Luke (1:39–56), and thus the feast has a scriptural basis.[178] He employed the same strategy that had previously been used by Johannes Leser and was used again some years later by Zwicker. All of them attest that the Catholic liturgy and other ecclesiastical practices, even recent ones, are essentially based on the Bible and divine inspiration and therefore are not human inventions.[179] To

---

[175] Weltsch, *John of Jenstein*, p. 84; I. Westergård, *Approaching Sacred Pregnancy: The Cult of the Visitation and Narrative Altarpieces in Late Fifteenth-Century Florence* (Helsinki, 2007), pp. 64–5; Loserth, 'Codex Epistolaris', pp. 351–9.

[176] Weltsch, *John of Jenstein*, p. 88; S. Mossman, 'Dorothea von Montau and the Masters of Prague', *Oxford German Studies* 39 (2010), 106–23 (p. 115).

[177] Weltsch, *John of Jenstein*, Appendix II, pp. 191–2: 'Hic enim murantes [*recte* murmurantes] detrahunt non me mea in dyocesi absque summi indultu pontificis festum instituere non [sic] posse, insuper, quod haut dubium erroneum est et sapit heresim, non debere me eciam supersticiosa festa indicere atque insolitas novitates invenire. [...] Et iterum diffitior eciam hoc festum supersticiosum fore et erroneum, sed econtra fateor id esse catholicum et contrarium dicere heresim sapere; nam huis qui supersticiosum id festum dicit, profecto et supersticiosum ewangelium affirmat.'

[178] Jan of Jenštejn eventually triumphed in this matter. He defeated the opposition by seeking apostolic sanction for the new feast, which was given after tedious investigation three years later, on 9 November 1389 by Boniface IX. The feast was instituted for the whole Church, and it was set on 2 July. As a minor setback it was not the liturgy written by Jenštejn that was accepted for the feast but that written by an English cardinal, Adam Easton. See Weltsch, *John of Jenstein*, pp. 88–91.

[179] Many prominent late medieval theologians, including William Ockham, Heinrich Totting von Oyta and Jean Gerson, would have shared the view that *determinationes et definitiones* of the Church are not a special category of Catholic truths but only define what is already prescribed in the Bible, apostolic tradition or special revelation: Lang, 'Das Verhältnis von Schrift', pp. 232–3.

question their validity is to undermine the word of God, and to fail to understand this is a failure in understanding the Scriptures.

Even though the call for the Bible's ultimate authority was common in late medieval religious debate, it is nevertheless remarkable that in the *Cum dormirent homines* Zwicker does not defend the right of the Church and the papacy to establish new decrees and regulations. He had done so in the *Refutatio errorum*, and the matter is likewise discussed in other anti-heretical treatises, including works known to Zwicker. The *Refutatio* has a whole chapter dedicated to the matter: 'they say that the things that are instituted by bishops and prelates of the Church are not to be observed, because they are human traditions, not of God'.[180] Its source is without any doubt Moneta of Cremona's treatise, which has a corresponding chapter. Zwicker uses the same arguments and Bible verses to counter heretical arguments that are already presented by Moneta, at times almost verbatim. Both claim that the Church inherited the right to give new ordinances from the apostles and the primitive church, and that if the 'Church of the Jews' (*Ecclesia de Judeis*) had the right to add something to the Law of God, so much more so had the present Church.[181] The defence of the 'new institutions' in the *Refutatio* is thus practically a paraphrase of the longer chapter in Moneta's work, but it is discarded as such from the *Cum dormirent homines*. Instead, the arguments are dispersed less obviously throughout the work. As we have seen, the canonical hours are defended with the assertion that what heretics regarded as human inventions were originally instituted by God. Moneta's treatise and the *Refutatio* also quote Christ's promise of the Holy Spirit (John 16:12–13) to support this continuous divine inspiration.[182] Zwicker uses the same verse in the same sense – not all that is according to divine law and God's plans is revealed plainly in the Bible – but it appears in a completely different location, in the chapter on purgatory.[183]

The disappearance of the chapter dedicated solely to the new constitutions

---

[180] 'Item dicunt quod ea que instituntur ab episcopis et ecclesie prelatis non sint seruanda, eo quod tradiciones hominium sint non dei', quoted here from Gdańsk, PAN MS Mar. F. 295, fol. 216va–vb (Redaction 1); cf. *Refutatio*, ed. Gretser, p. 305E–G. Cf. also Augsburg, StaSB MS 2° Cod 338, fol.164r–v (Redaction 4).

[181] Gdańsk, PAN MS Mar. F. 295, fol. 216vb; Moneta, *Adversus Catharos et Valdenses*, p. 445. See also n. 58 above in this chapter.

[182] Gdańsk, PAN MS Mar. F. 295, fol. 216va; Moneta, *Adversus Catharos et Valdenses*, p. 445.

[183] Zwicker, *Cum dormirent homines*, p. 286F: 'Sed, non sequitur, Christus hoc non dixit, ergo non est verum, non est credendum, nec faciendum: imo, multa vera, multa credenda, multa facienda reseruauit aduentui Spiritus sancti. Ioan.16 [John 16:12]. Adhuc multa habeo vobis dicere, sed non potestis portare modo etc.' (But it does not follow: 'Christ did not say this, therefore it is not true, is not to be believed, not to be done.' Rather, he reserved for the coming of the Holy Spirit many things that are true, many that are to be believed, many that are to be done. John 16: 'I have many things to say to you: but you cannot bear them now, etc.').

demonstrates an important feature in Zwicker's polemical biblicism, a feature that was polished when the *Refutatio* was reworked into the *Cum dormirent homines*: the argument is condensed into essentials, to be proved or disproved solely (or so it is made to appear) on the basis of biblical *auctoritas*. This method does not allow secondary argument on whether or not popes or bishops had the right to institute new feasts, make canon law decrees or doctrinal statements. In the spiritual atmosphere where not only Waldensians but also zealous reformers in Prague were critical of the Church's bureaucratic nature and promoted Christocentric piety, it was wiser to soften statements such as that still appearing in the *Refutatio*: 'From which it is obvious that the Church of God neither was nor is confined to those things that Christ taught in person, and therefore it was and is able to make constitutions inspired by Him.'[184] Defending the legitimacy of popes' decretals or decisions of an episcopal synod was not necessary, not because these must not be followed, but because they only explained the fundamental truth Zwicker's treatise tries to establish: Catholic cult in all its aspects, be it canonical hours, church bells, priests' garments or sacramentals, is firmly and solidly based in the Scriptures.

Sicut verba sonant: *monastic and scholastic versus literal dissident reading*

The struggle over the correct reading of the Scriptures in the *Cum dormirent homines* becomes a caricaturist collision of two ways of interpreting the Bible. Scholastic argumentation and meditative rumination of an intellectual schooled both at university and in a monastic milieu confronts a moralistic-literal dissident reading. It is caricaturist because it is at least partially, perhaps mostly, an imaginative construction of the first party. The many passages adopted from Moneta's approximately 150-year-old treatise raise suspicions that the heretical opinions cited in the *Cum dormirent homines* are not those of the Waldensians of the late fourteenth century.[185] Yet, even when one recognizes Zwicker's polemic as literary construction, one should not underestimate the opposing party or assume that they did not hold any of the views ascribed to them. There is more than enough evidence, from both Catholic and Waldensian sources, to demonstrate that there was continuity

---

[184] Gdańsk, PAN MS Mar. F. 295, fol. 216va–vb: 'Ex quibus patet quod ecclesia dei non fuit nec eciam est contenta hiis que christus docuit personaliter et ideo potuit et potest constituciones facere illo inspirante.'

[185] In addition to the examples above, see e.g. on ecclesiastical singing and countering the assertion that Paul ordained only silent, spiritual singing in his letter to the Ephesians, Zwicker, *Cum dormirent homines*, p. 293D; Moneta, *Adversus Catharos et Valdenses*, p. 458.

and doctrinal unity within the Waldensian movement.[186] It was not an invention of the Catholic polemicists that Waldensians denied the existence of purgatory or the power of the saints, and their denial of oath-taking was certainly based on a literal interpretation of Matthew 5:34–37: 'But I say to you not to swear at all, neither by heaven, for it is the throne of God.' Without doubt, Waldensians did subscribe to many of the opinions Zwicker refuted. That being said, he is nevertheless attacking a straw man, whose core beliefs might consist of what Zwicker had learned from converted Brethren and their followers he had interrogated, but which had stuffing borrowed from two centuries of learned polemic against heretics.

From Zwicker's perspective Waldensian biblical interpretation is based on a simplistic and overly literal reading of the Bible. According to him, Waldensians understand the Scriptures 'as words sound' (*sicut verba sonant*), which leads to heresy. They take the words at face value without delving below the surface to understand their true meaning. Thus they deny the existence of purgatory because Christ spoke only of two gates and roads, narrow and broad, that lead either to salvation or to damnation. For Zwicker this argument is unsound, as it does not automatically follow that because what Christ said and commanded is true and must be observed, what he did not mention does not exist. Even many commands should not be taken too literally:

> It is famously said, and he understood it this way, because in Matthew 18[:8–9]: 'And if thy hand, or thy foot scandalize thee, cut it off, and cast it from thee. And if thy eye scandalize thee, pluck it out, and cast it from thee.' This the Lord by no means understood as the words sound. So it is not to be observed literally, because this letter not only kills, but plucks out eyes and cuts off hand and feet, 'but the spirit quickeneth', 2 Corinthians 3[:6].[187]

Jesus's order to pluck out tempting eyes was commonly quoted by medieval theologians to show that not all New Testament commands need be read as they first appear.[188] The late medieval attitude towards literal sense was extremely nuanced, and the passage cited above shows that Zwicker shared the view of the contemporary biblical scholars. It was characterized by balancing the literal sense as the primary sense of Scripture and the only one

---

[186] See esp. Biller, 'Goodbye to Waldensianism?'.

[187] Zwicker, *Cum dormirent homines*, p. 286E–F: 'Et notanter dicitur, et ita intellexit, quia, Matt.18. dicit: Si manus, tua vel pes tuus scandalizat te, abscinde eum et proiice abs te. Et si oculus tuus scandalizat te, erue eum, et proiice abs te. Hoc Dominus nequaquam intellexit ita, sicut verba sonant. Ergo non est literaliter obseruandum: quia haec litera non solum occidit, imo oculos eruit, manus et pedes abscindit; Spiritus autem viuificat, 2. Corinth.3.' See also ibid., pp. 293G, 296D.

[188] K. Froehlich, '"Always to Keep to the Literal Sense in Holy Scripture Means to Kill One's Soul": The State of Biblical Hermeneutics at the Beginning of the Fifteenth Century', in *Literary Uses of Typology: From the Late Middle Ages to the Present*, ed. E. R. Miner (Princeton, 1977), pp. 20–48 (p. 31).

valid for arguing dubious points of doctrine, and the avoidance of overly literal reading in a grammatically rigorous way. By the late Middle Ages scholars had come to recognize four senses of Scripture (literal, allegorical (typological), moral (tropological) and anagogical), but especially since the rise of scholastic argumentation the literal sense was being seen as the foundation for the others. Basing his view on Augustine, the Franciscan Nicholas of Lyra – perhaps the most important late medieval exegete – commented thus on the importance of the literal sense: 'as only from literal sense, and not from mystical, can an argument be made for proving or declaration of something dubious'.[189] Thomas Aquinas had attested the same in *Summa Theologica*: 'But there is nothing lost in Sacred Scripture, for there is nothing contained under the spiritual sense necessary for the faith that Scripture does not also treat plainly elsewhere in its literal sense.'[190]

The literal sense was thus expanded in meaning and interpreted in such a way as to avoid the contradictions that would follow if every sentence of the Bible was read in a grammatically literal way. The literal sense of late medieval exegesis was the sense the author had intended – in the case of Scripture the author being God.[191] In some cases the parabolic sense was the intended sense. Nicholas of Lyra quotes the verse about cutting off the scandalizing body parts, just as Zwicker did, to give an example of how one must read according to the 'mystical' sense lest the sense of Scripture be false, which was obviously impossible.[192] This is the reason why Zwicker stresses how Christ 'understood' (*intellexit*) the words: it is the intention of Christ that guides the interpretation, not how a simple-minded heretic would understand the words when he reads them. At the same time it is clear that Zwicker saw himself as reading the primary plain sense of the Bible. After quoting 2 Maccabees to prove that prayer on behalf of the dead was effective, Zwicker challenges his opponent:

> Weigh this carefully, you Waldensian heresiarch, who accept what is stated in the Bible. Although the prayers for the dead are not elsewhere stated so

[189] Nicholas of Lyra, *Prologus de commendatione Sacrae Scripturae*, PL 113, 29C: 'maxime cum ex solo sensu litterali, et non ex mystico, possit argumentum fieri ad probationem vel declarationem alicuius dubii, secundum quod dicit Augustinus in epistola contra Vincentium Donatistam.'

[190] Thomas Aquinas, *Summa theologiae*, Ia, qu. I, art. 10 ra 1, cited and translated in F. van Liere, *An Introduction to the Medieval Bible* (New York, 2014), p. 135.

[191] A. J. Minnis, '"Authorial Intention" and "Literal Sense" in the Exegetical Theories of Richard Fitzralph and John Wyclif: An Essay in the Medieval History of Biblical Hermeneutics', *Proceedings of the Royal Irish Academy. Section C: Archaeology, Celtic Studies, History, Linguistics, Literature* 75 (1975), 1–31; C. Ocker, *Biblical Poetics before Humanism and Reformation* (Cambridge, 2002), pp. 142–9; Levy, *Holy Scripture*, pp. 11–23; van Liere, *Medieval Bible*, pp. 133–9.

[192] Nicholas of Lyra, *Prologus de commendatione Sacrae Scripturae*, PL 113, 34C; Levy, *Holy Scripture*, pp. 13–14.

expressly, here they are so clearly and plainly treated that they could not be expressed with more clear and open words.[193]

Overly literal reading was seen as a cause of heresy and error as early as the patristic era. Gregory the Great had remarked in his *Moralia in Job* that sometimes to read *iuxta litteram* led to error rather than to education.[194] These accusations were emphasized again in the late fourteenth and early fifteenth century, as Wyclif, Hus and their followers were accused of bypassing the authoritative tradition and reading literally the plain words of Scripture.[195] Although the earliest refutations of Wyclif both in England and in Prague predate Zwicker's career and literary work,[196] there is no reason to assume that he was directly influenced by them. It is all the more remarkable that the accusation of naïve, literal reading of Scripture was used in very similar ways to brand both university masters and unlearned Waldensian dissidents, as seems to have happened at this point (1390s), without apparent coordination between the accusers.[197]

Zwicker follows the opinion shared by medieval biblical scholars that reading every sentence in the Bible as it 'sounds' *prima facie* resulted in conflicts where it would seem that Scripture has mistakes, and he endeavours to catch Waldensians with this error. In order to show that images in churches were a devout practice instituted in the Bible, Zwicker first cites God's commandment to Moses to make two golden statues of cherubs facing the

---

[193] Zwicker, *Cum dormirent homines*, p. 288D–E: 'Hic, Waldensis haeresiarcha, perpende, qui ea, quae in Biblia ponuntur, accipis; quantumlibet alibi orationes pro defunctis non tam expresse ponuntur, tamen ita clare et lucide tanguntur, quod clarioribus et nudioribus verbis exprimi non valeant.' See also ibid., p. 286B: 'Sed Lucae 20 [20:36] clarissimam audi scripturam. Aequales enim Angelis sunt, et filii sunt Dei cum filii sint resurrectionis' (But Luke 20 [20:36], listen to the clearest Scripture: 'They are equal to angels, and are the children of God, being the children of the resurrection').

[194] Gregorius I, *Moralia in Iob*, PL 75, 513D; Levy, *Holy Scripture*, pp. 210–11.

[195] Ian Levy has argued, based on comprehensive reading of both Wyclif and Hus and their adversaries, that neither of the vilified masters proposed the naïve *sola scriptura* policy ascribed to them by their medieval opponents, most notably by William Woodford and Jean Gerson. Levy, *Holy Scripture*, pp. 55, 89, 93–4, 104, 106, 156, 190 and passim.

[196] The Franciscan William Woodford had made his case against Wyclif already in 1383; Levy, *Holy Scripture*, p. 92. The Dominican Nicolaus Biceps had attacked Wyclif's remanence doctrine as early as in 1378–9, and the Silesian Dominican master Heinrich Bitterfeld was aware of Wyclif's condemnation in England around 1385, see Šmahel, *Die Prager Universität im Mittelalter*, p. 259; see also M. Van Dussen, *From England to Bohemia: Heresy and Communication in the Later Middle Ages* (Cambridge, 2012), p. 68.

[197] Whereas in the fifteenth century Waldensianism was used to make Hussitism appear as a part of the continuum of 'old heresies'; see R. Välimäki, 'Old Errors, New Sects: The Waldensians, Wyclif and Hus in Fifteenth-Century Manuscripts', in *Golden Leaves, Burned Books*, ed. G. Müller-Oberhäuser and T. Immonen [forthcoming].

Ark of the Covenant (Exodus 25:18–20). Well aware that another chapter in Exodus includes the classic prohibition of images, Zwicker uses these verses to demonstrate the fragility of heretical reading:

> Mark this, you Waldensian heretic: the images <u>should</u> be made. Are not the images of golden Cherubs fashioned with faces turned to gaze upon each other? If not, then, you need to explain and understand this letter entirely not as it sounds. As it is written in Exodus 20[:4]: 'Thou shalt not make to thyself a graven thing, nor the likeness of any thing that is in heaven above, or in the earth beneath, nor of those things that are in the waters under the earth.' Or, you need to say that the Lord ordered contrary things, for here it is said, 'do not make', and there, 'make'. For are not the golden cherubs likenesses of those that are in heaven above?[198]

Zwicker makes use of this contradiction throughout the whole chapter. How is it possible that God, who prohibited likenesses of things that are in heaven, upon earth or under water, in other instances allows Solomon to order two rows of statues standing upon sculpted oxen for the temple (3 Kings 7:24–25), or orders Moses to make a bronze serpent 'and set it up as a sign' (Numbers 21:8). The solution to this contradiction is the intended meaning: the images are forbidden only if they are adored as pagan idolaters do. It is in the light of this intention that all image prohibitions in the Bible must be understood. If images are for the glory of God and the honour of his saints, they are 'optimal' (*optime*) and 'of divine will' (*voluntatis divine*). The blind Waldensian simply fails to see how the bronze serpent signifies Christ hanging on the cross, and if Christ can be expressed in the form of a serpent, why not in the form of a human?[199]

Although Zwicker borrowed much material for this chapter from Moneta, who, for example, remarks on the apparent contradiction of the image prohibition in Exodus and Moses' golden cherubs, and asks why it may not be permitted to serve the image of the crucifix if Jews were allowed to serve the bronze serpent,[200] it is far from a direct excerpt. Moneta collects the *auctoritates* in order to show that making and honouring images is legitimate, but it is Zwicker who underlines that the fundamental error is reading Scripture *sicut verba sonant*, not according to its intended sense. The originality and

---

[198] Zwicker, *Cum dormirent homines*, p. 296D–E: 'Ecce Waldensis Haeretice, faciendas esse imagines. An non sunt aurei Cherubim imagines versis vultibus ad se contuendum fabricati. Vel ergo oportet te illam literam exponere, et non omnino sicut sonat intelligere, sicut scribitur Exod. 20. Non facies tibi sculptile, neque omnem similitudinem, quae est in coelo desuper, et quae in terra deorsum, nec eorum, quae sunt in aqua sub terra, Vel, oportet te dicere, quod Dominus praecepit contraria; quia hic dicitur; non facies; illic, facies. An non sunt aurei Cherubim similitudines eorum, quae sunt in coelo desuper?'

[199] Ibid., pp. 296E–297C.

[200] Moneta, *Adversus Catharos et Valdenses*, p. 460.

extraordinary thoroughness of Zwicker's treatment becomes even more obvious when one compares it to earlier treatises in circulation in Zwicker's time. The standard German anti-heretical work of the previous century, the treatise of the Anonymous of Passau, remarks on the Waldensian condemnation of images in churches based on the above-mentioned Old Testament image prohibition and solves the problem by simply pointing out that images are made for the purpose of remembering, not adoring, and that they are the 'scripture of the laity'.[201] *Attendite a falsis prophetis* is likewise very concise, noting the same 'scripture of the laity' function and stressing that images are honoured not as such but because of what they represent.[202] Only Zwicker sees the need, in a way that is characteristic of the whole *Cum dormirent homines*, to go to the root of things and turn the veneration of images into a profound question of biblical interpretation.

Attacking the interpretation behind the propositions in addition to the propositions themselves is another example of reinventing the thirteenth-century disputational polemical style, outlined by Sackville. For example, Moneta accused the Cathars of misinterpreting Aristotle, and accusations about the heretic's erroneous interpretation and false learning were an essential layer of the polemical construct of heresy in the thirteenth century.[203] That heretics corrupt the sense of the Scriptures is of course embedded in the very definition of heresy,[204] but it is a different thing to proclaim that heretical interpretation of the Bible is false and actually to discuss the principles of interpretation, as Zwicker did. If Moneta indulged in the philosophical problems of thirteenth-century scholasticism, Zwicker was interested in the burning issue of his own day: the intended sense of the Scriptures. He could not, however, completely avoid logical hair-splitting, as the next example shows.

---

[201] *Quellen*, ed. Patschovsky and Selge, p. 96.

[202] St Florian, MS XI 152, fol. 49v: 'Item dicunt in ymaginum veneracione ydolatram committi. Cum tamen ymagines non propter se, sed propter eum, quem rep[rese]-ntant venerentur, sicut multe consuetudines in ecclesia fiunt, ut signa misse forma ecclesiarum, figuratio vasorum et disposicio ornamentorum, et sic de singulis non propter se, sed propter inclusa misteria sunt invente. Sic picture et ymagines maxime propter laycos quorum scripture sunt principaliter preparantur' (Item, they say that idolatry is committed in the veneration of images, although images should be venerated not for themselves but for Him whom they represent. Similarly, many customs arise in the Church, such as gestures in the mass, the shape of churches, the shaping of vessels and the arrangement of ornaments, and in each case these are devised not for themselves but for the mysteries contained within them. Thus pictures and images are prepared especially for lay people, as their principal scriptures).

[203] Sackville, *Heresy and Heretics*, pp. 30–1; cf. Moneta, *Adversus Catharos et Valdenses*, p. 23.

[204] See the definition of the *Decretum*, C. 24, q. 3, c. 27: 'Quicumque igitur aliter scripturam intelligit, quam sensus Spiritus sancti flagitat, a quo scripta est, licet ab ecclesia non recesserit, tamen hereticus appellari potest' (Whoever understands Scripture otherwise than the sense of the Holy Spirit – by whom it was written – demands, even though he may not have left the Church, nevertheless he can be called a heretic).'

While Zwicker's interpretation of image making rests heavily on the patristic and medieval commentary tradition,[205] he is still able to pursue his argument relatively smoothly, as if he is building solely upon Scripture. This becomes almost impossible in the last chapter of the *Cum dormirent homines*, where Zwicker refutes one of the most persistent points of dispute between the Catholic Church and its critics: the legitimacy of taking oaths.[206] Unlike some topics of the *Cum dormirent homines*, such as the jubilee, exorcisms or universities, which were in the context of Waldensianism only marginal issues with little practical importance for inquisitions of heresy, the denial of oaths was a problem faced repeatedly by an inquisitor who tried to impose judicial oaths on heretics who vehemently believed that any kind of oath was a grave sin.[207] Refusing to take any oath was also a very visible mark of heresy in medieval society, whose cohesion was to a large extent maintained by oath-taking, to the extent that popular perception of heresy could be synonymous with not swearing oaths.[208]

Therefore it is no wonder that the *Cum dormirent homines* treats the question in detail. Again Zwicker immediately bases his argument on the correct reading of Scripture:

And for confirmation of their error they corrupt the word of the Saviour in Matthew 5[:34] pointing out that the Lord said: 'But I say to you: "entirely do not swear" (*omnino non iurare*)', and wishing to take Christ as having

---

[205] For example Moses raising the brazen serpent was commonly interpreted as a type foreshadowing Christ's crucifixion; van Liere, *Medieval Bible*, p. 119.

[206] Oath-taking was deemed forbidden from the first phases of the Waldensian movement, and it became one of the characteristics of the group in the eyes of inquisitors. See e.g. Cameron, *Waldenses*, p. 24; Audisio, *The Waldensian Dissent*, pp. 48–9. On the general opposition of heretics to taking oaths, especially in trials, see A. Prosperi, 'Fede, giuramento, inquisizione', in *Glaube und Eid*, ed. P. Prodi and E. Müller-Luckner (Munich, 1993), pp. 157–71 (esp. p. 158); A. Vauchez, 'Le refus du serment chez les hérétiques médiévaux', in *Le serment II. Théories et Devenir*, ed. R. Verdier (Paris, 1991), pp. 257–63; Bueno, *Defining Heresy*, pp. 54–7.

[207] The long question list used by both Zwicker and Martinus of Prague includes commonplace warnings against heretics trying to avoid oaths, see Werner, Nachrichten', p. 271. One of the heretics Zwicker sentenced as relapsed, Gundel am Holzapfelberg, refused the inquisitor's requests to take an oath for a long time in his second trial in January 1398; BSB MS Clm 15125, fols. 206vb–207ra.

[208] One of the witnesses called by inquisitor Gallus of Jindřichův Hradec in 1340s, who, when asked about heretics he knew, referred to people in the suburbs of Prague who did not take oaths: 'Item dicit se audivisse, quod in Platea pannificum sunt aliqui, qui non iurant' (Item, he said that there are some in the Clothmakers' Square who do not swear). Another man was suspicious partly because his daughter did not swear or say 'trun' (verily). See *Quellen*, ed. Patschovsky, pp. 214, 217. Almost a century earlier the Franciscan preacher Berthold von Regensburg had tried to teach his audience that people who did not swear oaths were heretics; A. E. Schönbach, *Studien zur Geschichte der altdeutschen Predigt. 3: das Wirken Bertholds von Regensburg gegen die Ketzer* (Vienna, 1904), pp. 5, 11–12.

meant that one cannot swear in any manner or for any cause without sin. But the poor, illiterate, ignorant and asses, not knowing the construction of languages, do not understand that there is great difference between 'entirely do not swear' (*omnino non iurare*), as a heretic says, and 'do not to swear at all'[209] (*non iurare omnino*), as Christ says.[210]

The illiterate, unlearned heretics mistake the intended meaning of the author and ultimate authority of the Scripture, Christ. The true, intended meaning is then explained by Zwicker. *Omnino* in 'non iurare omnino' could be understood in three ways. Firstly, 'in all words' (*in omni verbo*); secondly, 'for all deeds' (*pro omni facto*); and thirdly, 'by all things' (*per omnem rem*). This last meaning is according to Zwicker 'more clearly to the point of the gospel' (*apertius ad propositum Euangelii*), and explains how *omnino* should be understood as applying to not swearing 'by all things – consequently not by the created but only by the Creator, or by the created thing sanctified by God. And such an oath is sworn principally by the sanctifying Creator rather than by the sanctified created thing.'[211] Thus Christ's seemingly unequivocal prohibition of oaths is more clearly or manifestly (*apertius*) to be understood as a command to swear oaths only by God or by things made holy by God – and the rest of the long chapter proceeds to demonstrate biblical examples for this.

Ecclesiastical courts, of course, employed oaths at every turn of the proceedings,[212] and the problem of oaths was thus solved in biblical commentary and canon law centuries before Zwicker, so he could resort to this tradition as well as to previous anti-heretical polemic. Moneta of Cremona had struggled with the legitimacy of oaths and had dedicated a long and convoluted chapter to arguing against Waldensian and Cathar interpretations.[213] While it includes some elements that are also to be found in the *Cum dormirent homines*, for example the idea that *omnino* refers to swearing 'by created things' (*per creaturam*),[214] Zwicker seems also to draw on other sources

---

[209] Aiming at fluency in English, *omnino* has been translated in two different ways in this passage; less fluent but less misleading would be 'entirely do not swear' and 'do not swear entirely'.

[210] Zwicker, *Cum dormirent homines*, p. 298B–C: 'Et ad suum errorem confirmandum peruertunt verbum Saluatoris Mathaei quinto dicentes Dominum dixisse; *Ego autem dico vobis; omnino non iurare*: volentes Christum intendisse, quod nullis modis, nullis ex causis, possit quis sine peccato iurare. Sed miseri, illiterati idiotae et asini, dictionum constructionem nescientes, non intelligunt, magnam esse differentiam inter, *omnino non iurare*, sicut dicit haereticus, et, inter *non iurare omnino*, sicut dicit Christus.'

[211] Ibid., p. 298C–D: 'id est, per omnem rem, quia non per creaturam, sed solum per creatorem, aut per creaturam per Deum sanctificatam. Et tale iuramentum fit principalius per creatorem sanctificantem, quam per creaturam sanctificatam.'

[212] H. Helmholz, *The Spirit of Classical Canon Law* (Athens, GA, 2010), pp. 145–6.

[213] Moneta, *Adversus Catharos et Valdenses*, pp. 463–75.

[214] Ibid., pp. 465–6.

for his exact formulations. Twelfth-century canonists had expanded the permitted oaths by God to things that were blessed by God, on the condition that it was God who was invoked, not the objects themselves.[215] The biblical commentators agreed, albeit with some reservations.[216] Zwicker's citation of the scriptural verses where God himself swears or patriarchs and apostles swear unpunished was also standard practice for medieval Bible commentators, used to show that taking oaths could not be illicit.[217]

There is, however, one unusual element in Zwicker's exposition. It is the grammatical hair-splitting of *omnino non iurare* versus *non iurare omnino*. First of all, there is no significant difference in meaning between the two. Augustine uses both interchangeably in his treatise *De mendacio* (*On Lying*).[218] Neither is this in any way a standard argument for the legitimacy of oaths. Its source seems to be Bonaventure, who in his *Collationes* proposes that there is a distinction between the two sentences and attributes this error to 'Manichees':[219]

> But Manichees taunt us and say we ought not to swear at all, because it says so in the New Testament. [...] The heretics do not pay proper attention to the force of the words for it is different to say 'do not swear at all' [*non iurare omnino*] and 'entirely do not swear' [*omnino non iurare*], as it is different to say: 'some man does not run' [*quidam homo non currit*] and 'no man runs' [*non quidam homo currit*].[220] 'Entirely do not swear' is the same as 'in no circumstances swear' and 'do not swear at all' is the same as 'do not swear in all circumstances', but only for certain reasons.[221]

[215] See e.g on swearing by the cross, Rufinus, *Summa decretorum*, ed. H. Singer (Aalen, 1963), p. 390. See also Helmholz, *The Spirit of Classical Canon Law*, pp. 150–1.

[216] L. Smith, *The Ten Commandments: Interpreting the Bible in the Medieval World* (Leiden, 2014), pp. 166–7. Bonaventure accepted swearing by created things, if the act referred to their creator; Bonaventure, *Commentaria in Quatuor Libros Sententiarum Magistri Petri Lombardi*, d. 39, art. 2, qu. 2.

[217] Smith, *The Ten Commandments*, p. 164.

[218] Augustine, *De mendacio* XV.28, PL 40, 507.

[219] Here Manichees are probably a simple theological straw man rather than a description of any particular dualist heresy. Cf. H. Chiu, 'Alan of Lille's Academic Concept of the Manichee', *Journal of Religious History* 35 (2011), 492–506.

[220] These are wordplays of medieval logic. See E. D. Buckner, 'Natalis on Equipollence', The Logic Museum (2006): 'Most medieval logicians seemed to agree that placing that "not some" (*non quidam*) was equivalent to "no" (*nullus*).' http://www.logic-museum.com/opposition/summatotiuslogicae.htm.

[221] Bonaventure, 'Collationes de decem praeceptis', Coll. 3.20: 'Sed Manichaei insultant nobis et dicunt, quod non debemus omnino iurare, quia dicitur in novo testamento [...] Haeretici autem non bene attendunt vim vocabulorum. Differt enim dicere: non iurare omnino, et dicere: omnino non iurare; sicut differt dicere: quidam homo non currit, et non quidam homo currit. Omnino non iurare idem est, quod nullo modo iurare, et non omnino iurare idem est, quod non omnibus modis iurare, sed ex certis causis.' My translation is based on Smith, *The Ten Commandments*, p. 98 (with some revisions). Smith translates Bonaventure's grammatical hair-splitting as follows: 'do

Zwicker does not quote Bonaventure directly, but the similarity of the wordplay and the fact that both Bonaventure and Zwicker mock heretics for not understanding how language works indicates that Bonaventure or some work copying him was Zwicker's source. This is not the only instance where such implicit sources can be found looming behind the ostensible biblicism. In the chapter treating purgatory and alongside it venial and mortal sins as well as their satisfaction, Zwicker compares penance with a board to which a drowning person clings and is saved after a shipwreck.[222] The comparison is common,[223] and Zwicker's formulation resembles that of Alain of Lille, who favoured the metaphor.[224]

My current purpose is not, however, to list sources for Zwicker's treatise, but to demonstrate how implicit references to commentary tradition are an essential part of Zwicker's biblicist argumentation. Only by realizing the long exposition on oath-taking in biblical and canonist commentaries can one understand how the sense proposed by Zwicker for Matthew 5:34 is 'more clearly to the point of the Gospel'. The literal, intended meaning of Scripture as it was understood at the end of the fourteenth century forms the basis of Zwicker's refutation of Waldensianism. Yet orthodox interpretation was possible only by dragging after it the heavy commentary tradition. The problems Zwicker faced are very much the same as those encountered by Richard FitzRalph half a century earlier, when he composed a theological treatise against the Armenian Church at the request of Pope Clement VI. Because Armenians did not accept Western fathers and traditions, FitzRalph

---

not swear in all cases' [non iurare omnino – the Gospel formulation] and 'in every case, do not swear' [omnino non iurare].

[222] Zwicker, *Cum dormirent homines*, p. 288B: 'eo quod innocentia baptismalis per actuale peccatum perdita, per poenitentiam, quasi per secundam tabulam post naufragium recuperatur.'

[223] Jerome, *Commentarii in Isaiam* 2.3 (LLT-A): 'secunda enim post naufragium tabula paenitentiae est et consolatio miseriarum' (for after a shipwreck the second plank and a consolation in miseries is the plank of penance); *Epistulae* 84.6 (LLT-A): 'secunda post naufragium tabula est culpam simpliciter confiteri' (after a shipwreck the second plank is simply to confess guilt); *Decretum*, D. 1 de pen. c. 72.

[224] Alain of Lille, *Distinctiones dictionum theologicalium*, PL 210, 965D: 'Tabula [...] Dicitur poenitentia, de qua dicitur quod est secunda tabula post naufragium; [...] sequitur aliud naufragium per actuale peccatum, in quo locum habet quasi secunda tabula poenitentiae' (A plank [...] is called penance, of which it is said that it is the second plank after a shipwreck; [...] another shipwreck follows through actual sin, where the second plank of penance has, as it were, a place). Cf. *Contra haereticos* i.48, PL 210, 353D: 'secundum naufragium est in actuali peccato, contra quod est secunda tabula, scilicet poenitentia' (There is a second shipwreck in actual sin, against which there is a plank, that is to say, penance). See also R. F. Yeager, 'Alain of Lille's Use of "Naufragium" in *De Planctu Naturae*', in *Through A Classical Eye: Transcultural and Transhistorical Visions in Medieval English, Italian, and Latin Literature in Honour of Winthrop Wetherbee*, ed. A. Galloway and R. F. Yeager (Toronto, 2009), pp. 86–106.

decided to base his arguments solely upon Scripture and what he defined as its literal sense – very much the same as the intended sense described above. Like Zwicker later, FitzRalph wanted to demonstrate how doctrines of the Roman Church such as *filioque* or papal primacy are clearly (*plane*), expressly (*expresse*) and evidently (*evidenter*) manifested in the Bible. However, according to Ian C. Levy, FitzRalph is only able to do so on the basis of certain theological presuppositions that he does not voice: 'Having committed himself to arguing from the text of Scripture, the biblical text is going to have to bear a substantial doctrinal load if it is to convey Catholic – and thus divinely intended – meaning.'[225] Although there is no reason to suppose that Zwicker was familiar with FitzRalph's treatise, only a few chapters of which treat questions relevant to the anti-Waldensian polemic, and which is very different in its style and composition,[226] Levy's remark could just as well describe Zwicker's biblical argumentation.

Zwicker mostly uses Scripture to build up arguments according to the expanded literal sense of Scripture, meticulously listing the quoted chapter. This corresponds to the argumentation in schoolroom disputations and scholastic theology. There are, however, also traces of monastic rumination on Scripture and of liturgical reading.[227] This monastic aspect is important for the *Cum dormirent homines* and it needs to be tackled to understand Zwicker's biblicist programme. Petrus Zwicker was, after all, a Celestine monk and provincial as well as a former schoolteacher with a university education in *artes liberales* (the liberal arts). The Celestine spirituality emphasized liturgy, which occupied a significant part of their daily programme.[228] According to the late medieval constitutions of the order, Celestine priors had important

---

[225] Levy, *Holy Scripture*, pp. 14–18, quotation 17.

[226] The crucial points of dispute between the Roman and Eastern Churches concerned the nature(s) of Christ, and the Waldensians never challenged the Catholic christology. FitzRalph's Book 13 on sin, penance and purgatory touches the same themes as Zwicker's polemics, but even similar questions like the requirement of satisfaction after the absolution of sins (13.2–6) are treated in such different ways that there is no hint of FitzRalph's influence on Zwicker. Richard FitzRalph, *Summa Domini Armacani in Questionibus Armenorum nouiter impressa Et Correcta a magistro nostro Iohanne Iudoris* (Paris, 1512), fols. 102rb–103vb; cf. Zwicker, *Cum dormirent homines*, p. 287C–F. FitzRalph's treatise is composed as a dialogue between 'Ricardus' and 'Iohannes', and single propositions are sometimes discussed over several chapters. On the dialogical style of FitzRalph's treatise, see Minnis, '"Authorial Intention" and "Literal Sense"', p. 5.

[227] On the difference between the scholastic *lectio* (reading) of Scripture, the objective of which is science and knowledge, and the monastic reading aimed at meditation, see J. Leclercq, *The Love of Learning and the Desire for God: A Study of Monastic Culture*, trans. C. Misrahi (New York, 1993), p. 72. Mary Carruthers invokes the language of the comparative study of religions and describes the division as one between orthodoxy and orthopraxis in her *The Craft of Thought: Meditation, Rhetoric, and the Making of Images, 400–1200* (Cambridge, 1998), p. 1.

[228] Borchardt, *Die Cölestiner*, pp. 222–31.

liturgical obligations.[229] Hence, it is no wonder that Zwicker ardently defended ecclesiastical singing, canonical hours and liturgical garments, as well as the validity of liturgical books.[230] The interplay of Scripture, liturgy and anti-heretical polemic is, however, much more fundamental than a mere congruence of subject matters.

At times scriptural quotations in the *Cum dormirent homines* betray a mental approach that is closer to monastic typological meditation on Scripture than schoolroom argumentation. When Zwicker confronts the secret ministry of the Waldensian Brethren, he offers multiple biblical quotations and apostolic examples, demonstrating that true faith must be public and manifest, even in the face of persecution. One of the quoted verses is: '"Matthew 5[:14]: A city seated on a mountain cannot be hid"; this mountain is Christ, this fat, this curdled mountain, in which God is well pleased to dwell.'[231] The quotation refers only to the Gospel of Matthew, but is a fairly transparent reference to Psalm 67:16–17.[232] This is not an example of similar theological presuppositions that were required to interpret, for example, the New Testament denial of oaths in a way compatible with prevailing praxis. Rather, it arises from very traditional typological exegesis where the prefiguration of the Old Testament – the mountain in which God is well pleased to dwell – is fulfilled in the life of Christ, whose words in turn are an allegory of the contemporary Church. The interpretation that the fat mountain of the psalm is Christ, of course, derives from commentary tradition.[233]

A passage in the *Cum dormirent homines* also reveals that we should not necessarily imagine Zwicker looking up passages in a manuscript of the bible or paraphrasing an earlier treatise – although he certainly did the latter. The Bible was omnipresent in medieval culture through various media, and even literate, learned clerics such as Zwicker were probably more familiar with it through liturgy and preaching than by reading Scripture itself.[234] An author

---

[229] Chapter 16.1–2, ed. in Borchardt, *Die Cölestiner*, pp. 462–3.

[230] Zwicker, *Cum dormirent homines*, p. 294F. Biller, in fact, has remarked that these features could point out to the 'inner life' of Zwicker, but has not singled out what it means. See Biller, *Waldenses*, pp. 273–4.

[231] Zwicker, *Cum dormirent homines*, p. 280E: 'Item, Matth. 5. Non potest ciuitas abscondi supra montem posita. Mons Christus est, ille pinguis, ille coagulatus, in quo beneplacitum est Deo habitare in eo.'

[232] Vulgate, Psalm 67:16–17: 'Mons Dei, mons pinguis: mons coagulátus, mons pinguis. Ut quid suspicámini, montes coagulátos? mons in quo beneplácitum est Deo habitáre in eo.' Cf. Douay-Rheims translation: 'The mountain of God is a fat mountain. A curdled mountain, a fat mountain. Why suspect, ye curdled mountains? A mountain in which God is well pleased to dwell.' Zwicker quotes the psalm text more closely on another occasion: *Cum dormirent homines*, p. 294H.

[233] Cf. Haymo of Halberstadt, *Commentaria in psalmos*, PL 116, 416C–D; *Biblia latina cum glossa ordinaria*, vol. 2 (1481), 268r; Bernard of Clairvaux, *Sermones de diversis* xxxiii.8, PL 183, 630A.

[234] Van Liere, *Medieval Bible*, p. 208.

could cite the Bible by heart, but the verse thus memorized might not even be compatible with contemporary Latin translation. As part of the same denunciation of the Waldensian Brethren and their secret pastoral care and preaching quoted above, Zwicker invoked Jesus's commission to preach and baptize. The citation is Matthew 28:19: 'ite, docete omnes gentes' (Go, teach all nations),[235] but the medieval Vulgate has 'euntes ergo docete omnes gentes' (Going therefore, teach all nations). The quotation in the *Cum dormirent homines* comes from the so-called *Vetus latina* version that preceded Jerome's translation.[236] The reason for this is simple but revealing. Certain verses of the *Vetus latina* prevailed in liturgical use, because it had already established itself in Gelasian and Gregorian sacramentaries, and the commission in the Gospel of Matthew belongs to them.[237] This version persisted in the liturgy until the late Middle Ages, and appears, for example, in William Durand's influential and widespread liturgical manual.[238] Zwicker may equally well have borrowed the verse from a source he used or memorized after years of liturgical repetition. Either way, it has a clear echo of the liturgy in it. The example is a small detail, yet it demonstrates how the word of God in medieval culture was not confined to the wording of Bible codices, but was ubiquitous, present in liturgy and images as well as on parchment or paper.[239]

This intimate, inseparable connection between Scripture and its ritual and material manifestations – liturgy, images, sacred objects, church buildings, consecrations and feast days – is the core message of the *Cum dormirent homines*. According to Zwicker, even practices that were not essential to one's salvation, such as visiting consecrated churches, were firmly founded in the Bible and in accordance with God's plan for his Church and people. As a response to the Waldensian claim that it is not 'better, holier or more dignified' (*meliorem, sanctiorem, vel digniorem*) to serve God in a church consecrated by Catholic bishop than in any other house, Zwicker admits that if someone is impeded from attending church for a good reason, he or she can adore God at home and that this is in no way condemned by

---

[235] This particular quotation is missing from Gretser's edition, where only Mark 16:15 is cited, although it is claimed to be from 'Matth. vltim'; Zwicker, *Cum dormirent homines*, p. 280H. I have instead used the following early manuscripts: Seitenstetten, MS 213, fol. 111vb; St Florian, MS XI 234, fol. 95rb, Gdańsk, PAN MS Mar. F. 295, fol. 193ra, all of which have 'Ite, docete omnes gentes', followed by the same quotation from the Gospel of Mark as in Gretser's text. The *Refutatio errorum* has the same quotation; *Refutatio*, ed. Gretser, p. 303H.

[236] For a brief introduction to Latin translations of the Bible, see van Liere, *Medieval Bible*, pp. 82–91.

[237] O. M. Phelan, *The Formation of Christian Europe: The Carolingians, Baptism, and the Imperium Christianum* (Oxford, 2014), p. 108.

[238] Guillaume Durand of Mende, *Rationale diuinorum officiorum* 1.6 (LLT-A).

[239] This current view of scholarship is well illustrated in Frans van Liere's recent introduction to the medieval Bible, where two chapters are dedicated to Scripture in liturgy, preaching, images and drama: van Liere, *Medieval Bible*, pp. 208–60.

the Catholic Church.[240] However, he immediately hurries to add: 'but that a material church consecrated by a Catholic bishop is more dignified than other houses, and that offerings and prayers made there are more pleasing to God, can be sufficiently proven from both Testaments'.[241] This statement is followed by one of the treatise's most impressive arrays of biblical quotations, designed to demonstrate how offerings made in the temple are pleasing to God, how he punishes those desecrating God's house and how Christ chased away vendors from the temple and himself taught in the temple and in synagogues.[242] For Zwicker consecrated churches were the equivalent and contemporary manifestation of the temple, of which Christ had said, 'Is it not written, my house shall be called the house of prayer to all nations?' (Mark 11:17). Zwicker continues: 'Thus you Waldensian heretics are nothing, for you are of no nation because you condemn the church of God.'[243]

Polemics for the Church in crisis

To conclude the analysis of Petrus Zwicker's two treatises, I will address a perennial problem in the study of anti-heretical polemic: how well do their representations of medieval dissenters correspond to their lived reality, and can they be used as sources for anything beyond the fantasies of medieval clerics? This problem is intimately linked to the nature of the treatises and the process of compilation, borrowing and original composition that was described above. In the last two decades especially, many scholars have stressed heresy as an invention, in other words constructing it primarily from Catholic prejudice, fears and literary conventions.[244] While some sects

---

[240] Zwicker, *Cum dormirent homines*, p. 289H.

[241] Ibid., p. 290A: 'Quod autem Ecclesia materialis consecrata ab Episcopo Catholico dignior sit aliis domibus; et oblationes et orationes ibi factae Deo (sint) acceptabiliores, hoc sufficienter potest probari ex vtroque Testamento.'

[242] Ibid., pp. 290A–291C.

[243] Ibid., p. 291B: 'Nonne scriptum est: quia domus mea domus orationis vocabitur omnibus gentibus? Ergo vos Waldenses haeretici nihil estis; quia, nullius gentis estis; quia Ecclesiam Dei contemnitis.'

[244] The 'invention of heresy' was coined in the collection of essays *Inventer l'hérésie?*, ed. Zerner; but the origins of this approach are in the studies of Herbert Grundmann, see esp. Grundmann, 'Der Typus des Ketzers in mittelalterlicher Anschauung'; H. Grundmann, 'Ketzerverhöre des Spätmittelalters als quellenkritisches Problem', *DA* 21 (1965), 519–60; perhaps more influential, at least in the English-speaking world, has been R. Lerner's classic study on the heresy of the Free Spirit: Lerner, *The Heresy of the Free Spirit*; for an overview of the battle against heresy in the High Middle Ages that stresses invention of heresy to the extreme, see Moore, *The War on Heresy*; Irene Bueno's recent study on Jacques Fournier stresses definition and redesigning of boundaries between heresy and orthodoxy over invention of heresy, see Bueno, *Defining Heresy*, p. 11.

that appeared very real to medieval authors, such as devil-worshipping Luciferans or debauched heretics of the Free Spirit, are now regarded as imaginary constructions by any serious scholar,[245] the debate on the existence and nature of the dualist heretics, the Cathars of southern France and northern Italy, continues to rage.[246] On the other hand, even polemical texts are (again) regarded as including some elements derived from heretics themselves, at least when the authors obviously were in contact with the textual community of the local dissenters.[247]

Waldensian heresy did not need to be invented. As already mentioned, Peter Biller has forcefully argued against such claims, and there is plenty of evidence of the existence of a Waldensian movement whose members, at least the leading strata of lay confessors and preachers, possessed a relatively uniform doctrinal system that was at odds with the established Catholic doctrine and the institutional Church of the late Middle Ages.[248] Regarding Petrus Zwicker's writing, Biller has also proposed that one can distinguish different layers of text in the *Cum dormirent homines*, and that below the layer of blackening heresy-*topoi* Zwicker expresses a more sympathetic view of the Waldensian followers.[249] Georg Modestin, on the other hand, has criticized this approach, deeming the work to be a composite text and the different layers more likely to reflect different sources than different voices of the author, 'various "Peter Zwickers"'.[250]

The composite nature is, in my interpretation, much more prominent in the *Refutatio errorum*, which (in its long redaction) includes long passages borrowed from earlier works. In comparison, the *Cum dormirent homines* is a much more polished and structured work, which presses Waldensianism into the framework of Catholicism, the former as negation of the latter. Zwicker encountered a heterodox group that was real enough, and his knowledge and understanding of its doctrine, customs and inner relationships were extremely nuanced. Particularly in the *Cum dormirent homines* Zwicker's own experience with the Waldensian Brethren and their followers is visible.[251]

---

[245] Utz Tremp, *Von der Häresie zur Hexerei*, pp. 311–82, provides an overview on the discussion about these two imagined heresies.

[246] Even described as 'the new Cathar wars' by J. H. Arnold, 'The Cathar Middle Ages as a Methodological and Historiographical Problem', in *Cathars in Question*, ed. A. Sennis (York, 2016), pp. 53–78 (p. 58). Among others, the collection includes the current views of the main sceptics M. G. Pegg, R. I. Moore and Julien Théry-Astruc, as well as those of scholars such as Jörg Feuchter, Caterina Bruschi, Claire Taylor, Lucy Sackville and Peter Biller, who defend the existence of the Cathars as a real, dualist dissident movement.

[247] Sackville, *Heresy and Heretics*, pp. 39–40.

[248] Biller, 'Goodbye to Waldensianism?'.

[249] Biller, *Waldenses*, pp. 273–85.

[250] Modestin, 'The Anti-Waldensian Treatise', pp. 225–6.

[251] See Biller, *Waldenses*, pp. 273–4, 288–90. See also Chapter 5, below.

Nevertheless, when reading his polemical treatises one has to realize that they discuss Waldensian heresy in terms central to late medieval piety: the authority of the Scriptures, penance and justification, the role of the clergy, the meditative power of the saints, indulgences and devotional objects and images. To do this successfully required extensive reworking, rearranging and rewriting of the material already circulating, not only in treatises against heresy, but in more unexpected sources as well, and the end product was a treatise that would significantly shape the perception of Waldensianism in the coming decades.

The probable reason for the popularity of Zwicker's treatise, in addition to its better structure and writing than most tracts in circulation, was that it touched on issues such as the role of the clergy and the laity or the Church's property and power that were current in the discussions facilitated by the Great Western Schism and calls for reform of the Church. I will return to these themes in Chapter 5. With regard to information about Waldensianism, the *Cum dormirent homines* is not actually terribly innovative: it presents existing Catholic knowledge on the Waldensian heresy – and arguments to refute it – in a systematic form, knowledge that was already circulating in Austrian and German manuscripts in texts such as the somewhat earlier, anonymous work *Attendite a falsis prophetis* and the correspondence of the Waldensians from the 1360s, and in the shorter lists and tracts on Waldensian errors probably composed in the early 1390s.[252] Even thirteenth-century works, such as the treatise of the Anonymous of Passau and the *De inquisitione hereticorum* falsely attributed to David of Augsburg, presented a picture of Waldensian heresy that was for the most part compatible with the view of the late fourteenth-century Catholic polemicists[253] – not to mention the richness of arguments and counter-arguments available to readers who had access to rarer works such the *Adversus Catharos et Valdenses* by Moneta of Cremona. Yet even when Zwicker reuses the same Bible verses to refute the same propositions as generations of authors before him, he demonstrates a remarkable ability to reduce the arguments to fundamentals about the authority and interpretation of the Scripture, as we have seen.

To grasp the significance of Zwicker's oeuvre one has to remember that by no means all inquisitors wrote polemics against heresy. There was a significant time lapse between the treatises of the early thirteenth century and the late fourteenth, a period of over a century when remarkably few theological refutations of heresy were written.[254] From the 1320s on, several

---

[252] For these texts, see Chapter 3.

[253] The most notable differences between the views of the thirteenth and late fourteenth centuries were that later authors had a more detailed knowledge of Waldensian history and mostly, if not always, abandoned the idea that Waldensian doctrine included the consecration of the sacrament by laymen. See Biller, *Waldenses*, 248.

[254] Jacques Fournier's, later Pope Benedict XII, commentary on the first ten chapters of

decades of Dominican inquisition in Bohemia produced legal manuals and commentaries,[255] but not expositions of heretical doctrines. More than two centuries of Polish inquisitors left behind a few documents and compilations of tracts, but hardly any contribution to anti-heretical literature.[256] In comparison, the last years of the fourteenth century are a period when literary, theological refutation of heresy by inquisitors again rose to prominence. Zwicker was not the only contemporary inquisitor of Waldensians to engage in such activity. The already mentioned Johannes Wasmud von Homburg, a canon of St Peter and altar chaplain of Mainz Cathedral, commissioned by the archbishop of Mainz to investigate Waldensians in 1392, also completed a treatise against various heresies, *Tractatus contra hereticos Beckardos, Lulhardos et Swestriones* in 1398. The work has survived in four manuscripts,[257] so its impact was significantly more limited than that of Zwicker's polemics.

The revival of anti-heretical polemics was part of a general late medieval expansion of literary culture. The great transition started well before the advent of printing, and manuscript books were both produced in unprecedented numbers and read by more diverse audiences, lay and religious alike, than ever before in medieval Western Europe. Perhaps the best example of a new author and writer emerging in this period is the much more famous contemporary of Petrus Zwicker, the chancellor of Paris University, Jean Gerson, who reflected on writing and saw its role in defending the Church in much more self-conscious ways than previous generations of medieval scholars. For Gerson, to fight against heresy was to write, and for him it was for the University of Paris to produce the doctors to defend the Church.[258] Zwicker was a much less reflective and self-conscious writer than Gerson, but no less determined in his call for learned clergy to rise to the task of combatting the threat of heresy. Because its impact lasted for decades the literature produced by the German inquisitors at the turn of the fifteenth century was at least as important a tool of persecution as the inquisitions and sentences imposed upon heretics.

---

the Gospel of Matthew written before his election as pope in 1334 is a remarkable exception, providing original exegetical refutation of heretics by a major inquisitor and prelate. See I. Bueno, 'False Prophets and Ravening Wolves: Biblical Exegesis as a Tool against Heretics in Jacques Fournier's Postilla on Matthew', *Speculum* 89 (2014), 35–65; Bueno, *Defining Heresy*, pp. 151–244. However, as only a few copies ever existed outside the apostolic library, the influence of the work beyond the curia must have remained modest. See also Introduction, above.

[255] Studied and edited in Patschovsky, *Anfänge*.

[256] P. Kras, 'Dominican Inquisitors in Medieval Poland (14th–15th c.)', in *Praedicatores, inquisitores I*, pp. 249–309 (p. 250).

[257] 'Tractatus contra hereticos', ed. Schmidt, p. 337; Deane, 'Archiepiscopal Inquisitions', p. 203.

[258] D. Hobbins, *Authorship and Publicity before Print: Jean Gerson and the Transformation of Late Medieval Learning* (Philadelphia, 2009), pp. 12–13.

Comparing the *Refutatio errorum* and the *Cum dormirent homines* has shown us the close affinity and similarity of the treatises, and brought Petrus Zwicker into the limelight and centre stage: in my view he is the author of both works. It has also revealed the remarkable change of paradigm that takes place in Zwicker's anti-heretical polemic. The *Refutatio errorum* is a practical, compilatory text, structured in twelve chapters divided according to different Waldensian propositions and arguments against them. The *Cum dormirent homines* is a fully-fledged polemical treatise, with a detailed description of Waldensian origins, an exhaustive array of arguments and counter-arguments concerning different issues of doctrine, occasional exemplary stories to support them and explain the issues and clever rhetorical devices to drive the arguments home. But the difference is not just in how refined and polished the texts are. The *Cum dormirent homines*'s exclusively biblicist argumentation is a remarkable, almost unique feature within the whole genre of the medieval anti-heretical polemical treatise. It also has wider religious and cultural implications at the turn of the fifteenth century.

Late medieval scholars shared the view that the perfect Christian life is revealed in the Bible. However, different conclusions were drawn from this conviction. John Wyclif's relentless criticism of the mendicant orders was based on this idea: after all, if God had seen mendicant orders as a more perfect way of pursuing a Christian life, he would not have failed to reveal it in Scripture.[259] Petrus Zwicker's defence of Catholic cult, from sacramentals to clerical vestments, from cemeteries to universities, is derived from the same principle: the Bible is the ultimate guide to the Christian *modus vivendi*. However, for Zwicker, as for many other clerics on the 'winning' side of late medieval controversies about authority and tradition, this principle was guided by a deep conviction that the Roman Church had not fundamentally failed, that despite its recent shortcomings it was still the caretaker of the apostolic legacy. Ergo, its customs and practices *must* be rooted in the Bible and God's revelation.

The reason for direct invocation of the Bible's authority lies in the crisis of the late fourteenth-century Church. The whole mass of canon law, papal constitutions, tradition, custom and authority had become so incredibly complex and burdensome in the years of the Great Schism that at the beginning of the fifteenth century completely orthodox and esteemed figures such as Jean Gerson would call for bypassing them in favour of truth contained in the Scriptures and interpreted by the universal Church represented by the general council.[260] While Moneta of Cremona, writing in

---

[259] Levy, *Holy Scripture*, p. 89.
[260] Especially in 'Conversi estis'; see Gerson, *Œuvres complètes* V, p. 178; J. B. Morrall, *Gerson and the Great Schism* (Manchester, 1960), pp. 76–7; Hamm, *Religiosität im späten Mittelalter*, p. 10. In addition to Gerson, such figures as Heinrich von Langenstein, Pierre d'Ailly and Francesco Zabarella turned directly to the Scriptures for the

the aftermath of the Fourth Lateran Council and belonging to the recently founded Order of Preachers supported by a medieval papacy at the height of its power, could with good conscience defend the Church's right to pass new resolutions, things were far more complicated for Petrus Zwicker, who lived within a Church ruled by two popes and in a realm riven by conflict. The authority of human tradition and law was so tarnished that it did not merit defence. Zwicker's project to find solid scriptural foundation to Catholic doctrine, custom and liturgy is not only an argumentation strategy against Waldensians, but one of many attempts to find unquestionable authority and absolute truth in times of prolonged insecurity.

There is also reason to suspect that Zwicker's meticulously listed scriptural evidence was intended to counter more than one opponent. On the literal, immediately manifest level the enemy was Waldensian heretics and heresiarchs. But Zwicker may also have intended to argue at the same time against those who though they were Christians in name, even prelates, nevertheless attacked Catholic truths in the same way the heretics did. One should never expect medieval religious polemics to be read only *sicut verba sonant*.

---

authority of the general council; T. M. Izbicki, 'The Authority of Peter and Paul. The Use of Biblical Authority during the Great Schism', in *A Companion to the Great Western Schism (1378–1417)*, ed. J. Rollo-Koster and T. M. Izbicki (Leiden, 2009), pp. 375–93.

3

The Inquisitor's Practice and his Legacy

Item possunt facere conscribi libros in quibus continentur inquisiciones facte et processus habiti contra hereticos.

They can order books to be made, which contain the completed inquiries and processes against heretics.

Lombard inquisitor's manual, Linz, OÖLB MS 177, fol. 79v.

Peter Zwicker was no ordinary inquisitor. He broke the mould. Or rather, he and his colleagues and assistants broke the mould. They utterly overhauled the models they had for inquisition and they produced new ones. They did this in the first instance by a complete updating of inquisitorial knowledge of Waldensian heresy, history and doctrine. They did it, secondly, through their introduction of a fundamental shift in the character of questions. There was a sea change. Even in the interrogation of ordinary believers or followers, there was now much more concentration on faith and doctrine. Furthermore, although these new questionnaires and formularies were used by later inquisitors, they circulated in a form that was accessible and useful to a wider circle of pastoral authorities. The framework Zwicker and his colleagues created for enquiry into Waldensian heresy was of course apt for judicial interrogation. But even more significant was its provision of aid to confessors, preachers and lecturers when they encountered heresy or criticism and doubt about Catholic doctrine and practices. This, as I shall argue, is the reason why the formularies composed by Zwicker's circle circulated in compilations notably different from the models Zwicker had at his disposal or the manual composed for his or his assistants' use – which has luckily survived. The great majority of copies containing Zwicker's question formulas, copies of sentences or short descriptions of Waldensians are not professional and specialized manuals for inquisitors but more general compilations on heresy. Thus, as I see them, these manuscripts are the products and vehicles of the pastoralization of heresy, and they addressed audiences beyond their courtroom use by inquisitors and their notaries.

In giving the various compilations of Zwicker's inquisitorial material a common name, I follow Peter Biller and call them the *Processus Petri*.[1] Even though in individual manuscripts the *Processus Petri* includes either the *Cum dormirent homines* or, more rarely, the *Refutatio errorum*, I treat these two polemical treatises as individual works and use the name *Processus Petri* for the collection of inquisitorial material. The name is a compressed form of the title given to the collection in some medieval manuscripts, such as in the late fifteenth-century codex in the collections of the Vatican Library: 'Processus domini petri de ordine celestinorum inquisitoris hereticorum etc.'.[2] Although not universally used, it is the only medieval attribution given to the texts, and proves that for at least some readers the authority of the contents was guaranteed by the name of the inquisitor Petrus Zwicker. Sometimes the reference to the inquisitor stayed in the text even though almost all contextual information was lost. In a very late (1490s) manuscript the list of Waldensian errors based on Zwicker's letter from 1395 was attributed to an unnamed *provinciali ordinis celefaccinorum* (Provincial of the Order of Celefacins), who had been an inquisitor of heretics *per Alamaniam* (for Germany).[3] The attribution had become so conventional that it lingered in the manuscripts even when the connection to the historical person was lost.

It is first necessary to define the contents and nature of the various collections of inquisitorial material pertaining to Zwicker's and his contemporary colleagues' procedure against the Waldensians in the 1390s, which ranged from question lists to the declarations of sentences. That these documents exist only in later collections is in no way unusual. Later copying and rearranging, and in the process creating confusion, duplicates and omissions in the inquisitorial material, is typical of the sources that have survived. As Biller, Bruschi and Sneddon have observed in their edition of the Toulouse inquisition depositions of 1273–82, the immediate process of inquisition resulted in exclusive and specialized collections. Later use required more general selections, even when the users themselves were professional inquisitors.[4] However, the rearrangement and compilation of the *Processus Petri* has been more a complex process than those of collections made within one inquisitorial archive, such as the Toulouse depositions. There was no single compilation that was copied to the preserved manuscripts. Rather it seems that the documents were compiled on various different occasions and stages from the early 1390s to the early 1400s. Nevertheless, even though the

---

[1] Biller, *Waldenses*, pp. 233, 263–9, 271; Biller, *Aspects*, pp. 355–6, 360, 368–9.

[2] BAV MS Pal. lat. 677, fol. 43r.

[3] Würzburg, UB I. t. f. 234, part 7, fol. 11r.

[4] P. Biller, C. Bruschi and S. Sneddon, 'Introduction', in *Inquisitors and Heretics in Thirteenth-Century Languedoc: Edition and Translation of Toulouse Inquisition Depositions, 1273–1282*, ed. P. Biller, C. Bruschi and S. Sneddon (Leiden, 2011), pp. 3–127 (p. 10).

different compilations formed from this inquisitorial material differ from each other in significant ways, they all share documents and formularies undeniably originating from the persecution of Waldensians in the 1390s, and they usually include references to Petrus Zwicker.

The earliest layer of the *Processus Petri* are the question formulas and short descriptions of Waldensians, which I see as composed at the beginning of the 1390s, probably combining the efforts of Petrus Zwicker and Martinus of Prague. These, together with the 195 original protocols of the Stettin trials and later copies of sentences in Austria and Hungary, illustrate the interaction between the inquisitor and those suspected of heresy. Zwicker's question lists are known to be among the most detailed and accurate formulas ever created to interrogate Waldensians,[5] and Zwicker's flexible use of this apparatus has been recognized.[6] However, although Biller has pointed out the emphasis on belief and doctrine in Zwicker's questionnaires in comparison to earlier French interrogatories,[7] the doctrinal and pastoral aspects of this framework have not been fully explored.

I shall also examine the transformation of the manuals used by Zwicker and his assistant inquisitors into compilations based on Zwicker's procedure. In a St Florian manuscript – MS XI 234 – there is a copy of an inquisitor's manual, and this is based on a manual used by Zwicker and his *familia* in the diocese of Passau in the 1390s. The manuscript has been known but its significance has not been recognized. The manuscript enables the exploration of previously unknown features of Zwicker's inquisitions. In addition it illustrates the contrast between the working manual in inquisitorial use in the 1390s and the later compilations based on it. As we shall see, the popularity and diversity of these latter compilations – the *Processus Petri* – were part and parcel of the demand for a pastorally oriented and general compilation on Waldensian heresy rather than a professional, legal inquisitor's manual.

The texts in the enigmatic collection Processus Petri

The bulk of the collection *Processus Petri* has been well known for over a century. Because of the interesting content and the availability of these sources in rather easily accessible nineteenth-century editions,[8] they are

---

[5] Kurze, 'Zur Ketzergeschichte', p. 76; Utz Tremp, 'Multum abhorrerem confiteri', pp. 154, 160, 169, 177.

[6] Kurze, 'Zur Ketzergeschichte', pp. 76–7; Biller, *Waldenses*, pp. 255, 275; Modestin, *Ketzer in der Stadt*, p. 124; Modestin, 'Zwicker', p. 28.

[7] P. Biller, '"Deep Is the Heart of Man, and Inscrutable" Signs of Heresy in Medieval Languedoc', in *Text and Controversy from Wyclif to Bale: Essays in Honour of Anne Hudson*, ed. H. Barr and A. M. Hutchison (Turnhout, 2005), pp. 267–80 (pp. 272–3).

[8] Esp. G. Friess, 'Patarener, Begharden und Waldenser in Österreich während des Mittelalters', *Österreichische Vierteljahresschrift für katholische Theologie* 11 (1872),

frequently referred to in scholarship, even in general surveys on medieval Waldensianism[9] and in studies only briefly referring to Waldensian opinions.[10] However, they are usually treated as individual sources, pieces of information about Zwicker's inquisition of German Waldenses, not as what they are: collections of texts that have their own history and interdependence between the different parts. These formulas, questionnaires and descriptions of heresy are as much the results and end-products of inquisitions in the 1390s as were the conversions and executions of heretics they facilitated. Previous editions and studies of the texts have made much of the existing material available, but have insufficiently addressed what these sources are actually about. As Leonard E. Boyle pointed out in his entertainingly polemical and learned critique of Le Roy Ladurie's *Montaillou*, 'Whatever one's source is [...] one should first appreciate it as a whole before turning it to one's own purposes.'[11]

When turning from the editions to the manuscripts of the texts, we quickly see that these sources cannot be used in a straightforward way. Different combinations of the inquisitorial materials appear in nineteen manuscripts together with the *Cum dormirent homines*, but almost every time in different selections or in a different order. Less frequently some parts of the collection appear together with the *Refutatio errorum*. The circulation of different texts with these two treatises is presented in Appendix 3 and in Table 2 below. Perhaps as a consequence of the cryptic nature of these compilations, they have been referred to in various vague terms. In his studies on the Bohemian inquisition Alexander Patschovsky has called them 'materials formed around the inquisition of Petrus Zwicker at the end of the fourteenth century'.[12] Georg Modestin has recently proposed that Zwicker's treatise was in its time considered a part of 'the inquisitorial material' with which it was copied.[13] Peter Segl has described these compilations as consisting of copies or revisions of certain parts of the written material formed in Zwicker's inquisitorial

---

209–72; Preger, *Beiträge*; Haupt, *Der Waldensische Ursprung des Codex Teplensis*; Haupt, 'Waldenserthum und Inquisition'; Döllinger, *Beiträge II*.

[9] For example Cameron, *Waldenses*, pp. 139, 142; Audisio, *The Waldensian Dissent*, p. 115; Gonnet and Molnár, *Les Vaudois au Moyen Âge*, pp. 150–3; A. Molnár, *Die Waldenser: Geschichte und europäisches Ausmaß einer Ketzerbewegung* (Göttingen, 1980), pp. 156–59; M. Schneider, *Europäisches Waldensertum im 13. und 14. Jahrhundert: Gemeinschaftsform, Frömmigkeit, sozialer Hintergrund* (Berlin, 1981), pp. 99, 129.

[10] B. Z. Kedar, *Crusade and Mission: European Approaches toward the Muslims* (Princeton, 1984), p. 174; W.-D. Schäufele, *'Defecit ecclesia': Studien zur Verfallsidee in der Kirchengeschichtsanschauung des Mittelalters* (Mainz, 2006), pp. 202, 207, 211, 220.

[11] L. E. Boyle, 'Montaillou Revisited: *Mentalité* and Methodology', in *Pathways to Medieval Peasants*, ed. J. A. Raftis (Toronto, 1981), pp. 119–40 (p. 119).

[12] *Quellen*, ed. Patschovsky, p. 92, n. 304: 'Materialen, entstanden im Umkreis der Inquisition des Peter Zwicker zu Ende des 14. Jahrhunderts'. Cf. p. 25, n. 38; Patschovsky, *Anfänge*, pp. 69, n. 267, 72.

[13] Modestin, 'The Anti-Waldensian Treatise', pp. 216–17.

processes.[14] Biller's most recent characterization of the *Processus Petri* is as 'an elementary inquisitor's guidance anthology'.[15] Any reader who is not familiar with the material will surely begin to wonder what the difference between such an anthology and an inquisitor's manual is, as the latter genre also includes works that are little more than compilations of formulas and copies of documents.[16] There is indeed a difference between a working inquisitor's manual and the majority of the preserved *Processus Petri* compilations, and as will become evident in the course of this chapter, this difference is an aspect of the increasingly pastoral and doctrinal approach to Waldensian heresy.

There is no thorough study of the contents and structure of the *Processus Petri*. Peter Biller prepared for his unpublished dissertation what he calls 'only a preliminary and brief survey of a body of literature which deserves and needs an independent study'.[17] This preliminary survey is still the best description of the manuscript tradition of the *Processus Petri*. Ernst Werner, Dietrich Kurze, Jarosław Szymański and Peter Segl have likewise shed light on different parts of the material.[18] It is, however, still unclear which texts are from the hand of Zwicker, what is old, recycled material and which parts were written by some contemporary. It is also debatable whether the existing manuscripts are derivations from a manual or manuals used by Zwicker, or whether they are compilations made for or by a third party. In other words, was it Zwicker's intention to compose an inquisitor's manual, or does the material in circulation reflect more the reception of the persecutions by contemporaries and the will to preserve the memory of the events and save some exemplary texts for later use? The second alternative is true in most cases: but there exists at least one manuscript, St Florian, MS XI 234, that is a copy of a manual Zwicker or his commissary used at the inquisitions in the diocese of Passau in the 1390s, and another manuscript, Würzburg University Library MS M. ch. f. 51, whose compiler must have had access to material that comes from the immediate circle around the inquisitor.

The texts that usually circulate in the *Processus Petri* manuscripts are listed below. The combinations of letters in parentheses refer to abbreviations in

---

[14] Segl, 'Die Waldenser in Österreich', p. 161, n. 1: 'Abschriften bzw. Überarbeitungen bestimmter Teile des bei seinen Prozessen angefallenen Schriftgutes'.

[15] Biller, 'Editions of Trials', p. 35; cf. Biller, 'Signs of Heresy', p. 271: 'the procedural anthology of the German inquisitor Peter Zwicker'.

[16] On the diversity of the genre of the inquisitor's manual, see L. J. Sackville, 'The Inquisitor's Manual at Work', *Viator* 44 (2013), 201–16 (p. 202).

[17] Biller, 'Aspects', pp. 354–6, quotation p. 354, n. 2; the analysis on the lists of the converted Waldensians has been published in updated form in Biller, *Waldenses*, ch. XIV.

[18] Werner, 'Nachrichten', esp. p. 215–25, 265–74; *Quellen*, ed. Kurze, pp. 17–18, 73–4; J. Szymański, '"Articuli secte Waldensium" na tle antyheretyckich zbiorów rekopismiennych Biblioteki Uniwersytetu Wroclawskiego', *Studia zródloznawcze* 42 (2004), 85–96; Segl, 'Die Waldenser in Österreich', esp. pp. 161, n. 1, 164.

Appendix 3 and Table 2. The relevant editions are mentioned in the footnotes, and the edition mentioned first is the best or the most easily accessible edition. Later references will be to these. The manuscripts of the *Processus Petri* are described in Appendix 1.

The short list of converted Waldensians (Ia). List of eleven converted Waldensian Brethren, dated 4 September 1391.[19]

The long list of converted Waldensians (Ib). Another list of twenty names, both brethren and Waldensian laity, dated 1391. It includes mention of Zwicker and Martin von Amberg (Martinus of Prague) converting heretics in Erfurt.[20]

Short question list with a formulary of oaths in German (iag) or in Latin (ial). A question list against Waldensians closely resembling the one used by Petrus Zwicker in Stettin, 1392–4.[21]

Long question list with German oaths (ibg), or with one or more oaths omitted (ib). A longer and more detailed list of questions with similar contents and likewise used by Zwicker.[22]

---

[19] Werner, 'Nachrichten', p. 265; M. F. Illyricus, *Catalogus testium veritatis, qui ante nostram aetatem pontifici romano ejusque erroribus reclamarunt* (Argentinae, 1562), p. 445; J. Chmel, 'Beilage zu dem Bericht über eine im Jahre 1831 unternommene kleine Reise zum Behufe der Oesterr. Geschichts-Quellen-Sammlung', *Oesterreichische Zeitschrift für Geschichts- und Staatskunde* 3 (1837), 127–8 (p. 127) (only the first lines); G. Friess, 'Die Häretiker des 14. Jahrhunderts im Erzherzogthume Österreich', *Hippolytus: theologische Quartalschrift der Diöcese St. Pölten* 5 (1862), 45–59; 129–46 (p. 131); Friess, 'Patarener, Begharden und Waldenser', p. 257; Döllinger, *Beiträge II*, p. 367; Kurze, 'Zur Ketzergeschichte', p. 94; R. Cegna, 'Il Valdismo del '300 come alternativa alla chiesa di Roma', *BSSV* 148 (1980), 49–56 (pp. 52–3); Cegna, 'La condizione del valdismo', pp. 45–6; Smelyansky, 'Self-Styled Inquisitors', pp. 254–5; On the list, see esp. Biller, *Waldenses*, ch. XIV. The version edited by Cegna from Wrocław, BU MS I F 230 (Silesian inquisitor's manual, 1399) has the date 19 April 1393, which is probably incorrect. Although the manual itself is an early copy, the short list of converts is a later addition, dated 1462. See K. K. Jażdżewski, *Catalogus manu scriptorum codicum medii aevi Latinorum signa 180–260 comprehendens* (Wratislaviae, 1982), p. 355.

[20] Haupt, *Der Waldensische Ursprung des Codex Teplensis*, pp. 35–6; Döllinger, *Beiträge II*, pp. 330–1; Smelyansky, 'Self-Styled Inquisitors', pp. 255–6.

[21] *Quellen*, ed. Kurze, 73–7; Chmel, 'Beilage', pp. 127–8 (only iag oaths); Friess, 'Die Häretiker des 14. Jahrhunderts', pp. 137–41 (iag); Friess, 'Patarener, Begharden und Waldenser', pp. 266–71 (iag).

[22] Werner, 'Nachrichten', pp. 271–4; *Scriptores contra sectam waldensium*, ed. Gretser, pp. 308H–310A; Döllinger, *Beiträge II*, pp. 332–5 (excerpt) (ibg).

Articuli Waldensium (a). A list of Waldensian errors, which resembles the long question list. It was most probably composed at the beginning of the 1390s.[23]

De vita et conversacione (vca/vcb/vcc). A Description of the Waldensian Brethren's way of living and their ordination. It is circulated in three different redactions. The one transmitted with the *Refutatio errorum* is indicated (vcb), and that with the *Cum dormirent homines* (vcc).[24]

Formulary for the inquisition in the diocese of Passau (fip). An unedited formulary preserved only in the manual of St Florian, MS XI 234, which relates to Zwicker's commission in the diocese of Passau, including formulas for institution of an inquisitor, his commissary and several forms for absolutions and citations.

Formulary of sentences (fa). A short compilation of anonymous model sentences, including a formula for absolution by a bishop, a sentence for the incarceration of a heretic whose conversion is doubtful and an order for releasing obstinate and relapsed heretics to the secular arm. Model for Zwicker's sentences in Austria.[25]

Formulary based on Zwicker's sentences in the diocese of Passau in 1398 (fb). The most common formulary of Zwicker's sentences, including the anonymous model sentence for incarceration from (fa).[26]

---

[23] Werner, 'Nachrichten', pp. 267–71; *Scriptores contra sectam waldensium*, ed. Gretser, 307F–308F; Friess, 'Patarener, Begharden und Waldenser', pp. 259–61; Döllinger, *Beiträge II*, pp. 338–41; R. Holinka, 'Sektářství v Čechách před revolucí husitskou', *Sborník filosofické fakulty University Komenského v Bratislavě* 52 (1929), 125–312 (pp. 176–9) (excerpt).

[24] Schmidt, 'Actenstücke', pp. 243–5 (vca); Molnár, 'La Valdensium regula du manuscrit de Prague' (vcb); H. Haupt, 'Waldensia', *Zeitschrift für Kirchengeschichte* 10 (1889), 311–29 (pp. 328–9) (vcb); Werner, 'Nachrichten', pp. 265–7 (vcc); Friess, 'Patarener, Begharden und Waldenser', pp. 257–9 (vcc); Döllinger, *Beiträge II*, pp. 367–9 (vcc, excerpt); Friess, 'Die Häretiker des 14. Jahrhunderts', pp. 135, 145–6 (vcc, excerpts). See below for further discussion on the different versions. An exception to the rule is Augsburg, StaSB MS 2°Cod 338, where the version (vcc) is copied with the *Refutatio*.

[25] The manuscript exemplars are St Florian, MS XI 234, fol. 87ra–vb; Berlin, Staatsbibliothek, MS Theol. lat. fol. 704, pp. 28b–30a; Prague, KMK MS K IX, fols. 94v–96r; KMK MS D LI, fols. 139v–140v; Wrocław, BU MS I F 230, fol. 234ra–vb; Ibid., MS Mil. II 58, fols. 233va–234rb. Based on the two Wrocław manuscripts, edited by Szymański, 'Articuli secte Waldensium', pp. 95–6.

[26] Haupt, 'Waldenserthum und Inquisition', pp. 404–8 (excerpt); Döllinger, *Beiträge II*, pp. 346–51. As Haupt edits only excerpts and Döllinger's edition is of poor quality, many references are to manuscripts.

Formulary based on Zwicker's sentences, compiled after 1403 (fc). This contains the formulas of (fb), adding three new sentences and formulas for absolution closely related to parts of (fi).[27]

Formulary, revised from the sentences of the diocese of Passau in 1398 (fd). It is based on (fb), but revised into anonymous model sentences by removing references to Zwicker and particular deponents. Not edited.

Zwicker's manifesto against Waldensians (Zm). A letter addressed to the Austrian Habsburg dukes Wilhelm and Albrecht IV, written in the autumn 1395,[28] asking for their support for an inquisition of heresy, but obviously intended for public circulation. It lists around ninety Waldensian errors. This open letter is perhaps the best-known text in the *Processus Petri* and is discussed extensively elsewhere.[29]

Summary of Zwicker's manifesto (Zms). A shortened version of the manifesto, included in three late manuscripts. Not edited.

Notes on the arson of priests' property (nar). Short notices reporting the arson of priests' houses in the diocese of Passau in 1396 and 1397. These are probably later additions to the *Processus Petri* based on local knowledge.[30]

Errores beghardorum et beginarum **(ebb).** Short description of Beghards and Beguines, circulating only in manuscripts with the *Refutatio errorum*. Not edited.

The order of the different texts is presented in two tables. The first table is Appendix 3, and it has the manuscripts that also include the *Cum dormirent*

---

[27] Excerpts in Haupt, 'Waldensrthum und Inquisition', pp. 101–3; Döllinger, *Beiträge II*, pp. 343–4; Haupt, *Der Waldensische Ursprung des Codex Teplensis*, pp. 34–5. The only manuscript exemplar is Würzburg, UB MS M. ch. f. 51, fols. 24r–34r.

[28] There has been some confusion concerning the date, perhaps due to the erronous dating of 1398 by Preger in his edition of the document, Preger, *Beiträge*, p. 246; cf. Schäufele, *Defecit ecclesia*, pp. 202, 207, 211, 220; most of the manuscripts have September 1395 as the date, and I fully agree with Segl that the letter was undeniably composed following the death of Duke Albrecht III of Austria on 29 August 1395, Segl, 'Die Waldenser in Österreich', pp. 163–4; see also Patschovsky, *Der Passauer Anonymus*, p. 145.

[29] Ed. in Preger, *Beiträge*, pp. 246–50; Chmel, 'Beilage', p. 128 (excerpts); Friess, 'Die Häretiker des 14. Jahrhunderts', pp. 141–5; Friess, 'Patarener, Begharden und Waldenser', pp. 262–6; Döllinger, *Beiträge II*, pp. 305–11; on the contents and context of the letter, Segl, 'Die Waldenser in Österreich', pp. 163–4; The manifest is a reference point for Modestin's survey of the doctrine of the Waldensians in Strasbourg, Modestin, *Ketzer in der Stadt*, pp. 125–37.

[30] Friess, 'Patarener, Begharden und Waldenser', p. 266. Friess mistakenly dates the notes to 1393, see below; Chmel, 'Beilage', p. 128.

homines. Table 2 below has the manuscripts that have the *Refutatio errorum* and sections of the *Processus Petri*. I have concentrated only on compilations that include either of Zwicker's polemical treatises. Some parts of the *Processus Petri* were also combined into other compilations, often incorporating both older and more recent anti-heretical material.[31] These are without any attribution to Zwicker or connection to his polemical works, or to particular inquisitions. They are discussed in relation to the individual texts but not taken into account in the comparison of the manuscripts. Excluded also are two fifteenth-century manuscripts where the *Cum dormirent homines* and the *Refutatio* are accompanied by a list of Waldensian errors that is not based on the inquisitions of the 1390s but on the earlier treatise by the Anonymous of Passau.[32] These are not taken into account because the primary objective is to explore how the compilation of Zwicker's inquisitorial formulas was composed and revised in the 1390s.

A great variety of manuscripts fall under our definition of *Processus Petri*. There are manuscripts that consist only of the *Cum dormirent homines* and a single text from Zwicker's inquisitions. Manuscript 61 of Vyšší Brod's Cistercian monastery has the short questionnaire with oath formulas followed by Zwicker's treatise, but nothing more, yet it is given the title 'Processus domini Petri de Ordine Celestinorum Inquisitoris hereticorum'.[33] I have also included such shorter manuscripts among copies of the *Processus Petri*. At the other end of the scale is the manual of St Florian, MS XI 234, which, because of material not transmitted elsewhere, forms the only proper inquisitor's manual. Several other manuscripts are manual-like, formed from various formularies, question lists and lists of errors. As the tables show, the different elements could be reorganized, and the polemical treatise could be placed either at the beginning, the middle or the end of the *Processus Petri*.

The division into groups in Appendix 3 is based on the contents, not on the genealogy of the manuscripts, which are all fifteenth-century copies. The division follows the accumulation of datable material in the course of the persecution of Waldensians in the 1390s and early 1400s. These texts include the two lists of the converted Waldensians (1391); the *Cum dormirent homines* (1395); the manifesto Zwicker wrote to the Habsburg dukes Albrecht IV and Wilhelm in the wake of the death of Duke Albrecht III, asking for their support in his campaign against heretics (September 1395); short notices

---

[31] See below, especially the *De vita et conversacione*, the long question list and the *Articuli Waldensium*.

[32] Gdańsk, PAN MS Mar. F. 294: *Cum dormirent homines*, fols. 203va–220va; *Refutatio*, fols. 220va–226vb; the list of errors, fol. 227ra–rb; Herzogenburg, Stiftsbibliothek, MS 22: the list of errors, fol. 162ra–va; *Cum dormirent homines*, fols. 162vb–183vb; the *Refutatio*, fols. 183vb–192ra. The error list is edited in Molnár, 'Les 32 errores Valdensium'.

[33] Full title has been since lost, but it was visible in the nineteenth century, see Appendix 1.

describing attacks against members of the clergy in Austria in 1396 and 1397; a formulary of sentences compiled after January/February 1398, and finally a further version of this formulary put together after 1403. The *terminus post quem* is the earliest possible date when each combination of texts could have been compiled.

The manual in the St Florian manuscript (Group A) is a singular case, as it is based on the manual used by Zwicker and will be discussed in detail below. Group B has mainly formularies and interrogatories that were put together at the latest in the early 1390s, but the *Cum dormirent homines* gives the *post quem* date 1395. The notices of heretics' attacks against the clergy in Upper Austria mean that Group C could only have been compiled after 1397. Group D has the formulary reworked from the sentences Zwicker imposed in early 1398. Group E has only one manuscript, Würzburg University Library MS M. ch. f. 51, which includes a further redaction of the formulary, the last sentence being in Vienna 1403. Group F is a relatively consistent later redaction, compiled after 1425. Here the date does not come from the *Processus Petri*. In the almost identical Augsburg and Salzburg manuscripts Zwicker's texts are part of a more extensive collection on heresy, compiled after the trial of the Hussite Johannes Drändorf in 1425.[34] Finally, Group G has four manuscripts with only a single text in addition to the *Cum dormirent homines* treatise. These could have been grouped together with Group B, but in order to facilitate the comparison of the more extensive compilations, they are given their own group.

A significant demarcation line needs to be drawn round the materials of Austrian provenance. Unlike the earlier pieces composed about the Waldensians, it is certain that these Austrian texts originate either from Zwicker's own hand or from trials led by him. The implications of this are demonstrated in Table 2, where the manuscripts with the *Refutatio errorum* are presented. None of them has any explicit references to inquisitions in Austria and they include only descriptions of Waldenses that originate from the beginning of the 1390s. The lack of Austrian formularies and thus explicit references to Zwicker's inquisitions in the *Refutatio errorum* manuscripts does not, however, undermine the case for Zwicker's authorship that was proposed in Chapter 2. Zwicker finished his major work, the *Cum dormirent homines*, right at the beginning of his sojourn in Upper Austria, and it is only to be expected that this new work was disseminated there instead of the less polished *Refutatio*.

---

[34] See manuscript descriptions in Appendix 1. Würzburg, UB I. t. f. 234 does not have the Drändorf trial documents, but it is a late (1490s?) copy, while the somewhat shortened *Cum dormirent homines* and the summary of Zwicker's manifesto resemble the other two manuscripts closely.

Table 2: The *Refutatio errorum* with the *Processus Petri*.

Augsburg, StaSB MS 2° Cod 338	BSB MS Clm 1329	Trier, Stadtbibliothek, MS 680/879	Wiesbaden, Landesbibliothek, MS 35	Michelstadt, Kirchenbibliothek MS I. Db. 685	Prague, NKCR MS XIII. E. 7
la	ibg (end)	vcb	vcb	vcb	vcb (end)
vcc	R4	a	a	a	a
a	a	ib	ib	ib	ib
luc	luc	ebb	ebb	ebb	ebb
ibg	ibg (begin.)	R1	R1	R1	R3
R4		Rc	Rc	Rc (shorter)	[x]
					vcb (begin.)

Note: Abbreviations additional to those listed above for the PP are: luc = a short note on Luciferans, unpublished; R1–4 = the *Refutatio* of the corresponding redaction. Rc = a penitential manual added to the end of the *Refutatio*, unpublished. [x] = material not part of the PP, either later additions to empty leaves or binding mistakes.

The six manuscripts can be roughly divided into two groups. The Augsburg and Munich manuscripts both come from the diocese of Augsburg and from the libraries of the Augustinian Canons. Both date to the second half of the fifteenth century, and in addition to the Redaction 4 *Refutatio*, they have a short description of Luciferans. The four other manuscripts have the same versions of the *De vita et conversacione* (vcb) and a short, anonymous treatise against Beghards and Beguines.[35] Three of them (Wiesbaden, Trier, Michelstadt) originate from the Rhine–Main area, the Trier manuscript dating to the 1430s, the Wiesbaden and Michelstadt manuscripts to the late fifteenth century. The Prague manuscript is probably earlier, but it cannot be the exemplar for the others, as its version of the *Refutatio errorum* is the shorter Redaction 3. As the group is otherwise relatively uniform, it seems that it is based on an earlier collection, possibly originating in Bohemia or eastern German dioceses and reaching its final form in western Germany. The *De vita et conversacione*, the *Articuli Waldensium* and the long questionnaire form a unit in a Lusatian (Zgorzelec) and in a Silesian compilation of heresy, both

[35] This may have some connection to Martinus of Prague, who is the probable author of a question formula against Beguines and Beghards, extant in one manuscript that also included a copy of the *Refutatio*. See Augsburg, Stadtbibliothek MS 2° Cod 185, fol. 242r. Martinus's question formula is edited in A. Patschovsky, 'Gli eretici davanti al tribunale. A proposito dei processi-verbali inquisitoriali in Germania e in Boemia nel XIV secolo', in *La parola all'accusato*, ed. J.-C. M. Vigueur and A. Paravicini Bagliani (Palermo, 1991), pp. 242–67 (pp. 264–5).

probably dating to the 1390s.[36] The same combination circulated in Czech lands in the fifteenth century, again without either of Zwicker's treatises. This conglomerate appears not only in the Olomouc codex edited by Werner,[37] but also in two manuscripts of the Prague Metropolitan Library, as well as in a manual copied in the 1450s in Erfurt.[38]

Most of the question lists, oath formulas and descriptions of Waldensianism had thus been circulating together by the time the manual of St Florian, MS XI 234 (or to be precise, its lost exemplar) was compiled, around 1395–6. Zwicker's own manual is not, however, a straightforward exemplar of the later collections. An important text in the *Processus Petri* is the manifesto of 1395, listing around ninety items of Waldensian doctrine and practice. It is very common, but it was added to the *Processus Petri* only later. In nine copies the manifesto opens the whole compilation. With its powerful opening, *Ego frater Petrus provincialis Ordinis Celestinorum* (I Brother Peter, Provincial of the Order of Celestines), it certainly helped to preserve the memory of Petrus Zwicker. The letter is a polemical warning against the threat the Waldenses posed to the Duchy of Austria, and it was without doubt intended for public circulation. It is easy to see why later compilers added it to Zwicker's *Processus*, and equally easy to understand why it is not transmitted among the procedural formularies and relatively neutral descriptions of Waldensianism in the manual of St Florian. All the information on the Waldensians contained in the manifesto of 1395 was already available in a more practical format in these tools intended for enquiries into heresy.

The earlier texts, such as the question formulas and lists of converted Waldensians, have a more extensive and geographically more diverse circulation, whereas the late additions are sometimes preserved only in a single manuscript, such as the sentence of Andreas Hesel in Vienna in 1403.[39] The availability of the texts was certainly a defining and limiting factor, as always in medieval compilations,[40] and it is only to be expected that question

---

[36] Wrocław, BU MS Mil. II 58, fols. 231va–233va (1393) and MS I F 230, fols. 231va–233vb (1399), both described in Szymański, 'Articuli secte Waldensium'. On MS Mil. II 58, see also S. Kądzielski and W. Mrozowicz, *Catalogus codicum medii aevi manuscriptorum qui in Bibliotheca Universitatis Wratislaviensis asservantur signa 6055–6124 comprehendens (Codices Milichiani, vol. 1)* (Wrocław, 1998), pp. 193–5. In MS Mil. II 58 these texts and the formulary (fa) are a later addition – in a different hand – to a larger anti-heretical compilation. This manuscript is a probable model for the group of similar compilations.

[37] Werner, 'Nachrichten', pp. 265–74.

[38] Prague, KMK, MS D LI, fols. 136v–139v; MS K IX, fols. 92r–94v (only the *Articuli* and the long questionnaire); Berlin, Staatsbibliothek MS Theol. lat. fol 704, pp. 22–8. On the dating, see P. J. Becker and T. Brandis, *Die theologischen lateinischen Handschriften in Folio der Staatsbibliothek Preussischer Kulturbesitz Berlin. 2. Ms. theol. lat. fol. 598–737* (Wiesbaden, 1985), p. 240.

[39] Würzburg, UB MS M. ch. f. 51, fols. 27v–28r.

[40] On 'exemplar poverty' as a limiting factor of manuscript production, M. Connolly,

formulas and error lists that travelled around central Europe with the inquisitors had more changes of transmission than sentences declared on a particular occasion. However, in the formation of the *Processus Petri* a development takes place that is not accidental or casual: the emergence of new question lists, descriptions of heresy and formularies that corresponded to the inquisitorial practice of Petrus Zwicker and Martinus of Prague. At the same time a genre of texts that was integral to the inquisitors' manuals disappears, namely legal consultations and certain important formularies. What was added and what was left out must be studied in order to understand why and for what purpose Zwicker's formularies, question lists and sentences were copied, and to explain what that tells us about changing attitudes towards Waldensian heresy.

Waldensians and how to interrogate them

The most widely disseminated texts of the *Processus Petri* are short descriptions of the conversion of several Waldensian preachers and their followers in 1391, as well as a description of a heretic's way of life, the *De vita et conversacione*, a list of Waldensian errors, the *Articuli Waldensium* and two question lists for the interrogation of Waldensian heretics, including the (usually) vernacular formularies for oaths required in the inquisition. These are counted among the *Processus Petri*,[41] but besides the shorter question list, which Dietrich Kurze has confirmed as that used by Zwicker in Stettin, 1392–4,[42] it has been unclear who composed the texts and for what occasion.[43] These texts embody the increasingly accurate knowledge of Waldensianism and innovations in interrogating the heretics emerging in the 1390s, and it is necessary to relate them to Zwicker's *modus operandi*.

The conversion of several prominent German Waldensians in 1391 is generally considered the incentive for the persecutions that lasted for a decade and in which both Petrus Zwicker and Martinus of Prague played central roles.[44] After the conversion two lists recounting the names of

---

'Compiling the Book', in *The Production of Books in England 1350–1500*, ed. A. Gillespie and D. Wakelin (Cambridge, 2011), pp. 129–49 (p. 129); R. Hanna, 'Miscellaneity and Vernacularity: Conditions of Literary Production in Late Medieval England', in *The Whole Book: Cultural Perspectives on the Medieval Miscellany*, ed. S. G. Nichols and S. Wenzel (Ann Arbor, 1996), pp. 37–51 (p. 47).

[41] Biller, 'Aspects', p. 354; *Quellen*, ed. Patschvosky, p. 92, n. 104; Segl, 'Die Waldenser in Österreich', p. 161, n. 1.

[42] Kurze, 'Zur Ketzergeschichte', p. 76, n. 121; *Quellen*, ed. Kurze, pp. 17–18, 73–7.

[43] For example, Modestin displays a more sceptical attitude towards Zwicker's role in composition of the lists of the converted Waldensians, suggesting only that Zwicker may have had access to the information; Modestin, 'Zwicker', p. 27.

[44] Kurze, 'Zur Ketzergeschichte', pp. 70–1; Kieckhefer, *Repression*, pp. 57–8; Utz Tremp,

converted Waldensian Brethren and their followers were composed. The lists are complementary, the shorter including eleven or twelve names and the longer twenty.[45] The shorter is dated to 4 September 1391,[46] while the longer refers more generally to the events in 1391. Unfortunately the circumstances leading to the conversion and the details of the trial remain a mystery, as these are not recorded in any surviving document. Katrin Utz Tremp and Georg Modestin have proposed that by the end of the fourteenth century the Waldensian lay apostolate had reached a crisis of legitimation leading to inner tensions, conversions and resorting to other religious authorities, for example mendicants.[47] Alexander Patschovsky has seen the period as a time of intellectual stagnation in the movement, making the Waldensians more susceptible to pressure from the Church.[48] These may well be the underlying causes, but it is unclear how they actually led to such a group conversion, and it is not known who reconciled the former heretics to the Church; some of them even became priests.[49] It seems that both Martinus of Prague and Petrus Zwicker were involved as inquisitors, at least in the aftermath. The longer list gives occasional details about the converts, and it mentions the heresiarch Conradus of Erfurt,[50] who after his conversion went to his home town, apparently as part of his penance, and 'in front of the heretics of the same sect spoke against his error, preaching to them the true faith of Christ Jesus'. However,

---

'Multum abhorrerem confiteri', p. 166; Cameron, *Waldenses*, p. 140; Modestin, *Ketzer in der Stadt*, p. 2.

[45] The two lists are best described in Biller, *Waldenses*, ch. XIV; and in Kurze, 'Zur Ketzergeschichte', pp. 79–80 and n. 152. The available editions are listed above in nn. 19 and 20.

[46] Kurze, 'Zur Ketzergeschichte', p. 94. The edition of Werner from Olomouc MS 69 has only 'die mensis Septembris'; Werner, 'Nachrichten', p. 265. A Silesian manuscript edited by R. Cegna has the date 19 April 1393, which is not supported by other manuscripts; Cegna, 'Il valdismo del '300', pp. 52–3; Cegna, 'La condizione del valdismo', pp. 45–6.

[47] Utz Tremp, 'Multum abhorrerem confiteri', pp. 166–7; Modestin, *Ketzer in der Stadt*, p. 3.

[48] Patschovsky, 'The literacy of Waldensianism from Valdes to c. 1400', pp. 135–6.

[49] The longer list names five heresiarchs who became Catholic priests after their conversion: 'primus Johannes de Wienna, item Claus de Brandenburg, item Fridericus de Hardeck, item Haynricus de Engelstat factus est crucifer. Item Petrus de septem castris Ungarie. Isti quinque post conversionem eorum facti sunt sacerdotes ecclesie katholice' (First John of Vienna; item, Claus of Brandenburg; item, Frederick of Hardegg; item Henry of Engelstadt [who] was made to wear a cross; item, Peter of Siebenbürgen [Romania] of Hungary. After conversion these five became priests of the Catholic Church); Haupt, *Der Waldensische Ursprung des Codex Teplensis*, p. 35. Claus de Brandenburg is the same person as Nikolaus Gotschalk, who is often mentioned in Stettin protocols; Kurze, 'Zur Ketzergeschichte', pp. 80–1.

[50] Possibly identical with Konrad von Thüringen, whose name appears among the heresiarchs who used to visit Pomeranian Waldensians; Kurze, 'Zur Ketzergeschichte', p. 80, n. 152.

117

apart from his sister, Conradus had little success in converting his former flock, and the list states that it was only after the two inquisitors arrived in Erfurt in 1391 that all were 'convicted, converted, abjured and sentenced to wear crosses'.[51]

Not only the two lists of converts but also the *Articuli Waldensium*, the *De vita et conversacione* and the long question list with a formulary of oaths can be linked to these events: that is, the conversion of Waldensian *magistri* and subsequent trials in Erfurt, where Petrus Zwicker and Martinus of Prague first co-operated in the inquisition of heresy. These texts represent the information acquired by the inquisitors from the converted Brethren. It has been suggested that the accurate knowledge of Waldensian doctrine, history and practices manifest in Zwicker's inquisitions and texts came partly from discussion with the converted Brethren,[52] yet only very tentatively and with reservations have these texts been linked to this acquisition of information.[53] This is at least partly due to the uncertain origin of the texts and their relation to each other.[54] A later date than that I am proposing has also been suggested for these texts. There is a tradition attributing the *Articuli Waldensium*, the list of Waldensian articles of faith, to Martinus of Prague and dating it to the second half of the 1390s or the beginning of the 1400s.[55] Following this, Ernst Werner has proposed that the longer interrogatory also comes from the hand of Martinus and dates the texts between 1394 and 1404.[56] So far I have been

---

[51] BAV MS Pal. lat. 677, fol. 54v: 'Item conradus de erfordia qui prius fuit sutor hic post conuersionem suam uenit erfordiam et coram hereticos eiusdem secte reclamauit errorem suum predicans eis ueram cristi iesu fidem, et nullus uoluit conuerti nisi soror eius que fuit uxor mathei uel mathie witeberg pileatoris. Postea tamen anno domini 1391 per dominum martinum de amberg, et fratrem petrum celestinum omnes in erfordia sunt conuicti et conuersi abiurati et cruce signati' (Item, Conrad of Erfurt, who earlier was a shoemaker. After his conversion he came to Erfurt and in front of the heretics of the same sect spoke against his error, preaching to the the true faith of Christ Jesus. And no one wanted to convert apart from his sister, who was the wife of Matthew or Matthias of Wittenberg, a hat-maker. Later however, AD 1391, all of them were convicted in Erfurt by Lord Martinus of Amberg and Lord Petrus the Celestine, and were converted, abjured and marked with the cross [made to wear the cross]). Cf. Haupt, *Der Waldensische Ursprung des Codex Teplensis*, p. 35.

[52] Kurze, 'Zur Ketzergeschichte', pp. 70–1; Biller, *Waldenses*, p. 272; Smelyansky, 'Self-Styled Inquisitors', p. 150.

[53] Biller proposed in his dissertation that the description of the Brothers' entry in the Waldensian order (the *De vita et conversacione*) originates either from the conversion of the 1360s or around 1390; Biller, 'Aspects', p. 367. Cf. Biller, 'Fingerprinting an Anonymous Description of the Waldensians', p. 163, where he relates the text to the inquisitions around 1400.

[54] Modestin, 'Zwicker', p. 27.

[55] A. Armand Hugon and G. Gonnet, *Bibliografia Valdese* (Torre Pellice, 1953), no. 719: 'Articuli Waldensium, scritti forse da Martino, prete della Chiesa del Tyn a Praga, tra il 1395 e il 1404'.

[56] Werner, 'Nachrichten', pp. 219–20. Before Werner, Holinka had considered Peter

unable to find any evidence for this conjecture and dating. On the contrary, it is certain that these pieces were written prior to the major inquisitions in Brandenburg-Pomerania and Austria, as the following analysis shows.

Some version of the *Articuli* existed already in 1391, because Martinus of Prague used a similar error list in Würzburg in 1391.[57] At the latest the *Articuli*, the *De vita et conversacione* and the long question list were composed by 1393, which is the dating of their earliest manuscript exemplar.[58] Here these texts, as well as the formulary (fa) which worked as the model for Zwicker's sentences in the diocese of Passau, form a unit that was added by a different hand into a compilation including earlier anti-heretical texts and formularies, such as the *Attendite a falsis prophetis* and excerpts from the treatise by the Anonymous of Passau. This early exemplar does not undermine Petrus Zwicker's involvement in the composition of these texts, quite the contrary. The manuscript in question belonged to the Franciscans in Zgorzelec, a town situated less than 50 kilometres from Oybin.[59] As already mentioned above, these texts circulated without Zwicker's treatises in Bohemian, Silesian and eastern German manuscripts, and it seems that this transmission had already started before 1395.

De vita et conversacione

The text *De vita et conversacione*, describing the ordination and way of life of Waldensian Brethren, has an enigmatic origin. It circulated in different versions, one of which was most probably written at the end of the fourteenth century, and it is perhaps the most important late medieval description of the Waldensian Brethren's *modus vivendi*. In the *Processus Petri* manuscripts it usually follows the short list of Waldensian Brethren, and is often copied directly after the names of the converts as if it were an explanation referring to the preceding names: 'predicti nominant inter eos apostoli, magistri et fratres, habent autem talem uitam et conuersacionem' (Among themselves the aforesaid name [themselves] apostles, masters and brethren, [and] they have this way of life and conduct).[60] Peter Biller has identified three different versions of the text. Although the division is somewhat arbitrary because

---

von Pillichsdorf to be the author of the *Articuli Waldensium*; Holinka, 'Sektářství v Čechách', pp. 130–2. As this is based on the outdated attribution of the *Cum dormirent homines* to Pillichsdorf, his arguments amount to a suggestion of Zwicker's authorship.

[57] *TIF*, 1. Abschnitt, 17. Heft, pp. 3263–6; see also Haupt, *Die religiösen Sekten*, pp. 23–6.

[58] Wrocław, BU MS Mil. II 58, fols. 231va–234rb. See also Szymański, 'Articuli secte Waldensium', p. 90.

[59] The geographical proximity, and a possible connection to Zwicker, have been pointed out by Szymański, 'Articuli secte Waldensium', p. 93.

[60] BAV MS Pal. lat. 677, fol. 47v.

of the great variation between different copies,[61] it nevertheless describes roughly the different versions of the text. The first version includes a list of Waldensian errors (different from those in the *Articuli Waldensium*, which is part of the *Processus Petri*) and a description of the way of living of the Brethren as well as their ordination, listing their vows and the seven articles of faith.[62] This version (for which I use the abbreviation vca) has a different circulation from the *Processus Petri*. In addition to Schmidt's edition from a lost manuscript and four other manuscripts listed by Biller, I have discovered that the text is incorporated in *Continuatio cimboli apostolorum* (*Continuation of the Apostles' Creed*), written by the bishop of Brandenburg, Stephan Bodecker, c. 1440–50.[63]

The second version described by Biller has a description of the Waldensian Brethren's way of living, clearly related to that in the first version, but the account of the ordination of a Brother is different and more detailed. The third version is very close to the second, but also has another list of vows and the seven articles of faith.[64] Of the versions listed by Biller the second and third are transmitted within the *Processus Petri* manuscripts: the second usually in the manuscripts with *Cum dormirent homines* and the *Processus Petri*, listed in Appendix 3, where it is incorporated in the short list of converts and the *Articuli Waldensium* (version vcc). In addition, one *Processus Petri* manuscript with the *Refutatio errorum* has this second version,[65] as does the compilation edited by Werner.[66] The version (vcc) also appears in four anti-heretical compilations without Zwicker's treatises.[67] A slightly different third version (vcb) is the one that accompanies the *Refutatio errorum* in the four manuscripts listed in Table 2 above.[68]

---

[61] For example Augsburg, UB MS II. 1. 2° 78, fols. 245va–246vb, counted by Biller as the same version with the lost Strasbourg manuscript (here: vca), has certain similarities with it, but also a different set of Waldensian errors and somewhat different disposition of the parts of the text.

[62] Biller, 'Aspects', p. 366. The earliest known exemplar of this version, Strasbourg City Library MS B 174, dated 1404, has been destroyed, but its contents have been edited by Schmidt, 'Actenstücke', pp. 243–5.

[63] The chapter has been edited by Kurze, but he does not recognize the source of the description; *Quellen*, ed. Kurze, pp. 280–1.

[64] Biller, 'Aspects', pp. 366–7.

[65] Augsburg, StaSB MS 2° Cod 338, fols. 153r–154r.

[66] Werner, 'Nachrichten, pp. 265–7.

[67] Wrocław, BU MS Mil. II 58, fols. 231va–234rb; Wrocław, BU MS I F 230, fols. 231va–234vb; Berlin, Staatsbibliothek, MS Theol. Lat. fol. 704, pp. 22a–25a; Prague, KMK MS D LI, fols. 136v–140v, where (vcc) is accompanied by the *Articuli Waldensium*, the long questionnaire and the anonymous formulary of sentences (fa). The earliest exemplar, MS Mil. II 58 (*c.* 1393), is a probable model for the other compilations. See above, p. 115, n. 36.

[68] In addition to these, Biller lists only one additional manuscript, Trier, Priester-Seminar MS 81. See Biller, 'Aspects', p. 368.

The *De vita et conversacione* was obviously incorporated in the *Processus Petri* and revised in the process. The origins and revisions of this short text are intriguing, and reveal a lot about how the Waldensians were perceived and presented at the turn of the fifteenth century. In some of its forms the text is an almost neutral description of a religious group, comparable in its sobriety to an earlier text known as the *De vita et actibus ... Pauperum de Lugduno*.[69] However, small revisions, omissions and adjustment of context in the version that circulated within the *Processus Petri* ensured that it represented the Waldensians as a heretical sect.

Peter Biller has connected the composition of the *De vita et conversacione* to the conversion of Waldensian Brethren in 1360s, or, in his later articles, more probably to Zwicker's inquisitions in the 1390s.[70] Given the contents of the text, the later date is extremely probable. I have found further manuscript evidence that suggests that the text was composed in the aftermath of the conversion of 1391. There is a manuscript in Weimar, Herzogin Anna Amalia Bibliothek, originally from the Salvatorberg Carthusian monastery in Erfurt, written around 1400 with some later additions.[71] In the last part of the manuscript there are several texts on heresy written by the same hand, including the *De vita et conversacione*. All the other texts, with the exception of a fragment from Isidore of Sevilla's *Etymologies*, concern local, fourteenth-century Thuringian heretics.[72] There are no other texts on Waldensians and no reason whatsoever to link this copy to the manuscript circulation of the *Processus Petri* or to the texts relating to the earlier conversion of Waldensian Brethren in the 1360s. Instead it seems to represent a local tradition of Erfurt, and can plausibly be linked to the inquisition of Waldensian Brethren in 1391 which featured Zwicker and Martinus of Prague in Erfurt. Thus it is more probable that the *De vita et conversacione* originated from the descriptions drawn up around 1391 than from the earlier 1360s conversion.

The text in the Weimar manuscript does not belong to any of the versions listed by Biller, but it more closely resembles the first version, edited by A.

---

[69] Biller, 'Fingerprinting an Anonymous Description of the Waldensians', p. 190.

[70] Biller, 'Aspects', pp. 48, 367; Biller, 'Fingerprinting an Anonymous Description of the Waldensians', p. 163; P. Biller, 'Heretics Doing Things Secretly', in *Secrets and Discovery in the Middle Ages: Proceedings of the 5th European Congress of the Fédération Internationale des Instituts d'Études Médiévales (Porto, 25th to 29th June 2013)*, ed. J. Meirinhos, C. López Alcalde and J. Rebalde (Barcelona, 2017), pp. 15–26 (pp. 17–19).

[71] Weimar, Herzogin Anna Amalia Bibliothek MS Fol 20. Described in B. C. Bushey, *Die lateinischen Handschriften bis 1600*, Bibliographien und Kataloge der Herzogin-Anna-Amalia-Bibliothek zu Weimar (Wiesbaden, 2004), pp. 86–92.

[72] The texts describe the so called Crypto-Flagellants following the prophesy of Konrad Schmid, including Konrad Schmid's *Prophetiae*, *Articuli heresis flagella-lorum*, and the inquisition protocol of Constantinus de Arenaco in Erfurt in 1350: Bushey, *Die lateinischen Handschriften bis 1600*, pp. 90–2. The most recent, comprehensive work on the Thuringian heresy, including these texts, is I. Würth, *Geißler in Thüringen: die Entstehung einer spätmittelalterlichen Häresie* (Berlin, 2012).

Schmidt, based on the lost Strasbourg manuscript, than those incorporated in the *Processus Petri*. The most striking feature is the absence of any polemic. In fact, it was too neutral in its description of Waldensians to satisfy a later reader. The original scribe had entitled the Waldensian articles of faith simply 'Thus follow the articles of faith'. A later hand struck through 'of faith', replacing it with 'of the error of this heresy'.[73] Other compilers and revisers also faced the same problem, but the later versions of the text are more subtle in 'hereticizing' its Waldensians, that is explaining or describing the ostensibly pious lifestyle of the Waldensians so that it does not appear too Christian. The Strasbourg manuscript adds concluding remarks that Waldensians ignore the learned masters of the scriptures, degrade members of the clergy by listing all their possible bad deeds and not remembering or believing anything good about them and by lying about those who convert from Waldensianism.[74] Likewise, both versions transmitted within the *Processus Petri* word their descriptions of the fasting practices of the Brethren so that they appear to a reader not as pious asceticism but as hypocrisy and the simulated sanctity of deceptive heretics: 'firstly, they fast three or four days in week, one on water and bread unless they are set to hard travel or work, and this they do among their followers so that they would appear holier in front of them'.[75] In the Weimar manuscript and in the version one (vca) the corresponding sentences are simply a description of the ascetic fasting regimen. It is obvious that the more polemical statement above was reworked from this:

> Firstly, that they fast four days in week, namely Monday, Wednesday, Friday and Saturday, and one of them on water and bread, namely Friday, unless they are travelling or working hard or prevented by a reasonable cause.[76]

An even more significant textual revision was the omission of the seven articles of faith,[77] subscription to which was required from the new brother

---

[73] HAAB MS Fol. 20, fol. 320vb: 'Secuntur articuli fidei [later hand:] erroris huius heresis'.

[74] Schmidt, 'Actenstücke', pp. 244–5.

[75] 'Primo ieiunant tres uel quatuor dies in ebdomada, unam in aqua et pane nisi sint in graui itinere uel labore constituti et hoc faciunt inter suos subditos, ut coram eis appareant sanctiores.' Werner, 'Nachrichten', p. 265. For the version with the *Refutatio*: Trier, Stadtbibliothek MS 680/879, fol. 88r: 'Primo ieiunant tres uel quatuor dies in septimana cum pane et aqua nisi sunt in graui Itinere uel labore constituti et hec faciunt inter suos subditos ut appareant coram ipsis sancciores.'

[76] 'Primo quod quatuor dies in ebdomada ieiunant; videlicet feriam secundam, quartam, sextam et sabbatum; et vnum illorum in aqua et pane scilicet feriam sextam; nisi in itinere uel aliquo graui labore siue casu rationabili impediantur.' HAAB MS Fol 20, fol. 320vb. Cf. Schmidt, 'Actenstücke', p. 243; Augsburg, UB MS II. 1. 2° 78, fol. 246ra.

[77] These can be regarded as a genuine Waldensian tradition, as they appear also in other Waldensian texts. The articles in the Weimar manuscript and Schmidt's edition correspond to the seven articles of faith in a Waldensian exposition of their

upon entering the brotherhood. All versions explain what the seven articles are except the version included in the *Processus Petri* manuscripts with the *Cum dormirent homines* (vcc). Although its description of the ordination of a new brother is otherwise longer and more thorough than, for example, those in the Weimar or Strasbourg manuscripts, the seven articles are dismissed with a short remark: 'then one of the more knowledgeable of them [the Brethren] proposes to him [the new brother] something about the sacraments and the seven articles of faith in which they notwithstanding believe'.[78] Nothing more is said about the articles. These omitted seven articles were, according to the Weimar manuscript:

1. There is one God who has a trinity of persons and a unity of essence.
2. The same God is the creator of all things visible and invisible.
3. He gave the Law to Moses at Mount Sinai.
4. He sent his son to be incarnated from an uncorrupted virgin.
5. He chose an immaculate church to himself.
6. Resurrection of the body.
7. He is to come to judge the living and the dead.[79]

Their omission from what I regard to be a finalized and publication-ready version of the *De vita et conversacione* is not accidental, but part of the process of dismissing the disturbingly orthodox features of Waldensianism. In the seven articles there is absolutely nothing that the medieval Church would not have approved of.[80] There were various lists of *Glaubensstücke* (*Articles of Belief*) in circulation, although the number was not settled in the medieval catechesis. Remarkably, in his *Gewissensspiegel* (*Mirror of Conscience*) Martin

---

doctrine influenced by the Hussites and written down in Occitan in the sixteenth century; R. Cegna, *Fede ed etica valdese nel quattrocento: il Libro espositivo e il Tesoro e luce della fede* (Torino, 1982), pp. 135–7; Molnár, *Storia dei valdesi (1)*, p. 259; A. Brenon, 'The Waldensian Books', in *Heresy and Literacy, 1000–1530*, ed. P. Biller and A. Hudson (Cambridge, 1994), pp. 144–5, 153–6.

[78] St Florian, MS XI 234, fol. 84vb: 'tunc sciencior ex ipsis proponit sibi aliquid de sacramentis et de vii articulis fidei quos tamen credunt'. In Werner, 'Nachrichten', p. 266, 'tantum' instead of 'tamen'.

[79] HAAB MS Fol 20, fol 321rb: 'Item tempore ordinacionis examinantur et interrogantur de septem articulis fidei, scilicet vtrum credat vnum deum in trinitate personarum et vnitatem essencie; Secundo quod idem deus sit creator omnium visibilium et invisibilium; Tertio quod tradidit legem moysi in monte synay; Quarto quod misit filium suum incarnandum de virgine incorrupta; Quinto quod elegit sibi ecclesiam immaculatam; sexto carnis resurrectionem; Septimo quod venturus est iudicare viuos et mortuos et sic de aliis articulis fidei nullam faciunt mencionem.' Cf. Schmidt, 'Actenstücke', p. 244.

[80] Brenon, 'The Waldensian Books', p. 154, regarding the sixteenth-century exposition: 'while the parts of the Exposé devoted to the article of the faith or the ten commandments are entirely orthodox'.

von Amberg, later known as Martinus of Prague when an inquisitor, lists seven articles on Christ's humanity and seven on his divinity that in their contents concur with the Waldensian articles (with the exception that the law given to Moses is not listed by Martinus).[81] These articles from the ordination of heresiarchs were left out because of their close and hence problematic resemblance to the Church's confession and catechesis.

In order to make the *De vita et conversacione* in all its complexity available for the scholars of Waldensianism, an edition with a full collation of the manuscripts is in preparation. Here, a preliminary interpretation of its textual history in relation to the formation of the *Processus Petri* is in order. First, the Weimar manuscript and version 1 recognized by Biller (here: vca) represent the oldest redaction(s) of the work, written at the latest in the early 1390s and possibly incorporating older material. Whether the writer was a convert or an inquisitor must remain forever unknown. There was a practical demand among inquisitors, polemicists and preachers for such a work, which explains why it started to spread, but the text, as it was, was dangerous. It could easily be misinterpreted (from the inquisitor's point of view). Therefore, in the circle of Petrus Zwicker and Martinus of Prague, a revised version (vcc, Biller's second) was produced. This was done by 1393, the date of the earliest manuscript exemplar. With omissions and additions, and with the surrounding texts, it was safe for publication. It soon formed a textual unit with the short list of converts, the *Articuli Waldensium* and the long question list. This is the most widely spread and at the same time the least contro-versial version. The revision process transformed an almost impartial and thus potentially dangerous description of the lifestyle of the Waldensian Brethren into a short treatise on the ordination of heresiarchs. This was done by deleting problematic passages, adding explanatory remarks and combining the *De vita et conversacione* with other texts that made its heretical content obvious. The end-product was a work that could be safely circulated without blurring the demarcation between heresy and orthodoxy.

Biller's third version (vcb), transmitted with the *Refutatio errorum* and with the *Articuli Waldensium*, remains a question mark. It has common features with both (vca) and (vcc). Further, it is the least coherent one. For example, it repeats the vows that are required from a new Brother. It could be an intermediate form between the two other versions, which started to spread before it was finalized. It is more likely that it was put together a bit later, at the beginning of the fifteenth century, by a compiler who had access to the two other versions. Different versions highlight the nature of this short tract on Waldensians: it consists of relatively independent sections of possibly

---

[81] Martin von Amberg, *Der Gewissensspiegel*, pp. 35–8; see also Haupt, *Der Waldensische Ursprung des Codex Teplensis*, p. 9.

different origin, such as the list of errors and the ordination of a new brother, which were rearranged, updated and revised at need.

Articuli Waldensium

The text that was often combined with the *De vita et conversacione*, the *Articuli Waldensium*, is one of the diverse lists of Waldensian errors that originated from the trials of the 1390s and early 1400s. It is among the more extensive lists of this kind, superseded only by the list in Zwicker's letter to the Austrian dukes in 1395, with its over ninety articles of faith. The *Articuli* and Zwicker's letter resemble each other closely. Both meticulously list how different aspects of religious practice, from church music to sacramentals and pilgrimages, were condemned by Waldensians. There is no doubt that the *Articuli* were known to Zwicker. This is evident from several manuscripts in which it was imbedded in the *Processus Petri*, including the manual of St Florian. Zwicker also used the *Articuli* when he composed the *Cum dormirent homines*. In the error list, there is a peculiar story about how some Waldensians consecrated bread and wine and celebrated communion. The practice was, however, disapproved of by the majority of the Waldensian Brethren, who instead recommended that their followers should take part in the Easter celebrations and the customary yearly Eucharist required of the faithful.

> Some of them have been accustomed to communicate to themselves at Easter in this way: one of them takes the unleavened bread, placing it on small board, and wine and water in a spoon, and he blesses these together and shares them with others. This being done he throws both the board and the spoon into the fire to burn. A great many of their masters, however, abhor this, not having much faith in such private communion, but when the pressure by the people is great, they go to a church for communion to avoid attention. Many of them, however, sometimes stay without communion for four to six years, hiding in villages or in cities at Easter time so that they would not be noticed by Christians.[82]

---

[82] 'Item quidam eorum consueverunt se ipsos communicare ad pascha isto modo: Aliquis eorum sumit panem azimum ponens eum super parvum asserem, vinum et ad [sic] aquam ad unum coclear et benedicit ista simul et communicat se et alios. Quo facto tam asserem quam coclear in ignem proicit comburendo. Plurimi tamen magistrorum suorum abhorrent hoc, non habentes multam fidem in huiusmodi communione proptera [sic, probably a mistake of the editor, cf. BAV MS Pal. lat. 677, fol. 49: propria] sed vadunt ad communicandum in ecclesiam, quando est populi maior pressura, ne notentur. Multi tamen ex ipsis quandoque manent sine communicatione ad quatuor uel sex annos, abscondentes se in villis uel in civitatibus paschali tempore, ne a christianis agnoscantur.' Werner, 'Nachrichten', pp. 268–9. On Waldensian attitudes to the Eucharist in the late fourteenth century, see esp. Biller, 'Aspects', pp. 100–1; Biller, *Waldenses*, pp. 246, 248, 273, 280–1, 290.

This anecdote is then repeated in the *Cum dormirent homines* in a briefer fashion but clearly deriving from the same story and referring to recent events:

> But recently it has been discovered that a certain heresiarch, even though he was a mere layman, prepared the Body of the Lord, as it appeared good to him, and shared it with some companions; although the legitimacy of this was to some extent contradicted by other heresiarchs.[83]

The concise remarks in the *Cum dormirent homines* could not have been the source of the more detailed paragraph in the *Articuli*, so it is likely that at least one version of the *Articuli* was at Zwicker's disposal in 1395, when he composed his treatise. This, together with the broad geographical dissemination of the *Articuli*, implies that they were compiled in the early 1390s, the context again probably the aftermath of the conversion of the Brethren in 1391. Martinus of Prague used some version of the *Articuli* in Würzburg in 1391.[84]

The *Articuli* and the long question list, which it often accompanied, contain essentially the same information about Waldensians, including some details that are not in similar and contemporary texts. The *Articuli* state that Waldensians pray for the members of their 'sect' and also that God 'would unleash upon us Christians, whom they call and believe to be "outsiders", war, hunger, pestilence or other forms of distress so that meanwhile we would stop the inquisitions and the fight against them'.[85] There is a corresponding question at the end of the long question list, enquiring of the deponent: 'Did you ever pray for a disturbance of the peace, so that you and your friends would be forgotten and we would not make enquiries, as done now?'[86] The *Articuli* and the long question list are thus opposite sides of the same coin, one presenting the Waldensian errors as a list, the other a ready formula of questions for the use of inquisitor or confessor.

The question remains as to whether it was Petrus Zwicker who composed the *Articuli Waldensium* and the long question list and reworked the *De vita et conversacione*, or Martinus of Prague, as proposed by Ernst Werner.[87] The existence of these texts in the *Processus Petri* does not exclude the latter option,

---

83 Zwicker, *Cum dormirent homines*, p. 278F: 'Nam nouiter compertum est, quod quidam haeresiarcha, licet fuerit purus Laicus, corpus Christi, vt sibi videbatur, confecerit, et se ipsum, et quosdam complices communicauerit; licet fuerit super hoc ab aliis haeresiarchis aliqualiter redargutus.'

84 See above, n. 57

85 Werner, 'Nachrichten', p. 269: 'et quo nobis christianis, quos inter se alienos, id est di ffremden, credunt et nominant, permittat advenire bella, famen, pestilentiam uel aliam incommoda, ut in medio tempore ab eorum inquisitione et impugnatione cessemus.'

86 Ibid., p. 274. 'Orasti ne aliquociens pro pacis disturbio, ut tu et tuorum amicorum obliuisceruntur, nec inquiremus, sicut iam factus.'

87 Ibid., pp. 219–20.

nor does Zwicker's use of them in composing his treatise. Given the close co-operation between the two inquisitors from 1391 onwards there would have been plenty of occasions for the transmission of texts between the two. In fact, Werner suggested that Martin could have used Zwicker's 'notes' (*Aufzeichnungen*) when composing his own texts.[88] Dietrich Kurze's proposition concerning the two lists of questions supports this conjecture. Kurze has proposed, contrary to previous nineteenth-century assumptions, that it was the short question formula that was closer to Petrus Zwicker's inquisitory practice in Stettin, not the longer list of questions.[89] This would neatly go together with the interpretation of Werner: the short question list would be the one composed by Zwicker, the longer by Martinus. However, the history, especially the history transmitted in the medieval manuscripts, is often much more complicated and more uncertain than the clear-cut interpretations of scholars, or their attempts to find authors of texts that were in a constant process of being reworked and re-edited. It is almost impossible to pinpoint the direction of influences between the two closely co-operating inquisitors and their assistants.[90] Nevertheless, as we shall see, there is clear evidence that Petrus Zwicker knew and used the long question formula from very early on.

I do not intend to dispute Kurze's conclusion that Zwicker used the short question list in Stettin – indeed, the short *interrogatorium* corresponds closely to the answers in the protocols – but I would suggest that he also occasionally used the longer, more extensive one to assist in the enquiry. The two question lists are not mutually exclusive but complementary. For example, the standard question about killing is very simple in the short list: 'Have you believed that all manslaughter is sin?'[91] However, most answers in Stettin are responses to more specific (and theologically more problematic) questions: can evildoers be punished through legal and judicial execution and does the judge in that case commit a sin?[92] The long question list addresses the problem with the question: 'Do not judges and jurors commit sin when condemning the impious to death and sentencing evildoers to death?'[93] It

---

[88] Ibid., p. 220.

[89] Kurze, 'Zur Ketzergeschichte', p. 76, esp. n. 121; See also Quellen, ed. Kurze, pp. 17–18, edition of the short questionnaire pp. 73–7. One has to point out that Kurze never proposed that the list of questions circulated in the Austrian manuscripts and the one Zwicker had used in Stettin were *identical*, only that they were very close to each other.

[90] When studying two manuscripts of the Wrocław, Biblioteka Uniwersytecka inculding parts of the *Processus Petri*, J. Szymański proposed similar shared authorsip for these texts: Szymański, 'Articuli secte Waldensium', pp. 92–4.

[91] *Quellen*, ed. Kurze, p. 74: 'Credidisti, omne homicidium esse peccatum?'

[92] Ibid., pp. 113, 115, 117, 120, 124, 173, 202, 231, 258. This was first remarked by Biller, *Waldenses*, p. 88, although without comparison between the two question lists.

[93] Quoted here from Werner, 'Nachrichten', p. 274: 'Peccant ne iudices et iurati, cond(?)empnando impios morte uel adiudicando maleficos morti.'

was certainly this question that Claws Zevecow de Kokstede answered on 19 February 1394: 'He believed that all killing, however done, even judicially, were a sin, and that the judge and the jurors sin mortally and cannot be saved.'[94] Hence, it seems that Petrus Zwicker used both question lists when interrogating the Waldensians in Brandenburg and Pomerania. There is also a detail in the long list which points to Zwicker's influence. Like the Pseudo-Ezekiel quotation in the *Refutatio errorum* discussed earlier, it points to a particular source in an inquisitor's manual. The question on the lack of belief in pilgrimages is formulated in a peculiar manner: 'Did you visit the houses of saints for indulgences? Have you been in Rome, Aachen and so on?'[95] The selection of these two cities probably derives from a similar formulation, in a consultation about beliefs that indicate a heretic, in the *Consilium* of Iacobus de Mediolano (James of Milan), included in the Bohemian inquisitorial manual Zwicker owned, a text he copied into his own manual.[96]

By contrast, it is the short question list – though doubtless used by Zwicker – that demonstrates the influence of Martinus of Prague. Patschovsky has divided the short list into four parts corresponding to the course of the trial, these being (1) questions relating to the background of the accused; (2) the level of involvement (for example confessions to the heretics, penances received, aid given to the Brethren); (3) doctrinal questions; and (4) questions relating to the end of the process (for example readiness to abjure, previous sentences for heresy). These stages are directly equivalent to those in a short formula of questions dealing with the Beghards, transmitted in one manuscript and attributed there to *dominus Martinus*. Patschovsky considers *dominus Martinus* to be Martinus of Prague, who had proceeded against the Beghards in Strasbourg in the 1370s.[97] The conceptual schema of the two question formulas is indeed surprisingly

---

[94] *Quellen*, ed. Kurze, p. 231: 'Item credidit, omne homicidium, qualitercunque fuerit, eciam factum iudicialiter, fore peccatum, et quod iudex et scabini peccantur mortaliter et salvari non possent.' A different word for jurors is used (*iurati/scabini*), but the contents of the question and answer match.

[95] 'Visitasti tu limina sanctorum pro indulgenciis; Fuisti rome, aquisgrani etc.', St Florian, MS XI 234, fol. 86va. The Olomouc manuscript edited by Werner has only Rome; Werner, 'Nachrichten', p. 273. Some other manuscripts have Rome, Aachen and Prague; see BAV MS Pal. lat. 677, fol. 52v.

[96] Parmeggiani, *Consilia*, p. 183: 'Secunda questio est, numquid ille qui dixit quod nullo modo credit quod Rome, Aquisgrani peccata dimittantur; item, quod non credit quod peccata dimictat, nisi solus Deus, possit dici hereticus' (The second question is, is it not the case that he who says that he does not believe that [visits] to Romen [and] Aachen in any way remit sins can be called a heretic? Item, [as also] he who does not believe that [anything] remits sins, only God?). Cf. Linz, OÖLB MS 177, fols. 114v–115r; St Florian, MS XI 234, fols. 124va–125ra.

[97] Patschovsky, 'Gli eretici davanti al tribunale', pp. 262–5. On Martinus of Prague in Strasbourg, Patschovsky, 'Straßburger Beginenverfolkungen im 14. Jahrhundert', pp. 89–91.

similar, even when the doctrinal contents under inquiry were totally different. This is a very non-standard form of questioning heretics. For example, Nicholas Eymerich, the Aragonese inquisitor a generation earlier than Zwicker, provides a formula that begins in a similar fashion by questioning the background of the accused and proceeds to questions on introduction to heresy and doctrine. But he does not offer a ready list of questions, and the whole process relies on a much more complicated use of witnesses, coercive imprisonment and multiple interrogations to elicit a confession unlike Zwicker's and Martinus's praxis.[98] The question formula of Bernard Gui for use against Waldensian believers is not built around the course of the trial but simply lists the questions an inquisitor should put to suspected Waldensians, emphasizing where and when the accused saw Waldensian preachers and what they taught.[99] The discrepancy in style undermines Kathrin Utz Tremp's argument that Gui's interrogatory inspired Zwicker's.[100] I prefer to accept Patschovsky's interpretation of the connection between the question list Zwicker used against the Waldensians and that Martinus used against the Beghards.

It is thus futile to try to identify the separate inputs of Petrus Zwicker and Martinus of Prague in the above-mentioned lists of Waldensian converts, descriptions of their way of living and doctrine, or formulas of questions. It is obvious that both these inquisitors participated in composing these texts and both used them in conducting their duties, sometimes alone, at other times together. Other possible contributors cannot be excluded, especially around the year 1391, as the details of the mass conversion are lost to us. Modestin has proposed that Dominican inquisitor Nicolaus Böckeler was somehow involved,[101] not to mention all the notaries and deputy or locum inquisitors assisting the inquisitors proper.

Did the question lists, and thus the interrogations based on them, differ from the previous practice of the inquisitors? It has been said that Zwicker's apparatus of questions was extremely detailed and systematic compared to that of other inquisitors of the time, or even of any medieval inquisitor.[102] He is also known for dismissing popular rumours that had also circulated around Stettin only few years earlier, and which had suggested that Waldensians assembled at night to worship Lucifer.[103] At the same time Zwicker has the reputation of having been a very flexible interrogator, varying his questions

---

[98] Nicolaus Eymericus, *Directorium inqvisitorum*, ed. F. Peña (Rome, 1578), part III, p. 286.

[99] Bernard Gui, *Practica inquisitionis*, 256–7.

[100] Utz Tremp, 'Multum abhorrerem confiteri', p. 163.

[101] Modestin, 'Zwicker', p. 27.

[102] Utz Tremp, 'Multum abhorrerem confiteri', pp. 154, 160, 169, 177.

[103] Biller, *Waldenses*, p. 255; see also Introduction above, p. 8, n. 21. The allegations about Luciferanism in Stettin are discussed in more detail in Chapter 5.

based on the deponents' expected level of understanding and involvement in heresy, and therefore formulating his questions in a rather neutral way, allowing answers that did not fit into his expectations.[104] An example is the interrogation of Herman Wegener on 16 March 1394 in Stettin; Zwicker did not ask him about the articles of faith 'because he was stupid and simple',[105] whereas the inquisitor clearly expanded his array of questions when encountering prominent members of the movement.[106]

However, flexibility in interrogation is not what makes Petrus Zwicker or Martinus of Prague special as inquisitors. While there certainly were medieval inquisitors who had no great ambitions in their duty but simply went through their list of accusations, there were many others who led extensive and varied interrogations and (seemingly) allowed the deponent even more freedom in telling their stories than Zwicker in Stettin. The most famous example of the latter is the bishop of Pamiers, Jacques Fournier, whose detailed registers have inspired not only Le Roy Ladurie's famous *Montaillou* but also numerous other studies.[107] Moreover, posing a different set of questions according to the suspects' degree of involvement in heresy was more standard than exceptional. In the Toulouse inquisition of 1273–82 the testimony of John of Torrena, who denied his own involvement in heresy but testified about others', is a fraction of the length of the detailed confession of the well-connected host of heretics, Raymond Hugh, whose brother-in-law was the heretical Good Man Bernard of Tilhol.[108] Even the trial in 1400 led by the Strasbourg city council, whose members, according to Georg Modestin, had little theological interest beyond showing that somebody had belonged to the Waldensians,[109] demonstrates this tendency. The leading figure of the local Waldensian community, die Alte zum Hirtze, is questioned in great detail, as is the habitual host of itinerant Brethren, Hartmann der Biermann.[110] In

---

[104] Kurze, 'Zur Ketzergeschichte', pp. 76–7; Biller, *Waldenses*, pp. 255, 275; Modestin, *Ketzer in der Stadt*, p. 124; Modestin, 'Zwicker', p. 28.

[105] *Quellen*, ed. Kurze, p. 245: 'sed quia stolidus fuit et simplex, ideo inquisitor alios articulos pertransiit.'

[106] Kurze, 'Zur Ketzergeschichte', pp. 76–7; Biller, *Waldenses*, p. 255.

[107] Although more recent scholarship has warned against giving too much credit to the individuality of Jacques Fournier and his methods, there is no denying that for whatever reasons his registers are among the most detailed among the medieval inquisitors' documents. See e.g. Arnold, *Inquisition and Power*, p. 164–7; Sparks, *Heresy, Inquisition and Life-Cycle*, pp. 22–3; Bueno, *Defining Heresy*, pp. 88–9.

[108] *Toulouse Inquisition Depositions*, ed. Biller, Bruschi and Sneddon, pp. 372–435 (Raymond Hugh), 458–65 (John of Torrena). On the importance of Raymond Hugh and his brother for the local Cathar community, see Biller, Bruschi and Sneddon, 'Introduction', p. 45; on the practice of skipping irrelevant questions in the Toulouse inquisition, ibid., p. 66.

[109] Modestin, *Ketzer in der Stadt*, pp. 17–27, 124.

[110] *Quellen*, ed. Modestin, pp. 110–18 (die Alte zum Hirtze), 118–20 (Hartmann der Biermann).

contrast, the depositions of average suspects are very short, sometimes only a few lines, stating only that they had believed as others and confessed their sins to heresiarchs.[111]

The crucial feature in Petrus Zwicker's and Martinus of Prague's question lists and inquisitorial practice is not that they adapted their questions or allowed the deponents to speak spontaneously, but that in the *Processus Petri* there is one of the most elaborate medieval apparatuses to facilitate a detailed inquiry into the beliefs of the dissident laity, not just into their heretical activities. Biller remarked on this when he compared Zwicker's short list to question lists from the *Ordo Processus Narbonensis* (late 1240s) and Bernard Gui's *Practica Inquisitionis* (1323). Of these, Zwicker's questionnaire is the most concerned with beliefs of individual *credens*, whereas the earliest formula concentrates on external actions. Biller was, with good grounds, cautious about seeing this as a linear development, pointing out that again in Fribourg in 1430 the majority of *credentes* were interrogated rather briefly, whereas Bernard Gui's contemporary Bishop Jacques Fournier was much more curious and interested in probing into details than the summary Gui.[112] Below I shall elaborate on Biller's observations and demonstrate that in late fourteenth-century Germany there was indeed a development in the inquisitorial practice and inquisitors' attitudes towards the laity's capacity to express and discern matters of faith. This development is significant, not only compared to the thirteenth-century French question formulas, but also to the immediate predecessors of the fourteenth-century Bohemian inquisitorial praxis.

When we evaluate inquisitors' attitudes towards laypeople's intellectual and spiritual abilities, the point is not that when the 'simple' Herman Wegener was unable to answer Zwicker's questions, the inquisitor could abandon his rigid formula. It is that a considerable number of questions pertaining to minute details of faith were asked from the majority of suspects and adequate answers proving either heresy or orthodoxy were expected. Even the simple-minded could be instructed and converted. Interrogating Aleyd Takken on 12 March 1394, Zwicker noted (he wrote this protocol himself, as he did with Herman Wegener): 'hearing that she is simple and not strongly rooted in other articles of the Waldensian sect, the inquisitor skipped these and turned himself to restore her to faith'.[113]

---

[111] For example, the depositions of Ellekint Huter and Metze Waser are very brief and simple: see *Quellen*, ed. Modestin, pp. 136, 140. Even among the characteristically terse records of mid-thirteenth-century inquisitions there are detailed documents when the witnesses are literate Franciscans; Arnold, *Inquisition and Power*, p. 106.

[112] Biller, 'Signs of Heresy', pp. 271–5.

[113] *Quellen*, ed. Kurze, p. 241: 'Et inquisitor, audiens, eam esse simplicem nec fortifer in aliis articulis secte Waldensium hereticorum radicatam, ipsos pertransiit et se ad reversionem ipsius ad fidem convertit.'

As already implied, this was not the obvious *modus operandi*. The earlier models for interrogation, based on the development of inquisitorial procedure in thirteenth- and early fourteenth-century France and Italy, did not assume meticulous interrogation of ordinary believers or followers on details of faith. A good example is a questionnaire transmitted in the fourteenth-century Bohemian manual that belonged to Zwicker.[114] The question list is of thirteenth-century French origin.[115] It focuses on asking if the suspect had known or seen any heretics, been in the same places on the same occasions, believed that they were good men, possessed their books or relics of burned heretics, or if she or he had in any way helped them or received anything from them. Only 'converts', referring here to those who taught heresy, were to be interrogated in detail about their errors.[116] Similar methods are proposed in other thirteenth-century questionnaires.[117] From the legal point of view acts constituted the firmest evidence, especially when sentencing those belonging to the difficult category of *credentes*, people sympathizing and believing in the heretics but not themselves preaching heresy, or in the case of Waldensians, those who were not Brethren but confessed to them and listened to their teachings.[118] When reflecting on the difficulty of discerning who was a *credens*, the French inquisitor Bernard Gui famously said, citing the consultation of Gui Foulques (Guido Fulcodii, later Pope Clement IV) that 'deep is the heart of man, and inscrutable', and that the most evident proof comes from the acts themselves.[119] Nicholas Eymerich instructed in his *Directorium inquisitorum* (*Inquisitors' Rulebook*) that simple laypeople should not be interrogated of the subtleties of faith, unless there is reason to assume that heretics have corrupted them.[120]

---

[114] Linz, OÖLB MS 177, fol. 4r–v.

[115] C. Douais, 'Les hérétiques du Midi au XIIIe siècle. Cinq pièces inédites', *Annales du Midi: revue archéologique, historique et philologique de la France méridionale* 3 (1891), 367–79. See pp. 367–8 for dating, pp. 376–7 for an edition.

[116] Linz, OÖLB MS 177, fol. 4r–v: 'Item a conuersis inquiratur in quibus errauerunt et si errores predicauerunt vel docuerunt et qui audiuerunt suam predicacionem siue doctrinam' (Item, there should be questioning of the converted: in what things they erred, and if they preached or taught their errors, and who heard their preaching or teaching).

[117] See esp. *Ordo processus Narbonensis* and *Doctrina de modo procedendi contra haereticos*, based on inquisitions around Carcassone and Toulouse. Their question lists are collated in Biller, Bruschi and Sneddon, 'Introduction', pp. 67–70; both include only one laconic question about faith: 'Whether they believed in a heretic or a Waldensian, or in their errors.' Ibid., p. 69. See also Biller, 'Signs of Heresy', pp. 271–7.

[118] On the formation of *credentes* and other categories of heresy, Arnold, *Inquisition and Power*, pp. 20–9, 35–47, 49–51.

[119] Bernard Gui, *Practica inquisitionis*, p. 224; cf. Consultation of Gui Foulques, Questio IX, ed. Bivolarov, *Inquisitoren-Handbücher*, p. 240. The Bohemian manual Linz, OÖLB MS 177 has the consultation at fols. 11r–20r.

[120] Nicolaus Eymericus, *Directorium inqvisitorum*, pars I, qu. 4.5, p. 47.

These principles were also implemented in practice: the deposition of Raymond Hugh, which fills dozens of folios and was made before the inquisitors Ranulph of Plassac and Pons of Parnac in April 1274, includes only a very short reference to Raymond's heretical beliefs.[121] The main point of the interrogation was to reveal who had consorted with heretics (Good Men), wanted to see them, gave them something, admired them or in general knew about heretics and their followers. That the thirteenth-century inquisitors were more interested in actions demonstrating affiliation with heretics than what the deponents actually believed is well attested in scholarship.[122] So is the shift from observing outward actions towards inquiring about the inner state of a deponent's soul, which John H. Arnold has called a 'construction of the confessing subject' and which, according to him, took place by the late thirteenth century.[123] With that came the need to inquire into the religious convictions of ordinary laypeople, and the interrogation methods of Bishop Jacques Fournier marked a turning point in southern France around 1320.[124]

But this shift was not uniform, linear or absolute,[125] and it was still very much in progress in the Bohemian-German inquisitorial practice in the fourteenth century. The copy of the thirteenth-century question list from the Linz manual quoted above contains a very clear example of this change in motion. After writing down two additional question lists, the same fourteenth-century scribe has added a short notice about what should be taken into account during the inquisition of heresy. This addition includes a question about believing and acting against Christian dogma and the teachings of the Roman Church.[126] It thus changes the emphasis from the deponent's relationship with heresiarchs towards his or her own beliefs and disbeliefs.

---

[121] *Toulouse Inquisition Depositions*, ed. Biller, Bruschi and Sneddon, pp. 414–15.

[122] W. L. Wakefield, 'Heretics and Inquisitors: The Case of Auriac and Cambiac', *Journal of Medieval History* 12 (1985), 225–37 (p. 225); Arnold, *Inquisition and Power*, p. 98; Pegg, *The Corruption of Angels*, p. 45; Biller, 'Signs of Heresy', pp. 272, 274–5; C. Taylor, '"Heresy" in Quercy in the 1240s: Authorities and Audiences', in *Heresy and the Making of European Culture: Medieval and Modern Perspectives*, ed. A. P. Roach and J. R. Simpson (Aldershot, 2013), pp. 239–55 (pp. 253–4).

[123] Arnold, *Inquisition and Power*, pp. 98–107.

[124] Bueno, *Defining Heresy*, pp. 112–18.

[125] Arnold never proposes that it was, and in fact warns against assuming so, *Inquisition and Power*, p. 50. See also Biller, 'Signs of Heresy', pp. 274–5.

[126] Linz, OÖLB MS 177, fol. 7r: 'Primo si vnquam et precipue postquam ad annos discrecionis peruenit, fecit, dixit, asseruit, tenuit, approbauit, credidit, commisit aliquid contra fidem catholicam et eius articulos vel ecclesiastica sacramenta aut contra id quod sacrosancta Romana ecclesia tenet, docet, predicat et obseruat' (First, if he ever – and especially after reaching the age of discretion – did, said, asserted, held, approved, believed [or] committed anything against the Catholic faith or its articles or ecclesiastical sacraments, or against what the sacrosanct Roman Church holds, teaches, preaches and observes).

Regarding the protocols of inquisition, the comparison with Zwicker's and his *familia*'s practice are the depositions from the inquisitions of Gallus of Jindřichův Hradec (Neuhaus) from the 1330s to the 1350s. Zwicker was familiar with the same Bohemian practice of inquisition, and an interrogatory most likely used by Gallus is transmitted in Linz, OÖLB MS 177.[127] It was a model available for Zwicker, yet had little direct influence. Gallus's question formula has questions about the deponent's beliefs, but unlike Zwicker's question lists, it is not aimed primarily against Waldensians, but tries instead to confirm if the deponent had dissident thoughts about the seven sacraments. Only the last questions about purgatory and intervention on behalf of the dead have clear anti-Waldensian implications.[128] The contrast between the Bohemian inquisitions of the early and mid-1300s and the late fourteenth-century proceedings against Waldensians is even more evident when one surveys the depositions from Gallus's inquisitions, which unfortunately have survived only in fragments. Yet even these fragments bear witness to intensive interrogations that were often recorded in greater length and detail than protocols produced by Zwicker's notaries in Stettin. The emphasis is, however, completely different. Gallus inquired minutely into the suspects' heretical connections and acquaintances, using contradictions in deponents' testimonies to catch them. What the deponents themselves thought about the Waldensian articles of faith is of marginal importance. A good example is a certain Henricus, who was interrogated in Prague (in December 1345 or 1349)[129] on at least four different days. Gallus asks only in passing and very briefly what the Waldensian Brethren had taught, and if Henricus thought that the Waldensian confessors had the power to bind and release from sins. But he makes a great effort to prove that contrary to Henricus's statement when he first confessed, his (then deceased) brother had visited him only a few years earlier.[130] In Gallus's protocols, the heresy is attested above all by connections to other heretics and contumacy is revealed by proving that the deponent had lied to the inquisitor.

Some of the differences can be explained through different conditions. Gallus and other mid-fourteenth-century Bohemian inquisitors operated in a hostile atmosphere trying to extract information from reluctant deponents, while Petrus Zwicker faced, with few exceptions, more or less submissive penitents. Nevertheless, even taking this into account the differences in principles and practice are obvious. Even when Zwicker started to acquire information about something unusual it did not alter his line of inquiry, which was still concentrated on an individual deponent's faith. A good example is the protocol of Gyrdrud Melsaw, who is the first to reveal the opposition to

---

[127] Patschovsky, *Anfänge*, pp. 104–5. Cf. Linz, OÖLB MS 177, fols. 76v–77v.
[128] Patschovsky, *Anfänge*, p. 105.
[129] On the dating, *Quellen*, ed. Patschovsky, p. 203.
[130] Ibid., pp. 204, 206, 212.

the inquisitor's office in the village of Klein-Wubiser. These acts of resistance were the strongest Zwicker encountered during his commission in the diocese of Cammin. Although the summary edition by Dieterich Kurze from Gyrdrud's deposition gives a prominent place to the extraordinary comments by the leading Waldensians of Klein-Wubiser about the inquisitor as the devil and their attempts to shame those going to confess, these clauses are actually only an afterthought in Gyrdrud's protocol, where the main point is her own confession of her heresy, along the lines of Zwicker's usual procedure.[131] She reveals a quite ordinary relationship to Waldensian Brethren (confessing to them yearly or whenever possible, and deeming them better confessors than members of the clergy as they obtained their authority directly from God) as well as standard opinions about not believing in the invocation of saints, purgatory and prayer on behalf of the dead. She nevertheless participated in the veneration of saints and masses for the dead, as was common among the Pomeranian Waldensians. Likewise she kissed the relics of the saints, but only in honour of God, not the saints, and did not believe that indulgences or pilgrimages had any salutary powers, no more than holy water, blessed candles, ashes or salt.

Her confession is thus very much a product of the questionnaire formulated by Petrus Zwicker and Martinus of Prague and used by Zwicker in Stettin: an inquiry into the faith of an ordinary believer, facilitated by the inquisitor's intimate knowledge of Waldensian doctrine, habits and relationships inside the group. The role of the deeds as evidence of the deponent's heresy never disappeared: whether or not one has confessed to a Waldensian Brother was a crucial factor when the inquisitor estimated the degree of an accused person's heresy, and if she or he had been a Waldensian or not. The two acquitted persons among the 195 surviving depositions from Stettin were able to convince Zwicker that they had never confessed to anyone but to consecrated priests of the Church.[132] Mere acts, however, were no longer sufficient as evidence. In addition to whether or not the accused celebrated the feast days of the saints, Zwicker was interested in whether he or she believed that the saints could intercede on behalf of the living, and to whose honour, the saints' or God's, the deponent fasted and feasted.[133] Zwicker's protocols

---

[131] *Quellen*, ed. Kurze, pp. 167–8; cf. the original in HAB MS Guelf. 403 Helmst, fols. 76v–77r. The edition by Kurze omits much of the 'standard' confession on heretical beliefs, unless the deposition includes singular or rare opinions. See Introduction, above.

[132] *Quellen*, ed. Kurze, pp. 153–4, 249–50.

[133] Ibid., p. 74: 'Ieiunasti vigilias sanctorum et celebrasti festa? Si fecisti, ad cuius laudem, fecisti secundum hereticos?' (Did you fast on the vigils of the saints and did you celebrate [their] feasts? If you did, in whose honour, [and] did you do so according to the heretics?). The second part of this refers to the late medieval Waldensian practice whereby celebrating feast days of saints was explained as acts done to honour God alone, not saints.

produced minute accounts of the Waldensian laity's beliefs, not only because he was a well-informed interrogator, but because his inquisitorial apparatus brought individual belief to the forefront of the inquisition of heresy in a way unanticipated by any of his immediate predecessors or models.

Petrus Zwicker and Martinus of Prague were not the only ones who questioned the Waldensian laity in detail. In the contemporary trials in the archdiocese of Mainz, the layman Henne Russeneyden was interrogated by a group of theologians from the University of Heidelberg in late 1392 or early 1393, led by the doctor of theology Konrad von Soltau and the Dominican inquisitor Nicolaus Böckeler.[134] According to the protocol drawn from the trial, Henne was 'heard and examined under oath for several days, and continuously and separately for hours by us, the above mentioned doctors, masters and clerics'.[135] When Henne was at first obstinate and unwilling to recant – although he had come to the court voluntarily – the interrogators and other theologians and clerics tried to convince him both publicly and privately with various arguments from the Scriptures.[136] Even if the notary had exaggerated the contribution of the theologians in order to legitimize the sentence, the trial demonstrates the conviction that even the laity's faith should be under meticulous scrutiny and every possible argument should be used to convert them from their heresy – a tendency that characterizes also Zwicker and Martin's inquisitions but is absent from the inquisitions against Waldensians earlier in the fourteenth century in Germany and Bohemia. Their question lists also spread. The fragments from an inquisition held in Prague at some time between 1389 and 1395 demonstrate close affinity to the question lists of Zwicker and Martinus.[137] As the name of the inquisitors is not preserved in them, it is possible that either man or both conducted the inquisition.[138] In 1394 Zwicker had the commission from the archbishop of Prague,[139] and in May 1396, when consulted concerning suspected relapsed

---

[134] On the trial, see Deane, 'Archiepiscopal Inquisitions', pp. 215–17.

[135] 'Per nos prefatosque doctores, magistros et clericos, pluribus diebus et horis continuis interpolatis, auditus et examinatus sub juramento'; Kolpacoff, 'Papal Schism', pp. 288–9.

[136] 'Et quamquam dictus Henne per nos et alios magistros doctores ac clericos peritos prefatos caritative fraternaliter et modeste fuerit monitus et pluries et sepius coniunctim et divisim publice nobis pro tribunali sedentibus ac eciam privatimet secrete variis exhortamentis et sacra scriptura et fidei catholice veritate fundatis.' Kolpacoff, 'Papal Schism', p. 290.

[137] Edited as 'Fragment B' in Hlaváček, 'Zur böhmischen Inquisition', pp. 127–30; for the dating based on the persons mentioned, p. 119; previously edited and dated to 1393 by J. Truhlář, 'Pabĕrky z rukopisů Klementinských Nr. 26', *Vestník Ceské akademie* 8 (1899), 353–7. The fragments nowadays have the shelfmark NKCR MS VII. A. 16/3.

[138] Soukup has tentatively speculated the possibility that Martinus was the inquisitor; Soukup, 'Die Waldenser in Böhmen', p. 140.

[139] *Quellen*, ed. Kurze, p. 235.

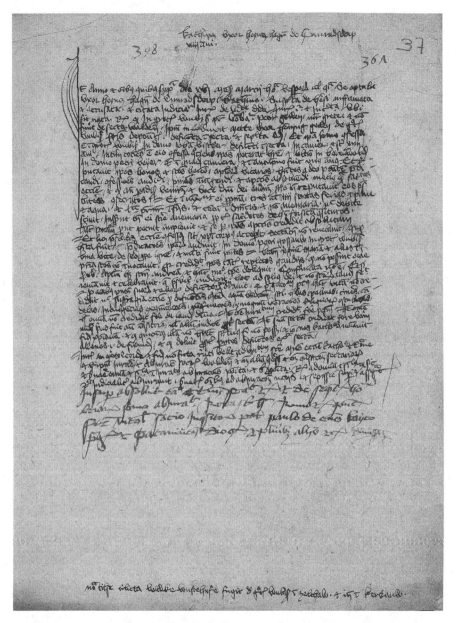

Figure 1. Petrus Zwicker wrote some of the protocols himself. The protocol from Katharina Hagen's interrogation (16 March 1394) shows Zwicker's handwriting; the eschatocol is written by an anonymous notary. Herzog August Bibliotek Wolfenbüttel, MS Guelf. 348 Novi, fol. 37r.

Waldensians in Regensburg, Martinus writes from Prague as 'heretice praui-tatis Inquisitor etc.'.[140] Whoever the inquisitor was, the fragments show that the use of these question formulas was not confined to the inquisitions in Stettin and Austria.

The conversion of the Waldensian Brethren in 1391 marked a shift in German inquisitorial practice as well as in the descriptions of Waldensians. It is justifiable to claim that Petrus Zwicker and Martinus of Prague possessed a more detailed and in many ways less prejudiced view of Waldensianism than many of their predecessors. This is reflected in the minute descriptions of the Waldensians and in the complex question formulas that were compiled and put to use from the early 1390s onwards. In addition, these inquisitors were of the opinion that laypeople were capable of making their own judgments in doctrinal matters. Consequently, they were held responsible for their beliefs in addition to their actions and their relationship to the heresiarchs – a view that spread as the *Processus Petri* started to circulate. The new lists of questions did not completely replace earlier ones: in some fifteenth-century compilations the above-mentioned thirteenth-century French question list was transmitted together with the long question list of Zwicker and Martinus.[141] As in many other areas of medieval culture, the new material accumulated and coexisted with earlier knowledge.

The conviction that the souls and beliefs of the laity must be under scrutiny, not only their actions, also had more sinister implications. It had the potential to bring more people under suspicion of heresy, as we shall see in Chapter 4. Moreover, despite the accuracy of the inquisitor's knowledge, even the question lists of Zwicker and Martinus did violence to the Waldensian followers' beliefs. This will be discussed in Chapter 5. Before that, however, it is necessary to explicate the difference between the earlier inquisitor's manuals and the *Processus Petri* compilations.

The remains of Zwicker's manual in Austria

Medieval titles such as *Processus domini petri de ordine Celestinorum Inquisitoris hereticorum* (*Procedures of Lord Peter of the Order of Celestines Inquisitor of Heretics*)[142] or *Processus inquisicionis ad hereticos* (*Inquisition Procedures for*

---

[140] ÖNB MS 3748, fols. 149v–150r. The letter is a later copy attached to the rest of the trial documentation. The episcopal officials of Regensburg describe Martinus as 'a sede apostolica deputati'. As this is the only occasion when his papal commission is mentioned, it might be an assumption by Regensburg's officials. Alternatively, Martinus really was a papal inquisitor in Prague for a while.

[141] Prague, KMK MS D LI, fols. 135r–v, 138v–139v; ibid., MS K IX, fols. 91r–92r, 93r–94v; Berlin, Staatsbibliothek, MS Theol. lat. fol. 704, pp. 20a, 25a–28a.

[142] Seitenstetten, MS 188, fol. 1r.

Heretics)[143] imply that a reader would find guidelines for the judicial process of inquisition of heresy.[144] In a narrow sense that is true for the manuscripts in question. The texts discussed above give basic instructions on how to interrogate Waldensian heretics, what oaths are required and how to give absolution, not forgetting the stricter punishments of imprisonment and being handed over to the secular arm. Yet they cover only a small part of the work required of an inquisitor of heresy operating within the administrative and legal system of the late medieval Church. The brevity of the *Processus Petri* becomes evident when one compares it to the manual on which Petrus Zwicker himself was basing his operations. This calls for an examination of the purpose of the *Processus Petri* compilations. As we shall see, they emerged because of the need for basic information on heresy and inquiring into it for parish priests supervising the penance of converts and other ecclesiastical officials operating in dioceses where heresy was suspected and suppressed.

There are two manuals combining French and Italian legal and procedural treatises on the *officium inquisitionis* (office of inquisition) that are extant in fourteenth-century copies of Bohemian and German provenance,[145] one in Linz and another now in the Vatican Library. The Vatican manuscript is a copy of the earlier Linz codex, and Patschovsky has described in detail the contents and relationship of the two manuscripts[146] – I have provided a concise description of the Linz manuscript in Appendix 1. Biller and Patschovsky followed A. Dondaine's classic study on the manuals of inquisitors when they recognized the central text of the collection as 'a French manual' from the thirteenth century,[147] though the form in which it appears in the German manuscripts is a later Italian version of the manual, dating to the turn of the fourteenth century.[148]

---

[143] Seitenstetten, MS 252, fol. 168va.

[144] On the development of the inquisitorial process and its application, particularly for the prosecution of heretics, as well as its abuses, see Trusen, 'Der Inquisitionsprozess'; W. Trusen, 'Von den Anfängen des Inquisitionsprozesses zum Verfahren bei der inquisitio haereticae pravitatis', in *Die Anfänge der Inquisition im Mittelalter*, ed. P. Segl (Cologne, 1993), pp. 39–76; Kelly, 'Inquisition and the Prosecution of Heresy'; Kelly, 'Inquisitorial Due Process'; Kelly, 'Inquisitorial Deviations and Cover-Ups'.

[145] In addition, there is the fourteenth-century Bohemian manual of the inquisitor of HAB MS 311 Helmst, ed. in Patschovsky, *Anfänge*, pp. 95–231. It includes some of the same material, but as a whole it is distinct from the two manuals discussed here.

[146] *Quellen*, ed. Patschovsky, pp. 130–54.

[147] Biller, 'Aspects', p. 368; *Quellen*, ed. Patschovsky, p. 139; A. Dondaine, 'Le Manuel de L'Inquisiteur (1230–1330)', in *Les hérésies et l'Inquisition, XIIe–XIIIe siècles: documents et études*, ed. Y. Dossat. Originally published in *Archivum Fratrum Praedicatorum* 17 (1947) (Aldershot, 1990), pp. 85–194 (pp. 106–7, 141–6).

[148] On the adaptation of the French manual in Italy, T. Scharff, 'Schrift zur Kontrolle – Kontrolle der Schrift. Italienische und französische Inquisitoren-Handbücher des 13. und frühen 14. Jahrhunderts', *DA* 52 (1996), 547–84 (pp. 554–5, 583–4); R. Parmeggiani, 'Un secolo di manualistica inquisitoriale (1230–1330): intertestualità

Linz, OÖLB MS 177 was once part of the library of the Benedictine monastery Garsten, Zwicker's base of operations in Upper Austria. Besides the Franco-Italian manuals, formularies and legal consultations, the Linz manuscript also includes material from Bohemian inquisitions: a question list probably compiled by Gallus of Jindřichův Hradec, a Bohemian inquisitor of heresy in the first half of the fourteenth century,[149] and two legal consultations on the case against the goldsmith Heynuš Lugner in late 1330s or early 1340s,[150] as well as a fragment of a German confession addressed to a Dominican inquisitor in the diocese of Prague, Swatibor of Langendorf.[151] Patschovsky has dated the manuscript to the first half of the fourteenth century, and established that it once belonged to Johannes Paduanus (d. 1358), one of the leading officials in the diocesan curias of Olomouc and Prague. Patschovsky likewise proposes that it ended up in Garsten through the agency of Petrus Zwicker, who would have acquired it from the library of the Bohemian inquisitors.[152]

The provenance is a strong enough indication that this manual was once in Zwicker's possession, but comparing the sentences Zwicker issued to the model of this manual leaves this beyond doubt. In a sentence declared in Ödenburg (Sopron) in 1401, Zwicker orders the houses of the heretics to be destroyed,[153] and repeats almost verbatim the wording of a thirteenth-century Italian formulary transmitted in the Linz codex.[154] The similarity, especially in declaring that the former lair of heretics should became a rubbish heap

---

e circolazione del diritto', *Rivista Internazionale di Diritto Comune* 13 (2002), 229–70 (pp. 234, 237–7).

[149] Linz, OÖLB MS 177, fols. 76v–77r. The question list has been edited in Patschovsky, *Anfänge*, pp. 104–5; see also *Quellen*, ed. Patschovsky, p. 146.

[150] Linz, OÖLB MS 177, fols. 100r–108r. The text in *Quellen*, ed. Patschovsky, pp. 256–312.

[151] Linz, OÖLB MS 177, fol. 57r; *Quellen*, ed. Patschovsky, pp. 313–17.

[152] *Quellen*, ed. Patschovsky, pp. 93–4. Patschovsky does not explain this. It is doubtful if such a physical library existed, although there is a solid tradition of inquisition in Bohemia. M. Tönsing, 'Contra hereticam pravitatem. Zu den Luccheser Ketzererlassen Karls IV. (1369)', in *Studia Luxemburgensia. Festschrift für Heinz Stoob zum 70. Geburtstag*, ed. F. B. Fahlbusch and P. Johanek (Warendorf, 1989), pp. 285–311 (p. 287) also refers to the existence of the library, based on Patschovsky, but Tönsing's note refers to Patschovsky, *Anfänge*, p. 116 (manifesto of Inquisitor Colda), where there is no mention of the library.

[153] On the implications of this sentence, especially its rhetoric of filth, see R. Välimäki, 'Imagery of Disease, Poison and Healing in the Late Fourteenth-Century Polemics against Waldensian Heresy', in *Infirmity in Antiquity and the Middle Ages: Social and Cultural Approaches to Health, Weakness and Care*, ed. C. Krötzl, K. Mustakallio and J. Kuuliala (Burlington, 2015), pp. 137–52 (pp. 142–4).

[154] The formulary has been edited in M. d'Alatri, 'L'inquisizione francescana nell'Italia centrale nel secolo xiii (finis)', *Collectanea Franciscana* 23 (1953), 51–169. I have used the reprint, M. d'Alatri, *L'inquisizione francescana nell'Italia centrale del Duecento* (Rome, 1996), pp. 171–206, destruction of the heretics' houses at p. 181.

(*receptaculum sordium*), shows that Zwicker's source was not any legislation ordering the destruction of heretics' houses, but the particular formula in the Linz manual.[155]

The extensive formularies and legal consultations of the manual, although the basis of Zwicker's practice of inquisition, were not transmitted further in the *Processus Petri* manuscripts, with one exception. St Florian, MS XI 234 includes material copied from the Linz manual in the same fascicule manuscript as the *Processus Petri*, also including the *Cum dormirent homines*. The manuscript was not known to the nineteenth-century scholars who edited parts of Zwicker's sentences and formularies, and consequently it has received relatively little comment in scholarship in spite of its extremely interesting and extraordinary content. Both Biller and Patschovsky have pointed out that it includes unedited and unique sections.[156] This unique part is a formulary pertaining specifically to the inquisition by Petrus Zwicker, Martinus of Prague and Zwicker's commissary Fridericus of Garsten in the diocese of Passau from 1395 onwards.

A collation of the two manuscripts is presented in Appendix 4. It shows that several parts of the older manual were copied after the compilation consisting of Zwicker's *Cum dormirent homines* and the 1390s descriptions of Waldensians and formularies regarding inquisition against them. The duplication of the texts from the Linz manual was done selectively, and I will return to this later. First we should take a look at the formularies for inquisition in Upper Austria after 1395.

The first formulary includes a sentence and an absolution by a bishop, a sentence of perpetual imprisonment and the relinquishment of the convicted to the secular arm.[157] It is purely a model, without reference to any particular persons or dioceses. As such the formulary is transmitted in Bohemian, Silesian and eastern German compilations on heresy, together with some parts of the *Processus Petri* but without Zwicker's treatises or references to

---

[155] Linz, OÖLB MS 177, fol. 38v: 'vt dicta domus nunquam reedifficanda in post[e]rum, funditus diruatur, et iuxta statutum apostolicum ibi sit perpetuo receptaculum sordium vbi fuit aliquando latibulum hereticorum' (so that the said house should never thenceforth be rebuilt, should be demolished from its foundations; and in accordance with papal statute there should be there a rubbish-heap where there was once a heretics' lair). Cf. Würzburg, UB MS M. ch. f. 51, fol. 24v: 'Et ubi cristi fidelium communitati magnum ex hac incomodum prouenerit funditus diruantur et in posterum nullatenus reedificerentur, ut ibi sit perpetuo receptaclium [sic] sordium ubi prius fuit aliquando latibulum hereticorum' (And where considerable inconvenience for the Christian community will have arisen from this, the [houses] should be demolished from their foundations and in no way thereafter be rebuilt; and that there should be a rubbish heap for ever – there where earlier there was for a while a heretics' lair).

[156] Biller, 'Aspects', pp. 354–5; *Quellen*, ed. Patschovsky, p. 92, n. 304.

[157] St Florian, MS XI 234, fol. 87ra–vb.

him,[158] and also without the material pertaining to inquisitions in Austria. The reason for this becomes evident when one compares the formulary and the Austrian sentences: the latter are based on the model of the former, and indeed comprise a new replacement formulary, updated with the examples from Austrian inquisitions.[159]

The second formulary is practically unknown to scholarship, and it is partially based on the mandate letters received and issued by Petrus Zwicker in Upper Austria in the mid-1390s. The first of these is the *Forma instituendi seu faciendi inquisitoris* (*Form for Instituting or Making an Inquisitor*), an episcopal mandate for the inquisition of heresy in the diocese, including an obligation on both spiritual and secular authorities to support the inquisitor.[160] It is issued by a canon and official of the diocese of Passau (his name is unfortunately not preserved) for both Petrus Zwicker and Martinus of Prague. Like most of the texts in the St Florian manual, the formula bristles with difficulties and outright scribal mistakes.[161] The inclusion of Martinus's name in the mandate is intriguing and puzzling, because he does not appear in any record of a sentence issued in the diocese of Passau. This is the only reference to his and Zwicker's co-operation there. The two following formulas, titled *Substitucio cooperari in absencia* (*Substitution to Operate during Absence*) and *Alia commissio* (*Other Commission*),[162] were both issued by Zwicker to delegate the powers of the inquisitor to his commissary Fridericus, a monk in Garsten and parish priest of Steyr. From the sentences issued in Steyr in 1398 it is known that Fridericus of Garsten was Zwicker's commissary,[163] but the mandates have been transmitted only in this manuscript. They are certainly from Zwicker's pen, replicating the rhetoric of his *Cum dormirent homines* when describing the threat of heresy in the diocese: 'especially as the people were sound asleep and the enemy would sow the most troubling tares amidst the

---

[158] In addition to the manuscripts listed at p. 120, n. 67 above, see Prague, KMK MS K IX, fols 88v–96r.

[159] See below.

[160] St Florian, MS XI 234, fol. 88ra–va.

[161] Ibid., fol 88ra: 'religioso viro fratri petro priori fratrum celestinorum I[n] Oywin ac Monasteriorum eiusdem ordinis per Alamaniam prouinciali, ac domino Martino rectori parochialis ecclesie Inpmetricem [?] pragensis diocesis'. Because of these difficulties, the translations of the St Florian MS given here and below should be regarded like the provisional maps drawn by early explorers: 'To the religious man Brother Petrus, Prior of the Celestine Brethren of Oybin and Provincial of the monasteries of the same Order for Germany, and to lord Martinus, rector of the parish church of ? in the diocese of Prague'. The name of the parish is corrupted. The wording implicates that Martinus was not yet altar priest of the Church of Our Lady before Týn ('altarista in ecclesia beate Marie Virginis ante Letam Curiam, Maioris civitatis Pragensis'), as he is described from 1399 onwards, see Neumann, *České sekty ve století 14. a 15*, pp. 6*–7*.

[162] St Florian, MS XI 234, fol. 88va–vb.

[163] See below.

wheat'.[164] These are followed by shorter formulas for citation of the suspects and penitents, for excommunication, aggravation of the penance, canonical purgation and different forms of absolution.[165] The short question list is placed after this formulary, followed by the *Cum dormirent homines*.

The material copied from the Linz manual is a very particular set of texts. Several of them are *consilia*, legal consultations given by experts in canon and civil law, sometimes popes, cardinals and papal legates, on questions that inquisitors faced in their proceedings. Their formation and compilation was part of the body of legislation and guidelines that progressively grew to regulate *inquisitio heretice pravitatis* from the 1230s onwards.[166] Many of the questions the consultations address are very specific, such as in the *consilia* of Forteguerra on whether the sons and grandsons of convicted heretics, who according to imperial law are deprived of all public offices and honours, could be automatically restored to these without specific dispensation after their (grand-) parents had completed their penance (the answer is no).[167] The *consilia* copied into the St Florian manual are early fourteenth-century Italian and French consultations, with the exception of two Bohemian consultations on the case of the goldsmith Heynuš Lugner of Brno, which Patschovsky has dated to between 1335 and 1343, and which are preserved only in these two manuscripts.[168] Other texts are also legal in nature, including definitions of concepts in canon law and excerpts from Guido de Baisio's treatise on the *Liber sextus*. Moreover, the two short inquisitors' manuals list the powers and privileges of inquisitors based on papal and imperial legislation. In particular the *De auctoritate et forma officii inquisitionis* (*On the Authority and Form of the Office of Inquisition*), written in Lombardy in the late thirteenth century, belongs to a group of manuals that attempted to organize and present in practical form the confusing number of different laws, degrees and privileges issued by different popes.[169] All in all the material originating from the Linz manuals consists of specialized professional texts covering the legal basis of inquisitions against heretics.

These legal consultations and the far more extensive formulary of citations, excommunications and absolutions set the manual of St Florian apart from

---

[164] St Florian, MS XI 234, fol. 88va: 'maxime cum dormiant homines et inimicus homo zizaniam grauissimam in medio tritici seminauerit'. Cf. Zwicker, *Cum dormirent homines*, p. 277H.

[165] St Florian, MS XI 234, fols. 88vb–93ra.

[166] Recently two studies and editions have considerably improved the state of our knowledge of the dating, circulation, effect and edition history of the thirteenth- and early fourteenth-century *consilia*: Parmeggiani, *Consilia*; Bivolarov, *Inquisitoren-Handbücher*. See also R. Parmeggiani, 'Formazione ed evoluzione della procedura inquisitoriale: i consilia', *BSSV* 200 (2007), 45–69.

[167] Linz, OÖLB MS 177, fol. 85r. Cf. edition in Parmeggiani, *Consilia*, p. 174.

[168] *Quellen*, ed. Patschovsky, pp. 256–8.

[169] Parmeggiani, *Explicatio*, p. lix; Sackville, 'The Inquisitor's Manual at Work', p. 213.

the other *Processus Petri* manuscripts. In fact, it is the only manuscript with Zwicker's formularies and question lists that contains a full working manual for an inquisitor. Therefore, if one wants to study the process of inquisition practised by Zwicker, the complete *Processus Petri Inquisitoris*, the manuals of St Florian, MS XI 234 and Linz, OÖLB MS 177 must serve as a starting point. Moreover, it is not only the content that makes the manual of St Florian such a practical text. There are also small remarks, written amongst the formulas, which are clearly meant to guide a notary or commissary in their duties. Between the formulas for sentencing heretics to perpetual imprisonment and relinquishment to the secular arm there is a notice: 'Note, from one sentence something can be taken to another, if it fits the deed.'[170] This probably means that the wording of one formula could be used for other sentences also, as long as it did not disturb the facts.

How did the St Florian manual come to be, and how did it arrive at this Augustinian house? Unlike the heavily annotated and glossed Linz manual, which had passed through the hands of several inquisitors and diocesan officials,[171] MS XI 234 is a copy for a monastic library, produced at St Florian itself.[172] The whole inquisitor's manual has been written by one scribe, who unfortunately was not very careful. From the *Cum dormirent homines*, sometimes shorter and sometimes longer passages are missing. A different hand belonging to a corrector, who obviously had access to the source manuscript, has tried to fill some gaps, but only in Zwicker's treatise and oath formulas.[173] Patschovsky has argued that the Linz manual was the model for those texts in the St Florian manual that are also included in the earlier manuscript.[174] It was, however, not the direct model. There was probably at least one intermediate manuscript combining material from Zwicker's commission and the Linz manual, from which the St Florian manual was copied. First of all, as the collation in Appendix 4 demonstrates, the material from the older manual was copied very eclectically. The treatises are not in their original order, and only very particular texts, namely legal consultations and definitions of canon law, were selected. Hence the selection was made by someone who knew what he was doing, unlike the scribe who produced the St Florian manual, who appears to have copied only

---

[170] St Florian, MS XI 234, fol. 87va: 'Nota, de vna sententia capere potes aliquid ad aliam, si facto congruit'. See also fol. 88va: 'Commissio domini episcopi scribatur in prima persona [or *pagina*]' (The commission of the lord Bishop should be written in the first person [*or* on the first page]).

[171] Unfortunately, none of the glossator or commentator hands in the Linz manual can be identified as Zwicker's handwriting with any certainty.

[172] See Appendix 1. On the physical differences between functioning handbooks and grand manuals that were used more as an archival resource than a practical manual to be carried around, see Sackville, 'The Inquisitor's Manual at Work', pp. 206–7.

[173] St Florian, MS XI 234, esp. fols. 93r, 96v and 96r, where an omission is only marked by a sign in the margin, but not corrected.

[174] *Quellen*, ed. Patschovsky, pp. 91–2, n. 304, p. 256.

mechanically and consequently made many omissions and mistakes. Moreover, the scribe combines into one textual unit texts that are separate in the Linz codex.[175] These combinations make sense from the user's point of view, but require careful reading and recompilation of the source text, and do not appear to have been the work of the rather careless scribe of MS XI 234.

My suggestion, therefore, is that the scribe was not directly copying from the older manual itself but instead working with an exemplar that already had a selection of texts from the Linz inquisitor's manual. This lost manuscript already included the *Processus Petri* and the *Cum dormirent homines*. There was a clear need for such a manual in Upper Austria around 1395, after Zwicker had instituted a local organization for an inquisition in the diocese of Passau with his own commissary. Not only Zwicker but his commissary Fridericus of Garsten and his notary Stephanus Lamp would have required guidelines about both the Waldensians and the legal basis of the inquisition of heresy, not to forget the particular privileges and commissions for the diocese of Passau. It is probably one of these three men who after 1395 compiled the manual whose later copy is St Florian, MS XI 234. They had not only the motivation but also access to all the required texts.

The question as to how this manual ended up in the library of St Florian still remains. Medieval texts, especially highly specialized texts like the inquisitor's manual, were not readily available for any willing copyist. In a manuscript culture that was characterized by the scarcity of available source texts, the transmission of texts and the creation of new ones required material mediations, the movement of the manuscript exemplars, which are often, according to Michael Van Dussen, localizable.[176] One can indeed find a particular moment and setting for the transmission of this collection of texts. The manual most likely arrived at St Florian when Zwicker was directing the inquisition of heresy in the nearby town of Enns, probably in 1396. We know of his presence from the sentencing of Jans von Pewg, declared by Zwicker in January 1398.[177] In his second trial Jans von Pewg admitted that he had been examined 'one and half years before' in Enns, and the wording of the sentence ('you came to us') implies that it was Zwicker himself who interrogated and absolved him.[178] Even if one must be extremely careful in trusting the dates

---

[175] *Interpretatio inquisitorum et prelatorum* (*The Interpretation of Inquisitors and Prelates*) is copied as if it were the last chapter of the Consultation of Forteguerra, St Florian, MS XI 234, fols. 132vb–133va, cf. Linz, OÖLB MS 177, fols. 84r–86r.

[176] Van Dussen, *From England to Bohemia*, p. 22; see also R. Hanna, *Pursuing History: Middle English Manuscripts and Their Texts* (Stanford, 1996), p. 5 and passim.

[177] For discussion on the dating, see below.

[178] St Paul im Lavanttal, MS 77/4, fol. 330va: 'recognouisti quod ante alterum dimidium annum ex nostro mandato per plebanum tuum vocatus ad nostrum veneris examen ad Anasium' (You admitted that when summoned by your parish priest, on our command, a year and a half ago, you came to our examination at Enns). *Ante alterum dimidium annum* is not easy to interpret, but according to the

presented in the documents of inquisition, let alone in copies of them, the sentence indicates that Zwicker was in Enns at some point in the year 1396. The nearby Augustinian house of St Florian would have been a convenient choice of residence.[179]

This would be a frail chain of deduction, were there not also another textual trace of Petrus Zwicker in St Florian. In MS XI 96 there is a short *Pater noster* treatise, where different clauses of the prayer are presented in a table collated with corresponding vices and virtues.[180] This method of explaining the *Pater noster* draws on patristic exegetics and acquired various forms of presentation in the Middle Ages,[181] and the text would be of little interest for the present study, if not for its title: 'Dicta magistri petri Inquisitoris'. Considering the possible time frame and geographical location, the only imaginable 'Petrus Inquisitor' is Petrus Zwicker. This is the only surviving copy of the work, in fact the only known text by Petrus Zwicker not treating heresy. Its presence in a manuscript without any other works of Zwicker or any other traces of the origin of this short treatise indicates that it somehow came from the local tradition of St Florian. The combination of the presence of Zwicker's unique manual in MS XI 234 and Zwicker's conducting of inquisitions in the vicinity justifies proposing that he visited St Florian in the year 1396. It is even possible that during his sojourn he taught at St Florian, and it is interesting that his theological teachings were passed on under the authorship of 'Petrus Inquisitor'. This is also the moment of transmission for his inquisitor's manual to St Florian, where the copies that have come to us were produced. This dating, *c.* 1396, for the arrival of these texts at St Florian fits with the contents of the inquisitor's manual: for it does not yet include the formulary based on the sentences from 1397–8, circulating in several Austrian and southern German manuscripts.[182]

Different sections of this manual are discussed further in the following chapters. Here there are three conclusions. First and most important, the manual of St Florian is a physical manifestation of the reforms in the inquisition against Waldensians initiated in the last years of the fourteenth century and promoted above all by Petrus Zwicker and Martinus of Prague, as discussed in the previous chapter. This becomes evident when one looks at

---

medieval Latin glossary of du Cange it means *alter dimidiu*, 'one and a half', a use that is recorded in late medieval Germany.

[179] The connection between the inquisition in Enns and the existence of Zwicker's texts at St Florian has been pointed out, but without exploring any further implications, by Modestin, 'The Anti-Waldensian Treatise', p. 223.

[180] St Florian, MS XI 96, fols. 298r–299r. The existence of this work was first recognized by Biller, *Waldenses*, p. 274; and recently Smelyansky, 'Self-Styled Inquisitors', pp. 168–76. See also Chapter 2 above.

[181] A. Lewis, 'Textual Borrowings, Theological Mobility, and the Lollard Pater Noster Commentary', *Philological Quarterly* 88 (2009), 1–23.

[182] Group D in Appendix 3.

what was left out and what was added. All descriptions of Waldensians and their doctrine, as well as the question lists for their interrogation, are texts composed at the beginning of the 1390s in Zwicker's and Martinus's circle. Linz, OÖLB MS 177 included several formulas, some of them intended for Waldensians.[183] None of them is copied into the manual of St Florian, neither did they have any significant influence on the two question lists used by Zwicker and Martinus. While the Linz manual, like most inquisitors' manuals, is a general manual offering guidelines against various heresies, the St Florian manual is specifically designed for action against the Waldensians. Therefore all descriptions of heresy and theological treatises in the Linz manual – which are relatively rare, it being largely a legal-practical manual – are similarly omitted. Instead, the *Cum dormirent homines* provides the necessary information about the nature of Waldensian doctrine and how to refute it.

The formularies for sentences, commission, citations and absolutions are partly based on earlier models, but it appears that only those applicable to the episcopal inquisition in the diocese of Passau are included here. The only texts received as such are legal consultations and commentaries as well as manuals treating the privileges of inquisitors. While these, based mainly on the French and Italian thirteenth- and early fourteenth-century legislation regulating papal inquisitors, were not completely valid for episcopal inquisitors in the 1390s, the general principles were nevertheless the same and one can easily understand why they were still used. The medieval canon law on heresy did not significantly change after the early fourteenth century,[184] and until the late fourteenth century the secular laws against heresy in the Empire were essentially based on the 1230s legislation of Frederick II.[185] The manual of St Florian reveals, in a sense, the essence of Petrus Zwicker's – and, as far as we can tell, Martinus of Prague's – inquisitorial practice: it amalgamated more than a century of canon-legal sources from specialized judges of heresy into an extremely pastorally and theologically oriented view of heretics, their interrogation, conversion and penance.

Secondly, the manuals link Petrus Zwicker to the Bohemian tradition of inquisitors of heresy. Although unlike his fourteenth-century Bohemian

---

[183] Linz, OÖLB MS 177, fols. 83r–84r, 86r–v (against Waldensians); 4r–5r, 6r–7r, 76v–77v (other question formulas).

[184] L. Paolini, *Il 'De officio inquisitionis': la procedura inquisitoriale a Bologna e a Ferrara nel Trecento* (Bologna, 1976), p. xxxiii; Bruschi, 'Familia inquisitionis'.

[185] Frederick's decrees against heresy in the Empire and in Sicily were repeated, for example, in the *Majestas Carolina* (1355) of Charles IV; Tönsing, 'Contra hereticam pravitatem', pp. 288, 303, 306–7; Ragg, *Ketzer und Recht*, p. 159. It is nevertheless notable that among the *Processus Petri* manuscripts there are no traces of more recent papal or imperial privileges for inquisitors, issued above all in the 1350s and 1360s. These are discussed in Tönsing's article. The reason for their absence is most likely that they were intended for individual inquisitors and bishops, and were neither valid nor available for the later inquisitors.

predecessors in that he was not a Dominican and had no papal mandate, Zwicker nonetheless inherited their canon-legal and practical-technical legacy. We have to remember that this link to Prague was not merely intellectual and textual: in his first major commission as inquisitor in Stettin Zwicker was authorized by Archbishop Jan of Jenštejn of Prague and the Pomeranian bishop of Cammin. The bishop was Johannes Brunonis, who in practice never went to his diocese but stayed in Prague as the Chancellor of King Wenceslaus.[186] Moreover, dispatching an inquisitor to combat the Waldensians was consistent with the anti-heretical policy of Jan of Jenštejn, who already in 1381 had ordered bishops to nominate inquisitors against Waldensians and who held Waldensian heretics in custody in 1384.[187] Pomerania and Austria were not the only territories outside the official control of the metropolitan see where Prague sent inquisitors of heresy. In 1390s Bohemian Dominican inquisitors operated in Silesia, which against the wishes of Emperor Charles IV and the archbishops of Prague had remained a part of the Polish diocesan structure. Alexander Patschovsky sees the Silesian inquisition as an instrument of control that was not possible for Prague at the level of conventional Church hierarchy.[188] Although Zwicker and his inquisitions were not straightforward political tools of the Bohemian Church and Crown, it is nevertheless important to realize that at least in the first half of 1390s Zwicker was an inquisitor from the archdiocese of Prague, commissioned by the archbishop and by the royal chancellor, equipped with the Bohemian inquisitor's manual and often accompanied by the secular cleric Martinus of Prague. This is important to keep in mind as a counterargument to the romanticizing interpretations of wandering inquisitors hunting Waldensians out of their own conviction and seeking authorization from local bishops.[189]

Thirdly, the singularity of the St Florian manual in comparison to the other *Processus Petri* manuscripts demonstrates that the fifteenth-century copies of Zwicker's *processus* are not functional inquisitors' manuals in the same sense as the ones used by Zwicker, Martinus and other inquisitors. These are only very limited views of the late medieval *officium inquisitionis*, concentrating on describing Waldensian heresy and questions that should be posed to Waldensian heretics, supported by a short formulary of vernacular or Latin oaths and some model sentences from Zwicker's and Martinus's proceedings. In particular, the lack of formulas for citation undermines their usefulness

---

[186] See above, Chapter 1.

[187] Loserth, 'Codex Epistolaris', p. 368; *Concilia Pragensia*, ed. Höfler, pp. 26–7; *Quellen*, ed. Patschovsky, 319–23.

[188] Patschovsky, 'Über die politische Bedeutung', pp. 240–2; Patschovsky, 'Spuren böhmischer Ketzerverfolgung', p. 363 and passim.

[189] Kieckhefer, *Repression*, pp. 67–73; Cameron, *Waldenses*, pp. 139–40; Biller, *Waldenses*, p. 103; Modestin, *Ketzer in der Stadt*, p. 3; Modestin, 'Zwicker', p. 25; Smelyansky, 'Self-Styled Inquisitors'. This view has been criticized by Deane, 'Archiepiscopal Inquisitions', pp. 205–6. See also the discussion in Chapter 1.

for inquisition of heresy, as the citation, together with examination and sentencing, belongs to the essential functions of inquisition. The inquisitors' manuals usually address all these themes, albeit with different emphasis.[190] The preservation of a more extensive procedural compilation in St Florian, MS XI 234 demonstrates that such texts were available, at least locally in Austria. Correspondingly, the greater popularity of the less technical anthologies on Waldensianism indicates that this doctrinal and pastoral version of the *Processus Petri* satisfied the needs of the monastic libraries, chapter houses and individual clergymen who owned these compilations in the decades following Zwicker and Martinus's inquisition. If not intended for inquisitors, what was the purpose of these manuals and for whom were the final versions of the *Processus Petri* compiled?

The transformation of the inquisitor's manual

Amadeo Molnár, in his history of the medieval Waldensians, proposed that Zwicker made extracts of his sentences available to the religious orders so that they could be used later, either to control (the converts) or in later inquisitions of heresy.[191] Molnár is very close to the mark in describing the uses of the *Processus Petri*. I shall now elaborate this view: Zwicker's inquisitorial material, in the form it acquired in Austria in the late 1390s and again after 1403, was intended more as an aid in the supervision of penances in the aftermath of inquisitions than as a proper inquisitor's manual.

The examples presented above of the different text layers or stages in the *Processus Petri*, have demonstrated, if nothing else, that there was no single compilation, but several different occasions of compilation and accumulation. Only a minority of the manuscripts were produced for the use of the inquisitor or other officials. There was certainly a need for those practical manuals among the inquisitor's *familia*, including Zwicker's commissary Fridericus and his notary Stephanus Lamp, who would become an inquisitor himself two decades later.[192] The St Florian manual discussed above is most likely based on such a manual composed for the immediate requirements of the inquisitions in Upper Austria in the 1390s. Decades later, new instances of heresy facilitated collections of older texts, even if these did not exactly describe the same doctrinal errors. The *Processus Petri* and Zwicker's polemical treatises circulated with tracts against the Hussites, mirroring the opinion of many fifteenth-century authors, according to which the Bohemians

---

[190] Sackville, *Heresy and Heretics*, pp. 140–1.
[191] Molnár, *Die Waldenser*, p. 157.
[192] Segl, 'Die Waldenser in Österreich', pp. 173, 182. Stephanus Lamp is mentioned as inquisitor in 1418; OÖLA, Stiftsarchiv Gleink, 1418 V 19; and in 1419, OÖLA, Stiftsarchiv Garsten, 1419 III 8.

had revived the old heresy of the Waldensians.[193] One of the important manuscripts including the *Cum dormirent homines* together with the *Processus Petri* is Würzburg, University Library MS M. ch. f. 51. The manuscript was produced in Würzburg, and together with Zwicker's texts there are parts of Pseudo-David von Augsburg's thirteenth-century anti-heretical treatise *De inquisitione hereticorum*, a list of John Wyclif's errors and other shorter descriptions of heresy (such as Konrad Hager's sentence from the 1340s). The fascicule including thirteenth- and fourteenth-century texts on heresy is followed by documents recounting the events around the Niklashäuser Pilgrimage of 1476 in the diocese of Würzburg, and the heresy of its prophet Hans Behem. These texts on heresy were produced at roughly the same time in the late 1470s, although they belong to different codicological units.[194] It thus seems that the fascicule about earlier heresies was produced either for reference in the trials of Hans Behem, or to satisfy a more general need for knowledge about heresy kindled by these events.

However, there was a call for texts on the Waldensians reaching beyond the inquisitor's close associates but nevertheless generated by the *officium inquisitionis*. A passage in the *Processus Petri* itself demonstrates why different excerpts from Zwicker's inquisitorial procedure were circulating in Austria in the last years of the century. In the long sentence against three relapsed and one obstinate heretic, declared by Zwicker in early 1398, the widow of Chunrad Fewr, Els of Tanbach, revealed something highly intriguing. In the previous year she had been sentenced for Waldensian heresy by Zwicker's *commissarius* Fridericus, had abjured heresy and received public penance by wearing crosses. In January 1398 she was again in court, this time interrogated by Zwicker himself. The inquisitor deemed Els to be a relapsed heretic. Among the proofs of her relapse is an episode where Els admits that her parish priest had questioned her on matters of faith. The priest had asked whether she wanted to swear an oath, and whether she had fasted on the feast days of the saints. She opposed the priest on both questions. The reasons for her sudden change of attitude are a mystery, but here the most important detail is that the parish priest participated in supervising the penance of the condemned heretic, and did so displaying accurate knowledge of Waldensianism:

> In the same examination you admitted that when asked again by your parish priest, if you had fasted on the vigil of [the feast of] All Saints in the preceding year only in honour of God and not the saints, you indeed asked your priest if a master was more powerful than his servant, intending to hint with that why the saints should not be invoked.[195]

---

[193] Välimäki, 'Old Errors, New Sects'.

[194] On the Niklashausen pilgrimage and heresy, K. Arnold, *Niklashausen 1476* (Baden-Baden, 1980), esp. pp. 67–74.

[195] BSB MS Clm 15125, fol. 208ra: 'Item in eodem examine recognouisti quod iterum per plebanum tuum interrogata, si vigiliam omnium sanctorum anni immediate

The late medieval Waldensians often explained the participation in feasts of saints in this way, and it could be regarded as a theological justification of a custom they in principle condemned but in practice followed. But for a parish priest to know how to ask such a question he needed more elaborate information about Waldensians than the common assumption that heretics despised saints. The information was readily available in the texts originating from Zwicker's inquisitions. In his manifesto of 1395 Zwicker expounded, among other things, the Waldensian interpretation of saints' feasts: 'And even though they fast at the vigils of the Holy Virgin and other saints, celebrating their feasts, they do this only for appearances' sake so that they are not recognized, or only for the praise and glory of God and not the saints.'[196] That a local priest was able to inquire into the details of Waldensian beliefs demonstrates that Zwicker had succeeded in his propaganda and attempts to promote awareness about Waldensians and their errors.

It was precisely for duties like this that the clergy in Austria required Zwicker's question lists, as well as lists of Waldensian articles and treatises on their doctrine. However, it was more the professional inquisitions led by Zwicker and his commissaries that had created the need than the mere fact that Waldenses existed in Austria. The penances imposed by inquisitors needed to be supervised and the orthodoxy of the flock sustained. As the case of Els Fewr exemplifies, the task fell to the parish clergy,[197] who consequently needed at least rudimentary guidelines for the task. Most of the extant *Processus Petri* compilations are more suited to this more general market than to the more technical market of actual inquisitors.

The latest additions to the *Processus Petri* come from the mainly Austrian trials in the second half of the 1390s and the turn of the fifteenth century. These additions are formularies compiled from Zwicker's sentences, including several from the diocese of Passau, one sentence (against several persons) from the diocese of Salzburg and one from the Hungarian diocese of Győr.[198] These were added to the *Processus Petri* in two stages, c. 1398 and after 1403,

---

preteriti ieiunaueris in honore solius dei et non sanctorum, ymmo quod ipsum tuum plebanum interrogaueris utrum dominus esset potencior seruo suo volens innuere per hoc quod sancti non sunt invocandi.'

[196] Preger, *Beiträge*, p. 247: 'et ideo licet beate virginis et aliorum sanctorum vigilias ieiunent, festa celebrent, hoc tamen vel ad ostentacionem, ne notentur, vel ad solius dei et non sanctorum laudem faciunt et honorem.'

[197] On parish clergy's role in supervising penances, see also Lentes and Scharff, 'Schriftlichkeit und Disziplinierung', pp. 245–6.

[198] Excluded from the analysis here are the sentences in Trnava in 1400 and Buda in 1404, the former a separate fragment and the latter part of a lost manuscript 99 of the Moravian State Archives, which disappeared during the transfer to the City Archives. Judging by the description in Biller, 'Aspects', pp. 370–3, and excerpts edited in Neumann, *České sekty ve století 14. a 15.*, pp. 6*–7*, the lost manuscript may have been a further compilation based on the inquisitorial procedure of Zwicker and Martinus of Prague, and exceptional for its emphasis on Martinus's sentences.

marking the last revisions to the compilation in Zwicker's lifetime. All the sentences in the earlier formulary were declared in the diocese of Passau in early 1398, but they recount the interrogations of accused persons from 1395 onwards.[199] These are transmitted together and in the same order in five medieval manuscripts, and in a revised, anonymous form in two further copies.[200] According to my interpretation, this formulary is based on a single *sermo generalis* (general sermon), an occasion for sentencing the heretics to perform a public penance and for relinquishing the impenitent and relapsed heretics to the secular arm.[201] This took place at the end of January or the beginning of February 1398. After that the declarations were reworked by Zwicker or by someone close to him into a formulary for sentencing the heretics. In the following decades, in Austria and southern Germany this formulary was copied with the *Cum dormirent homines* and other parts of *Processus Petri* (it never existed independently).

The formulary includes the sentences listed below. The orthography of the names varies from manuscript to manuscript. To maintain consistency, I follow here the forms used by Herman Haupt in his partial edition of the sentences.[202]

1. A formula for sentencing a penitent heretic whose conversion is dubious to perpetual imprisonment. This is only a formula, without references to any specific inquisitor or accused. Part of the anonymous formulary (fa) that is described above.
2. Sentence of Jans von Pewg, from the parish of Garsten, in 1398. Sentenced by Petrus Zwicker to public penance by wearing a hat with an image of a perjuring peasant whose tongue is drawn out by a devil, in front of the congregation on seven Sundays or feast days.
3. The sentence of five Waldenses from the parishes of Garsten, Weistrach, St Michael and Unterwolfern[203] (Els, widow of Chunrad Fewr; Dietrich Wagner; Salmon de Swammarn; Geysel, widow of Ulric am Rabenpüchel; and Henricus zum Dörfflein) to public penance by wearing crosses.

The extant descriptions do not, unfortunately, provide enough detail to enable a proprer comparison to the *Processus Petri* manuscripts. See also Introduction, above.
[199] These have been edited, but not in full, in Haupt, 'Waldenserthum und Inquisition', pp. 404–8; and Döllinger, *Beiträge II*, pp. 346–51.
[200] See Appendix 3, Group D.
[201] For a description of the *sermo generalis*, based on the Dominican inquisitor Bernard Gui's *Practica*, see J. B. Given, *Inquisition and Medieval Society: Power, Discipline, and Resistance in Languedoc* (Ithaca, 2001), pp. 73–6.
[202] Haupt, 'Waldenserthum und Inquisition', pp. 404–8.
[203] All these places are in the vicinity of Steyr and Garsten. The medieval orthography is compared to modern place names by Segl, 'Die Waldenser in Österreich'; Nickson, 'The "Pseudo-Reinerius" Treatise', p. 278; G. Gartner, *Geschichte der Pfarre Weistrach* (Steyr, 1973), p. 61; P. Segl, *Ketzer in Österreich* (Paderborn, 1984), p. 176.

The sentence is not dated, but it is based on the abjurations received by Fridericus of Garsten in May 1397, see below.

4. Sentence of three Waldensians (Kunegundis, widow of Frideric in der Aw; Gundel am Holzapfelberg; and the same Els Fewr as in 3, above) as relapsed heretics and their release to the secular arm, and the sentence of Dyemuet, widow of Mathel zu Hausleithen as an obstinate and impenitent heretic in January 1398.

An important distinction should be made between the original depositions of inquisition, such as the 195 protocols preserved from the trials in Stettin, and the sentences listed above. The latter are not notarial documents prepared during the interrogations, but copies of the final sentences read out publicly by the inquisitor when the penance was imposed on the repentant heretics and when the obstinate and relapsed heretics were delivered to the secular arm for execution. There was, of course, notarial documentation of the processes in Upper Austria. According to established scholarship based on a rather vague notice by the famous sixteenth-century church historian Matthias Flacius Illyricus, these were deposited in the library of Garsten.[204] Whether or not Illyricus's remark truly referred to Zwicker's protocols, these have since been lost.

What we have are documents that had gone through several revisions from the depositions to the final sentences and that were further reworked when they were compiled to work as a model for later inquisitors or other interested members of the clergy. The formulary nature of the sentence is well demonstrated by the medieval manuscripts, where the sentences are given titles such as 'See the sentences of the heretics who are assigned to wear the crosses'.[205] In two late manuscripts the sentences from the diocese

---

[204] Illyricus, *Catalogus testium veritatis*, p. 509. Matthias Illyricus's statement in notably vague third-hand information, mentioning neither Garsten nor Zwicker by name: 'Stier. Est ciuitas in finibus Austriae ac Bauarie hoc nomine dicta. Audiui ex Michaele Stifelio, ibi in quodam monasterio esse tria satis magna uolumina examinationum, aut confessionum multorum hominum à Romana Ecclesia dissentientium, qui iam olim fortè amplius ante ducentos annos sunt ab inquisitoribus examinati' (Steyr. Called by this name is a city within the confines of Austria and Bavaria. I have heard from Michael Stiefel that there are – in some monastery there – three pretty large volumes of examinations or confessions of many men dissenting from the Roman Church, [who] were one upon a time examined by inquisitors – now perhaps more than 200 years ago). See also F. X. Pritz, *Geschichte der ehemaligen Benediktiner-Klöster Garsten und Gleink, im Lande ob der Enns, und der dazu gehörigen Pfarren* (Linz, 1841), p. 32; Friess, 'Patarener, Begharden und Waldenser', p. 244, n. 4; Kurze, 'Zur Ketzergeschichte', p. 70; Biller, 'Aspects', p. 136; *Quellen*, ed. Patschovsky, p. 90 (Patschovsky takes the testimony of Illyricus with a grain of salt); and Segl, 'Die Waldenser in Österreich', p. 166.

[205] 'Nota sententie de hereticis qui cruce signantur'; Würzburg, UB MS M. ch. f. 51, fol. 24r.

of Passau are even stripped of all particular information about the inquisitor, the convicted and places and times, even though retaining the specifics of the crime of heresy.[206] Thus the textual core of Zwicker's sentences, themselves based on earlier formulas, became in turn models for newer manuals. This is a typical process. Inquisitors' manuals often included examples from earlier processes transformed into formularies.[207] In fact, the transmission of Zwicker's Austrian and Hungarian sentences resembles to a great extent the haphazard survival of thirteenth- and fourteenth-century Italian acts of the inquisition, which according to Thomas Scharff have mainly survived in copies outside the inquisitorial archives that were made to meet the interests of various communes and individual notaries.[208]

Keeping this formulary nature of the copies in mind is essential when using these copies as sources for heresy and its repression. For example, the dating of the Austrian trials is based almost solely on the dates given in these sentences. There is a danger here, not always duly recognized. The dates, times and places were important for the inquisitor and his officials. The dates of earlier confessions and penances were meticulously written down, as they could be and were used as aggravating evidence in cases of suspected relapse into heresy. The purpose is evident in Zwicker's sentences. When Kunegundis, widow of Frideric in der Aw, was declared a relapsed heretic in 1398, Zwicker opened the declaration by stating that from his own certain knowledge Kunegundis had abjured the heresy before him in 1395, 'as [these things] are this way more evidently contained in our documents'.[209] Petrus Zwicker was limited to his own and sometimes to his predecessor Henricus of Olomouc's archives,[210] but in areas and cities where the inquisition of heresy

---

[206] See group F in Appendix 3.

[207] Dondaine, 'Le Manuel de L'Inquisiteur', pp. 105–12; Parmeggiani, *Explicatio*, pp. xlvii–l, liii; Sackville, 'The Inquisitor's Manual at Work', pp. 208–9. A good example is the thirteenth-century formulary, parts of which are copied in Linz, OÖLB MS 177 (see above). The formulary has been edited in d'Alatri, *L'inquisizione francescana*, pp. 171–206.

[208] T. Scharff, 'Erfassen und Erschrecken. Funktionen des Prozessschriftguts der kirchlichen Inquisition in Italien im 13. und frühen 14. Jahrhundert', in *Als die Welt in die Akten kam: Prozeßschriftgut im europäischen Mittelalter*, ed. S. Lepsius and T. Wetzstein (Frankfurt am Main, 2008), pp. 255–73 (p. 259). Scharff makes a clear distinction between archival sources and the transmission outside the inquisitors' archives, and according to him, the latter should hardly be described 'im eigentlich Sinn als "Inquisitionsakten"'.

[209] BSB MS Clm 15125, fols. 205vb–206ra: 'licet dudum anno domini M° ccc° lxxxxv [1395] ex certa nostra scientia sectam hereticorum waldensium cum omnibus punctis et articulis […] coram nobis et testibus sufficientibus et ydoneis publice abiuraueris […] sicut hoc modo in actis nostris euidentius continentur'.

[210] There are several references to the sentences issued by Henricus of Olomouc; BSB MS Clm 15125, fols. 205ra–rb; 206va (cf. edition in Haupt, 'Waldenserthum und Inquisition', p. 404);‒St Florian, MS XI 234, fol. 90vb; Würzburg, UB MS M. ch. f.

was organized and regular the use of the inquisitorial archives produced impressive results by any standards of data retrieval. A well-known case is the posthumous trial of Armanno Pungilupo in Ferrara. In 1301, inquisitor Guido da Vicenza was able to prove, using archives stretching back to 1254, that Armanno, who died in 1269, had been a heretic in his lifetime.[211]

According to canon law the requirement to produce documents faithful to the hearings was legally binding for the judges.[212] Obviously this did not apply to the later formularies and manuals reworked from the sentences. However meticulous the scribes were, the copying process was always susceptible to errors, and numerals were especially problematic.[213] The provenance of the extant copies with the sentences is so far removed from the judicial proceedings in and around Steyr that it is hard to imagine any other purpose beyond use as illustrative examples in the collection.[214] An extreme example can be found in a manuscript in Augsburg University Library. There, in most cases the names and dates are simply left out, but there are other changes as well. 'Dietrich Wagner' of the 'original' sentence is replaced with the generalizing description *faber* (craftsman) and 'Salmon de Swammarn' with *scissor* (cleaver or carver).[215] This transformation from a legal document to a formulary does not mean that we cannot say anything about the actual trials that took place or that we should regard these sentences simply as fifteenth-century literary constructions. It is surprising how much trouble the copyists went to in recounting every detail of the inquisitor's title and the names of the persons involved. Quite likely when the formulary was first compiled it

---

51, fol. 29r (cf. edition in Haupt, *Der Waldensische Ursprung des Codex Teplensis*, pp. 34–5).

[211] Scharff, 'Erfassen und Erschrecken', p. 271.

[212] S. Lepsius, 'Kontrolle von Amtsträger durch Schrift. Luccheser Notare und Richter im Syndikatsprozess', in *Als die Welt in die Akten kam: Prozeßschriftgut im europäischen Mittelalter*, ed. S. Lepsius and T. Wetzstein (Frankfurt am Main, 2008), pp. 389–467 (pp. 389–92).

[213] This was already acknowledged by medieval scholars. Hugh of St Victor remarked of the Apocrypha: 'We certainly recognize that in these books there are many errors with regard to numbers due to scribal mistakes': Hugh of St Victor, 'The Diligent Examiner', in *Interpretation of Scripture: Theory. A Selection of Works of Hugh, Andrew, Richard and Godfrey of St Victor, and of Robert Melun*, ed. F. T. Harkins and F. van Liere (Hyde Park, 2013), pp. 231–52 (p. 244).

[214] The three manuscript of the Bayerische Staatsbibliothek, MS Clm 5338, 15125 and 22373, come from the Bavarian religious houses Chiemsee (Augustinian Canons), Rebdorf (Augustinian Canons) and Windberg (Praemonstratensians) respectively, all manuscripts probably dating to the first half of the fifteenth century. Würzburg, UB MS M. ch. f. 51 is significantly later, from the 1470s, and probably composed in Würzburg. The only Austrian copy is from the library of the Secular Canons in Spital am Pyhrn (founded in 1414), some 70 km south of Steyr, nowadays St Paul im Lavanttal, MS 77/4.

[215] Augsburg, UB MS II. 1. 2° 129, fols 150v–151r. Cf. also Salzburg, St Peter MS b VIII 9, fols. 305rb–307va.

functioned also as a repository for the names and sentences of those involved. Local authorities, both civil and ecclesiastical, would also have needed such copies, insofar as they participated in supervising the penances.[216] Moreover, often the sentences were read aloud in the local churches during masses on the feast days following the actual *sermo generalis*.[217]

One result of the failure to fully appreciate the nature of the preserved sentences from Zwicker's inquisitions in Upper Austria as a formulary is that the chronology of the Austrian trials has not been properly worked out. Previous scholars have suggested various dates for Zwicker's activity in Austria. Problems have arisen when individual manuscripts and, worse still, individual sections from them have been quoted as documentation of the course of Zwicker's inquisitions, without consideration of their context. A telling example is the dating of Els Fewr's first appearance in court, at that time represented by Zwicker's commissary Fridericus, Benedictine monk from Garsten and parish priest of Steyr. According to Haupt's edition:

> Likewise we discovered in our inquisition, that you Els, widow of Chunrad Fewr in Tampach, from the parish of Garsten, although you then, in the year of our Lord 1391, 4 May, in front of Lord Fridericus, commissary in the above-mentioned way, judicially, legally and solemnly, under the punishment of the relapsed, abjured the sect of the Waldensian heretics with each and all items and articles.[218]

Haupt followed here his reading of the Munich manuscript Clm 5338, but gave two optional datings, 1390 and 1398.[219] However, from his preferred dating he drew the conclusion that Zwicker, through his commissary, was leading the trials in the diocese of Passau from 1391 onwards, and this interpretation has been accepted until recently.[220] The dating is, however, erroneous. In the manuscript quoted by Haupt, the date actually reads: 'licet

---

[216] Also in some northern Italian towns there were books of inquisitors' sentences copied for the use of the local community, Scharff, 'Erfassen und Erschrecken', pp. 259–60.

[217] On this practice, Scharff, 'Schrift zur Kontrolle', p. 564; Lentes and Scharff, 'Schriftlichkeit und Disziplinierung', p. 242.

[218] Haupt, 'Waldenserthum und Inquisition', p. 407: 'Item eadem nostra inquisicione comperimus, quod tu Els relicta Chunradi Fewr in Tampach plebis in Garsten, licet dudum anno domini 1391 die 4 mensis Maji coram domino Friderico modo predicto commissario sectam hereticorum Waldensium cum omnibus et singulis punctis et articulis iudicialiter et legitime sollempniterque sub pena relapsorum abiuraveris [...].'

[219] Ibid., p. 407, from the Würzburg, UB MS M. ch. f. 51 and BSB MS Clm 22373 respectively.

[220] Ibid., p. 370; Molnár, *Storia dei valdesi* (1), p. 107; Biller, *Waldenses*, p. 255; Segl, 'Die Waldenser in Österreich', p. 177; Modestin, *Ketzer in der Stadt*, p. 4; Modestin, 'Zwicker', p. 28; Modestin, 'The Anti-Waldensian Treatise', p. 217.

dudum Anno domini M° ccc° 97° die quarta Mensis May',[221] that is 4 May 1397. The dates offered by other manuscript exemplars are:

BSB MS Clm 15125, fol. 207vb: 'anno domini M° ccc° 97 die quarta Mensis Maÿ' [4 May 1397]
BSB MS Clm 22373, fol. 259va: 'Anno domini Millesimo ccc° lxxxxviii° die quarta Mensis Maÿ' [4 May 1398]
St Paul im Lavanttal, MS 77/4, fol. 333va: 'anno domini M° ccc° 97 die quarta Mensis May' [4 May 1397]
Würzburg, UB MS M. ch. f. 51, fol. 33r: 'licet dudum anno domini 1390 die iiii mensis May' [4 May 1390]

The last date, attested only in the Würzburg manuscript from the 1470s, is obviously wrong. It is very unlikely that Zwicker had the whole apparatus of *officium inquisitionis*, including a commissary, up and running in the diocese of Passau before the conversion of Waldensians in 1391, commonly agreed to be the starting point of the persecutions,[222] especially when this is supported only by a single, late manuscript. Therefore I have decided to dismiss this as a possibility. May 1398 is not possible, because Els was sentenced as a *relapsa* in January of that year. The chronology becomes clearer when one looks at this collection as a whole. It seems that all these sentences relate to the co-operation of Petrus Zwicker and the Castellan of Steyr, Heinrich von Zelking, in January 1398 in capturing and sentencing relapsed or resisting heretics. All the final sentences refer to this co-operation between the secular and spiritual authority. Zwicker explicitly stated that von Zelking was commissioned by the dukes of Austria, Wilhelm and Albrecht IV, to help in the inquisition of heresy, when the castellan brought Gundel am Holzapfelberg to his trial by the orders of the inquisitor on 18 January 1398.[223] Kunegundis in der Aw was also cited to the court, but she came voluntarily a few days earlier, on

---

[221] BSB MS Clm 5338, fol. 243r. The misinterpretation probably arose from the Arabic numeral '97', as the fifteenth-century '7' sometimes resembles the numeral '1'. However, here it is clearly '7', and the reading is reinforced when one compares it to the fifteenth century folio numbering, see e.g. fol. 237r.

[222] See above, pp. 116–17, n. 44.

[223] BSB MS Clm 15125, fol. 206vb: 'cum nuper Anno domini M° ccc° 98° die vero xviii° Mensis Ianuarii [18 January 1398] per nobilem et Strennuum [sic] virum dominum henricum de Czelking, Castellanum in Styra, nostrum inquisitorem [sic] officis cooperatorem fidelissimum ab illustris dominis et principibus ducibus austrie Wilhelmo et Alberto ad premissa deputatum, tamquam de relapsu suspectus captiuatus fueras et ex nostri personaliter constituti mandato ad examen perductus et coram notario publico et testibus ÿdoneis per nos interrogatus' (Whereas recently, AD 1398, on the 18th day of the month of January, you – as someone suspected of relapsing [into heresy] – had been taken prisoner by the noble and steadfast man Lord Henry of Zelking, Castellan of Steyr, most faithful collaborator with our inquisitors' office [and deputed] to the aforesaid things by the illustrious Lords, Princes [and] Dukes of Austria, Wilhelm and Albrecht, and at the command of us

14 January.[224] Els Fewr, on the other hand, had to be captured and brought to the court, on 24 January,[225] and although the castellan is not mentioned here, he was almost certainly responsible for it. Finally, there is the sentence of Jans von Pewg, where only the year 1398[226] is given, no day or month. He is sentenced to undergo his public penance in the church of St Giles in Steyr under the threat of punishment 'made by you in front of the noble and steadfast knight Heinrich von Zelking and in front of us, with a certain bond and guarantee of good and proper men'.[227] It therefore seems likely that Jans von Pewg's trial took place in early 1398, and it was probably declared on the same occasion as the rest of the accused were relinquished to the secular arm.

The procedure described above would fit with the standard course of a *sermo generalis*. The inquisitor would wait until there was a sufficient number of heretics meriting stricter sanctions, either public penance or capital punishment, and then organize a public occasion after consulting legal and religious experts on the punishments.[228] In the well-recorded practice of Bernard Gui the inquisitor proceeded from milder penances such

---

(personally constituted [in this matter]) you were brought to examination and were questioned by us in the presence of a notary public and suitable witnesses).

[224] BSB MS Clm 15125, fol. 206ra: 'Cum nuper Anno domini M° ccc° 98° die 14 Mensis Ianuarii [14 January 1398] per pllebanum [sic] tuum legittime citata coram nobis comparueris' (Whereas [...] lawfully cited by your parish priest you appeared before us).

[225] BSB MS Clm 15125, fol. 207vb: 'Cum nuper Anno domini M° ccc° 98 xxiiiiᵃ die mensis Ianuarii ex nostra ordinacione tamquam de relapsa suspecta captiuata fuisti et ad examen perducta et per nos interrogata' (Whereas [...] at our command you were taken prisoner as someone suspected of relapsing and were brought to examination and questioned by us).

[226] Segl, 'Die Waldenser in Österreich', p. 173, n. 56, dates the sentence to 1399 or 1400, but 1399 is only supported by the Würzburg manuscript. The rest of the manuscript tradition agrees with the year 1398, except BSB MS Clm 22373, fol. 256va: 'anno domini millesimo ccc° lxxxviii° [1388]', obviously due to an omission of the Roman numeral 'x'. The year 1388 is also attested in the fragment of the formulary in HAB MS Guelf 431 Helmst, fol. 5r.

[227] BSB MS Clm 15125, fol. 204vb: 'sub pena coram nobili et Strennue milite domino heinrico de Czelkingen et coram nobis per te facta, cum certa proborum bonorum fideiussoria caucione.'

[228] At least the sentences claim that such a consultation also took place in Steyr. See e.g. before the handing over to the secular arm, BSB MS Clm 15125, fol. 208rb–va: 'quod secundum iura canonica talibus in heresim in iudicio abiuratam relabentibus aut expresse in sua heretica prauitate perdurare volentibus, non est ulterius ei[s] gracia facienda, de multorum bonorum virorum in sacra Theologia ac in vtroque iure peritorum maturo consilio super eiuscemodi habito et obtento' (that, after receiving and obtaining mature counsel on this matter from many good men learned in sacred theology and in both laws, according to canon law grace should no longer be granted to them: to such as relapse into heresy after abjuring it in law or such that expressly wish to persist in their heretical wickedness). These formulary expressions have been left out in the editions of Haupt and Döllinger.

as pilgrimages to perpetual imprisonments and finally to relinquishment to the secular arm. In each case the *culpa*, a summary account of the person's involvement in heresy, was read aloud in the vernacular.[229] Recounting each person's involvement in heresy also explains why the undated sentence of penitential crosses on five Waldensians, absolved by Zwicker's commissary Fridericus of Garsten, is in the same compilation. It includes the abjuration and penance of crosses ordered to Els Fewr, and consequently it was probably read aloud as a background for her final sentence. This mentions her former abjuration of heresy only briefly, in contrast to rather long narratives for the other two relapsed heretics Kunegundis in der Aw and Gundel am Holzapfelberg. The precise date for the *sermo generalis* in Steyr unfortunately remains unknown, as the notarial confirmation of the date, place and witnesses belonging to the sentences proper has been lost in the revision of the documents into a formulary. The *terminus post quem* comes from the trial of Els Fewr on 24 January 1398, the latest date mentioned.

Zwicker's presence in the diocese of Passau, however, can be redated. He was obviously present in 1395 when he wrote his letter to the dukes and finished the *Cum dormirent homines*, and received the abjuration of Kunegundis in der Aw.[230] The probable dating of summer 1396 for Jans von Pewg's inquisition in Enns has already been discussed above with regard to the inquisitor's St Florian manual. From May to July 1397 Fridericus of Garsten, as Zwicker's commissary, was responsible for the inquisition in the diocese of Passau. He received the abjuration of Els Fewr in May and absolved Gundel am Holzapfelberg for the first time on 21 July.[231] Then in January 1398 it was again Petrus Zwicker, now supported by the Castellan of Steyr, who concluded matters. The only question is whether Zwicker was also present in January 1397, as 23 January of that year is the most common date given for the trial of Dyemuet zu Hausleithen,[232] who, alongside the three *relapsi*, was condemned as an obstinate and impenitent heretic in January 1398, having refused to swear an oath at her trial. As an obstinate heretic was first excommunicated for a year before the final sentence and execution,[233] the first interrogation could indeed have happened on the suggested date a year earlier, and the appearance of Dyemuet's name together with those of the *relapsi* would then mark her final and definitive sentence. Unfortunately, as

---

[229] Given, *Inquisition and Medieval Society*, pp. 73–4.

[230] BSB MS Clm 15125, fols. 205vb–206ra.

[231] Ibid., fol. 206va–vb.

[232] 23 January 1397 is proposed by BSB MS Clm 5338, fol. 242v and Clm 15125, fol. 207rb as well as St Paul im Lavanttal, MS 77/4, fol. 333rb. 13 January 1398 appears only in Würzburg, UB MS M. ch. f. 51, fols. 32v–33r. BSB MS Clm 22373, fol. 259ra has again a clearly corrupted date, 23 January 1388.

[233] *De auctoritate et forma inquisicionis*, Linz, OÖLB MS 177, fol. 79v; X 5.7.13, according to the canons of the Fourth Lateran Council; see also, Ragg, *Ketzer und Recht*, pp. 69–70.

her name suddenly disappears from the records and is not mentioned among those relinquished to the secular arm, no more can be said about the matter.[234] However, based on the formulary one can propose the following time frame for Zwicker's commission in Austria: he was the inquisitor of heresy for the diocese of Passau only from 1395 onwards, and his recorded activity there ended in January or February 1398.

It is not only the date of the first abjuration of Els Fewr that is very doubtful, but other supposed evidence of the trials of Austrian Waldenses prior to 1395. It has been assumed that the persecution was going on when a certain Johannes, the vicar of Wolfern (filial church of Garsten), was burned along with his servants in his home by the heretics. Based on the nineteenth-century edition by G. Friess from the two manuscripts from the library of Seitenstetten, the event has often been dated to 1393.[235] Biller corrected this among the footnotes of his unpublished dissertation, pointing out that one manuscript used by Friess has the year 1390 and another 1396.[236] I have consulted the manuscripts and agree with Biller. As in the case of Zwicker's sentences discussed above, 1390 seems implausible. Moreover, the later dating, 1396 and 1397, appears in another manuscript that has been overlooked in this discussion,[237] and a manuscript that only mentions vicar Johannes's burning dates it to Lent 1396.[238] Therefore I am inclined to accept

---

[234] However, Zwicker was in the area in the autumn of 1397, as demonstrated by a passage in the annals of the Benedictine monastery of Gleink, discovered by Peter Segl, according to which Zwicker formed a *Gebetsbrüderschaft* with Abbot Udalrich and his monastery on 13 August 1397. OÖLA, Stiftsarchiv Gleink MS Nr. 2, p. 78; Segl, 'Die Waldenser in Österreich', p. 183; Modestin, 'Zwicker', p. 30.

[235] Friess, 'Patarener, Begharden und Waldenser', p. 266; Friess misread the first year as 1343; cf. Haupt, 'Waldenserthum und Inquisition', pp. 372–3; Nickson, 'The "Pseudo-Reinerius" Treatise', p. 281; Segl, 'Die Waldenser in Österreich', pp. 165, 183–4 (at p. 184, n. 92 Segl points out the difficulty in dating but ends up following Haupt's interpretation); Utz Tremp, *Von der Häresie zur Hexerei*, p. 298; Modestin, 'Zwicker', p. 28.

[236] Biller, 'Aspects', p. 354, n. 10.

[237] HAB MS Guelf 431 Helmst, fol. 2va: 'Anno domini M. ccc. 96 combustus est dominus Johannes in bolfaren cum familia sua ab hereticis de nocte; Item Anno etc 97 heretici fuerunt captiuati sicud pro fugi combusserunt dotem in bolfaren volentes combussisse dominum Iacobum tunc temporis vicarium ibidem cum sua familia sed dei gratia premuniente euasit cum suis' (AD 1396 lord John, together with his household in Wolfern, was burned by heretics during the night. Item, AD [13]97 heretics, as fugitives, were taken prisoner. They burned the [Church's] donation in Wolfern, intending to have burned lord James, then the vicar there, with his household. But through the grace of God, forewarning him, he escaped with his people).

[238] BSB MS Clm 22373, fol. 224vb: 'Nota quod in anno ab incarnatione domini nostri iesu christi m° c°c°c° lxxxx°vi° [1396] tempore ieiunii in ebdomana ante letare feria tertia qua canitur; combusserunt domum domini plebani in Wolfaren et dominum iohannem vicarium ibidem cum tota familia sua et sic in igne perierunt cum rebus et aliorum etc.'

the later dates, that is 1396 for the arson against the vicar Johannes and 1397 for the attempt on his household. The Waldensian opposition in Wolfern thus corresponds with the period of persecution by Zwicker and his associates as presented in the formulary of sentences.

In the seventeenth-century chronicle of Valentin Prevenhuber, based on the Annals of Garsten, Zwicker's arrival in Austria is likewise dated to 1395 and the major persecutions to around 1397. Although a post-medieval chronicle, the wording of Prevenhuber indicates that he had worked with sources describing the inquisition of heresy around Steyr:

> The Annals of the monastery of Garsten report about this – that after Duke Albrecht of Austria called a Celestine monk called Brother Petrus into Austria in the year 1395, and wanted to entrust him with the office of inquisition in the bishopric of Passau, the result from this was that in the year 1397 through this sort of inquisition of heretical wickedness more than a thousand were summoned here to the town of Steyr. Quite a lot were sentenced to wear the symbol of the cross. Many persons however, both men and women, were then handed over to secular justice, some placed in prison for ever. On the order of the secular princes, however, between eighty and a hundred were burned by the citizens of Steyr, on a field or pasture in Früxenthal [Kraxenthal], now a beautiful meadow below Bucholz. For this reason that spot, in the same place, is called to this day 'The Heretic Cemetery'.[239]

Moreover, the contemporary continuation to the *Österreichische Chronik von den 95 Herrschaften* (*Austrian Chronicle of 95 Lordships*), describing the death of Duke Albrecht III (29 August 1395), praises the duke's efforts to uproot the Waldensian heresy, but also explains that the burning of more than a hundred heretics in Steyr happened 'afterwards' (*hernach*).[240] This part of the chronicle

---

[239] V. Preuenhueber, *Annales Styrenses: sammt dessen übrigen historisch- und genealogischen Schrifften, zur Erläuterung der österreich. steyermärckischen und steyerischen Geschichten* (Nuremberg, 1740), p. 72: 'Davon meldten die Annales des Closters Garsten: Daß, nachdem Anno 1395 Herzog Albrecht zu Oesterreich, einen Coelestiner Muenchen, Fr. Petrus genannt, in Oesterreich beruffen, un im Bissthum Passau das Officium Inquisicionis ihme anbefohlen worden, so senen hierauf Anno 1397, durch solche Inquisitionem hareticae pravitatis in der Stadt allhie zu Steyer mehr dem tausend Persohnen eingezogen, etliche das Zeichen des Creutzes zu tragen verurtheilet, viele aber, sowohl Manns= als Weibs=Persohnen, dem weltlichen Gerichte uebergeben, theils in ewige Gefaegnisse gelegt, achtzig bis hundert aber auf der Weyde oder Au, im Frueren=Thal (so anjetzo eine schoene Wiese untern Puechholtz ist) auf Befehl der Landes=Fürsten, von denen Burgern zu Steyer verbrennet worden; Daher der Ort um selbige Revier noch auf den heutigen Tag der Ketzer-Freudhoff genennet wird.'

[240] *Österreichische Chronik von den 95 Herrschaften*, ed. J. Seemüller, MGH Deutsche Chroniken 6 (Hanover, 1909), p. 221: 'Auch schuf er bey seinen zeiten auch cze rewten die keczerhait, die da haisset Waldenses, darumb hernach mer denn hundert keczer ze Steyr wurden verprennet' (Also, in his days he managed to uproot heresy,

is dated to 1398 or soon after,[241] implying again that the inquisitions took place between 1395 and 1398.

The conclusive evidence that Zwicker was not acting as inquisitor in the diocese of Passau before 1395 comes not from Austria but from Stettin. When Zwicker started interrogating the Waldenses of the Polish diocese of Poznań in March 1394, a diocese outside of his mandate, he recounted all the bishops who had commissioned him, apparently in an attempt to boost his authority. These included the archbishop of Prague and the bishops of Lebus and Cammin,[242] but not the bishop of Passau. Thus it seems that it was only in 1395 when Petrus Zwicker was called to Upper Austria.

To return to the *Processus Petri*, the dating of the sentences also gives a *terminus post quem* of early 1398 for the compilation of the formulary, or rather to the updates made to an already existing formulary on which the sentences were based. This is demonstrated when one compares Zwicker's manual in the St Florian manuscript and the sentencing of relapsed heretics in Steyr.

St Florian, MS XI 234, fol. 87va–vb
Quod tu n. tam grauiter et tam multipliciter in crimine heresis primo in ipsum crimen labendo et postmodum in ipsum crimen heresis per te primitus abiuratum sicut canis ad vomitum rediens, miserabiliter relabendo diuersimode deliquisti sicut tibi lectum est hic et recitatum intelligibiliter in wulgari (That you N. have done wrong so gravely and in such various and diverse ways in the crime of heresy: first falling into that crime and later on, after first abjuring that same crime of heresy, like a dog returning to its vomit wretchedly falling back into it, as was read out here and recited to you clearly in the vernacular).

BSB MS Clm 15125, fol. 208ra–rb
Quia igitur vos kunegundis, Gundel et Els, vos inquam tres predicti tam grauiter et tam multipliciter primo in crimine heresis labendo et postea in ipsum crimen heresis per uos coram nobis uel certo nostro commissario legittime et Iudicialiter abiurastis, sicut canis ad vomitum redeuntes, miserabiliter relabendo diuersimode deliquistis [...] Sicut coram nobis omnibus lectum est hic et recitatum intelligibiliter in wulgari (Whereas you therefore, Kunegunde, Gundel and Els – the aforesaid three of you, I say – have done wrong so gravely and in such various and diverse ways in the crime of heresy: first falling into that crime and afterwards like a dog returning to its vomit wretchedly falling back into that same crime of heresy – [previously] lawfully and judicially abjured by you in our presence or that

---

which there was called 'Waldensians', so that afterwards more than one hundred heretics were burned at Steyr).

[241] F. P. Knapp, *Die Literatur des Spätmittelalters in den Ländern Österreich, Steiermark, Kärnten, Salzburg und Tirol von 1273 bis 1439*. Vol. 2.2, *Die Literatur zur Zeit der habsburgischen Herzöge Rudolf IV. bis Albrecht V. (1358–1439)* (Graz, 2004), p. 288.

[242] *Quellen*, ed. Kurze, p. 235.

of our designated commissary – [...] Just as was read out to all here, in our presence, and recited clearly in the vernacular).

The almost word-to-word congruence shows that this formula was used by the notary when drawing up the final sentence, and in turn the formulary itself was then updated with a fresh, more detailed example. Not everything was revised, though. The formula for sentencing a penitent heretic to perpetual imprisonment remained unchanged, meaning that it continued to circulate as a simple formula with no reference to particular persons or incidents. Apparently such sentences were not given in Steyr in 1398,[243] although Zwicker's mandate in the diocese of Passau included the customary powers to imprison heretics,[244] and although a decade later such sentences were implemented.[245] In any case, the compiler of the new formulary copied the anonymous model sentence without contemporary updates. What was left out was the formulary for the declaration of a final sentence by a bishop.[246] Finally, the imaginative penance of having to wear a ridiculous hat imposed on Jans von Pewg, as well as the crosses assigned to five Waldensians questioned by Fridericus of Garsten, were added as new components in the formulary.

Recognizing this process of updating a formulary is extremely important when reading these sources. They are not a bundle of sentences that have escaped the ravages of time by chance, nor are they a representative sample of Zwicker's inquisitions around Steyr. They are pieces that somebody participating in the inquisition of heresy considered exemplary and good for further use. There may have been more people sentenced at the same time, and there certainly were other similar occasions, but traces of these are lost. This formulary was then added to the older material belonging to the *Processus Petri*. This happened, according to my interpretation, in the diocese of Passau and quite soon after the *sermo generalis* in Steyr early in 1398. In

---

[243] Cf. Segl, 'Die Waldenser in Österreich', p. 182. Segl reaches the opposite conclusion from the formulary, i.e. that Zwicker sentenced heretics to imprisonment. In material relating to Zwicker, such sentences are, however, mentioned only in anonymous formularies.

[244] St Florian, MS XI 234, fol. 88rb: 'aut eciam de heresi suspectos citandi, examinandi, excommunicandi, arrestandi, capiendi, incarcerandi, tenendi etiam manibris et compedibus ferreis, et ad tempus uel perpetuo incarceratos tenendi ac quoscumque eorum si expedire videbitur ad questiones seu tormenta ponenda' (or also of citing those suspect of heresy, examining, excommunicating, arresting, capturing, incarcerating, also holding with manacles and leg-irons, holding the incarcerated for a period or for ever, and, if seems fit, putting any of them to the question or torture).

[245] Reinprecht II of Wallsee received oaths of truce from imprisoned heretics in 1408; Vienna, Österreichische Staatsarchiv, Haus-, Hof-, und Staatsarchiv, Allgemeine Urkundenreihe, 1408 II 17; Doblinger, 'Die Herren von Walsee', p. 399; Segl, 'Die Waldenser in Österreich', p. 175, n. 57.

[246] St Florian, MS XI 234, fol. 87ra–rb.

this form it also spread to the southern German religious houses, whose manuscripts are today in the Bayerische Staatsbibliothek.[247] This certainly happened before 1401. Of the manuscripts discussed above, only the codex in Würzburg University Library (E in Appendix 3) contains the sentences declared by Petrus Zwicker from 1401 to 1403, sometimes together with Martinus of Prague, thus forming the last revisions of the *Processus Petri* in Zwicker's lifetime.

The last revisions and a priest sentenced after a copying mistake

Most of the texts in the Würzburg manuscript are standard parts of the *Processus Petri* discussed above: two question lists, two lists of converted Waldensians, the *De vita et conversacione* and the *Articuli Waldensium*, accompanied by the *Cum dormirent homines*. Yet the formulary of sentences includes not only those originating from Passau, but incorporates three later sentences: crosses and the destruction of houses of heretics in Sopron, Hungary, in January 1401;[248] Zwicker and Martinus against relapsed heretics in Hartberg, Steiermark in February 1401;[249] and Zwicker against a heretic called Andreas Hesel in Vienna in March 1403.[250]

Even more intriguing are the three undated sentences against clerics of the diocese of Passau, whose names are not revealed. The sentences are, or so it has been thought, preserved only in this manuscript and edited by Haupt.[251] The first is against the parish priest 'N' from the diocese of Passau (*N plebanus pataviensis diocesis*), who is absolved from a sentence of excommunication imposed for not appearing before an inquisitor. The second is an absolution from excommunication of an anonymous canon, originally imposed by the episcopal commissary 'Johannes', declared by Zwicker because of contumacy, and an order to the inquisitor and clergy of the diocese to spread the news of

---

[247] Similar dating, *c.* 1400, for the compilation of this collection was actually proposed by G. Gartner, although based on very limited source material: G. Gartner, 'Mittelalterliche Ketzerprozesse in Steyr', in *Auftrag und Verwirklichung: Festschrift zum 200-jährigen Bestand d. Kirchenhist. Lehrkanzel seit d. Aufhebung des Jesuitenordens 1773*, ed. F. Loidl (Vienna, 1974), pp. 123–33 (p. 125). Gartner's essay, however, contains many fundamental errors, for example mixing up the identities of Petrus Zwicker and Peter von Pillichsdorf.

[248] Würzburg, UB MS M. ch. f. 51, fols. 24r–25r; ed. Haupt, 'Waldenserthum und Inquisition', pp. 401–3.

[249] Würzburg, UB MS M. ch. f. 51, fols. 25v–27r; ed. Haupt, 'Waldenserthum und Inquisition', pp. 408–11.

[250] Würzburg, UB MS M. ch. f. 51, fols. 27v–28v; ed. partially in Döllinger, *Beiträge II*, pp. 343–4. Döllinger falsely gives 'Cod. Bavar. Monac. 329' (= BSB MS Clm 1329) as the source. Döllinger's edition is, as always, to be used with great caution.

[251] Würzburg, UB MS M. ch. f. 51, fols. 28v–29r; ed. Haupt, *Der Waldensische Ursprung des Codex Teplensis*, pp. 34–5.

the absolution. The third is a judgment of Waldensian heresy, again against an unnamed parish priest (*plebanus*), who is absolved and released with private penance (*sub occulta penitencia dimissimus graciose*), even though he had professed the Waldensian errors from his childhood. This last intriguing sentence especially has caused speculation that Zwicker wished to cover and hide heretical tendencies within the clergy.[252] The sentence is indeed surprisingly short and briefly handled for the sentence of a priest, where one would expect meticulous documentation, not to speak of degradation from holy orders.[253]

The explanation is simple. The supposed parish priest was only 'sentenced' after a medieval copying error, *plebis* in place of *plebanus*. The absolution and secret penitence follow almost verbatim the formula for (judicial) absolution of a person previously sacramentally absolved and not relapsed since. This formula is from the manual of St Florian. It begins:

> Frater P etc. recognoscimus publice et per presentes. Quod ~ plebis ~ diocesis nostro se examini presentauit.[254]

This is the corresponding opening of the Würzburg formulary:

> Frater petrus etc, Recognoscimus publice per presentes, Quod N plebanus diocesis patauiensis nostro se examini presentauit.[255]

The same mistakes were made in the formula for absolution of simple excommunication, meaning here that those who are absolved were excommunicated because of opposition to an inquisition or the inquisitor's orders, without necessarily being heretics proper. Except for substituting *plebis* [of a parish] with *plebanus* [parish priest], the formulas are practically identical.[256] The error is understandable. Replacing a rare word with a more familiar one was a typical scribal error. Both words are habitually and similarly abbreviated,

---

[252] Segl, 'Die Waldenser in Österreich', p. 183.

[253] Cf. X 5.7.9; Bivolarov, *Inquisitoren-Handbücher*, pp. 306–7.

[254] St Florian, MS XI 234, fol. 90va: 'We, brother P etc. publicly and through those present, acknowledge, that [n] of the parish [x], of the diocese [y], presented himself for our examination.'

[255] Würzburg, UB MS M. ch. f. 51, fol. 29r: 'We, brother Petrus etc. publicly and through those present, acknowledge, that parish priest N of the diocese of Passau presented himself for our examination.'

[256] St Florian, MS XI 234, fol. 90rb: 'Secuntur quedam absoluciones et primo ab excommunicacione simplici: Quia n plebis […] pataviensis diocesis. In causa fidei per nos citatus et ob non paricionem mandatorum nostrum ymo uerius cuius etc. seu contumaciam excommunicatus […]'. Cf. Würzburg UB, M. ch. f. 51, f. 28v: '[Q]uia N Plebanus pat[aviensis] diocesis in causa fidei per nos citatus et ob non paricionem mandatorum nostrorum ymmo verius etc. cuius etc seu contumaciam excommunicatus […].'

and *plebanus* is a common word, while in our period and area parish is more often called *parochia* than *plebs*. The connection between the two formularies is further exposed when one compares them as units. Haupt edited only three of the six absolutions in the Würzburg manuscript, and changed their order. Collated with the formulary of absolutions in Zwicker's manual of St Florian, one sees that these six are repeated in the same order, omitting only a very short formula for absolving with private penance. The collation is presented in Appendix 5.

There is no reason to assume that the Würzburg formulary was a copy of the St Florian manual. In their overall contents and disposition the two manuscripts differ remarkably. Rather, they both represent separate manuscript traditions, both originating from Petrus Zwicker's compilations and formularies. Given that this is so, why should we prefer the version in the often negligently copied St Florian manual? The reason is that *plebs* was the intended form, which is confirmed in Zwicker's sentences, where both *parochia* and *plebs* are used when stating the home parish of the condemned. Thus Jans von Pewg is 'of the parish (*parochie*) of Garsten',[257] while Els is 'widow of Chunrad Fewr in Tampach, of the parish in Garsten (*plebis in Gĕrsten*)'[258] and Geysel, widow of Ulrich of Rabenpüchel, was at the time of her trial living 'at Lueg of the parish (*plebis*) of St Michael, the filial church of Seitenstetten Monastery'.[259] The list could easily be continued.

It thus seems justified to dismiss *plebanus* as a scribal corruption emerging at some point in the manuscript tradition leading to the Würzburg formulary. It is equally unjustifed to assume that the unnamed person absolved by the episcopal commissary 'Johannes' (whose name appears in both manuscripts) in another formula was a canon. Although called 'discreet man d. G. etc. and canon of the diocese mentioned above' in the Würzburg manuscript,[260] the

---

[257] BSB MS Clm 15125, fol. 204ra: 'quod tu Jans vom pewg parochie Gersten'; cf. Würzburg, UB MS M. ch. f. 51, fol. 30r.

[258] BSB MS Clm 15125, fol. 204vb: 'Te ells relictam Chunradi fewr ym Tanpach plebis in Gĕrsten'; cf. Würzburg, UB MS M. ch. f. 51, fol. 33r.

[259] BSB MS Clm 15125, fol. 205ra: 'Te Geÿsel relictam ulricis am Rabenpichel nunc ym lueg plebis sancti Michelis filialis ecclesie Monasterii Seitten steten'; cf. Würzburg, UB MS M. ch. f. 51, fol. 31r, where the place name is 'Wes' instead of 'Lueg'.

[260] The reading is grammatically tenuous. Würzburg, UB MS M. ch. f. 51, fol. 28v has 'discretum virum d. g. etc et canonicis [sic] diocesis predicte'. Cf. Haupt, *Der Waldensische Ursprung des Codex Teplensis*, p. 34: 'discretum virum d. G. etc. et canonicum diocesis predicte'. The episcopal commissary Johannes is possibly Johann von Rottau, who was the dean of Enns between 1394 and November 1398; R. Zinnhobler, 'Die Inhaber von Pfarre und Dekanat Enns im Mittelalter', in *Die Dechanten von Enns-Lorch*, ed. R. Zinnhobler and J. Ebner (Linz, 1982), pp. 24–52 (p. 38); the name Johannes might be a scribal corruption. It is equally possible that the commissary was Leonhard Schawr, canon in Regensburg and Passau and the official for the diocese of Passau at least in 1388–1401. He is almost certainly the 'Io[annes] [sic] t[alis] Rat[isponensis] et pat[auiensis] ecc[les]ia[rum] ca[noni]cus,

St Florian formula mentions only a 'discreet man d. G. of such church, of such diocese mentioned above'.[261] The three formulas for excommunicating a contumacious priest mention *vicarius seu conuentor* (vicar or rector) and appear to be general formularies not addressing a particular situation or person.[262] By contrast, the absolution formula has enough details to suggest that it was probably based on an actual document issued in the diocese of Passau during Zwicker's inquisitions. As such it hints at clerical (if not necessarily by a canon) obstruction of the inquisition of heresy, and implies that the inquisitions in Upper Austria were not universally supported by the local clergy.

The version of *Processus Petri* in the Würzburg manuscript was compiled after March 1403. This must have been done either by Zwicker himself or by someone with access to his documents and notes, otherwise it would have been very difficult to bring together sentences issued in different places in 1401 and 1403 in order to insert them into a formulary. The formulary of absolutions, although corrupted, further implies access to Zwicker's own manual(s), as it, unlike other texts of the *Processus Petri*, was not in general circulation. The latest knowledge we have of Zwicker is from June 1404 in Buda, where he received an abjuration of a heretic previously converted by Henricus of Olomouc.[263] This sentence is not included in the Würzburg manuscript, and soon after that we lose track of Zwicker. I would tentatively argue for 1403–4 for the compilation of this last version, although a slightly later date cannot be excluded. It never became popular, as it is only preserved in one manuscript. How it ended up in Würzburg in the 1470s cannot unfortunately be answered unless new manuscripts are found.[264]

The revision of the *Processus Petri* did not end with the close of Zwicker's career as an inquisitor. Already mentioned is the removal of references to particular persons from the formulary of Zwicker's sentences in Passau (1398). This was probably done after 1425, because both manuscripts with this

---

offic[ialis] cur[ie] pat[auiensis]' (Jo[hn], canon of the churches of Regensburg and Passau, official of the court of Passau) who gives Zwicker an inquisitorial mandate in Passau in the heavily abberviated formula at St Florian, MS XI 234, fol. 88ra. See R. Välimäki, 'Bishops and the Inquisition of Heresy in Late Medieval Germany', in *Dominus episcopus. Medieval Bishops in their Dioceses*, ed. A. J. Lappin and E. Balzamo (Stockholm, 2018), pp. 186–206 (pp. 199–200).

[261] St Florian, MS XI 234, fol. 90rb: 'discretum virum d. G. talis ecclesie talis diocesis predicte'.

[262] Ibid., fols. 89va–90ra.

[263] Biller, 'Aspects', p. 372. Biller refers to a lost manuscript; see Chapter 1, p. 23, n. 2 above.

[264] The bishops' chronicle of Würzburg mentions that Waldensians were persecuted there in 1446; F. Machilek, 'Ein Eichstätter Inquisitionsverfahren aus dem Jahre 1460', *Jahrbuch für fränkische Landesforschung* 34/35 (1975), 417–46 (p. 440). That could have created demand for anti-Waldensian texts, but no firm link between this persecution and the Würzburg copy of the *Processus Petri* can be established.

anonymous formulary also mention the sentencing of the Hussite Johannes Drändorf in Heidelberg.[265] Also in other instances parts of the *Processus Petri* were adapted to anti-Hussite propaganda. A manuscript in Prague has a list of errors by Waldensians and Pikards (or Pikarts),[266] titled *Articuli de Pikardis* (*Articles of Pikards*),[267] and a few pages later 'Articuli hereticorum Waldensium et decardorum [sic]' (*Articles of Waldensian Heretics and Beghards*).[268] The list is loosely but clearly based on the *Articuli Waldensium* and the *De vita et conversacione*, both taken from the *Processus Petri*. In 1420, a parish priest and bachelor of theology, Jiří of Těchnic (Georgius de Tyechnicz), compiled a manuscript against the 'heresiarchs of Constance', including the *Cum dormirent homines* and several works against Wyclif and Hus, some of them written by Jiří himself. His short refutation of Waldensianism starts with a list of errors based on the *Articuli Waldensium*.[269] These examples demonstrate how the memory and understanding of Waldensianism, of which Zwicker's texts by then constituted a significant part, were revitalized in the fifteenth century for polemical attacks on new heresies. The different compilations of the *Processus Petri* were not documents frozen in time, only telling about the events relating to their original composition, but texts adapted to new situations.

* * * * * * * * * * * * * * * *

[265] Augsburg, UB MS II. 1. 2° 129, fols. 150r–152v; Salzburg, St Peter, MS b VIII 9, fols. 305rb–307va. On the trial of Johannes Drändorf, H. Heimpel, *Drei Inquisitions-Verfahren aus dem Jahre 1425: Akten der Prozesse gegen die deutschen Hussiten Johannes Drändorf und Peter Turnau sowie gegen Drändorfs Diener Martin Borchard* (Göttingen, 1969); H. Haupt, 'Johann von Drändorfs Verurteilung durch die Inquisition zu Heidelberg (1425)', *Zeitschrift für Geschichte des Oberrheins* 54 (1900), 479–90.

[266] In the fifteenth century the name Pikards was used to refer to the radical group of Hussites following Martin Húska. They denied every form of the real presence of Christ's body in the Eucharist, and were defamed as immoral antinomians and condemned and persecuted by the moderate Utraquists in Prague as well as by the Taborites. The origin of the name and its usage is best described in A. Patschovsky, 'Der taboritische Chiliasmus. Seine Idee, sein Bild bei den Zeitgenossen und die Interpretation der Geschichtswissenschaft', in *Häresie und vorzeitige Reformation im Spätmittelalter*, ed. F. Šmahel (Munich, 1998), pp. 169–95 (pp. 175–80).

[267] The list has been edited and Czech parts translated into German in K. Höfler, *Geschichtschreiber der husitischen Bewegung in Böhmen*, 3 vols. (Vienna, 1856), I, 503–14; cf. Werner, 'Nachrichten', pp. 215–16; Kaminsky, *A History of the Hussite Revolution*, p. 178.

[268] NKCR MS XI. D. 8, fol. 95r; cf. Höfler, *Geschichtschreiber der husitischen Bewegung*, I, p. 505. *Decardorum* is obviously corrupted from *becardorum* (of the Beghards).

[269] Wrocław, BU MS I F 707, fols. 122ra–199va; the Waldensian articles at fols. 196rb–199va. These have been edited in J. Szymański, 'Hy sunt articuli secte waldensium hereticorum z kodeksu IF 707 Biblioteki Uniwersyteckiej we Wroclawiu', in *Historicae viae. Studia dedykowane Profesorowi Lechowi A. Tyszkiewiczowi z okazji 55-lecia pracy naukowej*, ed. M. Goliński and S. Rosik (Wrocław, 2012), pp. 51–62 (pp. 55–7). For these and other examples of the common circulation of anti-Waldensian and anti-Hussite treatises, see Välimäki, 'Old Errors, New Sects'.

Petrus Zwicker never composed a full inquisitors' manual, unlike two other famous inquisitors of the fourteenth century, Bernard Gui and Nicholas Eymerich. The texts he without doubt meant for public circulation, the *Cum dormirent homines* and the manifesto of 1395, are aimed at making the clergy aware of the dangers of the Waldensian heresy, its doctrine and how to counter it. Shorter texts compiled a few years earlier, such as lists of converted Waldensians, the *Articuli Waldensium* and the *De vita et conversacione*, were likewise intended to improve the clergy's knowledge of the Waldensians. Zwicker, together with Martinus of Prague, also completely revised the way of interrogating Waldensians, and through their trials they offered a new set of methods for how to question, absolve and punish heretics. As the inquisitors left behind them converted heretics obliged to undergo public penance, they also charged the parish clergy with the unfamiliar and extraordinary task of supervising the penitents. Therefore it is no wonder that there was a demand for Zwicker's question lists, and formulas for oaths, absolutions and model sentences. These were compiled on several occasions. The unusually extensive and specialized St Florian manual is derived from a compilation put together around 1396, and Zwicker's formulary of sentences was first updated after 1398 and again after 1403. The revisions in Zwicker's lifetime were done by Zwicker himself or by some member of his *familia*, but the different versions that were in circulation most likely resulted from copies made by local clerics and religious houses for their own purposes.

Treating the *Processus Petri* only as a compilation for inquisition of heresy satisfies the modern scholar's wish to see uniformity of genre and some kind of heuristic unity in a literary work, expectations which according to Marianne Børch create an understanding of medieval texts very different from that of their contemporary readers.[270] Thus we want to read and to analyse an inquisitorial treatise in the context of inquisition and persecution of heresy. While the underlying understanding of context may be correct, such a reading may mislead us if we fail to see that the changes in the manuscripts can signify textual innovations or even the moving of the text from one genre to another, the purpose of analysis according to the Überlieferungsgeschichtliche Methode.[271]

This chapter has focused closely on the texts produced by inquisitorial actions, revising points of precise detail and chronology. These technical issues, important in themselves, speak also to a fundamentally important point in the history of inquisition. The shift that takes place between Zwicker's main source on the *officium inquisitionis*, the fourteenth-century

---

[270] M. Børch, 'Preface', in *Text and Voice: The Rhetoric of Authority in the Middle Ages*, ed. M. Børch (Odense, 2004), pp. 7–20 (pp. 10–11).

[271] W. Williams-Krapp, *Überlieferung und Gattung: zur Gattung 'Spiel' im Mittelalter* (Tübingen, 1980); Williams-Krapp, 'Die überlieferungsgeschichtliche Methode. Rückblick und Ausblick', pp. 5–8.

manual in Linz, OÖLB MS 177, and the manuscripts transmitting the *Processus Petri* in its various forms is significant. The first represents the Franco-Italian and Bohemian tradition of the inquisition of heresy, and a manual-type text more focused on legal questions than doctrinal content. It is a manual for an inquisitor who has to use more time for wrestling with civic and ecclesiastical authorities than debating with heretics, as the Italian and Bohemian inquisitors of the fourteenth century were often forced to do. The second type is in a sense a description of the inquisitorial process, but it is focused the doctrinal and pastoral side of controlling the heresy, including only the most basic formulas for taking oaths and delivering an absolution. It is a manual, but one more useful for a parish priest or local official supervising the penance of heretics than for the inquisitor of heresy dealing with the legal problems involved in sentencing a person to death and confiscating his or her property. One should always bear in mind that one or other of the *Cum dormirent homines* and the *Refutatio errorum* was almost always included in these compilations, providing detailed theological refutations of heretical doctrine, while the Linz manual includes only short descriptions of heretics. The *Processus Petri* manuscripts concentrate on heresy, not inquisition, and the heresy they represent is Waldensianism as defined by Petrus Zwicker. Both the wide circulation of these texts and the example we discussed above – of a parish priest inquiring into heretical beliefs of a convert – indicate that the reformed, more faith-oriented approach to interrogating suspected heretics was not practised only by Petrus Zwicker, Martinus of Prague and their immediate companions. Their views spread more widely among the clergy and transformed their approach towards heresy and its repression in Austria, Bohemia and Southern Germany.

4

Communicating Faith

Debet igitur divinarum scripturarum tractator et doctor, defensor rectae fidei ac debellator erroris, et bona docere et mala dedocere.

So the interpreter and teacher of the divine scriptures, the defender of the true faith and vanquisher of error, must communicate what is good and eradicate what is bad.

Augustine of Hippo, *De doctrina christiana*, IV.4.[1]

In the previous chapters I have discussed the pastoralization of heresy in the inquisitorial procedure, in other words the change of paradigm in the approach to Waldensianism and its inquisition that emerged in the circle around Petrus Zwicker and Martinus of Prague in the 1390s. The present chapter demonstrates that the increasingly pastoral and doctrinal approach to heresy did not stay confined to a limited circle of inquisitors, but was both consciously promoted in the surrounding society and at times eagerly received by contemporaries.

First, I shall look at instances when inquisitors themselves were able to communicate their message to the laity and the parish clergy, first of all by preaching and the performance of sentences, and less obviously but no less importantly through summonses (*citationes*) to trials. Zwicker's summonses from the diocese of Passau, previously unknown to scholars, reveal that they were a carefully constructed and integral part of spreading the anti-heretical message. Read aloud in parish churches for several weeks, they, together with the public penances, made the accusations of heresy, guilt over transgression, as well as contrition and penitence, a visible, audible and tangible part of life in the areas where inquisitors operated. Zwicker preached to converted heretics and good Catholics alike, but his sermons have not been preserved. I shall, however, draw attention to certain homiletic passages in

---

[1] Augustine of Hippo, *De Doctrina Christiana*, ed. and trans. R. P. H. Green (Oxford, 1996), pp. 200–1.

the *Cum dormirent homines* that suggest the probable contents of Zwicker's anti-heretical sermons.

Secondly, I shall discuss the transmission of Zwicker's polemical language to contemporary devotional literature. Ulrich von Pottenstein's catechetic compilation includes a unique case of the translation of a Latin anti-heretical treatise, the *Cum dormirent homines*, into the vernacular in the lifetime of the work's author, and in the same geographical area where he had conducted inquisitions. It is not just an example of contemporary reception, for Ulrich's catechetic treatment develops further an important feature of Zwicker's refutation of heresy. The emphasis on the authority of the scriptures as a basis for the Catholic cult and for the dignity of the clergy meant that Waldensianism was less and less the demonic other – rather, to an ever greater degree it was a transgression that almost anyone could commit, for example by being overtly critical of sinful priests or Church ownership of property. A further contemporary example is provided by the postil of Johlín of Vodňany. Though probably not familiar with the *Cum dormirent homines* or the *Refutatio errorum*, he almost certainly knew parts of the *Processus Petri* and in his sermons and the postil he demonstrates the same tendency: heresy is not a corrupting influence of Satanic doctrine but an articulation of too radical and fundamental a criticism of the Church and its ministers – who at the same time were viciously attacked by Johlín for their failures.

Inquisitor as preacher and performer

In late January or early February 1401 Petrus Zwicker preached against the Waldensian heresy in Hartberg, in Steiermark, Austria. Zwicker was there, together with Martinus of Prague, to lead the inquisition against local Waldenses by the command of Gregor, papal legate and archbishop of Salzburg. After the sermon a woman called Peters, the wife of Frideric Reat de Stangendorff, made a demonstration of her conversion. She publicly declared on several different occasions that the inquisitor's sermon had converted her from heresy, saying: 'if I had not heard that sermon I would never have become Christian, I would never have converted'. In Peters's case the conversion, or rather performance of it, was probably the last attempt to save herself, as the inquisitors' noose was tightening around her neck. Peters had confessed and abjured heresy, but she had given a false confession under a false name. After her abjuration she had encouraged others to ignore Zwicker's summonses to court. Her conversion came too late to save her life, and she was released to the secular arm as a relapsed heretic. The whole incident is remarkable, which is probably the reason why it was copied into the last version of the *Processus Petri*'s formulary of model sentences in the first place.[2] Peters's story is told in detail elsewhere,[3] and in this chapter my interest lies in the references to the inquisitor's preaching and other instances of communication with the laity during inquisitions.

Peters's sentence serves as a clue to occasions when the inquisitor's views of true faith and heresy were publicly communicated to laymen and women through a sermon. At the turn of the fifteenth century, the Austrian laity held both orthodox and heterodox sympathies. The laypeople were more and more addressed in theological and devotional discourse, though it is perhaps better to say that the former distinction between laity and clergy and other members of religious orders as audiences for religious communication was being eroded.[4] In the later Middle Ages stories and *topoi* that had previously belonged to a narrow monastic culture found their way into vernacular texts, mystery plays and sermons.[5] We can thus assume that a preaching inquisitor addressed a mixed audience of secular clergy and laity who possessed varying degrees of theological knowledge but were nevertheless used to public discussions on doctrinal matters.

The message propagated in sermons, citations and declarations of sentences is important if we are to access the anti-heretical sentiment of the laity. We instinctively tend to see the laity, and sometimes local authorities, as opposing the inquisitors. True, there are more than enough examples of this opposition from the Italian communes and Languedocian towns, as well as from fourteenth-century Bohemia.[6] But the laity also supported the persecution of heretics. Richard Kieckhefer has referred to anti-heretical sentiments among the laity in late medieval Germany, though he does not give any specific examples.[7] A very illuminating example of this comes from the diocese of Passau, albeit some years after the Waldensian persecutions.

---

[2] Würzburg, UB MS M. ch. f. 51, fols. 25v–27r. The document is edited in Haupt, 'Waldenserthum und Inquisition', pp. 408–11.

[3] R. Välimäki, '*Bona docere et mala dedocere* – Inquisition of Heresy and Communication with the Lay Population', in *Modus vivendi: Religious Reform and the Laity in Late Medieval Europe*, ed. M. Heinonen, M. Kaartinen and M. Rubin [forthcoming]; Haupt, 'Waldenserthum und Inquisition', pp. 378–9.

[4] Cf. Mossman, *Marquard von Lindau*, pp. 27–30.

[5] A good example is the dissemination of the story of thirty Jews sold for one piece of silver each. See J. Hanska, 'Mendicant Preachers as Disseminators of Anti-Jewish Literary Topoi: The Case of Luca da Bitonto', in *From Words to Deeds: The Effectiveness of Preaching in the Late Middle Ages*, ed. M. G. Muzzarelli (Turnhout, 2014), pp. 117–38 (pp. 126–8).

[6] On both individual and collective resistance to the inquisitors in Languedoc, see Given, *Inquisition and Medieval Society*, pp. 90–191; in fourteenth-century Bohemia, Doležalová, 'The Inquisitions in Medieval Bohemia', pp. 302–9; in Renaissance Italy, M. M. Tavuzzi, *Renaissance Inquisitors: Dominican Inquisitors and Inquisitorial Districts in Northern Italy, 1474–1527* (Leiden, 2007), p. 75.

[7] Kieckhefer, *Repression*, pp. 70, 73.

In the papal penitentiary there are two applications by Benedictine monks of Melk Abbey from 1451. As young boys they had participated in the burning of heretics during the early Hussite revolt. One of them had been only 10 years old when he had carried wood for the pyre, and later as monks they were not sure if these acts of violence constituted an obstacle to their ecclesiastical careers – hence their application to the penitentiary for dispensation.[8] So, the persecution of heretics could be a common enterprise for prelates and inquisitors, parish clergy and laity.

What, or even when and to whom, the inquisitors preached is more difficult to grasp than many other aspects of their mission. In general, the role of preaching in the battle against heresy is well acknowledged, and from the thirteenth century onwards the Dominican order was the exemplar of the combination of the activities of preaching and persecuting heretics.[9] They were joined by Franciscans, from whose ranks rose, for example, Berthold von Regensburg, who preached against heresy both in Latin and German around the middle of the thirteenth century.[10] In late medieval Europe, the preachers were mobilized in the service of social and civil reforms in addition to religious education,[11] but anti-heretical preaching was also an incentive to persecution. The trial of Waldensians in Strasbourg in 1400 was instigated by the apparently spontaneous and uninvited sermons of a Dominican 'cursor from Basel', identified as Peter Mangold by Georg Modestin, during Advent 1399, forcing the city council to act in fear of their reputations.[12] Already in 1393 there had been a similar event in Augsburg. The prosecution of thirty-four heretics was initiated by a wandering preacher (*Pfaffe*) – revealed to be the same Heinrich Angermeyer who later came into conflict with the bishop of Würzburg in Rothenburg ob der Tauber – who turned his sermon on usury

---

[8] *Häresie und Luthertum*, ed. F. Tamburini and L. Schmugge (Paderborn, 2000), pp. 47–51.

[9] On the Dominicans and preaching against heresy, see Ames, *Righteous Persecution*, pp. 35–49.

[10] A. Czerwon, *Predigt gegen Ketzer: Studien zu den lateinischen Sermones Bertholds von Regensburg* (Tübingen, 2011), pp. 65–170.

[11] R. Rusconi, 'Public Purity and Discipline: States and Religious Renewal', in *Christianity in Western Europe c. 1100–c. 1500*, ed. M. Rubin and W. Simons (Cambridge, 2009), pp. 458–71; Soukup, 'Die Predigt als Mittel religiöser Erneuerung'; Ocker, 'Die Armut und die menschliche Natur', pp. 113–18; J. Nechutová, 'Reform- und Busssprediger von Waldhauser bis Hus', in *Kirchliche Reformimpulse des 14./15. Jahrhunderts in Ostmitteleuropa*, ed. W. Eberhard and F. Machile (Cologne, 2006), pp. 239–54.

[12] *Quellen*, ed. Modestin, pp. 58–63; Modestin, *Ketzer in der Stadt*, pp. 12–13; G. Modestin, 'La parole efficace ou le déclenchement du procès contre les vaudois de Strasbourg (1399–1400)', in *Mirificus praedicator: à l'occasion du sixième centenaire du passage de Saint Vincent Ferrier en pays romand: actes du colloque d'Estavayer-le-Lac, 7–9 octobre 2004*, ed. P.-B. Hodel and F. Morenzoni (Rome, 2006), pp. 233–45.

into an anti-heretical homily and persuaded Bishop Burkhard von Ellerbach to give him a commission to inquire into heresy in Augsburg.[13]

When inquisitors and the inquisitions themselves are studied, the educational and performative aspects of *inquisitio heretice pravitatis* are usually discussed in relation to the declaration of penances and sentences, the so-called *sermo generalis*. This has been analysed both as symbolic communication, performance and ritual,[14] and as a part of a Gramscian struggle for hegemony.[15] In comparison, relatively little has been said about preaching, or the sermon is said to have had a minor role in the *sermo generalis*.[16] Yet, the inquisitors were certainly expected to preach. Early fourteenth-century Italian manuals, such as the anonymous *Libellus* (*Little Book*) and *De officio inquisitionis*, advise inquisitors to preach weekly on faith either themselves or through a deputy preacher.[17] The formal requirements for papal inquisitors issued by the thirteenth-century popes included proficiency in preaching,[18] and the decrees of the Dominican General Chapter of 1401, held in Udine, ordered that inquisitors who were not competent preachers be dismissed from their offices.[19]

The sermon that Peters attended in Hartberg in 1401 was certainly a public sermon intended to educate laypeople on the dangers of heresy.[20] Perhaps it was part of her penance; the thirteenth-century guidelines for inquisitors already compel the penitent converts to be present at the *sermo generalis*.[21] But what did Petrus Zwicker preach on such occasions, and how was it related

---

[13] Modestin, 'Der Augsburger Waldenserprozess', pp. 51–3, 66–7 and passim; see also Smelyansky, 'Urban Order and Urban Other'; on the heresy accusations in Rothenburg, see Schnurrer, 'Der Fall Hans Wern'.

[14] T. Scharff, 'Die Inquisitoren und die Macht der Zeichen. Symbolische Kommunikation in der Praxis der mitteralterlichen dominikanischen Inquisition', in *Praedicatores, inquisitores I. The Dominicans and the Medieval Inquisition. Acts of the 1st International Seminar on the Dominicans and the Inquisition 23–25. February 2002* (Rome, 2004), pp. 111–43 (pp. 123–7); I. Forrest, *The Detection of Heresy in Late Medieval England* (Oxford, 2005), pp. 130–42; G. G. Merlo, 'Il sermo generalis dell'inquisitore: una sacra rappresentazione anomala', in *Vite di eretici e storie di frati*, ed. M. Benedetti, G. G. Merlo and A. Piazza (Milan, 1998), pp. 203–20.

[15] Given, *Inquisition and Medieval Society*, pp. 71–90.

[16] Ibid., pp. 73–78, esp. 73; Scharff, 'Die Inquisitoren und die Macht der Zeichen', p. 124; for the opposite view, see G. G. Merlo, *Inquisitori e inquisizione del Medioevo* (Bologna, 2008), ch. 5.2; Ames, *Righteous Persecution*, pp. 40–6.

[17] Ames, *Righteous Persecution*, pp. 40–6.

[18] Bivolarov, *Inquisitoren-Handbücher*, p. 262.

[19] Tavuzzi, *Renaissance Inquisitors*, p. 8.

[20] For more detail, see Välimäki, '*Bona docere et mala dedocere*'.

[21] See e.g. *Ordo processus Narbonensis*: 'his poenitentias iungatis: videlicet ut cruces portent [...] et intersint omni die Dominica Missae ac vesperis, et sermoni generali, si fiat in villa: nisi impedimentum habuerint sine fraude' (You are to enjoin penances on them: that is, that they must wear crosses [...] and that they must attend every Sunday mass and vespers, and the general sermon, if one takes place in the town:

to his anti-heretical works? The content of Zwicker's sermons was certainly critical of Waldensian errors, but can anything more specific be said about the message intended for the laity?

Even if the purpose was to inform the laity about dangerous opinions that should be avoided, not merely to demonize the opponent, there were many different levels at which the doctrine could be preached. The most rudimentary form of propagating the faith was to point out suspicious tenets. Berthold von Regensburg in one of his sermons bluntly stated that if one heard somebody claiming that all oath-taking, even truthful, was a sin, that person should be deemed to be the worst heretic.[22] We can assume that in the 1390s the most observable Waldensian beliefs were emphasized as deviant, either by inquisitors or other preachers. The various short documents listing Waldensian errors almost certainly had their oral equivalents, and it is obvious that Zwicker's manifesto of 1395 was meant for public propagation. However, more detailed and in-depth homilies were also delivered. Hints of the contents can be found above all in *Cum dormirent homines*. Biller has pointed out that in his treatise Zwicker gives some *exempla* that may reflect his pastoral activity.[23] Similarly, Cameron proposes that 'the homely and graphic quality of his imagery suggests strongly that he may have done so from the pulpit as well as on paper',[24] and recently Smelyansky has echoed this interpretation.[25] These authors give some example of this imagery, but no actual comparison of Zwicker's language and contemporary homiletic material has been made.

In addition to straightforward exempla, in several passages the language and argumentation of the *Cum dormirent homines* incorporate comparisons, metaphors and remarks that resemble homiletic style. At times these also break the rule of addressing the Waldensian heresiarch as the primary imagined audience. For example, the chapter handling Waldensian incredulity about the Virgin Mary and the saints begins:

> The Waldensian heretics think that the blessed Virgin Mary and the saints in Heaven are so full of joy that they cannot know anything that happens on earth, and consequently they are not to be invoked by us, because they cannot pray for us. Against this is twice set Luke 15: 'there shall be joy for the angels of God upon one sinner that doth penance'. If the angels have joy over us doing penance, they must by all means know that we do penance.

---

unless they have genuine difficulty): *Texte zur Inquisition*, ed. K.-V. Selge (Gütersloh, 1967), 60; see also, Merlo, *Inquisitori e inquisizione del Medioevo*, ch. 5.4.

[22] Berthold von Regensburg, Sermo XVIII, Schönbach, *Studien zur Geschichte der altdeutschen Predigt 3*, p. 12: 'quod nullus debet jurare etiam veritatem. considerate, si unquam audiatis talem, quia pessimus est hereticus'.

[23] Biller, *Waldenses*, p. 273.

[24] Cameron, *Waldenses*, p. 143.

[25] Smelyansky, 'Self-Styled Inquisitors', p. 166.

Nobody is joyful over things that they simply do not know. Never would you be joyful over your brother who is crowned king, if it never entered your mind that your brother would possibly be crowned king.[26]

The *waldenses heretici* are mentioned in the third person, as if addressing an audience other than the heretics, abandoning the basic structure where the arguments are directed to an imagined heretical opponent. The short biblical reference to Luke 15 – and the repetition ('twice') in verses 7 and 10 – is followed by an example of rejoicing over a brother who is elected king, which is intended to make the bible verse understandable and memorable, much in the style of late medieval sermons.[27] Zwicker continues by further expanding the proposition and explaining that knowing of a sinner's penitence includes knowing of his bad deeds and the good deeds left undone. Although constructed to counter the Waldensian proposition that saints were unable to know about our deeds and lives on earth, the form of the argument resembles a homily. The adjustment in the style of the treatise becomes even more evident when it is followed by a long and exhaustive list of biblical references to support the orthodox position. Even the list bears resemblance to preaching tools, *Summae auctoritatum*, lists of biblical materials intended to enable the preacher to prove or disprove doctrinal questions and organized under headings of doctrine.[28] The line between treatise and sermon was not clear, and in some manuscripts the *Cum dormirent homines* is in fact called a sermon.[29]

The appearance of oral features – such as a declamatory address to a person or persons – in a written text is not, however, necessarily an indication that

---

[26] Zwicker, *Cum dormirent homines*, p. 282: 'Tenent Waldenses haeretici B. Virginem Mariam et sanctos in Patria tantis impletos esse gaudiis, quod nihil possint cogitare de his, quae in terris fiunt, et per consequens, eos non esse inuocandos a nobis; quia non possunt orare pro nobis. Contra Luc. 15. bis ponitur: Gaudium erit Angelis Dei, super vno peccatore poenitentiam agente. Si gaudent Angeli de nobis poenitentibus, sciunt vtique penitere nos. Nihil enim gaudent de illo, quod simpliciter nescint. Nunquam enim gauisus de fratre tuo in regem coronato, si nunquam occurrerit menti tuae, fratrem tuum in regem fore possibile coronari.'

[27] An excellent example is the famous Dominican preacher Vincent Ferrer, who in his Lenten sermons in the diocese of Lausanne in 1404 used exempla at almost every turn but in a very entertaining way. The whole sermon cycle, preserved in a *reportatio* by the Franciscan Fridericus of Amberg, is edited in Vincent Ferrer, *Sermones de cuaresma en Suiza: 1404: Couvent des Cordeliers, ms 62*, ed. F. M. Gimeno Blay and M. L. Mandingorra Llavata (Valencia, 2009). Vincent Ferrer was invited to preach in the Swiss parts of the diocese of Lausanne by the bishop of Lausanne because of the heresy in the area, see P.-B. Hodel, 'D'une édition à l'autre. La lettre de saint Vincent Ferrier à Jean de Puynoix du 17 décembre 1403', in *Mirificus praedicator*, pp. 189–203 (p. 203).

[28] On *summae auctoritatum*, see Sackville, *Heresy and Heretics*, pp. 42–53.

[29] Göttweit, Stiftsbibliothek MS XV 245, fol. 221vb: 'et illud tu dampnas etc. Et sic est finis sermonis.'; BSB MS Clm 15125, fol. 174ra: 'Sermo factus per inquisitorem'.

the text was intended for oral performance. Particularly in sermon literature the orality of a text was a conscious literary strategy to convey the appeal of familiar, spoken homily in religious literature intended for private study.[30] It is nevertheless difficult to see a need for such literary strategy in a Latin polemic whose only audience was the clergy combatting heresy. A more likely explanation of its purpose is that the *exempla* and other homiletic elements were included to provide material for those composing sermons against heresy. It is noticeable that the parables and exempla in the *Cum dormirent homines* are placed to clarify difficult theological questions. The example quoted above is on the invocation of saints, and other *exempla* can be found on purgatory and deathbed penance, as well as on administration of the sacraments.[31] There is no reason to doubt that this is the material used by Zwicker himself and probably intended by him to be useful to other preachers.

Just how close the polemical refutation of heresy and sermons explaining it to the people could be is demonstrated in the homily by Master Matthew of Kraków just a few years before the outbreak of the great Waldensian persecutions. In January 1384 heretics, probably Waldensians (though they are never called such), were held in custody by Archbishop Jan of Jenštejn of Prague. While the heretics were awaiting their judgment, Matthew of Kraków exposed their errors to the citizens of Prague. Although the sermon has been preserved only in two later, Latin summaries,[32] we can assume it was preached to the laity, possibly in the native German of Matthew, as the report

---

[30] H.-J. Schiewer, 'Spuren von Mündlichkeit in der mittelalterlichen Predigtüberlieferung: ein Plädoyer für exemplarisches und beschreibend-interpretierendes Edieren', *Editio. Internationales Jahrbuch für Editionswissenschaft* 6 (1992), 64–79 (p. 65); K. Ruh, 'Deutsche Predigtbücher des Mittelalters', in *Beiträge zur Geschichte der Predigt* (Hamburg, 1981), pp. 11–30; V. Mertens, 'Predigt oder Traktat? Thesen zur Textdynamik mittelhochdeutscher geistlicher Prosa', *Jahrbuch für internationale Germanistik* 24 (1992), 41–3; Czerwon, *Predigt gegen Ketzer*, pp. 164–5. For the opposing view that the sermon genre was essentially oral, see B. M. Kienzle, 'Medieval Sermons and Their Performance: Theory and Record', in *Preacher, Sermon and Audience in the Middle Ages*, ed. C. Muessig (Leiden, 2002), pp. 89–124. A middle road is represented by B. Roest, who proposes that the sermon collections of Hartung von Erfurt were used as model sermons and communal reading texts as well as for private meditation; B. Roest, *Franciscan Literature of Religious Instruction before the Council of Trent* (Leiden, 2004), p. 44. This had already been suggested by V. Mertens, 'Theologie der Mönche – Frömmigkeit der Laien? Beobachtungen zur Textgeschichte von Predigten des Hartwig von Erfurt. Mit einem Textanhang', in *Literatur und Laienbildung im Spätmittelalter und in der Reformationszeit*, ed. L. Grenzmann and K. Stackmann (Stuttgart, 1984), pp. 661–83 (pp. 661–2).

[31] Zwicker, *Cum dormirent homines*, pp. 282A–B, 286G–7A, 288C. Cf. Smelyansky, 'Self-Styled Inquisitors', p. 158, who simultaneously but independently of my research noted 'Zwicker's ability to explain complex theological points with analogies that would make sense to a lay audience'.

[32] On the transmission of the text, see *Quellen*, ed. Patschovsky, pp. 318–19; edition pp. 319–23.

states that 'Master Matthew of Kraków declared these [errors] publicly giving a sermon to the people'.[33] The person who wrote the report was evidently more interested in the heretical opinions than the counter-arguments by the university theologian, as only some of the latter are recorded. The eight errors listed are common to the Waldensians: opposition to ecclesiastical baptism, the authority of the Church Fathers and later theologians, the legitimacy of capital punishment, purgatory, the validity of good deeds and charity on behalf of the dead, invocation and veneration of the saints and the Virgin Mary, the right of a priest living in mortal sin to administer the sacraments and finally indulgences.[34] The few counter-arguments noted show that Matthew's sermon against the Waldensians followed roughly the same structure as the polemical treatises: first the heretical proposition, then orthodox refutation based on the Scriptures. The fourth article on purgatory even bears traces of the sequence that predominates in Zwicker's works: heretical proposition – Catholic argument – heretical counterargument – Catholic refutation. Matthew explained that although the existence of Purgatory was attested in 2 Maccabees 12:46 ('it is therefore a holy and wholesome thought to pray for the dead, that they may be loosed from sins'),[35] the heretics dismissed the Books of the Maccabees as apocryphal, which according to Matthew was wrong, for the Church 'accepts the whole Bible'.[36]

Matthew's sermon in Prague is also a perfect example of the dangers of preaching about the errors of heretics in public, for there was a very real possibility of misinterpretation. The first error of the heretics is presented in a confusing sentence: 'that in our [Catholic] faith, by the power of our

---

[33] Ibid., p. 319: 'quos pronunciavit publice magister Matheus de Cracovia sermonem faciens ad populum'.

[34] Ibid., pp. 319–23.

[35] 'Sancta ergo et salubris est cogitatio pro defunctis exorare, ut a peccatis solvantur.' The verse in question was one of the main verses in support of the doctrine of purgatory; Le Goff, *The Birth of Purgatory*, p. 41.

[36] *Quellen*, ed. Patschovsky, p. 321; on the medieval canon of the Bible, van Liere, *Medieval Bible*, ch. 3. It is not out of the question that Master Matthew resorted to existing polemics. The treatise *Attendite a falsis prophetis*, circulating in Germany and Bohemia and possibly dating to before the sermon, discusses the status of the Books of Maccabees in a very similar way to Matthew's sermon; cf. St Florian, MS XI 152, fol. 49v: 'Nec obstat, quod libri Machabeorum dicuntur apocrifi, cum ab ecclesia recipiantur et aliis libris biblie apponantur.' The validity of Maccabees as proof of purgatory was questioned again during the formative years of Hussitism; see R. Cegna, 'Nicola della Rosa Nera detto da Dresda (1380?–1416?) De reliquiis et de veneratione sanctorum : de purgatorio', *Mediaevalia Philosophica Polonorum = Bulletin d'information concernant les recherches sur la philosophie médiévale en Pologne* 23 (1977), 3–171 (pp. 63–4); Cegna, 'La condizione del valdismo', p. 58, n. 54; P. Soukup, 'The Reception of the Books of the Maccabees in the Hussite Reformation', in *Dying for the Faith, Killing for the Faith: Old-Testament Faith-Warriors (1 and 2 Maccabees) in Historical Perspective*, ed. G. Signori (Leiden, 2012), pp. 195–207.

sacraments, only our small children are saved when baptized, not adults'.[37] As Patschovsky noted in the commentary in his edition, this must refer to the Waldensian critique of child baptism rather than to an opinion that only those baptized as children can be saved, as the text would suggest. The presupposition that Waldensians denied the validity of baptism probably comes from the thirteenth-century treatise by the Anonymous of Passau,[38] for baptism was not an issue in the late fourteenth century. Zwicker simply stated in the *Cum dormirent homines* that the Waldensians accept the sacrament of baptism from the ordained clergy.[39] The repetition of the same misapprehension over child baptism in both known manuscripts of Matthew's sermon summary demonstrates the danger in oral exposition of heresy: the message could easily be misunderstood. Here the confusion was created by educated, Latinate scribes, not by the laity!

The danger of misinterpreting the inquisitor's message must have been the reason why Zwicker uses *exempla* when dealing with particularly difficult and controversial theological issues. Purgatory, which had been incorporated into Catholic theology in the thirteenth century and had raised suspicion even among those intellectuals who systematized the innovation,[40] is explained through two *exempla*. The first of them clarifies a point about the number of to the afterlife that were available for the dead. The heretical proposition was that the implementation of purgatory in soteriology violated Christ's promise of the two ways in the Sermon on the Mount: the broad way to destruction and the narrow way to life.[41] Zwicker's counter-argument is that there are finally (*finaliter*) two ways leading to two permanent destinations, meaning that purgatory is part of the narrow way leading to salvation. He elaborates the explanation with a story about an emperor who orders all who have completely clear eyesight to go to Jerusalem and all who are completely blind to go to Babylon, whereas those whose eyes are not completely bright should go to Rome until their eyes are cleared. The clear-eyed are those without sin or who have atoned for their sins during their lifetimes, the blind are those who die in mortal sin without penitence, while those going first to Rome have committed sin and have not completed their penance in their lifetime.[42] The explanation of the roads and destinations is immediately followed by

---

[37] *Quellen*, ed. Patschovsky, p. 319: 'quod in fide nostra vi sacramentorum nostrorum non salvarentur nisi parvuli nostri baptizati et non adulti.'

[38] Ibid., pp. 319–20, n. 587. Cf. the treatise of the Anonymous of Passau, *Quellen*, ed. Patschovsky and Selge, p. 81: 'De baptismo errant quidam dicentes parvulos non salvari per baptismus' (On baptism some err, saying that babies are not saved through baptism).

[39] Zwicker, *Cum dormirent homines*, p. 291G–H; see also Biller, 'Aspects', p. 99.

[40] Le Goff, *The Birth of Purgatory*, pp. 239–40 and passim.

[41] Matthew 7:13–14; cf. Zwicker, *Cum dormirent homines*, p. 286E.

[42] Zwicker, *Cum dormirent homines*, p. 286G–H.

another example 'that often takes place',[43] meaning here that an example from everyday life is offered: somebody sins for thirty years and then becomes bedridden because of pestilence or a mortal wound. He recognizes or fears approaching death and with true penitence confesses his sins. He assumes penance with a genuine intention of fulfilling it but dies before completing it. He cannot be damned, because 'God does not despise a contrite and humbled heart.'[44] Neither can the soul ascend directly to heaven without sufficient penance. Thus purgatory is an expression of God's mercy and justice, as no good deed goes unpunished and nothing bad unpunished.[45]

The provision of a detailed explanation of heretical and Catholic doctrine in sermons in the way Matthew of Kraków did in Prague 1384, and as we can assume Zwicker did in the 1390s, was not as common as one might expect. The heretic was a common figure in medieval *exempla* and model sermons, but the character is more often used as a recognizable, much-reduced villain in the moral stories than as an object of actual theological exposition.[46] Some preachers, even the very famous ones, did not even bother to explain the doctrine of the heretics, instead simply inciting the people against them with horror stories. When Bernardino da Siena, in one of his sermons at Siena in 1427, referred to heretics in Piedmont – Waldensians, even though Bernardino did not use the name – he did not say anything about their heresy, but instead told a story about how once a year they toss a baby until it is dead, then grind it into powder in a wine keg to make a magic potion.[47] Even model sermons written specially for the inquisitors are very stereotypical in their descriptions of heretics. The exempla offered by Humbert of Romans in the model sermons for inquisition are general and include almost every biblical attribute given to the heretics, from ministers of Satan to sowers of tares and false

---

[43] 'Exemplum quod frequenter accidit', Zwicker, *Cum dormirent homines*, p. 286H.

[44] Cf. Psalms 50:19: 'cor contritum et humiliatum, Deus, non despicies.'

[45] Zwicker, *Cum dormirent homines*, pp. 286I I–287A.

[46] Sackville, *Heresy and Heretics*, pp. 60–75, 197–8. Sackville proposes that Stephen of Bourbon's chapter *De heresi* in his *Tractatus de diversis materiis predicabilibus* (*Treatise on Various Preachable Materials*) is an exception, discussing the Waldensian and Cathar heretics in much the same way as anti-heretical treatises. On the other hand, that part of the work was probably not intended to be preached as such, but to inform other Dominicans. Stephen himself says that 'I have inserted these things here, thinking it good for the brethren, defenders of the faith, not to be ignorant of them.' Trans. and cit., ibid., p. 69. Again, the *Tractatus* is an example of interplay between polemical treatises and homily.

[47] Bernardino da Siena, *Prediche volgari: sul campo di Siena 1427*, ed. C. Delcorno, 2 vols. (Milano, 1989), II, 793–4; F. Mormando, *The Preacher's Demons: Bernardino of Siena and the Social Underworld of Early Renaissance Italy* (Chicago, 1999), p. 86. Bernardino's strategy of demonizing the heretics was obviously very successful, as in Milan he almost managed to get a teacher of arithmetic, Amedeo de Landi, burned by the mob as a heretic without any formal accusations by the city officials or inquisitors of heresy. See ibid., pp. 82–4.

prophets.[48] This demonizing and generalizing style was at times developed into a conscious strategy to avoid the spread of heretical doctrine through its intended refutation. Ian Forrest has pointed out that in early fifteenth-century England the preachers against Lollards were instructed to avoid difficult theological questions such as the Eucharist. Instead, they concentrated on sneering at the heretics through analogies of disease and debauchery.[49] By contrast, in the battle against heresy in the late fourteenth- and early fifteenth-century German Empire the inquisitors, and quite possibly the preachers too, embraced rather than avoided exposition of doctrine.[50]

At times a preacher could integrate the anti-heretical message into more general pastoral education. The Dominican Vincent Ferrer preached in Switzerland during Lent 1404. There are surprisingly few direct attacks against heretics in his sermons, and in Fribourg his verbal offensive is aimed rather at Jews and usurers.[51] However, it would be strange if Vincent Ferrer had not preached against heresy, as he was specially invited to do so by Bishop Guillaume of Menthonay, who had also ordered the unsuccessful inquisition against Waldensians in Fribourg in 1399.[52] Nor it is possible that Vincent was ignorant of the Waldensian heresy, as he had recently preached against it on the other side of the Alps.[53] He did not dismiss heresy, but he chose an indirect approach to the problem. Vincent's sermons are general penitential sermons, as one should expect from a Lenten homily. He encourages his listeners to penitence and gives guidelines to proper ways of confessing and participating in the mass and other services. The anti-heretical message is embedded in the catechesis. On Tuesday before Palm Sunday Vincent preached in Avenches on the seven stairs that lead to heaven – an allusion to the vision of Jacob in

---

[48] Humbertus de Romanis, 'De eruditione predicatorum', ed. M. La Bigne, *Maxima bibliotheca veterum patrum et antiquorum scriptorum ecclesiasticorum* 25 (Lyon, 1677), pp. 424A–567E (p. 554); see also Ames, *Righteous Persecution*, pp. 41–42; Medieval preachers usually composed their personal sermons using the model sermons together with other sources; see N. Bériou, 'Les sermons latins après 1200', in *The Sermon*, ed. B. M. Kienzle (Turnhout, 2000), pp. 363–447 (pp. 423–30). On Humbert's collection and its nature as preaching aid rather than sermons proper, see ibid., pp. 392–3; see also the similar conclusions drawn from some heresy sermons of Berthold of Regensburg in Czerwon, *Predigt gegen Ketzer*, p. 160.

[49] Forrest, *The Detection of Heresy*, pp. 147–8, 150–7.

[50] This seems to have been the case also in fifteenth-century France, where the Eucharist was explicated in detail and with anti-heretical implications; M. Hervé, *Le métier de prédicateur en France septentrionale à la fin du Moyen Âge (1350–1520)* (Paris, 1988), pp. 312–15.

[51] This has led Utz Tremp to conclude that Vincent Ferrer probably regarded the local heretics as unlearned rustics and consequently was unaware of the endorsement of Waldensianism among the well-off merchant class of Fribourg; K. Utz Tremp, 'Predigt und Inquisition', in *Mirificus praedicator*, pp. 205–32 (pp. 206–8).

[52] The orders for the inquisitors are edited in *Quellen*, ed. Utz Tremp, pp. 585–7.

[53] See Vincent's own description in his letter to Jean de Puynoix, Hodel, 'D'une édition à l'autre', pp. 201–2.

Genesis 28:11–15 – saying that the first step is to believe in articles of faith as taught by the Church: 'because if a man accomplished all virtuous deeds in fasting, abstaining and so on and doubted the Catholic faith, he could not enter the heavenly kingdom'.[54] On at least three occasions, Vincent reminded his listeners that the excommunicated are totally excluded from God's mercy and absolution, which are channelled by the Church, and calls for their contrition and penitence.[55] Thus, Vincent did not preach against the heretics or call for the eradication of heresy, but instead delivered sermons on true faith and proper Christian conduct, spiced with jibes aimed at heretics and other dissidents.

Although the sources are very different in length, detail and nature, there is a palpable tendency in Matthew of Kraków's sermon against heretics in Prague in 1384, homiletic elements in Zwicker's treatise and the Lenten homilies of Vincent Ferrer in Switzerland 1404. All are aimed against heretics. Their emphasis may be different, but all share the view that heresy is an error from which one can convert, do penance and seek absolution. Likewise, all engage with doctrine, even difficult and complicated points of theology, in a way that tries to educate the listener – real or imagined – about the true faith. The same approach can be seen when the emphasis was on purgatory, at least in Fribourg in sermons by the Dominicans Bertrand Borgonyon and William of Vufflens and the Augustinian eremite Hans Erhart during the second wave of suppression of Waldensianism in the 1420s–30s.[56] Yet another example of the same view of heresy and conversion is the 'cursor from Basel', Peter Mangold, whose Advent sermons in 1399 initiated the persecution in Strasbourg in 1400. The content of Mangold's sermons remains unknown, but in the preliminary examination he explains that the reason for his sermons was the hope that somebody would convert of their own free will.[57] The preaching campaigns in Fribourg originated from a different direction and tradition from those in south-eastern parts of the Empire, and are probably not directly influenced by Zwicker's texts. Nevertheless, they are important contemporary examples of treating heresy as a pastoral problem.

---

[54] Vincent Ferrer, *Sermones de cuaresma en Suiza*, p. 108. 'Quia si homo plene omnia opera virtuosa perficeret in ieiunando, abstinendo, etc. et dubitaret de fide katholica, non posset intrare in regnum celorum.' The heretical examples given here are more against radical mysticism and general doubt about transubstantiation than specifically against Waldensians. They usually did not deny the Creed, Our Father or the sacraments.

[55] Vincent Ferrer, *Sermones de cuaresma en Suiza*, pp. 77, 116–17, 145.

[56] Utz Tremp, 'Predigt und Inquisition', pp. 219–21.

[57] *Quellen*, ed. Modestin, p. 153 [K115]: 'Und was er do gebrediget hette, daz hette er uß dem munde geton, und rette deste vúrbasser, daz er gedehte, ist jeman hie, der bessert sich villiht, wenne die materie, die er brediget, die rúrte vast ketzerie und den glöben.'

Citations and public penance

Summoning the accused to appear in front of the inquisitor was the action that launched the inquisition of heresy, and public penances imposed on converted heretics continued the performance of heresy and orthodoxy even after the inquisitor himself had left the neighbourhood. These two parts of the process were also the channels of communication that potentially reached the widest audience, as both spread to the parish churches of the area where inquisitors operated.

Although the citations were an integral part of the inquisition of heresy and the formulas for citations often occupied large sections of the inquisitors' manuals,[58] the citation has received much less attention than other parts of heresy prosecutions.[59] Even studies on inquisition procedure often dismiss the summoning of the accused as self-evident or treat it very briefly.[60] An exception is Ian Forrest, who in his study on the counter-measures against heretics in fifteenth-century England has recognized the potential influence of the citations. Forrest describes the citations as hybrid media, involving writing and speech in conjunction, and presented both at the homes of the accused and in their parish churches. The officials took care that the contents of the citations were read aloud carefully and in the vernacular.[61] Although England

---

[58] The Bohemian manual of the early fourteenth century included fifty-three different formulas for summonses, from general summonses for whole towns to special cases of fugitive heretics. These occupy sixteen of the total thirty-nine folios of the manual. See Patschovsky, *Anfänge*, pp. 14, 152–84, 237–41; on the summons as an essential part of the inquisition, Sackville, *Heresy and Heretics*, p. 140.

[59] See especially several recent and thorough studies of judicial consultations and papal legislation in inquisitors' manuals, Parmeggiani, 'Formazione'; Parmeggiani, *Consilia*; Bivolarov, *Inquisitoren-Handbücher*.

[60] H. C. Lea, *A History of the Inquisition of the Middle Ages*, 3 vols. (New York, 1956), I, 407. Trusen, 'Der Inquisitionsprozess', describes the citations simply: 'dort müsse sie zitiert und ihr der Grund der Ladung mitgeteilt werden'; see also Kelly, 'Inquisition and the Prosecution of Heresy', p. 448. Bivolarov in his otherwise detailed account of the procedure against heresy treats the citations only in the sense that the summary process allowed oral instead of written citation: Bivolarov, *Inquisitoren-Handbücher*, p. 302. A slightly more detailed account is given in T. A. Fudge, *The Trial of Jan Hus: Medieval Heresy and Criminal Procedure* (New York, 2013), p. 78. Generally on the importance of citations in late medieval criminal prosecutions, see J. Carraway, 'Contumacy, Defense Strategy, and Criminal Law in Late Medieval Italy', *Law and History Review* 29 (2011), 99–132 (pp. 105–6). Flade in his classic study dedicated a chapter to citations, but discussed there mostly fugitive suspects. The actual system of citations is very vaguely described; see P. Flade, 'Das römische Inquisitionsverfahren in Deutschland bis zu den Hexenprozessen', *Studien zur Geschichte der Theologie und der Kirche* 9 (1902), 1–122 (pp. 56–9). Bueno also discusses summonses to court but only in the context of forgery and fugitives; Bueno, *Defining Heresy*, pp. 47–9.

[61] Forrest, *The Detection of Heresy*, pp. 125–30.

was a special case in medieval Europe in many ways and in particular in heresy legislation, the practice of citation in Zwicker's inquisitions appears to be strikingly similar to the examples studied by Forrest.

The first call was at the opening sermon of the inquisition of heresy in a certain place, usually followed by the declaration of the period of grace (*tempus gratie/tempus indulgentie/tempus misericordie* – time of grace, of indulgence, of mercy), when the heretics and their associates could come to confess without fear of the most severe punishments.[62] There is no evidence of Petrus Zwicker declaring an actual *tempus gratie*, though in the Stettin protocols a clear distinction is made between those coming voluntarily (*spontanea voluntate*) and those summoned (*citatus/citata*).[63] There was another form of general citations in those read in parish churches or otherwise publicly, summoning everybody involved in heresy or with knowledge about heretics to come to the inquisitor. Finally, as the trials progressed persons with heretical *fama* were personally summoned, if need be repeatedly, under threat of excommunication, to appear in court within the assigned time.[64]

Previous scholars have commented on citations by Zwicker based on the protocols of Stettin, and the fundamental observations made by Wilhelm Wattenbach were later confirmed by Dietrich Kurze. The accused were cited either publicly in their parish churches, or individually orally or literally. Some arrived voluntarily (*spontanea voluntate*): Katherina, wife of Henningh Wideman, explained that she was instructed by a certain priest and ordered by her secular lords to follow the summons.[65] The arrival of the citations, at

---

[62] Though it was deemed as legal action, the period of grace was more based on custom than on law; Bivolarov, *Inquisitoren-Handbücher*, p. 293.

[63] There are actually two uses for the words *sponte* and *spontaneus* in Zwicker's material. The question 'Have you been called or judicially cited to come voluntarily?' (Fuisti vocatus vel iudicialiter citatus venire sponte) in the short question list reflects the more general and older meaning of 'voluntarily', as used, for example, by Lucius III in the *Ad abolendam* (1184): 'to return voluntarily to the faith after the discovery of the error' (post deprehensionem erroris ad fidei catholicae unitatem sponte recurrere); X 5.7.9. On the other hand, the use in the protocols follows the practice outlined in later manuals and consultations, referring to those arriving of their own accord without citation. See e.g. the protocol of Hans Spigilman, who arrived from the diocese of Poznań, outside Zwicker's jurisdiction: 'he arrived not cited but of his own free will' (se obtulit non citatus sed spontanea sua voluntate); *Quellen*, ed. Kurze, p. 236. On the meanings of 'sponte' see Bivolarov, *Inquisitoren-Handbücher*, p. 295. The more specific meaning of *sponte* was defined by Gui Foulques in his famous consultation, also known to Zwicker: 'sponte ergo venit, qui non venit admonitus nominatim' (therefore someone who comes – without being admonished by name to do so – comes 'voluntarily'); Bivolarov, *Inquisitoren-Handbücher*, p. 233.

[64] The fourteenth-century Bohemian manual includes four personal, peremptory citations; Patschovsky, *Anfänge*, Nr. 49–63, pp. 152–61. So does the Tuscan formulary; d'Alatri, *L'inquisizione francescana*, pp. 189–91.

[65] Wattenbach, 'Über Ketzergeschichte', pp. 24–6; Kurze, 'Zur Ketzergeschichte', p. 74.

least when they were aggravating summonses directed to specific persons, had the potential to generate conflict. When Zwicker cited the suspects from the Waldensian village of Klein-Wubiser, his envoy, a man called Fikke from the neighbouring village of Gross-Wubiser, was seized and imprisoned by the local Waldensians. Zwicker's second messenger was the priest of Gross-Wubiser, and this time the letter, which the local village magistrate Jacob Hokman knew to include 'bad words' (*mala verba*) about his relatives and neighbours, was allowed to be read out in Klein-Wubiser.[66]

These summonses can be explored via the manual used by Zwicker and composed him or by his subdelegates. The citation formulas by Zwicker have not been studied, as they are preserved only in the unedited manual of St Florian, XI 234, described in Chapter 3. The manual includes a collection of formulas made or revised from earlier manuals especially for the inquisition in the diocese of Passau. There are three formulas for citations, apparently based on citations for inquisitions in Steyr and Enns in 1395–6.[67] The first is a general citation for all who have had dealings with heretics to appear voluntarily in front of the inquisitor, the second a *citatio specialis* for named persons and the third a citation for those who have already confessed to the inquisitor to arrive on a certain day to receive their penance. These formulas not only complement our understanding of Zwicker's inquisitorial practice, but above all demonstrate how the inquisitor mobilized the parish clergy and let his message be heard in every village church.[68] Here, the general citation is used as an example of this propagation of the anti-heretical message.

The general summons was addressed to every parish priest or their vicars in the diocese of Passau who would receive the letter. By the episcopal authority granted to him and with the threat of excommunication should the recipient not comply, Zwicker ordered that:

> [I]n your churches at high masses when a larger number of people attend divine services, and on every Sunday and feast day from the day when the present letter was presented to you until the next resurrection Sunday [Easter Sunday] inclusively, you are to proclaim from your pulpits and have proclaimed by your vicars in a clear and fully intelligible voice: that each and every one of either sex and of whatever estate and condition who has ever in their life belonged to the sect of the Waldensian heretics – who in the vernacular and among themselves are called 'the known', that is 'di kunden låwt', a great multitude of whom, alas, have lain hidden amongst the faithful Catholic people, all the more dangerous for being deceitfully

---

The deposition of Katherina says: 'sed modo venit primo ex inductione alicuius presbiteri et ex iussu dominorum temporalium', *Quellen*, ed. Kurze, p. 227.

[66] *Quellen*, ed. Kurze, pp. 233–5; Cameron, *Waldenses*, p. 141.

[67] The manuscript exemplar on which the manual is based must have ended up in St Florian in 1396 when Zwicker was residing in the area. See Chapter 3, above.

[68] See also Välimäki, '*Bona docere et mala dedocere*'.

hidden! – should in no way dare or presume to go up to and receive the venerable sacrament of the Body of the Lord unless each and every one comes into our presence and – swearing solemnly and judicially in front of us – returns to the unity of the Catholic Church. If someone is caught, he or she will be punished very severely, through our definitive sentence, with the harshest penalty according to the rigour of the law.[69]

The core of the summons is typical of the beginning of inquisition: a general call for everybody involved in heresy to come forward voluntarily to seek absolution in order to avoid more severe penances and punishments. At the same time it displays an unusual sense of timing and familiarity with Waldensian practices. The citation was meant to be read out until Easter Sunday: thus it was issued during Lent, the time of annual repentance, confession and communion expected from every Christian. The admonition not to take part in communion in a heretical state of soul is intended to prevent the common late medieval Waldensian practice of double confession to both heresiarchs and priests. Whether from Pomerania, Strasbourg or Augsburg, the sources of the late fourteenth century attest that Waldensian followers confessed their sins to the parish priests in order to have communion at Easter – obviously not mentioning anything about their heresy.[70] This was well known to the inquisitors. The list *Articuli Waldensium* claims that the practice was recommended by the Waldensian Brethren to their followers.[71] Zwicker inquired into this practice in Stettin[72] and received depositions that confirmed

---

[69] St Florian, MS XI 234, fol. 88vb: 'quatenus omnibus diebus dominicis et festiuis a die qua presentes presentate vobis fuerint littere littere [sic] vsque in diem resurreccionis dominice proxime futurum inclusiue in vestris ecclesiis infra missarum solempnia quando maior populi multitudo ad diuina aderit congregata, viua expressa et plenariter intelligibili voce de vestris ambonibus proclametis ac proclamari per vestros vicarios faciatis, quod omnes et singuli sexus utriusque cuiuscumque status seu condicionis fuerint, qui umquam in tota vita sua fuerunt de secta waldens*ium* hereticorum qui wlgariter noti i.e. di kunden låwt inter se nominati sunt, quorum proch dolor nimia multitudo a plurimis annis in hiis partibus dilituit [r. dilatuit] in medio fidelis populi katholici tanto periculosus [sic] quanto fraudulencius occultata; ad venerabile sacramentum corporis dominici accede aut ipsum sumere nullatenus audeant et presumant nisi prius omnes et singuli ad nostram perueniant presenciam et coram nobis iudicialiter et solempniter ad*iurans* ecclesie katholice redeant vnitatem. Si quis uero repertus fuerit ille uel illa per nostram diffi*nitivam* [sententiam?] pena grauissima iuxta rigorem iuris durissime punietur.'

[70] Biller, 'Aspects', pp. 100–1, 112–17; Cameron, *Waldenses*, p. 132; Modestin, *Ketzer in der Stadt*, pp. 132–4.

[71] Cited from St Florian, MS XI 234, fol. 85rb: 'Item suadent credent[es] suis suis [sic] ire ad communionem ad ecclesiam solum tempore paschali et sic colorant se quasi sint eciam christiani' (Item, they persuade their believers to go to communion in church only at Easter time, and thus they give themselves an appearance as though they also are Christians).

[72] The short question list: 'Es eciam confessus presbiteris ecclesie? Sumpsisti corpus domini? Revelasti ipsis sectam? Fuisti prohibitus revelare sectam an non?' (Did you

it.[73] The citation in Upper Austria speaks directly to those Waldensians who Zwicker anticipated would go to church during Lent. Reading the citations aloud was more than a matter of a judicial summons. It was used to spread the Catholic message that receiving communion in a state of mortal sin such as heresy led to damnation rather than salvation. Vincent Ferrer was getting across the same thing in the Lenten sermons – discussed earlier – that he delivered in the Waldensian areas of Switzerland in 1404.

Petrus Zwicker knew exactly how to adapt his message to his audience. To the Austrian dukes he presented himself as 'brother Petrus, provincial of the Celestine Order for Germany and the inquisitor of heresy' – these are the opening words of his manifesto of 1395.[74] On the other hand, he addressed the converted Waldensians and other laypeople in Upper Austria as 'beloved children', here in the role of 'Petrus the Monk, inquisitor and auditor (*auditor*) of the *kundenlauten*'. This is the self-description in the summons to receive penance, also to be read publicly during mass. Like any professional performer attentive to matters of style, Zwicker demanded that his assistants follow instructions carefully. The parish priest or his vicar was 'to declare and have it declared thus, precisely, exactly and clearly in your vernacular idiom'. Understanding the message was very important. If the 'beloved children' failed to appear to receive their penances on the appointed date, the inquisitor would 'adjudge them publicly to be perjurers: and, as the crime demands, he will without fail or doubt subject them to the harshest penance'.[75]

---

also confess to priests in church? Did you receive the body of Christ? Did you reveal the sect? Were you prohibited or not?). Here from BAV MS Pal. lat. 677, fol. 43r.

[73] *Quellen*, ed. Kurze, pp. 80, 89, 113, 119, 130, 199, 205, 253, 258, 260.

[74] Preger, *Beiträge*, p. 246.

[75] St Florian, MS XI 234, fol. 89ra–rb: 'taliter expresse fideliter et intelligibiliter ydeomate vestro wlgari pronunccietis et pronuncciari faciatis: dilecti pueri, Petrus monachus Inquisitor et auditor der kundenlauten [89rb:] mandat uobis per me uirtute presentis littere suo sigillo sigillatis sub pena excommunicacionis et periurii, quod omnes illi qui siue in aneso [Enns] siue in Stira [Steyr] apud ipsum *illo anno* uel preterito ex parte fidei siue litteras eius habeant siue non habeant et signanter ac specialiter illi qui proximis preteritis suis vocacionibus ad ipsum non venierint [sic] uel si uenerent et suo mandato ulteriorem terminum receperunt ut proxima feria [versi?] hora tali ad ipsum veniant indilate ad locum talem ad suscipiendam gratiosam penitentiam quam ipse promittit omnibus volumptarie et beneuole venientibus humiliterque se disponentibus et deuote; si uero aliqui de predictis residuis non uenirent seu contumaciter venire contempserint, illos periuros publice iudicabit et durissima secundum exigenciam delicti penitentia subiciet sine fallo uel dubio' (You are to declare and have it declared thus, precisely, exactly and clearly in your vernacular idiom. Beloved children, Petrus, monk, inquisitor and hearer of the *kundenlauten* sends this command to you, through me, by virtue of the present letter, sealed with his seal: that all of those in Enns or in Steyr who – in relation to him – this year or the previous year have letters from him regarding faith, or those who do not have [letters], and particularly and especially those who did not come to him on the most recent past summonses, or if they did come and by his

The title 'Petrus monachus Inquisitor et auditor der kundenlauten' is a striking deviation from the formal inquisitorial title used in the sentences or protocols, listing the mandate and ecclesiastical rank of the inquisitor.[76] He is not only the inquisitor of heresy, but particularly a judge of the *kunden-lauten*, the 'known people', the Waldensians, stressing his mission against the Waldensian heresy and using the name Waldensians used of themselves.[77] Possibly Zwicker used similar formulas already in Stettin, for there he is twice called a monk by the local heretics. Beata, wife of Tyde Ruerbeke from Klein-Wubiser, the same village where citations would cause the calamity, testified that when her husband had left the village with some others, apparently to flee from the inquisitor, they had claimed that they 'wanted to go to the monk before thirteen days [have passed?]'.[78] Even more strange and cryptic is the deposition of Gyrdrud Melsaw from the same village. She revealed that when she was angered at her husband when he came back home full of praise for the inquisitor, Sybert Curaw, one of the leading opponents of Zwicker's inquisition in Stettin, said to her he wished 'that she would be in body and soul with the monk', and that she should bear the inquisitor's child.[79] Here, the scribe packs in many things: Gyrdrud being angry at her husband who praised the inquisitor, and Sybert saying something that was probably a bawdily humorous joke about priests' and monks' supposed celibacy, suggesting that Gyrdrud should try and compromise the inquisitor![80] Whatever the joke meant, it shows that a simple monk was probably more within the mental framework of the deponents than the grand 'provincial of the Celestine Order for Germany'. At the same time it is remarkable how precisely Zwicker's self-representation fits the moulds of the two roles that are explored in this book: a monk and an inquisitor.

From the citation formulas it is evident that they were not simply a routine part of judicial summons. They were part of a well-thought-out apparatus for

---

command received a later date, such as the next weekday at such and such an hour: they should come without delay to such and such a place to receive the gracious penance which he promises to all those who come voluntarily and with good will, comporting themselves humbly and devoutly. If however any of the rest of the aforesaid do not come, or contumaciously disdain coming, he will adjudge them publicly to be perjurers: and, as the crime demands, he will without fail or doubt subject them to the harshest penance).

[76] See e.g. Haupt, 'Waldenserthum und Inquisition', p. 404.

[77] See above, Introduction, p. 20, n. 83.

[78] 'Quod vellent ire ad monachum ante 13 dies.' *Quellen*, ed. Kurze, p. 144.

[79] 'Quod vellet, quod esset corpore et anima apud monachum, et quod deberet sibi puerum generari.' Ibid., p. 168. The sentence continues even more puzzlingly: 'et deberent fieri sanctos ultra omnes amicos et episcopos.'

[80] In his own deposition Sybert says that he said this 'jokingly' (*in ioco*); ibid., p. 260. Sexual rumours or accusations that tried to compromise an inquisitor were not unique to Stettin. The deponents in Bologna accused the inquisitor Guido da Vicenza of courting a local woman; M. Vise, 'The Women and the Inquisitor: Peacemaking in Bologna, 1299', *Speculum* 93 (2018), 357–86 (p. 367).

propagating the faith, calling on the services of far more than the inquisitor himself and his immediate assistants. It required mobilization of the parish clergy,[81] and Zwicker made an effort to make sure that his intended message was repeated in the correct form in the different parts of the diocese. The role of the local clergy did not end with the citations. Their duties in the implementation and supervision of the penances imposed upon converted heretics were at least as noteworthy as delivering the citations.

For if Zwicker had a sense of drama in his citations, he also displayed it here: the sentencing of a person for heresy was done with an impressive religious performance. This is the opening of one of the penitential psalms, Psalm 129 'De profundis', sung during the absolution and public penance of a heretic:[82]

> Out of the depths I have cried to thee, O Lord;
> Lord, hear my voice.
> Let thy ears be attentive to the voice of my supplication.

Everything in the sentence – the gestures, liturgy and penance imposed upon the penitent convert, or obstinate heretic – had a symbolic function, aimed at the reconciliation of a lost sheep.[83] It also extended the monastic corporal discipline of penance to laymen and women,[84] and even called on spectators to reflect upon their own sins and possible lapses from orthodoxy.[85] At a very fundamental level the penances were both atonement for sins and a sort of aversion therapy against the errors of which the heretic had been culpable. According to a fifteenth-century revision of Zwicker's formula for the assignment of penitential crosses the punishment could be modified 'by adding, if it is thought worthwhile, a pilgrimage to Saint Peter's in Rome, to be completed within a year, and thereby [bringing about the converts'] instruction in the things that are the opposite of the those matters in which they erred'.[86] Satisfaction was thus made by completing a tedious and expensive peregrination to the place that was the epitome of things Waldensians criticized or doubted: the Roman papacy, indulgences,

---

81 This may not always have happened without problems. Some formulas in Zwicker's manual may refer to clerical disobedience. See Chapter 3, above.

82 See Zwicker's formula for absolution, *Quellen*, ed. Kurze, p. 77: 'Primo dicatur psalmus "Miserere mei deus", vel "Deus miseratur nostri" vel "De profundis"'.

83 On inquisition of heresy as religious drama and symbolic communication, see Merlo, 'Il sermo generalis dell'inquisitore'; Merlo, *Inquisitori e inquisizione del Medioevo*, ch. 5; Scharff, 'Die Inquisitoren und die Macht der Zeichen'; Given, *Inquisition and Medieval Society*, p. 73.

84 Ames, *Righteous Persecution*, pp. 172–7.

85 Arnold, *Inquisition and Power*, pp. 62–3, 72–3.

86 Augsburg, UB MS II.1. 2° 129, fol. 151r: 'addendo prout videtur expedire ad sanctum petrum peregrinacionem romam infra annum faciendam, et sic precipere contraria horum in quibus errauerunt.'

pilgrimages, church buildings and decorations and sumptuous liturgy. It was both personal satisfaction and communal education.

To understand how this worked, one has to look beyond the *sermo generalis* and what an inquisitor could do personally. The declaration of sentences by the inquisitor in the presence of local prelates, community notables and parishioners was undeniably the most formidable spectacle of orthodoxy. Of course, the execution by the secular authorities of relapsed or obstinate heretics attracted great attention, but keen participation is recorded also on the occasions of less draconian punishments. When Petrus Zwicker condemned Andreas Hesel of Vienna to public penance in the cemetery of St Stephen's Cathedral in 1403, the occasion was followed not only by the official witnesses required by canon law, but also by 'very many other trustworthy witnesses both clerics and laymen, and a great multitude of people of this parish, assembled here to hear the word of God'.[87] But however great this audience was, it was much smaller than the multitudes of people who were reached by the performance of penance in large numbers of parish churches.

In early 1398 Zwicker sentenced Jans von Pewg from the parish of Garsten to wear a hat with an image of a perjuring peasant whose tongue is drawn out by a devil. Wearing the hat, he was to sit on ladders in front of the congregation for seven Sundays or feast days in the church of St Aegidius (Giles) of Steyr.[88] He was sentenced not only for heresy but also for perjury, hence the mocking hat. For Jans the sentence was a humiliation, but it also had a communal impact: Steyr was the main urban centre of the Waldensian area of Upper Austria and St Aegidius its major church. There the heresy and above all contrition and satisfaction were made visible and tangible for several weeks. Some penances even required the congregation's participation, such as the one Zwicker imposed on Els Fewr, an old Waldensian widow from Garsten. She had been absolved by Zwicker's predecessor Henricus of Olomouc several years before; later she relapsed into heresy, abjured again to Zwicker's commissary Fridericus of Garsten, and was sentenced to wear crosses for the rest of her life. In addition, and 'for the greater grace to follow from your conversion' (*ad maiorem tue conversionis consequendam graciam*), Zwicker ordered her to do public penance at her parish church in Garsten on seven Sundays. She was to go around the church in front of a priest, who would hit her hard with sticks or branches (*virgis*). After that, when she entered the church she was to prostrate herself in front of the doors, and be

---

[87] Würzburg, UB MS M. ch. f. 51, fol. 28r: 'et quampluribus fidedignis aliis testibus clericis et laicis ac maxima multitudine hominum plebis dicte parochie ibi ad audiendum verbum dei congregata.'

[88] The sentence is edited in Döllinger, *Beiträge II*, pp. 346–8. As stated earlier, Döllinger's editions must be used with caution. I have used these manuscripts: Würzburg, UB MS M. ch. f. 51, fol. 30r–v; BSB MS Clm 5338, fols. 240v–241r; MS Clm 15125, fol. 204ra–vb.

trodden under the entering parishioners' feet until told by the parish priest to stand up. On the same occasion similar public penances were imposed on two other Waldensians.[89]

These sentences are not extraordinary *per se*; the penitential system of Zwicker was firmly based on earlier Franco-Italian and Bohemian inquisitorial manuals.[90] However, the manual of St Florian again offers valuable insight into how the penances were forged into pastoral education. The manual includes a formula titled 'Mandatum ad recipiendum penitentiam', a letter addressed to a parish priest and ordering him to help the penitent in her public penance on the following Sunday. The penance is very much like the one ordered for Els and the two other Waldenses, and it is likely that instructional letters like this accompanied them when they returned to their parishes. The penitent has to circle the church carrying a burning candle in the right hand and a rod in the left hand. When entering the church the convert gives the candle and the branch to the priest and lays herself on the ground. The priest hits her with the rod thrice saying aloud a penitential psalm and after that the convert lies prostrated to be trampled until the majority of the parish has entered the church.[91] The penitent is ordered to continue her penance in another place, which she herself should know. Neither do the duties of the

---

[89] The best edition of the sentence is Haupt, 'Waldenserthum und Inquisition', pp. 404–5. Els later relapsed again and was finally sentenced to be burned at the stake.

[90] See the example of the demolition of heretics' houses in Chapter 3.

[91] The formula, like almost all texts in St Florian, MS XI 234, is heavily and inconsistently abbreviated and at times very difficult to interpret. See fol. 90ra: 'Mandatis [sic] vobis in virtute salutaris obediencie quatenus proxima die dominica ipsam dirigatis in sua penitentia facienda; debet namque statim post vexilla et ante clerum in processione circuire tenendo in manu dextra lumen cereum et in sinistra virgam et quando reintratur in ecclesiam conuersa ad vos dabit vobis lumen et virgam in manus vestras et confestim per^ti [?] se prosternet in terra vosque percucietis eam virga tribus plagis super dorsum eius et dicetis interea psalmum de profundis uel aliquem alium penitentialem psalmum. Ex tunc ipsa iacebit prostata ita ut atri*as* [?] euntibus si qui propter deum velint dimittere conculcetur uel valeat conculceri [sic] donec maior ingressa ecclesiam fuerit multitudo populi christiani; tunc ad vocem vestram ipsa surget, et statim altera uel eadem die ibit in lo[*cum*] talem ad penitentiam peragendam quam ipsa per se bene nouit' (By virtue of salutary obedience you are commanded (?) to direct her next Sunday in the carrying out of her penance. She is to go around in the procession immediately behind the banners and in front of the clergy, holding in her right hand a wax light and in her left hand a rod. And when there is re-entry into the church she is to turn to you and give the light to you and the rod into your hands, and immediately she is to prostrate herself on the ground [-] and you are to strike her with the rod with three blows on her back, meanwhile saying the psalm *De profundis*, or some other penitential psalm. Thereafter she will lie prostrate, such that she is trampled upon or can be trampled upon [by] those coming through the porch [or is not trampled upon] if some want to pass over this for the sake of God, until most of the numbers of Christian people have entered the church. Then at your call she is to get up. And immediately on that same day or another one she should go to such and such a place to carry out the penance that she knows herself).

local priest end here. Zwicker's instruction continues, that on the following Sunday the parish priest should explain the punishment to his congregation, saying that her penitential crosses are due to her false expurgation under oath and receiving communion in such a state. Moreover, the convert has to do the same penance on two other Sundays after she returns from another, unnamed location, and she must wear the crosses on her clothing always when outside her home. The priest is to supervise all this, under the threat of facing inquisitorial proceedings himself, and at the end he has to provide written testimony that the penance has been carried out, so that the inquisitor can absolve the penitent.[92] These detailed guidelines demonstrate how intense the period of penance was also for the local congregation. First the public performance; then, in the absence of the convert, the exposition of the reasons behind it; and finally a repeated theatre of penitence.

The inquisition of heresy, when conducted in a thorough manner and over several years as Zwicker did in Stettin or in Upper Austria, transformed the lands of heretics into a landscape of penance and contrition. The manuals and their formulas obviously describe the ideal, and we should not assume that inquisitor's mandates were always followed to the letter. On the other hand, neither should we think that they were ignored to any significant degree. In Upper Austria the considerable and close involvement of the local clergy and lay elite in inquisitions[93] means that we can assume that citations were read

---

[92] St Florian, MS XI 234, fol. 90ra–rb: 'Tandem vos proxima dominica dicetis ad populum in ambone quod illam penitentiam [90rb:] I*deo* sibi iniunxerimus quia falso se iuramento expurgauitque, taliter in excommunicacione christi corpus accepit, crucem uero portat quia huius ca[usa] est reperta. Et postquam de lo[co] predicto uenerit ip*sa* duabu*s* aliis diebus dominicis penitebit publice sicut prius. Et quocumque sub diuo i.e. sub celo transierit extra domorum tecta tot annos crucem portabit. Cauete siquidem ne quidquam premissorum obmittatur aut laxetur, al*ias* contra vos procederemus, Iuris iusticia me*dia*nte; post que qu*i*dem sic ut [sic] premittitur omnimode facta ipsa, si ad nos venerit vestro cum testimonio litterali prouidebimus ei de gratia facienda' (Later, the next Sunday, from the pulpit you are to say to the people that this penance [was imposed for these reasons]. 'We will have imposed it on her because she [something missing] and she purged herself on oath, falsely; and being this in a state of excommunication she received the body of Christ; actually she wears a cross because grounds for this were discovered.' And afterwards she will have come [back] from the aforesaid place, and she will do penance publicly on two other Sundays, just as she did earlier. And she will wear her cross for such and such a number of years, wherever she will have gone outside the roofs of houses into the open air, that is to say, under the sky. Look out lest any of the aforesaid things get left out or relaxed: otherwise we shall proceed against you, through the justice of the law. After these things, however, if there is news [that] all things [penances?] have been in every way carried out, if she comes to us with your testimonial letter, we shall provide for the grace that is to be granted to her).

[93] One has to remember that Fridericus of Garsten was Zwicker's commissary and Castellan of Steyr, and that Heinrich von Zelking was a representative of the secular arm and supervisor of penance. See Chapter 3 above.

out and that penances were supervised in the local churches. This all lasted from Sunday to Sunday and one from one feast to another: the first general citations were read out for several weeks, followed by specific citations. If the suspects did not show up, these were repeated, and after that the still contumacious heretics were excommunicated, this again to be announced aloud in surrounding parishes. After the trials were over the public penances followed, accompanied by declarations of absolution from excommunication. The inquisitor himself, or his assistant, toured the land conducting trials and holding sermons. All this affected the services in the local communities for weeks, months and even years. Of necessity, it required a local clergy that was up to these tasks and possessed an adequate understanding of heresy. This need was most likely behind the composition of the new theological polemics and their great popularity. It also generated pastoral literature and even vernacular translations based on Zwicker's texts, which are discussed next.

From polemics to pastoral theology: Ulrich von Pottenstein

So far the pastoralization of heresy has been traced in anti-heretical treatises, inquisitors' manuals, the process of inquisition and inquisitors' communication with the surrounding society through sermons, sentences and summonses. Apart from the sermon, where several issues and audiences could be addressed simultaneously, these were all media or genres specifically directed against heretics. In this section I am going to extend the net to include two works which had far more general themes and were not at first sight anti-heretical, but which were both influenced by Petrus Zwicker's texts and the anti-Waldensian atmosphere of the 1390s. Although their genre and tradition in no way required it, these works came to incorporate significant anti-heretical sections either taken directly from Zwicker's text or developed from Zwicker's themes. The texts are a massive catechetical treatise by Ulrich von Pottenstein, completed in the first decade of the fifteenth century and written in the Austrian-Bavarian dialect of Early New High German, and a Latin postilla by Johlín of Vodňany, parish priest of St Wenceslas at Zderaz, Prague, written in 1403–4. Both are representative of the new currents of pastoral care, preaching and lay education emerging around 1400, the former of the so-called *Wiener Schule* of religious literature, and the latter of the Prague reform movement.[94] They demonstrate how entangled the issues of church reform, lay education and the danger of heresy were around 1400. These texts also show that Zwicker's texts were eagerly received by his contemporaries, and that the discussions on Waldensian heresy touched people outside the relatively narrow circle of those directly involved in the inquisitions.

[94] These reform movements will be discussed in relation to each work.

Inquisitors were also priests, with pastoral obligations and other tasks beyond the business of inquiring into dissidents. In other words, being an inquisitor of heresy was not a full-time occupation.[95] So it is not surprising to find them engaged in writing pastoral works as well as anti-heretical treatises. Petrus Zwicker wrote a short exposition of the *Pater noster* that has been preserved at the library of St Florian. A piece of monastic meditation rather than an exercise in popular pastoralism, it nevertheless betrays an interest in explaining the main Christian prayer that laypeople were expected to know.[96] Martin von Amberg (Prague) composed a German manual of confession before 1382,[97] and a short introduction to Richard of Thetford's sermon manual is attributed to him.[98] Martinus's manual of confession is a general treatise, not directed against heresy or heretics. But what it presupposed of laypeople was just one aspect of the same general broadening of pastoral care and correction that we see at work in the expansion of the interrogatories of the inquisitors of Waldensianism in the late fourteenth century. Explicating the Apostles' Creed, Martinus twice stresses that every adult Christian should know the articles addressing Christ's human nature, and that there is no excuse for not knowing them.[99]

This view is mirrored in the depositions from the 1390s. The episcopal tribunal in Regensburg noted down flaws in the way the deponents pronounced the Lord's Prayer, the Creed and the Hail Mary,[100] and in Stettin Zwicker remarked on the various and to him unsatisfactory ways of saying

---

[95] The office of inquisitor was one title and duty among many for perhaps a majority of late fifteenth-century Italian friars acting as inquisitors; Tavuzzi, *Renaissance Inquisitors*, pp. 79–119; see also Kieckhefer, *Repression*, pp. 5–8.

[96] St Florian, MS XI 96, fols. 298r-299r. The existence of this work was first recognized by Biller, *Waldenses*, p. 274; recently, Smelyansky, 'Self-Styled Inquisitors', pp. 168–76. Unlike Smelyansky, I am inclined to interpret the tract as a monastic, not an anti-heretical or pastoral work. As I have argued in Chapter 3, there are very good reasons to assume that the treatise ended up at St Florian through Zwicker's visit there, and that the uniqueness of the extant copy indicates local tradition rather than wider circulation.

[97] Martin von Amberg, *Der Gewissensspiegel*

[98] BSB MS Clm 3764, fol. 35ra–vb: 'Incipiunt modi predicandi boni ualde. Et primo modus generalis editus a domino martino Inquisitori hereticorum Amberge' (Here begin very good ways of preaching. And the first way was produced by lord Martin of Amberg, inquisitor of heretics). Cf. H. Hauke and A. Freckmann, *Mittelalterliche lateinische Handschriften aus Augsburger Bibliotheken. Band II: Dominikaner- und Dombibliothek (Clm 3680-3830)*, in preparation. Description available at *Manuscripta Mediaevalia*.

[99] Martin von Amberg, *Der Gewissensspiegel*, pp. 36–7: 'Die stück di do gehorn zw einer bewerung seyner heyligen menscheit ist ein yegleicher mensche der zw wissen und zw chunnen seynem nachsten auz zu legen [...] Die syben stuck ist ein iczleicher schuldich czw wissen und zw gelawben und der mag sich auch nyemand von unwissenheit enschuldigen.'

[100] ÖNB MS 3748, fols. 145r–v, 153r, 155r.

the Hail Mary.[101] All this was only marginally important in deciding whether the accused was a heretic. Ignorance of the basic articles of faith cannot have helped the accused, but it was poor judicial evidence of heresy. Rather, it revealed the need for pastoral correction and education. At times this was done by the inquisitor and on the spot, as when Zwicker assigned Simon and Jude as patrons to a certain Jacob in Stettin, who in his interrogation claimed not to have a patron apostle,[102] but we can assume that in the majority of cases this duty fell to the clergy who supervised the penance. Those who came under suspicion of heresy received special attention, but the correction of heretics was not a separate phenomenon to the general admonition or imposition on the laity to follow a good Christian life, it was simply the most extreme aspect of it.

In relation to the pastoralization of heresy, the works of Ulrich von Pottenstein and Johlín of Vodňany are even more fascinating than the inquisitors' schooling of erring souls. Unlike inquisitors, these two clerics were not expected to write or preach against heresy, but they did. Explicitly anti-heretical sections were not standard features of catechetical literature or postils, both of which usually addressed general matters of faith and morals. Consequently, the devotion of significant attention to attacking heresy – in two such works written at the same time and in the same geographical area where Waldensians were persecuted – demonstrates that Zwicker's call to arms in this cause had got a response and had found new champions. As we shall see later, both authors must have been informed of the persecutions taking place since the early 1390s and may well have had some direct experience of Waldensians.

Ulrich von Pottenstein (*c.* 1360–1416) made his ecclesiastical career and rose among the ranks of the Austrian clergy at the turn of the century, and he could not have done that without coming across the heretics. As parson of Pottenstein (early 1390s–1404) he was a member of the chapter of St Stephen's in Vienna. Ulrich was closely connected to the ducal court as their chaplain.[103] Since Ulrich was a canon at the Cathedral of St Stephen, he could hardly have remained unaware of the trial of Andreas Hesel – nor of his punishment

---

[101] *Quellen*, ed. Kurze, pp. 97, 99, 227, 239.

[102] Ibid., p. 99: 'et quod non habeat apostolum, sed inquisitor ei dedit Symonem et Judam pro apostolis.' Not to have had a patron apostle at all was exceptional among the Waldensians interrogated in Stettin, although the degree of commitment to their veneration varied remarkably.

[103] G. Baptist-Hlawatsch, 'Einführung', in *Dekalog-Auslegung: das erste Gebot: Text und Quellen*, ed. G. Baptist-Hlawatsch (Tübingen, 1995), pp. 1*–64* (pp. 1*–4*); Baptist-Hlawatsch, *Das katechetische Werk*, pp. 2–4; P. Ernst, 'Ulrich von Pottenstein. Leben und Werk nach dem Stand der neueren Forschung', *Unsere Heimat* 58 (1987), 203–13 (p. 206); Menhardt, 'Funde zu Ulrich von Pottenstein', pp. 146–7. On Ulrich in the service of Albrecht IV, the most recent is C. Lackner, *Hof und Herrschaft: Rat, Kanzlei und Regierung der österreichischen Herzoge (1365–1406)* (Vienna, 2002), p. 157.

by Petrus Zwicker, the wearing of penitential crosses in the cemetery of St Stephen's in the presence of what is described a great multitude of clergy and laity in March 1403, even if Ulrich is not specifically named as having been part of this crowd.[104]

For decades scholars have speculated about the possibility that Ulrich got hold of some property confiscated from the Waldensians. As parson and dean of Enns-Lorch he did indeed create new benefices, and in his testament (1416) he donated significant property to a new chapel, whose building he had personally initiated, in the Church of St Mary at Enns, property which he had acquired during the preceding years in Upper Austria. Ulrich's noble patron Reinprecht II von Wallsee, whom Ulrich also persuaded to make donations, had been *Landeshauptmann* (governor) at Enns since 1380, and would thus have been responsible for dispensing secular justice in the inquisitions of heresy, including possible confiscations of property.[105] Reinprecht is indeed mentioned as a persecutor of Waldensians in a document from 1408.[106] Unfortunately the references to inquisitions at Enns are vague remarks in Zwicker's later sentences, and we cannot even be sure that property was confiscated there.[107] In any case Ulrich received the offices at Enns only in 1411 or 1412, well after he had finished his catechetic *summa*,[108] so there is no need to attribute his anti-heretical views to a desire for personal gain. There were several points in Ulrich's life when he could easily have encountered suspected, convicted or converted Waldensians, and in general it is clear that

---

[104] Würzburg, UB M. ch. f. 51, f. 28r: 'presentibus honorabilibus et discretis viris et dominis petro Schulderwerem plebanus in stewestarff [?], ulrico de gretz et henrico dicto albus predicatoribus apud dictam ecclesiam sancti Stephani et quampluribus fidedignis aliis testibus clericis et laicis ac maxima multitudine hominum plebis dicte parochie ibi ad audiendum verbum dei congregata' (present being the honourable and worthy men and lords Peter Schulderwerem parish priest in Stewestarff (?), Ulric of Graz and Henry called 'White', preachers at the said church of St Stephen; and very many other trustworthy witnesses, clerical and lay, and a great multitude of men of the parish, gathered there to hear the word of God).

[105] Menhardt, 'Funde zu Ulrich von Pottenstein', p. 147; Ernst, 'Ulrich von Pottenstein', p. 207; Segl, 'Die Waldenser in Österreich', pp. 173–5. On Ulrich's and Ruprecht's donations and foundations, but without any speculation about Waldensian origin, see Baptist-Hlawatsch, 'Einführung', pp. 5*–7*.

[106] Doblinger, 'Die Herren von Walsee', p. 399; Segl, 'Die Waldenser in Österreich', p. 175, n. 57.

[107] The only person certainly convicted at Enns was Jans von Pewg, whose sentence for perjury in January 1398 refers to his first abjuration at Enns 'one and half year earlier'; see pp. 145–6 above. In all probability many more were sentenced at Enns, because Zwicker's formulary of citations refers to past inquisition at Enns and Steyr. See above, pp. 188–9, n. 75. In theory the property was confiscated from all who did not come voluntarily to confess and convert; Bivolarov, *Inquisitoren-Handbücher*, pp. 306–7. However, the sources do not reveal anything about the practice Zwicker followed.

[108] Baptist-Hlawatsch, 'Einführung', pp. 5*–6*.

a clergyman forging a career in Austria in the 1390s and early 1400s did not need to seek out heretics to meet them, but was bound to encounter or at the very least hear of them. In one way or another they were part of the common or garden experience of contemporary clergymen, and it is this fact that explains the popularity of Zwicker's texts in Austria and southern Germany, as well as Ulrich's decision to translate the *Cum dormirent homines* and incorporate it into his catechetical treatise.

The campaigns against Waldensians in Reinprecht von Wallsee's territory may have facilitated Ulrich's translation work at a more general level. Ulrich was a representative of the *Wiener Schule* of authors, translators and compilers, and a central characteristic of this group was a practical rather than speculative scholarly bent when it came to theology and other academic disciplines. And, as Klaus Wolf has emphasized, the literary production and other activities of these academics connected to the Habsburg court – which had founded the University of Vienna – were fundamentally in support of the state (*staatstragende*). For theologians this meant defending the unity of faith in the realm. While Wolf devotes much time to the university's anti-Jewish and anti-Hussite endeavours, as well as the struggle against lay superstition in the fifteenth century, by contrast the political dimension of fighting Waldensians gets only brief attention, in relation to Ulrich von Pottenstein and Reinprecht von Wallsee.[109] Yet, in the 1390s no one could have foreseen the Hussites, and it was the Waldensians who were the heretics that threatened the Church in Austria. After Duke Albrecht III's death in 1395, a contemporary chronicle praised his faith and his efforts to uproot heresy, because of which more than a hundred heretics were later burned in Steyr – an obvious reference to Petrus Zwicker's inquisitions starting in 1395.[110] After the sudden death of the duke at the age of 45, Zwicker seems to have been afraid of losing the support of secular rulers. The point of his manifesto of 1395 was to convince the new dukes Albrecht IV and Wilhelm of the seriousness of the danger of heresy in Austria. His call was answered only after some delay. At Pentecost 1397 the ducal cousins issued a letter to their subjects ordering the arrest of all heretics and those impeding the work of inquisitors. In January 1398 the Castellan of Steyr, Heinrich von Zelking, featured as *cooperator* with the inquisitor by order of the said dukes.[111] The concern for the lack of secular support Zwicker expressed in his letter and the delay in replying are both probably the result of

---

[109] K. Wolf, *Hof – Universität – Laien: literatur- und sprachgeschichtliche Untersuchungen zum deutschen Schrifttum der Wiener Schule des Spätmittelalters* (Wiesbaden, 2006), pp. 118–30 (in general), 193–4 (on Waldensians).

[110] *Österreichische Chronik von den 95 Herrschaften*, ed. Seemüller, p. 221: 'Auch schuf er bey seinen zeiten auch cze rewten die keczerhait, die da haisset Waldenses, darumb hernach mer denn hundert keczer ze Steyr wurden verprennet.'

[111] For Zwicker's manifesto, see Preger, *Beiträge*, pp. 246–50. The letter of Albrecht IV and Wilhelm has been published in Preuenhueber, *Annales Styrenses*, pp. 72–3; and Friess, 'Patarener, Begharden und Waldenser', pp. 271–2. See also Haupt,

the extremely unstable political situation in which the cousins were vying for power.[112] However, after they had settled their accounts, the next generation of Habsburgs certainly saw themselves as protectors of the Catholic faith and persecutors of dissidents.

It was in this political environment that Ulrich von Pottenstein wrote his catechetical treatise. Rather than a practical guide to the Christian life, this was a German compendium of theological knowledge translated from Latin sources.[113] The treatise was so huge that it never circulated as a complete work. It consists of seventy chapters divided into four parts; *Pater noster* (chapters 1–13), *Ave Maria* (14–20), *Credo* (21–42) and *Magnificat/Decalogus* (43–70). The full work would have covered around 1,200 folios, but despite its huge size the internal references between different parts imply that Ulrich von Pottenstein intended it to be a unit.[114] However, he never intended his work to be read as a whole: rather it was to be browsed thematically. For this purpose he prepared an index to the whole work, containing Latin/German keywords (for example: *Aqua/Wasser* – water) in alphabetical order, and providing references by chapter number and letter. The index for the whole work has not been preserved, only indices for individual parts, but the *Gesamtregister* (complete index) has been reconstructed by Gabriele Baptist-Hlawatsch.[115] The exact dating of the catechetic treatise is not known, and Ulrich must have toiled for years in compiling a work of that size. It is clear that Ulrich was at work within a few years of the *Cum dormirent homines*'s composition and Zwicker's inquisitions in Upper Austria. Baptist-Hlawatsch's view is that the compilation of the catechetical treatise began around 1395 and the whole work was finished before Ulrich received the deaconate at Enns-Lorch in 1411/12.[116] Whatever the exact dates, we can be confident in talking about the 'contemporary' reception of the *Cum dormirent homines*.

The connection between the *Cum dormirent homines* and Ulrich von Pottenstein's *oeuvre* was pointed out by Hermann Menhardt in 1953, although he followed the false attribution of the *Cum dormirent homines* to Peter von

---

'Waldenserthum und Inquisition', p. 374, Kieckhefer, *Repression*, p. 56; Segl, 'Die Waldenser in Österreich', p. 146; Modestin, 'The Anti-Waldensian Treatise', p. 217.

[112] On the power struggle between the Habsburg cousins, see Lackner, *Hof und Herrschaft*, pp. 23–4; C. Lackner, 'Des mocht er nicht geneissen, wiewol er der rechte naturleich erbe was …: Zum Hollenburger Vertrag vom 22. November 1395', *Jahrbuch für Landeskunde von Niederösterreich* 65 (1999), 1–16.

[113] T. Hohmann, '"Die recht gelerten maister". Bemerkungen zur Übersetzungsliteratur der Wiener Schule des Spätmittelalters', in *Die Österreichische Literatur: ihr Profil von den Anfängen im Mittelalter bis ins 18. Jahrhundert (1050–1750)*, ed. F. P. Knapp and H. Zeman (Graz, 1986), pp. 349–65 (p. 356).

[114] Baptist Hlawatsch, 'Einführung', p. 17*.

[115] Baptist-Hlawatsch, *Das katechetische Werk*, pp. 209–322; see also Wolf, *Hof – Universität – Laien*, p. 193.

[116] Baptist-Hlawatsch, 'Einführung', pp. 20*–2*.

Pillichsdorf.[117] Menhardt also presented a collation of Zwicker's treatise and the *Credo* part of Ulrich's treatise according to its earliest and most complete manuscript copy, in MS 3050 of the Österreichische Nationalbibliothek.[118] He noticed that Ulrich had translated almost the complete text of Zwicker's treatise, but despite his meticulous work Menhardt was unable to locate the last chapter of the *Cum dormirent homines*, the chapter on denial of oaths. This led him to speculate whether it had been lost with the last, ripped-off quire of MS 3050, or whether Ulrich never used it.[119] Ulrich did indeed translate Zwicker's defence of oath-taking, but not, unlike all other chapters, its *Credo* part, only its exposition of the Decalogue.[120] This fits with the thematic, encyclopaedic disposition of Ulrich's treatise, but it also demonstrates that Ulrich worked with Zwicker's text for a long time instead of simply translating and inserting it into his work in one block.

Ulrich von Pottenstein shared Zwicker's pastoral approach to heresy. Waldensians were not an unfathomable demonic other. Instead Waldensian heresy was a failure in good Christian practice and represented doubt about the Church and the clergy's authority. It was a negative image of the Christian *modus vivendi*, but not in the mysterious and diabolical way that was commonly represented in the fourteenth-century rumours about heretics as devil worshippers. Such representations would dominate the clergy's imagination some decades later as the demonizing imagery formerly attached to heretics was transferred to witches.[121] Waldensian heresy did not seep into the Church through fundamental denial of God, nor was it a metaphysical error such as the ancient heresies of Mani and Arius, which Ulrich likewise discusses in the *Credo* part.[122] Neither was it idolatry and superstition, whose various and numerous forms Ulrich, like many others before him, regarded as disobeying the First Commandment.[123]

---

[117] Menhardt, 'Funde zu Ulrich von Pottenstein', pp. 159–70.

[118] Ibid., pp. 167–8. Cod. 3050, copied by a professional scribe, Albrand von Suntra, in Vienna at the beginning of the fifteenth century, is considered to be the most trustworthy exemplar of the *Credo* part, and closest to the author's text. See Baptist-Hlawatsch, *Das katechetische Werk*, pp. 13–20.

[119] Menhardt, 'Funde zu Ulrich von Pottenstein', p. 167.

[120] Ulrich von Pottenstein, *Dekalog*, 2. Gebot, Cap. L. Transcription of Kalocza, Föszékesegyházi Könyvtár MS 629 by SFB 226.

[121] See especially Utz Tremp, *Von der Häresie zur Hexerei*, pp. 311–53, 383–531.

[122] Manicheans and their dualist universe were quite naturally brought up right at the beginning of the Creed, where belief in one God as creator of all things was handled; Ulrich von Pottenstein, *Credo*, cap. 22A (ÖNB MS 3050, fol. 45rb). Correspondingly, Arians are presented as a warning example of not believing in Christ's two natures; ibid., 23A (fol. 59va).

[123] The First Commandment has been edited; see Pottenstein, *Dekalog-Auslegung*. Ulrich's opinions on superstition have been examined by E. Lasson, *Superstitions médiévales: une analyse d'après l'exégèse du premier commandement d'Ulrich de Pottenstein* (Paris, 2010). Some twenty years earlier Martinus of Prague also listed 'ungelawben'

Waldensianism manifested itself in different and manifold lapses from the doctrine of the Church, which – following the model of Zwicker's biblicist polemical prose – was firmly founded on the word of God. Ulrich employs the schema and further develops it. The *Cum dormirent homines*'s chapter about burial in consecrated ground is inserted into the *Credo* part's chapter 27, treating different aspects of Christian burial according to the example set by Christ's tomb after his crucifixion. Refutation of the Waldensians' beliefs begins directly after a discussion on whether executed criminals can be given Christian burial, and if women who died while pregnant could be buried with their foetuses. Just a short introduction leads the reader to different topic:

> However much burial has a deep and solid foundation in the Old and New Testaments and in holy laws, nevertheless the impious Waldensian heretics speak against it and suppose in their error that a corpse of a dead person is not better buried in a church or in a graveyard than in a field or some other place.[124]

This topical rearrangement of the chapters translated from the *Cum dormirent homines* brings Waldensian heresy closer to everyday pastoral problems. As in the case of problems such as burial of criminals or pregnant women, Waldensian doubts about the necessity of consecrated cemeteries are presented as issues that the reader of the catechetical treatise might face in relation to which Ulrich's treatise offers the requisite authorities and correct interpretation. Burial is not the only such case. The chapters on the consecration of churches (*Cum dormirent homines*: 23) and altars (24) as well as on the veneration of Mary and the saints (19) and of God (20) are all dispersed within Ulrich's chapter 33 on the verse 'Ich gelaub in die heyligen gemainen kyrchen, gemainschafft der heyligen' (I believe in the holy catholic church and the communion of saints).[125] The criticism of consecrations is presented as denial of the material church, which is a manifestation of the universal church. The question of whether God alone or Mary and the saints as well can be venerated quite obviously relates to the communion of saints. The anti-Waldensian sections are interspersed with others on completely different

---

(unbelief) as deviation from the First Commandment; Martin von Amberg, *Der Gewissensspiegel*, pp. 40–3.

[124] Ulrich von Pottenstein, *Credo*, cap. 27M (ÖNB MS 3050, fol. 103va–vb): 'Wie wol die begrebnuss aus der alten ee vnd aus der newen ee vnd aus den heyligen rechten ainen tewffen vnd vesten grunt haben, dannoch widersprechen ir die vnseligen keczer Waldenses vnd halden daz in irem irrsal, daz aines toten menschen leichnam nicht paz begraben werd in ainer kirchen oder in ainem freythof denn in ainem akcher oder an ainer andern stat.'

[125] Ulrich von Pottenstein, *Credo*, cap. 33 (ÖNB MS 3050 fols. 244ra–260ra). Consecration of churches is addressed in 33C, of altars in 33E, on Mary and the saints in 33H and the veneration of God alone in 33I.

issues, such as judicial privileges of the clergy and church space.[126] The *Cum dormirent homines* had already looked at Waldensianism through a structure that stressed certain themes, for example ecclesiastical singing, doing this more in accordance with their importance in contemporary Catholicism than their prominence in heretical criticism. Ulrich simply went further down the same path.

Ulrich does not, however, completely break up the structure of the *Cum dormirent homines*. The main part of Zwicker's treatise is translated almost without interruptions, and constitutes Ulrich's chapter 35.[127] Ulrich explains how the Waldensians in many ways oppose what he has written, that only properly ordained priests can consecrate the Eucharist, and that the Waldensians try to deprive the clergy of their dignity (*wirdichait*).[128] Here, Waldensianism is presented explicitly and primarily as an anticlerical heresy. This view is prominent also in the *Cum dormirent homines*, and will be discussed in more detail in Chapter 5 below, but it is nowhere so openly stated as in Ulrich's treatise. Only at the end of his long chapter 35 does Ulrich give the fundamental explanation for why he has written so much about heresy:

> But that I have written at such length and so much about heretics in this chapter: I am driven to this, because they are those who in so many ways, so deceitfully and mischievously oppose the universal holy Christian Church, which is the only dove which alone is beautiful, which alone is transcendent (*auszerwelt*), which alone is without wrinkle and without blemish; and they defile her (the Church) in all her parts, her glory and order, where and how often they are capable.[129]

The Waldensians attack the Church in such diverse ways that Ulrich feels he has been forced to counter them. This is pretty standard rhetoric against heresy, and Ulrich's originality does not lie in his words, but in his organization of his

---

[126] Cap. 33D in between of consecration of churches and altars.

[127] Ulrich von Pottenstein, *Credo*, cap. 35 (ÖNB MS 3050, fols. 276ra–289va). It covers chapters 1–18, 25–9, and 31–5 of the *Cum dormirent homines*, though not in that exact order. See also Menhardt, 'Funde zu Ulrich von Pottenstein', pp. 161, 167–8.

[128] Ulrich von Pottenstein, *Credo*, cap. 35A (ÖNB MS 3050, fol. 276ra): 'Als man nu gehöret hat von dem heyligen sacrament des altar, wy daz niem gesegen mag denn ain priester, der da rechtleich geweicht ist nach den sluszeln der kirchen die Christus Ihesus den czwelifpoten verlichen hat vnd iren nachkomen. Daz widersprechen die keczer waldenses manichueltichlich vnd encziehen priesterleicher wirdichait an manigen stukchen.'

[129] Ulrich von Pottenstein, *Credo*, cap. 35N (ÖNB MS 3050, fol. 289va]: 'Daz aber ich so lang vnd so uil in dem capitel von den keczern geschriben han, darczu hat mich geübt, wann si sind dÿ, die der gemainen heyligen christenleichen kirchen, die ain ainige tawbe ist, die allain die schön ist, die allain die auszerwelt ist, die allain an alle runczen ist vnd an mail, so gar manigueltichleich, listichleich vnd schalkchleich widersprechen vnd si lestern in iren glidern vnd in irer czir vnd ordnung, wa vnd wie offte si daz volbringen mügen.'

materials, how he presents the manifold threat that the heretics represented. By dispersing the chapters of the *Cum dormirent homines*, and by integrating the negative image of heretics within chapters that give positive, normative guidelines for a good Christian life, Ulrich juxtaposes the heretical and the orthodox in a way that was not possible in conventional anti-heretical polemic. Ulrich's motivation for writing against heresy was the same as that of the apologists, to defend Christianity. But the pastoral and didactic text that was his chosen genre was better adapted than theirs – straight anti-heretical polemic – for the job of presenting the Waldensians as a negative image of the Church.[130]

The analysis of Ulrich von Pottenstein's translation principles, not to speak of a systematic comparison of Zwicker's Latin and Ulrich's vernacular, is beyond the scope of the present study.[131] However, there is one feature in Ulrich's translation methods that concerns us here. At times, Ulrich clarifies Zwicker's refutation of heresy in order to make the meaning utterly unambiguous to the laity and lower clergy. Menhard noted that at times Ulrich translates the *Cum dormirent homines* almost word for word, with occasional lapses into 'latinities', but often also expands Zwicker's prose.[132] More recently, both Baptist-Hlawatsch and Wolf have noted how Ulrich tried to follow his Latin models very closely. This occasionally resulted in almost incomprehensible sentences, but on the other hand allowed non-Latinate readers as intimate access to Latin learning as possible.[133] Although Baptist-Hlawatsch and Wolf were commenting on Ulrich's translation of Gratian's *Decretum* and the *Summa de vitiis et virtutibus* by William Perald, their remarks are equally applicable to his Zwicker translation. At times clarifications and additions were necessary simply in order to convert the at times very condensed Latin of the treatise into a vernacular that a less erudite reader could follow. To be intelligible, the references to the Bible in the *Cum dormirent homines* often require a reader to be familiar with the verse in question. When translating Ulrich tried, if not always very successfully, to adapt the scholastic refutation of heresy for a reader who was not fully aware of the medieval commentary tradition.[134]

In addition to these minor clarifications, there is a significant addition by Ulrich in chapter 35A, which opens the longest almost uninterrupted section on Waldensians. Ulrich gives a relatively accurate translation of Zwicker's

---

[130] See also R. Välimäki, 'Transfers of Anti-Waldensian Material from a Polemical Treatise to a Didactic Text', *Medieval Worlds* 7 (2018), 153–69.

[131] This was the goal of the unfinished dissertation project by Christine Wolf, whose transcriptions I have been able to consult; see pp. 16–17 above.

[132] Menhardt, 'Funde zu Ulrich von Pottenstein', pp. 160–6.

[133] Baptist-Hlawatsch, 'Einführung', pp. 38*–9*; Wolf, *Hof – Universität – Laien*, p. 350.

[134] An example of this is discussed in detail in Välimäki, 'Transfers of Anti-Waldensian material', pp. 161–2.

opening with the parable of the wheat and the tares (Matthew 13:24–30). But whereas Zwicker gives only a very short explanation – that the good sower is Christ, while the enemy sowing tares among the wheat is Satan, the sleeping men being negligent prelates – Ulrich gives a complete homily on the Bible verse. This gives further explanations of the parable, such as expounding the field as the human heart and adding as *auctoritates* Ambrose, Augustine, Remigius and Chrysostom.[135] This section somewhat resembles contemporary moral sermons on the parable, such as Vincent Ferrer's homily on the spiritual negligence and intellectual ignorance of men,[136] or Cardinal Bertrand de la Tour's interpretation, made some decades earlier, that the field was divided into four, consisting of the human conscience, the Church, the religious orders (*religio sacra*) and the Scriptures. Each had its corresponding tares, namely evil deeds and vices for individual conscience, 'tares of the heretics' (*zizania hereticorum*) for the Church, hypocritical brothers for religious order, and false commentary for Scripture.[137]

Unlike the authors of these 'general' homilies, Ulrich concentrates on the tare of heresy. It is remarkable is that he also takes up the ambiguous relationship to heresy and its persecution that is inherent in the parable. Even though wheat and tares was a metaphor commonly used in anti-heretical texts, at least after Bernard of Clairvaux revived the Augustinian tradition in Albi in 1145,[138] it could be read as forbidding persecution and requiring tolerance until the Last Judgment, because Christ warned against gathering tares lest the wheat should also be rooted out. Only in the time of harvest are the bundles of tares to be burned (Matthew 13:28–30).[139] Ulrich takes up this question as a 'doubt' (*dubium*) interpretation:

---

[135] Zwicker, *Cum dormirent homines*, p. 277G–H. Cf. Ulrich von Pottenstein, *Credo*, cap. 35A (ÖNB MS 3050, fol. 276ra–rb). Ulrich's own homily is at fols. 276rb–277rb, where the translation from Zwicker continues from where it was interrupted. Menhardt had already pointed out the homily-like character of this passage; Menhardt, 'Funde zu Ulrich von Pottenstein', p. 162.

[136] Sermo XXXVIII. Dominica V, post Epiphaniam. Sermo I, in Vincent Ferrer, *Opera seu sermones de tempore et sanctis, cum Tractatu de Vita Spirituali*, ed. C. Erhard (Augsburg, 1729), p. 121.

[137] BAV MS Vat. lat. 1240, fol. 140v. On the controversial and nuanced life-story of a Franciscan cardinal at the court of Pope John XXII, P. Nold, 'Bertrand de la Tour, O.Min. Life and Works', *Archivum Franciscanum Historicum* 94 (2001), 275–323; P. Nold, *Pope John XXII and his Franciscan Cardinal: Bertrand de la Tour and the Apostolic Poverty Controversy* (Oxford, 2003).

[138] B. M. Kienzle, *Cistercians, Heresy, and Crusade in Occitania, 1145–1229: Preaching in the Lord's Vineyard* (York, 2001), pp. 100–1, 165–6; Ames, *Righteous Persecution*, p. 25; Sackville, *Heresy and Heretics*, pp. 155, 171; E. Mitre Fernández, 'Muerte, veneno y enfermedad, metáforas medievales de la herejía', *Heresis: revue d'histoire des dissidences européennes* 25 (1995), 63–84 (p. 81).

[139] On the liberal implications of the parable, R. H. Bainton, 'The Parable of the Tares as the Proof Text for Religious Liberty to the End of the Sixteenth Century', *Church History* 1 (1932), 67–89.

Also, what is 'tare' today can become wheat tomorrow. 'Suffer both to grow until the harvest', that is the tares and the wheat, the evil and the good, till the day of the Last Judgment. Dubium. From this passage it could be said, that one cannot separate heretics from the church; moreover, one should not correct them with the sword.[140]

The medieval understanding of tolerance, especially tolerance of heretics, was not one the modern Western world would recognize as such. Ulrich shares the common high and late medieval opinion that only secret heretics who do not cause damage to the Church should be tolerated,[141] whereas 'the [obvious open] heretics, who drag others away from faith, these should be separated from the church with both swords [i.e. spiritual and secular], so that a rotten member does not corrupt the others'.[142]

The more extensive and explicit interpretation that Ulrich attaches to Zwicker's prologue demonstrates the demands of different audiences, or at least what the authors deemed these audiences to be capable of understanding. Ulrich's expansion is all standard interpretation of the parable, offering implications that anyone capable of reading the *Cum dormirent homines* should also have been able to draw. However, Ulrich, writing for laypeople and the lower clergy, obviously felt the need for a more thorough explication to avoid potentially dangerous misunderstandings of this verse. This method was congruent with the general principle of the *Wiener Schule*, to offer lay readers only content free of heresy and speculation.[143] Perhaps the continuing trials and executions in Austria had also created a need to justify the Church's position in detail, and to make it clear that the Church unambiguously approved the executions of obstinate, relapsed and impenitent heretics.

The actuality of the Waldensian problem was without doubt a reason for Ulrich von Pottenstein's decision to translate the whole of Zwicker's *Cum dormirent homines*. Beyond that, the works also shared a fundamentally similar view about the Church, the clergy and the laity. Although the pastoral theology of the *Wiener Schule* was intended for the education of laity, it did not by any means signify their emancipation. Quite the contrary. As Werner

---

[140] Ulrich von Pottenstein, *Credo*, cap. 35A (ÖNB MS 3050, fol. 277ra): 'Auch waz hewte raten ist, daz mag morgen waicz werden. Lasset sy pede wachsen hincz czu dem snyt, daz ist den raten vnd den waicz, die pösen vnd die guten, hincz an den tag des iungisten gerichtes. [Marg: Dubium] Aus der schrifft möcht man sprechen, daz man die keczer nicht von der kirchen tailen sulle; michelsmer schol man si mit dem swerte nicht pessern.'

[141] See esp. Thomas Aquinas, *Summae theologiae* 2a 2ae q. 11, art. 3. The parable of the tares is interpreted similarly in a Bohemian Franciscan postil, written around 1380; see the edition in Neumann, 'Výbor z předhusitských postil', pp. 97–8.

[142] Ulrich von Pottenstein, *Credo*, cap. 35A (ÖNB MS 3050, fol. 277ra): 'Wann die offembaren keczer die die andern czïehen von dem gelauben die schol man von der kirchen taylen mit peden swerten, daz ain fawles gelid die andern icht fawl mache.'

[143] Wolf, *Hof – Universität – Laien*, pp. 188–9.

Williams-Krapp and Klaus Wolf have stated, the *Wiener Schule* marked a sharpening of the division between the clergy and the laity. Its message emphasized the doctrinal authority of the Church. The vernacular devotional literature avoided controversial questions and guided the laity to orthodox piety as defined and instructed by the clergy.[144] Zwicker's confident, biblicist polemic supported this mission, as it firmly explicated the foundation of the Church's teachings in the Scriptures and required absolute obedience to the consecrated clergy instead of lay confessors and preachers. Latin anti-heretical polemic was not in itself a genre suitable for lay consumption, but when Zwicker's trenchant polemic met the *Wiener Schule*'s translation ideals it could become such.

One could argue that the importance of Ulrich's translation is qualified by its modest success. The manuscript tradition of the catechetic *summa* is indeed very small, only eleven extant manuscripts (and one very short fragment),[145] none of which comprises the whole treatise. Consequently the vernacular tradition of *Cum dormirent homines*, integrated into Ulrich's work, is significantly thinner than the Latin manuscript circulation. However, the translation in itself is a demonstration of the *Cum dormirent homines*'s rapid success in Austria. In just a few years it had become *the* work on Waldensianism, and Ulrich preferred it to both older anti-heretical texts and the contemporary anti-Waldensian tract by Peter von Pillichdorf (who was Ulrich's fellow canon at St Stephen's in Vienna). It is also worth noting that the chapters on Waldensians are overrepresented in the preserved copies of Ulrich's treatise: seven out of eleven manuscripts include at least one whole chapter translated from the *Cum dormirent homines*, a not insignificant number, especially as the translation covers fewer than 30 folios within a work of 1,200 folios, most of them in the *Credo* part.[146] We should also note a scribe and a later commentator of the Österreichische Nationalbibliothek, MS 3050, who manifested a special interest in Waldensians. Rubrics and marginalia are relatively rare in this manuscript, but several point to Waldensians in the index of the work and help the reader

---

[144] W. Williams-Krapp, 'Observanzbewegungen, monastische Spiritualität und geistliche Literatur im 15. Jahrhundert', *Internationales Archiv für Sozialgeschichte der Literatur* 20 (1995), 1–15 (pp. 14–15); W. Williams-Krapp, 'Konturen einer religiösen Bildungsoffensive. Zur literarischen Laienpastoration im 15. und frühen 16. Jahrhundert', in *Kirchlicher und religiöser Alltag im Spätmittelalter. Akten der internationalen Tagung in Weingarten, 4.–7. Oktober 2007*, ed. A. Meyer (Ostfildern, 2010), pp. 77–88 (pp. 81–3); Wolf, *Hof – Universität – Laien*, p. 137.

[145] On the manuscript circulation, Baptist-Hlawatsch, *Das katechetische Werk*, pp. 13–73; Baptist-Hlawatsch, 'Einführung', p. 16*–18*. I have checked the currently known manuscript circulation at *Handschriftencensus* (20 February 2018).

[146] In addition to the main exemplar of the *Credo*, ÖNB MS 3050, these are ÖNB MS 2952; Salzburg, St Peter MS a X 13; Budapest, Magyar Tudományos Akadémia Könyvtár MS K. 532; Eger, Főegyházmegyei Könyvtár MS D.II.1; Kalocsa, Főszékesegyházi Könyvtár MS 322 (101) and ibid., MS 629. See descriptions at Baptist-Hlawatsch, *Das katechetische Werk*, pp. 13–62.

to locate the anti-Waldensian chapters.[147] Had Ulrich von Pottenstein not buried his translation in his gargantuan catechetical encyclopaedia, it could have been much more popular. Both the wide circulation of Zwicker's Latin treatise and the greater number of surviving texts of the Waldensian sections in Ulrich's treatises imply that there was demand for such a work.

Johlín of Vodňany: preaching and propaganda against Waldensians in Bohemia

Outside Austria and southern Germany, Zwicker's treatises attracted most readers in Bohemia.[148] This is no wonder, as Prague was Zwicker's home diocese, the University of Prague his alma mater and his co-inquisitor Martinus altar priest in the city. There was also a demand for anti-Waldensian literature. Although the Bohemian inquisitions in the 1390s did not reach the intensity of the persecution led by Gallus of Jindřichův Hradec in the second quarter of the fourteenth century,[149] and are not comparable to the contemporary trials in Pomerania and Austria, Waldensians were prosecuted in the archdiocese of Prague. Fragments of inquisition documents provide evidence of interrogations and abjurations of Waldensians from the north Bohemian town of Chomutov and the nearby village of Sušany.[150] These cannot be dated exactly, but Hlaváček gives a time frame of 1389–95 for the abjuration of Wenceslaus de Czussan (of Sušany).[151] Two protocols of trials held in Prague at some point in the 1390s against two women both named Margaretha and living in Chomutov bear a striking resemblance to Zwicker's interrogatory and the Stettin protocols.[152] It is not out of the question that he was the anonymous inquisitor of the document.[153] If not, the inquisitor was certainly

---

[147] ÖNB MS 3050, fols. 8v, 9r, 103v, 276v, 277r, 277v, 346vb.

[148] See Appendix 1 for the numerous copies of the *Cum dormirent homines* and the *Refutatio errorum*. The earliest datable *Cum dormirent homines* manuscript of Bohemian origin is Gdańsk, PAN MS Mar. F. 295, written in 1404.

[149] The full scope of these persecutions became acknowledged through the studies and editions by A. Patschovsky; Patschovsky, *Anfänge*, pp. 55–65; *Quellen*, ed. Patschovsky, pp. 173–255; A. Patschovsky, 'Ketzer und Ketzerverfolgung in Böhmen im Jahrhundert vor Hus', *Geschichte in Wissenschaft und Unterricht* 32 (1981), 261–72. For recent summaries of the fourteenth-century Bohemian inquisitions, see Soukup, 'Die Waldenser in Böhmen', pp. 133–40; Doležalová, 'The Inquisitions in Medieval Bohemia'.

[150] Truhlář, 'Paběrky z rukopisů Klementinských Nr. 26'; Hlaváček, 'Zur böhmischen Inquisition', pp. 124–31. Hlaváček re-edits the fragment edited by Truhlář and gives the first edition of two additional protocols. Cf. also Soukup, 'Die Waldenser in Böhmen', p. 140.

[151] Hlaváček, 'Zur böhmischen Inquisition', pp. 118–19.

[152] Ibid., pp. 124–7.

[153] Ibid., p. 115 recognizes the resemblance but dismisses the possibility that Zwicker

influenced by the interrogatories of the *Processus Petri*. It is therefore unsurprising to find a wide circulation of Zwicker's works in Bohemia. In addition, there are traces of his impact in contemporary Bohemian literary production.

In 1403–4 Johlín of Vodňany, priest of St Wenceslas at Zderaz, Prague, and canon of the Order of the Holy Sepulchre with Double Cross,[154] wrote a sermon collection which is counted among the most influential Latin postils and *exempla* collections of its time.[155] Johlín claims in his prologue that his postil is based on sermons he preached to the laity in the vernacular, a statement that is certainly a literary convention, but probably has some truth in it.[156] In their Latin literary form his homilies were certainly successful. The postil resembled and for a time even competed for popularity with contemporary collections by Jan Hus. Divided into three parts according to the ecclesiastical calendar and consisting of 145 sermons, it has survived in approximately twenty manuscripts.[157] It has been only partially edited. In two studies published at the beginning of the 1920s, A. Neumann edited excerpts from all three parts, relating them above all to heresy, schism and Johlín's assault on the poor morals of his times.[158] Neumann's publication

---

was the inquisitor. Soukup, 'Die Waldenser in Böhmen', p. 140 carefully speculates on the possibility.

[154] For Johlín's biography, R. Říčan, 'Johlín z Vodňan, křižovník kláštera zderazského', *Věstník Královské české společnosti nauk. Třida filosoficko-historicko-filologická* 2 (1929), 1–150; Machilek, 'Beweggründe, Inhalte und Probleme', p. 56; Marin, *L'archevêque, le maître et le dévot*, p. 52. The church and monastery of Zderaz belonged to this minor chivalric order, influential mainly in Silesia. On the history of the order, see W. Hermann, *Zur Geschichte der Neisser Kreuzherren von Orden der regulierten Chorherren und Wächter des Heiligen Grabes zu Jerusalem mit dem doppelten roten Kreuz* (Breslau, 1938).

[155] Nechutová, *Die lateinische Literatur*, pp. 220–1.

[156] Neumann, 'Výbor z předhusitských postil', p. 250: 'quatenus sermones, quos in vulgari ad populum ore proprio deprompsi, memorie traderem literat[or]um' (so that I would consign to the remembrance of the literate the sermons that I uttered to the people with my own mouth in the vernacular). There is an additional Bohemian collection of Lenten sermons, *Quadragesimale Admontense*, written down by a listener in Latin with occasional Czech words. It bears a resemblance to some of Johlín's sermons, and the editors of the collection have proposed that it is based on sermons delivered by Johlín in Prague, see *Quadragesimale Admontense – Quadragesimale admontské*, ed. H. Florianová, D. Martínková, Z. Silagiová and H. Šedinová (Prague, 2006), pp. xci–cii; cf. Nechutová, *Die lateinische Literatur*, pp. 220–1. Nechutová disagrees and proposes that the work was written in the 1370s. The relationship between the compilations is yet to be settled. The sections about Waldensians discussed here are not contained in the *Quadragesimale*.

[157] A. Vidmanová, 'Autoritäten und Wiclif in Hussens homiletischen Schriften', in *Antiqui und Moderni: Traditionsbewußtsein und Fortschrittsbewußtsein im späten Mittelalter*, ed. A. Zimmermann (Berlin, 1974), pp. 383–93 (p. 391); Marin, *L'archevêque, le maître et le dévot*, p. 52.

[158] Neumann, *České sekty ve století 14. a 15.*, pp. 2*–4*; Neumann, 'Výbor z předhusitských postil', pp. 250–5, 287–90, 319–26, 356–60, 366–76.

gives an overview of these themes, but is frustratingly fragmentary. In places where Johlín discusses Waldensians, I have compared Neumann's edition to manuscripts.[159]

In the studies on heresy in Bohemia and Waldensianism, Johlín's postil is usually quoted as evidence of Waldensian activity in the Czech lands.[160] It has been proposed that Johlín is the same person as the priest Johlín, who in 1381 as priest of Písek was accused of having heretical parents and grandparents, and who sought and was given dispensation for his heretical ancestry. He would thus have had intimate knowledge of the Waldensians and also the motivation to demonstrate his orthodox opinions.[161] Patschovsky considers this assumption very doubtful,[162] but the possibility cannot be excluded. Whatever Johlín's family history was, it was certainly not necessary to be a descendant of heretics to harbour anti-Waldensian opinions. It is also difficult to imagine that a person who had achieved a position as priest and canon in a locally significant religious house would have had to give reassurances that he was not Waldensian. Still, attacking Waldensians may have been useful as a guarantee of orthodoxy in Johlín's postil, given its expression of critical opinions of corrupt prelates and impious secular lords.

Though lamenting the vices of worldly priests and simony in the Church was common, especially during the Schism, vehement attacks against clerical malpractices always carried a risk of heresy accusations. This was felt by the earlier generations of reform preachers in Prague. Konrad Waldhauser (d. 1369), Milíč of Kroměříž (d. 1374), and Matěj of Janov (d. 1393) were all suspected of heresy, although in the end none of them was sentenced as a heretic.[163] If the difference between a fiery but theologically conventional reform sermon or tract and heretical opinion could only be established at the episcopal or papal court, it is no wonder that the distinction was difficult for the laity to grasp. When Johlín disparaged prelates, saying

This is a great abuse, that men who are in a higher estate want to live so luxuriously: these are not prelates according to the order of the apostles [...] but according to the order of scribes and Pharisees, imposing heavy

---

[159] For the postil parts II and III I have been able to use the same manuscripts as Neumann, Prague, NKCR MS I. D. 43 (part II) and I. D. 44 (part III). Folio numbers are given as they are counted in the Manuscriptorium Digital Library. There is slight variation between the numbering used by Neumann and the contemporary numbering.

[160] Kaminsky, *A History of the Hussite Revolution*, p. 174; Gonnet and Molnár, *Les Vaudois au Moyen Âge*, pp. 157–8; Molnár, *Die Waldenser*, pp. 165–6.

[161] Říčan, 'Johlín z Vodňan', pp. 3–4; Gonnet and Molnár, *Les Vaudois au Moyen Âge*, pp. 157–8; Molnár, *Die Waldenser*, p. 165.

[162] *Quellen*, ed. Patschovsky, pp. 127–8.

[163] Nechutová, *Die lateinische Literatur*, pp. 253–4, 257–9; Soukup, 'Die Predigt als Mittel religiöser Erneuerung', pp. 240–6. The accusations against Janov are discussed in Chapter 2, pp. 79–80 above.

and intolerable burdens on the shoulders of those under them while being unwilling to lift a finger themselves.[164]

he is using language that could very well come from the mouth of a Waldensian preacher. Given that accusations of heresy were commonly voiced in the polemics of the Schism,[165] and Waldensianism was topical thanks to contemporary persecutions, it was especially important to distinguish between righteous and orthodox critique and dangerous heretical corruption. Johlín uses a sermon on Matthew 7:15, 'Beware of false prophets', to make this difference clear.[166] The biblical image of false prophets, who come as sheep in wolves' clothing, was an integral part of the medieval heresy *topos*,[167] and an opening verse of a relatively popular, short treatise on Waldensians, written prior to 1390.[168] Characteristically for Bohemian reform preachers, Johlín is preoccupied with the end of times,[169] and he produces a combination of Christ's warning against false prophets, contemporary Waldensians and the first of the four horsemen of the Apocalypse. Johlín interprets the white horse as the false faith that the heretics claim to be true and the bow of the horseman as their false exposition of the Scriptures.[170] From all the diverse heresies Johlín selects the Waldensians:

[164] Neumann, 'Výbor z předhusitských postil', p. 255: 'Hec est abusio valde magna, quod homines, qui sunt in statu sublimiori sic volunt vivere delicate, non isti prelati secundum ordinem apostolorum [...] sed secundum ordinem scribarum et pharizeorum, qui imponunt onera gravia et inportabilia in humeros subditorum, digito autem suo nolunt ea movere.'

[165] See e.g. the accusations against the Prussian preacher Johannes Malkaw after his sermons in Strasbourg in 1390; M. Tönsing, *Johannes Malkaw aus Preussen (ca. 1360–1416): ein Kleriker im Spannungsfeld von Kanzel, Ketzerprozess und Kirchenspaltung* (Warendorf, 2004), pp. 25–7, 64–110. See also Chapter 5, below.

[166] NKCR MS I. D. 44, fols. 94va–98rb, excerpts edited in Neumann, *České sekty ve století 14. a 15.*, pp. 2*–3*; Neumann, 'Výbor z předhusitských postil', pp. 371–2.

[167] See esp. Sackville, *Heresy and Heretics*, pp. 161–71; Bueno, 'False Prophets and Ravening Wolves', pp. 44–54.

[168] I have discussed the dating and attribution of this treatise in the Introduction, p. 18, n. 74.

[169] Especially prominent in the thought of Milíč of Kroměříže and Matěj of Janov, see Nechutová, *Die lateinische Literatur*, pp. 252, 257, 260–1; in the following century the troubled times inspired a significant amount of apocalyptic prophecy in German, F. C. Kneupper, *The Empire at the End of Time: Identity and Reform in Late Medieval German Prophecy* (Oxford, 2016).

[170] NKCR MS I. D. 44, fol. 96rb–va: 'de quibus prophetis habuit visionem b. Iohannes Apok. vi° vbi scribitur de quotur equis et eorum sesoribus et dicitur quod vna ex illius equs [sic] fuit albus, et qui sedebat super eum habebat arcum. Iste sesor cum suo equo significat hereticos qui sedent in albo equo, dicunt enim quod nullus saluari potest nisi sit in eorum fide, quam dicunt esse albam, i.e. veram et bonam. Sed attendite ne per eos decipiamini et wlneremini, quia habent arcum acutum ex quo sagitant i.e. falsam scripturarum expositionem, et ideo vocantur falsi prophete quia prophetias false exponunt' (blessed John had a vision about these prophets in the 6th

There are numerous sects of these heretics and therefore it would take too long to speak about them all, but hear something about the sect of the Waldensian heretics who, alas, are greatly multiplying, namely how you can recognize them, and how not to believe them, but rather how to avoid them: about whose error you should hear thus.[171]

This introduction is followed by a list of errors that is basically Zwicker's *Articuli Waldensium* with a few omissions.[172] It seems that this is the source about Waldensians Johlín is tapping into, as there are no quotations that can be traced back to the *Cum dormirent homines* or the *Refutatio errorum*. Johlín's adaptation of the *Articuli* is revealing on the question of the purpose and reception of such an error list. It serves as a brief and to-the-point presentation of Waldensian doctrine. After all, Johlín had to follow the limitations of his genre, the model sermon, and cannot go into too much detail. He complains about this, but also states that he wants to name all Waldensian errors so that the listener/reader can learn to discern them:

Their first error is that they deny purgatory, saying that there are only two roads after death for each human, namely that a dying human being either immediately flies up to heaven or descends to hell. But this is not true, and it can be refuted in many ways with Scriptures and rational arguments. But it would be too tedious, so listen briefly to other errors so that you can recognize them.[173]

Because Johlín's description of Waldensians is based on an existing list of errors, some have regarded it as untrustworthy testimony about Waldensian

---

[chapter] of the Apocalypse, where it is written about four horses and their riders. And it is said that one of the horses was 'white, and he that sat on him had a bow'. That rider signifies heretics who sit on a white horse. For they say that no one can be saved except in their sect, which they say is white, that is to say, true and good. But beware lest you be deceived and wounded by them, because they have a sharp bow with which they shoot, that is to say, the false exposition of Scripture. And for this reason they are called 'false prophets', because they expound false prophecies).

[171] NKČR MS I. D. 44, fol. 96va: 'Sunt autem illorum hereticorum plures secte et ideo dicere de omnibus esset nimis longum; de secta tamen valdensium hereticorum qui proch dolor satis multiplicantur aliquid audiatis quo modo videlicet possitis eos cognoscere et eisdem non credere, sed eos devitare de quorum errore sic audiatis.'

[172] Neumann noticed this and compared Johlín's postil to the *Articuli* as printed by Döllinger, Neumann, *České sekty ve století 14. a 15.*, pp. 10–12; cf. Döllinger, *Beiträge II*, pp. 338–41. On the *Articuli*, see Chapter 3, above.

[173] NKČR, MS I. D. 44, fol. 96va: 'Primus eorum error est quia negant purgatorium dicentes tantum esse duas vias post mortem cuiuslibet hominis scilicet quod homo moriens statim evolat ad celum uel descendat [sic] ad infernum, sed hoc verum non est, quod multipliciter posset inprobari scripturis et rationibus; Sed esset nimis longum, breuiter igitur de aliis eorum erroribus ut eos cognoscere possitis sic audiatis.'

activity in Bohemia.[174] The issue of how widespread Waldensianism was in pre-Hussite Bohemia is beside the point here, although there is no reason to doubt that Waldensians enjoyed a certain following there around the turn of the century.[175] If there were Waldensian Brethren in the surroundings of Prague at the beginning of the fifteenth century, after a decade of intense inquisition and prosecution of them and their followers they were probably lying low rather than broadcasting their presence on street corners. The crucial issue is that Johlín warns his audience that there are people around who criticize the same vices as righteous preachers, avarice of the clergy, corruption of the religious orders and abuse of indulgences, but they do it in a wrong, heretical way, which must be shunned. The heretic that stands closest is the most threatening one, and most effort is required to refute the heresy that resembles call for reform. This is the reason behind the repeated cries that Waldensians were the most dangerous heretics. The outcry of the Anonymous of Passau is (in)famous:

> This [sect] of the Leonistas [= Waldensians] has a great appearance of piety, because in front of the people they live justly and believe well all the things about God and all the articles that are included in the Creed. They blaspheme only the Roman Church and clergy: something which is easy for the multitude of the laity to believe.[176]

Johlín's postil is a manifestation of the same fear. It is also a clear statement of where the writer stands: I am a fervent critic of corruption in the Church, but by no means a heretic or suspect of heresy.

More remarkably, the postil facilitates the attribution of the heretical stigma of Waldensianism, established and enforced for two centuries, to those who were more radical than Johlín himself. One has to remember that in the first years of the fifteenth century, Prague was the centre of a reform movement searching for its direction, and diverse and extreme ideas about clerical authority, frequent communion, Church property and the validity of the indulgences were voiced, among other concerns.[177] On some of these opinions

---

[174] Říčan, 'Johlín z Vodňan', pp. 116–17; but criticized by Kaminsky, *A History of the Hussite Revolution*, p. 174.

[175] Soukup, 'Die Waldenser in Böhmen', p. 140; Hlaváček, 'Zur böhmischen Inquisition'.

[176] *Quellen*, ed. Patschovsky and Selge, p. 73: 'Hec Leonistarum magnam habens speciem pietatis – eo quod coram hominibus iuste vivant et bene omnia de deo credant et omnes articulos, qui in symbolo continentur – solummodo Romanam ecclesiam blasphemant et clerum, cui multitudo laicorum facilis est ad credendum.' For similar expressions, see eg. Preger (ed.), 'Der Tractat des David von Augsburg', p. 211; Zwicker, *Cum dormirent homines*, p. 278A; see also Sackville, *Heresy and Heretics*, pp. 144–5.

[177] On the reform movement in Prague before the Hussite wars, see especially Marin, *L'archevêque, le maître et le dévot*; Kaminsky, *A History of the Hussite Revolution*, pp. 7–35; G. Denzler, 'Reform der Kirche um 1400', in *Die hussitische Revolution:*

Johlín casts a shadow of doubt. He explains that the bishop's vestments and ornaments, which are more sumptuous than those of other priests, 'are not for display but signify things beyond themselves' (*non sunt ad ostentacionem, sed sunt signa signatorum*). Then he warns that there are people who are either fools (*insipientes*) or familiar with heresy (*vel eciam heresim sapientes*), who ridicule the Church by claiming that the precious paraphernalia of the bishops is for human show only. He then proceeds to explain the correct meaning 'in order to root out the insanity of such disbeliefs from their hearts and to kindle devotion in believers'.[178] The rest of the sermon is an exposition of the symbolism of the bishop's liturgical vestments, following the standard handbook *Rationale divinorum officiorum* by William Durand of Mende.[179] Johlín speaks only of heresy in general and does not name the Waldensians, but it is clear that they are the heretics he means. The doubt over the necessity of clerical vestments and paraphernalia appears in Johlín's own adaptation of Zwicker's *Articuli*.[180] All in all, the Waldensians are Johlín's default heretics.

---

religiöse, politische und regionale Aspekte, ed. F. Machilek (Cologne, 2012), pp. 9–24; on reform preaching, Ocker, 'Die Armut und die menschliche Natur'; Nechutová, 'Reform- und Bussprediger von Waldhauser bis Hus'; Soukup, 'Die Predigt als Mittel religiöser Erneuerung'; on frequent communion in Bohemia, Holeton, *La Communion des tout-petits enfants*, pp. 19–27; Holeton, 'The Bohemian Eucharistic Movement in its European Context'.

[178] NKCR MS I. D 43, fol. 145ra–rb: 'Quod colligi potest ex eorum ornamentis quibus ornantur ultra alios sacerdotes, hec autem ornamenta non sunt ad ostentacionem sed sunt signa signatorum. Sunt enim quidam homines insipientes uel eciam heresim sapientes qui contra sanctam ecclesiam garriunt et locuuntur, uidentes apparatum preciosum quo utuntur episcopi in diuinis celebratis; credentes quod ad ostentacionem humanam, et [non?] ad diuini cultus ministerium nec ad edificacionem populi illud fiat; Sed ut talium infidelium uesania de cordibus eorum exstirpetur et in fidelibus deuocio accendatur; Quid apparatus episcoporum significet ad eorum laudem et gloriam modicum audiatis' (What can be gathered from their ornaments, with which they are ornamented to a degree beyond that of other priests, is that these ornaments are not for display but signify things beyond themselves. For there are some people who are either fools or familiar with heresy who ridicule and speak against the Church when seeing the precious paraphernalia used by bishops when celebrating divine services: believing that this happens for human ostentation, [not] for the sake of divine worship or the edification of the people. You should listen to this, so that madness may be uprooted from the hearts of such infidels and devotion kindled in the faithful: the apparatus signifies their moderate praise and honour). Cf. Neumann, 'Výbor z předhusitských postil', p. 360.

[179] Johlín admits this at the end of his sermon: 'O tu predicator scias premissa esse extracta de secunda parte rationalis libri' (And know, you preacher, that the previous things were extracted from the second part of the *Rationale* book); NKCR MS I. D 43, fol. 145vb. The clerical vestments and ornaments are treated in the *Rationale diuinorum officiorum* 3.1 (LLT-A).

[180] NKCR MS I. D. 44, fols. 96va–97ra: 'Item omnia preparamenta episcoporum sicut infulas, cirotecas, anullos etc vocant supersticionem.' Cf. *Articuli Waldensium*: 'Item omnia apparamenta episcoporum, infulas, cyrothecas, turnamenta [r. ornamenta?], annulos etc. vocant superstitionem', Werner, 'Nachrichten', p. 270.

In another sermon they are the contemporary equivalent of the ancient Jews, who believed that because they had their Temple only they would be saved. Waldensians make the same mistake when they claim that only those in their sect enjoy salvation.[181]

If Johlín only hints that those having doubts about the necessity of bishop's sumptuous liturgical garments are heretics, people who are not paying respect to their pastors are certainly suspected of Waldensianism:

> And of such people there is great suspicion that they have part in Waldensian heresy. These incessantly slander priests on street corners and in their meetings, always condemning their habits and way of living. But we should honour them as fathers, and follow their good example.[182]

Although Johlín uses here some literary conventions usually attached to Waldensians, such as preaching on street corners and in private meetings, it is worth noting that here and elsewhere his description of heretics is devoid of demonizing metaphors. The suspected heretics are not malign figures corrupting the simple-minded in secrecy with their doctrines, but people voicing doubts about the clergy and church services.

We must remember that this was not the usual way of describing Waldensians (or heretics in general) in the late fourteenth and early fifteenth centuries. One has only to recall the popular rumours about heretics worshipping Lucifer that Zwicker encountered and dismissed in Stettin,[183]

---

[181] NKCR, MS I. D. 43, fol. 96r: 'Et pro certo tales sunt multi qui ad suas sectas quosdam trahunt per sua mendacia dicentes quod in aliis statibus homo saluus esse non potest nisi in eorum statu sicut faciunt valdenses. Quod autem salus in templo non fuit scilicet quod ipsi predicabant patet per principium misse hodierne; In qua dicitur per cristum: Salus populi ego sum. Ego sum inquam salus; non templum lapidem; non secte quorumcumque hominium sed ego sum salus' (And certainly there are many such, who draw some people into their sects with their lies, saying a man cannot be saved in other conditions, only in theirs, as the Waldensians do. That there was not salvation in the temple, that is to say as they were preaching there was, is made plain at the introit of the daily mass, in which it is said by Christ, 'I am the salvation of the people'. 'I am', I say, 'the salvation'. Not a stone temple, not the sects of any sorts of men, but 'I am the salvation'). Cf. Neumann, 'Výbor z předhusitských postil', p. 359.

[182] Neumann, 'Výbor z předhusitských postil', p. 321: 'Et de talibus est magna suspicio, ne habeant partem heresis Waldensis. Tales enim sacerdotibus saltem in angulis et in suis conventiculis detrahere non cessant, vitam eorum et mores semper condempnantes. Nos vero eos honoremus, ut patres et sequamur consilia eorum bona.'

[183] See above all the interrogation of Herman Gossaw on 6/7 December 1392, where the notary writes of the rumours of Lucifer worship: 'quod inquisitor noverat, predictos articulos non esse de secta Waldensium', *Quellen*, ed. Kurze, pp. 88–9. See also Biller, *Waldenses*, pp. 258, 279; Utz Tremp, *Von der Häresie zur Hexerei*, pp. 285–6, 297.

contemporary descriptions of a sinful 'synagogue' of heretics in Piedmont[184] and a few decades later Bernardino da Siena's fantastical sermons about heretics, likewise in Piedmont, who once a year tossed a baby from one to the other until it died and made magic powder out of its body.[185] The late medieval descriptions of heresy in general were no more progressive, rational or free from literary conventions than their predecessors in the twelfth and thirteenth centuries. But the descriptions of Waldensians written and circu- lating in German and Bohemian areas at the turn of the fifteenth century are exceptional in being confined to minute descriptions of the doctrine. This is especially true of the texts originating from the circle of Petrus Zwicker and Martinus of Prague. It is within their sphere of influence in Upper Austria and Bohemia, where their writings were in circulation, that this pastoral approach to heresy spread beyond inquisitorial texts.

* * * * * * * * * * * * * * *

This chapter has explored how the pastoral theological approach to the Waldensian heresy spread from Zwicker's circle into the surrounding society. The inquisitor's own preaching addressed the same theological issues that were discussed in his Latin treatises, and in general the anti-heretical sermon in the late fourteenth- and early fifteenth-century Empire did not shun difficult doctrinal questions. Yet direct communication to the laity was only the first step. Crucial to the dissemination of the anti-heretical message during and immediately after the inquisitions was the mobilization of the parish clergy. The priests and rectors read out summonses to trials in the churches or in the homes of the heretics. Zwicker's citations were not arid judicial orders but original, thought-out and flexible parts of the inquisitor's communication with the local communities – not to mention the part of the inquisitor's message that reached the widest audience. After the penance was issued by the inquisitor, the supervision of it fell to the local clergy, as did the task of explaining the reasons for the punishment to the parishioners. As both the citations and the public penances were performed for a minimum period of several weeks and in several parishes, they were the occasions when ordinary lay people encountered anti-heretical propaganda.

A more profound dissemination, and also revision, of Zwicker's concept of Waldensianism took place in the translation of the *Cum dormirent homines* by Ulrich von Pottenstein and in the preaching of Johlín of Vodňany. They both take pastoralization of heresy further than Zwicker did; he, despite his originality, wrote within the tradition of the Latin anti-heretical polemical treatise. Ulrich and Johlín undoubtedly attacked Waldensians, whom they saw as undermining the Church. At the same time their refutation, structured

---

[184] Utz Tremp, *Von der Häresie zur Hexerei*, pp. 237–9.
[185] See above in this chapter, p. 181.

around individual doctrines, was directed beyond the learned elite: it was generalized and popularized. In Ulrich's catechism Waldensianism becomes an exact inversion, a negative image of good Christian conduct. He treats Waldensianism as a serious threat to the Church's mission, authority and catechesis, not as a demonized other but as an erroneous interpretation of a whole range of subjects. Johlín of Vodňany attacked Waldensians within the framework of sermons, and saw them as the worst of heretics that people should learn to recognize – and as a tool for this recognition he offered the *Articuli Waldensium* from the *Processus Petri*. Like Ulrich, Johlín discusses heresy as a critique of established Catholic cult and ritual practices, for example clerical ornaments. He explicitly hints in his sermons that those who do not respect their priests might be guilty of Waldensian heresy.

This approach was a further transition from the conventional and legal understanding of a *credens* as one who believes heretics, someone who attended their sermons and confessed at them. Those who savoured of heresy were upholders and utterers of particular opinions, but not necessarily confined to people who followed heresiarchs. Like Petrus Zwicker and Martinus of Prague in their interrogations, Ulrich and Johlín saw the laity as capable of individual belief and understanding of doctrine – and consequently able to make misjudgements. Beyond that, approaching heresy as a range of lapses from a proper Christian *modus vivendi* made the stigma of Waldensianism applicable to radicals and reformers who criticized the Church and those of its practices they considered to be vain, novel additions or corruptions, but who did not necessarily belong to any particular dissident or heretical group. The conception of heresy was diluted, but widened to cover more transgressions. When heresy was reduced to lack of belief in the necessity of liturgical vestments or disrespect of the clergy, everyone became a possible heresy suspect.

5

The Dissidents, the Clergy and the Church

Olim enim dum suborta essent scismata, cicius apponebantur remedia nedum per patres spirituales sed eciam principes seculares.

Once upon a time, when schisms would spring up, the remedies were more quickly applied, not only by spiritual fathers but also by secular princes.

Thomas Ebendorfer, *Tractatus de schismatibus*, after 1451.[1]

Petrus Zwicker lived in times that were profoundly characterized by the Great Schism (1378–1417), a division that occurred in the papal election of 1378, leading to the election of two (and eventually three) rival popes in Rome and Avignon. In 1395, when Zwicker wrote the *Cum dormirent homines*, there were no foreseeable prospects of unification. Indeed, it seemed possible that the Church would remain permanently divided.[2] In previous chapters I have suggested that certain features in Zwicker's writing, above all the endeavour to find a basis for the Church's doctrine and practices in the Scriptures alone, were a reaction to the uncertainty of the times. In this chapter I explore how Zwicker contributed to dealing with this uncertainty.

Even the fundamental principles of the Church and its hierarchy were undermined and questioned in the course of the Schism: the floor was open to both radical and revisionist opinions. People, laity and the clergy alike, without any connection to dissident groups, criticized practices they considered to be vain, novel additions or corruption in the Church. The translation of Zwicker's treatise by Ulrich von Pottenstein and the anti-Waldensian declarations in Johlín of Vodňany's sermons in particular are directed at such practices. There was a danger of slipping into Waldensian heresy when overtly criticizing the Church and the clergy. The refutation of heretical beliefs was thus more than an attack on an enemy of the late medieval Church. It

---

[1] T. Ebendorfer, *Tractatus de schismatibus*, ed. H. Zimmermann, MGH Scriptores Rerum Germanicarum NS 20 (Munich, 2004), p. 3.

[2] R. N. Swanson, 'A Survey of Views on the Great Schism, c. 1395', *Archivum Historiae Pontificiae* 21 (1983), 79–103.

was part of a process of keeping intact and in their right place the constituent elements of its wobbling spiritual geography, the dissidents, the good Catholic laypeople, the clergy and Mother Church herself.

Virgin Mary venerated and denigrated

The Virgin Mary had been honoured and loved by Christians from the earliest centuries of the Church, but in late medieval piety she acquired a status almost comparable to that of her son. From the late fourteenth century onwards, Mary takes a new position in the depictions of God's judgment. She appears together with Christ as the primary intercessor for humanity, asking for mercy from the Father. *Maria misericordiae* (Mary of mercy) becomes, together with the merciful rather than judgemental Christ, the loving defender of humanity and the individual soul.[3]

Not all forms of Marian devotion were, however, universally approved, as we shall see. And despite Petrus Zwicker's attempts to present Catholicism as firmly founded in the Scriptures and united against fractured heresy, even the clergy were hardly presenting a united front. The example of honouring and dishonouring the Virgin Mary, her images and statues demonstrates that the Waldensians were not the most fervent and certainly not the most dangerous critics of the Church in the 1390s. Consequently the refutation of some Waldensian errors in Zwicker's and others' treatises may have been facilitated by dissident voices from the ranks of fellow clerics as much as by the Waldensians.

Since the thirteenth century Catholic polemicists had claimed that the Waldensians condemned the cult of saints, pilgrimages and relics, but in these early works Mary is hardly mentioned. In his *Adversus Catharos et Valdenses*, Moneta of Cremona handles the Waldensian condemnation of the cult of saints, but the treatise is surprisingly terse when it comes to Marian piety. She is not specified in the defence of the invocation of saints,[4] and when she is mentioned, it is in relation to the carnality of Christ's birth, not because of her own sanctity and the veneration that was her due.[5] Likewise the description of Waldensians by the Anonymous of Passau in Austria *c.* 1260 is rather general on this topic: Waldensians do not believe in saints except those mentioned in the gospels, nor do they approve of relics, miracles and pilgrimages. The Virgin Mary does not play any prominent role in this work either. She is mentioned only in the sentence '[T]hey do not invoke any saints

---

[3] Hamm, *Religiosität im späten Mittelalter*, esp. pp. 429–34; M. Rubin, *Mother of God: A History of the Virgin Mary* (London, 2009), pp. 121–351.

[4] Moneta, *Adversus Catharos et Valdenses*, IV.ix.4, p. 374.

[5] Ibid., III.iii.7–8, pp. 250–6.

or the blessed Mary but only God.'[6] Also the *Attendite a falsis prophetis*, written in Germany sometime before 1390, has only one relatively concise chapter on the intercession of the saints in general, and makes no mention of the Virgin.[7]

The condemnation of honouring and invoking saints and especially the Virgin rises to occupy a central place in Zwicker's polemics. In both the *Refutatio errorum*[8] and the *Cum dormirent homines* the questions of whether saints can act on behalf of those living on earth and whether God alone is to be served, and the arguments for and against the honouring and invoking of the saints, are dealt with in meticulous detail.[9] But it is Mary who is the pivotal saint, and her praising and honouring that are the chief signs of orthodoxy. Zwicker hurls the accusation, 'that because Waldensians do not praise the blessed Mary, they are not the generations [cf. Luke 1:48], but corruptions, even mortifications'.[10] In addition to being the primary intercessor, Mary has a special place in Zwicker's indulgence theology as the stream of merit flowing from Christ.[11]

Mary occupies a special position among the saints in the error lists and questionnaires compiled in the 1390s: the Waldensians do not pray to Mary or saints or believe that they can in any way help the living.[12] The inquisitors asked if the deponents knew their *Ave Maria*, and if they knew it properly. The episcopal tribunal in Regensburg in 1395 noted down flaws in the way the deponents pronounced the Lord's Prayer, the Creed and the *Ave Maria*,[13] and in Stettin Zwicker remarked how poorly some deponents knew their *Ave Maria*.[14]

Were the German Waldensians more hostile towards the cult of the Mary at the end of the fourteenth century than earlier? Probably not. The inquisitorial documents from the 1390s reveal how the average followers of the Waldensian Brethren were fully aware from the teachings of their confessors

---

[6] *Quellen*, ed. Patschovsky and Selge, pp. 97, 98–101.

[7] St Florian, MS XI 152, fol. 50r.

[8] *Refutatio*, ed. Gretser, pp. 303E–304G, see esp. p. 304C–F. The chapter on the saints and Mary is common to all redactions.

[9] See chapters XIX, XX and XXX, Zwicker, *Cum dormirent homines*, pp. 282F–286D, 294F–296B.

[10] Ibid., p. 283E: 'Quod, quia Waldenses non laudant beatam Mariam, non sunt generationes, sed corruptiones, imo mortificationes.'

[11] Ibid., p. 294F–G.

[12] These include Zwicker's manifesto from 1395, Preger, *Beiträge*, pp. 246–7; *Articuli Waldensium* and the long question list, Werner, 'Nachrichten', pp. 267, 273; Waldensians accused in Bingen in 1393, Kolpacoff, 'Papal Schism', p. 285; and in Fribourg in 1399, *Quellen*, ed. Utz Tremp, pp. 590–1.

[13] ÖNB MS 3748, fols. 145r–v, 153r, 155r.

[14] *Quellen*, ed. Kurze, pp. 97, 99, 227, 239. Cf. Zwicker's short questionnaire, ibid., p. 74; and especially the long questionnaire, Werner, 'Nachrichten', p. 273: 'Scis Ave Maria, dicas qualiter scis!' (Do you know the Hail Mary? Say how you know it!).

that it was pointless to invoke the saints.[15] Yet the same protocols tell us that their lived religion was sufficiently diverse to combine elements of Catholic and Waldensian practices. Thus, when a suspected Waldensian, Mathias Joris, was interrogated by Zwicker in Stettin in 1393, he answered thus regarding Mary and other saints:

> That he had heard and believed that blessed Mary and the saints are so full of joys in heaven, that they do not pray for sinners, but yet he believed, that blessed Mary could pray for him.[16]

Furthermore, several other Waldensian followers interrogated in Stettin said that they invoked Mary and believed that she, but not the other saints, could pray for them.[17] The earliest and least polemical version of the *De vita et conversacione*, a description of the Waldensian Brethren's ordination and lifestyle, states that Waldensians do not use the *Ave Maria* or the Creed, and that they believe the veneration of saints to be idolatry, that saints cannot intercede on behalf of the living or the dead and that 'Gregory, Nicholas, Martin, Catherine and so on' are not saints.[18] Mary is not, however, mentioned except in the rejection of the *Ave Maria*.

The Waldensians in Strasbourg in 1400 demonstrated a comparable attitude towards honouring and invoking the Virgin.[19] One of the key witnesses and informers in the Strasbourg process in 1400 was Kunigund Strussin senior. She was originally from Nördlingen and had escaped the Waldensian persecutions in Augsburg in 1393.[20] She opens her survey of the Waldensian tenets by saying 'that God alone could help them, not Our Lady nor the saints, however worthy Our Lady might be'.[21] In Stettin one of the deponents said

---

[15] See e.g. *Quellen*, ed. Kurze, pp. 212, 227, 236.

[16] Ibid., p. 145: 'Item quod audiverit et crediderit, beatam Mariam et sanctos in celo ita plenos esse gaudiis, quod non orent pro peccatoribus, attamen crediderit, beatam Mariam pro se posse orare.'

[17] Ibid., pp. 124, 226, 258. The syncretism regarding Mary among the Pomeranian Waldensians has been noted before. See Wattenbach, 'Über Ketzergeschichte', pp. 55–6; Kurze, 'Zur Ketzergeschichte', p. 85; Cameron, *Waldenses*, p. 135; M. Goodich, *Miracles and Wonders: The Development of the Concept of Miracle, 1150–1350* (Aldershot, 2007), p. 64.

[18] HAAB MS Fol 20, fols. 320vb–321rb: 'sed simbolum et Aue mariam non orant. [...] Item veneracionem sanctorum dicunt esse ydolatriam; Item nec concedunt sanctos posse intercedere pro nobis siue pro viuis siue pro mortuis [...] non credunt sanctum gregorium; Nycolaum, Martinum, Kather*inam* et ceteros esse sanctos.'

[19] Modestin, *Ketzer in der Stadt*, p. 146.

[20] Ibid., pp. 32–3.

[21] 'Daz in Gotte alleine gehelffen múge, und nit Unßer Frȯwe noch die heiligen, wiewol daz Unßer Frowe wurdig were', *Quellen*, ed. Modestin, p. 154 [K116]; cf. the second revision, p. 168 [139] where both Mary and the saints are 'wurdig'.

he believed that the Blessed Virgin was a chaste child-bearer, but that he did not invoke her or the saints.[22]

The Waldensians interrogated in the 1390s do not display any notable hostility towards the Virgin Mary. Their attitude could better be described as varying from distanced reverence to intimate devotion. The condemnation of venerating saints and Mary becomes prominent because the inquisitors and polemicists, above all Petrus Zwicker, combine and generalize the Waldensian dismissal of various practices they considered to be superfluous or erroneous: relic cults, pilgrimages, indulgences and intercession on behalf of the dead and the living. Above all, in the *Cum dormirent homines* these come together as a universal denial of the veneration of the saints and Mary especially, and the Waldensians are portrayed as undermining even her worth and dignity when they refuse to praise her.

The question remains: why did Zwicker emphasize Waldensian rejection of the Virgin? To understand this we have to revisit the case that was briefly mentioned in Chapter 2 in relation to the legitimacy of the 'new constitutions': the Feast of the Visitation of the Blessed Virgin Mary. There I argued that when Mary was more ardently defended against the Waldensians at the turn of the fifteenth century, it was Catholic theology and pious practices that had changed, not their enemies.[23] The heated polemics against the Waldensian position were connected to the enhanced status of Mary in late medieval devotional life, and particularly to the attempts to reform the schismatic Church through the Marian cult and the installation of the feast of the Visitation, confirmed by the Roman pope Boniface IX in 1389. The centre of this attempted and failed reform was the archdiocese of Prague, the home diocese of Petrus Zwicker and Martinus of Prague. The feast of the Visitation was not itself free from accusations of error and heresy in the heated atmosphere of the Schism. The crucial figure in the development of the Feast of the Visitation was Archbishop Jan of Jenštejn, a controversial character in the metropolitan see of Prague (1378–94, d. 1400). He was an adamant supporter of obedience to Rome to the bitter end, and one of those who believed that the Schism would be ended and the Church renewed through faith and devotion. In his plans it was the Virgin in particular who played a pivotal role.

In 1378 the archbishop had seen a vision of Satan and an antipope, which he later interpreted as a prefiguration of the Schism. In his vision, the Virgin Mary was the only hope for reconciliation. The Visitation of Mary had for some time appealed to the archbishop, who had adorned both the chapel window in his previous diocese of Meissen and his palace in Prague with

---

[22] *Quellen*, ed. Kurze p. 237: 'quod bene crediderit, beatam virginem esse castam puerperam, sed ipsam et sanctos non invocavit.'

[23] Cf. Cameron, *Waldenses*, p. 134. On the late fourteenth-century Waldensians, Cameron has remarked that 'it was the scope of popular Catholicism that had increased, not the depth of Waldensian hostility to it'.

pictures of the gospel story. The institution of a new feast to celebrate this biblical event seemed to be an appropriate way to appease the Virgin. In 1386 he proceeded with the adoption of the feast, and having consulted some theologians and canonists he composed the office for the feast himself.[24] His efforts were confirmed by another vision, but this time seen by a devout woman, introduced to Jenštejn by Matthew of Kraków. Mary had appeared to this woman and instructed her to tell the archbishop that he should remain firm in installing the new feast, and that this would grant him eternal life. Resolve was required, because the none-too-popular archbishop was attacked by some of the higher clergy after he announced the new feast in the diocesan synod in June 1386. The opposition in the cathedral chapter was led by Master Vojtěch Raňkův of Ježov.[25] The opposing party claimed that the archbishop had instituted novelties that had no foundation in tradition or in Scripture, and Jenštejn retaliated by accusing his critics of heresy because they doubted a feast that was founded in the gospels.[26] The archbishop countered the opposition by seeking apostolic sanction for the new feast, which was granted after laborious investigation three years later, on 9 November 1389, by Boniface IX. The feast was set for 2 July, but as a minor setback it was not the liturgy written by Jenštejn that was accepted for the feast, but one written by an English cardinal, Adam Easton.[27] Nevertheless Jan of Jenštejn exulted. He composed a sermon full of triumph to his clergy, praising the Virgin Mary, 'who alone destroys all the heresies', and who would crush the schismatics.[28]

But something else relating to the Blessed Virgin was going on. A few weeks before, on 18 October 1389, a synod of the Prague archdiocese had forced three men – Matěj of Janov, Jakub of Kaplice and a priest called Andreas – to revoke heretical, erroneous or controversial articles that incorporated popular opposition to excesses or malpractices in the cult of the saints, and particularly the cult of the Virgin.[29] In front of the synod, Janov merely admitted that he had preached some things that perhaps were not right and could be misunderstood. He therefore confirmed his Catholic faith by reassuring everyone there that he upheld Catholic doctrine and practices, among them the veneration of relics and that the saints in heaven could intercede on behalf of sinners, and that the images of Christ and saints did not constitute a danger of idolatry. Perhaps Janov's great popularity and the former favour of the archbishop protected him, because all that happened

---

[24] Weltsch, *John of Jenstein*, pp. 84, 87–8.
[25] Mossman, 'Dorothea von Montau and the Masters of Prague', p. 115; Weltsch, *John of Jenstein*, p. 88.
[26] Weltsch, *John of Jenstein*, appendix II, pp. 191–2. See also Chapter 2, pp. 82–3.
[27] Weltsch, *John of Jenstein*, pp. 88–91.
[28] The sermon is cited ibid., p. 90, n. 51.
[29] Discussed also above, Chapter 2, p. 80.

was a half-year suspension from preaching and hearing confessions outside his own parochial church.[30]

Much more radical was Jakub of Kaplice, who according to the synod had preached things that were outright heretical, savoured of heresy or were erroneous, scandalous and wrong. The first of the outright heretical articles was 'that the Blessed Virgin cannot help us in anything', and the first of those articles which savoured of heresy, 'that the Blessed Virgin cannot deliver any mercy to the faithful'.[31] The most striking accusation is, however, the libel against the Virgin's image:

> And not only did I transgress gravely in words against the glorious Virgin, but also in deeds – I insulted the Blessed Virgin, making an obscene gesture of male genitalia to her image, and I said, that I would like to cook peas with such a statue and with others.[32]

Jakub had thus claimed that the wooden statue was not any holier because it represented a saint, and consequently burning it was not a sacrilege. A similar opinion, but concerning the sanctity of the wooden cross, was attributed to Andreas Hesel, whom Zwicker sentenced in Vienna in 1403.[33]

These clergymen thus expressed open suspicion and sometimes even graphic criticism of certain forms of devotion that were popular and promoted by the higher clergy. When discussing Prague and Mary, we have to remember that there was a long tradition of Marian devotion that could have been dubious in the eyes of the reformers. The Cathedral of St Vitus in Prague claimed to possess Mary's bloodied veil (*peplum cruentatum*), supposedly worn by her at the crucifixion. A ritual for the display of the relic had also developed by the mid-fourteenth century.[34] Thus, some of the criticism was quite probably aimed against existing practices in the cathedral and parishes, not necessarily innovations by Jan of Jenštejn. Nevertheless – taking into account the timing of the event – it is pretty obvious that the institution of

---

[30] *Documenta Mag. Joannis Hus*, ed. Palacký, pp. 699–700.

[31] Ibid., pp. 700–1: 'quod ego Jacobus talis x [sic] praedicavi aliqua non praedicanda: inter quae sunt aliqua haeretica, aliqua sapiunt haeresim, aliqua sunt erronea, scandalosa, praesumtuosa, fatua et falsa [...] primum, quod beata virgo non possit nobis in aliquot subvenire [...] primo, quod beata virgo non possit fidelibus aliquam gratiam facere.'

[32] Ibid., p. 702: 'Etiam non solum excessi graviter in verbo contra virginem gloriosam, sed etiam in facto feci unam contumeliam beatae virgini, ostendo ficum, Čípek rukú, [Ms. czýpek ruku] ejus imagini, et dixi, quod cum tali imagine ac cum aliis vellem pisum decoquere.' Cf. NKCR MS XIII. E. 7, fol. 190r–v.

[33] Würzburg UB, MS M. ch. f. 51, fol. 27v: 'Item quod lignum sancte crucis alio ligno non sanccius sit, ex quo cum illo carnes et caules excoqui possint' (Item, that the wood of the holy cross is not holier than other wood, from which it follows that meat and cauliflower can be cooked with it).

[34] Rubin, *Mother of God*, p. 248.

the Feast of the Visitation and the indulgences[35] granted by the archbishop to those visiting the shrines of Mary were connected to the disciplinary actions against those attacking the worship of saints, their images and relics.

How was all this connected to the Waldensians and polemical writing and preaching against them? There were Waldensians in Bohemia, and they played a role in the popular support of Hus and his followers two decades later,[36] but they probably had nothing to do with this trial, nor are Waldensians mentioned in the accusations. What Janov and the two other priests had preached was quite probably derived from their own reform programmes and perception of corruption and malpractice in the Church. Janov was at that time writing his *Regulae veteris et novi testamenti*, which called for Christocentric reform and lamented that relics, images and other holy objects diverted the faithful from the genuine devotion that should be directed towards Christ and the Eucharist.[37]

When commenting on the similar principles but different goals of Janov's and Zwicker's biblicism in Chapter 2, I pointed out that Zwicker could hardly have been ignorant of the former's opinions and the accusations levelled against him and other radical reformers in Prague. Again, it is possible that Zwicker did not have only the Waldensians in mind as targets of his criticism. The accusations against Janov and his accomplices include the very things that the Waldensians were claiming to condemn: the cult of saints, intercession by the saints and Mary, images of saints, the liturgy and indulgences. And their attack on these practices was much more intense and of course public than that of the clandestine Waldensians. From the mouths of popular, educated preachers and clergymen[38] like Matěj of Janov the message was much more dangerous, and more difficult to control.

If reforming preachers were advocating similar changes to the Waldensians, their opponents had more means to attack the former. A few years earlier, the sinister reputation of Beghards and Beguines was used to blacken the followers of Jan Milíč of Kroměříž, who campaigned for frequent lay communion.[39] The anti-Waldensian polemic provided a tool of refutation at least as effective. From the accusations against the Prussian preacher Johannes Malkaw in Strasbourg in 1391 we know that inquisitors tried to brand their

---

[35] Attacks on the indulgences granted by Jan of Jenštejn were explicitly mentioned in the revocation of Jakub of Kaplice; *Documenta Mag. Joannis Hus*, ed. Palacký, pp. 701–2.

[36] Doležalová, 'The Inquisitions in Medieval Bohemia', p. 310; on Bohemian Waldensians in general, Soukup, 'Die Waldenser in Böhmen'.

[37] See Chapter 2, pp. 79–80.

[38] There is a fragment from a deposition of one of Janov's followers in front of an inquisitior or an episcopal court at the beginning of the 1390s. The deponent was likely an Augustinian eremite; Hlaváček, 'Zur böhmischen Inquisition', pp. 116–17, 124–7.

[39] Weltsch, *John of Jenstein*, p. 170.

opponent as a Waldensian, even when they almost certainly knew that the accused was not a proper Waldensian but a clergyman like themselves.[40] Johlín of Vodňany used insinuations about Waldensianism against reformers more radical than himself. Later, probably after the Council of Constance, Janov's confession and Zwicker's texts were physically brought together: the copies of the 1389 trial documents were bundled together with texts on Waldensians and Hussites, including Zwicker's *Refutatio errorum* and parts of the *Processus Petri*.[41] As well as being a refutation of Waldensianism, the long discussions on the veneration of saints in the *Cum dormirent homines* should be interpreted as a reflection of the debates that were fought within the Church and the ranks of the clergy. Given these conflicts, it is no wonder that Zwicker also made profound declarations about the clergy and their position.

The clergy devalued, the clergy elevated

The previous chapters have demonstrated that at the turn of the fifteenth century the Waldensians were accused of devaluing practically all aspects of the Catholic cult, from intercession on behalf of the dead to church buildings and the invocation of saints. Of all the Waldensian errors, however, one stood out in the eyes of their opponents. The Waldensians were first and foremost seen as an anticlerical heresy undermining the authority and powers of the consecrated and ordained clergy and the hierarchy of the Church. Throughout Zwicker's works the inviolable dignity of the clergy and the public proclamation of faith by the Church are contrasted with the illicit secret ministry of the Waldensian lay Brethren. Yet it is Ulrich von Pottenstein who best expresses the contemporary sentiments in the introductory clauses to his translation of Zwicker's *Cum dormirent homines*:

> So: one has now heard of the holy sacrament of the altar, and how nobody can consecrate it but a priest who is properly ordained according to the keys of the Church, which Christ Jesus has granted to the Apostles and their followers. Against this the Waldensian heretics speak in many ways, and in many articles they detract from clerical dignity.[42]

---

[40] Tönsing, *Johannes Malkaw*, pp. 70–1, 225–6; the inquisitor in Malkaw's case, Nikolaus Böckeler, was in charge of the contemporary Waldensian trials in Mainz; Deane, 'Archiepiscopal Inquisitions', pp. 215–17. See also below.

[41] See the manuscript description of NKCR MS XIII. E. 7 in Appendix 1.

[42] Ulrich von Pottenstein, *Credo*, cap. 35A (ÖNB MS 3050 fol. 276ra): 'Als man nu gehöret hat von dem heyligen sacrament des altar, wy daz niem gesegen mag denn ain priester, der da rechtleich geweicht ist nach den slußeln der kirchen, die christus ihesus den czwelifpoten verlichen hat vnd iren nachkomen. Daz widersprechen die keczer Waldenses manichueltichlich vnd encziehen priesterleicher wirdichait an manigen stukchen.'

Much of the intention behind Petrus Zwicker's mission was to undermine the authority of the Waldensian Brethren in the eyes of their followers and supporters. Kathrin Utz Tremp has remarked that the will to impose a clear divide between clergy and illegitimate lay confessors is prominent in the questions Zwicker put to the Waldensians in Stettin. He was eager to determine whether the deponents had believed that the heresiarchs were priests sent by the pope or a bishop, and if not, where they had received their authority to preach and to hear confessions. The purpose was not only to discern heretics but to educate the Waldensian sympathizers about this fundamental division between laity and clergy. Of the contemporaries, only Zwicker inquired into the deponents' opinion about heresiarchs in such detail.[43] Georg Modestin has recently expanded Utz Tremp's analysis to Zwicker's polemical writing and has pointed out that denigration of the Waldensian Brethren from this priestly standpoint is central to the polemical strategy of the *Cum dormirent homines*.[44]

Discrediting the Waldensian lay apostolate and the claim to be the true church was a continuation of a debate that took place in the 1360s' correspondence between converted Austrian (ex-)Waldensians and the Lombard Brethren, which itself drew on the arguments of the thirteenth-century polemics.[45] Refuting the authority of the Waldensian ministry also has a central role in both the *Refutatio errorum* and the *Cum dormirent homines*.[46] However, despite his vehement onslaughts on the heresiarchs, such as deprecating their status as pastors when they flee and leave their followers to face inquisitors alone,[47] Zwicker actually says more about the clergy and their functions than about Waldensian Brethren, especially in the *Cum dormirent homines*. The dignity of the ordained and consecrated priests and

---

[43] Utz Tremp, 'Multum abhorrerem confiteri', pp. 153–60, 169, 177. Cf. Zwicker's short questionnaire, quoted from St Florian, MS XI 234, fol. 91ra: 'Putabas eos bonos et sanctos homines; Vice apostolorum in terris ambulantes et quod haberent potestatem a deo verbum dei predicandi; confessiones audiendi; penitentias iniungendi et a peccatis absoluendi melius quam sacerdotes ecclesie uel equales' (Did you think of them as good and holy men; walking the earth in the place of the apostles; and that they had power from God to preach the word to God; to hear confessions, impose penances and absolve from sins – better than the Church's priests or equally?).

[44] Modestin, 'The Anti-Waldensian Treatise', pp. 219–20.

[45] The texts edited in Biller, 'Aspects', pp. 264–353. See also Biller, *Waldenses*, chs. XI–XII; Gonnet, 'Valdesi d'Austria', pp. 27–8; Molnár, *Storia dei valdesi (1)*, pp. 103–4; Utz Tremp, 'Multum abhorrerem confiteri', pp. 164–6; Cameron, *Waldenses*, pp. 118–25.

[46] Both treatises start with this; see the *Refutatio*'s first chapter: 'Primo dicunt heresiarchas, quos apud se fratres nominant et in confessione dominos appellant, esse veros discipulorum Christi successores' (First they [heretics] say that the heresiarchs – who among themselves are named 'Brethren' and in confession are called 'lords' – are the true successors of Christ's disciples). Redactions 1, 3 and 4, and in the *Cum dormirent homines*, esp. chs I, V–XI, XIII.

[47] Zwicker, *Cum dormirent homines*, p. 281E.

the Waldensians' (alleged) hatred of the clergy permeates the treatise. The theme is not confined to the chapters that expressly concern matters such as the obligation to obey even bad priests. For Zwicker, the Waldensians' hatred and envy of the clergy is the ultimate reason for their falling into heresy. Having told his version of 'Petrus Waldensis's' conversion, probably adapted from the Waldensian historical text *Liber electorum* or directly from the Waldensian Brethren,[48] Zwicker complains about how the Waldensians had first disobeyed the papal curia's prohibition of preaching and then

> in hatred of the clergy and true priesthood they began, from the ancient errors of old heretics and adding new and pernicious articles, to destroy, condemn and reject everything – with the sole exception of the Sacraments – through which the clergy like a pious mother collects her children, just as a mother hen collects chicks under her wings. Their errors and some ways to refute them are presented in the following [chapters].[49]

This sets the framework. Zwicker's treatise is not just an apologia for true faith and its articles. It is an apologia for the Catholic cult as administered, supervised and represented by the ordained clergy. There is an anti-Waldensian literary tradition in the background. For example the Anonymous of Passau lamented that the Waldensians condemned the Roman Church and its clergy while otherwise appearing good Christians.[50] In the *De inquisitione hereticorum*, the lay ministry of the Waldensians was perceived as undermining the authority of the clergy and Church's hierarchy.[51] Nevertheless, Zwicker's firm stand in defence of the clergy should be read as reflecting and participating in contemporary debates about clerical authority far broader than the problem posed by the Waldensians, much as his biblicist style and the defence of the Virgin Mary and the cult of saints were a commentary on the reformist ideas of late fourteenth-century Prague.

Although lamentations about the state of the Church and the morals of the clergy had been constant since at least the High Middle Ages,[52] one can say

---

[48] Biller, *Waldenses*, p. 257; on the *Liber Electorum* in general, see ibid., ch. XII. A critical edition of the text is in Biller, 'Aspects', pp. 264–70.

[49] Zwicker, *Cum dormirent homines*, p. 278E: 'Vnde in odium clericorum et veri Sacerdotii ex antiquis erroribus veteranorum haereticorum, et superadditis nouis et damnosis articulis, inceperunt, solis exceptis Sacramentis, omnia destruere et condemnare, et reprobare, per quae Clerus, velut pia mater, filios eius congregat, sicut gallina congregat pullos suos sub alis. Quorum errores, cum suis aliqualibus reprobationibus in sequentibus apparebunt.'

[50] *Quellen*, ed. Patschovsky and Selge, p. 73.

[51] 'Der Tractat des David von Augsburg', ed. Preger, p. 206.

[52] F. Graus, 'The Church and its Critics in Time of Crisis', in *Anticlericalism in Late Medieval and Early Modern Europe*, ed. P. A. Dykema and H. A. Oberman (Leiden, 1993), pp. 65–81 (pp. 68–71); K. Elm, 'Antiklerikalismus im deutschen Mittelalter', ibid., pp. 3–18 (pp. 5–10).

without exaggeration that when Zwicker wrote the *Cum dormirent homines* in 1395 the authority of the Church, the papacy and the clergy was approaching its low point. The traditional view of the 'crisis of the late Middle Ages' and the relations between the laity and the clergy around 1400, especially prevalent in German scholarship, has been softened by studies on reform and renewal, but there is no denying that the inner conflict of the Church severely taxed its dignity.[53] The Great Schism had not been resolved through the death of the Roman pope Urban VI, as many had hoped. Instead, the election of Boniface IX in November 1389 had reinforced the division of Christendom into two obediences, undermining the prestige of the papal see. By the 1390s there was a real fear that the state of schism would become permanent.[54] Although there are conflicting interpretations of the extent to which the Schism was a reality at the local level,[55] there is no doubt that the mutual excommunications and heresy accusations by the rival obediences did little to promote the dignity of the prelates. In the eyes of contemporaries, parish priests, vicars and members of the religious orders did no better. The Bohemian reform preacher Milíč of Kroměříž criticised prelates, priests, friars and nuns alike in his letter to Pope Urban V in 1367. The clergy are accused above all of simony and avarice:

> What would I say about canons? Some of them fight and joust in arms more than sing in churches; some have their prebends established purely on the basis of usuries or contracts made through the fraud of usuries; some

[53] It is not possible to go into details of the crisis discussion here. It has been summed up in H. Müller, *Die kirchliche Krise des Spätmittelalters: Schisma, Konziliarismus und Konzilien* (Munich, 2012), pp. 59–61. See also Kneupper, *The Empire at the End of Time*, pp. 11, 139–40; Machilek, 'Beweggründe, Inhalte und Probleme', pp. 46–7; P. Segl, 'Schisma, Krise, Häresie und Schwarzer Tod. Signaturen der "Welt vor Hus"', in *Jan Hus – Zwischen Zeiten, Völkern, Konfessionen*, ed. F. Seibt (Munich, 1997), pp. 27–38; important attempts to go beyond the narratives of lateness, decline or reform are essays by H. Kaminsky, 'From Lateness to Waning to Crisis: The Burden of the Later Middle Ages', *Journal of Early Modern History* 4 (2000), 85–125; and J. H. Van Engen, 'Multiple Options: The World of the Fifteenth-Century Church', *Church History* 77 (2008), 257–84. Despite its bleak title, F. Graus, *Pest – Geissler – Judenmorde : das 14. Jahrhundert als Krisenzeit* (Göttingen, 1987), pp. 118–43, is a balanced overview of the fourteenth-century crisis that also takes into account the emerging reform movements and lay devotion.

[54] É. Delaruelle, E.-R. Labande and P. Ourliac, *L'Église au temps du grand schisme et de la crise conciliaire (1378–1449)* (Paris, 1962), pp. 66–7; Swanson, 'A Survey of Views on the Great Schism, c. 1395'; Graus, *Pest – Geissler – Judenmorde*, p. 143; Müller, *Die kirchliche Krise des Spätmittelalters*, pp. 6–10.

[55] Earlier the prevailing interpretation was that the Schism touched above all the prelates, clergy and rulers, not laity, see e.g. Graus, *Pest – Geissler – Judenmorde*, p. 126; more recently P. Daileader, 'Local Experiences of the Great Western Schism', in *A Companion to the Great Western Schism (1378–1417)*, ed. J. Rollo-Koster and T. M. Izbicki (Leiden, 2009), pp. 89–121, argued that the Schism was felt at every level of society, but proposed also that factual coexistence of the rival obediences often meant minimal consequences for ordinary laypeople.

borrow money, and whatever is repaid beyond the original sum is given for the buying of masses.[56]

A little more than a decade later, around 1380, the visitation protocols from over 300 parishes in the archdiocese of Prague by Archdeacon Pavel of Janovic reveal widespread abuses and malpractices, ranging from open drunkenness to concubines and the running of a brothel by a priest – to the extent that these vices are taken for granted by parishioners.[57] Greed comes up again, and accusations of priests asking for illicit payments for sacraments and other services are common. A witness even said that a priest asked for money to be put on the altar when he was ministering the Eucharist, and when the deponent did not have any, the priest threw the wafer back onto the altar.[58]

Waldensians interrogated in the 1390s also had firsthand experience of clerical abuses. An extreme example of opportunism and corruption is the story that Heyne Vilter the Elder from Prenzlau told Zwicker in the first stage of the Stettin inquisitions in December 1392. When Zwicker asked if the deponent had been previously accused of heresy, he learned that Heyne, together with four other Waldensian men and their wives, had been *infamati* (defamed) of heresy six or eight or six years earlier – the depositions are inconsistent about the date of the previous proceedings. They had been called to an official of the diocese of Cammin, known only as Burch in the protocols, but who was probably Borke de Lobeze, archdeacon of Stolp.[59] He certainly confirmed Waldensian presumptions about the avarice and corruptibility of prelates. When the accused appeared before him and declined to swear an oath, he simply wanted to delegate the problem to another official, but not before trying to extort some money from the accused, threatening to 'throw

---

[56] F. Mcnčik, 'Milič a dva jeho spisy z i. 1367', *Věslník Královské české společnosti nauk. Třída filosoficko-historicko-filologická* (1890), 309–36 (p. 321): 'Quid dicam de canonicis? Quidam plus pugnant et hastiludunt in armis, quam cantant in ecclesiis; quidam praebendas suas habent fundatas mere super usuras sive contractus factos in fraudem usurarum; quidam mutuant pecunias, et quidquid ultra sortem redditur, hoc datur pro missis comparandis.'

[57] Summarized by Fudge, 'The "Law of God": Reform and Religious Practice in Late Medieval Bohemia', p. 49; from the edition of I. Hlaváček and Z. Hledíková, *Protocollum visitationis archidiaconatus Pragensis annis 1379–1382 per Paulum de Janowicz Archidiaconum Pragensem factae* (Prague, 1973). See also F. Šmahel, 'The Hussite Critique of the Clergy's Civil Dominion', in *Anticlericalism in Late Medieval and Early Modern Europe*, ed. P. A. Dykema and H. A. Oberman (Leiden, 1993), pp. 83–90 (pp. 84–5).

[58] *Protocollum visitationis*, ed. Hlaváček and Hledíková, p. 319; cited in I. Hlaváček, 'Beiträge zum Alltagsleben im vorhussitischen Böhmen. Zur Aussagekraft des Prager Visitationsprotokolls von 1379-1391 und der benachbarten Quellen', *Jahrbuch für fränkische Landesforschung* 34/35 (1975), 865–82 (p. 875, n. 27).

[59] *Quellen*, ed. Kurze, p. 89, n. 1a.

them into the fire' unless they agreed to pay three marks in gold. In the end they paid one, which seemed to satisfy Borke.[60]

Starting with this extortion, the whole process became a farce. The accused were questioned on two further occasions in Stettin and Cammin, and there was confusion over whether they had already exculpated themselves. Finally they were ordered to appear before the dean of Gramzow. Because of an ongoing war, with the dean's consent they did not have to come to him, but the dean arrived at a lay synod (*sinodum laycalem*) that convened in the parochial church of Prenzlau. There Heyne Vilter and his companions were accused of worshiping Lucifer,[61] a popular rumour about Waldensians, which Zwicker methodically dismissed in his inquisitions.[62] In addition to not believing the local rumours about heretics, the inquisitor and his *familia* were clearly displeased with the previous tribunal. The enumerator of the protocols wrote in the margin of Heyne Vilter's protocol, 'Note this strange and abominable process',[63] and Zwicker sentenced the deponents not as relapsed heretics but as first offenders – literally a matter of life and death in heresy tribunals. Against this background it is no wonder that Waldensians were generally distrustful towards the clergy. In Stettin, on 26 February 1393 Mechtyld, wife of Jacob Philippus, did not believe in intercession on behalf of the dead or purgatory because they were invented by priests out of their greed,[64] and on 27 January 1393 Tylls, wife of Hans Sleyke, replied thus to Zwicker's question on whether she regarded indulgences as beneficial: 'that no, because they [the Waldensian Brethren] say that that they are invented because of the avarice of the priests, and similarly about the excommunications'.[65]

---

[60] Ibid., p. 90: 'Interrogatus, quare ditaverit eos vel de quo culpaverit eos, respondit, quod inputaverit, eo quod non dicerent trwen, et respondentibus ipsis, quod hoc dimisissent propter deum, ipse [Burch] remisit eos in Stetyn ad dominum Nicolaum dictum Darczaw, et postulante (a) nominatis tres marcas denariorum Stetinensium dictorum Vynkenawgen, et minante eis ad ignem proicere, si non darent, tandem pactantes dederint unam marcam.'

[61] In addition to Heyne Vilter the Elder's deposition, the story is pieced together from the protocols of Heyne Vilter the Younger (nephew of the older Heyne), Claus Hufener, brothers Jacob and Zacharias Welsaw and the latter's wife Katherina Welsaw. See *Quellen*, ed. Kurze, pp. 89–96, 111–12; the events have been described in Kurze, 'Zur Ketzergeschichte', pp. 55–6; and in detail in Utz Tremp, *Von der Häresie zur Hexerei*, pp. 283–92.

[62] See above all the interrogation of Herman Gossaw in December 6/7, 1392, where the notary writes concerning the rumours of Lucifer-worship: 'quod inquisitor noverat, predictos articulos non esse de secta Waldensium' (that the inquisitor had known, that the aforesaid articles were not of the Waldensian sect): *Quellen*, ed. Kurze, pp. 88–9. See also Biller, *Waldenses*, pp. 258, 279 and p. 8, n. 21 above.

[63] *Quellen*, ed. Kurze, p. 90: 'Nota hic mirabilem et abhominandum processum.'

[64] Ibid., p. 201: 'Nec crediderit eis prodesse nec aliqua alia suffragia etc. ecclesiastica, [...] et quod nullum esset purgatorium, quia hec solum prespbiteri excogitasset ex avaricia sua.'

[65] Ibid., p. 124: 'Interrogata de indulgenciis an crediderit esse utiles, respondit, quod

Doubt concerning indulgences and their effect was not confined to Waldensians but was shared by non-heretical laity as well. Zwicker grudgingly acknowledges this, and the fault of the clergy, in the *Cum dormirent homines*:

> Why not only Waldensian heretics but also many Catholics are at times perplexed about indulgences: that is due to the pronouncement without any distinction made by priests seeking profit, who indiscriminately promise indulgences to all people doing this or that. And this is not according to the intention of the pope or other prelates, who do not give these [indulgences] except to those who are truly penitent, confessed and contrite.[66]

The fault is thus not in the system but in the failure of a few corrupt priests. That the failures of some or even most of its members did not mean that the Church as a whole failed was an opinion shared by virtually all medieval thinkers, but in the years of the Schism even the loyal sons of the Church were prone to see more corruption than virtue in the *ecclesia militans* (church militant).[67] Zwicker, however, continued to be positive about the dignity and sanctity of the clergy. Notable in the quotation above is the conviction that only individual priests, not the papacy or bishops, are slack in granting indulgences. This was after all the time when Boniface IX launched an extensive indulgence campaign which was widely disapproved of as simony, among others by the Dominican Heinrich von Bitterfeld, who opposed it in Prague in 1393/4.[68] Instead of joining the chorus lamenting the deplorable state of

---

non, quia dixerint excogitatum propter avariciam clericorum, et de excommunicacionibus similiter.' Almost identical opinion can already be found among the Waldensians in Mainz: 'Sextus, quod indulgencie concesse ab ecclesia sint trufe et invente propter pecunias' (Sixth, that indulgences granted by the Church are ridiculous trifles, invented for the sake of money), Kolpacoff, 'Papal Schism', p. 283. The somewhat earlier treatise *Attendite a falsis prophetis* claims that Waldenses regard canonical hours to be inventions due to the clergy's greediness: 'quia hore canonice sint invenciones sacerdotum, propter avariciam adinvente' (St Florian, MS XI 152, fol. 50r). More examples can easily be found.

[66] Zwicker, *Cum dormirent homines*, pp. 295H–296A: 'Quare autem non solum Waldenses haeretici, immo multi Catholici, quandoque titubant de Indulgentiis, hoc facit indiscreta pronunciatio quaestuosorum sacerdotum, qui indifferenter omnibus hominibus, hoc et illud facientibus, indulgentias promittunt. Et hoc non est de mente Domini Papae, aut aliorum Praelatorum; qui non dant eas, nisi vere poenitentibus et confessis, et contritis.'

[67] Levy, *Holy Scripture*, pp. 4, 7, 36 and passim; Graus, *Pest – Geissler – Judenmorde*, p. 126. A perfect example is the Parisian theologian and later cardinal Pierre d'Ailly, who regarded the Schism as divine punishment caused by failure at all levels of the ecclesiastical hierarchy; L. B. Pascoe, *Church and Reform: Bishops, Theologians, and Canon Lawyers in the Thought of Pierre d'Ailly (1351–1420)* (Leiden, 2004), pp. 15–16, 25–6.

[68] Machilek, 'Beweggründe, Inhalte und Probleme', p. 45. Bitterfeld was otherwise a defender of indulgences, opposing Wyclif's teachings on the topic since the 1380s;

the Church, Zwicker chose to stress that the system was fundamentally in accordance with God's plan and that the failings of a few individuals did not change this fundamental truth.

The rationale for glorifying the clergy is only partly rooted in the literary form of anti-heretical polemic. Certainly the juxtaposition of heretical lay ministers and consecrated priests required the presentation of the clergy in a better light than, for example, in the *gravamina* (complaints) detailing the plight of the Church. There was no need, however, to refrain from berating the clergy in anti-heretical literature. The failure of the clerics, especially parish priests, was often seen as a major reason for the appeal of heresy. In the early thirteenth century both the papal curia and the early Dominicans saw the cause of the heretics' success as the poor morals and education of the secular clergy.[69] The thirteenth-century treatise of the Anonymous of Passau finds more to blame in the failure, negligence, and scandalous lifestyle of priests and doctors than in the pride and ignorance of the heretics.[70]

Those who followed Zwicker's example in writing against the Waldensians did not hold back from criticizing the contemporary clergy. Johlín of Vodňany berates his fellow churchmen more fiercely than he ever does heretics. They greedily hunt for benefices and offices, they attend carnal feasts, they are negligent in their ignorance, and their bad example destroys the laity's faith in the sacraments. Prelates living luxuriously and voluptuously, giving favours to their relatives and acting as secular princes are the sign of the approaching Antichrist. In the lower clergy there are many who hardly ever read the Scriptures and other devout texts. Others (probably mendicants are meant) show papal bulls that give them the right to extract money.[71] Ulrich von Pottenstein was unquestionably a solid defender of the church hierarchy and the clergy's dignity, but when he writes about the qualities of the good prelates in chapter 7 of the *Pater noster* part of his work, he inserts a long *exemplum* complaining about the prelates of his own days, comparing bad priests to vultures and blind bats, in language not unlike the words he and Zwicker used against the Waldensians.[72]

In comparison, Petrus Zwicker's complaints about the morals of the clergy

Šmahel, *Die Prager Universität im Mittelalter*, pp. 259–60; Koudelka, 'Heinrich von Bitterfeld', pp. 44–8.

[69] Ames, *Righteous Persecution*, pp. 137–8.

[70] *Quellen*, ed. Patschovsky and Selge, pp 71–2, 94–5, 99, 101; see also the part titled 'De occasionibus errorum hereticorum', ed. Preger, *Beiträge*, pp. 242–5. For a detailed survey of the reasons for heresy in the Anonymous of Passau, see Segl, *Ketzer in Österreich*, pp. 247–70; A. Patschovsky, 'Wie wird man Ketzer? Der Beitrag der Volkskunde zur Entstehung von Häresien', in *Volksreligion im hohen und späten Mittelalter*, ed. P. Dinzelbacher and D. Bauer (Paderborn, 1990) pp. 145–62.

[71] Neumann, 'Výbor z předhusitských postil', pp. 251–2, 254–5, 290, 320.

[72] Ulrich von Pottenstein, *Pater Noster*, cap. 7D in Hayer, 'Paternoster-Auslegung II', pp. 154–7; Välimäki, 'Transfers of Anti-Waldensian Material', pp. 160–1.

are modest. The opening sentence 'but while men were asleep' (Matthew 13:25) includes a rebuke to prelates who should be 'living reasonably and in a civil way' but 'are sleeping in the body of negligence' while the heresiarchs devour their flock.[73] This is a typical exposition of the sleeping men in the parable of the wheat and the tares. The negligence of the prelates and doctors of the Church, more than anyone else's, is to blame when sin, vice and heresy multiply in the Church. This explanation for the verse was given, for example, by Vincent Ferrer and by the Franciscan cardinal Bertrand de la Tour in the early fourteenth century.[74]

Choosing Matthew 13:25 for the opening of his treatise, Zwicker guides his readers towards the interpretation that the clergy are to blame for the spread of heresy, but it remains a general allusion. Zwicker dwells on the vices of the clergy far less than an average sermon on the verse. In fact, when translating this passage, Ulrich von Pottenstein expands the exposition of the parable and makes it clear that heresy and error spread when the prelates are negligent, obscene or weighed down by sins.[75] Zwicker, however, returns only in passing to the shortcomings of the priests. The laxity in promising indulgences has already been mentioned. In addition, Zwicker admits that the many vices of the clergy, especially carnal ones, are the reason why the Waldensian followers think that their own confessors have more authority to absolve from sins than the priests. Moreover, he warns that if the prelates are not inspired to greater vigilance it has to be feared that the heresiarchs will usurp even more power for themselves. He concedes that there are some bad priests, but immediately accuses Waldensians of generalizing the vices of one to all and staying silent about the virtues of good clerics.[76]

The fundamental question for Zwicker is the sacral status of the priesthood (*sacerdotium*), while the moral status of the clergy is secondary. Zwicker proceeds uncompromisingly to prove two points. Firstly, the validity of

---

[73] Zwicker, *Cum dormirent homines*, p. 277H G: 'Maxime vero inimici sunt, qui omnium virtutum fundamentum, quod est fides Christiana, impugnare conantur sicut sunt haeresiarchae, quis [r. qui] Praelatis Ecclesiae, velut hominibus rationabiliter et humane viuere debentibus, in corpore negligentiae dormientibus, illas pauculas, & utinam non multas ouiculas rapiunt, inficiunt et fura[n]tur' (Above all there are enemies who try to impugn the foundation of all virtues, which is the Christian faith, such as the heresiarchs. While the prelates of the Church sleep in the body of neglect, like men entitled to live reasonably and humanly, the heresiarchs attack – how I wish it were not many of them! – little lambs, infecting and stealing them).

[74] Bertrand de la Tour, 'Sermo primus, dominica quarta post octavias Epiphanie', BAV MS Vat. lat. 1240, fols. 140v, 142v; Sermo XXXVIII. Dominica V, post Epiphaniam. Sermo I, in Vincent Ferrer, *Opera seu sermones de tempore et sanctis*, p. 121; on Bertrand de la Tour and his works, Nold, *Pope John XXII and his Franciscan Cardinal*.

[75] Ulrich von Pottenstein, *Credo*, cap. 35A (ÖNB MS 3050, fol. 276rb–va); Välimäki, 'Transfers of Anti-Waldensian Material', p. 163.

[76] Zwicker, *Cum dormirent homines*, pp. 278F, 281F, 282E.

sacraments and dignity of the priesthood do not depend on the virtues or vices of the individual. Secondly, all prelates, even bad and negligent, must be obeyed. The validity of sacraments regardless of the minister's status was based on Augustine's refutation of Donatism, and it had been deeply grounded in medieval canon law and theology since the twelfth century.[77] Here the tension between tradition and biblicist argumentation is evident. Zwicker cannot muster any direct Bible quotations to support his position; neither would he resort to the authority of the doctors of the Church, glosses or canon law, although he was committed to them. Therefore the chapter on clerical dignity, discussed in more detail below, consists mainly of *exempla*.[78] For his second main argument, that even bad and evil priests and prelates must be honoured and obeyed, Zwicker can again draw from the Scriptures, using various examples of Christ chastising but at the same time honouring Pharisees because of their sacerdotal dignity.[79] Obedience to priests was, of course, prescribed in canon law and catechesis, and the laity was expected to honour the clerics by virtue of their office even when their knowledge and conduct did not meet their expectations.[80]

Given that the dignity of the clergy was difficult to demonstrate within scriptural argumentation, it is no wonder that Zwicker eliminated the more complicated (and from a biblical perspective dubious) matters of ecclesiastical hierarchy and religious orders from the *Cum dormirent homines*, whereas in the *Refutatio errorum* there is a whole chapter defending the papacy and bishops,[81] and in his letter to the Austrian dukes Zwicker mentions that Waldensians condemn the holy orders of the clergy, religious orders of any rule and papal authority.[82] In the *Cum dormirent homines*, the emphasis is on proving the

---

[77] D. C.1, q. 1 cc. 30–3. See also Helmholz, *The Spirit of Classical Canon Law*, pp. 206–9; H. Vorgrimler, *Sakramententheologie* (Düsseldorf, 1987), p. 68.

[78] Zwicker, *Cum dormirent homines*, pp. 281F–282B.

[79] Ibid., p. 282B–C.

[80] See especially the decretal *Quum ex iniuncto* by Innocent III in X 1.7.12. On honouring the clergy and their priestly status, see also Martin von Amberg, *Der Gewissensspiegel*, pp. 48–9. In practice the laity were often discontented with their parish priests and attempted to regulate them, R. N. Swanson, 'Apostolic Successors: Priests and Priesthood, Bishops, and Episcopacy in Medieval Western Europe', in *A Companion to Priesthood and Holy Orders in the Middle Ages*, ed. G. Peters and C. C. Anderson (Leiden, 2016), pp. 4–42 (pp. 21–2); R. Cossar, *The Transformation of the Laity in Bergamo, 1265–c. 1400* (Leiden, 2006), pp. 141–2.

[81] *Refutatio*, ed. Gretser, p. 305D–E: 'Sexto dicunt, quod papa, archiepiscopi, episcopi non habeant maiorem auctoritatem, quam sacerdotes' (Sixthly, they say that the pope, archbishops and bishops do not have greater authority than priests). In the *Cum dormirent homines* the ecclesiastical hierarchy is explicitly mentioned only in the chapter on indulgences; Zwicker, *Cum dormirent homines*, p. 295G–H. There Zwicker argues that the pope, cardinals, patriarchs and bishops can give indulgences based on their position as successors of Peter (pope), the apostles (cardinals), *principales patres in dominico grege* (patriarchs) and *perfecti iusti* (bishops).

[82] Preger, *Beiträge*, p. 248 (nos. 58, 67, 69).

dignity and sanctity of the consecrated clergy, and thus to rebut any claims to lay apostolate. In theory this was a simple and unambiguous matter in light of the tradition of the medieval Church, its exegesis and law. But, like the authority of the Scriptures, the authority and dignity of the clergy were also under scrutiny in the late fourteenth century. The focus on the priesthood, its dignity, sanctity and legitimacy means that Zwicker's treatise participates in and was read as part of the heated debate about authority in the late medieval Church. The discussions would culminate twenty years later at the Council of Constance and involve figures such as Matthew of Kraków, Pierre d'Ailly, Jean Gerson and Jan Hus. What Zwicker says about clerical dignity and obedience to bad priests was not as self-evident and uncontroversial as he presented it.

The worst priest and the holiest layman

The priestly office and dignity are not conferred by birth or virtue but by ordination and apostolic succession. That is the principle behind Zwicker's self-referential statement: 'Not therefore is that Petrus a priest, because he is son of sinner Catherina, but because he is properly ordained through a Catholic bishop inside the bowels of Mother Church.'[83] He continues to explain that the virtue, sanctity and righteousness of a layman, however great they might be, do not raise him to priestly status; neither does the greatest vice unmake a priest. And although administering sacraments in a state of mortal sin is pernicious to the priest, it does not make those sacraments invalid for the receiver. As noted already, this conviction was embedded in medieval canon law, and, however much they complained about the performance of individual priests, virtually all late medieval reformers shared this view. It was even reinforced by the Oxford theologian John Wyclif and the Bohemian reformer Jan Hus, who were branded as heretics because they supposedly thought otherwise.[84] Questioning it would have shaken the

---

[83] Zwicker, *Cum dormirent homines*, p. 281F: 'Non enim est ille Petrus ideo Sacerdos; quia Catherinae peccatricis filius, sed quia per Episcopum Catholicum intra viscera matris Ecclesiae rite ordinatus.' The sentence seems to lack something, and it was probably corrupted very early in the transmission of the treatise.

[84] John Wyclif and Jan Hus were both accused of Donatist heresy, i.e. denying the validity of sacraments of a wicked priest. However, modern scholarship has interpreted their writings as more conservative in this regard. Wyclif maintained the view – except perhaps very late in his life – that even an unworthy priest could administer sacraments: S. Penn, 'Wyclif and the Sacraments', in *A Companion to John Wyclif: Late Medieval Theologian*, ed. I. C. Levy (Leiden, 2006), pp. 241–91 (pp. 244, 278); I. C. Levy, 'Was John Wyclif's Theology of the Eucharist Donatistic?', *Scottish Journal of Theology* 53 (2000), 137–53; On Hus's opinion, see Levy, *Holy Scripture*, pp. 164, 168, 174.

whole apparatus of salvation and led to a state of profound uncertainty, as nobody could have been sure if the absolution from sins or the body of Christ they had received was effective, or even if the priests administering the sacraments were properly ordained.

This is also the reason why Waldensians were perceived to be such dangerous heretics. Zwicker does not say this explicitly, but Ulrich von Pottenstein does do so in his slightly expanded translation of Zwicker's chapter on priesthood:

> Therefore the priest who does not possess the Holy Spirit, who is indecent or sinning greatly – he may not forgive sins. As little may the pope do that, if he is in sin. So speak up, you wily fox, and if what you say is true, then our salvation is in great doubt and greatly damaged.[85]

The doubt and fear were acute. In the years of the Schism there was increasing uncertainty over the status of the priests of the opposing papal party. One of the troublemakers of the time, the provocative preacher and in every way controversial character Johannes Malkaw from Prussia, tapped into this fear when he preached against Avignonese and neutral parties in Strasbourg in 1390, claiming them to be *ipso facto* excommunicated and their sacraments invalid. The claim was in opposition to canon law, as explained above. Indeed, in the following year Malkaw was accused by the Dominican inquisitor Nikolaus Böckeler of various heresies, including irreverence towards the Eucharist and disobedience to ecclesiastical authorities. The provocative claim about sacramental validity was not itself in the error list.[86] Interestingly, Johannes Malkaw was accused, among other things, of lapsing into the error of the Waldensians because he had preached and administered sacraments without the permission of the local bishop.[87] The commission, which included Johannes Arnoldi, the inquisitor who had led the trials of Waldensians in Strasbourg a few years earlier, certainly did not think the troublesome cleric Malkaw a Waldensian proper, but wanted to

---

[85] Ulrich von Pottenstein, *Credo*, cap. 35E (ÖNB MS 3050, fol. 281ra): 'Darumb welicher priester den heiligen geist nicht hat, der ain vnkewscher ist oder sust sundig, der mag die sünde nicht vergeben. Als wenig mag es der pabst tun ob er süntig ist. Also sprichst du, du listiger fuchs vnd ist dein rede war so stet vnser hail in grossem zweyuel vnd in grossen schäden.' Cf. Zwicker, *Cum dormirent homines*, p. 281H. Peter von Pillichsdorf voices similar concern over the uncertainty of salvation arising from the demand that priests be sinless; Peter von Pillichsdorf, *Fragmentum ex Tractatu*, pp. 301H–302A.

[86] Tönsing, *Johannes Malkaw*, pp. 25–7, 64–110. On Böckeler, see also G. Modestin, 'Ein Mainzer Inquisitor in Straßburg: Ketzerverfolgung und Ordensreform auf dem Lebensweg von Nikolaus Böckeler OP (1378–1400)', *Mainzer Zeitschrift. Mittelrheinisches Jahrbuch für Archäologie, Kunst und Geschichte* 102 (2007), 167–73.

[87] See especially the consultation on Malkaw's case given in Strasbourg in 10 March 1391, ed. Tönsing, *Johannes Malkaw*, 225–6.

brand him as a heretic, and for that purpose Waldensians were a suitable and well-known category.[88] In Malkaw's case the plan failed, and he was able to continue what became a successful ecclesiastical career.[89] But the incident demonstrates how Waldensianism became synonymous with usurpation of clerical authority, and how their name could be used to defame enemies in the quarrels of the Schism.

Zwicker's claims about clerical dignity, on the other hand, are much more controversial than his basically conformist statements about the validity of sacraments. Nowhere in Zwicker's text is the juxtaposition of the priesthood and the laity more clear than in the provocative sentence: 'Thus the worst person who is a priest is worthier than the holiest person who is a layman.'[90] Hence the most sinful fornicator and usurer would by the grace of his office be worthier (*dignior*) than the most modest, pious and obedient layperson. The proposition is bold, almost absurd in the anticlerical climate of the late fourteenth century and in relation to the reputation for sanctity that surrounded many pious laypeople in the late Middle Ages.[91] In his claims about the priesthood's inherent dignity Zwicker is also on shaky ground in relation to his biblicist argumentation strategy. He is not able to adduce a single quotation from the Scriptures but has to rely on *exempla* and comparisons.[92]

Zwicker's argument holds only through careful separation of worthiness (*dignitas*) and sanctity (*sanctitas*), and by attaching the former to the office itself and the latter to personal qualities. Zwicker offers concrete examples. He asks if anyone can doubt that a king living a life is worthier and more dignified than a chaste knight, or if the same applies to a fornicating bishop in

---

[88] Ibid., pp. 70 1. The inquisitor of Malkaw's case, Nikolaus Böckeler, was also in charge of the contemporary Waldensian trials in Mainz, Deane, 'Archiepiscopal Inquisitions', pp. 215–17; Modestin, 'Ein Mainzer Inquisitor', pp. 169–70.

[89] Tönsing, *Johannes Malkaw*, pp. 110–13. The end of the process and the circumstances surrounding Malkaw's release are unclear, but already in November 1393 the Roman pope Boniface IX had nominated Johannes Malkaw as his chaplain of honour.

[90] Zwicker, *Cum dormirent homines*, p. 281F: 'Pessimus ergo homo, qui est sacerdos, dignior est sanctissimo homine, qui est laicus.'

[91] Such as the merchant Pier Pettinaio of Siena, D. Webb, 'Pier Pettinaio of Siena [Introduction]', in *Saints and Cities in Medieval Italy* (Manchester, 2007), pp. 191–3; or Birgitta of Sweden, on whom see e.g. P. Salmesvuori, *Power and Sainthood: The Case of Birgitta of Sweden* (New York, 2014), pp. 23–39; or Dominican lay penitent women, on whom see M. Lehmijoki-Gardner, *Worldly Saints: Social Interaction of Dominican Penitent Women in Italy, 1200–1500* (Helsinki, 1999).

[92] Therefore the assertions on dignity are supported by the requirement of obedience to prelates regardless of their virtue. Here the biblical basis is much firmer, and Zwicker throws in the example of Christ, who both rebuked scribes and Pharisees for their hypocrisy and in other instances displayed respect towards them, as well as the instructions in apostolic letters to be obedient to one's prelates and superiors: Zwicker, *Cum dormirent homines*, p. 282B–E.

comparison to a simple, chaste priest. Finally he proposes: 'Often it happens, that a simple monk is discovered to be more holy than his abbot, but never worthier.'[93] Thus dignity or worthiness were in Zwicker's thought connected to the hierarchy of office, both in the Church and in secular life. Especially when the office-holder performed his duties there was no need to doubt his worthiness. From the perspective of political scandals, Zwicker's view on the relationship of morals and performance in office is interesting:

> Just as fornication or adultery do not remove royal dignity from a king, if he is otherwise a good justiciar [administrator of justice], doing judgment and justice in his land, neither can priestly dignity be removed, if the priest otherwise administers the sacraments properly, preaches the word of God or does other things pertaining to a priest.[94]

There is a probable source text, or rather group of texts, for the impeccable dignity of the clerical office. The dignity or worthiness (*dignitas*) of the priesthood was discussed at length in a short treatise that was extremely popular, especially in central Europe: *Stella clericorum* (*The Star of Clerics*). It was first written around 1200 and its various versions circulated in numerous manuscripts throughout the later Middle Ages and thereafter in early printed editions.[95] It presents a very similar view of a priest's worthiness to Zwicker's. The goodwill of God and the dignity of the clergy are so great that sometimes God does good things through bad priests, 'because if some priests do not have dignity from merit, they have it from the office'.[96] Although the proposition that the worst priest is better or worthier than the best layman is not found as such in the edited text of *Stella clericorum*, it is certainly within this tradition and spirit that Zwicker wrote.

The work was definitely known to Jan Hus, who refers to it when refuting a proposition made by a certain priest in a sermon during the ordination of a new priest in Plzeň, Bohemia. The proposition was that the priest is 'creator of his creator' when he consecrates the sacrament, and Hus correctly recognized its origin in the *Stella clericorum*.[97] The polemic in which Hus engaged took place fifteen years after the publication of the *Cum dormirent homines*, but

---

[93] Ibid., p. 281G: 'Contingit frequenter simplicem monachum suo Abbate reperiri sanctiorem, nunquam autem digniorem.'

[94] Ibid.: 'Sicut ergo fornicatio, aut adulterium, non tollit a Rege regalem dignitatem, si alias est bonus Iustitiarius, faciens in terra iudicium et iustitiam, ita nec potest tollere dignitatem sacerdotalem, si alias rite Sacramenta ministrat, Verbum Dei praedicat, aut alia sacerdotalia faciat.'

[95] There are over 450 extant manuscripts, 60 references to lost manuscripts and more than 80 printed editions of the work before 1559, *Stella clericorum*, ed. E. H. Reiter (Toronto, 1997), p. 1.

[96] *Stella clericorum*, ed. Reiter, cap. 19:16–20.

[97] Joannes Hus, 'Replica contra Praedicatorem Plznensem, M. Joannis Hus, Anno M.CCCC.XII', in *Historia et monumenta Joannis Hus* [...] *recensita omnia juxta antiquam*

it relates directly to Zwicker's bold remark that the worst priest is worthier than the holiest layman. In late 1411 Hus wrote a letter to his supporters in the Bohemian city of Plzeň, where he mentioned that he had received tidings about a priest who, preaching at the ordination of a new priest, praised the dignity of the priesthood and among other things claimed that the worst priest was better than the best layman.[98] Shortly afterwards, Hus wrote a short treatise in Latin to revoke the errors of the preacher in Plzeň and found the proposition – which closely resembles the wording in *Cum dormirent homines* – outrageous. To him it was incomprehensible that a fornicating or simoniacal priest could claim greater worthiness than a pious and chaste layman, or even the Virgin Mary.[99] The propositions Hus refutes sound exaggerated, but are probably based on a real inaugural sermon, *sermo de novo sacerdote* (sermon about a new priest), and like any speech in honour of the promoted person it was supposed to praise them and their new status. A significant number of such sermons have survived, but as usual with late medieval sermons, the great majority of them are unpublished.[100] Sometimes the eulogy was rather unabashed, and rhetoric very similar to that of the sermon that irritated Hus, including the statement that priests are worthier than the Virgin Mary, can be found in a sermon *de novo sacerdote* written in 1454 and transmitted with a copy of the *Cum dormirent homines*.[101] It is, indeed, not out of the question that the *Cum dormirent homines* had served as the model for the assertion that the worst priest was better than the best layman. The wording, which we have only as secondhand information from Hus, resembles the admittedly very sharp formulation of Zwicker, and one has to remember that Bohemia was an

---

anni MDLVIII editionem norimbergensem Joannis Montani et Ulrici Neuberi (Nuremberg, 1715), pp. 179 85 (p. 181). Cf. *Stella clericorum*, ed. Reiter, cap. 21:1–3; 22:6–8.

[98] For the Czech letter with a Latin translation, see *Documenta Mag. Joannis Hus*, ed. Palacký, pp. 24–30. See also M. Spinka, *John Hus: A Biography* (Princeton, 1968), pp. 143–4; C. C. Anderson, 'The Six Errors. Hus on Simony', in *Reassessing Reform: A Historical Investigation into Church Renewal*, ed. C. M. Bellitto and D. Z. Flanagin (Washington, DC, 2012), p. 119.

[99] Joannes Hus, 'Replica contra Praedicatorem Plznensem', 182–3.

[100] For an example of a published sermon for a new priest, see *epistola ad novum sacerdotem*, written by Matthew of Kraków in 1418 and edited in M. Nuding, *Matthäus von Krakau: Theologe, Politiker, Kirchenreformer in Krakau, Prag und Heidelberg zur Zeit des Grossen Abendländischen Schismas* (Tübingen, 2007), pp. 329–31. Matthew's sermon praises priestly authority and power, but also encourages the ordained to be worthy of this responsibility and not distracted by anything else.

[101] BSB MS Clm 19539, fols. 252va–256rb, esp. fol. 256ra: 'Nam beata virgo pro magno habuit quod christum semel generauit sed sacerdos longe in hac parte dignior est; quia quem virgo semel genuit, Sacerdos per verba consecracionis cottidie conficit, corpus et sangwinem christi iesu' (For the blessed Virgin held it to be a great thing that she generated Christ; since through the words of consecration a priest confects every day the body and blood of Christ Jesus, whom the virgin Mary generated once [ergo etc.]). It was common for medieval sermons to circulate as single texts amid compilation manuscripts; Bériou, 'Les sermons latins après 1200', p. 386.

area where Zwicker's treatise circulated very soon after he wrote it.[102] Hus, on the other hand, most probably did not draw upon the *Cum dormirent homines*. If he had, he would without doubt have mentioned it, as he mentioned the *Stella clericorum*.

Nevertheless, Petrus Zwicker and Jan Hus both commented on the same discussion about the dignity and worthiness of the priestly office, albeit reaching opposite conclusions. Although Jan Hus was sentenced as a heretic at Constance in 1415, and Petrus Zwicker was an inquisitor whose treatise would continue to circulate as justification of true faith for a century, one should not be too hasty to draw the conclusion that in the eyes of their contemporaries the positions held by these men were undeniably orthodox or heretical. The dignity of the clergy was an issue that was all but solved during the decades these men were writing and preaching. The view presented by Zwicker on the worthiness of priests and obedience towards wicked prelates is the one that would prevail at the Council of Constance. It was enforced above all by the influential chancellor of the University of Paris, Jean Gerson, who maintained that the clergy deserved respect regardless of the quality of their personal lives.[103]

Both Ian Levy and Colt Anderson have argued that we must not let the winning side blur our vision, for the outcome was not certain. In some ways the theologians condemned at the council, John Wyclif and Jan Hus, were more conservative and conventional in their ecclesiology than their judges, while on the so-called orthodox side there were men whose views were practically identical to theirs, such as Dietrich of Niem, whose orthodoxy was never questioned.[104] Although Levy's and Anderson's reading of Wyclif and Hus is very sympathetic, almost to the point of being an apologia, their remark that the result of this debate was not settled before the council is important also in understanding Zwicker's assertions in their proper sense: as arguments made in an ongoing dispute, not as final words supported by the uncontested canon of the Church.

An example of the opposite view on the worthiness and unworthiness of priests was presented by a man who would become one of the foremost theologians in the time of Schism and the councils, and in the presence of the highest authority. In the sermon preached in the presence of Pope Urban VI on the feast of St Peter and Paul (29 July) in 1382, Matthew of Kraków spoke

---

[102] The matter was discussed also in a contemporary postilla, possibly written by Johlín of Vodňany, *Quadragesimale Admontense*, ed. Florianová et al., p. 128, which states in a way very similar to Zwicker that 'Hec fuit heresis: Bonus laycus esset dignior quam malus sacerdos' (This was the heresy: a good layman is worthier than a bad priest). On this work, see p. 208, n. 156 above.

[103] Gerson's opinions on the subject are summed up by L. B. Pascoe, *Jean Gerson: Principles of Church Reform* (Leiden, 1973), p. 156.

[104] Levy, *Holy Scripture*, pp. xii–xiii, 190–2 and passim; Anderson, 'The Six Errors', esp. p. 107.

about prelates, as was fitting on the day of the principal apostles. In many instances he warned against elevating persons of dubious morals or abilities to become prelates lest their example cause damage to the Church and the faith. Among other things ignorance of God's law would render a person unworthy (*indignus*) for his office:

> Thus, whoever has no notion of truth or a very modest one, he is unworthy of a position of authority, nor is it thought fit for him to be called with the priest's name, as holy Jerome testifies on this in Aggeus 2 (12): 'Ask the priests the law. You should think,' he says, 'that the priesthood is the office of giving answers about the law to him who asks.' If he is a priest, he should know the law of God. If he is ignorant, he himself argues that he is not a priest of the Lord.[105]

There is no fundamental division between the positions of Matthew and Zwicker, but there is a difference of emphasis. After all, Matthew does not go as far as to propose that such an unworthy priest should be *ipso facto* deposed from his office or have his sacraments declared invalid. He merely says that he does not merit the name of priest and that such persons should not be raised to priestly status. Correspondingly Zwicker, however much he stresses the dignity of the office as independent of personal qualities, is forced to admit that the person can be unworthy (*indignus*) in order to drive through the main argument of the sacrament's validity. 'Thus the value, dignity and nobility of the sacraments is the same whether they are ministered by a worthy or by an unworthy priest.'[106]

Yet when hairs were split as the Schism dragged on, the emphases became crucial. Waldensians, or rather the idea of them, played a small but not insignificant part in these disputes. They were heretics who were commonly known to usurp priestly authority and give it to laymen and to deny the sacramental powers of wicked priests. The way Petrus Zwicker and Ulrich von Pottenstein in his footsteps portrayed Waldensians only reinforced this aspect.

As anticlerical heretics *par excellence* the name of the Waldensians was useful when anyone wanted to cast the suspicion of heresy on opponents. We have already seen how 'Waldensian error' was used in the attempt to smear

---

[105] 'Quisquis ergo nullam vel nimis modicam habet veritatis noticiam, indignus principatu, immo nec sacerdos nomini nominandus esse censetur, testante beato Ieronimo super illud Aggei 2 (12): *Interrogate sacerdotes legem. Considera*, inquit, *sacerdotum esse officium de lege interroganti respondere*. Si sacerdos est, sciat legem domini. Si ipse ignorat, ipse arguit se non esse sacerdotem domini', ed. Nuding, *Matthäus von Krakau*, pp. 302–12, at 307. Cf. Jerome, *Commentaria in Aggaeum*, PL 25, 1406B.

[106] Zwicker, *Cum dormirent homines*, p. 281H: 'Et ergo idem valor Sacramentorum, dignitas et nobilitas, siue a digno, siue indigno presbytero conferantur.' Cf. also ibid., p. 282B. 'Indignus' was also the term Stephan Páleč used of priests living in sin when he argued against Hus at the council; Levy, *Holy Scripture*, pp. 168–9.

Johannes Malkaw in 1391. Even laypeople were familiar with the potential. In 1394–5 accusations about Waldensianism were employed in what Ludwig Schnurrer revealed to have been a personal feud between two leading burghers of Rothenburg ob der Tauber.[107] In 1404, Johlín of Vodňany declared that those who slandered priests were suspected of Waldensian heresy.[108] In 1408 Jan Hus defended Abraham, a priest at the Church of the Holy Spirit in Prague, who had been called in front of an episcopal inquisition. Hus accused the inquisitors of wanting to condemn Abraham for holding 'the error of the Waldensians' because he did not want to take an oath.[109] Though the last accusation is not about anticlericalism, it demonstrates how radical Bohemian reformers could be labelled as Waldensians before the name Hussite emerged – and how Waldensianism had become a sort of jack-of-all-trades heresy in the German-Bohemian area.

In order to see how the threat of Waldensianism was applied in the debates on the clergy's authorship at the Council of Constance, we turn to Jean Gerson. In May 1418 Gerson discussed the possibility of a pope's deposition due to heresy in relation to Wyclif's doctrines condemned at the council:

> Just as sanctity, however great, does not constitute anyone in papal or episcopal status, unless [he is chosen] by human election according to common law, contrary to the opinion of the Waldensians, so too no iniquity removes anyone from episcopal or papal rank according to common law if there is no intervention by a human act of deposition.[110]

This is not the only text where Gerson sees Waldensians as the precursors of Wyclif and the Hussites. In *De potestate ecclesiastica*, written in February 1417, he says that Wyclif and his followers had revived the 'old error of the Waldensians and the Poors of Lyon' by requiring a state of grace from true prelates. In Gerson's opinion this endangered the whole hierarchy of the Church and could not be a prerequisite for ecclesiastical power, as no one could be sure if he was counted among the predestined.[111] In another work he compares the condemnation of ecclesiastical property by Wyclif's and Hus's followers to the old heresies of the Waldensians and Albigenses.[112] The Waldensians served also as a warning example of the stupidity and defiance

---

[107] Schnurrer, 'Der Fall Hans Wern'.

[108] Neumann, 'Výbor z předhusitských postil', p. 321. See also Chapter 4, above.

[109] *Documenta Mag. Joannis Hus*, ed. Palacký, pp. 184–5. See also Fudge, *The Trial of Jan Hus*, p. 123.

[110] Gerson, *Œuvres complètes*, VI, 286: 'Sicut enim nulla sanctitas quantumcumque magna constituit aliquem in statu papali vel episcopali nisi per electionem humanam de lege communi, contra opinionem Valdensium, ita nulla iniquitas removet aliquem ab episcopali gradu vel papali de communi lege, si non interveniat humana depositio.'

[111] Ibid., VI, 212.

[112] Ibid., IX, 449.

of those who dared to preach without the authorization of their prelates.[113] Daniel Hobbins has suggested that Wyclif's doctrine alarmed Gerson because it targeted the Church's property and through that revived the two old heresies.[114] I am, however, inclined to see Gerson's primary point as the threat the Waldensians had caused to the ecclesiastical hierarchy, a threat echoed by Wyclif and Hus from Gerson's point of view. The frightening thing was not the demand that clerics should lead a virtuous life – this was after all what every single author discussed in this chapter wanted to enforce – but making virtue a precondition of sacramental and ecclesiastical power. Proposing virtue as an ideal was not a problem, but asserting that clerical actions and authority were invalid without it put the salvation of everyone in great doubt, as Ulrich von Pottenstein expressed it.

Gerson's statement on Waldensians is too general to identify any particular text as its source, either Zwicker's or anyone else's. Nevertheless, I argue that the use of the label of Waldensianism in the ecclesiastical quarrels of the 1390s and early 1400s, as well as its appearance in Gerson's writings during the Council of Constance, was a result of the persecutions of the 1390s. More importantly, it was a product of the pastoralization of heresy, of the specific approach to heresy taken by Petrus Zwicker and his circle. The strong assertions Zwicker makes about the dignity of the priesthood and obedience to wicked clerics were first and foremost intended to counter any possibility of a lay apostolate being comparable to ordained clerics. Zwicker's tendency to go into the doctrinal foundations, to reduce the argument to absolutes such as the worst priest being more worthy than the holiest layman, enabled other applications of the label of heresy. As in the case of the Virgin Mary and the cult of saints, when the refutation of Waldensians concentrated on certain points of doctrine – and the dignity of the ordained clergy was certainly a focal point – Waldensianism could be used to discern, explain and condemn persons and movements expressing similar ideas. In effect, Waldensianism in the form it was redefined and rewritten by Zwicker and other inquisitors from the early 1390s onwards gave the ecclesiastical elite tools to label emerging radical tendencies before any other names were thought up. Waldensianism was by no means the only tool in the toolbox, but it was a useful one, and it was used.

The absence of the Schism

The Great Schism touched Europeans in varying degrees, but the higher a person was in the ecclesiastical hierarchy the more profoundly his life and

---

[113] Ibid., VIII, 132.
[114] Hobbins, *Authorship and Publicity*, p. 13.

career were affected.[115] The Schism earned Zwicker a promotion, albeit a largely nominal one. In 1394 at the latest he became the provincial of the German Celestines, consisting only of the monastery in Oybin and a smaller house in Prague, a province that was created under the Italian main monastery, S. Spirito del Morrone, to prevent the German Celestines from falling under the influence of the French party.[116] Those churchmen whose offices and careers were not directly disturbed (or advanced) by the Schism nevertheless experienced the division as a menacing phenomenon that marked their whole cultural and intellectual environment. The Schism became one of the major polemical quarrels and textual battles of the Middle Ages.[117] The lawyer Dietrich of Niem famously said in his treatise *De schismate* (1409/10) that if all the treatises complaining about the state of the Church could be assembled, a hundred camels could hardly carry them.[118]

Bemoaning the division of Christendom was so commonplace that it is no surprise to find it in the *Cum dormirent homines*, where whole chapters are devoted to the continuity and unity of the faith. However, a striking feature that has gone practically unnoticed in scholarship is the absence of any direct reference to the Schism. Zwicker represents the Church as one and undivided, a situation wholly at odds with what in fact prevailed in 1395. Of course, the imagined unity of the Church was required for the juxtaposition of heretics and Catholics, the representation of Waldensianism as a negative image of Catholicism that permeates Zwicker's treatise. I argue that through this comparison the disunity of the heretics became a way of handling the trauma caused by the Schism, a way to find consolation in a situation where no imminent solution for the division was in sight. The question of the true Church is obviously entangled with the debates about the clergy's worthiness and sacramental powers, discussed above, but the unity of the Church and continuation of faith are in the context of the Schism such fundamental problems that they merit a separate treatment.

Contrasting the unity and continuity of the Church with the division and short history of the heretics was a response to the Waldensian interpretation of history, formulated by the mid-fourteenth century in the Waldensian history *Liber electorum*, and representing Waldensians as the true heirs of the apostles and a continuing tradition that began after the Church fell into error with the Donation of Constantine.[119] One finds the discussion at the beginning

---

[115] Disputes over nominations to offices between different obediences in various European regions are surveyed in Daileader, 'Local Experiences of the Great Western Schism', pp. 90–108.

[116] See p. 23 above.

[117] R. N. Swanson, 'Academic Circles: Universities and Exchanges of Information and Ideas in the Age of the Great Schism', in *Religious Controversy in Europe, 1378–1536*, ed. M. Van Dussen and P. Soukup (Turnhout, 2013), pp. 17–43 (p. 19).

[118] Machilek, 'Beweggründe, Inhalte und Probleme', pp. 5–6.

[119] On the Waldensians' own historiography and the *Liber electorum*, see Biller,

of the *Cum dormirent homines*, amongst the chapters discussing Waldensian origins, ordination and lay ministry.[120] The refutation of the Waldensian claim of continuity and constituting a true church is not unique to Zwicker. In late fourteenth-century German-speaking Europe Waldensian discussions on their history circulated in the polemical correspondence between the Lombard Brethren and Austrian converts from Waldensianism in the 1360s,[121] as well as in the *Liber electorum*, copies of which existed in southern German and Austrian libraries.[122] The Viennese scholar Peter von Pillichsdorf, who was familiar with the *Liber electorum*, also commented on the topic.[123]

The correspondence from the 1360s includes many of the central arguments regarding the unity of the Church and faith. The *Liber electorum* and the Lombard Brethren claimed that the true Church and its priesthood can be small and exist in secrecy, as Waldensians had done under persecution.[124] To the Austrian converts Johannes Leser and Seyfridus, and to Zwicker and Peter von Pillichsdorf later, the paucity of the elect and their operation in secrecy automatically constituted proof that Waldensians were a sect, not a church. Leser gleefully points out that the Lombards speak of 'our church' as if there were others, while he and his companions only know one Catholic Church.[125] Seyfridus declares his faith in one true Church where the whole clerical hierarchy has different functions and duties in declaring the word of God and administering his sacraments – and outside of which the Waldensians have placed themselves.[126]

Peter von Pillichsdorf, who unlike Zwicker does not hesitate to cite extra-biblical authorities, refutes the Waldensian presumption of being the true Church and successors of the apostles by relating it to Haymo of Halberstadt's commentary on Apocalypse 21:16: 'And the city lieth in a foursquare'. This foursquare represents the Church, 'because it is robust in faith, patient in hope, abundant in love and effective in action'.[127] Whichever

---

Waldenses, chs XI–XII; J. Oberste, 'Le pape Sylvestre en Antéchrist. Pauvreté et ecclesiologie dans le débat sur l'hérésie au bas Moyen Âge', in *Les Cathares devant l'histoire. Mélanges offerts à Jean Duvernoy*, ed. A. Brenon and C. Dieulafait (Cahors, 2005), pp. 389–405 (pp. 401–3); Tolonen, 'Medieval memories'; Schäufele, *Defecit ecclesia*, pp. 221–30, 232–46; Gonnet, 'Valdesi d'Austria', pp. 7–11.

[120] Especially chs II–VI, XII.

[121] See below.

[122] Biller, *Waldenses*, p. 248, n. 40; Biller, 'Aspects', pp. 215–22.

[123] Peter von Pillichsdorf, *Fragmentum ex Tractatu*, p. 300G–1F; Biller, *Waldenses*, pp. 248–9.

[124] Biller, 'Aspects', pp. 267–9, 286, 289, 295–6.

[125] Ibid., p. 308. Cf. pp. 312–13.

[126] Ibid., pp. 323–4.

[127] 'Bene Ecclesia in quadro posita memoratur, quia est robusta per fidem, longanimis per spem, ampla per charitatem, efficax per operationem.' Peter von Pillichsdorf, *Fragmentum ex Tractatu*, p. 300H. Cf. Haymo of Halberstadt, *Expositio in Apocalypsin*, PL 117, 1201C.

group best meets these conditions must be the Church of Christ. The 'multitude following Sylvester', who have martyrs and preach publicly, await the future glory trustingly without constant complaint, have spread throughout the world and administer effectively all sacraments through ordained priests, fulfil these preconditions more perfectly than the persecuted and secretive Waldensians: thus the Catholic Church must be the Church of Christ.[128] Both the converted Waldensians and Peter von Pillichsdorf follow the conventions of anti-Waldensian polemics. The scarcity of Waldensians as proof of their erroneous ways is by no means a fourteenth-century invention. As Jean Gonnet has pointed out, Johannes Leser and Seyfridus reapplied the arguments of the thirteenth-century polemics to repudiate the Waldensian claim to constitute the Church of Christ,[129] and 'the multitude who preach openly contrasted with the secretive few' reasoning appears, for example, in Moneta of Cremona's treatise.[130] Moneta is also a probable source for Zwicker's chapters on unity and continuity, but because of the disintegration caused by the Great Schism these claims were much more controversial in the 1390s than they had been in the 1240s or 1360s.

The unity of the Church appears in the *Cum dormirent homines* in a twofold way. The first is the assertion that the same faith has continued since the days of the patriarchs of the Old Testament. Zwicker presents it as a precondition for the refutation of Waldensian errors. 'In order to cast back, to fight against, to repair and to condemn their erroneous tenets one first has to note that the Catholic faith is one faith of all the elect both preceding and following the coming of Christ.'[131] The list of the elect preceding Christ starts from Abel. The chapter is probably influenced by Moneta's treatise, although it is no direct loan. Moneta also takes the Church as beginning with Abel and proposes that the unbroken chain of the just begins from him.[132] For Moneta's purposes the question of continuity between the Old and New Testaments was much more crucial than to Zwicker, because Moneta argued not only against Waldensians but also Cathar dualists who regarded the God of the Old Testament as evil and all people before Christ as damned, and consequently did not accept the authority of the Old Testament. The broader debate on the validity of

---

[128] Peter von Pillichsdorf, *Fragmentum ex Tractatu*, pp. 300H–301F.

[129] Gonnet, 'Valdesi d'Austria', pp. 23, 27–8.

[130] Moneta, *Adversus Catharos et Valdenses*, pp. 395, 405–6, 413, 442–3.

[131] 'Ad retorquendum igitur, repugnandum, resarciendum et reprobandum ipsorum erroneos articulos est primo notandum, Quod fides [katholica] una est omnium electorum tam praecedencium Christi adventum quam sequentium.', Zwicker, *Cum dormirent homines*, p. 278G. The word *catholica/katholica* is missing from Gretser's edition but it is to be found in several manuscripts, see e.g. Seitenstetten, MS 213, fol. 109va; St Florian, MS XI 234, fol. 93vb; Gdańsk, PAN MS Mar. F. 295, fol. 191vb; Salzburg, St Peter, MS b V 1, fol. 40r.

[132] Moneta, *Adversus Catharos et Valdenses*, pp. 408–9; see also Biller, *Waldenses*, pp. 259–60.

the Old Testament, the goodness of the God of Moses and the justness of the patriarchs takes up the greater part of Book Two in Moneta's work.[133] For anti-Waldensian polemic the continuity from old to new law was not such a fundamental question, since Waldensians generally accepted the authority of the Old Testament.

Zwicker's biblicist argumentation, however, required that both Testaments were presented as part of the same continuum, that both described the same Church. His justification, for example, of church buildings, decorations and images relies heavily on Old Testament examples. Zwicker thus felt the need to underline that all the books of Scripture speak equally about the Church of Christ. While this may all sound self-evident, we should bear in mind that many fundamental tenets that were previously accepted almost without question became the subject of open controversy during the Schism and contemporary councils. Ian Levy has pointed out that while the *ecclesia ab Abel* was a conventional, ultimately Augustinian concept, because John Wyclif subscribed to it, it was repudiated in 1420 by the English Carmelite friar Thomas Netter, who placed the beginning of the Church in Christ's public ministry.[134] It is characteristic of the entanglement of the discussions in the late fourteenth century that one of the greatest inquisitors of the time, Petrus Zwicker, would have agreed completely with the primary heresiarch of the late medieval Church, John Wyclif, when he wrote in his gospel prologues that 'the old and new law are of equal authority, utility and reverence, because the two are one, because they are of the one Church'.[135] Zwicker's statement about the continuity of faith may have been made to support his extensive Old Testament citations, but it also demonstrates that his treatise is a product of an era when the fundamentals of existence – in this case the Church – were reflected upon and to some extent rearranged. The will to resort to biblical authority only, and the inherent continuity in the community of faithful, are both part of this rearrangement.

The second aspect of unity Zwicker presents is even more closely intertwined with the Schism: the paucity of Waldensians and disunity of the heretics in contrast to the Church. According to Zwicker, Waldenses were wrong in claiming that they were the elect few destined for salvation, because Scripture testifies to the multitude of the saved. They come from east and west to sit with Abraham, Isaac and Jacob in the heavenly kingdom (Matthew 8:11) and are uncountable numbers, of all nations, tribes and peoples, speaking all languages (Apocalypse 7:9). Zwicker compares this multitude to the few scattered Waldensians and even produces a list of

---

[133] Moneta, *Adversus Catharos et Valdenses*, pp. 143–221.

[134] Levy, *Holy Scripture*, pp. 56, 126.

[135] 'Eiusdem auctoritatis, utilitatis, et reverencie est lex vetus cum nova, quia iste due sunt una, quia unius ecclesie', G. A. Benrath, *Wyclifs Bibelkommentar* (Berlin, 1966), p. 112, n. 91; cit. in Levy, *Holy Scripture*, p. 249, n. 7.

all nations known to him that are free of their heresy, including England, Flanders, Brabant, Westphalia, Denmark, Sweden, Norway, Prussia and the kingdom of Kraków.[136] Peter Biller has drawn attention to this minimizing feature in Zwicker's polemical writing, a feature that complemented the more generally acknowledged tendency of medieval authors to exaggerate the spread and power of heresy.[137] The paucity of Waldensian followers stressed the sectarian nature of the movement as opposed to the universal Church, and strengthened the accusation that the Waldensians were guilty of pride and harsh judgement when they presumed that they alone constituted the elect: 'You, who make the greatest injustice to the divine clemency, as if the blood of Christ would be efficiently shed only for you.'[138]

In addition to the paucity of Waldensians, heresy in general is discussed in terms of division, internal quarrel and mutual condemnation. The *Cum dormirent homines* has a short chapter dedicated to how different sects curse each other.[139] It is usually cited as a proof of how Zwicker distinguished between different heresies, above all between Waldensianism and Luciferanism.[140] Despite the scholarly tendency to read it in this way, the function of this section is not to demonstrate Zwicker's clear-sightedness or expertise in heresiology, as Georg Modestin has recently pointed out.[141] When read together with the end of the preceding chapter, the passage constructs a scattered heresy–united church juxtaposition:

> Upon this mountain a city is placed, that is, the Catholic faith which is the unity of citizens. Because all Catholics from four corners of the world concord in the unity of faith. [chapter break] Not like this the heretics, of whom some disapprove and condemn others, just like Waldensians disapprove of, even feel nauseated by, the *Runcaros* and Beghards, and Luciferans and various others. But still they all are sons of the devil, because they are not yet collected together by Christ, John 11[:52]: Christ was not only to die for the nation, but to gather together in one the children of God, that were dispersed.[142]

---

[136] Zwicker, *Cum dormirent homines*, p. 281C–E.

[137] Biller, *Waldenses*, pp. 282, 287–8; Biller, 'Bernard Gui, Peter Zwicker', pp. 31–2, 41–2.

[138] Zwicker, *Cum dormirent homines*, p. 281C: 'Qui etiam nimiam iniuriam facitis diuinae clementiae, quasi Christi sanguis pro solis vobis efficienter effusus sit.'

[139] Cap. XII. 'Quod haeretici diuersarum sectarum damnant se mutuo'.

[140] Biller, *Waldenses*, p. 279; Biller, 'Bernard Gui, Sex and Luciferanism', p. 455; Utz Tremp, *Von der Häresie zur Hexerei*, pp. 307–10.

[141] Modestin, 'The Anti-Waldensian Treatise', p. 220.

[142] Zwicker, *Cum dormirent homines*, p. 280E–F: 'Super hunc montem posita est ciuitas; id est, fides Catholica que est ciuium vnitas. Nam omnes Catholici de quatuor plagis mundi concordant in fidei vnitate. [chapter break] Non sic haeretici, quorum quidam alios reprobant, et condempnant; sicut Waldenses reprobant, imo nauseant Runcaros et Beghardos, et Luciferianos, et alios diuersos; illi adhuc omnes sunt filii diaboli; quia nondum sunt per Christum in vnum congregati. Ioan 11: Christus non

If this were a polemical treatise written in the thirteenth or early fourteenth century the passage would hardly stand out. But in 1395 the sentence 'all Catholics from four corners of the world concord in the unity of faith' could not have been further from the lived experience of Catholics in different corners of Europe. This is an aspect of Zwicker's polemical writing that has gone almost unnoticed by scholars.[143] Only Modestin briefly remarks that Zwicker's image of *unitas* in the time of the Great Schism 'seems intentionally overstated'.[144] I argue that the context of schism is the key to understanding the ecclesiology of Zwicker's work. What Zwicker is effectively doing is reflecting onto heretics the distressing schism, internal quarrelling and mutual condemnation that had become commonplace in ecclesiastical life. At the same time he represents the Church as universal and united in faith.

How could Zwicker's claim of the Church's unity be even remotely credible to his contemporaries, who had witnessed almost two decades of profound division in Western Christendom? There was no option. As E. L. Saak has put it: 'For the fourteenth century, the myth of Christendom was a joke, and would have been seen as such if the situation had not been so serious, and if the stakes had not been so high.'[145] This was why it was so important for Zwicker to separate the Church of the elect and their present state. The proposition that follows the quotation from John 11:52, cited above, reflects this: 'But how are they children of God, if not yet gathered together, but dispersed? I answer: Christ speaks of those who are children of God according to eternal predestination, who are finally saved, however evil they might be at the moment.'[146] The Church eternal and its essential, metaphysical unity is the unity Zwicker is writing about, sometimes in a way that appears only remotely related to the anti-Waldensian argumentation. One such disconnected passage is the short chapter 'From which the unity is proven' (*Ex quibus probetur vnitas*), which explicates the fundamental connection of the Church to its creator:

> Unity of the Catholic faith can be proven from the unity of God, who created us all; from the unity of the first parent, who fathered us all; from

---

tantum moriturus erat pro gente, sed, vt filios Dei, qui erant dispersi, congregaret in vnum.'

[143] Recently E. Smelyansky has even proposed that the contrast between the universal Church and fragmented heretical sects 'was losing its force' in the Schism; Smelyansky, 'Urban Order and Urban Other', p. 12. This does not apply to Zwicker, as the analysis below shows.

[144] Modestin, 'The Anti-Waldensian Treatise', p. 220.

[145] E. L. Saak, *High Way to Heaven: The Augustinian Platform between Reform and Reformation, 1292–1524* (Leiden, 2002), p. 43.

[146] Zwicker, *Cum dormirent homines*, p. 280F: 'Sed quomodo filii Dei, si nondum congregati, sed dispersi? Respondeo: Christus loquitur secundum aeternam predestinationem, filios Dei esse, qui finaliter sunt saluandi quantumcumque temporaliter sunt mali.'

the unity of Christ, who redeemed us all; from the unity of baptism, which cleansed us all from original sin; from the unity of the realm, of which to be worthy, the master of the house called, constituted and placed us all into the vineyard of the present Church, as if to earn our daily coin.[147]

This chapter could be interpreted as part of Zwicker's refutation of Waldensian historiography, which proposed that a great division had taken place at the Donation of Constantine and that Waldensians were the true heirs of the apostles. In Moneta's treatise, which was Zwicker's probable source of inspiration, claims of continuity and unity are much more explicitly used to argue against the Waldensian reading of history. Moneta devotes whole chapters to demonstrating that after the Church had been instituted it never failed, and that Waldensians were not the chosen people prefigured in prophecies.[148]

The difference between Zwicker and Moneta, and indeed between Zwicker and more contemporary polemics in the correspondance of the 1360s and in Peter von Pillichsdorf's treatise, is that Zwicker is much more confident in proclaiming the Waldensians as a sect. In the first chapter of the *Cum dormirent homines* Zwicker rather briefly revokes any claim that owning property condemns the Church or the clergy, and then explains how Waldensians were founded by 'Petrus Waldensis' in France, 800 years after Pope Sylvester, and how he and his followers in their pride and error usurped priestly authority.[149] Although recounting the Waldensian story of origin, Zwicker does not consider it a serious possibility and threat to the Church's authority, and does not continue to expose it in detail, unlike the other polemical authors. For Zwicker, the Waldensians are undeniably a novel sect and their propositions about the fall of the Church with Pope Sylvester not even remotely credible.

Why then write powerful declarations about the Church's unity such as that quoted above, when their relationship to arguments against Waldensians is so tenuous? Again, the reason is the Great Schism. While the division of the Church in the time of Pope Sylvester was not really a threat, the ongoing division, which by 1395 had become a lasting state of affairs, was a menacing prospect. Hence Zwicker's need to stress that the Church he was defending was fundamentally united, that the present division was not essential in nature, only political, and that the Church was still the mystical body of Christ, the communicator of grace.

---

[147] Zwicker, *Cum dormirent homines*, p. 279E: 'Vnitas etiam fidei Catholicae potest probari ex vnitate Dei, qui nos omnes creauit, ex vnitate primi parentis qui nos omnes propagauit; ex vnitate Christi, qui nos [omnes] reparauit; ex unitate Baptismi, qui nos omnes ab originali crimine mundauit; ex vnitate regni, ad quod promerendum, Paterfamilias nos omnes, velut ad denarium diurnum accipiendum, in vineam praesentis Ecclesiae vocauit, constituit et locauit.'

[148] Moneta, *Adversus Catharos et Valdenses*, pp. 412–16.

[149] Zwicker, *Cum dormirent homines*, p. 278A–G.

Zwicker was not alone in formulating the fundamental unity of the Church. On the contrary, his treatise is but one manifestation of a turn that took place when the Schism became prolonged and started to seem unresolvable. If one clung to an absolute form of papalism, it meant that those supporting the opposing side were among the forces of the Antichrist, and that there was no room for neutrality or impartiality.[150] The Prussian priest Johannes Malkaw, discussed above, was one such stubborn figure, who preached against the Avignon party and neutrals in Strasbourg in 1390. He vehemently attacked those who circulated letters proposing that neither pope need be chosen for salvation. According to Malkaw, neutrals were even worse than the antipope's supporters and all of them, even down to simple priests, were *ipso facto* excommunicated and their sacraments invalid.[151] Such extreme notions were of course perilous to all attempts at unification and compromise, and would have meant that *cura animarum* (the care of souls) had ceased among the supporters of whichever obedience was wrong.

Therefore it is not surprising to find different explanations of how schism affected the unity of the Church. Matěj of Janov, the reform-minded theologian in Prague, who was undeniably one of the more radical thinkers of his time, devoted a whole tract to the unity and corporation of the Church in his Christocentric exposition *Regulae veteris et novi testamenti*, written c. 1387–92.[152] For Matěj the schism took place only among the hypocritical prelates and popes and did not affect the Church of the elect that was essentially (not only in metaphor) united by Christ. 'The elected member of Christ' only appeared divided and diminished, but the schism was in the body of the Antichrist and in the *ecclesia malignancium* (church of evil-doers).[153] It was not only radicals like Matěj who harboured such thoughts in the 1390s. When the hierarchical organization that had manifested the unity and order in the Church ruled by the pope in his plenitude of power was burdened by the division, even conventional scholars would turn to the more inherent unity of the *congregatio fidelium* (congregation of the faithful) for a foundation that remained untainted by the schism of popes and prelates, and that could form the basis upon which the Church could be reunited and reformed. The whole of conciliar thought was founded on this concept of unity based on the congregation of the faithful – and reluctance to admit that the unity could have been broken.[154] Reassurance of the essential wholeness of the Church

---

[150] Kaminsky, *A History of the Hussite Revolution*, pp. 27–8.

[151] Johannes Malkaw expresses his views in an apology written to charges raised against him by inquisitors, ed. Tönsing, *Johannes Malkaw*, pp. 247–50. Malkaw's views on the topic are summarized ibid., pp. 24–6.

[152] 'Tractatus quartus. De unitate et universitate ecclesie', in Matěj of Janov, *Regulae* II, pp. 140–308.

[153] Ibid., pp. 156–61. Matěj's opinions, his treatise and his clash with archiepiscopal officials have already been treated above, pp. 79–80, 222–4.

[154] Kaminsky, *A History of the Hussite Revolution*, p. 28; B. Tierney, *Foundations of the*

is the reason why Zwicker stresses the continuation of faith and unity of the Catholic Church at the very beginning of his treatise.

Turning away from hierarchical ecclesiology to the more mystical, incorruptible unity of faith also explains why the ecclesiastical hierarchy is hardly mentioned in the *Cum dormirent homines*,[155] whereas in the *Refutatio errorum* Zwicker defends the papal plenitude of power and compares the ecclesiastical offices with the celestial order. The long redactions of the *Refutatio* include comparison of the pope to 'the first and highest king, whose vicar he is on earth', and of different prelates to different grades of angels, beginning from seraphim, cherubim and thrones as cardinals and ending up with ordinary priests corresponding to ordinary angels. This 'propriety of ordination in the spiritual realm is an example and similitude, or reappearance (*relucescencia*) or designation or sign of the celestial realm which is incomparably more preeminent'.[156]

Conciliar Theory: The Contribution of the Medieval Canonists from Gratian to the Great Schism (Cambridge, 1955), pp. 221–2.

[155] In the *Cum dormirent homines* the ecclesiastical hierarchy is explicitly mentioned only in the chapter on indulgences (Zwicker, *Cum dormirent homines*, p. 295G–H). There Zwicker argues that the pope, cardinals, patriarchs and bishops can give indulgences based on their position as successors of Peter (pope), apostles (cardinals), *principales patres in dominico grege* (principal fathers in the Lord's flock = patriarchs), and *perfecti iusti* (the perfect just = bishops.)

[156] Only the papal plenitude of power is mentioned in the edited text, see *Refutatio*, ed. Gretser, p. 305D–E. The comparison to the ecclesiastical hierarchy is transmitted in Redactions 1 and 2. There is no edition of it. The following transcript is from Gdańsk, PAN MS Mar. F. 295, fol. 216va: 'Summus igitur enim pontifex similitudinem tenet primi ac summi regis cuius vices agit in terris, quam [quem?] tamen ad gubernacionem spiritualem cum debent assistere tres ordines clericorum, quorum primus adinstar Seraphyn debet esse feruentissimorum et totaliter et ardencium amore creatoris. Secundus adinstar cherubyn debet esse sapientissimorum et in rebus diuinalibus eruditissimorum. Tertius adinstar thronorum siue sedium debet esse iudicum, qui iura spiritualium et leges ecclesiasticas nouerunt ad profectum, ut penitentibus iura reddant, et illa ierarchia horum trium ordinum dicitur, i.e. sacri cetus cardinalium; dominacionibus aptantur patriarche siue primates qui post tres ordines preeminent in clero, principalibus archiepiscopi siue metropolitani adaptantur, potestatibus episcopi, virtutibus archidiaconi, archangelis archipresbiteri, angelis presbiteri. Ecce quomodo decencia ordinacionis in regno spirituali exemplum et similitudo siue relucescencia siue designacio siue signum est regni celestis inconparabiliter preeminencius' (The highest pontiff therefore possesses similarity to the first and highest king, whose vicar he is on earth, since three orders of clergy should help him in spiritual government. The first of them – the equivalent of the Seraphim – should be of the most fervent, totally and burning with love of the Creator. The second – the equivalent of the Cherubim – should be of the wisest and most learned in divine things. The third – the equivalent of the Thrones or Seats – should be of judges, who know the laws of spiritual matters and ecclesiastical matters for the good, so that they render law to the penitent. And this is said to be the hierarchy of the three orders, that is to say of the holy college of cardinals; the patriarchs or primates, who after the three orders are pre-eminent among the

This was a very conventional representation. The fourteenth-century canonists had universally enforced the papal plenitude of power and stressed that it was the source of all inferior authority in the Church.[157] The idea of the Church's government as an image of celestial hierarchy was likewise widespread in medieval culture, stemming from the late-fifth-century Pseudo-Dionysian *De coelesti hierarchia* (*On the Celestial Hierarchy*), and medieval authors designed various versions of the angelic hierarchy as they tried to depict the Church of their own times.[158] The hierarchical model survived even the Schism. The hierarchies, grades and levels would flourish in the fifteenth-century religious literature as steps to personals salvation.[159] Strict commitment to the ecclesiastical hierarchy was, however, problematic when the Church was deep in schism. The comparison had lost its credibility as a literary device and example. One could hardly see the two rival popes with their competing colleges of cardinals as a similitude of harmonious choirs of angels surrounding almighty God. Consequently Zwicker abandoned this irreconcilable parable when he composed the *Cum dormirent homines*.

The shift from the divine hierarchy to the inherent continuity and unity of faith and communion of the faithful is a significant intellectual leap that Zwicker takes from the *Refutatio errorum* to the *Cum dormirent homines*. It is comparable – and compatible – with the overall biblicist programme of the latter treatise (see Chapter 2). Both features are also very much a product of the spiritual atmosphere and anxiety of the Great Schism. They express a need to go to the foundations, to overcome the contemporary insecurity by seeking the most fundamental, immutable principles of faith. Together they also redefine anti-heretical polemic and its basis of argumentation. The Scriptures, the unity of faith and the communion of the faithful are what stand against heresy more firmly than all the consultations of canonists or opinions of doctors. The innovations Zwicker made within the traditional genre of anti heretical treatise arose from the atmosphere of crisis and reform in the 1390s, and consequently addressed the problems of the age of Schism and councils: unity of the Church, dignity of the clergy and legitimation of practised religion through the authority of the Scriptures. This is one of the reasons for the remarkable success of the *Cum dormirent homines* in the fifteenth century.

---

clergy, correspond to the Dominations, the archbishops and metropolitans to the Principals, the bishops to the Powers, the archdeacons to the Virtues, the archpriests to the Archangels, the priests to the Angels. Behold the propriety of ordination in the spiritual realm: example and similitude, or reappearance or designation or sign of the celestial realm, which is incomparably more preeminent).

[157] Tierney, *Foundations of the Conciliar Theory*, pp. 212, 218 and passim.

[158] Pascoe, *Jean Gerson*, pp. 17–18; D. Luscombe, 'The Hierarchies in the Writings of Alan of Lille, William of Auvergne, and St. Bonaventure', in *Angels in Medieval Philosophical Inquiry: Their Function and Significance*, ed. I. Iribarren and M. Lenz (Aldershot, 2008), pp. 15–28.

[159] Hamm, *Religiosität im späten Mittelalter*, p. 152.

One last aspect of Zwicker and the Great Schism has to be discussed, namely that he never mentions it in his treatise. The Church stands united in Christ, armed with the testimony of the Scriptures and the continuation of faith from the age of the patriarchs. Of course, not all texts written between 1378 and 1417 talk about the Schism. On the other hand, references to the deplorable state of the Church were extremely common, often in works that did not treat the schism *per se*. If one considers only the authors contemporary with Zwicker discussed in this and previous chapters, one easily finds examples.[160] Writing against heresy in no way required keeping quiet about the Schism – on the contrary, the two often went together. It is in fact surprising that with all the references to the unity of all Catholics and continuity of faith in both Testaments, Zwicker devotes even one word to the current schism. It is especially peculiar given the overall structure of the work, composed around heretical arguments and counter-arguments and responses to them. One almost expects a sentence like 'but if you heretic say that Catholics are also dispersed by the present schism, you are wrong', yet such counter-argument is never presented. By contrast, Matěj of Janov, who a few years earlier wrote about the unity of faith and of the elect of Christ in similar terms to Zwicker, constantly compares the unity of true Christians to the division among the hypocrites. The whole definition of the unity in the congregation of the faithful is formulated against the schism of prelates.[161] Why then did Zwicker remain silent about the contemporary calamities of the Church?

The silence cannot be accidental. The Schism was too profound an experience for all Zwicker's contemporaries, and his propositions about unity and continuity were so bold and so topically relevant to the debates of the Great Schism that the omission is clearly intentional. The easiest explanation is of course that the juxtaposition of heretical sects and the universal Church was built upon absolutes, and mentioning the division within the Church would have weakened the argument. There was, however, no obvious need to construct this comparison in the first place. As stated above, Zwicker does not use it as straightforward argument against the Waldensian interpretation of history, which he easily refutes on other grounds. Nor was there any Waldensian proposition against the unity of the Church that Zwicker had to counter. Therefore I would like to propose another possible way of interpreting the silence.

The silence about the Schism and its absence from the texts and speech might be a more widespread and influential phenomenon than recognized in modern scholarship – which for obvious reasons has concentrated on the

---

[160] Peter von Pillichsdorf, *Fragmentum ex Tractatu*, p. 299; Johlín of Vodňany in Neumann, 'Výbor z předhusitských postil', pp. 287, 323–4, 359, 373; Ulrich von Pottenstein, *Credo*, cap. 33B (ÖNB MS 3050, fols. 245vb–246ra); Jean Gerson, sermon 'Fulcite me' (1402) in Gerson, *Œuvres complètes*, V, 337.

[161] Matěj of Janov, *Regulae* II, 144, 158–61.

Great Schism's expressions and manifestations. Yet sometimes silence and silencing can be more significant than representation, as the cultural historical study of marginal groups has well demonstrated.[162] The absence of schism in public discourse was in certain cases a conscious strategy to avoid the disintegration of communities. J. Pacquet found in his study on the Great Schism's effects on the cities of Louvain, Brussels and Antwerp examples of indifference or conscious silence about the schism. The laity and clergy of Antwerp, belonging to the Roman obedience, simply cut off communication with the Avignon-minded bishop of Cambrai for a decade. When the whole county of Flanders, and Antwerp with it, declared itself neutral in 1390, the bishop, apparently ungrudgingly, allowed it. Moreover, one bishop of Cambrai in the 1390s, André of Luxembourg, forbade preachers in Brussels to mention the Schism in their sermons to avoid the disturbances it might cause.[163] Philip Daileader argued in his re-evaluation of the Schism's regional effects that such an approach, silencing the different parties and accepting the *de facto* coexistence of rival obediences, was due to recognizing the disastrous potential of the Schism. The solution was a wary pragmatism that gave priority to the unity of the communities.[164]

Zwicker's praise of the Church's unity and continuity cannot be described as wary or pragmatic, but it must be understood as an expression of the same anxiety over disintegration and insecurity. The possibility that the Catholic Church itself was divided was so terrifying that it is simply not brought up. Pandora's box must remain shut. The prospect of the disintegration of the Church was at least as devastating as was the option that sacraments ministered by wicked priests were invalid.

The Schism, however, may have a shadowy presence in Zwicker's treatise, but only as a reflection in a mirror. The treatise includes a chapter 'That the heretics of various sects condemn each other', that contrasts the division and mutual condemnation of different sects – Waldenses, Beghards, *Runcarii* and Luciferans – with the unity of all Catholics. It has no direct source, but seems to be original to Zwicker. Here, then, the reader can find division, dispersion and schism. But these are the traits of heretical sects: implying that those who were truly schismatics were to be counted among the heretics, not the church of the elect.

Corruption, division and malpractices among the prelates made Zwicker abandon the image of harmonious hierarchy as the basis of stability and

---

[162] See above all the discussion on explicit silencing of same-sex sexuality in late medieval culture, T. Linkinen, *Same-Sex Sexuality in Later Medieval English Culture* (Amsterdam, 2015), pp. 85–7, 107–9.

[163] J. Pacquet, 'Le schisme d'Occident à Louvain, Bruxelles et Anvers', *Revue d'histoire ecclésiastique* 59 (1964), 401–36; Daileader, 'Local Experiences of the Great Western Schism', pp. 114–15.

[164] Daileader, 'Local Experiences of the Great Western Schism', pp. 115, 120.

unity in the Church. This did not mean denying the authority of the pope or bishops, any more than the argumentation based on the scriptures alone meant discarding the commentaries of the doctors of the Church. These all prevailed, but the apology for the Church and its doctrine had to be founded on a firmer basis: in the unity of the faithful through time and in the words of Scripture. Writing about the inviolability of the Church eternal and its ultimate victory over the heretics must also have been a sort of consolation in the crisis of the Church. In 1395 there was no foreseeable solution to the Great Schism, and very little hope of initiating major reforms. In this context, Waldensianism, itself a movement weakened and shattered by conversions of its leaders, was actually an enemy that one could hope to conquer – and that was indeed by and large overcome by 1400.

Epilogue: The Consolation of Inquisition

> Harsh punishment, deserved by the criminal, afflicts the innocent. Immoral scoundrels now occupy positions of power and unjustly trample the rights of good men.[1]
>
> Boethius, *The Consolation of Philosophy*, 1.poem 5.

We return finally to Boethius, whose *De consolatione Philosophiae* was the only work besides the Bible to which Petrus Zwicker referred in all his anti-heretical and theological works. I found this detail extremely intriguing when it became clear to me. It seemed that history had a sinister sense of irony. A man who interrogated and convicted probably thousands of heretics, some of them to death, had as his favourite reading a book written by a convict awaiting his execution. Anicius Manlius Severinus Boethius, a Roman senator in sixth-century Italy, then ruled by the Ostrogothic king Theoderic, fell into disfavour and was sentenced to death for treason. He met his end in a prison in Pavia in 524, by blows from a club.[2] While waiting for his sentence he penned a consolatory philosophical and theological essay on human nature, evil and strokes of fate – and how to accept it all and find consolation in greater and eternal truths. His book would retain its popularity in centuries to come, especially in times of crisis.

Thinking of Zwicker and Boethius led me to reconsider the meaning of the repression of heresy to the persecutors: inquisitors, polemicists, bishops, parish clergy, secular rulers and, at times, ordinary laypeople. I have suggested that the refutation of heresy enabled reflection on the Church, the clergy and the Scriptures. All these became controversial matters in the late fourteenth century, suddenly and alarmingly open to debate as the Church entered a long period of internal division in the Great Schism (1378–1417). When reflected in the distorted mirror of Waldensianism, a heresy that had been condemned already in the twelfth century and that had a sinister reputation among both conventional and reformist churchmen, the polemicists were able defame and blacken some of the more radical opinions that were voiced in the debates on the Schism. After all, the most dangerous opponents were not the secretive, dispersed and by the late fourteenth century stagnant Waldensians, but zealots from the ranks of the clergy.

The Waldensians were a good choice of enemy. As the Schism prolonged and deepened, so also the desire and demand increased for unification and

---

[1] Boethius, *The Consolation of Philosophy*, trans. Green, p. 15.
[2] J. Matthews, 'Anicius Manlius Severinus Boethius', in *Boethius: His Life, Thought and Influence*, ed. M. Gibson (Oxford, 1981), pp. 15–43 (p. 15).

reform of the Church at all levels. Yet, in the mid-1390s, when Zwicker was writing his *magnum opus* against the heretics, the prospects for reform and ending the Schism were bleak. The Schism had stabilized itself, and the conciliarism that would eventually reunify the Church was merely a topic of academic debates. The threat that the Schism would become permanent was very real. For a churchman anxious over this state of affairs, there was very little to be done to improve the situation and bring solace to his soul. Through the conversion, persecution and condemnation of the Waldensians, however, there opened a front to defend Mother Church, one where results could be achieved. If heretics could be brought back to the fold, some cracks in the mutilated body of the Church would be sealed. For devout sons of the Church, there was consolation in the inquisition of heresy.

Such an approach would not have been possible if heresy had remained in the professionalized, specialized field of judicial inquiry that the *inquisitio heretice pravitatis* had become in the course of the thirteenth and early fourteenth centuries, or if the heretics had been described as licentious devil-worshippers as was common in fourteenth-century Germany. The heresy needed to be generalized into questions of beliefs, doctrine and individual failure to follow God's law. I have called this process the pastoralization of heresy, and in the preceding chapters I have traced its formation in polemical treatises, inquisitorial practice and manuals and in sermons, postils and catechetical works.

It meant mapping out the changing spiritual geography of the Empire at the turn of the fifteenth century, especially the positions of heresy, dissent, disbelief and orthodoxy. This journey proceeded from small circles to wider spheres. The study began in Petrus Zwicker's polemical texts and the formation and reform of the inquisition on Waldensianism in the last decade of the fourteenth century. Chapter 2 first established Petrus Zwicker's authorship over the treatise known as the *Refutatio errorum*, previously considered an anonymous work. Comparing the structure, argumentation, sources, and manuscript tradition of this treatise to the *Cum dormirent homines*, Zwicker's main work, I was able not only to prove that they have the same author, but I was also able to analyse the writing process and development of Zwicker's remarkable polemical style. The compilatory *Refutatio errorum* developed into the polished, well-structured *Cum dormirent homines*, which was to be the most popular late medieval text on the Waldensian heresy. Zwicker's polemical writing could be described as a revival of the debating polemical style of the thirteenth century, influenced above all by Moneta of Cremona, but equally characterized by late medieval disputes over authority and tradition.

The most original feature of the *Cum dormirent homines* is its almost exclusive biblicism: defence of the Catholic cult based on the Scriptures alone, without (explicitly) resorting to the commentary tradition or canon law. Zwicker's treatise is not only representative of late medieval reform biblicism, it is one of the most extreme manifestations of the *sola scriptura* principle in medieval literature. Unlike some contemporary works, such as the writings of Matěj of Janov, it is not extremist in its contents, but deeply conservative and conventional. In addition to an ingenious anti-Waldensian strategy, the *Cum dormirent homines*'s biblicism should be read as a profoundly orthodox response to the more general contemporary criticism levelled at the cult of saints, indulgences, relics and other practices that were, on equally biblical grounds, deemed superfluous later additions to Church practice, or even corruption. The *Cum dormirent homines* offers a reflection of the Catholic cult based on the only authority that all parties in the late medieval religious controversies accepted: the Bible. It is a defence of the established Church and proper Christian lifestyle, from honouring priests to veneration of holy images. This explains the popularity of Zwicker's treatise in the fifteenth century, when the same matters were disputed between the Roman Church and the Hussites, and when reform theologians struggled to produce unambiguous, orthodox guidelines for an emerging lay audience.

Another aspect of the pastoralization was the reform of the inquisitorial procedure. Petrus Zwicker and Martinus of Prague compiled new question-naires and error lists based on the inside information provided by the converted Waldensian Brethren in 1391, as well as on earlier descriptions of Waldensianism that had been circulating in German-speaking Europe. They created an apparatus that enabled inquiry into the individual beliefs of the deponent instead of simply striving to establish the heretical connections and actions of the accused. The change was not unlike the one John H. Arnold perceived in the Languedocian inquisition in the late thirteenth and early fourteenth centuries,[3] but in the German-Bohemian area the change took place only at the very end of the century, in the interrogatories of Zwicker and Martinus.

Chapter 3 traces the textual history of the formularies, questionnaires, and short descriptions of heresy that formed the *Processus Petri* collection, concluding that the probable purpose of most of the preserved manuscripts was not to function as an inquisitor's manual. Instead, they represent the need to compile simpler, more pastorally oriented manuals that were required by the parish clergy in their task of supervising the penance of converted heretics. The exception is the manual preserved in the compilation manuscript St. Florian, MS XI 234, which includes not only unique and up until now practically unknown formularies for Zwicker's inquisition in the diocese of Passau, but also legal consultations copied from an older Bohemian inquisi-tor's manual. The development was, however, much more profound than the adjustment in the characteristics of extant manuscripts. Petrus Zwicker and Martinus of Prague discarded earlier, action-oriented questionnaires

---

[3] Arnold, *Inquisition and Power*, pp. 98–107.

and created their own interrogatories, which, when put into use, produced detailed accounts of the Waldensian laity's beliefs. These questionnaires did not remain in the limited use of few inquisitors, but because of the wide circulation of the *Processus Petri* were transmitted among both secular clergy and religious houses.

From the confrontation with heretics in polemical treatises and in inquisitions, I proceeded to the interaction of the inquisitor and other propagators of the anti-heretical message in the surrounding society. A significant step in the observed process of pastoralization was the dissemination of anti-heretical polemic beyond the Latin treatise. When Ulrich von Pottenstein translated the *Cum dormirent homines* into early New High German, the result was not only a translation of inquisitorial discourse into the vernacular. Ulrich reorganized the chapters and redistributed them according to his own, thematic schema of pastoral theology. This further emphasized a feature that was nascent in Zwicker's Latin treatise: heresy was not complete otherness but a set of transgressions against particular doctrines and practices. Significantly, the inclusion of large anti-heretical sections in a manual of pastoral education, at least nominally intended for lay readers, implies the possibility of encountering and refuting heresy, disbelief and doubt within the framework of pastoral care, not only legal action. Above all, Ulrich presented Waldensianism as an anticlerical heresy. This created further possibilities for the generalization and use of Waldensianism as a label for other kinds of dissidents or radical reformers. This was indeed done, though almost certainly without Ulrich's influence, in Prague. Canon Johlín of Vodňany preached and composed his postil, where he tried to cast suspicion of Waldensian heresy over those who went too far in their criticism of the ordained clergy.

Finally, I explored the applications that the pastoralization of Waldensian heresy offered: discernment and labelling of dissidence in the grey area that was lived religion in the late Middle Ages, thus reinforcing the conventional understanding of the Church and the clergy. By widening the perspective from Waldensians it is possible to see that, despite their reputation as the worst enemies of the Church, on some issues they were not the most radical or the loudest critics of the Church. Marian devotion, the new feast of the Visitation and relating distribution of indulgences had far more vehement and influential opponents in the ranks of the clergy than among the Waldenses. I do not suggest that Waldensians approved of these practices, rather that in the 1390s they were not in a position to muster any significant opposition to them. Although the Brethren certainly disapproved of the cult of saints, and taught this to their followers, their disbelief was realized as general doubt about the possibility that saints could interact on behalf of the living, not as consistent scorn for Mary. On the contrary, Waldensian followers honoured and at times also invoked Mary, even when other saints were discarded. The emphasis on the Virgin above other saints in both questionnaires and polemics thus had more to do with the enforced status of Mary in late fourteenth-century Catholic devotion than with Waldensian teachings.

When Waldensianism increasingly became a transgression against a set of doctrines, the error and disbelief of an individual practised in addition to listening to sermons and confessing to lay ministers, it also became a tool to blacken various critics with the label of heresy. There were accusations of Waldensianism against persons who were not Waldenses, such as the Prussian priest Johannes Malkaw or the Franconian merchant Hans Wern, whose accusers almost certainly knew that their opponents were not truly Waldensians. In addition to offering a way to smear opponents, the image of Waldensianism created in the 1390s became a framework for understanding rising dissident groups when other labels were not available.

This has been a history of concepts, practices, techniques, discourses and ideas rather than events and causalities. It was driven originally by the question of why the persecution of Waldensians began and why it reached such proportions precisely at the end of the fourteenth century. I have not provided a definite answer, and I do not believe there is one to be found: there are many explanations for individual trials and instances of persecution, some of them mundane, some spiritual. Some are attainable for the historian, but many will always be lost in silence. Nevertheless, I am confident that I am on firm ground when I argue that the repression of Waldensian heresy would not have spread so far and wide, or acquired such great support from both ecclesiastical and secular authorities, or made such a significant impact on the anti-heretical literature of the Middle Ages without the processes I described: pastoralization of the battle against heresy in a way that was compatible with the emerging lay catechesis, and generalization of doctrinal questions to a level that was applicable in the debates during the Schism.

A successful inquisition of heresy was a consolation to the clergy, who otherwise saw little success in the years of the Schism. But did Petrus Zwicker's inquisition, where rumours of a Satanical 'other' were dismissed, also offer any relief to the accused? Zwicker was relatively lenient towards those he deemed to have been accused on dubious grounds, and as inquisitor he sought converts rather than martyrs. But as his 'pastoral' view of what constituted heresy spread to other churchmen, it produced yet another layer of 'otherness', as constructed by normative orthodoxy: disbelief in and criticism of the Church, faults which potentially lurked inside every good Catholic soul. From such a point of view, someone who had never so much as met a Waldensian Brother could nonetheless bear the taint of heresy.

Appendix 1: Manuscript Descriptions

The purpose of the manuscript descriptions is to provide basic information on the transmission history of the analysed works of Petrus Zwicker: the *Refutatio errorum*; the *Cum dormirent homines*; the *Processus Petri*; and the two inquisitors' manuals Zwicker used. The descriptions cover the parts relevant to these texts and provide references to the most up-to-date codicological descriptions of each manuscript. Appendix 1 is also meant to serve as an update to the listing of the *Cum dormirent homines* manuscripts published by Biller in 2001. Current shelfmarks are provided, and I have redated some manuscripts and described the contents in more detail. The manuscripts of the *Refutatio errorum* are comprehensively listed for the first time. Because the text has four different redactions, I have provided incipits and explicits for the *Refutatio*. Otherwise incipits and explicits are given only when it is necessary for the evaluation of the text version, for example in fragmentary copies.

Abbreviations: CDH = *Cum dormirent homines*; PP = *Processus Petri*. R1–4 = *Refutatio errorum*, redactions 1–4; Abbreviations of the *Processus Petri* according to Appendix 3 and the list in Chapter 3, pp. 109–11. The editions of the works of Petrus Zwicker have been presented in Chapters 1–3, and are not repeated here.

Manuscripts with the Refutatio errorum

Augsburg, Staats- und Stadtbibliothek (StaSB) MS 2° Cod 185
(215 × 150) Paper. 277 fols. C. 1400–60s. Theological compilation, different, originally independent fascicules. The fascicule with R2 (fols. 227r–242v) belongs to the oldest material.[1] It is written by one hand and forms a compilation on heresy.
Provenance: Augustinian Canons of the Holy Cross in Augsburg.
Contents: (227r) *Nomina mendicancium*; (227v–228r) various short notices and excerpts (canon law; Pseudo-Augustine); (228r) Four sects of the heretics in Germany. Similar text printed in Schmidt, 'Actenstücke', pp. 245–7; (228r) Short notice on Mathew 26:52; (229r–238r) R2 [inc.] *Nota quod erroribus*

---

[1] The watermark in the fascicule fols. 227–242, an oxhead with simple five-pointed star, has the closest equivalents in Piccard Findbuch 2, VI 187 (1397–8, Frankfurt am Main, Arnhem, Venlo) and 190 (1408–15, Frankfurt am Main, Munich, Innsbruck, etc.), see G. Piccard, *Die Ochsenkopfwasserzeichen*, Die Wasserzeichenkartei Piccard im Hauptstaatsarchiv Stuttgart, Findbuch 2, vols. 1–3 (Stuttgart, 1966).

hereticorum waldensium est istis et aliis scripturis obviandum [...] [expl.] *specialem ymmo spiritualem vtilitatem viderit expedire*; (238v–242r) Proceedings against the Beghard Johannes de Bruna (Brno). Unpublished. See Lerner, *The Heresy of the Free Spirit*, pp. 108–12; (242r–v) Interrogatory of *dominus Martini* (Martinus of Amberg/Prague?) against Beghards. Ed. Patschovsky, 'Gli eretici davanti al tribunale', pp. 264–5; (242v) Note on heresy of the Free Spirit. Ed. Schmidt, 'Actenstücke', pp. 248–50.

Remarks: The fascicule fols. 227–242 appears to be a compilation made for personal use. The hand is casual and the text heavily abbreviated. Between different excerpts and texts there is space left for notes.

Descriptions: H. Spilling, *Die Handschriften der Staats- und Stadtbibliothek Augsburg. 2° Cod 101–250* (Wiesbaden, 1984), pp. 129–36.

Augsburg, StaSB MS 2° Cod 338

(285 × 210) Paper. 357 fols. After mid-fifteenth century. Theological compilation, bound together from thirteen different parts. R4 and PP in part VI, fols. 153–176.

Provenance: Augustinian Canons of St Gregory in Augsburg. Donation by the doctor of medicine Johannes Hörlin to the monastery in 1474.

Contents: R4 + PP: (153r) the short list of converted Waldensians (la); (153r–154r) *De vita et conversacio* (vcc); (154r–156v) *Articuli Waldensium* (a); (156v) a short note on Luciferans (luc); (157r–158v) long question list (ibg); (159r–170r) R4 [inc.] *Erroribus hereticorum waldensium est sub sequentibus et aliis* [...] [expl.] *sed habes vt bene vtaris videas etc*; (170v–176v) empty.

Remarks: The only complete copy of R4. Possibly an exemplar from which BSB MS Clm 1329 was copied. The only *Refutatio errorum* manuscript with the version vcc of the *De vita et conversacione*.

Descriptions: W. Gehrt, *Die Handschriften der Staats- und Stadtbibliothek Augsburg. 2° Cod 251–400e* (Wiesbaden, 1989), pp. 140–4.

Augsburg, Universitätsbibliothek MS II. 1. 2° 127

(300 × 210) Paper. 198 fols. Fifteenth century (2nd quarter). Theological compilation, two columns, fifteenth-century binding.

Provenance: St Magnus in Füssen. German sections written in Swabian dialect.

Contents: CDH + R1: (131ra–158vb) CDH; (158vb–170va) R1 [inc.] *Notandum quod erroribus hereticorum waldensium est istis et aliis* [...] [expl.] *ymo spiritualem vtilitatem viderit expedire etc. etc. Explicit tractatus contra errores Waldensium*; (170vb–172ra) *Index rerum* for Nicolaus Magni de Jawor: *De superstitionibus*; (172va–173rb) Wernherus de Friedberg, revocation of his errors, Heidelberg 1405; (173rb–176va) Nicolaus Magni de Jawor: Refutation of Wernherus de Friedberg's errors; (177ra–198va) Nicolaus Magni de Jawor: *De superstitionibus*.

Remarks: Revocation of heresy by Wernherus de Friedberg and his refutation by Nicolaus Magni de Jawor (1405) are copied by a different hand from that of

Zwicker's treatises, but the texts belong to the same codicological unit. These texts also in Wiesbaden, Hessische Landesbibliothek MS 35, fols. 137v–144v. Descriptions: H. Hilg, *Lateinische mittelalterliche Handschriften in Folio der Universitätsbibliothek Augsburg: Cod. II. 1.2° 91–226* (Wiesbaden, 1999), pp. 122–5; Biller, *Waldenses*, pp. 267–8 (as Schloss Harburg II, 1, fol. 127).

Gdańsk, Polska Akademia Nauk Biblioteka (PAN) MS Mar. F. 294

(295 × 210) Paper. 276 fols. C. 1410. Theological compilation, two columns. Fifteenth-century leather binding.

Provenance: Marienkirche, Danzig. Belongs probably to the oldest collection, first half of the fifteenth century. Old shelfmark D 3.

Contents: CDH + R1: (203va–220va) CDH; (220va–226vb) R1 [inc.] *Notandum quod erroribus hereticorum waldensium est istis et aliis scripturis katholicis obuiandum* […] [expl.] *ymo spiritualem vtilitatem viderit expedire. Deo laus nunc et semper*; (227ra–rb) a list of Waldensian errors. Ed. Molnár, 'Les 32 errores Valdensium'. Cf. Herzogenburg, Stiftsbibliothek, MS 22, fol. 162ra–va.

Remarks: CDH and R1 are copied as one treatise, neither of the texts has a clear chapter division.

Descriptions: O. Günther, *Die Handschriften der Kirchenbibliothek von St. Marien in Danzig* (Danzig, 1921), pp. 393–8; Biller, *Waldenses*, p. 264.

Gdańsk, PAN MS Mar. F. 295

(295 × 210) Paper. 233 fols. 1404 (fols. 191r–218v). Theological compilation, fascicules of various provenance. Late fifteenth-century leather binding.

Provenance: fols. 191r–218v written in Bohemia in 1404. See a colophon and Czech words 'Rink slesz atÿ nemcze' at fol. 218ra. The codex was bound together before 1479, when it was donated to the library of Marienkirche by Johannes Steling, canon at Kolberg. See the notice inside the front cover.

Colophon: (218ra) *Expliciunt articuli hereticorum waldensium et reprobaciones eorumdem Sub anno dominice incarnacionis millesimo quadringentesimo quarto. Ante domine ne longe facias. In die sancte Gertrudis. Pro quo sit benedictus dominus noster ihesus cristus* […] *amen.*

Contents: CDH + R1: (191ra–211ra) CDH; (211ra–218ra) R1 [inc.] *Notandum quod erroribus hereticorum waldensium est istis et alijs scripturis katholicis obuiandum* […] [expl.] *et specialem, ymmo spiritualem vtilitatem viderit expedire etc. Rink slesz atÿ nemtze*; (218ra–vb) Jacobus de Sarapone, *Aurissa* (fragment).

Remarks: CDH and R1 copied as one treatise.

Descriptions: Günther, *Die Handschriften der Kirchenbibliothek von St. Marien*, pp. 398–9; Biller *Waldenses*, p. 264.

Herzogenburg, Stiftsbibliothek MS 22

(300 × 216) Paper. 193 fols. First half of the fifteenth century. *Sermones de sanctis; Errores Waldensium.*

Provenance: Augustine Canons of Herzogenburg

Contents: CDH + R1: (162ra–va) a list of Waldensian errors. Cf. Gdańsk, PAN, Mar. F. 294 fol. 227ra–rb; (162vb–183vb) CDH; (183vb–192ra) R1 [inc.] *Notandum quod erroribus hereticorum waldensium est istis et aliis scripturis katholicis obuiandum* [...] [expl.] *ymmo spiritualem vtilitatem viderit expedire. Sic est finis inquisicionum hereticorum waldensium. Sit laus et gloria deo. Amen. Etc.*
Remarks: CDH and R1 copied as one treatise.
Descriptions: G. Winner, 'Katalog der Handschriften der Stiftsbibliothek Herzogenburg', [handwritten catalogue] (St Pölten, 1978), pp. 29–31; Biller, *Waldenses*, p. 264.

Leipzig, Universitätsbibliothek MS 602

(300 × 210) Paper. 335 fols. Early fifteenth century (1421). Theological compilation.
Provenance: Probably the Dominican convent in Leipzig. Fols. 289ra–335vb written by Johannes Budaczsch in 1421.
Contents: CDH + R1: (289ra–314va) [old 303ra–328va] CDH [Title:] *Waldensium articulos*; (314va–322va) [old 328va–336va] R1 [inc.] *[N]otandum quod erroribus hereticorum waldensium est istis et alijs scripturis katholicis obviandum* [...] [expl.] *et specialem vtilitatem viderit expedire. Et sic est finis. Sit laus deo etc. Expliciunt articuli hereticorum Waldensium et reprobaciones earundem etc.*
Remarks: CDH and R1 copied as one treatise
Descriptions: Burkhart, *Die lateinischen und deutschen Handschriften der Universitäts-Bibliothek Leipzig*, pp. 247–52; Biller, *Waldenses*, p. 265.

Michelstadt, Kirchenbibliothek MS I. Db. 685[2]

(290 × 210) Paper. 366 fols. C. 1460.
Provenance: Speyer, probably in the possession of Magister Nicolaus Matz, who founded the Michelstadt library in 1499
Contents: PP + R1: (211ra–213va) *De vita et conversacione* (vcb) + *Articuli Waldensium* (a); (213va–214vb) long question list (ib?); (214vb–216rb) *De erroribus Beghardorum et Begutarum* [sic] (ebb); (216rb–228vb) R1 + a manual of confession (cf. Trier, Stadtbibliothek MS 680/879 fols. 104v–108r and Wiesbaden, Hessische Landesbibliothek MS 35, 132v–137v). [Inc.] *De erroribus Waldensium. Erroribus hereticorum Waldensium est istis et aliis scripturis obviandum* [...] [expl.] *ubi cessat penitencia ibidem cessabit eciam venia. Et sic est finis de ista meteria* [sic].
Remarks: Staub and Staub treat R1 and the manual of confession following it as one text. Cf. Wiesbaden, Hessische Landesbibliothek MS 35 and Trier, Stadtbibliothek MS 680/879. See also Table 2.
Descriptions: J. Staub and K. H. Staub, *Die mittelalterlichen Handschriften der Nicolaus-Matz-Bibliothek (Kirchenbibliothek) Michelstadt* (Michelstadt, 1999).

---

[2] Despite repeated attempts, I was unable to obtain a reproduction of the manuscript. The description is based on the catalogue.

Munich, BSB MS Clm 1329

(395 × 210) Paper. 233 fols. Late fifteenth– early sixteenth century. Theological compilation.
Provenance: Augustinian Canons of Diessen. German dialect in the oaths of PP is Swabian (information from W. Williams-Krapp). Old Diessen Cod. 141.
Contents: Parts of PP and R4: (215r–216r) long question list (ibg, ending); (216r–222v) R4 [inc.] *Nota Errores hereticorum waldensium. Erroribus hereticorum waldensium est subsequentibus et aliis subscriptis obuiandum* [...] [expl.] *Ad idem prima Cor. 14. Si mortui*; (223r–224r) *Articuli Waldensium* (a, fragmentary); (224v) a short note on Luciferans (luc); (224v) long question list (ibg, beginning).
Remarks: In the binding process some leaves were lost or their order was changed, leading to the loss of the end of R4 and the beginning of the *Articuli Waldensium*. The manuscript used by Gretser and Döllinger (see Chapter 2). Closely related to Augsburg, StaSB MS 2° Cod 338, possibly a copy from it.
Descriptions: Halm, *Catalogus codicum*, III.1, 252.

Philadelphia, Kislak Center for Special Collections, Rare Books and Manuscripts, University of Pennsylvania (UPenn) MS Codex 76

(302 × 206) Paper. 361 fols. Fifteenth century (2nd half). Theological compilation. Provenance: German.
Contents: CDH + R1: (308r–345v) CDH [Title:] *Incipit Tractatus contra errores Waldenses* [sic] *hereticorum compositus Anno Domini m ccc lxxxxv*; (345v–362r) R1 [inc.] *Notandum quod erroribus hereticorum Waldensium est istis et alijs scripturis katholicis obuiandum* [...] [expl.] *ymo spiritualem vtilitatem viderit expedire. Explicit tractatus contra errores Walden[sium] Hereticorum, et sunt duo tractatus. Doxa in rama theos*; (362v) empty [end of the codex]. Folio numbers according to the medieval numbering.
Remarks: CDH and R1 copied as one treatise.
Descriptions: Biller, *Waldenses*, p. 266 (as Pennsylvania, University Library MS Lea 22 (Lat.); Kislak Center: <http://hdl.library.upenn.edu/1017/d/medren/1545598>.

Prague, KMK MS C LX

(315 × 210) Paper. 300 fols. (?). Fifteenth century. Theological compilation.
Provenance: The Metropolitan Chapter Library of Prague. In the late fifteenth-century library of Magister Johannes Herttemberger.
Contents: CDH + R1: (248va–267ra) CDH; (267ra–274ra) R1 [inc.] *Notandum quod erroribus waldensium hereticorum est istis et aliis scripturis katholicis obuiandum* [...] [expl.] *ymmo spiritualem vtilitatem viderint expedire etc.*
Remarks: CDH and R1 copied as one treatise.
Descriptions: A. Patera and A. Podlaha, *Soupis rukopisů Knihovny Metropolitní kapitoly Pražské. A–E*, 2 vols. (Prague, 1910), I, 278–80; Biller, *Waldenses*, p. 266.

Prague, NKCR MS X. B. 2

(300 × 210) Paper. 338 fols. Fifteenth century. Theological compilation.
Provenance: Bohemia.
Contents: (141va–168ra) CDH; (168rb) R (excerpt) [inc.] *Notandum quod erroribus hereticorum waldensium est istis et aliis scripturis katholicis obuiandum.* […] [expl.] *Ego palam locutus sum mundo Amen*; (168rb–169va) an anonymous treatise *De mendacio*.
Remarks: Only the beginning of the first chapter of R.
Descriptions: J. Truhlář, *Catalogus codicum manu scriptorum latinorum qui in C.R. Bibliotheca Publica atque Universitatis Pragensis asservantur*, vol. II, *Codices 1666–2752 forulorum IX–XV et bibliothecae Kinskyanae* (Prague, 1906), p. 42; Biller, *Waldenses*, p. 267; Manuscriptorium.

Prague, NKCR MS XIII. E. 7

(210 × 150) Paper. 304 fols. Fifteenth century. Theological compilation.
Provenance: Bohemia.
Contents: PP + R3: (175r) *De vita et conversacione* (vcb), ending. [Inc.] *more apostolorum et quamvis retrahatur* […] [expl.] *nisi ad vnum annum uel ad duos*; (175r–176v) *Articuli Waldensium* (a); (176v–178r) long question list (ib); (178r–179v) *Errores beghardorum et beginarum* (ebb); (179v–187r) R3 [inc.] *Quomodo sit obuiandum erroribus predictis. Erroribus Waldesium et istis aliis omnibus est obuiandum* […] [expl.] *non summe mali in limbum, ergo assimili etc. Et sic est finis huius Tractatus*; (187r–v) various short notes, continues at fol. 194r; (187bis r–187ter v) an interrogatory according to decrees of Council of Constance. Excerpt, continues at fol. 192r; (188r–190v) Revocations of Matěj of Janov and priests Jacobus (Jakub of Kaplice) and Andreas at archiepiscopal synod in Prague, 18 October 1389. Ed. *Documenta Mag. Joannis Hus*, ed. Palacký, pp. 699–700; (191r–v) *De vita et conversacione* (vcb), beginning, fragmentary. [Inc.] *Valdensium regula. Nota quomodo ordinantur heresiarche* […] [expl.] *ordinatus in sede nostra*; (192r–193r) an interrogatory according to decrees of Council of Constance, continuation from fol. 187ter v; (193v) empty; (194r) various short notes, continuation from fol. 187v; (194v) empty.
Remarks: Fols. 175r–194v consist of three different fascicules on heresy, bound together and mixed up in the process. Three different hands (A: R2 and PP, fols. 175r–187v, 191r–v; B: an interrogatory according to Council of Constance, fols. 187 bis r–187 ter v, 192r–193r; C: the revocations of 1389, fols. 188r–190v).[3]
Descriptions: Truhlář, *Catalogus codicum*, p. 239; Manuscriptorium.

---

[3] Watermark analysis or counting the quires was not possible as the digital edition was used.

Appendix 1

Trier, Stadtbibliothek MS 680/879

(138 × 207) 294 fols. 1434–6. Theological compilation.

Provenance: Several texts copied by 'Iohannem Riisrock de Grymelscheich pastorem in Wiiss' (see fols. 87v, 293r). In the sixteenth century: 'Ad liberariam conventus Treverensis ex parte fratris Friderici'. Latest at the Chapter of St Simeon.

Contents: PP + R1: (87v–88v) *De vita et conversacione* (vcb); (88v–90r) *Articuli Waldensium* (a); (90r–91v) long question list (ib); (91v–93r) *Errores beghardorum et beginarum* (ebb); (93r–104v) R1 [inc.] *Erroribus hereticorum waldensium est istis et aliis scripturis obuiandum* [...] [expl.] *publicamque et spiritualem validitatem videris expedire*; (104v–108r) a manual of confession, unpublished. [Inc.] *Nota quod in extremo mortis periculo* [...] [expl.] *peccat in ecclesiam ut xxiii q ii; Et sic est finis de ista materia etc etc*. Cf. Wiesbaden, Hessische Landesbibliothek MS 35, fols. 132v–137v and Michelstadt, Kirchenbibliothek MS I. Db. 685; (108v) (in a different hand) short text on the mass.

Remarks: Cf. Wiesbaden, Hessische Landesbibliothek MS 35 and Michelstadt, Kirchenbibliothek MS I. Db. 685. See also Table 2.

Descriptions: G. Kentenich, *Die ascetischen Handschriften der Stadtbibliothek zu Trier (Abt. 2): Nr. 654–804 des Handschriften-Katalogs und Nachträge* (Trier, 1910), pp. 20–3.

Vienna, ÖNB MS 1588

(247 × 172) Parchment. 211 fols. Compilation of polemical treatises. Two parts: I, fols. 1r–80v, beginning of the fifteenth century; II, fols. 81r–211v, 1430/32.

Provenance: Library of the bishops of Ermland: Heinrich IV Heilsberg von Vogelsang (1401–15), only part I, and Franz Kuhschmalz (1424–57), the whole codex.

Colophons: (80v) *Iste liber spectat ad librariam quem comparavit dominus heinricus episcopus warmiensis*; (190v) *Scriptus est presens liber sub anno domini Millesimo Quadringentesimo Tricesimo secundo* (1432); 211v: *Hunc librum scribi fecit dominus [Franciscus episcopus (?)]* [diocese invisible, also name scraped off] Anno domini M° cccc^{mo} xxx (1430).

Contents: (1r–78r) Bartholomaeus Constantinopolitanus: *Libellus contra precipuos errores Graecorum*; (78v–80v) empty; (81r–190v) Peter of Pulkau et al. *Tractatus contra quattuor articulos Hussitarum*; (191r–211v) R1 [Title:] *Contra errores waldensium* [inc.] *Primo quia dicunt heresiarchas suos quos fratres nominant* [...] [expl.] *et specialem ymmo spiritualem utilitatem viderit expedire*. [In a different hand:] *Notandum quod erroribus hereticorum waldensium est istis et aliis scripturis supra scriptis catholicis obviandum*.

Remarks: The treatise of Peter of Pulkau against the Hussites and R written by the same hand, but on two different occasions, see the colophons.

Descriptions: *Tabulae codicum manu scriptorum praeter graecos et orientales in Bibliotheca Palatina Vindobonensi asservatorum*, 10 vols. (Vienna, 1864),

I, 257; Hill Museum and Manuscript Library: <http://www.vhmml.us/research2014/catalog/detail.asp?MSID=14915>; ÖNB: <http://data.onb.ac.at/rec/AL00174192>.

Wiesbaden, Hessische Landesbibliothek MS 35

(205 × 145) Paper. 380 fols. Late fifteenth century (fols. 149r–155v written in 1479–82). Theological compilation.

Provenance: Cistercian monastery of Eberbach

Contents: PP + R1: (113r–114r) *De vita et conversacione* (vcb); (114r–116r) *Articuli Waldensium* (a); (116r–117v) long question list (ib); (117v–119r) *De erroribus begardorum et beginarum* (ebb) (119r–132v) R1 [inc.] *Erroribus hereticorum waldensium est istis et aliis scripturis obuiandum* [...] [expl.] *et specialem ymmo spiritualem vtilitatem videris expedire*; (132v–137v) a manual of confession, unpublished. [Inc.] *Nota in extremo mortis periculo* [...] [expl.] *peccat in ecclesiam ut xxiii q ii; Et sic est finis de ista materia.* Cf. Trier, Stadtbibliothek MS 680/879, fols. 104v–108r and Michelstadt, Kirchenbibliothek MS I. Db. 685; (137v–140r) Wernherus de Friedberg, revocation of his errors, Heidelberg 1405; (140r–144v) Nicolaus Magni de Jawor: Refutation of Wernherus de Friedberg's errors; (144v–146r, 147v) a manual of confession, unpublished; (146v–147r) various theological questions, fragment; (148r–v) empty; (149r–155v) process against doctor of theology, Johannes de Wesalia, suspected of heresy, 1479–82 (156r) empty.

Remarks: Fols. 113r–144v written by the same hand; fols. 144v–147v probably later additions to the same fascicule; fols. 149r–155v form likely an independent fascicule. The texts relating to Wernherus de Friedberg (fols. 137v–144v) also in Augsburg, UB MS II. 1. 2° 127, fols. 172va–176va. Cf. also Trier, Stadtbibliothek MS 680/879 and Michelstadt, Kirchenbibliothek MS I. Db. 685. See also Table 2.

Descriptions: G. Zedler, *Die Handschriften der Nassauischen landesbibliothek zu Wiesbaden* (Leipzig, 1931), pp. 46–50.

Wrocław, Biblioteka Uniwersytecka (BU) I F 707

(310 × 215) Paper. 271 fols. 1420, 1433. Theological compilation. CDH and R are part of an anti-Hussite compilation collected in 1420.

Provenance: The first owner and compiler of the codex was the Bohemian parist priest of Těchnic (modern Solenice), and bacchelor of theology Jiří z Těchnic (Georgius de Tyechnicz), see owner mark on the back cover: *Liber domini georgii De curia oriundi nec non plebani In tyechnycz baccalarii sacre theologie per ipsum comparatus et partim collectus ante postilla et in vltimis sexternis. Anno domini M° cccc° xx° eciam Collecta contra heresiarchas Constancienses per multos doctores vbi interfui compilacionibus.* Later: Augustinan Canons of Żagań. Old shelfmark of Żagań, U.II.56.

Contents: (122ra–153vb) CDH [Title/prologue:] *Ego tantillus considerans et perlegens omnis cursus heresiarcharum primo Waldensium et aliorum plurimorum hereticorum scilicet wycleficcorum, hussitarum, Coptorum, nicolaytarum, arrianorum, yssmitarum, casiudeopotarum, duplicium, Georgianorum, Machometarum, plurimorum aliorum quos transcuri perlegi quorum hic nomina contineri non possint et sic accepi predicto waldenses feci sub horum nomine quantum mihi videbatur.* [Inc.] *Cvm dormirent homines venit inimicus eius et superseminat* [...]; (154ra) R, excerpt from the first chapter. [Inc.] *Notandum quod herroribus* [sic] *hereticorum waldensium est istis et alii scripturis katholicis obuiandum* [...] [expl.] *Ego palam locutus sum et enim* [?] *ab sanctorum*; (154ra–156vb) Jiří z Těchnic, treatise on ecclesiastical privileges, unedited; (156vb–164ra) Mařík Rvačka (Mauritius de Praga), *Tractatus contra Hussitas de sumpcione venerabilis sacramenti ewkaristie sub utraque specie*; (164rb–169ra) Jean Gerson, *De necessaria communione laicorum sub utraque specie.* Ed. Gerson, *Œuvres complètes*, X, 55–68; (169ra–vb) continuation to Gerson's treatise, unedited; (169vb–180vb) Jiří z Těchnic, a compilation against the Hussites, unedited. [Title, 180va, lower margin:] *Diversa contra heresiachas contradicentes sacre Romane ecclesie facta congregata per Georgium baccalaureum sacre theologie plebanum in Tyechnycz*; (181ra–182vb) Jacques de Nouvion (Jacobus de Noviano), *Disputacio cum Hussitis* (1408); (183vb–191ra) anonymous treatise against the Hussites, unedited; (191ra–193ra) Ondřej z Brodu (Andreas de Broda)?, *Tractatus de corpore Cristi*, unedited; (193ra–va) *Epistola wykleph ad apostolicum in extremis directa etc.*; (193va–196ra) various notes on the condemnation of Wicklef's doctrine in Prague; (196rb–199va) Waldensian articles collected by Jiří z Těchnic. [Title:] *Hy synt articuli Secte waldensium hereticorum* [inc.] *Primo oraciones, Ieiunia, elemosinas, celebraciones* [...] [expl.] *sacerdotium offerencium non aliorum. Explicit argumenta optima domini Georrii* [sic].

Literature: Szymański, 'Hy sunt articuli secte waldensium'; Välimäki, 'Old Errors, New Sects'.

Remarks: The anti-Hussite compilation seems to have been compiled in the aftermath of the Council of Conctance, consisting of text against the Hussites published in the council, works by Jiří z Těchnic, and Zwicker's treatises. For the anti-Hussite works and their editions, see Pavel Soukup, *Repertorium operum antihussiticorum, on-line database*, <www.antihus.eu>.

Descriptions: J. C. Friedrich, 'Catalogus codicum scriptorum qui in Bibliotheca Regia ac Academica Wratislaviensi servantur', 4 vols. [handwritten catalogue] Biblioteka Uniwersytecka Wrocław, Akc. 1967/1 (Wrocław, 1821–3), I, 208; W. Goeber and J. Klapper. 'Katalog rękopisów dawnej Biblioteki Uniwersyteckiej we Wrocławiu, t.5 (I F 661–778)', 26 vols. [handwritten catalogue], Biblioteka Uniwersytecka Wrocław. Akc. 1967/2 (Wrocław, *c.* 1920–44), V, 688–91; Biller, *Waldenses*, p. 269.

Wrocław, BU MS I Q 43

(210 × 150) Paper. 396 fols. 1439-50.[4] Theological compilation, fols. 42r–77v form an independent fascicule, written by one hand.

Provenance: Dominican convent of Wrocław?

Contents: (42r–73v) CDH; (73v–77v) R1, fragment [inc.] *Notandum quod erroribus waldensium hereticorum est istis* […] [expl.] *Item si peccatum nullum sit veniale, nullus erit absque peccato mortali. Ps. Omnis.* [text breaks off at the end of fol. 77v].

Remarks: R1 includes only chapters 1–4 and beginning of chapter 10 (Purgatory, cf. Table 1). Probably a loss of folios after fol. 77.

Descriptions: Friedrich, 'Catalogus codicum', I, 46; Goeber and Klapper, 'Katalog rękopisów', XIII, 63–5; Biller, *Waldenses*, p. 269.

Würzburg, Universitätsbibliothek, MS M. ch. f. 186

(294 × 212) Paper. 260 fols. First half of the fifteenth century; 1455. Theological compilation.

Provenance: Southern Germany. In the 18th century, Monastery of St Stephen in Würzburg.

Contents: (223ra–229vb) R1 [inc.] *Dicunt heresiarche quos apud se fratres nominant* […] [expl.] *et specialem ymmo spiritualem vtilitatem uidetur expedire.*

Remarks: In R1, the end of chapter 3, chapter 4 and the beginning of chapter 5 missing due to loss of leaves after fol. 223. The chapter on homicide (7) has revisions not found elsewhere. Thurn (p. 45) has misidentified the R1 as 'Tractatus contra Duodecim Errores Fratrum Bohemorum'. R1 begins at the same folio where the condemnation of Wyclif's articles at the Council of Constance (209v–223r) ends, but it is written in a different hand.

Descriptions: H. Thurn, *Handschriften aus benediktinischen Provenienzen. Hälfte 2: Die Handschriften aus St. Stephan zu Wurzburg. Die Handschriften der Universitatsbibliothek Würzburg* 2.2 (Wiesbaden, 1986), pp. 44–6. Biller, *Waldenses*, p. 269, mentions the manuscript, but gives the wrong shelfmark, M.ch.f. 86.

Manuscripts with the Processus Petri and the Cum dormirent homines

Augsburg, Universitätsbibliothek MS II. 1. 2º 129

(290 × 210) Paper. 277 fols. First half of the fifteenth century. Pastoral-theological and canon-legal compilation

Provenance: south-western Germany. Donation of Johannes Kautsch to St Magnus in Füssen, *c.* 1460.

Contents: (121r–133r) *De immunitate clericorum*; (133r–135r) Inquisition against Johannes Drändorf (1425). Ed. Heimpel, *Drei Inquisitions-Verfahren*, pp. 68

---

[4] Watermark dating, information from A. Poznański.

ff., 89–93, 95 ff., from this manuscript; (135v–138r) John Wyclif's forty-five articles condemned at the Council of Contance; (138r–v) Petrus de Alliaco: *Conclusiones de communione sub utraque specie* (against Jacobellus de Misa, 1415); (138v–139r) *De efficentia orationis* (continuation to the previous text); (139r–152v) PP + CDH [Title:] *Errores Waldensium prout eos ponit quidam frater petrus prouincialis ordinis celestinorum inquisitor heretice prauitatis per Alamaniam*; (139r–v) summary of Zwicker's manifest (Zms); (140v–141r) short question list with Latin oaths (ial); (141r–150r) CDH, shorter [inc.] *Incipit tractatus contra articulos waldensium hereticorum. Cum dormirent homines uenit inimicus homo* [...] [expl.] *Angelus iurauit per uiuentem in eternum quia in tempus et tempora et dimidium temporis*; (150r–152v) formulary of sentences, revised (fd); (153–155) empty.

Remarks: Fols. 121–155 from a codicological unit, on the basis of the darkening at fol. 121r, probably an independent fascicule before it was bound with the rest of the manuscript. Written after 1425 (trial of Johannes Draendorff). Almost identical to Salzburg, St Peter MS b VIII 9 and similar to Würzburg, UB I. t. f. 234, part 7.

Descriptions: Hilg, *Lateinische mittelalterliche Handschriften*, pp. 127–37, Biller, *Waldenses*, p. 268 (as Schloss Harburg II, 1, fol. 129).

Budapest, National Széchenyi Library MS 106[5]

(300 × 210) Paper. 31 fols. Fifteenth century. A fascicule codex, nineteenth-century binding.

Provenance: unknown, German/Austrian, reference to bishop of Passau, see oath formula, fol. 1v.

Contents: (1r–2v) short question list (iag); (3r–31r) CDH; (31v) An excerpt from a sermon.

Descriptions: E. Bartoniek, *Codices manu scripti Latini 1. Codices Latini medii aevi* (Budapest, 1940), pp. 99–100; Biller *Waldenses*, p. 264.

Göttweig, Stiftsbibliothek MS XV 250

(290 × 222) 290 fols. Paper. 1450–75.[6] Theological compilation.

Provenance: Benedictine monastery, Göttweig.

Contents: (257ra–284vb) CDH; (284vb–287ra) short question list (iag); (287ra–rb) short list of converted Waldensians (la); (287rb–vb) *De vita et conversacione* (vcc); (287vb–289rb) *Articuli Waldensium* (a); (289rb–290vb) long question list (ib).

Remarks: The MS has also an old folio numbering, fols. 257–290 = old fols, 194–227.

---

[5] This description is based on the description in Bartoniek, *Codices manu scripti Latini 1*, pp. 99–100.

[6] Watermark dating: AT6200-MC52_211 [http://www.wzma.at/9637]. Codicological information from A. Poznański.

Descriptions: V. Moeli, 'Manuscripten-Catalog der Stiftsbibliohek zu Göttweig', 3 vols. [handwritten catalogue], I, 476–8; Biller, *Waldendes*, p. 264, where only CDH is mentioned.

Munich, BSB MS Clm 5338

Paper. 399 fols. Fifteenth century. Theological compilation.
Provenance: Chiemsee, Augustinian Canons (Chiemsee ep. 38.)
Contents: (213r–248r) CDH + PP [Title:] *Incipit Tractatus contra errorem waldensium et contra eosdem waldenses de modo inquirendi*; (213r–239v) CDH; (239v–244r) formulary of sentences, Passau 1398 (fb); (244r–246r) Zwicker's manifesto (Zm); (246r–238r) short question list (iag).
Remarks: CDH + PP form an independent fascicule.
Descriptions: Halm, *Catalogus codicum*, III.3, 7–8; Biller, *Waldenses*, p. 265.

Munich, BSB MS Clm 15125

(305 × 195) Paper. 238 fols. 1420s. Theological compilation.
Provenance: Augustinian Canons of Rebdorf, old Rebdorf Cod. 25. The dialect in German oaths is Middle/North Bavarian (information from W. Williams-Krapp).
Contents: (170ra–208vb) PP + CDH [Title:] *Incipit tractatus Waldensium magistri petri*; (170ra–172ra) Zwicker's manifesto (Zm); (172ra–174ra) short question list (iag); (174ra–203vb) CDII [Title:] *Sermo factus per inquisitorem*; (203vb–208vb) formulary of sentences, Passau 1398 (fb) [expl.] *Explicit tractatus waldensium magistri petri etc.*
Descriptions: Halm, *Catalogus codicum*, IV.3, 1; Biller, *Waldenses*, p. 265.

Munich, BSB MS Clm 22373

Paper. 318 fols. First half of the fifteenth century. Theological compilation.
Provenance: Praemonstratensian monastery of Windberg, old Windberg Cod. 173. The dialect in German oaths is Middle Bavarian (information from W. Williams-Krapp).
Contents: (222va–224vb) Zwicker's manifesto (Zm) (224vb) Notes on the arson of priests' property (nar); (224vb–227ra) short question list (iag); (227ra–256rb) CDH [Title:] *Incipit tractatus contra articulos secte Waldensium hereticotum*; (256rb–260ra) formulary of sentences, Passau 1398 (fb).
Descriptions: Halm, *Catalogus codicum*, IV.4, 45; Biller, *Waldenses*, p. 266.

Salzburg, Erzabtei St Peter MS b V 1

(220 × 150) Paper. 252 fols. fifteenth century (2nd quarter or later). Theological compilation.
Provenance: Origin unknown, later Benedictine monastery of St Peter.
Contents: (1r–11r) *Erronei articuli baronum Bohemiarum regi Sigismundo in concilio Constantiensi traditi*; (12r–32r) *Eorum consultatio in concilio Constantiensi*; (33r) same text as at fol. 32r, crossed out as correction; (33v–73v) PP + CDH

Appendix 1

[Title:] *Vita et conuersacio Waldensium et Inquisicio et Reprobacio erroneorum Articulorum ipsorum*; (33v–34r) the first sentence of the short list (la) + *De vita et conversacione* (vcc). [Inc.] *Anno domini Millesimo tricentesimo nonagesimo primo die quarta mensis septembris infrascripti sunt Rectores pro nunc Secte Waldensium; primo a b c; etc. predicti nominantur inter eos apostoli magistri et fratres* [...] [expl.] *nisi ad vnum uel ad duos annos*; (34r–35v) *Articuli Waldensium* (a); (35v–37v) long question list (ibg); (37v–38r) long list of converted Waldensians (lb); (38v–73v) CDH [inc.] *Dum dormirent homines venit inimicus illius* [...] [expl.] *et ea que in eo sunt quia amplius tempus non erit; Item Ier.*; (74r–78v) empty.

Remarks: CDH ends abruptly at the end of fol. 73v, the rest of the last chapter (*de iuramento*) missing, probably due to the loss of a manuscript leaf. Fols. 1–73 are a separate unit from the rest of the manuscript.

Descriptions: A. Jungwirth, 'Beschreibung der Handschriften des Stiftes St. Peter in Salzburg', 6 vols. [handwritten catalogue] (Salzburg, 1910–12), IV; Biller, *Waldenses*, p. 267.

Salzburg, Erzabtei St Peter MS b VIII 9

(290 × 210) Paper. 341 fols. Late fifteenth century. Compilation of canon law.
Provenance: Ex Libris Martin Hattinger, OSB, abbot of Salzburg, 1584–1615. Hattinger was professed in Tegernsee. Hattinger possibly brought the codex with him, no signs of the MS in Salzburg before the sisteenth century.
Contents: (284ra–292va) *De immunitate clericorum*; (292va–294va) Inquisition against Johannes Drändorf (1425). Ed. Heimpel, *Drei Inquisitions-Verfahren*, pp. 68 ff., 89–93, 95 ff., but without knowledge of this manuscript; (294va–296va) John Wyclif's forty-five articles condemned at the Council of Contance; (296va–vb) Petrus de Alliaco: *Conclusiones de communione sub utraque specie* (against Jacobellus de Misa, 1415); (296vb–297ra) *De efficentia orationis* (continuation to the previous text); (297ra–307va) PP + CDH: (297ra–vb) summary of Zwicker's manifesto (Zms); (297vb–298va) short question list with Latin oaths (ial) (298va–305rb) CDH, shorter. [Title:] *Incipit tractatus contra articulos waldensium hereticorum.* [Inc.] *Cum dormirent homines venit inimicus homo* [...] [expl.] *Angelus Iurauit per uiuentem in eternum, quia in tempus et in tempora et dimidium temporis etc*; (305rb–307va) formulary of sentences, revised (fd).
Remarks: Almost identical to Augsburg, UB MS II. 1.2° 129, similar to Würzburg, UB I. t. f. 234, part 7.
Descriptions: Jungwirth, 'Beschreibung der Handschriften', IV; Biller, *Waldenses*, p. 267.

St Paul im Lavanttal, Stift St Paul MS 26/4

Paper. 243 fols. First half of the fifteenth century (1420?). Theological compilation.
Provenance: Spital am Pyhrn, secular canons. Written in Gravenwöhr, Oberpfalz (at least to fol. 213r).
Colophon: (213r) *Comparatus est iste liber per dominum Iacobum de Hederstorff*

et finitus per Ekhardum tunc temporum eruditor parvulorum in Gravenwoerd anno 1420.

Contents: (226ra–228ra) Zwicker's manifesto (Zm); (228v) empty; (229ra–243vb) CDH [Title:] *hic nota de heresi Waldensium.*

Remarks: Zwicker's manifesto and CDH written by different hands. The dating and localization (1420, Gravenwöhr) do not necessarily apply for PP + CDH.

Descriptions: C. Glaßner, 'Inventar der Handschriften des Benediktinerstiftes St. Paul im Lavanttal' (2002), <http://www.ksbm.oeaw.ac.at/stpaul/inv/index.htm>; Biller, *Waldenses*, p. 267.

St Paul im Lavanttal, Stift St Paul MS 77/4

Paper. 334 fols. Fifteenth century. Theological compilation.

Provenance: Spital am Pyhrn, secular canons.

Contents: (300ra–302ra) Zwicker's manifesto (Zm); (302ra–304ra) short question list (iag); (304ra–330ra) CDH [Title:] *Incipit tractatus contra articulos secte waldensium hereticorum*; (330ra–334rb) formulary of sentences, Passau 1398 (fb).

Remarks: Inside front cover: *Dicta fratris petri ordinis celestinorum de erroribus waldensium.*

Descriptions: Glaßner, 'Inventar (St. Paul im Lavanttal)'; Biller, *Waldenses*, p. 267.

Seitenstetten, Stift Seitenstetten MS 188

Paper. 234 fols. First half of the fifteenth century.[7] Theological compilation.

Provenance: Old medieval collection of Seitenstetten;[8] fol. 1r: *Ex libris Georgij Ardingeri.*

Contents: (1r–62r) PP + CDH [Title:] *Processus domini petri de ordine Celestinorum Inquisitoris hereticorum*; (1r–4v) short question list (iag); (4v–56v) CDH; (56v–57r) Sermon for a new priest. Later addition in a different hand; (57v–59v) Zwicker's manifesto (Zm); (59v, lower margin) notes on the arson of priests' property (nar); (60r) short list of converted Waldensians (la); (60r–61r) *De vita et conversacione* (vcc); (61r–62r) *Articuli Waldensium* (a); (62r) Beginnings of the two question lists (ia and ib): *producitur aliquis suspectus de heresi, queritur primo, scis quare es captiuatus etc. Item Vbi es natus etc. V. S. Est autem episcopus in loco premoninato ita quod non.*

Remarks: PP written by two different hands, change of hand after fol. 56v. The sermon for a new priest by a later hand than the rest of the compilation.

---

[7] Watermark dating: AT5000-725_199 [http://www.wzma.at/7871], Prague, 1406–15. Information from A. Poznański.

[8] Cf. H. Cerny, 'Beiträge zur Geschichte der Wissenschaftspflege des Stiftes Seitenstetten im Mittelalter', *Studien und Mitteilungen zur Geschichte des Benediktinerordens und seiner Zweige* 78 (1967), 68–143 (p. 74).

Descriptions: C. Glaßner, 'Inventar der mittelalterlichen Handschriften des Benediktinerstiftes Seitenstetten' (2005), <http://www.ksbm.oeaw.ac.at/ seit/inv/>; Biller, *Waldenses*, p. 268.

Seitenstetten, Stift Seitenstetten MS 252

Paper. 193 fols. 1415? Theological compilation. At least three different hands. Mathias de Mairhof (25ra–135va; 146va–167vb); Anonymous A (1ra–10rb; 11va–21rb (?); 168ra–193ra); Anonymous B (136ra–145vb).

Provenance: Old medieval collection of Seitenstetten (cf. Cerny, 'Beiträge zur Geschichte', p. 74).

Colophon: (134va) *Explicit summa bona de confessione et penitencia thome de aquino finita feria proxima post Egidii per mathiam de mairhof dictus Chetzel Anno etc. Quintodecimo* [1415].

Contents: (168ra–va) a note on hypocrisy; (168va–192vb) PP + CDH [Title:] *Processus inquisicionis ad hereticos balden*[ses]: (168va–169vb) Zwicker's manifesto (Zm); (170ra) Notes on the arson of priests' property (nar); (170ra) short list of converted Waldensians (la); (170ra–va) *De vita et conversacione* (vcc); (170va–171va) *Articuli Waldensium* (a); (171va–172vb) short question list (iag); (172vb–192vb) CDH; (193ra) a short excerpt from CHD, chapter XX, crossed out.

Remarks: A new fascicule with PP and CDH, written by Anonymous A begins at fol. 168ra.

Descriptions: Glaßner, 'Inventar (Seitenstetten)'; Biller, *Waldenses*, p. 268.

Vatican City, BAV MS Pal. lat. 677

(195 × 135) Paper. 106 fols. 1460s.[9] Compilation of anti-heretical treatises. Written by one scribe, Leonard Regel, intended as one volume. Binding of the Palatine Library of Heidelberg, dated 1558.

Provenance: Regensburg? (cf. oath formulas fols. 44r–56v, bishop of Regensburg mentioned); since the 1550s: Palatine Library of Heidelberg.

Colophon: (106r) *Per me leonardum Regel de ingolstat.* Unrecognized coat of arms at fol. 106v.

Contents: (1r–40v) Treatise of the Anonymous of Passau (pseudo-Reinerius redaction); (41r–42v) Articles against John Wyclif; (43r–106r) PP + CDH [Title:] *Processus domini petri de ordine celestinorum inquisitoris hereticorum etc*; (43r–47r) short question list (iag); (47r–v) short list of converted Waldensians (la); (47v–48v) *De vita et conversacione* (vcc); (48v–51r) *Articuli Waldensium* (a); (51r–54r) long question list (ib); (54r–55r) long list of converted Waldensians (lb); (55r–106r) CDH.

Remarks: The only preserved CDH and PP copy that is a

---

[9] Watermark dating, closest equivalents Piccard, Waage, V, 388–90, dated 1465–7. See G. Piccard, *Wasserzeichen Waage, Die Wasserzeichenkartei Piccard im Hauptstaatsarchiv Stuttgart*, Findbuch 5 (Stuttgart, 1978).

one-volume anti-heretical compilaton with other texts of the genre. Descriptions: H. Stevenson and G. B. de Rossi, *Codices Palatini latini Bibliothecae Vaticanae* I (Rome, 1886), p. 240; Biller, *Waldenses*, p. 268.

Vienna, ÖNB MS 5393

(295 × 210) Paper. 351 fols. First half of the fifteenth century with some later additions. Compilation on the topics of the Councils of Constance and Basel. The part with the PP + CDH probably from the late 1390s.[10]
Provenance: Austria, probably in possession of Prior Leonhard Petraer (d. 1435), Carthusian monastery of Gaming.
Contents: (286ra–287rb) short question list (iag); (287va–305vb) CDH.
Remarks: CDH written by two different hands, abrupt change of hand at the end of fol. 297v. According to Rischpler and Haltrich, 'Der Codex 5393', p. 315, the part with the questionnaire and CDH possibly belonged to Leonhard Petraer.
Description: Rischpler and Haltrich, 'Der Codex 5393', pp. 317–20.

Vyšší Brod (Hohenfurt), MS 61

Paper. 65(67) fols. Fifteenth century.
Provenance: Cistercian monastery of Vyšší Brod (Hohenfurt).
Contents: PP + CDH [Title:] (1v) [...] *Celestinorum Inquisitoris hereticorum.* According to descrip. by Pavel: *Processus domini Petri de Ordine Celestinorum Inquisitoris hereticorum*; (1v–5v) short question list (iag); (5v–65v) CDH [inc.] *[C]vm dormirent homines venit inimicus eius* [...] [expl.] *eleuauit manum suam ad celum et iurauit per* [end of my microfilm copy].
Remarks: According to Pavel, CDH ended at fol. 64v: *iurant veritatem et illud tu dampnas – Explicit hoc totum non plus hic est michi notum.* Fols. 65r–66r included medical recipes. Possibly the medical recipes have been torn from the end of the manuscript, together with the ending of the CDH.
Descriptions: Pavel, 'Beschreibung der im Stifte Hohenfurt befindlichen Handschriften', p. 261; Biller, *Waldenses*, pp. 264–5.

Wolfenbüttel, HAB MS Guelf. 431 Helmst

(285 × 215) Paper. 48 fols. Fifteenth century, CDH and PP *c.* 1405–15. Theological compilation.
Provenance: Upper Austria and northern Germany. Belonged to Mathias Flacius Illuricus in the sixteenth century.
Contents: (1ra–2va) Zwicker's manifesto (Zm), part missing from the middle; (2va) notes on the arson of priests' property (nar); (2vb) short list of converted Waldensians (la); (3ra–4rb) excerpts from oaths belonging to the

---

[10] Watermark dating: AT3760-320205_141 [http://www.wzma.at/183] Information of A. Poznański.

short questionnaire (iag); (5ra–6va) excerpts from the formulary of sentences, Passau 1398 (fb); (6vb) empty; (7ra–8rb) CDH, excerpt. [Inc.] *Cum dormirent homines venit inimicus eius* […] [expl.] *cum enim fueras sartor faber;* (8v) empty; (9ra–vb) excerpt from the treatise of the Anonymous of Passau; (10ra–14rb) CDH, excerpt. [Inc.] *Item b.h. reprobant Indulgencias* […] [expl.] *et illud tu dapnas; Huf daz feur in churz; Laus deo / pax viuis/ eterna defunctis;* (14v) empty; (15ra–vb) excerpt from the treatise of the Anonymous of Passau; (16rb–25vb) Excerpts from various theological treatises (Jean Gerson? Heinrich Totting von Oyta?); (26ra–48vb); CDH, excerpt. [Inc.] *nam nouiter compertum quod quidam heresiarca* […] [expl.] *et tu illud dampnas.*

Remarks: PP and CDH excerpts compiled from different sources, written by four different hands. The sections of CHD overlap each other, three different copies. The year 1410 in Zwicker's manifesto, fol. 1r: *et istis temporibus videlicet anno domini M cccc xus [1410] de mense Ianuarii.* Supported by watermark dating, see the description of HAB.

Descriptions: O. von Heinemann, *Die Handschriften der Herzoglichen Bibliothek zu Wolfenbüttel. Abth. 1: Die Helmstedter Handschriften* I (Wolfenbüttel, 1884), pp. 336–7; Biller, *Waldenses*, p. 268; HAB Handschriftendatenbank <http://diglib.hab.de/?db=mss&list=ms&id=431-helmst&catalog=Lesser>.

Würzburg, Universitätsbibliothek I. t. f. 234, part 7

(250 × 190) Paper. 12 fols. End of the fifteenth century. A fascicule MS bound behind a collection of incunabula.

Provenance: Eastern Franconia?

Contents: (1r–11r) CDH, shorter. [Title:] *Incipit Tractatus Contra heresim Waldensium.* [Inc.] *Cum dormirent homines venit inimicus homo* […] [expl.] *Angelus iuravit per viuentem in eternum quia in tempus et tempora et dimidium temporis etc;* (11r–12r) Summary of Zwicker's manifesto (Zms); (12r–v) short question list with Latin oaths (ial), excerpt.

Remarks: The summary of Zwicker's manifest, shorter version of CDH and beginning of the questionnaire similar to Augsburg UB, MS II. 1. 2° 129 and Salzburg, St Peter MS b VIII 9 (cf. Appendix 3). Here, the end of the question list and the formulary (fd) are missing, possibly due to a loss of leaves.

Descriptions: H. Thurn, *Die Handschriften der kleinen Provenienzen und Fragmente,* Die Handschriften der Universitätsbibliothek Würzburg 4 (Wiesbaden, 1990), p.13. The whole incunabula compilation described at INKA, <http://www.inka.uni-tuebingen.de>, no. 48002622.

Würzburg, Universitätsbibliothek MS M. ch. f. 51

(300 × 210) Paper. 427 fols. Last third of the fifteenth century. Historical and theological compilation.

Provenance: Würzburg, in the eighteenth century the Jesuit library of Würzburg.

Contents: (2r–5r) confession and abjuration of Conradus Hager of Dinkelsbühl;

(5v–7v) confession and abjuration of Hermannus dictus Kuchener; (7r–9v) privileges and notes concerning Würzburg (10r–16v) excerpts from the treatise of Anonymous of Passau; (17r–21r) excerpts from the *De inquisitione hereticorum* (pseudo-David of Augsburg); (21v–67v) PP + CHD: (21v–23v) short question list (iag); (24r–34r) Formulary based on Zwicker's sentences, compiled after 1403 (fc); (34v) short list of converted Waldensians (la); (34v–35r) *De vita et conversacione* (vcc); (35r–36r) *Articuli Waldensium* (a); (36r–38r) long question list (ib); (38r) long list of converted Waldensians (lb); (39v–67v) CDH; (68v–69v) articles against John Wyclif; (70r–v) *Der anspruch zwyschen unnserm genedistemm herenn kayserlichen maiestet kayser Fryderich und Herzogn Albrechtn von Münchnen.*

Remarks: Fols. 2–70 form a fascicule, mostly on heresy and written by one hand, with the exception of the short German text at fol. 70r–v. The same hand has written the account on the Niklashausen heresy 1476 (fols. 75r–83v). The texts against Waldensians were probably compiled in the context of these proceedings. On the Niklashausen heresy, see Arnold, *Niklashausen.*

Descriptions. H. Thurn, *Bestand bis zur Säkularisierung: Erwerbungen und Zugänge bis 1803*, Die Handschriften der Universitätsbibliothek Würzburg 5 (Wiesbaden, 1994), pp. 67–74; Biller, *Waldenses*, p. 269.

Manuscripts with only the Cum dormirent homines

Manuscripts marked * have been consulted for this study.

Dubrovnik, Dominican Convent MS 30

(300 × 214) Paper. 213 fols. Fourteenth and fifteenth century. Theological compilation.
Provenance: Germany, later Dominicans of Dubrovnik.
Contents: (147va–168ra) CDH (up to chapter XXII).
Descriptions: T. Kaeppeli and H.-V. Shooner, *Les manuscrits médiévaux de Saint-Dominique de Dubrovnik: catalogue sommaire* (Rome, 1965), pp. 62–5; Biller, 'Aspects', p. 217; Biller, *Waldenses*, p. 264.

*Kraków, Bibliotheca Jagellonica MS DD X 22 (cat. 2471)**

Paper. 12 fols. Fifteenth century. Excerpt.
Provenance: Unknown.
Contents: (1r–12v) CDH, excerpt. [Inc.] *Dum dormirent homines venit inimicus eius* […] [expl.] *Erras. Christus enim est in plenissimo gaudio et tamen orat pro toto mundo. I. Io ii⁰.* (chapter XX).
Description: W. Wisłocki, *Katalog rękopisów Bibljoteki Uniwersytetu Jagiellońskiego*, 2 vols. (Kraków, 1881), II, 591; Biller, *Waldenses*, p. 265.

Appendix 1

Munich, BSB MS Clm 5614*

Paper. 339 fols. Second half of the fifteenth century (1460s). Theological compilation.

Provenance: Augustinian Canons of Diessen, old shelfmark Diessen 114.

Contents: (247ra–260rb) anonymous anti-Hussite treatise *Eloquenti viro* [expl.] *Per me fratre Johannes dorum anno d. m⁰ 469 Eterna requies sit mea merces Amen;* (260va–284ra) CDH [Title:] *Obuiaciones contra hereticos waldensium.* [Expl.] *quando iurant vertitatem. et tu illud dampnas etc.* *Explicunt obuiationes sacre scripture errorum waldensium anno d. m. cccc⁰ xliiii⁰* [1444]; (284va–297va) *Disputatio capituli ecclesiae pragensis cum Rokyzana.* [Inc.] *Anno domini m⁰ cccc⁰ 64 In die purificationis beate marie virginis facta est magna congregatio* […] *Et est finis huius positionis contra rockizanam anno domini M⁰ lxviiii⁰* [1469].

Remarks: A manuscript used by Gretser. The dating 1444 given at the end of CDH is obviously wrong. CDH is copied between two anti-Hussite treatises, both finished in 1469, and by the same scribe (Brother Johannes Dorum). For the anti-Hussite works and their editions, see Soukup, *Repertorium operum antihussiticorum.*

Descriptions: Halm, *Catalogus codicum*, III.3, 30; Biller, *Waldenses*, p. 265

Munich, BSB MS Clm 8680*

Paper. 228 fols. Second half of the fifteenth century. Theological compilation.

Provenance: Carmelite Friars, Munich.

Contents: (176ra–202vb) CDH.

Descriptions: Halm, *Catalogus codicum*, IV.1, 45; Biller, *Waldenses*, p. 265.

Munich, BSB MS Clm 16170*

Paper. 402 fols. Fifteenth century. Theological compilation.

Provenance: Augustinian Canons, St Nicholas-prope-Passau.

Colophon: (289ra) *Explicit tractatus contra hereticos waldenses qui intitulatur Dum dormirent homines etc per manum mathei sundermair de ampfing. Sit nunc laus deo et sancto nicolao.*

Contents: (250ra–289ra) CDH.

Remarks: The manuscript 'M.S.S. Nic.' used by Gretser.

Description: Halm, *Catalogus codicum*, IV.3, 55; Biller, *Waldenses*, p. 265

Munich, BSB MS Clm 17562*

Parchment and Paper. 233 fols. Fourteen to fifteenth century (1460). Theological compilation.

Provenance: Augustinian Eremites of Schöntal.

Colophon: (181r) *Expliciunt obviationes sacre scripture errorum waldensium hereticorum script*[e] *finiteque in die sancti cristofferi Anno domini etc lx⁰* [1460].

Contents: (154r–181r) CDH.

Description: Halm, *Catalogus codicum*, IV.3, 107; Biller, *Waldenses*, pp. 265–6.

Munich BSB MS Clm 19539*

(290–300 × 190–200) Paper. 271 fols. Fifteenth century (1454). Theological compilation.

Provenance: Benedictine monastery of Tegernsee, fols. 223–257 written in Feltmaching.

Colophon: (252ra) *Expliciunt obuiationes sacre scripture errorum waldensium hereticorum scriptum Anno domini Liiii* [1454] *In die Sancti wenceslay martiris et In vigilia Sancti Michaelis In Feltmaching.*

Contents: (223ra–252ra) CDH; (252va–256rb) *Sermo de pastoribus et de nouo sacerdote.*

Descriptions: Halm, *Catalogus codicum*, IV.3, 255; Biller, *Waldenses*, p. 266.

Munich, BSB MS Clm 26756*

(160 × 110) Paper. 251 fols. Fifteenth century. Theological compilation.

Provenance: Dominican convent of Regensburg.

Contents: (2r–33r) CDH.

Descriptions: Halm, *Catalogus codicum*, IV.4, 210; Biller, *Waldenses*, p. 266.

Olomouc, Zemský archiv v Opavě, poboča Olomouc, Metropolitní kapitula Olomouc MS 57*

Provenance: Metropolitan chapter, Olomouc.

Contents: (157ra–174vb) CDH.

Description: J. Bistřický, F. Drkal and M. Kouřil, *Seznam Rukopisu Metropolitní Kapituly v Olomouci* (Prague, 1961), p. 109; Biller, *Waldenses*, p. 266.

Paris, Bibliothèque Mazarine MS 1683 (1185)*

(309 × 220) Paper. 193 fols. Second quarter of the fifteenth century. Compilation of material on the Councils of Constance and Basel.

Provenance: College of Navarre, compiled by the dean of Cambrai, Gilles Carlier.

Contents: (6r–33r) CDH [Title:] *scriptum d. p. C. contra Walden*[ses] *et eorum articulos*; (33v) *Articuli Waldensium et pauperum de lugduno.* A list of eighteen Waldensian articles based on the CDH, corresponding to the titles of this manuscript.

Descriptions: Biller, *Waldenses*, p. 266; Calames, <http://www.calames.abes.fr/pub/#details?id=MAZB11348>.

Prague, KMK MS C LXIX*

(310 × 210) Paper. 214 fols. First half of the fifteenth century (1415). Theological compilation.

Provenance: Bohemia.

Colophon: (75ra) *Explicit symbolum apostolorum Anno domini M⁰ CCCC vi; Per Manus Martini de Kluczow; Anno Domini M⁰ CCCC xv⁰* [1415] *eciam est finitum feria secunda post Mathei apostoli beatissimi.*

Contents: (75ra–101vb) CDH.
Remarks: *Symbolum apostolorum* and CDH written by Martinus of Kluczow.
Descriptions: Patera and Podlaha, *Soupis rukopisů*, I, 288; Biller, *Waldenses*, p. 266.

*Prague, NKCR MS X. B. 7**

(290 × 215) Paper. 178 fols. First half of the fifteenth century. Theological compilation.
Provenance: Bohemia
Contents: (72ra–98rb) CDH.
Descriptions: Truhlář, *Catalogus codicum*, pp. 44–5; Biller, *Waldenses*, p. 266; Manuscriptorium.

*Prague, NKCR MS XIII. E. 5**

(220 × 155). Paper. 290 fols. 1427–8. Theological compilation.
Provenance: In the fifteenth century in possession of Martinus, parish priest of Plana. CDH written in Cheb (Eger).
Contents: (153v–183v) CDH [expl.] *quando iurauit veritatem, et tu illud condempnas. Anno domini M°cccc xxviii° finita est reprobacio waldensium hereticorum in Egra feria secunda in vigilia Epiphanie domini Amen*; (183v–184v) thirty-nine Waldensian errors. Ed. Werner, *Nachrichten*, pp. 275–6.
Descriptions: Truhlár, *Catalogus codicum*, p. 237; Biller, *Waldenses*, p. 267; Manuscriptorium.

*Seitenstetten, Stift Seitenstetten MS 106**

Paper. 154 fols. First half of the fifteenth century.[11] Theological compilation.
Provenance: Old medieval collection of Seitenstetten (Cerny, 'Beiträge zur Geschichte', p. 74).
Contents: (109ra–132vb) CDH, a copy mixed up in the production. [Inc., from the middle of chapter I] *apostoli velud talia sed eciam omnes christiani* [...] (132va) *quando iurauit veritatem et tu illud dampnas.* The prologue and the beginning of chapter I copied at the end: (132va) *[C]Um dormirent homines uenit inimicus eius* [...] (132vb) *Item tempore primitive ecclesie non solum*; (144vb) CDH, part of chapter XXIII (information from A. Poznański).
Descriptions: Glaßner, 'Inventar (Seitenstetten)'; Biller, *Waldenses*, p. 268.

*Seitenstetten, Stift Seitenstetten MS 213**

Paper. 134 fols. 1400. Theological compilation.
Provenance: The scribe and previous owner, the priest Johannes Hofmüllner von Weitra.

---

[11] Watermark dating: AT5000-315_35, <http://www.wzma.at/3792>, 1410–20. Information from A. Poznański.

Colophon: (106rb) *Explicit summa Innocencii Iohannis dictus Rumph presbyteri de Weytra per proprias manus scriptam anno ab incarnacione domini quadringentesimo in die sancte Barbare virginis* [4 December 1400].

Contents: (108va–133ra) CDH.

Remarks: CDH written in the hand of Johannes von Weitra. MS 213 is the earliest dated copy of the *Cum dormirent homines*.

Descriptions: Glaßner, 'Inventar (Seitenstetten)'; Biller, *Waldenses*, p. 268.

Vienna, ÖNB MS 4219*

Paper. 359 fols. Fifteenth century (1444). Theological compilation, fifteenth-century leather binding.

Provenance: Austrian.

Colophon: (233ra) *Expliciunt obuiationes sacrae scripturis erroribus Waldensium. Anno Domini 1444.*

Contents: (212ra–233ra) CDH.

Descriptions: *Tabulae codicum manu scriptorum praeter graecos et orientales in Bibliotheca Palatina Vindobonensi asservatorum*, 10 vols. (Vienna, 1869), III, 207; H. Menhardt, *Verzeichnis der altdeutschen literarischen Handschriften der Österreichischen Nationalbibliothek* 1 (Berlin, 1960), p. 1014; Biller, *Waldenses*, p. 268.

Vienna, ÖNB MS 4511*

Paper. 219 fols. First half of the fifteenth century.[12] Theological compilation/ Hussitica.

Provenance: Unknown.

Contents: (159r–160v) Summary based on CDH, unedited. [Inc.] *Quidam scribitur contra valdenses quod ortus eorum est malus, progressus peior, exitus pessimus* [ ] [expl.] *primo in omni verbo; secundo pro omni facto; tertio per omnem rem.*

Descriptions: *Tabulae codicum*, III, 293; Biller, *Waldenses*, p. 268.

Zwettl, Stiftsbibliothek MS 185*

(294 x 205) Paper. 274 fols. 1406/1519. Theological compilation.

Provenance: Cistercian monastery of Zwettl. CDH written in Zwettl's scriptorium *c.* 1406.

Contents: (121rb–141rb) CDH.

Descriptions: C. Ziegler and J. Rössl, *Zisterzienserstift Zwettl: Katalog der Handschriften des Mittelalters Teil 2; Codex 101–200* (Vienna, 1985), pp. 233–7; Biller, *Waldenses*, p. 269; Manuscripta.at <http://manuscripta.at/?ID=31796>.

---

[12] Watermark dating: AT4000-625_123 <http://www.wzma.at/1537>. Information from A. Poznański.

Appendix 1

The inquisitors' manuals

The inquisitors' manuals Linz, Oberösterreichische Landesbibliothek (OÖLB) MS 177 and St Florian, MS XI 234 have already been described by A. Patschovsky but the new descriptions give more accurate information about Zwicker's formularies in the manual of St Florian, and offer references to recent editions of the *consilia* and other legal texts included in these manuals. Especially in relation to the Linz manual, the reader is advised to consult the detailed description by Patschovsky. His numbering of the texts is followed to allow easy comparison. Appendix 4 presents the comparison of the two manuals in a table.

Linz, OÖLB MS 177

(200 × 135–140) Parchment. 120 fols. Fourteenth century. An inquisitor's manual.

Provenance: Bohemian manual, probably owned by Johannes Paduanus (d. 1358), later in the ownership of Petrus Zwicker, since the early fifteenth century at the Benedictine monastery of Garsten. Old shelfmark of Garsten K 23.

Contents:

1   (1r) Short notices on absolution, etc., based on canon law.
2   (1r) Excerpts from the beginnings of the four gospels.
3   (1v–3v) a list of contents on fols. 11r–51r.
4   (3v) Short notice on Beghards.
5   (3v) Two short notices (on usury and inquisitorial process).
6   (4r–5r) Two question lists on heresy and witchcraft, French, thirteenth century, ed. Douais, 'Les hérétiques du Midi', pp. 376–9.
7   (5v) John XXII, decretal *Cum Mattheus* (*Extrav. Comm.* 5.3.3.).
8   (6r–7r) Questionnaire presented to the Dominican Venturino of Bergamo in Avignon (1335).
9   (7r) Short consultation relating to the preceding questionnaire. Unedited.
10 (7va–9rb) Isidore of Seville's list of heresies, according to *Decretum*, C. 24. q. 3 c. 39.
11 (10r) Image of crucified Christ, beginnings of the four gospels. John and Matthew written twice, the second time by a fourteenth-/fifteenth-century hand (not identifiable as Zwicker's handwriting). (10v) empty.
12 (11r–51r) French inquisitor's manual (Dondaine Manual no. 5), see Dondaine, 'Le Manuel de L'Inquisiteur', pp. 106–7.
   a   (11r–20r) Consultations of Guido Fulcodii (Gui Foulques) for Dominican inquisitors in Provence (September 1238–August 1243), version I. See Bivoralov, *Inquisitoren-Handbücher*, pp. 206–24, ed. 225–55.
   b   (20r–21r) Consultation of Avignon (21 June 1235). Descriptions:

Bivolarov, *Inquisitoren-Handbücher*, p. 186; Parmeggiani, *Consilia*, pp. 10–11, ed. 11–13.

c (21r–22v) Anonymous consultation (1249/55, southern France?). Descriptions: Bivolarov. *Inquisitoren-Handbücher*, p. 187; Parmeggiani, *Consilia*, pp. 47– 8, ed. 49–51.

d (22v–23r) Consultation of Jean de Bernin, archbishop of Vienne (10 May 1235). Descriptions: Bivolarov, *Inquisitoren-Handbücher*, p. 186; Parmeggiani, *Consilia*, pp. 8–9; ed. 10.

e (23r–28v) Consultation of the Council of Narbonne (1243). Descritions: Bivolarov, *Inquisitoren-Handbücher*, pp. 188–9; Parmeggiani, *Consilia*, pp. 22–4; ed. 24–32; *Texte zur Inquisition*, ed. Selge, pp. 60–9.

f (28v–29v) Ordinance of the papal legate Petrus de Collemedio (1244–53). Descriptions: Bivolarov, *Inquisitoren-Handbücher*, pp. 189–90; Parmeggiani, *Consilia*, pp. 32–3; ed. 33–4.

g (29v–36r) Consultation of the Council of Béziers (19 April 1246). Descriptions: Bivolarov, *Inquisitoren-Handbücher*, pp. 190–1; Parmeggiani, *Consilia*, pp. 34–6; ed. 36–46.

h-i (36r–48v) Formulary of Italian inquisitors (thirteenth century).[13] Fols. 36v–46r; ed. d'Alatri, 'L'inquisizione francescana', pp. 141–52 (nos. 11–31), reprinted in d'Alatri *L'inquisizione francescana*, pp. 178–96.

j (48r–51r) Excerpt from the statutes of the Council of Toulouse (1229).

13 (51r–v) Excerpts from canon law on excommunication and absolution.

14 (52r–57r) *De hereticorum inquisitione* (post 1267). See Parmeggiani, 'Un secolo di manualistica inquisitoriale', pp. 255–6; ibid., *Explicatio*, pp. liii–lviii.

15 (57r) Fragment of the German confession of episcopal inquisitor of Prague, Swatibor of Langendorf.

16 (57r–58v) Four papal letters.

17 (59r–69v) Excerpts from canon law.

18 (70r) *Ad reprimenda multorum facinora*, Henry VII (2 April 1313, Pisa).

19 (70r) Excerpt from *Liber sextus*, 5.2.7 with glossa

20 (70v) A verse of the Marian hymn 'Tu virens mundi lilium'.

21 (71r) Treatise *Quatuor dicunt secte hereticorum*. A similar text ed. Schmidt, 'Actenstückc', pp. 245–6.

22 (71v–72r) Excerpts from legislation against heretics by Louis IX of France (April 1229).

23 (72v–74r) Consultation of Conte Casati (1281–7). Descriptions: Bivolarov, *Inquisitoren-Handbücher*, p. 202; Parmeggiani, *Consilia*, pp. 130–1; ed. 131–6.

24 (74v–76v) Five papal bulls.

25 (76v–77v) Interrogatorium, Bohemian origin (Gallus of Jindřichův Hradec). Ed. Patschovsky, *Anfänge*, pp. 104–5.

---

[13] Patschovsky divided the formulary into two, letters h–i in his description.

26 (77v–83r) *De auctoritate et forma officii inquisitionis* (Lombardy, end of thirteenth century). See Parmeggiani, *Explicatio*, pp. lvii–lix.

27 (83r–v) Formulary/question list against Waldensians (French, Arles), unedited.

28 (83v–84r) Formula for abjuration of Waldensians, unedited.

29 (84r–v) A short consultation: *Interpretatio inquisitorum et prelatorum super quibusdam capitulis ex constitutionibus papalibus.* Unedited. See Parmeggiani, 'Un secolo di manualistica inquisitoriale', p. 253, n. 73.

30 (84v–85r) Decretal of Innocent III, *Litteras vestras.*

31 (85r–86r) Consultation of Forteguerra (3 March 1298, Tuscany?) Descrition: Parmeggiani, *Consilia*, pp. 173–4; ed. 174–7.

32 (86r) Excerpt from Bernard Gui's treatise on Beguines. Cf. Bernard Gui, *Practica inquisitionis*, pp. 267–8.

33 (86r–v) Interrogatory on Waldensians, unedited.

34 (86v–99v) Fragment of an unpublished manual of inquisitor, German/Austrian provenance (*c.* 1318–34).

35 (99v–100r) Guido de Baisio, *Lectura super Sexto*, an excerpt from the commentary on *Liber Sextus*, 5.2.11 ad v. 'Testium'. See Parmeggiani, *Consilia*, pp. lxx–lxxi.

36 (100r–108r) Two consultations on the case of goldsmith Heynuš Lugner of Brno (1335–43). See *Quellen*, ed. Patschovsky, pp. 256–8, ed. 259–312.

37 (108v–114r) Thomas Aquinas, Excerpt from *De articulis fidei et ecclesiae sacramentis.*

38 (114v–115r) Consultation of Jacobus of Milan (1306/13). Description: Parmeggiani, *Consilia*, pp. 180–2, ed. 182–5.

39 (115v–119r) Legal definitions of various terms and concepts.

40 (119r–120v) Consultation of Oldradus de Ponte on witchcraft accusations (1327–35). See *Quellen*, ed. Patschovsky, pp. 150–1.

Descriptions: *Quellen*, ed. Patschovsky, pp. 130–51; Parmeggiani, *Consilia*, pp. lxvii–lxxi.

St Florian, Stift St Florian MS XI 234

(285 × 200) Paper. 277 fols. C. 1400.[14] Theological compilation.
Provenance: St Florian, part of the medieval library collection and almost certainly copied at the monastery. See the fifteenth-century ownership mark of at fol. 1r, and a letter formula referring to St Florian at fol. 173v.
Contents: (84v–135v/138v) Zwicker's manual on inquisition of heresy: *Se[quitur] modus inquisicionis se[cte] heresi waldensium.*

---

[14] Watermark AT8500-14461_7 [http://www.wzma.at/10273], Wiener Neustadt, 1402. Information from A. Poznanski.

1 (84va) The short list of converted Waldensians (la) [inc.] *Anno domini M°
ccc° lxxxxi° die iiii mensis septembris* [...] [expl.] *in swicz rasor pannorum.*

2 (84va–85ra) *De vita et conversacione* (vcc) [inc.] *Predicti nominantur magistri
inter eos, apostoli et seniores* [...] [expl.] *nis ad vnum uel ad duos annos etc.*

3 (85ra–vb) *Articuli Waldensium* (a) [inc.] *De articulis hereticorum. Sunt autem
hii articuli quibus fidei katholice contrariantur* [...] [expl.] *extra quam nullus
possit saluari. Hec de Erroneis articulis.*

4 (85vb–87ra) Long question list (ib). [inc.] *Sequitur ordo examinationis suspectorum. Quando producitur suspectus aliquis de heresi, queratur primo* [...]
[expl.] *in quibus penitentie signa visa fuerint euidenter.*

5 (87ra–vb) Anonymous formulary of sentences (fa).

   a (87ra–rb) Declaration of sentence by a bishop. [Inc.] *In nomine domini
Amen. Nos H dei et apostolice sedis gratia episcopus* [...] [expl.] *ponendo
ordinarium in titulo.*

   b (87rb–va) Sentence for incarceration. [Inc.] *Sententia ad Inmurandum
seu incarcerandum hereticos* [...] [expl.] *Nota: de vna sententia capere potes
aliquod ad aliam, si facto congruit.*

   c (87va–vb) Sentence of relapsed heretics. [Inc.] *Sententia ad reliquendum
brachio seculari* [sic] *curie hereticos obstinatos uel relapsos* [...] [expl.] *et
eucharistie ministrentur. Lecta et lata hec sententia etc.*

6 (87vb–88ra) The long list of converted Waldensians (lb) [inc.] *Nota quod isti
fuerunt waldensium hereticorum magistri* [...] [expl.] *recognoscentes errorem
suum sunt conuersi etc.*

7 (88ra–90vb) Formulary for the inquisition in the diocese of Passau (fip).

   a (88ra–va) Episcopal commission for Petrus Zwicker and Martinus
of Prague by Georg von Hohenlohe, bishop of Passau (1389–
1423) through an unnamed official. Undated. [Inc.] *Forma
instituendi seu faciendi inquisitoris. Vniuersis et singulis abbatibus,
prepositis, prioribus* [...] [expl.] *recipere faciet retribucionem. Datum.
Commissio domini episcopi scribitur in prima persona* [?].

   b (88va) Mandate for Fridericus of Garsten to function as Zwicker's
commissary. [Inc.] *Substitucio cooperari in absencia. Nos frater P[etrus]
prouinc[ialis] fratrum ordinis celestinorum per alemaniam* [...] [expl.]
*nostrum sigillum officii inquisicionis, presentibus duximus appendendum.
datum etc.*

   c (88va–vb) Another mandate for Fridericus of Garsten. [Inc.] *Alia
commissio. Frater P[etrus] etc* [...] [expl.] *nostri officii sigillum appresso est
testimonio litteralis.*

   d (88vb) *Citatio suspectorum generalis.*

   e (88vb–89ra) *Citacio specialis ad examinacionem.*

   f (89ra–rb) *Citacio ad recipiendam penitentiam.*

   g (89rb–va) *Excommunicatio contumacis.*

   h (89va–vb) *Alia* [excommunicatio contumacis].

   i (89vb–90ra) *Reaggrauatio siue interdictum post premissa iam facta.*

j (90ra) *Forma littere expurgacionis.*

k (90ra–rb) *Mandatum ad recipiendam penitentiam.*

l (90rb) *Secuntur quedam absoluciones et primo ab excommunicacione simplici.*

m (90rb–va) *Absolucio excommunicacionis et aggrauacionis facta per delegantem.*

n (90va) *Absolucio totalis ferentis sententiam.*

o (90va–vb) *Absolucio dimissorum sub occulta penitencia prius per inquisitorem. Absolutorum sacramentaliter et non relapsorum.*

p (90vb) *Absolucio dimissorum sub penitencia occulta nunquam per inquisitorem absolutorum.*

q (90vb) *Absolucio crucis.*

r (90vb) *Absolucio creptorum* [sic] *de perpetuo carcere visis signis uere conuersionis.*

8 (91ra–93ra) Short question list (iag) [inc.] *Interrogatoria de fidei articulis aduersus hereticos waldenses; Vbi es natus* […] [expl.] *In nomine patris et filij et spiritus sancti. Amen.*

9 (93ra–112rb) CDH [Title:] *Incipit tractatus contra articulos secte waldensium hereticorum.*

10 (112va–115vb) *De auctoritate et forma officii inquisitionis,* cf. OÖLB MS 177, fols. 77v–83r.

11 (115vb–124rb) A fragment of an unpublished manual of an inquisitor, German/Austrian provenance (*c.* 1318–34). [Inc.] *Incipit alter tractatus de officio inquisicionis* […] [expl.] *extra de iure iurando; Etsi christus etc.* Cf. OÖLB MS 177, fols. 86v–99v.

12 (124rb–va) Guido de Baisio, *Lectura super Sexto,* an excerpt from the commentary on *Liber Sextus,* 5.2.11 ad v. 'Testium'. [Inc.] *Item nota in capitulo ut officium li vi° in glossa* […] [expl.] *excommunicamus etc glossa. Gwidonus archidiaconus Bononien*[sis]. Copied here directly after the preceding manual. Cf. OÖLB MS 177, fols. 99v–100r.

13 (124va–125ra) Consultation of Jacobus of Milan (1306/13), cf. OÖLB MS 177, fols. 114v–115r.

14 (125ra–126vb) Legal definitions of various terms and concepts, cf. OÖLB MS 177, fols. 115v–119r.

15 (126vb–127vb) Consultation of Oldradus de Ponte on witchcraft accusations (1327–35). Copied here directly after the preceding text. Cf. OÖLB MS 177, fols. 119r–120v.

16 (127vb–132va) Two consultations on the case of goldsmith Heynuš Lugner of Brno (1335– 43) [Title:] *Questiones bone contra hereticos.* Cf. OÖLB MS 177, fols. 100r–108r.

17 (132vb–133rb) Consultation of Forteguerra (3 March 1298, Tuscany?), cf. OÖLB MS 177, fols. 85r–86r.

18 (133rb–va) *Interpretatio inquisitorum et prelatorum super quibusdam capitulis ex constitutionibus papalibus.* Copied here directly after the consultation of Forteguerra. Cf. OÖLB MS 177 fol. 84r–v.

19 (133vb–135ra) Consultation of Conte Casati (1281–7), cf. OÖLB MS 177, fols. 72v–74r.

20 (135va–138vb) Sermon on sleep and vigilance. The sermon is written in the same fascicule, but in a different hand from the inquisitor's manual. Probably an addition at the end of a fascicule.

Descriptions: A. Czerny, *Die Handschriften der Stiftsbibliothek St. Florian* (Linz, 1871), pp. 99–100; *Quellen*, ed. Patschovsky, pp. 91–2; Biller, *Waldenses*, p. 267; Parmeggiani, *Consilia*, p. xcix.

Appendix 2: Chapters and Titles of the *Cum dormirent homines* according to Jacob Gretser (1613/77)

[Prologue] Cum dormirent homines, venit inimicus eius...	Prologue
I. Nota ortum & originem haereticorum Waldensium	I. Note the beginning and origin of the Waldensian heretics
II. De fidei vnitate & identitate	II. On the unity and identity of faith
III. De continuatione fidei	III. On the continuity of faith
IV. De perpetuitate fidei	IV. On the perpetuity of faith
V. Vnde pri[m]us Waldensis ordinatus fuerit?	V. By whom was the first Waldensian ordained?
VI. Ex quibus probetur vnitas	VI. By which the unity is proven
VII. Quod fides debeat esse manifesta probatur de Christo	VII. That faith ought to be manifest is shown by Christ
VIII. Argumenta Waldensium cum solutionibus	VIII. Waldensian arguments with solutions
IX. Probatio eiusdem per Apostolos	IX. Proof of them [solutions] through the Apostles
X. Quod Waldensis non praedicat mundialiter viuentibus	X. That the Waldensian does not preach to those leading a wordly life
XI. Quod haeresiarcha Waldensis non primo inducit aliquem, nec, per se	XI. That the Waldensian heresiarch does not lead anyone [to his sect], and not by himself
XII. Quod haeretici diuersarum sectarum damnant se mutuo	XII. That heretics of different sects condemn each other
XIII. Quod Waldensis haereticus timet publice praedicare	XIII. That the Waldensian heretic is afraid of preaching publicly
XIV. De temerario iudicio Waldensium	XIV. On the rash judgement of the Waldensians
XV. De multitudine saluandorum; contra eosdem Waldenses loquitur	XV. On the multitude of the saved: he [the author] speaks against those Waldensians

XVI. De obtrectationibus Waldensium contra presbyteros Ecclesiae, etc.	XVI. On the disparagement of the Church's priests by the Waldensians
XVII. Exempla familiaria de Sacramentis a quibuscunque collatis	XVII. Familiar examples of sacraments administered by whomever
XVIII. De obedientia exhibenda malis presbyteris	XVIII. On the obedience that should be shown to bad priests
XIX. De incredulitate B. Virginis & aliorum sanctorum	XIX. On disbelief in the Blessed Virgin and other saints
XX. Dicunt haeretici (Waldenses), quod solus Deus sit laudandus, etc	XX. Waldensian heretics say that only God is to be praised, etc.
XXI. Quod solum sint duae viae	XXI. That there are only two ways
XXII. De sepultura in coemeterio	XXII. On burial in the cemetery
XXIII. De incredulitate consecrationis Ecclesiae	XXIII. On disbelief in church consecration
XXIV. De incredulitate altaris consecrati	XXIV. On disbelief in altar consecration
X[X]V. De incredulitate vestium sacerdotalium, salis & aquae, cinerum & aliorum.	XXV. On disbelief in priests' vestments, salt, water, ashes and so on
XXVI. De incredulitate dedicationis Ecclesiarum	XXVI. On disbelief in church dedication
XXVII. De incredulitate cantus Ecclesiae	XXVII. On disbelief in ecclesiastical singing
XXVIII. De incredulitate Horarum Canonicarum	XXVIII. On disbelief in canonical hours
XXIX. Probatio Horarum Canonicarum	XXIX. Proof of canonical hours
XXX. De incrudelitate [sic] indulgentiarum	XXX. On disbelief in indulgences
XXXI. De anno Iubilaeo	XXXI. On jubilee years
XXXII. De excommunicatione	XXXII. On excommunication
XXXIII. De incredulitate imaginum	XXXIII. On disbelief in images
XXXIV. De incredulitate omnium que sacerdotes faciunt circa obsessos	XXXIV. On disbelief in all that priests do with people who are possessed
XXXV. De studiis priuilegiatis	XXXV. On universities
XXXVI. De incredulitate iuramenti quantumcunque iudicaliter facti	XXXVI. On disbelief in oath-taking, however judicially done

Appendix 3: The Circulation of the *Processus Petri* together with the *Cum dormirent homines*

A: Zwicker's manual in Austria, c. 1395–6	B: Compilations with *terminus post quem* 1395			C: *terminus post quem* 1397		D: *terminus post quem* 1398					E: *terminus post quem* 1403	F: *terminus post quem* 1425			G: CDH together with a single text of PP			
St Florian, MS XI 234	Salzburg, MS b V 1	BAV MS Pal. lat. 677	Göttweig, MS XV 250	Seitenstetten MS 188	Seitenstetten MS 252	BSB MS Clm 5338	BSB MS Clm 15125	BSB MS Clm 22373	St Paul im Lavanttal, MS 77/4	Wolfenbüttel, HAB MS Guelf. 431 Helmst	Würzburg, UB MS M. ch. f. 51	Augsburg, UB MS II. 1.2° 129	Salzburg, MS b VIII 9	Würzburg, UB I. t. f. 234	Budapest, NSL MS 106	Vyšší Brod, MS 61	Vienna, ÖNB MS 5393	St Paul im Lavanttal, MS 26/4
		iag	CDH	iag	Zm	CDH	Zm	Zm	Zm	Zm*	iag	Zms	Zms	CDH	iag	iag	iag	Zm
la	la*	la	iag	CDH	nar	fb	iag	nar	iag	nar	fc	ial	ial	Zms	CDH	CDH	CDH	CDH
vcc	vcc	vcc	la	[x]	la	Zm	CDH	iag	CDH	la	la	CDH	CDH	ial*			CDH	
a	a	a	vcc	Zm	vcc	iag	fb	CDH	fb	iag*	vcc	fd	fd					
ib	ibg	ib	a	nar	a			fb		fb*	a							
fa		CDH	ib	la	iag					CDH*	ib							
lb	lb		ib	vcc	CDH					[x]	lb							
fip				a						CDH*	CDH							
iag	CDH			ib/ia*						[x]								
CDH										CDH*								
[x]*																		
*Material copied from Linz, OÖLB MS 177	*Only the first sentence			*Only the first sentences						*Fragmentary				*only de dicenda veritate'				

Note: The sections of PP are indicated by the abbreviations described in Chapter 3. In addition: CDH = the *Cum dormirent homines*; [x] material not part of the PP, either later additions to empty leaves or binding mistakes. See Appendix 1 for detailed manuscript descriptions.

Appendix 4: Inquisitors' Manuals of St Florian and Linz

The texts of St Florian, MS XI 234 are collated with the respective sections of Linz, OÖLB MS 177. The St Florian manual is a combination of (a) descriptions of Waldensians and question lists on their errors, composed in the beginning of the 1390s (texts 1–4, 6, 8); (b) formulas relating to the beginning of the inquisition by Petrus Zwicker, Martinus of Prague and Zwicker's commissary Fridericus of Garsten in the diocese of Passau (texts 5, 7); (c) Zwicker's treatise *Cum dormirent homines* (text 9); and (d) material copied from the Linz inquisitor's manual (shaded). For a more accurate description of the texts see the manuscript descriptions in Appendix 1.

	St Florian, MS XI 234	Linz, OÖLB MS 177 (numbers refer to the MS description)
1	Short list of converted Waldensians	Short notices, questionnaires and excerpts (1-11)
2	*De vita et conversacione*	French inquisitor's manual (12)
3	*Articuli Waldensium*	Excerpts from canon law on excommunication and absolution (13)
4	Long question list without oaths	*De hereticorum inquisitione* (14)
5	Anonymous formulary of sentences	Fragment of the German confession of Swatibor of Langendorf (15)
6	Long list of converted Waldensians	Four papal letters (16)
7	Formulary for the inquisition in the diocese of Passau	Excerpts from canon law (17)
8	Short question list with German oaths	*Ad reprimenda multorum facinora* (Henry VII, 2 April 1313) (18)
9	*Cum dormirent homines*	Excerpt from VI 5.2.7 with glossa (19)
10	*De auctoritate et forma officii inquisitionis*	A verse of a Marian hymn (20)
11	Fragment of an unpublished inquisitor's manual, German/Austrian	*Quatuor dicunt secte hereticorum* (21)
12	Guido de Baisio, *Lectura super Sexto*, excerpt	Excerpts from legislation against heretics (22)
13	Consultation of Jacobus of Milan	Consultation of Conte Casati (23)

	St Florian, MS XI 234	Linz, OÖLB MS 177 (numbers refer to the MS description)
14	Legal definitions of various terms and concepts	Five papal bulls (24)
15	Consultation of Oldradus de Ponte	Bohemian interrogatorium on heresy (25
16	Two consultations of Brno	*De auctoritate et forma officii inquisitionis* (26)
17	Consultation of Forteguerrra	French question list against Waldensians (27)
18	*Interpretatio inquisitorum et prelatorum super quibusdam capitulis [...]*	Formula of abjuration of Waldensians (28)
19	Consultation of Conte Casati	*Interpretatio inquisitorum et prelatorum super quibusdam capitulis [...]* (29)
20		Decretal of Innocent III, *Litteras vestras* (30)
21		Consultation of Forteguerra (31)
22		Excerpt from Bernand Gui on Beguines (32)
23		Interrogatory on Waldensians (33)
24		Fragment of an unpublished inquisitor's manual, German/Austrian (34)
25		Guido de Baisio, *Lectura super Sexto*, excerpt (35)
26		Two consultations of Brno (36)
27		Thomas Aquinas, Excerpt from *De articulis fidei et ecclesiae sacramentis* (37)
28		Consultation of Jacobus of Milan (38)
29		Legal definitions of various terms and concepts (39)
30		Consultation of Oldradus de Ponte (40)

Appendix 5: Collation of Formularies in St Florian, MS XI 234 and Würzburg, UB MS M. ch. f. 51

Title in St Florian, MS XI 234	St Florian, MS XI 234, fols.	Würzburg, UB MS M. ch. f. 51, fols.	Haupt, *Der Waldensische Ursprung des Codex Teplensis*
Secuntur quedam absoluciones et primo ab excommunicacione simplici	90rb	28v	Nr. 3, p. 35
Absolucio excommunicacionis et aggravacionis facta per delegantem	90rb–va	28v	Nr. 1, p. 34
Absolucio totalis ferentis sententiam	90va	28v–29r	–
Absolucio dimissorum sub occulta penitencia prius per inquisitorem absolu-torum sacramentaliter et non relapsorum	90va–vb	29r	Nr. 2, p. 34–5
Absolucio dimissorum sub penitencia occulta nunquam per inquisitorem absolutorum	90vb	–	–
Absolucio crucis	90vb	29r	–
Absolucio creptorum [sic] de perpetuo carcere visis signis uere conuersionis	90vb	29r–v	–

Bibliography

Primary sources

Manuscripts

Augsburg, Staats- und Stadtbibliothek (StaSB)
MS 2° Cod 185
MS 2° Cod 338

Augsburg, Universitätsbibliothek (UB)
MS II. 1. 2° 78
MS II. 1. 2° 127
MS II. 1. 2° 129

Berlin, Staatsbibliothek zu Berlin – Preußischer Kulturbesitz
MS Theol. lat. fol. 704

Gdańsk, Polska Akademia Nauk Biblioteka (PAN)
MS Mar. F. 294
MS Mar. F. 295

Göttweig, Stiftsbibliothek
MS XV 250
MS 811 (rot)

Herzogenburg, Stiftsbibliothek
MS 22

Kraków, Bibliotheca Jagellonica
MS DD X 22 (cat. 2471)

Leipzig, Universitätsbibliothek (UB)
MS 602

Linz, Oberösterreichisches Landesarchiv (OÖLA)
Stiftsarchiv Gleink, MS Nr. 2
Stiftsarchiv Gleink, 1418 V 19
Stiftsarchiv Garsten, 1419 III 08

Linz, Oberösterreichische Landesbibliothek (OÖLB)
MS 177
MS 292
MS 296

Munich, Bayerische Staatsbibliothek (BSB)
MS Clm 1329
MS Clm 3764
MS Clm 5338
MS Clm 5614
MS Clm 8680
MS Clm 14959
MS Clm 15125
MS Clm 16170
MS Clm 17562
MS Clm 19539
MS Clm 22373
MS Clm 26756

Paris, Bibliothèque Mazarine
MS 1683 (1185)

Paris, Bibliothèque nationale de France,
MS Lat. 4224

Philadelphia, Kislak Center for Special Collections, Rare Books and
    Manuscripts, University of Pennsylvania (UPenn)
MS Codex 76

Prague, Knihovna Metropolitní kapituly (KMK)
MS C LX
MS C LXIX
MS D LI
MS K IX

Prague, Národní knihovna České republiky (NKCR)
MS I. D. 43
MS I. D. 44
MS IV. B. 4
MS VII. A. 16/3
MS VII. A. 16/4
MS X. B. 2
MS X. B. 7
MS XI. D. 8

MS XIII. E. 5
MS XIII. E. 7

Salzburg, Erzabtei St Peter
MS b V 1
MS b VIII 9

St Florian, Stift St Florian
MS XI 96
MS XI 152
MS XI 234

St Paul im Lavanttal, Stift St Paul
MS 26/4
MS 77/4

Seitenstetten, Stift Seitenstetten
MS 106
MS 188
MS 213
MS 252

Trier, Stadtbibliothek
MS 680/879

Vatican City, Biblioteca Apostolica Vaticana (BAV)
MS Pal. lat. 677
MS Vat. lat. 1240
MS Vat. lat. 4265

Weimar, Herzogin Anna Amalia Bibliothek (HAAB)
MS Fol 20

Vienna, Österreichische Nationalbibliothek (ÖNB)
MS 1588
MS 3050
MS 3748
MS 4219
MS 4511
MS 5393

Vienna, Österreichische Staatsarchiv (ÖStA), Haus-, Hof- und Staatsarchiv
    (HHStA)
Allgemeine Urkundenreihe 1408 II 17

Wiesbaden, Hessische Landesbibliothek
MS 35

Wolfenbüttel, Herzog August Bibliothek (HAB)
MS Guelf. 403 Helmst
MS Guelf. 431 Helmst
MS Guelf. 348 Novi

Wrocław, Biblioteka Uniwersytecka (BU)
MS I F 230
MS I F 707
MS I Q 43
MS Mil. II 58

Würzburg, Universitätsbibliothek (UB)
I. t. f. 234, part 7
MS M. ch. f. 51
MS M. ch. f. 186

Vyšší Brod (Hohenfurt)
MS 61

Zwettl, Stiftsbibliothek
MS 185

Transcriptions and handwritten catalogues

Friedrich, J. C., 'Catalogus codicum scriptorum qui in Bibliotheca Regia ac
Academica Wratislaviensi servantur', 4 vols. [handwritten catalogue]
Biblioteka Uniwersytecka Wrocław, Akc. 1967/1 (Wrocław, 1821–3).
Goeber W., and J. Klapper. 'Katalog rękopisów dawnej Biblioteki
Uniwersyteckiej we Wrocławiu', 26 vols. [handwritten catalogue]
Biblioteka Uniwersytecka Wrocław. Akc. 1967/2 (Wrocław, c. 1920–44).
Jungwirth, A., 'Beschreibung der Handschriften des Stiftes St. Peter in
Salzburg', 6 vols. [handwritten catalogue] (Salzburg, 1910–12).
Moeli, V., 'Manuscripten-Catalog der Stiftsbibliohek zu Göttweig', 3 vols.
[handwritten catalogue, undated].
Segl, P. 'Manifest des Inquisitors Peter Zwicker'. Collation of Zwicker's
manifest of 1395, undated. Used with the permission of Peter Segl.
SFB 226 Würzburg/Eichstätt. Teilprojekt 5: Ulrich von Pottenstein,
Ketzerstellen: Dekalog. Unpublished transkription from Kalocsa,
Föszékesegyházi Könyvtár, MS 629.
Ulrich von Pottenstein, excerpts from his translation of the *Credo* part of *Cum
dormirent homines*. Unpublished transcription by Christine Wolf, 2000.

Winner, G., 'Katalog der Handschriften der Stiftsbibliothek Herzogenburg' [handwritten catalogue] (St Pölten, 1978).

Printed primary sources

Alain of Lille, *Distinctiones dictionum theologicalium*, PL 210.

———, *Contra haereticos*, PL 210.

D'Alatri, M., *L'inquisizione francescana nell'Italia centrale del duecento* (Rome, 1996).

———, 'L'inquisizione francescana nell'Italia centrale nel decolo xiii (Finis)'. *Collectanea Francescana* 23 (1953), 51–169.

Augustine, *Contra epistolam Manichaei*, PL 42.

———, *De doctrina christiana*, ed. and trans. R. P. H. Green (Oxford, 1996).

———, *De mendacio*, PL 40.

Bernard of Clairvaux, *Sermones de diversis*, PL 183.

Bernard Gui, *Practica inquisitionis heretice pravitatis*, ed. C. Douais (Paris, 1886).

Bernardino da Siena, *Prediche volgari: sul campo di Siena 1427*, ed. C. Delcorno, 2 vols. (Milan, 1989).

Bible: see Vulgate.

Boethius, *Philosophiae consolatio*, LLT-A.

———, *The Consolation of Philosophy*, trans. R. Green, 4th edn (Indianapolis, 1962).

Bonaventure, 'Collationes de decem praeceptis', in *Opera Omnia* 5 (Quaracchi, 1891).

———, *Commentaria in Quatuor Libros Sententiarum Magistri Petri Lombardi*. Opera Omnia 3 (Quaracchi, 1887).

Carpzov, J. B., *Analecta Fastorum Zittaviensium Oder Historischer Schauplatz Der Löblichen Alten Sechs-Stadt des Marggraffthums Ober-Lausitz Zittau*, 5 vols. (Zittau, 1716).

Decretum magistri Gratiani (Concordia discordantium canonum), LLT-A.

Deutsche Reichstagsakten unter König Wenzel, Abt. 1–3 (1376–1400), 2nd edn (Göttingen, 1956).

Döllinger, J. J. I. von, *Beiträge zur Sektengeschichte des Mittelalters. Zweiter theil. Dokumente vornehmlich zur Geschichte der Valdesier und Katharer* (Munich, 1890).

Douais, C., 'Les hérétiques du Midi au XIIIe siècle. Cinq pièces inédites', *Annales du Midi* 3 (1891), 367–79.

Ebendorfer, T., *Tractatus de schismatibus*, ed. H. Zimmermann, MGH Scriptores Rerum Germanicarum NS 20 (Munich, 2004).

Emler, Josef, ed., 'Kronica Beneše z Weitmile', *FRB* IV (1884), 439–548.

Eymericus, Nicolaus, *Directorium Inqvisitorum*, ed. Francesco Peña (Rome, 1578–9).

FitzRalph, Richard, *Summa Domini Armacani in Questionibus Armenorum nouiter impressa Et Correcta a magistro nostro Iohanne ludoris* (Paris, 1512).

Ferrer, Vincent, *Sermones de cuaresma en Suiza, 1404: Couvent des Cordeliers, ms 62*, ed. F. M. Gimeno Blay and M. L. Mandingorra Llavata (Valencia, 2009).

——, *Opera seu sermones de tempore et sanctis, cum Tractatu de Vita Spirituali*, ed. C. Erhard (Augsburg, 1729).

Florianová, H., Martínková, D., Silagiová, Z. and Šedinová, H., eds., *Quadragesimale Admontense – Quadragesimale Admontské*, Fontes Latini Bohemorum 6 (Prague, 2006).

Friess, G., 'Patarener, Begharden und Waldenser in Österreich während des Mittelalters', *Österreichische Vierteljahresschrift für katholische Theologie* 11 (1872), 209–72.

Friedberg, A., ed., *Corpus iuris canonici: editio Lipsiensis secunda post Aemilii Ludouici Richteri curas ad librorum manu scriptorum et editionis romanae fidem recognouit et adnotatione critica*, Pars 1, *Decretum magistri Gratiani*, 2nd edn (Graz, 1959).

——, *Corpus iuris canonici: editio Lipsiensis secunda post Aemilii Ludouici Richteri curas ad librorum manu scriptorum et editionis romanae fidem recognouit et adnotatione critica*, Pars 2, *Decretalium collectiones*, 2nd edn (Graz, 1959).

Gerson, Jean, *Œuvres complètes*, ed. P. Glorieux, 10 vols. (Paris, 1960–73).

Gregory I, *Moralia*, PL 75.

Gretser, J., ed., *Lucae Tvdensis episcopi, Scriptores aliqvot svccedanei contra sectam waldensivm*, in *Maxima bibliotheca veterum patrum et antiquorum scriptorum ecclesiasticorum*, ed. M. de La Bigne, 27 vols. (Lyon, 1677), XXV, 252–312.

——, 'Refvtatio Errorvm, Quibus Waldenses distinentur, incerto auctore', in *Lucae Tvdensis episcopi, Scriptores aliqvot svccedanei contra sectam waldensivm*, in *Maxima bibliotheca veterum patrum et antiquorum scriptorum ecclesiasticorum*, ed. M. de La Bigne, 27 vols. (Lyon, 1677), XXV, 302G–307F.

Guilelmus Peraldus (William Perald), *Summa virtutum ac vitiorum* (Lyon, 1554).

Guillaume d'Auvergne (William of Auvergne), *Opera omnia*, 2 vols. (Paris, 1674).

Guillaume (William) Durand of Mende, *Rationale diuinorum officiorum*, LLT-A.

Hamesse, J., *Les Auctoritates Aristotelis: une florilège médiéval* (Louvain, 1974).

Hayer, G., 'Paternoster-Auslegung: nach der Handschrift a X 13 des Erzstiftes St. Peter zu Salzburg kritisch herausgegeben und eingeleitet. 1, I. und III. Teil' (unpublished Ph.D. dissertation, University of Salzburg, 1972).

——, 'Paternoster-Auslegung: nach der Handschrift a X 13 des Erzstiftes St. Peter zu Salzburg kritisch herausgegeben und eingeleitet. 2, II. Teil' (unpublished Ph.D. dissertation, University of Salzburg, 1972).

Haymo of Halberstadt, *Commentaria in psalmos*, PL 116.

———, *Expositio in Apocalypsin*, PL 117.

Heimpel, H., *Drei Inquisitions-Verfahren aus dem Jahre 1425: Akten der Prozesse gegen die deutschen Hussiten Johannes Drändorf und Peter Turnau sowie gegen Drändorfs Diener Martin Borchard* (Göttingen, 1969).

Hlaváček, I., and Hledíková, Z., eds., *Protocollum visitationis archidiaconatus Pragensis annis 1379-1382 per Paulum de Janowicz Archidiaconum Pragensem factae* (Prague, 1973).

Höfler, C., ed., *Concilia Pragensia = Prager Synodal-Beschlüsse* (Prague, 1862).

Höfler, K., *Geschichtschreiber der husitischen Bewegung in Böhmen*, 3 vols. (Vienna, 1856).

Hostiensis, *Summa Aurea*, 5 vols. (Venice, 1574).

Hugh of St. Victor, 'The Diligent Examiner', in *Interpretation of Scripture: Theory. A Selection of Works of Hugh, Andrew, Richard and Godfrey of St Victor, and of Robert Melun*, ed. F. T. Harkins and F. van Liere (Hyde Park, 2013), pp. 231–52.

Humbertus de Romanis, *De eruditione predicatorum*, ed. M. La Bigne, *Maxima bibliotheca veterum patrum et antiquorum scriptorum ecclesiasticorum*, 27 vols. (Lyon, 1677), XXV, 424A–567E

Hus, Joannes (Jan Hus), 'Replica contra Praedicatorem Plznensem, M. Joannis Hus, Anno M.CCCC.XII', in *Historia et monumenta Joannis Hus [...] recensita omnia juxta antiquam anni MDLVIII editionem norimbergensem Joannis Montani et Ulrici Neuberi* (Nuremberg, 1715), pp. 179–85.

Illyricus, Mathias Flacius, *Catalogus testium veritatis, qui ante nostram aetatem pontifici romano ejusque erroribus reclamarunt [...]* (Strasbourg, 1562).

Jerome, *Commentaria in Aggaeum*, PL 25.

———, *Commentarii in Isaiam*, LLT-A.

———, *Epistulae*, LLT-A.

Kurze, D., ed., *Quellen zur Ketzergeschichte Brandenburgs und Pommerns* (Berlin, 1975).

Liber decanorum facultatis philosophicae universitatis Pragensis, ab anno Christi 1367, usque ad annum 1585, 2 vols. (Prague, 1830), I.

Library of Latin Texts – Series A and Series B (LLT-A; LLT-B). Accessed in Brepolis, Brepols Publishers, http://clt.brepolis.net/llta/Default.aspx.

Loserth, J., 'Beiträge zur Geschichte der husitischen Bewegung I. Der Codex Epistolaris des Erzbischofs von Prag Johann von Jenzenstein', *Archiv für österreichische Geschichte* 55 (1877), 267–400.

Martin von Amberg, *Der Gewissensspiegel*, ed. S. N. Werbow (Berlin, 1958).

Matěj of Janov, *Mathiae de Janov dicti Magister Parisiensis Regulae veteris et novi testamenti*, ed. V. Kybal, 5 vols. (Prague, 1907–26).

Menčik, F., 'Milič a dva jeho spisy z r. 1367', *Věstník Královské české společnosti nauk. Třida filosoficko-historicko-filologická* (1890), 309–36.

Modestin, G., ed. *Quellen zur Geschichte der Waldenser von Straßburg*

(1400–1401), MGH Quellen zur Geistesgeschichte des Mittelalters 22 (Hanover, 2007).

Moneta (Cremonensis), *Monetae Adversus Catharos et Valdenses: libri quinque*, ed. T. A. Ricchini (Rome, 1743).

Neumann, A. A., 'Výbor z předhusitských postil', *Archiv literární* 2 (1922), 60–75, 94–102, 121–43, 184–9, 216–22, 233–40, 250–5, 287–90, 319–26, 356–60, 366–76.

Nicholas of Lyra, *Prologus de commendatione Sacrae Scripturae*, PL 113.

Oefele, A. F., von, *Rerum Boicarum scriptores*, 2 vols. (Augsburg, 1763).

Palacký, F., ed., *Documenta Mag. Joannis Hus vitam, doctrinam, causam in Constantiensi concilio actam et controversias de religione in Bohemia anni 1403-1418 motas illustrantia* (Prague, 1869).

Parmeggiani, R., *I consilia procedurali per l'Inquisizione medievale (1235–1330)* (Bologna, 2011).

Patrologia Latina (= PL), *Patrologiae: cursus completus series Latina*, ed. J.-P. Migne, 221 vols. (Paris, 1844–64). Accessed in *Corpus Corporum repositorium operum Latinorum apud universitatem Turicensem*. University of Zürich, <http://www.mlat.uzh.ch/MLS/index.php?lang=0>.

Patschovsky, A., ed., *Quellen zur böhmischen Inquisition im 14. Jahrhundert* (Weimar, 1979).

Patschovsky, A, and Selge, K-V., eds., *Quellen zur Geschichte der Waldenser* (Gütersloh, 1973).

Paulhart, H., ed., *Mittelalterliche Bibliothekskataloge Österreichs. Band 5. Oberösterreich* (Vienna 1971).

Peter von Pillichsdorf, 'Fragmentvm ex Tractatv Petri de Pilichdorff contra pauperes de Lugduno. Ex M.S.C. Monasterij Tegernseensi', in *Lucae Tvdensis episcopi, Scriptores aliqvot svccedanei contra sectam waldensivm*, ed. J. Gretser, in *Maxima bibliotheca veterum patrum et unliquorum scriptorum ecclesiasticorum*, ed. M. de La Bigne, 27 vols. (Lyon, 1677), XXV, 299E–302F.

Polc, J. V., and Hledíková Z., eds., *Pražské synody a koncily předhusitské doby* (Prague, 2002).

Preger, W., *Beiträge zur Geschichte der Waldesier im Mittelalter* (Munich, 1877).

———, ed. 'Der Tractat des David von Augsburg über die Waldesier', *Abhandlungen der historischen Classe der koniglich bayrischen Akademie der Wissenschaften* 14 (1879), 203–35.

Preuenhueber, V., *Annales Styrenses: sammt dessen übrigen historisch- und genealogischen Schrifften, zur Erläuterung der österreich. steyermärckischen und steyerischen Geschichten* (Nuremberg, 1740).

Prochno, J., 'Regesten zur Geschichte der Stadt und des Landes Zittau 1234-1437', *NLM* 114 (1938), 1–421.

Reiter, E. H., ed., *Stella Clericorum*, Toronto Medieval Latin Texts 23 (Toronto, 1997).

Ruf, Paul, ed., *Mittelalterliche Bibliothekskataloge Deutschlands und der Schweiz*, vol. 3, parts 3–4 (Munich, 1961).

Rufinus, *Summa Decretorum*, ed. H. Singer (Aalen, 1963).

Schmidt, A. ed., 'Tractatus contra hereticos Beckardos, Lulhardos et Swestriones des Wasmud von Homburg', *Archiv für mittelrheinische Kirchengeschichte* 14 (1962), 336–86.

Schmidt, C., 'Actenstücke besonders zur Geschichte der Waldenser', *Zeitschrift für die historische Theologie* 22 (1852), 238–62.

Scriptores Rerum Lusaticarum, n.s. 1 (Görlitz, 1839).

Seemüller, J., ed., *Österreichische Chronik von den 95 Herrschaften*, MGH Deutsche Chroniken 6 (Hanover, 1909).

Selge, K-V., ed., *Texte zur Inquisition* (Gütersloh, 1967).

Tamburini, F., and Schmugge, L., eds., *Häresie und Luthertum* (Paderborn, 2000).

Truhlář, J., 'Inkvisice Waldenských v Trnavě r. 1400', *Česky časopis historický* 9 (1903), 196–8.

———, 'Pabĕrky z rukopisů Klementinských Nr. 26', *Vestník Ceské akademie* 8 (1899), 353–7.

Thesaurus Iuris Franconici Oder Sammlung theils gedruckter theils ungedruckter Abhandlungen, Dissertationen, Programmen, Gutachten, Gesätze, Urkunden etc. etc., welche das Fränkische und besonders Hochfürstlich-Wirzburgische Geistliche, Weltliche, Bürgerliche, Peinliche, Lehen-, Polizey- und Kameralrecht erläutern etc, ed. J. M. Schneidt, 12 vols. (Würzburg, 1787–94).

Thomas Aquinas, *Summa theologiae* 2a 2ae, LLT-A.

Uiblein, P., ed., *Acta facultatis artium universitatis Vindobonensis 1385–1416* (Graz, 1968).

Ulrich von Pottenstein, *Dekalog-Auslegung: das erste Gebot: Text und Quellen*, ed. G. Baptist-Hlawatsch (Tübingen, 1995).

Utz Tremp, K., ed., *Quellen zur Geschichte der Waldenser von Freiburg im Üchtland (1399–1439)*, MGH Quellen zur Geistesgeschichte des Mittelalters 18 (Hanover, 2000).

Vulgate [Latin Bible], *Biblia Sacra Vulgatae editionis*. The Clementine Vulgate Project, online text and VulSearch 4.2. <http://vulsearch.sourceforge.net/index.html>. Translations accroding to Douay-Rheims translation. Electronic version produced from printed edition of the John Murphy Company, Baltimore, MD, USA (1899), by John Houston.

Wakefield, W. L. and Evans, A. P., eds., *Heresies of the High Middle Ages* (New York, 1969).

Zwicker, Petrus, [*Cum dormirent homines*] '[Pseudo]-Petri de Pilichdorf contra Haeresin Waldensium Tractatus', in *Lucae Tvdensis episcopi, Scriptores aliqvot svccedanei contra sectam waldensivm*, ed. J. Gretser, in *Maxima bibliotheca veterum patrum et antiquorum scriptorum ecclesiasticorum*, ed. M. de La Bigne, 27 vols. (Lyon, 1677), XXV, 277F–299G.

Secondary works

Ames, C. C., *Righteous Persecution: Inquisition, Dominicans, and Christianity in the Middle Ages* (Philadelphia, 2009).

Anderson, C. C., 'The Six Errors. Hus on Simony', in *Reassessing Reform: A Historical Investigation into Church Renewal*, ed. C. M. Bellitto and D. Z. Flanagin (Washington, DC, 2012), pp. 105–23.

Armand-Hugon, A., and Gonnet, G., *Bibliografia Valdese*, BSSV 63 (Torre Pellice, 1953).

Arnold, J. H., 'Benedict of Alignan's *Tractatus fidei contra diversos errores*: A Neglected Anti-Heresy Treatise' [forthcoming].

———, 'The Cathar Middle Ages as a Methodological and Historiographical Problem', in *Cathars in Question*, ed. A. Sennis (York, 2016), pp. 53–78.

———, *Inquisition and Power: Catharism and the Confessing Subject in Medieval Languedoc* (Philadelphia, 2001).

———, 'Inquisition, Texts and Discourse', in *Texts and the Repression of Medieval Heresy*, ed. C. Bruschi and P. Biller (York, 2003), pp. 63–80.

———, 'Responses to the Postmodern Challenge; or, What Might History Become?', *European History Quarterly* 37 (2007), 109–32.

Arnold, K., *Niklashausen 1476* (Baden-Baden, 1980).

Audisio, G., 'Le Sentiment de supériorité dans les minorités: l'exemple vaudois (xve–xvie siècle)', *BSSV* 194 (2004), 25–36.

———, *The Waldensian Dissent: Persecution and Survival, c. 1170–c. 1570* (Cambridge, 1999).

Bailey, M. D., *Battling Demons: Witchcraft, Heresy, and Reform in the Late Middle Ages* (University Park, 2003).

Bainton, R. H., 'The Parable of the Tares as the Proof Text for Religious Liberty to the End of the Sixteenth Century', *Church History* 1 (1932), 67–89.

Baptist-Hlawatsch, G. 'Einführung', in *Dekalog-Auslegung: das erste Gebot: Text und Quellen*, ed. G. Baptist-Hlawatsch (Tübingen, 1995), pp. 1*–64*.

———, *Das katechetische Werk Ulrichs von Pottenstein: sprachliche und rezeptionsgeschichtliche Untersuchungen* (Tübingen, 1980).

Barrow, J., *The Clergy in the Medieval World* (Cambridge, 2015).

Bartoniek, E., *Codices manu scripti Latini 1. Codices Latini medii aevi* (Budapest, 1940).

Bartoš, F. M., 'Husitika a bohemika několika knihoven německých a švýcarských', *Vestník královské ceské spolecnosti nauk. Trída filosoficko-historicko-jazykozpytná* 5 (1932), 1–92.

Benrath, G. A., *Wyclifs Bibelkommentar* (Berlin, 1966).

Bériou, N. 'Les sermons latins après 1200', in *The Sermon*, ed. B. M. Kienzle, Typologie des sources du Moyen Âge occidental 81–83 (Turnhout, 2000), pp. 363–447.

Biller, P. 'Aspects of the Waldenses in the Fourteenth Century, including
an Edition of their Correspondence' (unpublished Ph.D. dissertation,
University of Oxford, 1974).

———, 'Bernard Gui, Peter Zwicker, and the Geography of Valdismo or
Valdismi', *BSSV* 200 (2007), 31–43.

———, 'Bernard Gui, Sex and Luciferanism', in *Praedicatores, inquisitores
I. The Dominicans and the Medieval Inquisition. Acts of the 1st International
Seminar on the Dominicans and the Inquisition 23–25 February 2002*,
Dissertationes Historicae 29 (Rome, 2004), pp. 455–70.

———, '"Deep Is the Heart of Man, and Inscrutable": Signs of Heresy in
Medieval Languedoc', in *Text and Controversy from Wyclif to Bale: Essays
in Honour of Anne Hudson*, ed. H. Barr and A. M. Hutchison (Turnhout,
2005), pp. 267–80.

———, 'Editions of Trials and Lost Texts', in *Valdesi medievali. Bilanci e
prospettive di ricerca*, ed. M. Benedetti (Turin, 2009) 23–36.

———, 'Fingerprinting an Anonymous Description of the Waldensians',
in *Texts and the Repression of Medieval Heresy*, ed. C. Bruschi and P. Biller
(York, 2003), pp. 163–207.

———, 'Goodbye to Waldensianism?', *Past and Present* 192 (2006), pp. 3–33.

———, 'Heretics Doing Things Secretly', in *Secrets and Discovery in the
Middle Ages: Proceedings of the 5th European Congress of the Fédération
Internationale des Instituts d'Études Médiévales (Porto, 25th to 29th June
2013)*, ed. J. Meirinhos, C. López Alcalde and J. Rebalde (Barcelona, 2017),
pp. 15–26.

———, 'Intellectuals and the Masses. Oxen and She-Asses in the Medieval
Church', in *The Oxford Handbook of Medieval Christianity*, ed. J. H. Arnold
(Oxford, 2014), pp. 323–39.

———, 'Moneta's Confutation of Heresies and the Valdenses', *BSSV* 219
(2016), 27–42.

———, *The Waldenses, 1170–1530: Between a Religious Order and a Church*,
Variorum CS 676 (Aldershot, 2001).

———, 'Waldensians by the Baltic', in *Companion to the Waldenses*, ed. M.
Benedetti and E. Cameron (Leiden, 2018) [forthcoming].

———, 'Why no Food? Waldensian Followers in Bernard Gui's *Practica
inquisitionis* and *culpe*', in *Texts and the Repression of Medieval Heresy*, ed. C.
Bruschi and P. Biller (York, 2003), pp. 127–46.

Biller, P., Bruschi, C. and Sneddon S., eds., *Inquisitors and Heretics in
Thirteenth-Century Languedoc: Edition and Translation of Toulouse Inquisition
Depositions, 1273–1282* (Leiden, 2011).

———, 'Introduction', in *Inquisitors and Heretics in Thirteenth-Century
Languedoc*, ed. P. Biller, C. Bruschi and S. Sneddon (Leiden, 2011),
pp. 3–127.

Bistřický, J., Drkal, F. and Kouřil, M., *Seznam Rukopisu Metropolitní Kapituly v
Olomouci* (Prague, 1961).

Bivolarov, V., *Inquisitoren-Handbücher. Papsturkunden und juristische Gutachten aus dem 13. Jahrhundert mit Edition des Consilium von Guido Fulcodii*. MGH Studien und Texte 56 (Wiesbaden, 2014).

Børch, M., 'Preface', in *Text and Voice: The Rhetoric of Authority in the Middle Ages*, ed. M. Børch (Odense, 2004), pp. 7–20.

Borchardt, K., *Die Cölestiner: eine Mönchsgemeinschaft des späteren Mittelalters* (Husum, 2006).

Boyle, L.-E., 'Montaillou Revisited: Mentalité and Methodology', in *Pathways to Medieval Peasants*, ed. J. Ambrose Raftis, Papers in Mediaeval Studies 2 (Toronto, 1981), pp. 119–40.

Brenon, A., 'The Waldensian Books', in *Heresy and Literacy, 1000–1530*, ed. P. Biller and A. Hudson (Cambridge, 1994), pp. 137–59.

Bruschi, C., '*Familia inquisitionis*: A Study on the Inquisitors' Entourage (XIII–XIV Centuries)', *Mélanges de l'École française de Rome – Moyen Âge* 125 (2013). <http://journals.openedition.org/mefrm/1519>.

———, *The Wandering Heretics of Languedoc* (Cambridge, 2009).

Buckner, E. D., 'Natalis on Equipollence', The Logic Museum [webpage], 2006. <http://www.logicmuseum.com/opposition/summatotiuslogicae.htm>.

Bueno, I., *Defining Heresy: Inquisition, Theology, and Papal Policy in the Time of Jacques Fournier*, trans. I. Bolognese, T. Brophy and S. Rolfe Prodan (Leiden, 2015).

———, 'False Prophets and Ravening Wolves: Biblical Exegesis as a Tool against Heretics in Jacques Fournier's Postilla on Matthew', *Speculum* 89 (2014), 35–65.

Bürckstümmer, C., 'Waldenser in Dinkelsbühl', *Beiträge zur bayerischen Kirchengeschichte* 19 (1913), 272–75.

Burkhart, P., *Die lateinischen und deutschen Handschriften der Universitäts bibliothek Leipzig. Band 2, Die theologischen Handschriften; Teil 1 (MS. 501–625)*, Katalog der Handschriften der Universitätsbibliothek zu Leipzig 5 (Wiesbaden, 1999).

Bushey, B. C., *Die lateinischen Handschriften bis 1600*, Bibliographien und Kataloge der Herzogin-Anna-Amalia-Bibliothek zu Weimar (Wiesbaden, 2004).

Cameron, E., *Waldenses: Rejections of Holy Church in Medieval Europe* (Oxford, 2000).

Carraway, J., 'Contumacy, Defense Strategy, and Criminal Law in Late Medieval Italy', *Law and History Review* 29 (2011), 99–132.

Carruthers, M., *The Craft of Thought: Meditation, Rhetoric, and the Making of Images, 400–1200* (Cambridge, 1998).

Cegna, R., 'La condizione del valdismo secondo l'inedito "Tractatus bonus contra haereticos" del 1399, attribuibile all'inquisitore della Silesia Giovanni di Gliwice', in *I Valdesi e l'Europa* (Torre Pellice, 1982), pp. 39–66.

——, *Fede ed etica valdese nel quattrocento: il Libro espositivo e il Tesoro e luce della fede* (Turin, 1982).

——, 'Nicola della Rosa Nera detto da Dresda (1380?–1416?), De reliquiis et de veneratione sanctorum: de purgatorio', *Mediaevalia Philosophica Polonorum = Bulletin d'information concernant les recherches sur la philosophie médiévale en Pologne* 23 (1977), 3–171.

——, 'Il Valdismo del '300 come alternativa alla chiesa di Roma', *BSSV* 148 (1980), 49–56.

Chiu, H., 'Alan of Lille's Academic Concept of the Manichee', *Journal of Religious History* 35 (2011), 492–506.

Classen, A., 'Introduction: The Authority of the Written Word, the Sacred Object, and the Spoken Word: A Highly Contested Discourse in the Middle Ages. With a Focus on the Poet Wolfram von Eschenbach and the Mystic Hildegard von Bingen', in *Authorities in the Middle Ages: Influence, Legitimacy, and Power in Medieval Society*, ed. S. Kangas, M. Korpiola and T. Ainonen (Berlin, 2013), pp. 1–24.

Cohn, N., *Europe's Inner Demons: The Demonization of Christians in Medieval Christendom*, revised edn (London, 2000).

Connolly, M., 'Compiling the Book', in *The Production of Books in England 1350–1500*, ed. A. Gillespie and D. Wakelin (Cambridge, 2011), 129–49.

Conrad, K., 'Herzogliche Schwäche und städtische Macht in der zweiten Hälfte des 14. und im 15. Jahrhundert', in *Deutsche Geschichte im Osten Europas*, ed. W. Buchholz (Berlin, 1999), pp. 127–202.

Cossar, R., *The Transformation of the Laity in Bergamo, 1265–c. 1400* (Leiden, 2006).

Cropp, Glynnis M., 'Boethius in Translation in Medieval Europe', in *Translation: An International Encyclopedia of Translation Studies*, ed. H. Kittel, J. House and B. Schultze (Berlin, 2007), pp. 1329–37.

Czerwon, A., *Predigt gegen Ketzer: Studien zu den lateinischen Sermones Bertholds von Regensburg* (Tübingen, 2011).

Daileader, P., 'Local Experiences of the Great Western Schism', in *A Companion to the Great Western Schism (1378–1417)*, ed. J. Rollo-Koster and T. M. Izbicki (Leiden, 2009), pp. 89–121.

Deane, J. K., 'Archiepiscopal Inquisitions in the Middle Rhine: Urban Anticlericalism and Waldensianism in Late Fourteenth-Century Mainz', *Catholic Historical Review* 92 (2006), 197–224.

——, *A History of Medieval Heresy and Inquisition* (Lanham, 2011).

Delaruelle, É., Labande, E.-R. and Ourliac, P., *L'Église au temps du grand schisme et de la crise conciliaire (1378–1449)*, Histoire de l'Église depuis les origines jusqu'à nos jours 14 (Paris, 1962).

Denzler, G., 'Reform der Kirche um 1400', in *Die hussitische Revolution: religiöse, politische und regionale Aspekte*, ed. F. Machilek (Cologne, 2012), pp. 9–24.

Doblinger, M., 'Die Herren von Walsee. Ein Beitrag zur österreichischen Adelsgeschichte', *Archiv für österreichische Geschichte* 95 (1906), 335–578.

Doležalová, E., 'The Inquisitions in Medieval Bohemia: National and International Contexts', in *Heresy and the Making of European Culture: Medieval and Modern Perspectives*, ed. A. P. Roach and J. R. Simpson (Aldershot, 2013), pp. 299–311.

Dondaine, A., 'Le Manuel de L'Inquisiteur (1230–1330)', in *Les hérésies et l'Inquisition, XIIe–XIIIe siècles: documents et études*, ed. Y. Dossat (Aldershot, 1990), pp. 85–194. Originally published in *Archivum Fratrum Praedicatorum* 17 (1947), 85–194.

Dreyer, M., '... Rationabiliter infirmare et ...rationes quibus fides [innititur] in publicum deducere: Alain de Lille et le conflit avec les adversaires de la foi', in *Alain de Lille, le docteur universel: philosophie, théologie et littérature au XII siècle*, ed. J.-L. Solère, A. Vasiliu and A. Galonnier (Turnhout, 2005), pp. 429–42.

Driscoll, M. J., 'The Words on the Page: Thoughts on Philology, Old and New', in *Creating the Medieval Saga: Versions, Variability, and Editorial Interpretations of Old Norse Saga Literature*, ed. J. Quinn and E. Lethbridge (Odense, 2010), pp. 85–102.

Elders, L. J., 'Thomas Aquinas and the Fathers of the Church', in *The Reception of the Church Fathers in the West: From the Carolingians to the Maurists*, ed. Irena Backus, 2 vols. (Leiden, 1996), I, 337–66.

Elm, K., 'Antiklerikalismus im deutschen Mittelalter', in *Anticlericalism in Late Medieval and Early Modern Europe*, ed. P. A. Dykema and H. A. Oberman (Leiden, 1993), pp. 3–18.

Ernst, P., 'Ulrich von Pottenstein. Leben und Werk nach dem Stand der neueren Forschung', *Unsere Heimat* 58 (1987), 203–13.

Finke, H., 'Waldenserprocess in Regensburg, 1395', *Deutsche Zeitschrift für Geschichtswissenschaft* 4 (1890), 345–46.

Flade, P., 'Das römische Inquisitionsverfahren in Deutschland bis zu den Hexenprozessen', *Studien zur Geschichte der Theologie und der Kirche* 9 (1902), 1–122.

Forrest, I., *The Detection of Heresy in Late Medieval England* (Oxford, 2005).

Fries, J. E., 'Ausgrabungen in der mittelalterlichen Burg- und Klosterruine Oybin', *Arbeits- und Forschungsberichte zur Sächsische Bodendenkmalpflege* 44 (2002), 179–90.

Froehlich, K., '"Always to Keep to the Literal Sense in Holy Scripture Means to Kill One's Soul": The State of Biblical Hermeneutics at the Beginning of the Fifteenth Century', in *Literary Uses of Typology: From the Late Middle Ages to the Present*, ed. E. R. Miner (Princeton, 1977), pp. 20–48.

Fudge, T. A., *Jan Hus: Religious Reform and Social Revolution in Bohemia* (London, 2010).

———, 'The "Law of God": Reform and Religious Practice in Late Medieval Bohemia', in *The Bohemian Reformation and Religious Practice 1*, ed. D. R. Holeton (Prague, 1996), pp. 49–72

———, *The Trial of Jan Hus: Medieval Heresy and Criminal Procedure* (New York, 2013).

Fuhrmann, H., *Ignaz von Döllinger: ein exkommunizierter Theologe als Akademiepräsident und Historiker* (Leipzig, 1999).

Garber, R. L. R., *Feminine Figurae: Representations of Gender in Religious Texts by Medieval German Women Writers, 1100–1475* (New York, 2003).

Gartner, G., *Geschichte der Pfarre Weistrach* (Steyr, 1973).

———, 'Mittelalterliche Ketzerprozesse in Steyr', in *Auftrag und Verwirklichung: Festschrift zum 200-jährigen Bestand d. Kirchenhist. Lehrkanzel seit d. Aufhebung des Jesuitenordens 1773*, ed. F. Loidl (Vienna, 1974), pp. 123–33.

Gärtner, T., 'Die Zittauer Schule bis zur Gründung des Gymnasiums', in *Festschrift zur dreihundertjährigen Jubelfeier des Gymnasiums zu Zittau am 9. und 10. März 1886* (Zittau, 1886), pp. 1–24.

Gehrt, W., *Die Handschriften der Staats- und Stadtbibliothek Augsburg. 2° Cod 251–400e* (Wiesbaden, 1989).

Given, J. B., *Inquisition and Medieval Society: Power, Discipline, and Resistance in Languedoc* (Ithaca, 2001).

Glaßner, C., 'Inventar der Handschriften des Benediktinerstiftes St. Paul im Lavanttal' [webpage] (2002). <http://www.ksbm.oeaw.ac.at/stpaul/inv/index.htm>.

———, 'Inventar der mittelalterlichen Handschriften des Benediktinerstiftes Seitenstetten' [webpage] (2005). <http://www.ksbm.oeaw.ac.at/seit/inv/>.

Gonnet, G., 'I Valdesi d'Austria nella seconda metà del secolo XIV', *BSSV* 111 (1962), 5–41.

Gonnet, J., and Molnár A., *Les Vaudois au Moyen Âge* (Turin, 1974).

Goodich, M., *Miracles and Wonders: The Development of the Concept of Miracle, 1150–1350* (Aldershot, 2007).

Gramsch, R., *Erfurter Juristen im Spätmittelalter: die Karrieremuster und Tätigkeitsfelder einer gelehrten Elite des 14. und 15. Jahrhunderts* (Leiden, 2003).

Grane, L., *Modus loquendi theologicus: Luthers Kampf um die Erneuerung der Theologie (1515–1518)* (Leiden, 1975).

Graus, F., 'The Church and Its Critics in Time of Crisis', in *Anticlericalism in Late Medieval and Early Modern Europe*, ed. P. A. Dykema and H. A. Oberman (Leiden, 1993), pp. 65–81.

———, *Pest – Geissler – Judenmorde: das 14. Jahrhundert als Krisenzeit* (Göttingen, 1987).

Grundmann, H., 'Ketzerverhöre des Spätmittelalters als quellenkritisches Problem', *DA* 21 (1965), 519–60.

————, 'Der Typus des Ketzers in mittelalterlicher Anschauung', in *Ausgewählte Aufsätze*, 3 vols. (Stuttgart, 1976), I, 313–27.

Günther, F., *Die Klosterkirche Oybin* (Berlin, 1959).

Günther O., *Die Handschriften der Kirchenbibliothek von St. Marien in Danzig* (Danzig, 1921).

Halm K., von Laubmann, G. and Meyers, W., *Catalogus codicum latinorum*. Catalogus codicum manuscriptorum Bibliothecae Regiae Monacensis, vols. III.1–3 and IV.1–4 (vols. III.1–2, 2nd edn) (Munich, 1873–94).

Hamm, B., 'Normative Centering in the Fifteenth and Sixteenth Centuries: Observations on Religiosity, Theology, and Iconology', trans. J. M. Frymire, *Journal of Early Modern History* 3 (1999), 307–54.

————, *The Reformation of Faith in the Context of Late Medieval Theology and Piety: Essays by Berndt Hamm*, trans. R. J. Bast (Leiden, 2004).

————, *Religiosität im späten Mittelalter: Spannungspole, Neuaufbrüche, Normierungen*, ed. R. Friedrich and W. Simon (Tübingen, 2011).

Hanna, R., 'Miscellaneity and Vernacularity: Conditions of Literary Production in Late Medieval England', in *The Whole Book: Cultural Perspectives on the Medieval Miscellany*, ed. S. G. Nichols and S. Wenzel (Ann Arbor, 1996), pp. 37–51.

————, *Pursuing History: Middle English Manuscripts and Their Texts* (Stanford, 1996).

Hanska, J., 'Mendicant Preachers as Disseminators of Anti-Jewish Literary Topoi: The Case of Luca da Bitonto', in *From Words to Deeds: The Effectiveness of Preaching in the Late Middle Ages*, ed. M. G. Muzzarelli (Turnhout, 2014), pp. 117–38.

Haupt, H., 'Ein Beghardenprozess in Eichstädt vom Jahre 1381', *Zeitschrift für Kirchengeschichte* 5 (1882), 487–98.

————, 'Johann von Drändorfs Verurteilung durch die Inquisition zu Heidelberg (1425)', *Zeitschrift für Geschichte des Oberrheins* 54 (1900), 479–90.

————, *Die Religiösen Sekten in Franken vor der Reformation* (Würzburg, 1882).

————, 'Waldenserthum und Inquisition im südöstlichen Deutschland seit der Mitte des 14. Jahrhunderts', *Deutsche Zeitschrift für Geschichtswissenschaft* 3 (1890), 337–411.

————, 'Waldensia', *Zeitschrift für Kirchengeschichte* 10 (1889), 311–29.

————, *Der Waldensische Ursprung des Codex Teplensis* (Würzburg, 1886).

Heinemann, O. von, *Die Handschriften der Herzoglichen Bibliothek zu Wolfenbüttel. Abth. 1: Die Helmstedter Handschriften* I (Wolfenbüttel, 1884).

Helmholz, H., *The Spirit of Classical Canon Law* (Athens, GA, 2010).

Hermann, W., *Zur Geschichte der Neisser Kreuzherren von Orden der regulierten Chorherren und Wächter des Heiligen Grabes zu Jerusalem mit dem doppelten roten Kreuz* (Breslau, 1938).

Hervé, M., *Le métier de prédicateur en France septentrionale à la fin du Moyen Âge (1350–1520)* (Paris, 1988).

Bibliography

Hilg, H., *Lateinische mittelalterliche Handschriften in Folio der Universitätsbibliothek Augsburg: Cod. II. 1.2° 91–226* (Wiesbaden, 1999).

Hlaváček, I., 'Beiträge zum Alltagsleben im vorhussitischen Böhmen. Zur Aussagekraft des Prager Visitationsprotokolls von 1379–1391 und der benachbarten Quellen', *Jahrbuch für fränkische Landesforschung* 34/35 (1975), 865–82.

――――, 'Zur böhmischen Inquisition und Häresiebekämpfung um das Jahr 1400', in *Häresie und vorzeitige Reformation im Spätmittelalter*, ed. F. Šmahel (Munich, 1998), pp. 109–31.

Hledíková, Z., 'Die Prager Erzbischöfe als ständige Päpstliche Legaten. Ein Beitrag zur Kirchenpolitik Karls IV', *Beiträge zur Geschichte des Bistums Regensburg* 6 (1972), 221–56.

Hobbins, D., *Authorship and Publicity before Print: Jean Gerson and the Transformation of Late Medieval Learning* (Philadelphia, 2009).

Hodel, P.-B., 'D'une édition à l'autre. La lettre de saint Vincent Ferrier à Jean de Puynoix du 17 décembre 1403', in *Mirificus praedicator: à l'occasion du sixième centenaire du passage de Saint Vincent Ferrier en pays romand: actes du colloque d'Estavayer-le-Lac, 7–9 octobre 2004*, ed. P.-B. Hodel and F. Morenzoni (Rome, 2006), pp. 189–203.

Hohmann, T., '"Die recht gelerten maister". Bemerkungen zur Übersetzungsliteratur der Wiener Schule des Spätmittelalters', in *Die Österreichische Literatur: ihr Profil von den Anfängen im Mittelalter bis ins 18. Jahrhundert (1050–1750)*, ed. F. P. Knapp and H. Zeman (Graz, 1986), pp. 349–65.

Holeton, D. R., 'The Bohemian Eucharistic Movement in its European Context', in *The Bohemian Reformation and Religious Practice 1*, ed. D. R. Holeton (Prague, 1996), pp. 23–47.

――――, *La communion des tout-petits enfants: étude du mouvement eucharistique en Bohême vers la fin du Moyen-Âge* (Rome, 1989).

Holinka, R., 'Sektářství v Čechách před revolucí husitskou', *Sborník filosofické fakulty University Komenského v Bratislavě* 52 (1929), 125–312.

Immonen, T., 'Building the Cassinese Monastic Identity: A Reconstruction of the Fresco Program of the Desiderian Basilica (1071)' (unpublished Ph.D. dissertation, University of Helsinki, 2012).

Izbicki, T. M., 'The Authority of Peter and Paul. The Use of Biblical Authority during the Great Schism', in *A Companion to the Great Western Schism (1378–1417)*, ed. J. Rollo-Koster and T. M. Izbicki (Leiden, 2009), pp. 375–93.

Jażdżewski, K. K., *Catalogus manu scriptorum codicum medii aevi Latinorum signa 180–260 comprehendens* (Wrocław, 1982).

Kadlec, J., *Studien und Texte zum Leben und Wirken des Prager Magisters Andreas von Brod* (Münster, 1982).

Kądzielski, S., and Mrozowicz W., *Catalogus codicum medii aevi manuscriptorum qui in Bibliotheca Universitatis Wratislaviensis asservantur signa 6055-6124 comprehendens* (*Codices Milichiani*, vol. 1) (Wrocław, 1998).

Kaminsky, H., 'From Lateness to Waning to Crisis: The Burden of the Later Middle Ages', *Journal of Early Modern History* 4 (2000), 85–125.

———, *A History of the Hussite Revolution* (Berkeley, 1967).

Kedar, B. Z., *Crusade and Mission: European Approaches toward the Muslims* (Princeton, 1984).

Kelly, H. A., 'Inquisition and the Prosecution of Heresy: Misconceptions and Abuses', *Church History* 58 (1989), 439–51.

———, 'Inquisitorial Deviations and Cover-Ups: The Prosecutions of Margaret Porete and Guiard of Cressonessart, 1308–1310', *Speculum* 89 (2014), 936–73.

———, 'Inquisitorial Due Process and the Status of Secret Crimes', in *Inquisitions and Other Trial Procedures in the Medieval West* (Aldershot, 2001), pp. 407–27.

Kentenich, G., *Die ascetischen Handschriften der Stadtbibliothek zu Trier (Abt. 2): Nr. 654–804 des Handschriften-Katalogs und Nachträge* (Trier, 1910).

Kieckhefer, R., 'The Office of Inquisition and Medieval Heresy: The Transaction from Personal to Institutional Jurisdiction', *JEH* 46 (1995), 36–61.

———, 'Repression of Heresy in Germany, 1348–1520' (unpublished Ph.D. dissertation, University of Texas at Austin, 1972).

———, *Repression of Heresy in Medieval Germany* (Liverpool, 1979).

Kienzle, B. M., *Cistercians, Heresy, and Crusade in Occitania, 1145–1229: Preaching in the Lord's Vineyard* (York, 2001).

———, 'Medieval Sermons and Their Performance: Theory and Record', in *Preacher, Sermon and Audience in the Middle Ages*, ed. C. Muessig (Leiden, 2002), pp. 89–124.

Knapp, F. P., *Die Literatur des Spätmittelalters in den Ländern Österreich, Steiermark, Kärnten, Salzburg und Tirol von 1273 bis 1439*, vol 2.2, *Die Literatur zur Zeit der habsburgischen Herzöge Rudolf IV. bis Albrecht V. (1358–1439)* (Graz, 2004).

Kneupper, F. C., *The Empire at the End of Time: Identity and Reform in Late Medieval German Prophecy* (Oxford, 2016).

Kolpacoff, J. M., 'Papal Schism, Archiepiscopal Politics and Waldensian Persecution (1378–1396): The Ecclesio-Political Landscape of Late Fourteenth-Century Mainz' (unpublished Ph.D. dissertation, Northwestern University, 2000).

Koudelka, V. J., 'Heinrich von Bitterfeld OP († c. 1405), Professor an der Universität Prag', *Archivum Fratrum Praedicatorum* 23 (1953), 5–65.

Kras, P., 'Dominican Inquisitors in Medieval Poland (14th–15th C.)', in *Praedicatores, inquisitores I. The Dominicans and the Medieval Inquisition. Acts of the 1st International Seminar on the Dominicans and the Inquisition 23–25 February 2002*, Dissertationes Historicae 29 (Rome, 2004), pp. 249–309.

Kurze, D., 'Bemerkungen zu einzelnen Autoren und Quellen', in *Quellen zur Ketzergeschichte Brandenburgs und Pommerns*, ed. D. Kurze (Berlin, 1975), pp. 12–56.

———, 'Zur Ketzergeschichte der Mark Brandenburg und Pommerns vornehmlich im 14. Jahrhundert: Luziferianer, Putzkeller und Waldenser', *Jahrbuch für die Geschichte Mittel- und Ostdeutschlands* 16/17 (1968), 50–94.

Lackner, C., 'Des mocht er nicht geneissen, wiewol er der rechte naturleich erbe was …: Zum Hollenburger Vertrag vom 22. November 1395', *Jahrbuch für Landeskunde von Niederösterreich* 65 (1999), 1–16.

———, *Hof und Herrschaft: Rat, Kanzlei und Regierung der österreichischen Herzoge (1365–1406)* (Vienna, 2002).

Lambert, M., *Medieval Heresy: Popular Movements from the Gregorian Reform to the Reformation*, 3rd edn (Oxford, 2009).

Lang, A., *Die Entfaltung des apologetischen Problems in der Scholastik des Mittelalters* (Freiburg im Breisgau, 1962).

———, 'Das Verhältnis von Schrift, Tradition und kirchlichem Lehramt nach Heinrich Totting von Oyta', *Scholastik* 40 (1965), 214–34.

Larson, A. A., *Master of Penance* (Washington, DC, 2014).

Lasson, E., *Superstitions médiévales: une analyse d'après l'exégèse du premier commandement d'Ulrich de Pottenstein* (Paris, 2010).

Lauterbach, K. H., *Geschichtsverständnis, Zeitdidaxe und Reformgedanke an der Wende zum sechzehnten Jahrhundert: das oberrheinische 'Buchli der hundert capiteln' im Kontext des spämittelalterlichen Reformbiblizismus* (Freiburg-im-Breisgau, 1985).

Le Goff, J., *The Birth of Purgatory* (Chicago, 1986).

Lea, H. C., *A History of the Inquisition of the Middle Ages*, 3 vols. (New York, 1956).

Leclercq, J., *The Love of Learning and the Desire for God: A Study of Monastic Culture*, trans. C. Misrahi (New York, 1993).

Lehmijoki-Gardner, M., *Worldly Saints: Social Interaction of Dominican Penitent Women in Italy, 1200–1500* (Helsinki, 1999).

Lentes, T., and Scharff, T., 'Schriftlichkeit und Disziplinierung. Die Beispiele Inquisition und Frömmigkeit', *Frühmittelalterliche Studien* 31 (1997), 233–52.

Lepsius, S., 'Kontrolle von Amtsträger durch Schrift. Luccheser Notare und Richter im Syndikatsprozess', in *Als die Welt in die Akten kam: Prozeßschriftgut im europäischen Mittelalter*, ed. S. Lepsius and T. Wetzstein (Frankfurt-am-Main, 2008), pp. 389–467.

Lerner, R. E., *The Heresy of the Free Spirit in the Later Middle Ages* (Berkeley, 1972).

Levy, I. C., *Holy Scripture and the Quest for Authority at the End of the Middle Ages* (Notre Dame, 2012).

———, 'Was John Wyclif's Theology of the Eucharist Donatistic?', *Scottish Journal of Theology* 53 (2000), 137–53.

Lewis, A., 'Textual Borrowings, Theological Mobility, and the Lollard Pater Noster Commentary', *Philological Quarterly* 88 (2009), 1–23.

Liere, F. van, *An Introduction to the Medieval Bible* (New York, 2014).

Linkinen, T., *Same-Sex Sexuality in Later Medieval English Culture* (Amsterdam, 2015).

Luscombe, D., 'The Hierarchies in the Writings of Alan of Lille, William of Auvergne, and St. Bonaventure', in *Angels in Medieval Philosophical Inquiry: Their Function and Significance*, ed. I. Iribarren and M. Lenz (Aldershot, 2008), pp. 15–28.

Machilek, F., 'Beweggründe, Inhalte und Probleme kirchlicher Reformen des 14./15. Jahrhunderts (mit besonderer Berücksichtigung der Verhältnisse im östlichen Mitteleuropa)', in *Kirchliche Reformimpulse des 14./15. Jahrhunderts in Ostmitteleuropa*, ed. W. Eberhard and F. Machilek (Cologne, 2006), pp. 1–121.

———, 'Ein Eichstätter Inquisitionsverfahren aus dem Jahre 1460', *Jahrbuch für fränkische Landesforschung* 34/35 (1975), 417–46.

———, 'Praga caput regni: zur Entwicklung und Bedeutung Prags im Mittelalter', *Studien zum Deutschtum im Osten* 17 (1982), 67–125.

Marin, O., *L'archevêque, le maître et le dévot: genèses du mouvement réformateur pragois: années 1360–1419* (Paris, 2005).

Matthews, J., 'Anicius Manlius Severinus Boethius', in *Boethius: His Life, Thought and Influence*, ed. M. Gibson (Oxford, 1981), pp. 15–43.

Menhardt, H., 'Funde zu Ulrich von Pottenstein (etwa 1360–1420)', in *Festschrift für Wolfgang Stammler: zu seinem 65. Geburtstag dargebracht von Freunden und Schülern* (Berlin, 1953), pp. 146–71.

———, *Verzeichnis der altdeutschen literarischen Handschriften der Österreichischen Nationalbibliothek* 1 (Berlin, 1960).

Merlo, G. G., *Inquisitori e inquisizione del Medioevo* (Bologna, 2008).

———, 'Il sermo generalis dell'inquisitore: una sacra rappresentazione anomala', in *Vite di eretici e storie di frati*, ed. M. Benedetti, G. G. Merlo and A. Piazza (Milan, 1998), pp. 203–20.

Mertens, V., 'Predigt oder Traktat? Thesen zur Textdynamik mittelhochdeutscher geistlicher Prosa', *Jahrbuch für internationale Germanistik* 24 (1992), 41–3.

———, 'Theologie der Mönche – Frömmigkeit der Laien? Beobachtungen zur Textgeschichte von Predigten des Hartwig von Erfurt. Mit einem Textanhang', in *Literatur und Laienbildung im Spätmittelalter und in der Reformationszeit*, ed. L. Grenzmann and K. Stackmann (Stuttgart, 1984), pp. 661–83.

Minnis, A. J., '"Authorial Intention" and "Literal Sense" in the Exegetical Theories of Richard Fitzralph and John Wyclif: An Essay in the Medieval History of Biblical Hermeneutics', *Proceedings of the Royal Irish Academy. Section C: Archaeology, Celtic Studies, History, Linguistics, Literature* 75 (1975), 1–31.

Mitre Fernández, E., 'Muerte, veneno y enfermedad, metáforas medievales de la herejía', *Heresis: revue d'histoire des dissidences européennes* 25 (1995), 63–84.

Modestin, G., 'The Anti-Waldensian Treatise *Cum dormirent homines*: Historical Context, Polemical Strategy, and Manuscript Tradition', in *Religious Controversy in Europe, 1378–1536*, ed. M. Van Dussen and P. Soukup (Turnhout, 2013), pp. 211–29.

———, 'Der Augsburger Waldenserprozess und sein Straßburger Nachspiel (1393–1400)', *Zeitschrift des Historischen Vereins für Schwaben* 103 (2011), 43–68.

———, *Ketzer in der Stadt: der Prozess gegen die Straßburger Waldenser von 1400*. MGH Studien und Texte 41(Hanover, 2007).

———, 'Ein Mainzer Inquisitor in Straßburg: Ketzerverfolgung und Ordensreform auf dem Lebensweg von Nikolaus Böckeler OP (1378–1400)', *Mainzer Zeitschrift. Mittelrheinisches Jahrbuch für Archäologie, Kunst und Geschichte* 102 (2007), 167–73.

———, 'La parole efficace ou le déclenchement du procès contre les vaudois de Strasbourg (1399–1400)', in *Mirificus praedicator: à l'occasion du sixième centenaire du passage de Saint Vincent Ferrier en pays romand: actes du colloque d'Estavayer-le-Lac, 7–9 octobre 2004*, ed. P.-B. Hodel and F. Morenzoni (Rome, 2006), pp. 233–45.

———, 'Peter Zwicker (gest. nach dem 7. Juni 1404)', in *Schlesische Lebensbilder* 10, ed. F. Andreae (Breslau, 2010), pp. 25–34.

Molnár, A., 'Les 32 Errores Valdensium', *BSSV* 115 (1964), 3–4.

———, *Storia dei valdesi 1. Dalle origini all'adesione alla Riforma (1176–1532)*, 2nd edn (Turin, 1989).

———, 'La Valdensium regula du manuscrit de Prague', *BSSV* 123 (1968), 3–6.

———, 'Les Vaudois en Bohême avant la Révolution hussite', *BSSV* 116 (1964), 3–17.

———, *Die Waldenser: Geschichte und europäisches Ausmaß einer Ketzerbewegung* (Göttingen, 1980).

Moore, R. I., 'The Cathar Middle Ages as an Historiographical Problem', in *Christianity and Culture in the Middle Ages: Essays to Honor John Van Engen*, ed. D. C. Mengel and L. Wolverton (Notre Dame, 2014), pp. 58–86.

———, *The War on Heresy* (London, 2012).

Mormando, F., *The Preacher's Demons: Bernardino of Siena and the Social Underworld of Early Renaissance Italy* (Chicago, 1999).

Morrall, J. B., *Gerson and the Great Schism* (Manchester, 1960).

Mossman, S. 'Dorothea von Montau and the Masters of Prague', *Oxford German Studies* 39 (2010), 106–23.

———, *Marquard von Lindau and the Challenges of Religious Life in Late Medieval Germany: The Passion, the Eucharist, the Virgin Mary* (Oxford, 2010).

Müller, H., *Die kirchliche Krise des Spätmittelalters: Schisma, Konziliarismus und Konzilien*, Enzyklopädie deutscher Geschichte 90 (Munich, 2012).

Müller, J., 'Die Anfänge des sächsischen Schulwesens', *Neues Archiv für sächsische geschichte und Altertumskunde* 8 (1887), 1–40, 243–71.

Mutke, K., 'Die schlesischen Besitzungen des Coelestinerklosters Oybin', *Zeitschrift des Vereins für Geschichte Schlesiens* 48 (1914), 34–73.

Nechutová, J., *Die lateinische Literatur des Mittelalters in Böhmen* (Cologne, 2007).

———, 'Matěj of Janov and his Work *Regulae Veteris et Novi Testamenti*: The Significance of Volume VI and its Relation to the Previously Published Volumes', in *The Bohemian Reformation and Religious Practice 2*, ed. Z. V. David and D. R. Holeton (Prague, 1998), pp. 15–24.

———, 'Reform- und Bussprediger von Waldhauser bis Hus', in *Kirchliche Reformimpulse des 14./15. Jahrhunderts in Ostmitteleuropa*, ed. W. Eberhard and F. Machilek (Cologne, 2006), pp. 239–54.

Neddermeyer, U., *Von der Handschrift zum gedruckten Buch: Schriftlichkeit und Leseinteresse im Mittelalter und in der frühen Neuzeit: quantitative und qualitative Aspekte*, 2 vols. (Wiesbaden, 1998).

Němec, Richard, 'Architektur als identitätstragendes Herrschaftsinstrument. Kunsthistorische Betrachtungen der Residenzanlagen Karls IV. am Fallbeispiel der Burg- und Klosteranlage Oybin', *NLM* 128 (2006), 9–30.

———, 'Die Burg- und Klosteranlage Oybin. Die Entwicklung der Handelswege im Lausitzer Gebirge im Lichte der Territorialpolitik Karls IV. und ihre Bedeutung für die Erbauung des Kaiserhauses und die Stiftung des Coelestinerklosters', *Burgen und Schlösser* 44 (2003), 241–51.

———, 'Die Burg- und Klosteranlage Oybin im Kontext der regionalen und höfischen Architektur Karls IV. zur Verbreitung des Stils der Prager Veitsdomhütte', *Umění* 59 (2011), 102–25.

Neumann, A. A., *České sekty ve století 14. a 15. : Na základě archionich pramenů podává* (Velehrad, 1920).

Nickson, M., 'The "Pseudo-Reinerius" Treatise, the Final Stage of a Thirteenth-Century Work on Heresy from the Diocese of Passau', *Archives d'histoire doctrinale et littéraire du moyen âge* 42 (1967), 255–314.

Nold, P., 'Bertrand de la Tour, O.Min. Life and Works', *Archivum Franciscanum Historicum* 94 (2001), 275–323.

———, *Pope John XXII and his Franciscan Cardinal: Bertrand de la Tour and the Apostolic Poverty Controversy* (Oxford, 2003).

Nuding, M., *Matthäus von Krakau: Theologe, Politiker, Kirchenreformer in Krakau, Prag und Heidelberg zur Zeit des Großen Abendländischen Schismas* (Tübingen, 2007).

Oberste, J., 'Le pape Sylvestre en Antéchrist. Pauvreté et ecclesiologie dans le débat sur l'hérésie au bas Moyen Âge', in *Les Cathares devant l'histoire. Mélanges offerts à Jean Duvernoy*, ed. A. Brenon and C. Dieulafait (Cahors, 2005), pp. 389–405.

Ocker, C., 'Die Armut und die menschliche Natur: Konrad Waldhauser, Jan Milíč von Kroměříž und die Bettelmönche', in *Die 'neue Frömmigkeit' in Europa im Spätmittelalter*, ed. M. Derwich and M. Staub (Göttingen, 2004), pp. 111–29.

———, *Biblical Poetics before Humanism and Reformation* (Cambridge, 2002).

Pacquet, J., 'Le schisme d'Occident à Louvain, Bruxelles et Anvers', *Revue d'histoire ecclésiastique* 59 (1964), 401–36.

Paolini, L., *Il 'De officio inquisitionis': la procedura inquisitoriale a Bologna e a Ferrara nel Trecento* (Bologna, 1976).

———, 'Inquisizioni medievali: il modello italiano nella manualistica inquisitoriale (XIII–XIV secolo)', in *Negotium Fidei. Miscellanea di studi offerti a Mariano d'Alatri in occasione del suo 80 compleanno*, ed. P. Maranesi (Rome, 2002), pp. 177–98.

———, 'Italian Catharism and written culture', in *Heresy and Literacy, 1000–1530*, ed. P. Biller and A. Hudson (Cambridge, 1994), pp. 83–103.

Papini, C., *Valdo di Lione e i poveri nello spirito* (Turin, 2002).

Parmeggiani, R., *Explicatio super officio inquisitionis: origini e sviluppi della manualistica inquisitoriale tra Due e Trecento* (Roma, 2012).

———, 'Formazione ed evoluzione della procedura inquisitoriale: i consilia', *BSSV* 200 (2007), 45–69.

———, *La manualistica inquisitoriale (1230–1330): alcuni percorsi di lettura', *Quaderni del Mediae Aetatis Sodalicium* 6 (2003), 7–25.

———, 'Un secolo di manualistica inquisitoriale (1230–1330): intertestualità e circolazione del diritto', *Rivista Internazionale di Diritto Comune* 13 (2002), 229–70.

Pascoe, L. B., *Church and Reform: Bishops, Theologians, and Canon Lawyers in the Thought of Pierre d'Ailly (1351–1420)* (Leiden, 2004).

———, *Jean Gerson: Principles of Church Reform* (Leiden, 1973).

Patera A., and Podlaha A., *Soupis rukopisů Knihovny Metropolitní kapitoly Pražské. A–E*, 2 vols. (Prague, 1910).

Patschovsky, A., 'Ablaßkritik auf dem Basler Konzil: Der Widerruf Siegfried Wanners aus Nördlingen', in *Husitství – Reformace – Renesance. Sborník k 60. narozeninám Františka Šmahela*, ed. J. Pánek, M. Polívkaand and N. Rejchrtová (Prague, 1994), pp. 537–48.

———, *Die Anfänge einer ständigen Inquisition in Böhmen. Ein Prager Inquisitoren-Handbuch aus der ersten Hälfte des 14. Jahrhunderts* (Berlin, 1975).

———, 'Gli eretici davanti al tribunale. A proposito dei processi-verbali inquisitoriali in Germania e in Boemia nel XIV secolo', in *La parola all'accusato*, ed. J.-C. M. Vigueur and A. Paravicini Bagliani (Palermo, 1991), pp. 242–67.

———, 'Der Ketzer als Teufelsdiener', in *Papsttum, Kirche und Recht im Mittelalter. Festschrift für Horst Fuhrmann zum 65. Geburtstag*, ed. H. Mordek (Tübingen, 1991), pp. 317–34.

————, 'Ketzer und Ketzerverfolgung in Böhmen im Jahrhundert vor Hus', *Geschichte in Wissenschaft und Unterricht* 32 (1981), 261–72.

————, 'The Literacy of Waldensianism from Valdes to c. 1400', in *Heresy and Literacy, 1000–1530*, ed. P. Biller and A. Hudson (Cambridge, 1994), pp. 112–36.

————, *Der Passauer Anonymus: ein Sammelwerk über Ketzer, Juden, Antichrist aus der Mitte des 13. Jahrhunderts*, MGH Schriften 22 (Stuttgart, 1968).

————, [Review] 'Quellen zur Ketzergeschichte Brandenburgs und Pommerns. Gesammelt, herausgeben und eingeleitet von Dietrich Kurze', *DA* 34 (1978), 589–90.

————, 'Spuren böhmischer Ketzerverfolgung in Schlesien am Ende des 14. Jahrhunderts', in *Historia docet. Sborník prací k poctì šedesátých narozenin prof. PhDr. Ivana Hlaváèka*, ed. M. Polívka and M. Svatoš (Prague, 1992), pp. 357–87.

————, 'Straßburger Beginenverfolkungen im 14. Jahrhundert', *DA* 30 (1974), 56–198.

————, 'Der taboritische Chiliasmus. Seine Idee, sein Bild bei den Zeitgenossen und die Interpretation der Geschichtswissenschaft', in *Häresie und vorzeitige Reformation im Spätmittelalter*, ed. F. Šmahel (Munich, 1998), pp. 169–95.

————, 'Über die politische Bedeutung von Häresie und Häresieverfolgung im mittelalterlichen Böhmen', in *Die Anfänge der Inquisition im Mittelalter*, ed. P. Segl (Cologne, 1993), pp. 235–51.

————, 'Waldenserverfolgung in Schweidnitz 1315', *DA* 36 (1980), 137–76.

————, 'Wie wird man Ketzer? Der Beitrag der Volkskunde zur Entstehung von Häresien', in *Volksreligion im hohen und späten Mittelalter*, ed. P. Dinzelbacher and D. Bauer (Paderborn, 1990) pp. 145–62.

Pavel, R., 'Beschreibung der im Stifte Hohenfurt befindlichen Handschriften', in *Xenia Bernardina, Pars Secunda: die Handschriften-Verzeichnisse der Cistercienser Stifte. Zweiter Band· Wilhering, Schlierbach, Osegg, Hohenfurt* (Vienna, 1891), pp. 165–461.

Pegg, M. G., *The Corruption of Angels: The Great Inquisition of 1245–1246* (Princeton, 2001).

————, 'On Cathars, Albigenses, and Good Men of Languedoc', *Journal of Medieval History* 27 (2001), 81–95.

Penn, S., 'Wyclif and the Sacraments', in *A Companion to John Wyclif: Late Medieval Theologian*, ed. I. C. Levy (Leiden, 2006), pp. 241–91.

Pérez, J., *The Spanish Inquisition: A History* (New Haven, 2005).

Pescheck, C. A., *Geschichte der Cölestiner des Oybins* (Zittau, 1840).

Peters, E., *Inquisition* (New York, 1988).

Petersohn, J., 'Bistum Kammin', in *Die Bistümer des Heiligen Römischen Reiches*, ed. E. Gatz (Freiburg im-Breisgau, 2003), pp. 267–72.

————, 'Johann Brunonis', in *Die Bischöfe des Heiligen Römischen Reiches 1198 bis 1448. Ein biographisches Lexikon*, ed. E. Gatz (Berlin, 2001), p. 263.

———, *Die Kamminer Bischöfe des Mittelalters: Amtsbiographien und Bistumsstrukturen vom 12. bis 16. Jahrhundert* (Schwerin, 2015).

Phelan, O. M., *The Formation of Christian Europe: The Carolingians, Baptism, and the Imperium Christianum* (Oxford, 2014).

Piccard, G., *Die Ochsenkopfwasserzeichen*, Die Wasserzeichenkartei Piccard im Hauptstaatsarchiv Stuttgart, Findbuch 2, vols. 1–3 (Stuttgart, 1966).

———, *Wasserzeichen Waage*, Die Wasserzeichenkartei Piccard im Hauptstaatsarchiv Stuttgart, Findbuch 5 (Stuttgart, 1978).

Poznański, A., 'Ad retorquendum erroneos articulos: środki retoryczne w późnośredniowiecznych pismach antyheretyckich', in *Kultura pisma w średniowieczu: znane problemy nowe metody*, ed. A. Adamska and P. Kras (Lublin, 2013), pp. 243–54.

———, Reakcja Kościoła na kryzys ortodoksji w średniowieczu Piotra Zwickera traktat Cum dormirent homines', in *Ecclesia semper reformanda: kryzysy i reformy średniowiecznego Kościoła*, ed. T. Gałuszka, T. Graffand and G. Ryś (Kraków, 2013), pp. 195–210.

———, 'Traktat Piotra Zwickera Cum dormirent homines – uwagi wstepne', in *Fortunniejszy byl jezyk, bo ten i dzis mily*, ed. I. Bogumil and Z. Glombiowska (Gdańsk, 2010), pp. 98–105.

Pritz, F. X. *Geschichte der ehemaligen Benediktiner-Klöster Garsten und Gleink, im Lande ob der Enns, und der dazu gehörigen Pfarren* (Linz, 1841).

Prosperi, A., 'Fede, giuramento, inquisizione', in *Glaube und Eid*, ed. P. Prodi and E. Müller-Luckner (Munich, 1993), pp. 157–71.

Ragg, S., *Ketzer und Recht: die weltliche Ketzergesetzgebung des Hochmittelalters unter dem Einfluss des römischen und kanonischen Rechts*, MGH Studien und Texte 37 (Hanover, 2006).

Říčan, R., 'Johlín z Vodňan, křižovník kláštera zderazského', *Věstník Královské české společnosti nauk. Třida filosoficko-historicko-filologická* 2 (1929), 1–150.

Rischpler, S., and Haltrich, M., 'Der Codex 5393 der Österreichischen Nationalbibliothek und seine lokalhistorische Verortung', *Mitteilungen des Instituts für Österreichische Geschichtsforschung* 120 (2012), 307–20.

Roest, B., *Franciscan Literature of Religious Instruction before the Council of Trent* (Leiden, 2004).

Rubin, M., *Mother of God: A History of the Virgin Mary* (London, 2009).

Ruh, K., 'Deutsche Predigtbücher des Mittelalters', in *Beiträge zur Geschichte der Predigt* (Hamburg, 1981), pp. 11–30.

Ruland, A., *Die Ebracher Handschrift des Michael de Leone*, Besonderen Abdruck aus dem 'Archiv des historischen Vereines dür Unterfranken und Aschaffenburg' Band XIII. Heft 1 (Würzburg, 1854).

Rusconi, R., 'Public Purity and Discipline: States and Religious Renewal', in *Christianity in Western Europe c. 1100–c. 1500*, ed. M. Rubin and W. Simons (Cambridge, 2009), pp. 458–71.

Saak, E. L., *High Way to Heaven: The Augustinian Platform between Reform and Reformation, 1292–1524* (Leiden, 2002).

Sackville, L. J., *Heresy and Heretics in the Thirteenth Century: The Textual Representations*, Heresy and Inquisition in the Middle Ages 1 (York, 2011).

———, 'The Inquisitor's Manual at Work', *Viator* 44 (2013), 201–16.

———, 'The Textbook Heretic: Moneta of Cremona's Cathars', in *Cathars in Question*, ed. A. Sennis (York, 2016), pp. 185–207.

Salmesvuori, P., *Power and Sainthood: The Case of Birgitta of Sweden* (New York, 2014).

Sauppe, M. O., 'Geschichte der Burg und des Coelestinerklosters Oybin [I]', *NLM* 62 (1886), 88–110.

———, 'Geschichte der Burg und des Coelestinerklosters Oybin [II]', *NLM* 79 (1903), 177–240.

———, 'Geschichte der Burg und des Coelestinerklosters Oybin [III]', *NLM* 83 (1907), 110–95.

———, 'Regesta castri et monasterii Oywinensis', *NLM* 63 (1888), 370–7.

———, 'Zur Geschichte des Klosters Oybin im 15. Jahrhunder', *Neues Archiv für Sächsische Geschichte* 13 (1892), 315–22.

Scharff, T., 'Erfassen und Erschrecken. Funktionen des Prozeßschriftguts der kirchlichen Inquisition in Italien im 13. und frühen 14. Jahrhundert', in *Als die Welt in die Akten kam: Prozeßschriftgut im europäischen Mittelalter*, ed. S. Lepsius and T. Wetzstein (Frankfurt-am-Main, 2008), pp. 255–73.

———, 'Die Inquisitoren und die Macht der Zeichen. Symbolische Kommunikation in der Praxis der mitteralterlichen dominikanischen Inquisition', in *Praedicatores, Inquisitores I. The Dominicans and the Medieval Inquisition. Acts of the 1st International Seminar on the Dominicans and the Inquisition 23–25 February 2002*, Dissertationes Historicae 29 (Rome, 2004), pp. 111–43.

———, 'Schrift zur Kontrolle – Kontrolle der Schrift. Italienische und französiche Inquisitoren Handbücher des 13 und frühen 14. Jahrhunderts', *DA* 52 (1996), 547–84.

Schäufele, W-D., *'Defecit ecclesia': Studien zur Verfallsidee in der Kirchengeschichtsanschauung des Mittelalters* (Mainz, 2006).

Schiewer, H.-J., 'Spuren von Mündlichkeit in der mittelalterlichen Predigtüberlieferung: ein Plädoyer für exemplarisches und beschreibend-interpretierendes Edieren', *Editio. Internationales Jahrbuch für Editionswissenschaft* 6 (1992), 64–79.

Schilling, H., *Martin Luther: Rebell in einer Zeit des Umbruchs*, 2nd edn (Munich, 2012).

Schmid, A., 'Georg von Hohenlohe', in *Die Bischöfe des Heiligen Römischen Reiches 1198 bis 1448. Ein biographisches Lexikon*, ed. E. Gatz (Berlin, 2001), pp. 560–1.

Schmidtke, D., 'U. v. Pottenstein', in *Lexikon des Mittelalters* VIII (Munich, 1997), 1200–1.

Schmutz, J., *Juristen für das Reich: die deutschen Rechtsstudenten an der Universität Bologna 1265–1425* (Basel, 2000).

Schneider, M., *Europäisches Waldensertum im 13. und 14. Jahrhundert: Gemeinschaftsform, Frömmigkeit, sozialer Hintergrund* (Berlin, 1981).

Schnurrer, L., 'Der Fall Hans Wern. Ein spätmittelalterlicher Elitenkonflikt in der Reichstadt Rothenburg ob der Tauber', *Jahrbuch für fränkische Landesforschung* 61 (2001), 9–53.

Schönbach, A. E., *Studien zur Geschichte der altdeutschen Predigt 3: Das Wirken Bertholds von Regensburg gegen die Ketzer* (Vienna, 1904).

Schulze, M., 'Martin Luther and the Church Fathers', in *The Reception of the Church Fathers in the West: From the Carolingians to the Maurists*, ed. I. Backus, 2 vols. (Leiden, 1997), II, 573–626.

Scott, J., 'Theologians vs Canonists on Heresy', William of Ockham: Dialogus Latin Text and English Translation [webpage], <http://www.britac.ac.uk/pubs/dialogus/frmIntro1d1.html.>.

Segl, P., *Ketzer in Österreich* (Paderborn, 1984).

———, Schisma, Krise, Häresie und Schwarzer Tod. Signaturen der "Welt vor Hus"', in *Jan Hus – Zwischen Zeiten, Völkern, Konfessionen*, ed. F. Seibt (Munich, 1997), pp. 27–38.

———, 'Die Waldenser in Österreich um 1400: Lehren, Organisationsform, Verbreitung und Bekämpfung', in *Friedrich Reiser und die 'waldensisch-hussitische Internationale' im 15. Jahrhundert*, ed. A. de Lange and K. Utz Tremp (Heidelberg, 2006), pp. 161–88.

———, 'Zwicker, Peter', in *Lexikon des Mittelalters* IX (Munich, 1998), pp. 732–3.

Segl, P., ed., *Die Anfänge der Inquisition im Mittelalter. Mit einem Ausblick auf das 20. Jahrhundert und einem Beitrag über religiöse Intoleranz im nichtchristlichen Bereich* (Cologne, 1993).

Seibt, F., *Karl IV: ein Kaiser in Europa 1346–1378*, 4th edn (Munich, 1979).

Sennis, A., ed., *Cathars in Question*, Heresy and Inquisition in the Middle Ages 4 (York, 2016).

Šmahel, F., 'The Hussite Critique of the Clergy's Civil Dominion', in *Anticlericalism in Late Medieval and Early Modern Europe*, ed. P. A. Dykema and H. A. Oberman (Leiden, 1993), pp. 83–90.

———, *Die Prager Universität im Mittelalter: gesammelte Aufsätze* (Leiden, 2007).

Smelyansky, E., 'Self-Styled Inquisitors: Heresy, Mobility, and Anti-Waldensian Persecutions in Germany, 1390–1404' (unpublished Ph.D. dissertation, University of California, Irvine, 2015).

———, 'Urban Order and Urban Other: Anti-Waldensian Inquisition in Augsburg, 1393', *German History* 34 (2016), 1–20.

Smith, L., *The Ten Commandments: Interpreting the Bible in the Medieval World* (Leiden, 2014).

Soukup, P., 'Die Predigt als Mittel religiöser Erneuerung: Böhmen um 1400', in *Böhmen und das Deutsche Reich: Ideen- und Kulturtransfer im Vergleich*

(13.–16. Jahrhundert), ed. E. Schlotheuber and H. Seibert (Munich, 2009), pp. 235–64.

———, 'The Reception of the Books of the Maccabees in the Hussite Reformation', in *Dying for the Faith, Killing for the Faith: Old-Testament Faith-Warriors (1 and 2 Maccabees) in Historical Perspective*, ed. G. Signori (Leiden, 2012), pp. 195–207.

———, 'Die Waldenser in Böhmen und Mähren im 14. Jahrhundert', in *Friedrich Reiser und die 'waldensisch-hussitische Internationale' im 15. Jahrhundert*, ed. A. de Lange and K. Utz Tremp (Heidelberg, 2006), pp. 131–60.

Sparks, C., *Heresy, Inquisition and Life-Cycle in Medieval Languedoc*, Heresy and Inquisition in the Middle Ages 3 (York, 2014).

Speer, C., 'Die Bedeutung der Cölestiner für die Frömmigkeitspraxis städtischer Eliten im Spätmittelalter', in *Česká koruna na rozcestí. K dějinám Horní a Dolní Lužice a Dolního Slezska na přelomu středověku a raného novověku (1437–1526)*, ed. L. Bobková (Prague, 2010), pp. 294–338

———, *Frömmigkeit und Politik: Städtische Eliten in Görlitz zwischen 1300 und 1550* (Berlin, 2011).

Spijker, I. van 't, 'Beyond Reverence. Richard of Saint-Victor and the Fathers', in *Les réceptions des Pères de l'Église au Moyen Âge: le devenir de la tradition ecclésiale*, ed. N. Bériou, R. Berndt, M. Fédou, A. Oliva and A. Vauchez, 2 vols. (Münster, 2013), I, 439–64.

Spilling, H., *Die Handschriften der Staats- und Stadtbibliothek Augsburg. 2° Cod 101–250* (Wiesbaden, 1984).

Spinka, M., *John Hus: A Biography* (Princeton, 1968).

Staub, J., and Staub, K. H., *Die mittelalterlichen Handschriften der Nicolaus-Matz-Bibliothek (Kirchenbibliothek) Michelstadt* (Michelstadt 1999).

Stevenson, H., and de Rossi, G. B., *Codices Palatini latini Bibliothecae Vaticanae* I (Rome, 1886).

Stoob, H., 'Kaiser Karl IV. und der Ostseeraum', *Hansische Geschichtsblätter* 88 (1970), 163–214.

Swanson, R. N., 'Academic Circles: Universities and Exchanges of Information and Ideas in the Age of the Great Schism', in *Religious Controversy in Europe, 1378–1536*, ed. M. Van Dussen and P. Soukup (Turnhout, 2013), pp. 17–43.

———, 'Apostolic Successors: Priests and Priesthood, Bishops, and Episcopacy in Medieval Western Europe', in *A Companion to Priesthood and Holy Orders in the Middle Ages*, ed. G. Peters and C. C. Anderson (Leiden, 2016), pp. 4–42.

———, 'A Survey of Views on the Great Schism, c. 1395', *Archivum Historiae Pontificiae* 21 (1983), 79–103.

Szpiech, R., *Conversion and Narrative: Reading and Religious Authority in Medieval Polemic* (Philadelphia, 2013).

Szymański, J., '"Articuli secte Waldensium" na tle antyheretyckich zbiorów rekopismiennych Biblioteki Uniwersytetu Wroclawskiego', *Studia zródloznawcze* 42 (2004), 85–96.

———, 'Hy sunt articuli secte waldensium hereticorum z kodeksu IF 707 Biblioteki Uniwersyteckiej we Wroclawiu', in *Historicae viae. Studia dedykowane Profesorowi Lechowi A. Tyszkiewiczowi z okazji 55-lecia pracy naukowej*, ed. M. Goliński and S. Rosik (Wrocław, 2012), pp. 51–62.

Tabulae codicum manu scriptorum praeter graecos et orientales in Bibliotheca Palatina Vindobonensi asservatorum, 10 vols. (Vienna, 1864).

Tavuzzi, M. M., *Renaissance Inquisitors: Dominican Inquisitors and Inquisitorial Districts in Northern Italy, 1474–1527* (Leiden, 2007).

Taylor, C., 'Evidence for Dualism in Inquisitorial Registers of the 1240s: A Contribution to a Debate'. *History* 98 (2013), 319–45.

———, '"Heresy" in Quercy in the 1240s: Authorities and Audiences', in *Heresy and the Making of European Culture: Medieval and Modern Perspectives*, ed. A. P. Roach and J. R. Simpson (Aldershot, 2013), pp. 239–55.

Thurn, H., *Bestand bis zur Säkularisierung: Erwerbungen und Zugänge bis 1803*, Die Handschriften der Universitätsbibliothek Würzburg 5 (Wiesbaden, 1994).

———, *Handschriften aus benediktinischen Provenienzen. Hälfte 2: Die Handschriften aus St. Stephan zu Würzburg*. Die Handschriften der Universitatsbibliothek Würzburg 2.2 (Wiesbaden, 1986).

———, *Die Handschriften der kleinen Provenienzen und Fragmente*, Die Handschriften der Universitätsbibliothek Würzburg 4 (Wiesbaden, 1990).

Tierney, B., *Foundations of the Conciliar Theory: The Contribution of the Medieval Canonists from Gratian to the Great Schism* (Cambridge, 1955).

Tolonen, P., 'Medieval Memories of the Origins of the Waldensian Movement', in *History and Religion: Narrating a Religious Past*, ed. B.-C. Otto, S. Rau and J. Rüpke (Berlin, 2015), pp. 165–85.

Tönsing, M., 'Contra hereticam pravitatem. Zu den Luccheser Ketzererlassen Karls IV. (1369)', in *Studia Luxemburgensia. Festschrift für Heinz Stoob zum 70. Geburtstag*, ed. F. B. Fahlbusch and P. Johanek (Warendorf, 1989), pp. 285–311.

———, *Johannes Malkaw aus Preussen (ca. 1360-1416): ein Kleriker im Spannungsfeld von Kanzel, Ketzerprozess und Kirchenspaltung* (Warendorf, 2004).

Truhlář, J., *Catalogus codicum manu scriptorum latinorum qui in C.R. Bibliotheca Publica atque Universitatis Pragensis asservantur*, vol. II, *Codices 1666–2752 forulorum IX–XV et bibliothecae Kinskyanae* (Prague, 1906).

Trusen, W., Der Inquisitionsprozess. Seine historischen Grundlagen und frühen Formen', *Zeitschrift der Savigny-Stiftung für Rechtsgeschichte. Kanonistische Abteilung* 105 (1988), 168–230.

———, 'Von den Anfängen des Inquisitionsprozesses zum Verfahren bei der inquisitio haereticae pravitatis', in *Die Anfänge der Inquisition im Mittelalter*, ed. P. Segl (Cologne, 1993), pp. 39–76.

Ubl, K., 'Die Österreichischen Ketzer aus der Sicht zeitgenössischer Theologen', in *Handschriften, Historiographie und Recht: Winfried Stelzer zum 60. Geburtstag*, ed. W. Stelzer and G. Pfeifer (Munich, 2002), pp. 190–224.

Uiblein, P., 'Die ersten Österreicher als Professoren an der Wiener Theologischen Fakultät (1384–1389)', *Wiener Beiträge zur Theologie* 52 (1976), 85–101.

Utz Tremp, K., 'Multum abhorrerem confiteri homini laico. Die Waldenser zwischen Laienapostolat und Priestertum, insbesondere an der Wende vom 14. zum 15. Jahrhundert', in *Pfaffen und Laien, ein mittelalterlicher Antagonismus? Freiburger Colloquium 1996*, ed. E. C. Lutz and E. Tremp (Freiburg, 1999), pp. 153–89.

———, 'Predigt und Inquisition. Der Kampf gegen die Häresie in der Stadt Freiburg (erste Hälfte des 15. Jahrhunderts)', in *Mirificus praedicator: à l'occasion du sixième centenaire du passage de Saint Vincent Ferrier en pays romand : actes du colloque d'Estavayer-le-Lac, 7–9 octobre 2004*, ed. P.-B. Hodel and F. Morenzoni (Rome, 2006), pp. 205–32.

———, *Von der Häresie zur Hexerei: 'wirkliche' und imaginäre Sekten im Spätmittelalter*, MGH Schriften 59 (Hanover, 2008).

———, *Waldenser, Wiedergänger, Hexen und Rebellen. Biographien zu den Waldenserprozessen von Freiburg im Uchtland (1399 und 1430)* (Fribourg, 1999).

Välimäki, R., 'Bishops and the Inquisition of Heresy in Late Medieval Germany', in *Dominus Episcopus. Medieval Bishops between Diocese and Court*, ed. A. J. Lappin and E. Balzamo (Stockholm, 2018), 186–206.

———, '*Bona docere et mala dedocere* – Inquisition of Heresy and Communication with the Lay Population', in *Modus vivendi: Religious Reform and the laity in Late Medieval Europe*, ed. M. Heinonen, M. Kaartinen and M. Rubin [forthcoming].

———, 'Imagery of Disease, Poison and Healing in the Late Fourteenth-Century Polemics against Waldensian Heresy', in *Infirmity in Antiquity and the Middle Ages: Social and Cultural Approaches to Health, Weakness and Care*, ed. C. Krötzl, K. Mustakallio and J. Kuuliala (Burlington, 2015), pp. 137–52.

———, 'Old Errors, New Sects: The Waldensians, Wyclif and Hus in the Fifteenth-Century Manuscripts', in *Golden Leaves, Burned Books*, ed. G. Müller-Oberhäuser and T. Immonen (Turku, 2019) [forthcoming].

———, 'Transfers of Anti-Waldensian Material from a Polemical Treatise to a Didactic Text', *Medieval Worlds* 7 (2018), 153–69.

Välimäki, R., Vesanto, A., Hella, A., Poznański, A. and Ginter, F., 'Manuscripts, qualitative analysis and features on vectors. An attempt for a synthesis of conventional and computational methods in the attribution of late medieval anti-heretical treatises', in *Digital, Computational and Distant Readings of History: Emergent Approaches within the New Digital History*, ed. M. Fridlund, M. Oiva and P. Paju (Helsinki, 2019) [forthcoming].

Van Dussen, M., *From England to Bohemia: Heresy and Communication in the Later Middle Ages* (Cambridge, 2012).

Van Engen, J. H., 'Multiple Options: The World of the Fifteenth-Century Church', *Church History* 77 (2008), 257–84.

Vasoli, C., Il "Contra haereticos" di Alano di Lilla', *Bullettino dell'Istituto storico italiano per il medio evo e Archivio muratoriano* 75 (1963), 123–72.

Vauchez, A., 'Le refus du serment chez les hérétiques médiévaux', in *Le serment II. Théories et Devenir*, ed. R. Verdier (Paris, 1991), pp. 257–63.

Vidmanová, A., 'Autoritäten und Wiclif in Hussens homiletischen Schriften', in *Antiqui und Moderni: Traditionsbewußtsein und Fortschrittsbewußtsein im späten Mittelalter*, ed. A. Zimmermann (Berlin, 1974), pp. 383–93.

Vorgrimler, H., *Sakramententheologie* (Düsseldorf, 1987).

Wakefield, W. L., 'Heretics and Inquisitors: The Case of Auriac and Cambiac', *Journal of Medieval History* 12 (1985), 225–37.

———, 'Notes on Some Anti-Heretical Writings of the Thirteenth Century', *Franciscan Studies* 27 (1967), 285–321.

Wattenbach, W., 'Über Ketzergeschichte in Pommern und der Mark Brandenburg', *Sitzungsberichte der Preussichen Akademie der Wissenschaften*, Philos.-histor. Klasse 1 (1886), 47–58.

Webb, D., 'Pier Pettinaio of Siena' [Introduction], in *Saints and Cities in Medieval Italy* (Manchester, 2007), pp. 191–3.

Weltsch, R. E., *Archbishop John of Jenstein (1348–1400): Papalism, Humanism and Reform in Pre-Hussite Prague* (The Hague, 1968).

Werbow, S. N., 'Einleitung', in *Der Gewissensspiegel*, ed. S. N. Werbow (Berlin, 1958), pp. 9–31.

———, 'Martin von Amberg', in *Die deutsche Literatur des Mittelalters: Verfasserlexikon*, 2nd edn, 14 vols (Berlin and New York, 1987), VI, 143–50.

Werner, E. 'Nachrichten über spätmittelalterliche Ketzer aus tschechoslowakischen Archiven und Bibliotheken', *Wissenschaftliche Zeitschrift der Karl-Marx-Universität Leipzig. Gesellschafts- und sprachwissenschaftliche Reihe* 12 (1963), 215–84.

Westergård, I., *Approaching Sacred Pregnancy: The Cult of the Visitation and Narrative Altarpieces in Late Fifteenth-Century Florence* (Helsinki, 2007).

Wetter, E., 'Die Lausitz und die Mark Brandenburg', in *Karl IV., Kaiser von Gottes Gnaden: Kunst und Repräsentation des Hauses Luxemburg 1310–1437*, ed. J. Fajt, M. Hörsch, A. Langerand and B. D. Boehm (Munich, 2006), pp. 341–9.

Williams-Krapp, W., 'Konturen einer religiösen Bildungsoffensive. Zur literarischen Laienpastoration im 15. und frühen 16. Jahrhundert', in *Kirchlicher und religiöser Alltag im Spätmittelalter. Akten der internationalen*

Tagung in Weingarten, 4.–7. Oktober 2007, ed. A. Meyer (Ostfildern, 2010), pp. 77–88.

———, 'Observanzbewegungen, monastische Spiritualität und geistliche Literatur im 15. Jahrhundert', *Internationales Archiv für Sozialgeschichte der Literatur* 20 (1995), 1–15.

———, *Überlieferung und Gattung: zur Gattung 'Spiel' im Mittelalter* (Tübingen, 1980).

———, 'Die überlieferungsgeschichtliche Methode. Rückblick und Ausblick', *Internationales Archiv für Sozialgeschichte der Deutschen Literatur* 25 (2000), 1–21.

Wisłocki, W., *Katalog rękopisów Bibljoteki Uniwersytetu Jagiellońskiego*, 2 vols. (Kraków, 1881).

Wolf, K., *Hof – Universität – Laien: literatur- und sprachgeschichtliche Untersuchungen zum deutschen Schrifttum der Wiener Schule des Spätmittelalters* (Wiesbaden, 2006).

Wriedt, K., 'Schule und Universitätsbesuch in norddeutschen Städten des Spätmittelalters', in *Bildungs- und schulgeschichtliche Studien zu Spätmittelalter, Reformation und konfessionellem Zeitalter*, ed. H. Dickerhof (Wiesbaden, 1994), pp. 75–90.

Würth, I., *Geißler in Thüringen: Die Entstehung einer Spätmittelalterlichen Häresie* (Berlin, 2012).

Yeager, R. F., 'Alain of Lille's Use of "Naufragium" in *De Planctu Naturae*', in *Through a Classical Eye: Transcultural and Transhistorical Visions in Medieval English, Italian, and Latin Literature in Honour of Winthrop Wetherbee*, ed. A. Galloway and R. F. Yeager (Toronto, 2009), pp. 86–106.

Zedler, G., *Die Handschriften der nassauischen Landesbibliothek zu Wiesbaden* (Leipzig, 1931).

Zerner, M., ed., *Inventer l'hérésie? Discours polémiques et pouvoirs avant l'Inquisition* (Nice, 1998).

Zinnhobler, R., 'Die Inhaber von Pfarre und Dekanat Enns im Mittelalter', in *Die Dechanten von Enns-Lorch*, ed. R. Zinnhobler and J. Ebner (Linz, 1982), pp. 24–52.

Zobel, J. G., 'Beitrag zur geschichte des Klosters Oybin bei Zittau', *Neue Lausizische Monatsschrift*, Part 2, 8th section (1802), 102–24.

Ziegler C., and Rössl, J., *Zisterzienserstift Zwettl: Katalog der Handschriften des Mittelalters Teil 2: Codex 101–200* (Vienna, 1985).

Index

Adalbertus Ranconis de Ericinio (Vojtěch Raňkův of Ježov) 83
Albrecht III, duke of Austria 111 n. 28, 112, 161, 198
Albrecht IV, duke of Austria 111, 112, 157, 196 n. 103, 198
Alain of Lille 73 n. 129, 74, 94
Ambrose 69, 73 n. 129, 77, 204
Anderson, Colt 240
Antichrist 17, 232, 251
Anti-heretical polemics 7–9, 19, 39–41, 74, 84, 96, 98–101, 168, 179, 181 n. 46, 203, 204, 215–16, 232, 256, 261
    Anonymous of Passau 7, 17, 50, 52–3, 57, 73, 90, 119, 180, 212, 218, 227, 232, 276, 278, 279
    Attendite a falsis prophetis 18, 31, 56, 58, 77–8, 90, 100, 119, 179 n. 36, 219, 231 n. 65
    Benedict of Alignan OFM, *Tractatus fidei* 59
    De inquisitione hereticorum 17, 50, 77, 100, 150, 227, 279
    Summae auctoritatum 40, 177
    Use of *auctoritates* and *rationes* 61, 67–70, 71–8, 89, 204
    Wasmud von Homburg, *Contra beckardos, lulhardos et swestriones* 72, 101
    See also under Berthold von Regensburg, *Cum dormirent homines*, inquisitors' manuals, Moneta of Cremona, Peter von Pillichsdorf, Petrus Zwicker, *Refutatio errorum*, Ulrich von Pottenstein
Aquila 24
Arnold, John H. 2, 6, 21, 59 n. 67, 133, 259
Augsburg 20, 46, 174, 187
    Inquisition in, *see under* inquisition of heresy
    Bishop, *see under* bishops and archbishops
Augustine 69, 72, 73, 76, 77, 87, 93, 171, 204, 234, 247
Augustinians
    Canons regular 42, 46, 66 n. 94, 114, 144, 146, 155 n. 214, 262, 263, 266, 273, 280
    Eremites 183, 224 n. 38, 280

Baptist-Hlawatsch, Gabriele 16, 199, 203

Bernard of Clairvaux OCist 73, 96 n. 233, 204
Berthold von Regensburg OFM
    Sermons against heretics 91 n. 208, 174, 176
Bertrand de la Tour OFM 61 n. 57, 204, 233
Bible
    Authority 38, 71–4, 77, 82, 84, 92, 100, 102–3, 172, 235, 247, 253, 259
    Old testament against heretics 78, 246–7
    Canon 78, 179
    Commentaries 69–70, 73–4, 76, 91–4, 96, 256
    Interpretation 6, 55, 67, 70
        Literal sense 85–6, 95
        Waldensian interpretation 67, 77, 86, 87–92, 179
    In Zwicker's works, *see also under Cum dormirent homines*
    Misquotation of 63–4
    Omnipresence 96–7
Biller, Peter 8 n. 20, 10, 11, 13, 15, 17, 18, 20, 28–9 n. 28, 32, 39, 47, 49, 52, 53, 56, 61, 64, 65 n. 88, 66–7, 68, 96 n. 230, 99, 105–6, 108, 118 n. 53, 119–21, 124, 131, 139, 141, 160, 167 n. 263, 176, 248, 262
Bishops and archbishops 23, 84–5, 97–8, 110, 141, 148, 163, 226, 231, 235, 236, 257, 287
    Augsburg
        Burkhard von Ellerbach 175
        Authority and dignity 234–5, 237–8, 252, 256
    Bamberg 32, 35
    Cambrai 255
    Cammin 34, 162
        Bogislaw of Pommern-Volgast (contestant) 34–5
        Johannes Brunonis 34–5, 148
    Brandenburg 34
        Dietrich II 34 n. 61, 35
        Stephan Bodecker 120
        Heinrich von Bodendieck 34 n. 61
    Ermland 268
    Lausanne 177 n. 27
        Guillaume of Menthonay 182
    Lebus 34–5, 162
    Mainz 101
        Conrad von Weinsberg 36
    Meissen 32, 35, 221

Passau 162, 272
  Georg von Hohenlohe 37, 287
  Prague 34, 136, 162, *see also under*
    Prague
  See also Jan of Jenštejn
  Regensburg 32, 276
  Salzburg
    Gregor Schenk 172
  Vestments 43, 102, 213–14, 216
  Würzburg 36, 167 n. 264, 174
    Gerhard von Schwarzburg 33
  See also Jacques Fournier
Boethius 60–2, 68, 73 n. 129, 257
Bonaventure 93–4
Børch, Marianne 169
Borke de Lobeze, archdeacon of Stolp
  229–30.
Bohemia 10, 25, 28–30, 33–5, 173, 207–9,
  211–12, 215, 224, 238–9, 259
  kingdom of 35, *see also* Charles
    IV, Holy Roman Emperor,
    Wenceslaus, King of Bohemia
  inquisition in, *see under* inquisition
    of heresy
  reform movement 29, 45, 69,
    210, 212, 222–4, 242, *see also*
    Hussites, Jan Hus, Jan Milíč of
    Kroměříž, Matěj of Janov, Konrad
    Waldhauser
Boyle, Leonard E. 107
Bruschi, Caterina 3, 105
Burial 49, 50, 52–3, 76 n. 147, 201

Cameron, Euan 39–40, 176, 221 n. 23
Canon law 30 n. 37, 71–2, 82, 85, 92, 102,
  143–4, 155, 234–6, 258, 262, 271, 274,
  284, 285
  Against heresy 5, 7, 40, 72, 73 n. 131,
    147–8, 191
  Legal consultations, *see under*
    inquisitors' manuals
Carpzov, Johannes B. 24 n. 7, 26–7
Celestines 29, 95
  foundation of the order 23
  members
    Ulrich von Rorbach, subprior of
      Oybin 24
    see also Nicolao d'Aversa, Petrus
      Zwicker, Pietro da Morrone, *see*
      also under inquisitors
  Oybin, monastery 15 n. 56, 22–3,
    24–7, 29–30, 199, 244
  S. Spirito del Morrone, monastery
    23, 24, 29, 244
Cemeteries, *see* Burial
Charles IV, Holy Roman Emperor 28,
  34–5, 148
  as patron of the Church 22, 29–30

Church
  Armenian 94–5
  Buildings 43, 81, 97, 191, 201, 225,
    247
    Altars 201, 229
  Hierarchy 1, 43, 71, 217, 225, 227,
    232, 234, 238, 242–3, 245, 252–3,
    255
  Malpractices in 80, 209, 222, 224,
    227, 229–30, 231–2, 255
  Property of 1, 43, 73 n. 131, 100, 172,
    212, 242–3, 250
  Unity of the Roman Church 35, 67,
    187, 244–56
  Secular power of 100
Church fathers 62, 69–70, 76–7, 179, *see*
  also Ambrose, Augustine, Jerome, *see*
  also Gregory I *under* popes
Church Councils 71, 102, 247, 253
  Conciliarism 102, 258
  Of Basel 65, 277, 281
  Of Constance 45, 225, 235, 240, 242–3,
    267, 270, 271, 272, 274, 277, 281
Classen, Albrecht 71
Clergy
  Anticlericalism 9, 36, 225, 227–9, 230,
    237, 241–2, 260
  Assisting inquisitors 139, 150–1,
    186–8, 190–4, 215, 257, 259
  Dignity 8, 172–3, 202, 225–8, 231–43,
    253
  Malpractices, *see under* Church
  Obedience to wicked clerics 206,
    234–5, 237 n. 92, 240, 243
  Opposition to inquisitors 165, 167
  Stella clericorum 238, 240
  Waldensian opinions 229–231, 241
  See also under Sacraments
Confession 2, 140, 195, 223
  In inquisitions 6, 129, 130, 135, 154,
    172, 182
  Waldensian double confession 186–8
Conversion 63, 110, 147, 152, 172,
  183, 191, 227, 258, *see also under*
  Waldensians
Creed 183 n. 54, 195, 200 n. 122, 212, 219,
  220
Cropp, Glynnis M. 62
Cum dormirent homines
  Authorship 10, 15, 66
  Biblicism 61–2, 68–71, 73–81, 84–5,
    90, 94–8, 102–3, 247, 258–9
    See also under Bible
  Dating 68
  Disputational style 67–8
  Homily and *exempla* 74–5, 102,
    176–8, 180–1, 183, 234, 237
  Manuscripts 3, 13, 65–6, 263–7,

269–83, 286–9, *see also under Processus Petri, Refutatio errorum.*
Sources
  Anonymous of Passau 52–3
  Boethius 60–2, 68
  Moneta of Cremona 17, 53, 68–9, 73, 75–6, 84–6, 89–90, 92, 246–7, 250, 258
  Waldensian sources 17–18, 49–50, 56, 68, 82, 227
  Structure 48–9, 67
  Summary 57, 65 n. 88
  Translation, *see under* Ulrich von Pottenstein

Daileader, Philip 255
Deane, Jennifer Kolpacoff 10, 36, 148 n. 189
Dietrich of Niem 240, 244
Donation of Constantine 49, 244, 250
Dominicans 2, 8, 9, 17, 22, 23, 34, 101, 148, 174, 175, 181 n. 46, 182, 183, 231, 232, 237 n. 91, 265, 271, 279, 281, 284
Döllinger, J. J. Ignaz von 42, 110 n. 26, 164 n. 250, 191 n. 88, 266

Eucharist 29, 79, 125, 168 n. 266, 182, 202, 224, 229, 236
  Waldensian lay commnion, *see under* Waldensians
Excommunication 182, 185, 186, 194, 228, 236, 251
  Formulas 143, 164–5, 287
  Waldensian opposition 43, 230

Forrest, Ian 182, 184
Franciscans 22, 23, 36, 87, 119, 131 n. 111, 174, 204, 205 n. 141, 233

Garsten, monastery 4, 17–18, 33, 36, 50, 53, 56–7, 68, 140, 153, 160–1, 284
Gdańsk 43
Gleink, monastery 24, 37, 160 n. 234
Gonnet, Jean 34 n. 59, 246
Gretser, Jakob OSJ 13–14, 39, 42–3, 48–9, 51, 58, 63 n. 81, 65 n. 88, 66–7, 81, 97 n. 235, 246 n. 131, 266
Gui Foulques (Guido Fulcodii), pope Clement IV 132, 185 n. 63, 284

Hamm, Berndt 70
Haupt, Herman 28 n. 26, 110 n. 26, 152, 156, 158 n. 228, 164, 166
Haymo of Halberstadt 245
Heinrich Totting von Oyta 69, 75, 83 n. 179, 278
Heinrich von Bitterfeld OP 9, 88 n. 196, 231

Heinrich von Zelking, castellan of Steyr 157–8, 193 n. 93, 198
Heresy
  Definition 90, 98 n. 244, 133, 137, 172, 176, 200–1, 216, 258, 260–1
  Demonization 8, 65 n. 93, 172, 181–2, 200, 214–15, 216
  Donatism 234, 235 n. 84
  Fama 129, 185, 200, 214, 229–30, 261
  Hypocrisy 204, 212, 227, 254
  Pastoralization of 5–6, 38–9, 104, 106, 108, 116, 146–7, 148–9, 170, 171–2, 183, 194, 196, 200–1, 215–16, 243, 258–61.
  Niklashäuser Pilgrimage 150
  Tolerance of 9, 204–5
  topos 18–19, 99, 173, 181, 210, 214, 232
  Secular legislation 7 n. 16, 147
Heretics
  Beguines and Beghards 32, 72, 111, 114, 128–9, 168, 224, 248, 255, 263, 265, 267, 268, 284, 286
  Cathars (Albigenses) 9, 17, 18 n. 75, 40, 73, 78, 90, 92, 99, 130, 133, 181 n. 46, 242, 246
    Raymond Hugh 130, 133
  Credentes 131–2, 187, 216
  Crypto-Flagellants 121 n. 72
  Free Spirits 99, 263
  Hussites 69, 113, 149, 168, 179 n. 36, 198, 225, 242, 259, 268, 269–70, 280, *see also* Jan Hus
  Lollards (Wycliffites) 37, 72, 182, *see also* John Wyclif
  See also Luciferans, Waldensians
Hobbins, Daniel 243
Horace 73
Humbert of Romans OP 181–2

Idolatry 60, 80, 90, 200, 220, 222
Images 61, 78 n. 154, 79–81, 88–91, 97, 100, 218, 222–4, 259
Indulgences 9, 100, 128, 212, 219, 224, 231, 234 n. 81, 259–60
  Waldensian criticism 43, 50, 135, 179, 190, 221, 230–1
Illyricus, Matthias Flacius 153
Inquisition of heresy
  against Waldensians
    Augsburg 20, 36 n. 68, 174–5, 220
    Bamberg 33
    Bohemia 134, 136, 140, 178, 207
    Brandenburg 37, 119, 128 see also Stettin
    Buda 32, 36, 151 n. 198, 167
    Erfurt 23, 30, 36, 109, 117–18, 121
    Fribourg 10, 20, 36, 131, 182–3, 219 n. 12

Mainz 10, 101, 136, 225 n. 40
Nuremberg (Nürnberg) 33
Ödenburg (Sopron) 33, 140, 164
Passau, diocese 4, 15, 24, 32–3,
    37, 50, 57, 106, 108, 110–11, 119,
    141–2, 145, 147, 151–64, 165–7,
    171, *see also under* summonses
    (*citationes*)
Regensburg 12, 32, 140, 195, 219
Stettin 1, 4, 10, 14, 20, 32, 34–5,
    127–31, 134–5, 137, 148, 162,
    185–7, 189, 195–6, 219–21, 226,
    230, *see also* Luciferans
Steiermark 33, 164, 172–3, 175
Strasbourg 36, 130, 174, 183, 220,
    236
Trnava 15 n. 56, 33, 151 n. 198
Vienna 36, 115, 164, 191, 196–7,
    223
Würzburg 167 n. 264
Definition 2, 6–7
Opposition to 134–5, 160–1, 165, 173,
    189
Preaching 8, 171–2, 174–5, 178–83,
    215
    Sermo generalis 152, 156, 158–9,
        163, 175, 191
    Zwicker's sermons 172–3, 175–8,
        181, 183, 215, *see also* Homily
        and *exempla under Cum dormirent
        homines*
Summonses (*citationes*) 171, 173,
    184–5, 215
    Zwicker's summonses 110, 143,
        147, 172, 185–90, 193–4, 215
Tempus gratie 185
Toulouse 105, 130
Inquisitiors
    Aymo of Taninges OFM 36
    Bernard Gui OP 129, 131, 132, 152 n.
        201, 158, 169, 286
    Fridericus of Garsten OSB 4, 33, 141,
        142, 145, 149, 150, 153, 156, 159,
        163, 191, 193 n, 93, 287
    Gallus of Jindřichův Hradec
        (Neuhaus) OP 91 n. 208, 134, 140,
        207, 285
    Guido da Vicenza OP 155, 189 n. 80
    Heinrich Angermeyer 11, 30, 36, 174
    Henricus of Olomouc 32, 154, 167,
        191
    Humbert Franconis OP 36
    Itinerant inquisitors 11, 30 1, 35–6,
        148
    Johannes Arnoldi OP 236
    Johannes of Gliwice OP 18 n. 74
    Konrad von Soltau, doctor of
        theology 136

Nicholas Eymerich OP 129, 132, 169
Nikolaus Böckeler OP 129, 136, 225
    n. 40, 236–7
Nikolaus von Wartenberch OSBCel
    4, 23
Swatibor of Langendorf OP 140, 285
Stephanus Lamp 4, 37, 145, 149
Walter Schubel, vicar-general *in
    spiritualibus* in Würzburg 36
See also Jacques Fournier, Martinus
    of Pague, Petrus Zwicker
Inquisitors' manuals 104–6, 108, 132,
    139, 144, 148–9, 169–70, 175
    *De auctoritate et forma officii
        inquisitionis* 143, 159 n. 233, 286,
        288
    *Doctrina de modo procedendi contra
        haereticos* 132 n. 117
    Linz OÖLB MS 177 57, 63, 72, 104,
        128, 132, 134, 139–41, 143–5, 147–8,
        169–70, 284–6
    Legal consultations 7, 63–4, 72, 116,
        140–1, 143–4, 147, 259
    Ordo processus Narbonensis 131, 132
        n. 117, 175 n. 21
    St Florian, MS XI 234 15, 63, 72, 106,
        108, 110, 112, 115, 141–9, 165–7,
        169–70, 186–9, 286–9
    Würzburg, UB MS M. ch. f. 51 108,
        164–7, 278–9
    See also Processus Petri

Jacques Fournier OCist, inquisitor,
    bishop of Pamiers, Pope Benedict XII
    98 n. 244, 100 n. 254, 130–1, 133
Jakub of Kaplice, priest accused of
    heresy 80, 222–4, 267
Jan Hus 80, 160, 200, 221, 235, 238 40,
    241 n. 106, 242–3
Jan Milíč of Kroměříž 78, 209–10, 224,
    228–9
Jan of Jenštejn, Archbishop of Prague 24,
    35, 82–3, 223–4
    against Waldensians 32, 34, 148, 178
    see also Visitation, feast of
Jean Gerson 72, 83 n. 179, 88 n. 195,
    101–2, 235, 240, 242–3, 270, 278
Jerome 70, 73 n. 128, 76 n. 147, 77, 97, 241
Jerome of Prague 37
Jews 17, 56 n. 58, 73, 78, 84, 89, 173 n. 5,
    182, 198, 213–14
Jiří of Těchnic 168, 269–70
Johann von Rottau, dean of Enns 166 n.
    260
Johannes Malkaw, preacher 210 n. 165,
    224 5, 236 7, 251, 261
Johannes Paduanus, Bohemian prelate
    140, 284

Johlín of Vodňany, regular canon at
Zderaz, Prague 194, 208, 209, 240 n.
102
  Sermons against Waldensians 4, 25,
  172, 196, 208–16, 225, 232, 242, 254,
  260
John Wyclif 37, 69, 72–3, 88, 102, 150,
168, 231 n. 68, 235, 240, 242–3, 247,
271–2, 274, 276, 279

Kurze, Dietrich 10, 14, 66 n. 98, 108, 116,
120 n. 63, 127, 135, 185
Konrad Waldhauser 18 n. 74, 78, 209

Le Roy Ladurie, Emmanuel 107, 130
Levy, Ian C. 73, 88 n. 195, 95, 240, 247
Liturgy 29, 61, 80, 83, 95–7, 103, 190,
222
  Waldensian condemnation 43, 190–1,
  202, 216, 224
Luciferans 8, 99, 114, 129, 214, 229–30,
248, 255, 263, 266

Martin von Amberg 30, 109, *see also*
  Martinus of Prague
  Das Gewissensspiegel 3 n. 10, 123–4,
  195, 200–1 n. 123, 234 n. 80
Martinus of Plana, Bohemian priest 76,
282
Martinus of Prague, inquisitor and
  secular cleric
  Identity 3–4 n. 10, 207
  Inquisitor 11, 30–4, 36–7, 109, 117–8,
  121, 138, 141–2, 148–9, 164, 172,
  263, 287
  Co-author of the *Processus Petri*
  5–6, 91 n. 207, 106, 114 n. 35, 116,
  118–19, 124, 126–31, 135–6, 138,
  147, 151, 169, 171, 215, 259
Mary (Virgin) 239
  Ave Maria 81, 195–6
  Cult 218–19, 223
  Criticism by Catholics 222–4, 227
  Intercessor 218–19
  Waldensian opinion 43, 47, 49, 67,
  176, 179, 201, 218–21, 223, 260
  See also Visitation, feast of
Matěj of Janov 75 n. 143, 80, 209, 210 n.
169, 222, 224, 267
  Regulae veteris et novi testamenti
  79–80, 251, 254, 259
Menhardt, Hermann 16, 199–200, 204
n. 135
Modestin, Georg 10, 11, 36, 66, 68, 99,
107, 116 n. 43, 117, 129, 130, 146 n. 179,
174, 226, 248, 249
Moneta of Cremona OP 8
  Adversus Catharos et Valdenses 40,

50, 57, 73–4, 77–8, 90, 102–3, 218,
246–7, *see also under Cum dormirent
homines, Refutatio errorum*

Nicholas of Lyra OFM 87
Notaries 3, 25, 27–8, 129, 136, 144, 153–4,
163
  Stettin inquisitions 4, 134, 137, 214 n.
  183, 230 n. 62
  See also Stephanus Lamp *under*
  inquisitors

Oaths 37, 176
  Canon law 92–3
  In inquisition of heresy 91, 109, 112,
  115, 116, 118, 136, 139, 144, 148,
  150, 169–70, 193
  In *Cum dormirent homines* 91–4, 200
  Waldensian condemnation 43, 86,
  91–92, 159, 229, 242
Olomouc 32, 140
Our Father, prayer 183, n. 54, 195
  Waldensian practice 81, 195, 219

Pacquet, Jacques 255
Patschovsky, Alexander 18 n. 74, 34, 40,
57 n. 61, 107, 117, 128, 129, 139–41,
143–4, 148, 153 n. 204, 180, 209, 284
Penance 94, 100, 178, 196
  After death, *see* purgatory
  Punishment for heresy 6–8, 33,
  117–18, 139, 143, 147, 149–54, 156,
  158–9, 163, 165–6, 169–70, 171,
  175–6, 183, 184, 186–94, 196, 215, 259
  Waldensian practice 128, 226 n. 43
Peter Mangold OP 174, 183
Peter von Pillichsdorf 13, 16, 39, 66,
118–9 n. 56, 164, 199–200
  Anti-Waldensian treatise 39, 50, 236
  n. 85, 245–6, 250, 254
Petrus Zwicker OSBCel, inquisitor of
  heresy, provincial
  Celestine prior and provincial 22–3,
  24–5, 95–6, 244
  Education and entry to the Celestine
  Order 25–30, 95
  Inquisitor of heresy 23–4, 30–7,
  136–8, 147–8
  Familia 3–4, 64, 106, 134, 149, 169,
  230 *see also* notaries, *see also*
  Fridericus of Garsten, Nikolaus
  von Wartenberch, Stephanus
  Lamp *under* inquisitors
  Individual trials, *see* Brandenburg,
  Buda, Erfurt, Ödenburg, Passau,
  Stettin, Steiermark, Trnava,
  Vienna *under* inquisition of
  heresy

Interrogator 104, 129–38
 See also Processus Petri and
 summonses *under* inquisition of
 heresy
Polemicist, *see under* anti-heretical
 polemics, Bible, *Cum dormirent*
 homines, Refutatio errorum
Preacher *see under* inquisition of
 heresy
View on the Church and clergy, *see*
 under bishops and archbishops,
 Church, clergy, popes
Views on heresy, *see* Luciferans, *see*
 pastoralization of heresy *under*
 heresy
Works
 Commentary on the *Pater noster*
  25, 28, 62, 146, 195
 See also Cum dormirent homines,
  Processus Petri, Refutatio errorum
Philipp von Helpte, provost of Cammin
 35
Pietro da Morrone, pope Celestine V 23,
 24
Pierre d'Ailly, cardinal 102 n. 260, 231 n.
 67, 235
Popes 143, 175, 217, 251
 Alexander III 77
 Authority 9, 95, 102–3, 228, 231, 234,
  242, 251–3, 256
  Right to institute new laws and
   practices 82, 84–5
 Benedixt XII, *see* Jacques Fournier
 Boniface IX 9, 25, 83 n. 178, 221–2,
  228, 231, 237 n. 89
 Celestine V, *see* Pietro da Morrone
 Clement IV *see* Gui Foulques
 Clement VI 94
 Gregory I 70, 73, 74 n. 136, 76, 77,
  88, 220
 Innocent III 234 n. 80, 286
 John XXII, 204 n. 137, 284
 Lucius III 185 n. 63
 Urban V 228
 Urban VI 34, 228, 240
 Sylvester I 49, 73 n. 131, 82 n. 174,
  246, 250
 See also donation of Constantine
Poznań, dioecese 162, 185 n. 63
Poznański, Adam 11, 61, 65 n. 90, 66, 74
 n. 138, 271–2, 275, 277, 282–3, 286
Prague 4, 9, 22, 25, 32–3, 34, 77, 91 n. 208,
 128 n. 95, 138, 148, 194, 208–9, 231, 244
 Archdiocese 28, 34, 78, 80, 83, 148,
  207, 221, 222, 229
 Churches 29, 30, 223–4
 Relics 29, 80, 223–4
 University 26, 28, 79, 207

Preger, Wilhelm 17, 66 n. 98, 68 n. 108,
 111 n. 28
Prevenhuber, Valentin 161
Processus Petri 15–16, 104–8, 259–6
 Authorship 105, 116–19, 126–9, *see*
  also under Martinus of Prague
 Audience 148–51, 169–70
 Dating 106, 112–13, 115, 116–19,
  155–64, 167
 Editions 15, 106–7, 109–11
 Manuscripts 57, 107–8, 111–16, 263,
  265–9, 271–9, 286–9
 Together with *Cum dormirent*
  homines 105, 107, 112–3, 120,
  122–3
 Together with *Refutatio errorum*
  105, 107, 111, 112–14, 120, 225
 Structure 108–16
 Parts 108–11
  Articuli Waldensium 41, 110,
   114–15, 116, 118–19, 124, 125–7,
   168, 169, 186–7, 211, 216
  De vita et conversacione 40, 110,
   114–15, 118–25, 164, 168, 169, 220
  Errores beghardorum et beginarum
   111, 114
  Formularies for inquisitors 33,
   110–11, 141–3, 151–4, 155–60,
   162–4, 164–8, 186–9
  Long list of converted Waldensians
   109, 112, 115–17, 165, 169
  Long question list 91 n. 207, 106,
   109, 112, 114–15, 116–19, 124,
   126–31, 164, 169, 207–8
  Notes on the arson of priests'
   property 111, 160–1
  Short list of converted
   Waldensians 30, 109, 112,
   115–17, 164, 169
  Short question list 109, 106, 112,
   116–19, 127–31, 164, 169, 185 n.
   63, 207–8
  Zwicker's manifesto 111, 112, 115,
   125, 151, 169, 176, 188, 198
 See also St Florian MS XI 234,
  Würzburg, UB MS M. ch. f. 51
  under inquisitors' manuals
Pseudo-Dionysius, *De coelesti hierarchia*
 253
Purgatory 50–1, 55–6, 76, 84, 86, 94, 95 n.
 226, 134–5, 179, 183, 211, 230
 In *Refutatio errorum* 43–5, 49–59, 75
 Penance after death 50–2, 55, 58–9,
  63, 178, 180–1

Refutatio errorum 38–41, 99–100
 Authorship 12, 13–14, 17, 38–9, 48–9,
  56–8, 61–4, 102, 258

Editions 13, 41–2
Manuscripts 40, 43, 44–8, 80, 225,
    262–71
  Together with *Cum dormirent*
    homines 46–8
  Together with *Processus Petri see*
    under Processus Petri
Redactions 41–8
Sources
  Anonymous of Passau 52–3
  Benedict of Alignan 59
  Boethius 60–2
  Linz, OÖLB MS 177 63–4
  Moneta of Cremona 52–7
  William of Auvergne 58–9
Structure 48–9
  See also under purgatory, *see also* use
    of *auctoritates* and *rationes under*
    anti-heretical polemics
Reinprecht II of Wallsee,
    Landeshauptmann at Enns 37, 163 n.
    245, 197–8
Richard FitzRalph, 94–5
Rothenburg ob der Tauber 36, 174–5,
    242

Saak, Eric L. 249
Sackville, Lucy 8 n. 20, 17, 19, 40, 90, 99
    n. 256, 181 n. 46
Sacramentals 9, 85, 102, 125
Sacraments 133 n. 126, 134, 245–6, 251
  Ministered by a sinful priest 178,
    179, 229, 232, 233–4, 235–8, 241,
    243, 255
  Waldensian opinion 123, 179–80, 183
    n. 54, 225, 227, 234, 236, 243
  See also confession, Eucharist
Saints 237
  Invocation and veneration 50, 53 n.
    52, 60, 62, 67, 75, 79–80, 178, 201,
    224–5, 259
  Patron apostles 196
  Relics 79–80, 132, 135, 218, 221–2,
    224, 259 *see also under* Prague
  Statues 80, 88–9, 218, 223
  Waldensian opinion 43, 49, 77, 86,
    89, 135, 150–1, 176–7, 179, 196,
    218–20, 260
  See also idolatry, indulgences, Mary
    (Virgin)
Schawr, Leonhard, canon in Regensburg
    and Passau 166 n. 260
Schism 208, 217
  Compared to heresy 210, 222
  Great Western 4, 5, 8, 12, 23, 69, 72,
    100, 217–18, 221, 228, 231, 236–7,
    Silence about the Great Schism
    244, 248–52, 254–6

See also anticlericalism, Church
    councils, popes, *see also* unity
    under Church
Schnurrer, Ludwig 36 n. 68, 242
Scholasticism 74, 85, 87, 90–4, 95, 203
Segl, Peter 11, 13–4, 16, 24–5, n. 9, 36 n.
    74, 37 n. 75, 39, 68, 107–8, 111 n. 28, 158
    n. 226, 160 n. 234–5, 163 n. 243
Seneca 73
Sermons, anti-heretical, *see* Berthold von
    Regensburg, Vincent Ferrer, *see under*
    Cum dormirent homines, inquisition of
    heresy
Seitenstetten, monastery 160, 166, 275–6,
    282
Silesia 34, 46, 114, 119, 141, 148, 208 n.
    154
Singing, *see* liturgy
Smelyansky, Eugene 176, 195 n. 96
Sneddon, Shelag 105
St Florian, Augustinian house 25, 72,
    144–6, *see also under* inquisitors'
    manuals
Stanislaus of Znoyma 45
Steyr 142, 152 n. 203, 153, 155, 157–9,
    161–3, 191, 198, *see also* Heinrich von
    Zelking
Szymański, Jarosław 108, 127 n. 90

Überlieferungsgeschichtliche Methode
    15–16, 169
Ulrich von Pottenstein 4, 196–9
  Catechetic treatise 12, 16, 199
    Audience 205–7
    Dating 197, 199
    Editions 16
    Manuscripts 16–17, 199–200,
      206–7
    Translation of the *Cum dormirent*
      homines 76, 172, 199–203,
      215–16, 260
    Translation principles 196, 203–5
      see also Wiener Schule
    Views on clergy 232–3, 236, 243
    Views on Waldensians 200–3,
      205–6, 215–16, 225, 236, 241, 260
Utz Tremp, Kathrin 10, 117, 129, 182 n.
    51, 226

Thomas Aquinas OP 87, 205 n. 141, 286
Thomas Netter OCarm 74 n. 137, 247
Torture 163 n. 244

Vincent Ferrer OP 177 n. 27, 182–3, 188,
    204, 233
Visitation, feast of 29, 82–4, 221–2
Vojtěch Raňkův of Ježov *see* Adalbertus
    Ranconis de Ericinio

Waldensians
  Brethren 1, 20, 41, 86, 96, 99, 119, 130, 212
  Lay apostolate 43, 49, 96–7, 134, 135, 225–7, 233, 243, 245, 250
  Conradus of Erfurt / Konrad von Thüringen 117–18
  Conversion of the 1360s 10, 18, 31–2, 73, 77, 82, 121, 245–6
    Johannes Leser 82, 83, 245–6
    Seyfridus (Siegfried) 245–6
  Conversion of 1391 31, 109, 116–8, 121, 126, 138, 259
    Frederick of Hardegg 117 n. 49
    Henry of Engelstadt 117 n. 49
    John of Vienna 117 n. 49
    Ordination 120, 122–5, 220
    Peter of Siebenbürgen 117 n. 49
    Klaus (Nikolaus) von Solothurn 20 n. 81
    Konrad von Saxony 20 n. 81
    Nikolaus Gotschalk, / Claus de Brandenburg 117 n. 49
  De vita et actibus 40, 121
  Doctrine 20, 67, 68 n. 106, 85–6, 99, 118, 122–4, 179, 211, 243, 261
    Child baptism 179–80
    Lay communion 100 n. 253, 125–6
    Sinfulness of killing 43, 64, 127–8
    see also burial, idolatry, images, purgatory, sacramentals, *see also under* Bible, clergy, confession, excommunication, indulgences, liturgy, Mary (Virgin), oaths, Our Father, sacraments, saints
  Followers 99, 104, 132, 187, 212, 219–20, 233, 260
    Aleyd Takken 131
    Andreas Hesel 23 n. 2, 36, 115, 164, 191, 196–7, 223
    Die Alte zum Hirtze 130
    Beata Ruerbeke 189
    Claus Hufener 230 n. 61
    Claws Zevecow 128
    Dietrich Wagner 152, 155
    Dyemuet zu Hausleithen 153, 159
    Els Fewr 150–1, 152–3, 156, 158, 159, 160, 162, 166, 191
    Geysel am Rabenpüchel 152, 166
    Gundel am Holzapfelberg 91 n. 207, 153, 157, 159, 162
    Gyrdrud Melsaw 134–5, 189
    Hans Spigilman 185 n. 63
    Hartmann der Biermann 130
    Henne Russeneyden 136
    Henricus zum Dörfflein 152

  Heyne Vilter, the Elder 229–30
  Heyne Vilter, the Younger 230 n. 61
  Herman Gossaw 214 n. 183, 230 n. 62
  Herman Wegener 130–1
  Jacob Hokman 186
  Jacob, Katherina and Zacharias Welsaw 230 n. 61
  Jans von Pewg 145, 152, 158, 159, 163, 166, 191, 197 n. 107
  Katharina Hagen 137
  Katherina Wideman 185–6
  Kunegundis in der Aw 153, 154, 157, 159, 162
  Kunigund Strussin senior 220
  Mathias Joris 220
  Mechtyld Philippus 230
  Peter Beyer 1
  Peters de Stangendorff 172–3, 175
  Petrus Lavbruch 34 n. 61
  Salmon de Swammarn 152, 155
  Sybert Curaw 189
  Tylls Sleyke 230
  Wenceslaus de Czussan 207
  Inquisitions *see under* inquisitions of heresy
  Paucity and division 245–8
  History and origin 49–50, 67, 100 n. 253, 227, 244–6, 250
    Liber electorum 17–18, 49, 56, 68, 227, 244–5
    Valdesius ('Petrus Waldensis') 49, 77, 227, 250
    See also donation of Constantine
  See also under Processus Petri
Wattenbach, Wilhelm 185
Werner, Ernst 51 n. 46, 108, 115, 118, 120, 126–7
Wiener Schule 194, 198, 205–6, *see also* Ulrich von Pottenstein
Wilhelm, duke of Austria 111, 112, 157, 198
William Durand of Mende 97, 213
William Ockham OFM 83 n. 179
William Perald OP 72, 203
William Woodford OFM 88 n. 195–6.
Williams-Krapp, Werner 15 n. 59, 205–6, 266, 273
Witchcraft 65 n. 93, 200, 284, 286, 288
Wenceslaus, King of Bohemia 34–5, 148
Wolf, Christine 17, 203 n. 131
Wolf, Klaus 198, 203, 204–5

Zittau 24 n. 7, 26–8, 29
  Conradus Wiszinbach, town notary 27

YORK MEDIEVAL PRESS: PUBLICATIONS

Heresy and Inquisition in the Middle Ages

1 *Heresy and Heretics in the Thirteenth Century: The Textual Representations*, L. J. Sackville (2011)

2 *Heresy, Crusade and Inquisition in Medieval Quercy*, Claire Taylor (2011)

3 *Heresy, Inquisition and Life Cycle in Medieval Languedoc*, Chris Sparks (2014)

4 *Cathars in Question*, ed. Antonio Sennis (2016)

5 *Late Medieval Heresy: New Perspectives*, ed. Michael D. Bailey and Sean L. Field (2018)

Details of other York Medieval Press volumes are available from Boydell & Brewer Ltd